# Estate and Trust Planning

Jeffrey N. Pennell
Alan Newman

Section of Real Property,
Probate and Trust Law

Defending Liberty
Pursuing Justice

Cover design by ABA Publishing.

Printed in the United States of America.

09 08 07 06 05    5 4 3 2 1

Library of Congress Cataloging-in-Publication Data
    Estate and trust planning / authors Jeffrey N. Pennell, Alan Newman
       p. cm.
    Includes index.
    ISBN: 1-59031-566-9
    1.   Estate planning—United States. 2. Trusts and trustees--United States. 3. Wills--United States. I. Pennell, Jeffrey N., 1949 - II. Newman, Alan 1951 -

KF750.E89 2005

346.7305'2--de22
2005014472

# TABLE OF CONTENTS

# ABOUT THE AUTHORS

Professor Newman is at the University of Akron School of Law. A graduate of the University of Oklahoma School of Law, he clerked for the late Honorable Thomas Gibbs Gee of the United States Court of Appeals for the Fifth Circuit. He practiced trusts and estates law and estate planning from 1981 until 1995 in Oklahoma City. He is a Certified Public Accountant, an Academic Fellow of the American College of Trust and Estate Counsel, and a past chair of both the Taxation Section and the Estate Planning and Probate Law Section of the Oklahoma Bar Association. He is the Reporter for the Ohio Uniform Trust Code Joint Committee of the Ohio Bankers League Legal, Legislative, and Regulatory Committee, and the Ohio State Bar Association Estate Planning, Trust, and Probate Law Section. He is a member of the Real Property, Probate and Trust Law Section of the American Bar Association, and the Estate Planning, Trust, and Probate Law Section of the Ohio State Bar Association.

Professor Pennell is the Richard H. Clark Professor of Law at Emory University School of Law in Atlanta. A graduate of Northwestern University School of Law, he is a Member of the American Law Institute, an Adviser for its Restatement of the Law (Third) of Property — Wills and Other Donative Transfers, an Associate Reporter for its Restatement of the Law (Third) of Trusts, a Group Chair and former member of the Council of the Real Property, Probate and Trust Law Section of the American Bar Association, an Academic Fellow and Former Regent of the American College of Trust and Estate Counsel, and an Academician of The International Academy of Estate and Trust Law. His major publications exceed five dozen law review articles, institute chapters and nine books, including Income Taxation of Trusts, Estates, Grantors and Beneficiaries (West 1987), Federal Wealth Transfer Taxation (West 2003), Wealth Transfer Planning and Drafting (West 2005), a Trusts and Estates monograph (Aspen 2000), the Tax Management Portfolios on Estate Tax Apportionment (BNA 2001) and on the Marital Deduction (BNA 2004), and the three volume Casner & Pennell on Estate Planning (6th ed., CCH).

# GLOSSARY

**Abatement**  is the situation in which a testator's estate is inadequate to finance all the bequests under the will, in which case the order of abatement specifies the gifts that will be funded first and those that will abate or fail to provide therefor.

**Acceleration**  is an event that causes a future interest to become possessory, such as on disclaimer or application of a slayer statute.

**Accessions**  are growth in assets, typically between execution of a will and the testator's death and then between death and distribution of the estate. The accessions rules govern who gets these extra assets.

**Acknowledgement**  is a testator's affirmation that a signature is the testator's own and that the testator made it with the intent to validate a will or other document.

**Ademption by extinction**  is the testate circumstance by which the subject of a specific bequest is not found in the estate at death and cannot be replaced.

**Ademption by satisfaction**  is the testate counterpart to Advancement, involving a beneficiary's receipt during life of property or a bequest that was meant to be conveyed by the donor's will.

**Administrative infinality**  is one of the fantastic presumptions under the Rule Against Perpetuities.

**Administrator**  is the personal representative of a decedent's probate estate appointed by a court.

**Administrator cum testamento annexo**  is an administrator with the will attached, meaning of a testate estate. Administrators may be appointed by the probate court because the will did not nominate an executor, or because the person appointed is not willing or able to act.

**Administrator de bonis non**  is an administrator of goods not administered, which means a successor appointed because the predecessor executor or administrator was unable to complete the administration.

**Adoption**  statutes regard adopted children as natural born, and allow children to inherit from and through their adoptive parents only (and vice versa), with certain exceptions in the case of step-parent adoptions.

**Advancement**  describes an heir's receipt of property from an ancestor who subsequently dies intestate, the property being regarded as part of— it counts against—the heir's ultimate inheritance. The testate counterpart is ademption by satisfaction.

**Affinity** means relationship by marriage.

**Alien land laws** relate to the right of a nonresident not a citizen heir to inherit real property in the United States, usually limited in the number of acres or the duration the property may be retained.

**All-or-nothing rule** under the Rule Against Perpetuities relates to class gifts, in which all members' interests must be valid or they all must fail.

**Alternative contingencies doctrine** is a Rule Against Perpetuities convention that attempts to validate a disposition if one set of facts would make it valid and another invalid.

**Ambiguity** comes in several versions: patent and latent, and latent ambiguity comes in three varieties: equivocations, misdescriptions, and inaccuracies. These usually raise the question whether extrinsic evidence may be used to resolve questions of intent.

**Ambulatory** means it does nothing until death. Generally, wills are ambulatory during the testator's life.

**Ancillary administration** is probate administration in a jurisdiction other than the decedent's domicile.

**Annuity** is a contractual arrangement by which the issuer agrees to make certain payments, typically over the life (or lives) of the annuitant(s), in exchange for consideration. It is a nonprobate asset.

**Antenuptial agreements** are the same as prenuptial agreements.

**Anticipatory breach** is possible in a will contract setting in which one party proposes to violate their agreement and it is discovered before that person dies.

**Antilapse** statutes override or preclude certain lapsed gifts and usually apply also to void gifts, in each case by substituting representatives in the place of a deceased named beneficiary.

**Anti-netting rule** precludes a fiduciary who invested imprudently from netting gains from prudent investments (and also may preclude netting gains from imprudent investments) against losses from imprudent investments in an effort to avoid liability.

**Apportionment** usually is applied to describe the method by which a tax liability—typically the federal estate tax—is shared by the beneficiaries of an estate.

**Assignment** allows a potential heir to transfer an expectancy to a third party for consideration.

**Assistance** is a third party helping a testator with execution, such as guiding the hand through a signature. Compare Proxy signature.

**Atom bomb provision**   directs distribution of property undisposed of in a trust when all the named beneficiaries are deceased.

**Attestation**   is the witness signature procedure for a will. An attested will means the will was witnessed (as opposed to holographic).

**Augmented probate estate**   is a Uniform Probate Code concept by which certain nonprobate property dispositions are regarded as part of the decedent's probate estate for purposes of computing and satisfying a surviving spouse's elective share entitlement.

**Beneficial interest**   is the entitlement of a trust beneficiary.

**Blending exercise** of a power of appointment commingles the powerholder's own assets with the appointive assets.

**Blockbuster will**   is a concept not yet accepted that a will should be able to make changes to the disposition of nonprobate property, such as to change the beneficiary of life insurance.

**Cancellation** is a form of physical revocatory act to a will that traditionally affects the words on the paper.

**Capacity.**   See Mental capacity.

**Capture**   is a possible consequence of an invalid attempt to exercise a general power of appointment.

**Cessure provision**   is one form of spendthrift trust provision. Also known as a forfeiture provision.

**Cestui que trust**   is a hugely outdated term for beneficiary of a trust.

**Claflin doctrine**   refers to the existence of an unfulfilled purpose of the trust that would prevent voluntary termination of the trust, even with the consent of all trust beneficiaries.

**Class gift**   is a disposition to a group of beneficiaries defined by a common characteristic, usually with each member of the class taking an equal share. Class closing rules relate to these gifts.

**Codicil**   is a document executed with all the formalities required of a will and that amends or supplements an existing will.

**Collaterals**   are nonlineal blood relatives, including natural born, adopted, nonmarital, and half-bloods.

**Commingling**   is the function of a fiduciary mixing fiduciary assets with its own, rather than clearly marking them as subject to the fiduciary relation. It is the converse of earmarking or segregation and constitutes a fiduciary breach of duty.

**Community property**   is the system of intra-spousal property ownership that regards earnings from onerous activity during marriage as owned 50/50 by spouses.

**Commutation** is the process by which the value of a present and a future interest is determined and each is immediately satisfied by distribution of the underlying property in the proper proportions as between the two owners.

**Concurrent ownership** comes in several forms: joint tenancy, tenancy by the entireties, and tenants in common. It entails undivided mutual ownership of property, sometimes with probate avoidance and rights of survivorship at death, but not necessarily.

**Conditional revocation** is contingent on (non)occurrence of an event or fact. Basically the same as dependent relative revocation.

**Conditional will** is contingent on (non)occurrence of an event or fact to be intended as the maker's final wishes. "If I do not recover from surgery" would be a classic conditional will.

**Conflict of laws** describes the issue of which state law will be selected to resolve the substance of an issue, and which state's choice of law rules will be applied to make that selection.

**Consanguinity** means relationship by blood. The "degrees of consanguinity" is a method of determining how closely or distantly related an individual is to another.

**Conservator** is a court-appointed fiduciary who represents an incompetent individual during life. Also known in some jurisdictions as a guardian.

**Construction** is the process by which a court construes a document, looking to discern intent. As compared to Interpretation this is more about what the maker meant to say, instead of the meaning of what the maker did in fact say. Sometimes referred to as "reading between the lines."

**Constructive trust** is remedial, a creature of equity, usually to prevent unjust enrichment.

**Contingent beneficiary provision** directs distribution of property undisposed of in a trust when all the named beneficiaries are deceased.

**Convenience joint tenancy** is created as a means of providing property management without intending to create property rights in the other joint tenant(s), usually because the property owner did not know to use a durable power of attorney, and usually can be undone because of the lack of intent to make a gratuitous transfer of ownership rights.

**Corpus** is one name for the principal or res of a trust—the underlying property owned.

**Curtesy** is the largely antiquated and usually defunct common law entitlement of a surviving widower in the decedent's property, replaced in most jurisdictions with the elective share.

**Cy pres** refers to the authority to reform a trust, for example to avoid violation of the Rule Against Perpetuities, to comply with the likely intent of the settlor or prevent failure of a trust the purposes of which no longer are legal or achievable, or to generate a charitable deduction.

**Dead hand** refers to the prejudice of the common law to respect the wishes of the decedent who settled a trust for future generations. See the Rule Against Perpetuities.

**Declaration of trust** is a trust in which the settlor is also the initial trustee and "declares" that the settlor holds property as trustee, usually for the benefit of the settlor as well, at least until the settlor's death. A valid nonprobate property management and transfer device.

**Deeds** may serve as nonprobate dispositions if the property form used entails the right of survivorship.

**Deferred compensation** comes in many forms, such as qualified pension plans or stock option plans, that delay income taxation of salary or other forms of compensation for services, usually in a retirement benefit context. Often these are nonprobate assets, similar to insurance, annuities, and other contractual arrangements, and may constitute income in respect of a decedent if the employee dies before receiving the benefit.

**Deficiency** often refers to diminished mental capacity.

**Demonstrative bequest** is one of a particular asset or source of funds but, if that source is inadequate, from other funds, such as "$100, to be satisfied first from the balance of my account at the XYZ bank." It is essentially a combination of Specific and General bequests.

**Dependent relative revocation** is a legal fiction that an act of revocation did not occur if it was based on a mistake of fact or law and the testator would not have wanted the will revoked if the testator had known of the mistake.

**Derangement** usually refers to mental aberrations versus diminished capacity.

**Disclaimer** is a renunciation of property, and may be "qualified" by meeting certain requirements under the Internal Revenue Code.

**Discretionary trust** reposes authority in the trustee to choose among a group of beneficiaries in determining who will receive what amounts of income or principal.

**Dispensing power** under the Uniform Probate Code is authority for a court to admit a will to probate notwithstanding that it lacks certain formalities.

**Divorce** operates as a partial revocation by operation of law of dispositive provisions in favor of the former spouse and sometimes the spouse's relatives. It may revoke the entire document.

**Doctrine of infectious invalidity** is part of the result of violating the Rule Against Perpetuities that may invalidate otherwise valid interests that are closely tied to invalid interests.

**Doctrine of worthier title** converts a reversion to the heirs of the transferor into a remainder to the transferor.

**Donee** usually is the term used to describe a person receiving a gift of property, but in the context of powers of appointment it describes the person who may exercise the power, not the persons in whose favor the power may be exercised. See Objects or Permissible appointees, and Powerholder.

**Donor** usually is the term used to describe a person making a gift of property, and in the context of powers of appointment it describes the person who created the power.

**Dower** is the largely antiquated and usually defunct common law entitlement of a surviving widow in the decedent's property, replaced in most jurisdictions with the elective share.

**Dry trust** is one with no remaining corpus and that therefore will terminate.

**Duplicate original wills** are multiple copies each executed with the requisite formalities.

**Durable power of attorney** relies on the law of agency. Durable means that it survives the maker/principal's incapacity. The authorized agent is the attorney in fact. Durable powers may relate to property management or health care decision making, which might instead be called a health care proxy, health care directive, or medical directive. A living will is different.

**Earmarking** is the function of a fiduciary segregating fiduciary assets from its own and clearly marking them as subject to the fiduciary relation. It is the converse of commingling.

**Elective share** of a surviving spouse is the right in most jurisdictions to reject the decedent's estate plan in favor of a statutory entitlement. It exists only in the noncommunity property states and is their modern alternative to dower and curtesy.

**Equitable election** is the technique by which a testator leaves property to an individual by a will that at the same time purports to dispose of property that individual owns, putting the individual to an election to challenge the will and keep the individual's own property or to accept the validity of the will and the benefits it brings to the individual in exchange for permitting the will to dispose of the individual's own property. It also is used to describe the choice a surviving spouse must make between taking the elective share under state law or taking under the decedent's estate plan.

**Equitable interest/title**  is what the beneficiary of a trust is deemed to possess. The fiduciary owns the legal interest/title.

**Equivocation**  is a latent ambiguity that is an accurate description of more than one asset, person, event, etc. and creates ambiguity because it is not clear which of them was intended.

**ERISA**  is the acronym for the Employee Retirement Income Security Act, largely tax rules that govern qualified deferred compensation retirement benefits.

**Escheat**  is when the estate of an intestate decedent passes to the decedent's domiciliary state.

**Executor**  is the personal representative appointed by a valid will.

**Executory interest**  is the future interest created in the same document as a present interest and following any but a particular estate. The two varieties are springing and shifting executory interests.

**Exoneration**  is the rule dealing with payment of a decedent's debts, usually with respect to realty in the probate estate.

**Expectancy**  is what a potential heir expects to receive from a potential decedent.

**Express trust**  is the standard issue variety, in juxtaposition to an implied (resulting or constructive) trust. Some varieties are living or inter vivos trusts, insurance trusts, funded and unfunded trusts, testamentary trusts, divorce and tort settlement trusts, and employee benefit trusts.

**Extrinsic evidence**  is alleged proof of intent, not within the "four corners" of a document.

**Family allowance**  typically applies only for a limited duration, during probate administration of an estate, to provide support to surviving dependents.

**Fertile octogenarian**  is one of the fantastic presumptions under the Rule Against Perpetuities.

**Fictional eraser**  is a technique by which a court may ignore words in a document that create an ambiguity, in an effort to properly interpret the document. Usually applied in latent ambiguities of the inaccuracy, and less often the misdescription, variety.

**Fiduciary**  is the term for any of a number of property owners who hold property for the benefit of others, such as trustees, guardians, conservators, and personal representatives (executors and administrators).

**Forced election estate plan**  is the same as the widow's election.

**Forced heir share**  is another term for the elective share or a pretermitted heir share.

**Forfeiture provision**  is one form of spendthrift provision. Also known as a cessure provision.

**Formalities**   are the rules for valid execution.

**Four corners**   is the way of referring to a document and taking cues only from what actually was said "within the four corners" rather than implied or suggested by evidence extrinsic to the document.

**Fraud**   is a will contest ground that entails deception. In the exercise of a power of appointment it involves an effort to appoint to an impermissible appointee.

**Fraud in the execution**   relates to deceit regarding the terms or nature of a document.

**Fraud in the inducement**   relates to deception in the facts underlying the testator's formulation of intent.

**Funded trust**   means that the trust owns assets during the settlor's life, usually to provide asset management and probate avoidance, and is a valid nonprobate will substitute.

**General bequest**   is one of an unparticular fungible asset, such as "50 shares of XYZ stock" or "$100" or "a pecuniary amount equal to the smallest sum needed to reduce my estate taxes to zero." Compare Specific, Demonstrative, and Residuary bequests.

**General power of appointment**   permits the powerholder to appoint in favor of any one or more of the powerholder, the powerholder's estate, or creditors of either. Additional appointees are permissible but do not change the classification of the power. Compare Nongeneral, Limited and Special powers of appointment.

**Guardian**   is a fiduciary who represents a legally incompetent individual, either because of lack of capacity or lack of legal age. There are guardians of the person and of the property, who may be and frequently are different people.

**Health care proxy.**   See Durable power of attorney.

**Heirs**   are determined at the designated ancestor's death as those who take by intestacy. Heirs apparent are certain to take if they survive the designated ancestor and heirs presumptive are first in line presently but could be displaced.

**Holograph**   is a handwritten will that need not be attested. Not valid in the majority of states.

**Homestead**   is personal residence property exempt from creditor claims.

**Honorary trusts**   have no living person to enforce the trustee's duties and therefore frequently are regarded as invalid unless the trustee voluntarily chooses to comply. The most common is a trust for a pet.

**Imperative power**   is one that the law treats the powerholder as having to exercise, usually because there is no default beneficiary. Failure may result in distribution to the permissible appointees in equal shares under an implied default provision. Also known as Power in trust.

**Implied default** is the equitable disposition of power of appointment property as to which there is no effective default provision. See Imperative power.

**Implied gifts** are an equitable device to fill gaps in a disposition to accomplish what a court believes the maker of the document meant to provide.

**Implied trusts** are a creature of equity, either resulting or constructive trusts.

**Inaccuracy** is a latent ambiguity that is an inaccurate description of only one asset, person, event, etc. Compare Equivocation and Misdescription.

**Incapacity** is the state of being unable to manage your own affairs, or lacking the mentality to validly execute a document.

**Inconsistency** in a subsequent instrument revokes the prior document to the extent the differences cannot be reconciled.

**Incorporation by reference** is one document treating another as if it was fully reproduced in the one. "Read the attached list as if it was a part of this will."

**Independent legal significance** implies that something else stands on its own—has its own independent legal significance—and is valid notwithstanding its indirect effect on a will.

**In hand payment** provisions require a trustee to make distribution directly to the beneficiary, constituting a form of spendthrift protection.

**Insurance trust** may own the policy of insurance or may be only the designated beneficiary of the death proceeds of the policy, and may be funded or unfunded during the insured's life. A valid nonprobate will substitute.

**Integration** is the coordination of multiple pages of a single document, which may include those validly executed at different times, such as a will and codicils to it.

**Intent** usually is associated with will execution or revocation. It also may arise in construction cases.

**Interest** or an interested witness means taking more under a document than if it was not signed or valid, such as because the witness is a beneficiary under a will.

**Interpretation** is the process by which a court seeks to translate or define what a document means. As opposed to construction, which is more about what the maker meant to say, this is about what it does in fact provide. Sometimes referred to as "reading the lines" instead of "reading between the lines."

**In terrorem** or "in terror of" is a provision that disinherits any beneficiary who contests a will.

**Inter vivos power** of appointment is one exercisable by deed or other instrument executed during the powerholder's life.

**Inter vivos trust** is the same as a living trust.

**Intestate property** is probate property not validly disposed of by a will. Dying intestate means to die without a valid will. "Partial intestacy" occurs if a will exists but does not validly dispose of all the decedent's probate property.

**Joint and mutual will** is one document serving as the will of several people, with reciprocal or mirror image provisions for each of them. It need not be contractual.

**Joint tenancy** is concurrent ownership by several owners/tenants who enjoy undivided entitlement to the property, typically with the right of survivorship at the death of any but the last tenant to die. It is a nonprobate asset.

**Joint will** is one that several testators sign. It is the will of each.

**Lapse** refers to failure of a gift because the named beneficiary is deceased. See Antilapse and compare Void.

**Latent ambiguity** is one that is not clear from the face of the document but only when the terms are applied to the facts at hand. These come in three varieties: equivocations, misdescriptions, and inaccuracies. Compare Patent ambiguity.

**Legal list** is a list of approved investments for fiduciaries.

**Life in being** for Rule Against Perpetuities purposes is someone who was alive when the transfer became irrevocable.

**Life insurance** is a contract by which the policy owner pays premiums to an insurer that agrees to pay a death benefit to a beneficiary upon the death of an insured. It is nonprobate property.

**Limited power of appointment** is the old term to describe a nongeneral power.

**Lineals** are ancestors and descendants in the blood line, natural born, adopted, nonmarital, and half-bloods.

**Living trust** is the name of a trust created and typically funded during the settlor's life.

**Living will** is a very limited document that establishes the maker's wishes regarding end of life or heroic medical techniques, usually articulating the desire to be allowed to die. See also Durable power of attorney.

**Marital property** is used under the Uniform Marital Property Act to describe what would be community property in a community property state.

**Marshaling** is the technique by which a blending exercise of a power of appointment as to which a portion is valid will direct appointive assets to the valid portions to the extent possible, such as to avoid violation of the Rule Against Perpetuities.

**Medical directive.** See Durable power of attorney.

**Mental Capacity or Mentality** usually is referred to as "of sound mind" for will or other document execution validity.

**Merger** is the legal combination of titles, either life estate or term of years with the remainder or legal and equitable titles, resulting usually in a fee simple entitlement and potentially causing a trust to terminate because the combination of legal and equitable titles destroys the nature of a trust.

**Misdescription** is a latent ambiguity that is an inaccurate description that could apply to more than one asset, person, event, etc. and creates controversy because it is not clear which is the intended reference. Compare Equivocation and Inaccuracy.

**Mistake** is an issue in execution, revocation, or understanding the law or facts as they relate to a document. Mistake of this last variety comes in four varieties: mistakes of law, of fact, in the inducement, and of omission. The common law said there was no remedy for mistake. See also Ambiguity.

**Mortmain statutes** are found in only a small number of states and relate to dispositions in favor of charity, usually under a will or codicil executed close to death.

**Mutilation** is one form of physical revocatory act to a will that affects the paper on which the will is written.

**Mutual will** is one with reciprocal or mirror image provisions. It need not be contractual.

**Negative will** does not dispose of property but, instead, merely disinherits an heir. Authorized only in a minority of jurisdictions.

**Nongeneral power of appointment** is the modern term for a limited or special power, meaning that permissible appointees may not include the powerholder, the powerholder's estate, or creditors of either.

**Nonmarital** is the nonpejorative term used to describe a child born out of wedlock, also sometimes referred to as illegitimates or bastards.

**Nonprobate property** passes by operation of law pursuant to various will substitutes, such as a life insurance policy contract or retirement plan beneficiary designation, joint tenancy with right of survivorship or tenancy by the entireties, other payable on death arrangements, or pursuant to a trust.

**Nuncupative**   is an oral will, recognized as valid in only a few states.

**Objects**   of a power of appointment are the permissible appointees.

**Obliteration**   is a form of physical revocatory act to a will that affects the words on the paper.

**Oral trust**   of personal property usually is valid, but   may be invalid for real property because it fails to comply with the Statute of Frauds.

**Parentelic**   is a system of determining which of several collateral heirs is entitled to inherit in intestacy. Rather than the degree of consanguinity being determinative, it is based on the relation of the nearest lineal ancestor in common with the decedent.

**Particular estates**   are life estates, life estates per autre vie, and terms of years.

**Passive trust**   is one with no unfulfilled duties and therefore that will terminate.

**Patent ambiguity**   is one that is apparent from the face of the document. Compare Latent ambiguity.

**Payable on death (POD)**   is a form of contract provision that creates an entitlement in a third party when someone dies. These usually are nonprobate assets.

**Pennsylvania rule**   is one of the resolutions to the issue addressed by the Rule in *Wild's Case.*

**Permissible appointees**   are those persons or institutions who are within the class of recipients of property under a proper exercise of a power of appointment. See also Objects.

**Personal representative**   (either an Executor or Administrator) performs probate administration.

**Per capita, or per capita at each generation,**   are two alternative systems of representation among descendants.

**Per stirpes**   is the common law form of representation among descendants. There are classic and modified versions.

**Plain meaning**   is the presumption that terms should be given their everyday meaning.

**Possibility of reverter**   is the future interest retained by a transferor following a fee simple determinable.

**Posthumous heirs**   are those conceived before the decedent's death but treated as alive at the time of conception if subsequently born alive.

**Postnuptial agreement**   is a marital property contract entered by spouses that usually settles and waives elective share rights.

**Pour back trust** is a funded inter vivos trust that distributes at the settlor's death back to the settlor's probate estate.

**Pour over will** is a disposition in favor of a free standing trust, often unfunded during the testator's life, that contains the testator's primary estate planning provisions. The receptacle trust sometimes is known as a pour over trust.

**Powerholder** is the modern term for the holder of a power of appointment—historically called the donee of the power.

**Power in trust** is a power of appointment that the powerholder is regarded as obliged to exercise. See Imperative power.

**Power of appointment** is the right to select, within parameters set by the creator of the power, who will receive property subject to the power.

**Power of attorney** is an authorization allowing an "attorney in fact" to act on behalf of the "principal" who is delegating the task or authority to act.

**Power of termination** is the future interest retained by a transferor following a fee simple subject to a condition subsequent. Also known as Right of entry for condition broken.

**Precocious toddler** is one of the fantastic presumptions under the Rule Against Perpetuities.

**Prenuptial agreement** is a marital property contract entered by persons before they marry that usually settles and waives elective share rights.

**Presence** is a requirement of both execution and revocation, if a witness or proxy act is involved. Compliance may entail a line of sight test or a conscious presence standard.

**Presumption of revocation** exists if a will cannot be found, if the testator had exclusive control and access to it.

**Pretermitted heir** is an individual—usually a child or surviving spouse—who is not mentioned in the decedent's will and entitled to claim a statutory share of the estate. It is based on the assumption that the decedent "forgot" the heir and therefore differs from the elective share entitlement of a surviving spouse.

**Principal** is one name for the corpus or res of a trust—the underlying property owned. Also the person giving a power of attorney.

**Probate** means admitting a will to probate by proving the will is valid after the testator's death. The term also is used to refer to the property subject to probate administration (as opposed to nonprobate property that passes by operation of law or contract). The term also is a shorthand expression for probate administration.

**Probate administration** is the estate administration functions of marshaling assets, paying debts and expenses, and making distribution of the decedent's probate property.

**Probate avoidance** is the notion that delay, cost, and other disadvantages of probate administration should be avoided by use of will substitutes and nonprobate property devices.

**Proxy** signature is the testator authorizing someone to act on the testator's behalf to sign a will. Proxy revocation is the testator requesting that someone destroy the testator's will. Other forms of proxy refer to durable powers of attorney, such as a health care proxy.

**Prudent investor/person rules** are two versions of the standard to which a fiduciary will be held in investing trust corpus.

**Publication** is a testator's affirmation or declaration that the document being signed is a will.

**Reciprocity** statutes relate to the right of a nonresident not a citizen heir to inherit property if the law of her domicile would permit a citizen of our country to inherit from her decedent.

**Relation back doctrine** treats certain events, such as a disclaimer, as occurring at a previous time, such as when the transfer of an interest was made, when appointive property was placed in trust, or when a posthumous child was conceived.

**Release** allows a potential heir to receive early distribution of a share of a property owner's estate, in exchange for a release of the potential heir's expectancy.

**Remainder** is the future interest created in the same document as a present interest and following any particular estate.

**Remarriage** may restore or revive provisions or documents revoked by divorce.

**Remedies** usually are relevant in will contract cases involving breach. Specific performance is not an option.

**Renunciation** is another term for a disclaimer.

**Representation** is the division of property that an ancestor would have received if living, that instead passes to his or her descendants, either per stirpes, per capita, or per capita at each generation.

**Republication by codicil** is a means of (re)validating a will by subsequent execution of a codicil to that will.

**Res** is one name for the corpus or principal of a trust—the underlying property owned.

**Residuary bequest** is one of the residue of an estate. Compare Specific, General, and Demonstrative bequests.

**Residuary clauses** in a will dispose of property not specifically transferred under preresiduary provisions of the will—the residue. Absence or failure of a residuary clause causes that undisposed of property to pass by intestacy.

**Residue** is what remains in a probate estate after all debts, expenses, taxes, and prior preresiduary distributions have been satisfied.

**Resulting trust** is an equitable creature usually created to fill a gap in a trust document, the effect of which being to preserve the trust property for the settlor's benefit.

**Retention** statutes relate to the right of a nonresident not a citizen heir to inherit property if the law of her domicile will allow her to retain the property.

**Reversion** is the future interest retained by a transferor following any particular estate.

**Reverter.** See Possibility of reverter.

**Revival** is a fiction that a document previously revoked is restored in certain events, such as revocation of a second document that revoked the first document.

**Revocable trusts** are nonprobate property management and transfer devices that are not invalid as will substitutes.

**Revocation by operation of law** is automatic negation of a dispositive document or certain provisions in it under certain circumstances, such as divorce or murder.

**Revocation by subsequent instrument** usually involves a will or codicil that expressly or by inconsistency overrides a prior will.

**Revocation, partial** by physical act performed on only a portion of a will; not universally valid.

**Right of entry for condition broken.** See Power of termination.

**Rule Against Perpetuities** is the lives-in-being plus 21 years formulation that restricts the imposition of dead hand control.

**Rule in Clobberie's Case** addresses the question of required survivorship in a future interest.

**Rule in Shelley's Case** converts a remainder to the heirs of a life tenant into a remainder to the life tenant, which may be followed by a merger of the two interests.

**Rule in Wild's Case** addressed the meaning of a gift "to A and A's children."

**Rule of convenience** is a timing rule by which a class gift is determined by closing the class.

**Rule of destructibility of contingent remainders** is a now defunct preference treating remainder interests not yet vested when the preceding interest terminated as being invalid.

**Satisfaction.** See Ademption by satisfaction.

**Savings clause** is a provision, such as under the Rule Against Perpetuities, that attempts to make a disposition valid to the fullest extent possible or avoid invalidity to the fullest extent possible simply by stating the intent and calling for interpretation or application in a manner consistent with that intent.

**Second look doctrine** under the Rule Against Perpetuities tests the validity of a power of appointment or its exercise at the time the power is exercised or lapses.

**Secret trust** involves a transfer that on its face appears to be outright but that extrinsic evidence purports to show was meant to be restricted with fiduciary duties.

**Self-proving affidavit** is essentially a form of deposition, executed to avoid having to produce witnesses to affirm what they saw in a will execution.

**Self-trusteed declaration of trust.** See Declaration of trust.

**Semi-secret trust** is one that clearly is meant to be held subject to fiduciary duties but the nature of the trust or the identity of the beneficiaries is not disclosed.

**Settlor** is one name for the person who creates or settles a trust.

**Simultaneous death** is the circumstance when the order of several deaths cannot be established by proof. Seldom are they exactly simultaneous.

**Small trust termination** provisions permit a trustee to determine that continued administration of the trust will be uneconomic or counterproductive and collapse the trust with an outright distribution.

**Special power of appointment** is the old term to describe a nongeneral power.

**Specific bequest** is one of a particular asset or source of funds, such as "my watch" or "the balance of my account at the XYZ bank." Compare General, Demonstrative, and Residuary bequests.

**Spendthrift** provisions/trusts are those that protect a beneficiary's interest in trust from certain creditor claims.

**Spousal annuity** is the same as the survivor annuity under ERISA.

**Spousal election** is the same as the elective share.

**Springing power** is a durable power of attorney that by its terms does not become effective until a defined event, such as determination of the principal's incapacity.

**Standing** in a will contest context is the authority to prosecute the case because the contestant will be adversely affected by admission of the will to probate.

**Statute of Frauds** is that rule requiring agreements with respect to realty to be in writing.

**Stranger to the adoption rule** treated adopted children as natural born only vis-á-vis the adopting parent and not anyone—the stranger to the adoption—who was not a party to the adoption.

**Substantial compliance** in will execution is modern horseshoes: close is good enough.

**Succession** is the division of property among heirs.

**Superwill.** See Blockbuster will.

**Support trust** is a trust providing for the beneficiary's support or maintenance.

**Surcharge** is one of several remedies to redress a fiduciary breach by holding the fiduciary personally accountable for any loss incurred.

**Survivor annuity** is the ERISA-mandated entitlement of a participant's surviving spouse, also known as the spousal annuity.

**Survivorship** is the requirement that a named beneficiary must be alive at a certain time to take.

**Takers in default** are the beneficiaries who receive appointive property to the extent a power of appointment is not effectively exercised.

**Testamentary power** is a power of appointment exercisable by the powerholder's will.

**Testamentary trust** is one created by a will (testament).

**Testate** means there is a valid will.

**Testator** is the maker of a will.

**Thelluson Acts** relate to accumulation of income in trusts for the period of the Rule Against Perpetuities.

**Tortious interference** is a cause of action against anyone who intentionally and wrongfully influenced a decedent's making, revoking, or modifying a will.

**Totten trust** is a special form of bank account with payable on death provisions that essentially provides that the depositor is entitled to the funds during life and whatever remains at death is payable to a designated beneficiary. A valid nonprobate will substitute.

**Trustee** is the fiduciary who administers trust property.

**Trustor** is one name for the settlor who creates or settles a trust.

**Trust pursuit rule** permits beneficiaries to follow assets that were the subject of a fiduciary breach to recover them from a holder who is not a bona fide purchaser for value.

**Unborn widow** is one of the fantastic presumptions under the Rule Against Perpetuities.

**Undue influence** is one of several will contest grounds, meaning that the testator's free will was overcome and the will is that of the influencer, not the testator.

**Unfunded trust** means the trust has no corpus, or only a nominal corpus that just barely supports the legal existence of the trust, usually used in conjunction with life insurance or a pour over will.

**Validating lives** are individuals by whose life or death it can be proven that a gift of a contingent interest does not violate the Rule Against Perpetuities. They are not necessarily lives in being.

**Virtual adoption** permits a person who was not formally adopted to be treated as adopted in fact. This is a minority doctrine.

**Void** gifts are those that lapse because the named beneficiary predeceased the testator. Compare Lapse and see Antilapse.

**Wait-and-see** is the modern approach under the Rule Against Perpetuities that measures validity of interests not by the what-might-happen rule but by what in fact does transpire.

**Widow's election** can apply to a surviving spouse of either gender, and implies that the decedent put the survivor to an election, usually to give up property in exchange for benefits under the decedent's will, typically giving up a remainder in the survivor's property in trade for a life estate in the decedent's property.

**Will** is a document that may be handwritten by the testator (holograph), oral (nuncupative), or otherwise. It is revocable and ambulatory (it does nothing until death).

**Will contest** is an action challenging a will's validity.

**Will contract** is part of an agreement relating to terms or revocability of a document. Usually found with joint or mutual wills, but neither of these documents alone constitutes a contract.

**Will substitutes** are nonprobate forms of ownership that avoid the need for a will to convey ownership following a property owner's death. E.g., an inter vivos trust, or joint tenancy with the right of survivorship.

CHAPTER 1

# INTRODUCTION TO PROPERTY TRANSFERS AT DEATH

This Chapter introduces you to the study of wills, trusts, and estates, including much of the terminology you need and the distinction between probate and nonprobate property. Also addressed are sources and limitations on the power to dispose of property at death.

## Emphasis

We practiced estate planning prior to becoming professors, and we tend to teach on the assumption that our students are going to practice law in this area as well. Although we teach the substantive rules, we emphasize how to do certain tasks and what problems to avoid. We also don't often linger on policy or history lessons unless those help to understand a rule or how and why it works.

To illustrate, lawyers prepare wills and trust agreements to accomplish personal, family, tax, and other objectives. Often a serious dispute (maybe attributable to a glitch in the law or a lawyer's drafting mistake) shows us how to avoid similar problems in practice. We thus look closely at estate planning uses of the rules we study and tend to focus on alternative thinking. When we think in terms of policy, our objective is to consider how wise practitioners avoid flawed or problematic applications under the law as it is. We encourage you to focus on those elements too.

Less emphasis is devoted in this material to probate administration and procedure, because the probate of wills and the administration of estates are particularly jurisdiction-specific endeavors. Certain principles of fiduciary administration are equally applicable to trusts and estates, however, and those that are relatively universal in their formulation and application are discussed in Chapter 18.

The applicable exclusion amount under the Federal wealth transfer tax is such (in 2005, $1.5 million for the estate and generation-skipping transfer taxes; $1 million for the gift tax) that less than one percent of the decedent population is subject to these federal taxes. Thus, we discuss those laws only in broad brush and mostly just in Chapter 19. Many states also have an estate or an inheritance tax and many states have moved away from the federal tax regime in what is known as "decoupling" that now makes it impossible to generalize about the local tax burden on decedents. Fortunately the income tax rules that apply to trusts and estates have been relatively stable; they are reported in Chapter 20.

Many lawyers who practice in the wills, trusts, and estates area find it an especially rewarding practice. Regardless of the tax aspects, it is largely a family oriented undertaking. Family disputes can be more emotional than many others, but most practitioners in this area report that such disputes account for only a small portion of their practice. For the most part estate planning is a cooperative, constructive, and nonadversarial specialty. For clients of some wealth, estate planning may offer the opportunity to do sophisticated and creative tax planning work, and for those clients who own interests in closely held businesses the estate planner also may have the opportunity to engage in related business planning (e.g., succession planning for who will run the business when Mom or Dad dies). We try to focus in this book on these positive aspects of this area of concentration.

### The Future of Estate Planning

The future of estate planning as a specialty is likely to be influenced by a number of predominant trends. Perhaps the most important is demographics and the aging of America. People are growing older and living longer. Many of them will be concerned about wealth transfer planning for many years before they actually die. Most of them will be as concerned with planning for the rest of their lives as they will be about planning for their successors.

It also appears that the trend of high divorce and remarriage rates will continue. A large number of litigated wills and trusts cases arise in the context of second and subsequent marriages, particularly when there are children from prior relations. Those circumstances, with their potential for serious disputes, present difficult challenges in both planning and postmortem administration, for clients and lawyers alike.

Increases in the "applicable exclusion amount" permit a decedent to leave property (up to $1.5 million in 2005) to anyone free of federal estate tax, making transfer tax planning a nonissue for over ninety-nine percent of the population. Although tax planning may continue to be significant to an important segment of some estate planners' clientele (even if most of the wealth transfer tax is repealed), the need for other tax planning (e.g., income tax planning for IRA and retirement benefits) will remain for many others.

Another important dynamic is the amount of property that does not pass either under a decedent's will or by intestacy. Such property (typically referred to as "nonprobate property") includes assets held in trust, joint tenancy, or other contractual ownership forms that pass at a person's death by operation of law, and assets that pass pursuant to a beneficiary designation like life insurance proceeds, employee benefits, and other annuities.

Finally, we are an increasingly litigious society, and there is an unfortunate amount of malpractice being committed in this area (predominantly by lawyers who are not adequately educated or experienced and who believe that "anyone can draft a simple will" or act as a fiduciary). You will learn that there is no such thing as a *simple* will anymore: there are short wills, and lawyers who think about wills in simple ways, but there are no simple wills. Even straightforward drafting jobs can hold substantial risk of liability. This means that some successful estate and trust lawyers will be litigators who know enough about this area of the law to specialize in reformation of inept plans, or who spot and then seek redress for other lawyers' mistakes, or who defend professionals against such claims.

## Terminology

Historically, different terms have been used to deal with realty and personalty, and to describe the passage of property at death.

### *Intestacy: Real and Personal Property*

*Intestate property* is any property of a decedent (other than nonprobate property, defined below) that is not validly disposed of by a will. A person who dies without a valid will is said to have died *intestate*. *Escheat* is the term that applies if the decedent's estate passes to the state, usually because no one within a certain degree of relation survived the decedent. *Succession* is another term that applies to the division of an intestate decedent's estate among heirs.

*Descent* is the intestate entitlement of *heirs at law* to realty. *Distribution* is the intestate entitlement of *next of kin* to personalty. These days most people refer to statutes of descent and distribution and to heirs (rather than heirs at law or next of kin), and most state laws no longer distinguish between realty and personalty.

Because heirs are those who take from an intestate decedent, they cannot be determined until the death of the designated ancestor. Thus, a living person does not have heirs. Rather, we refer to *potential heirs*, and they fall into several categories. *Heirs expectant* (or *prospective heirs*) are those persons who ultimately *might* be entitled to the wealth. While their ancestor is still alive they cannot yet be true heirs, but they expect to inherit in the future. Of these, *heirs apparent* are those in the closest degree to the designated ancestor: these persons definitely will inherit if they survive the designated ancestor. *Heirs presumptive* are those individuals who presently are living and who currently are in the closest degree of relationship to the designated ancestor, but who can be preempted if a closer heir is born or otherwise qualifies. For example, if you have neither a spouse nor children your parents are your heirs presumptive, but they are not your heirs apparent because they could be supplanted if you marry or have descendants before you die.

*Lineals* are ancestors and descendants in the direct blood line, such as parents, grandparents, children, and grandchildren (including individuals who were adopted and who state law regards as natural born). Note that descendants are sometimes also referred to as "issue," although we avoid that term because it sometimes is thought to mean only children and therefore it creates confusion.

*Collaterals* are non-lineal relatives who are related by blood (*consanguinity*), and also may include adopteds. By contrast, *affinity* is relation by marriage. Thus, an aunt who is a sister of your parent is related to you by consanguinity; that aunt's husband (who most of us would refer to as an uncle) is related to you by affinity. The husband of your spouse's sister is your spouse's brother-in-law (a relationship by affinity) but is not related to you at all (notwithstanding that you also probably refer to him as your brother-in-law). As we will see in Chapter 2, relatives by affinity generally are not heirs. As a result, in the first example above, if you died without a will your aunt could be your heir, but your aunt's husband could not. An exception that actually creates confusion is your own spouse. As a statutory taker many rules treat the spouse as an heir, but your relation is by affinity only and in some regards your spouse is not treated as an heir. Finally, note that the term *relative* usually includes persons related by affinity or by consanguinity. Thus, not all "relatives" can be heirs and the term is not a good one to use because its meaning also is not clear.

### *Transfers by Will*

*Testate* means a valid will applies. *Testator* (or, if you still are living in the dark ages in which gender-based distinctions in terminology were popular, testa*trix*) refers to the person who makes a will. Assuming the will is valid, such a person is said to have died testate. A testator can be partially intestate to the extent the will does not dispose of all the testator's property. *Attested* wills are wills that are witnessed. *Holographs* are unwitnessed wills that are signed by the testator and either entirely or at least the material portions of which are handwritten by the testator. They are not valid in all states. *Nuncupative* wills are oral wills.

A *devise* is a gift of realty under a will; the recipient is called a *devisee*. A *bequest* is a gift of personalty under a will, and a *legacy* is a gift of cash under a will; in each case the recipient is called a *legatee* (there is no such thing as a *bequeathee*). Because of the lack of symmetry in this terminology, the Uniform Probate Code has determined to call all gifts of either realty or personalty "devises" and all beneficiaries of these gifts "devisees." Because of older case law that still distinguishes between these, you probably should learn and remember the separate designations.

To be a will, the document must be both revocable during the testator's life and *ambulatory*—which means that it has no legal effect before the maker dies. So, a will *ain't nothin' 'til you die.* Documents that have legal effect, or that are irrevocable, before the maker dies are not wills. This is important when we study in Chapter 6 the impact of the law of wills on instruments and arrangements (called *will substitutes*) under which property passes at a person's death other than under the terms of a will or the statutes of descent and distribution.

*Codicils* must be executed with all the formalities of a will (either a traditional attested will or, if the jurisdiction permits them, a holographic will) and add, delete, or otherwise change provisions in a prior existing will that is referred to in the codicil.

*Probate* is the process of proving after a testator's death that the will is valid (signed in the right place, by the right persons, and such), meaning that it is "admitted to probate." *Administration* of an estate (which often is mislabeled as probate because this is "probate administration" under the auspices of a probate court) is the process of marshalling and distributing the decedent's property and is performed by a personal representative, of which there are several flavors. *Executor* (not execu*trix*, unless you're stuck in the dark ages) refers to a personal representative who is appointed by the will. *Administrator* (not administra*trix*) refers to a personal representative who is appointed by the court, sometimes because there was no will, or because the will did not designate a personal representative, and sometimes because the executor designated by the will is unable or unwilling to act (or continue to act). *Administrator CTA* (cum testamento annexo—there is a will) means an administrator who is serving for an estate that is testate. *Administrator DBN* (de bonis non—of goods not administered) is a successor to some personal representative (either executor or administrator) that began but did not finish administration. *Administrator CTA DBN* means a successor to administer a testate estate. In many jurisdictions, including those in which the Uniform Probate Code has been adopted, the fiduciary charged with administration of the estate is simply referred to as the *personal representative*, without regard to gender or whether the appointed fiduciary was designated under a probated will of the decedent.

*Will contests* may be a third separate judicial proceeding (probate and administration being the other two), brought to challenge the validity of a will—not for lack of formalities of execution that would preclude its admission to probate—(although challenges to the probate of a will also are sometimes inaccurately referred to as will contests) instead, for things like fraud, undue influence, lack of testamentary capacity, and so forth. A will contest can take place at the same time the estate is being administered, with only the ultimate distribution being delayed until the contest issues can be resolved. In some states probate judges need not be lawyers, which explains why a legal action such as a contest is conducted in another, more formal court.

## Sources of the Law of Wills and Trusts

Before *Hodel v. Irving*, 481 U.S. 704 (1987), the right to transfer property at death was generally viewed as arising solely out of statute, without benefit of constitutional protection. In *Hodel*, the Supreme Court held a federal statute invalid under the taking (without just compensation) clause of the Fifth Amendment to the U.S. Constitution. Under that invalidated statute small, undivided interests in certain Indian lands could not pass on the owner's death by descent (intestacy) or devise (by will), but instead automatically escheated to the tribe. The Court acknowledged Congress' broad power to regulate Indian lands, but held that the Constitution prohibited Congress from totally abolishing both descent and devise of the interests involved. In the process, however, we are reminded that inheritance is not an unlimited entitlement but rather a function of legal authority established and regulated by law, much of which today is statutory.

By way of example, the modern law of wills in the United States is derived in large part from three English statutes: the Statute of Wills (1540), the Statute of Frauds (1677), and the Wills Act (1837). Historically, different rules applied to testamentary gifts of personal and real property. Today, the same requirements apply to each. The Uniform Probate Code, promulgated in 1969 and often simply referred to as the UPC, is a comprehensive set of statutes dealing with the law of wills and estates, and with other areas of the law such as nontestamentary transfers (e.g., life insurance, trusts, and bank deposit arrangements) that are testamentary in effect. It also has provisions that deal with future interests, guardianships and conservatorships, powers of appointment, and powers of attorney. The UPC has been adopted in whole or in part by about one third of the states. The UPC has been amended on numerous occasions, including a substantial substantive amendment in 1990. Although most states have enacted at least some parts or sections of the UPC, its influence is not limited to those provisions of the various states' laws that have been taken directly from the UPC. Rather, it also represents a statement of modern policy that is relied on by courts in construing non-UPC statutes and the common law.

In addition, a new Uniform Trust Code (UTC) was promulgated in 2000. It has been adopted in a number of states and is "making the rounds" for consideration in many others. It focuses attention on appropriate changes that in many cases will import UPC concepts into the similar but separate law of trusts.

Finally, Restatements of the law are comprehensive statements of the law that also influence courts and legislatures. Restatements are promulgated by the American Law Institute, the members of which include practicing lawyers, judges, and law professors. There are two Restatements that directly apply to wills and trusts, the Restatement (Third) of Property—Wills and Other Donative Transfers, and the Restatement (Third) of Trusts. Each is currently under revision, but both already are having an impact on wills, trusts, and estates law.

## Taxation, Improvidence, and Inheritance

Testamentary freedom is most disrupted by the government through taxation of wealth transfers (under estate, gift, generation-skipping, and inheritance taxes). This interference is well accepted as constitutional, almost without limit. Aside from the impact of the tax laws, experts argue about the relative merits of redistributing wealth, and the reality is that no system does as effective a job of redistribution as improvidence, which far and away is more efficient than taxation. Far more concentrated family wealth is dissipated by inheritors than is fragmented by taxation. Efficient estate planning seeks to minimize the effect of both taxation and improvidence on the transmission and preservation of wealth.

Also note that patterns of inheritance are changing, particularly for the middle class. For example, a large chunk of the wealth of many Americans is held in life insurance, which is a form that typically is not, and in some cases cannot, be enjoyed during life. Further, a sizeable portion of the accumulated wealth of an increasing number of Americans is invested in a form that cannot be squandered during life: annuities, particularly deferred compensation retirement benefits. In addition, a substantial portion of accumulated wealth is divested during life in the form of education provided to children, and health care expenses. Thus, for a topic that has been around for a very long time, we are engaged in a study of laws that are in a constant state of development. It is an exciting and important subject.

## Competing Interests

Any study of wills, trusts, and estates will reveal that this law is about classic tensions, often between living beneficiaries and decedents who had certain objectives and desires with respect to the disposition of their wealth. A small form of this tension is generated by planning that is designed to reduce the impact of direct taxes on wealth transfers. Federal wealth transfer taxes generate only about one percent of the money raised by all federal taxes in any given year. With increased frequency, there are calls for repeal of the wealth transfer taxes, but this conflict is not nearly as problematic as a second form of tension found in this arena, which is among beneficiaries. Most commonly this involves life income recipients who are adverse to the interests of remainder beneficiaries, but it also may involve the conflict between concurrent beneficiaries, some of whom received more than might seem "normal" or predictable.

For example, assume that the decedent (D) died survived by a spouse (S), and by two children (C1 and C2), and that D devised D's entire estate to T, in trust, to pay income to S for life, remainder to C1. There is an obvious conflict between both S and C1, on the one hand, and C2, who is disinherited, on the other. See Chapter 3 for a discussion of will contest grounds. There also is a potential for conflict between S and C1 because it is in S's interests for the trust assets to be invested to maximize income; C1 would prefer investments that result in growth of principal. See Chapter 18 for a discussion of the trustee's duty of impartiality with respect to the administration of the trust for S and C1.

A third form of tension involves "predators" who seek to tap into the wealth of decedents. Depending on the decedent's views, these might include creditors of beneficiaries, spouses of beneficiaries, greedy children, and even charities or others with their hands out. Many estate plans are drafted with an eye to minimizing the exposure to outsiders.

A fourth form of tension is the "dead hand" desire of some decedents to control the lives of their beneficiaries (or at least the beneficiaries' enjoyment of the decedent's wealth) from the grave, typically through restrictive provisions in the dispositions that benefit those individuals. The Rule Against Perpetuities, discussed in Chapter 17, is the essential (and now a fading) limitation imposed by the law of a declining number of jurisdictions on the duration of this form of control. It may surprise you that, as discussed in Chapter 13, for the most part the dead hand is respected in this area of the law for as long as a trust may validly exist. The UTC makes several inroads on this that are designed to level the playing field as between the decedent whose wealth is involved and the beneficiaries. But in large part the "golden rule" of American wills, trusts, and estates law is that "those who have the gold get to make the rules."

For example, in *Shapira v. Union National Bank*, 315 N.E.2d 825 (Ohio Ct. Com. Pleas 1974), a father's will conditioning his son's inheritance on the son being married to (or marrying within seven years after the father's death) a woman who was Jewish and whose parents both were Jewish was upheld. The condition would have been void as against public policy if it had been that the son not marry at all. But reasonable restrictions on marriage are regarded as valid. The hard issue in a case like *Shapira* is what constitutes a "reasonable" restriction. For example, it would be regarded as too restrictive if the son had been required to marry a Jewish woman whose birthday was an even numbered Tuesday in a leap year, but what if the restriction had been an Orthodox Jewish woman? The dividing line between too restrictive and permissible dead hand control always is a question of fact and degree. What if the son had strong religious, but non-Jewish, convictions? According to the Restatement (Third) of Property—Wills and Other Donative Transfers §6.2, the test of reasonableness is whether a marriage within the religion is likely to occur. Thus, the type and strength of the transferee's religious beliefs may affect whether a condition *to marry within* a specified religious faith is reasonable. And note that new Restatement (Third) of Trusts §29, comment j, illustration 3, says that a restriction conditioning a gift on *not marrying outside* a religious faith generally is an invalid restraint on marriage.

A fifth tension is between the desires of some testators and the rights of certain individuals to a portion of a decedent's estate. In the form of an elective share, a surviving spouse in most states (and in rare cases a child or other descendant) may reject the decedent's dispositive provisions and instead claim a guaranteed portion of the decedent's wealth. Those statutes typically are based on concepts of fairness and a perceived need to prevent certain individuals from becoming wards of the state while others enjoy a decedent's largess. They are in a state of some flux as society re-evaluates these notions. See Chapter 10.

### Probate and Nonprobate Transfers

### *Nonprobate Transfers: Will Substitutes*

Much of a person's wealth may not pass under the terms of a will (if the decedent died testate) or under the laws of intestate succession (if the decedent died without a will). Examples of nonprobate property (which is discussed in greater detail in Chapter 6) include the following:

- Life insurance. The owner of a policy of life insurance usually is the insured, but often a trust or other third party is an owner to allow the proceeds to escape estate taxation at the insured's death. The policy owner may designate a beneficiary (and one or more contingent beneficiaries) to receive the proceeds of the policy on the insured's death, when the policy "matures." The proceeds typically are payable by the contract terms to the designated beneficiary without regard to the terms of the insured's will (or the intestate succession statutes, if the insured died intestate). Consistent with its policy of honoring a decedent's intent to the extent it can be ascertained reliably, new Restatement (Third) of Property—Wills and Other Donative Transfers §7.2 comment e permits an insured to change the beneficiary of an insurance policy by will (rather than just by the policy beneficiary designation).

- Retirement plan interests. The participant/employee in an employer's retirement plan and the owner of an individual retirement account (an IRA) usually may designate one or more persons to receive benefits from the plan or IRA. Typically the designated beneficiary will receive these contractual benefits without regard to the terms of a will or the governing intestacy laws.

- Concurrent ownership property. Property the decedent owned with one or more others as joint tenants with rights of survivorship, or owned with a spouse as tenants by the entireties, will pass on the decedent's death by operation of law to the surviving concurrent owner(s) without regard to the terms of the decedent's will or the applicable intestacy statute.

- Other payable (or transfer) on death (POD or TOD) arrangements. Many states allow bank accounts, some states allow securities such as stocks and bonds, and a few states allow real estate, to be owned by one person, but payable (or transferable) on that person's death directly to one or more designated other persons. The designated beneficiary usually will become the new owner without regard to the owner's will or the laws of intestacy.

- Property held in trust. A decedent may have been the beneficiary of a trust that the decedent or another person created for the decedent's benefit. Depending on the terms of the agreement, the decedent may or may not have the right to affect who will benefit from the property following the decedent's death. The trust property will pass to, or continue in trust for, persons designated in the trust agreement without regard to the decedent's will or the laws of intestate succession. An exception might apply if the decedent had (and exercised) a testamentary power of appointment (discussed in Chapter 14) over the trust property, in which case it would pass on the decedent's death in accordance with any exercise of that power. Even then, however, the property will not pass as a part of the decedent's probate estate, but will instead pass directly from the trustee of the trust to the persons named to receive the trust property in the decedent's exercise of the power.

It is critical to consider nonprobate property carefully when doing estate planning for a client. All too common is a client's well drafted will that fails to accomplish the client's objectives because beneficiary designations, survivorship arrangements, and powers of appointment were not considered and coordinated with the terms of the client's will during the planning process.

### Probate Property

Probate property passes under the terms of the decedent's will, or under the laws of intestate succession to the extent a will does not effectively dispose of that property. To say that probate property consists of property titled in the decedent's individual name is not entirely accurate. For example, life insurance policies often are owned by the insured, individually, yet the policy proceeds are not probate assets unless they are paid to the estate, which is neither common nor advisable (they usually pass to designated beneficiaries outside of probate).

The distinction between probate and nonprobate property cannot be overemphasized. Generally, a decedent's nonprobate property will not pass under the terms of a will, if the beneficiary died testate, or under the jurisdiction's law of descent and distribution, if the beneficiary died intestate. The distinction also can be critical with respect to the application of many of the ancillary rules of the law of wills (e.g., lapse, discussed in Chapter 8). Nonprobate property, which is said to pass by "will substitute," is discussed in some detail in Chapter 6, but it is important to distinguish it from probate property from the outset of your study of the law of gratuitous transfers.

### Probate Administration

Remember, this sometimes is referred to as "probate" but better is called "administration" if a shorthand expression is needed. This is the process by which title to probate property of a decedent is transferred to heirs, if the decedent died intestate, or to devisees, if the decedent died testate, in each case after payment of all legitimate charges against the estate (such as taxes, debts, and costs of administration itself). "Probate" is the streamlined process of validating the will by establishing that it was validly executed and constitutes the last will of the decedent. A will usually can be admitted to probate without delay. By contrast, probate administration almost always will extend for a period of months and, depending on the circumstances, can continue for years.

A common question is whether a probate administration is necessary. A probate administration will not be needed if the decedent died owning no probate property, having arranged for all property to pass by will substitute. In addition, in some circumstances the estate of a decedent who died owning probate property will not need to be administered. For example, an administration probably would not be required if (1) the decedent's probate property consisted only of tangible personal property, such as household furnishings, (2) there is no dispute among the decedent's surviving family members and other beneficiaries, if any, and (3) the claims of any creditors of the decedent can be resolved without dispute. If the decedent's probate property included real estate, however, a probate administration probably will be necessary without regard to the beneficiaries being harmonious and all creditors' claims being resolved. This is because in most states the devisees of a testate decedent or the heirs of an intestate decedent will be unable to prove clear title to the real estate (so that it could be sold or encumbered in the future) without administration. Similarly, if the decedent's probate property included an asset controlled by a third party, such as cash in a bank account or securities in a brokerage account, the third party may require a probate administration to release the asset. Otherwise the third party might release the asset to the person who appeared to be entitled to receive it and only later learn that the decedent had a will leaving the property to others. In many states the third party could be held liable to the devisees of the property under the will if this happened.

If probate administration is required, the form it takes will vary widely depending on the nature and extent of the probate property owned by the decedent and the probate laws and procedures of the jurisdiction in which the administration occurs. At one time the probate administration of an estate in most states was cumbersome, time consuming, and expensive, but today in most states extensive reforms have simplified administration so that it is not particularly onerous or costly. The administration of an estate is the responsibility of a personal representative. Traditionally, the probate court appointed the personal representative and closely supervised administration of the estate. For example, personal representatives were required to file and have approved by the court an inventory and various accountings; sales of assets were required to be approved in cumbersome proceedings involving various notices and hearings; and the payment of creditors' claims required court sanction. The UPC is illustrative of the more streamlined and flexible approach many states now embrace if no one interested in the decedent's estate requests formal proceedings. In large part probate of the will, appointment of a personal representative, and administration of the estate can occur without prior notice and without formal judicial involvement.

In choosing the personal representative, clients commonly designate individual family members, banks, trust companies, and business associates or advisors, such as lawyers or accountants. Although the personal representative is charged with administration of the estate, it is common for inexperienced personal representatives to delegate much of that work to an attorney, and it also is common for attorneys who practice regularly in the estates and trusts area to have paraprofessionals on their support staffs who do much of the administration for personal representatives they are hired to represent.

The personal representative serves the beneficiaries of the estate, *and* estate creditors. To facilitate the prompt administration of a decedent's estate, most states have special statutes of limitation ("nonclaim statutes") that require creditors of a decedent to submit their claims to the personal representative within a relatively short period of time. Their claims are barred if they fail to timely file. In *Tulsa Professional Collection Services, Inc. v. Pope*, 485 U.S. 478 (1988), the Supreme Court held unconstitutional under the due process clause of the Fourteenth Amendment a state statute requiring only publication notice of the decedent's death to trigger the nonclaim statute. Rather, due process requires actual notice to known or reasonably ascertainable creditors to provide them with an adequate opportunity to file their claims. There may be a similar constitutional duty to notify other potential claimants against the estate, in the form of beneficiaries (either under intestacy or under prior wills that may be valid) who may have an interest in or a cause of action against the estate. This is a developing theory in estate administration law.

# CHAPTER 2

# INTESTACY

Probate property of a decedent who dies without a valid will passes to heirs by intestate succession. A decedent's intestate takers include a surviving spouse, who may be entitled to receive the entire estate and for most purposes is regarded as an heir. Most states have abandoned *dower* and *curtesy* (common law rights of a widow or widower, respectively, to a life estate in part or all of a decedent's realty). For easy understanding here, we assume that they are not the law or that the portion of the estate subject to dower or curtesy has been peeled off the top and that we are dealing with the balance of the estate. The decedent's descendants take what the spouse does not and, if there are no descendants, other heirs include parents, descendants of parents, and other ancestors or collaterals. Intestate succession necessarily raises questions of "status," such as whether the claimant *was* a spouse or a child of the decedent. And in limited circumstances (such as misconduct), a person who *is* an heir is barred or chooses not to benefit from the estate.

## Intestate Succession in General

Intestate succession is the statutory estate plan. It is the legislature's guesstimate of what the average decedent would want done with probate property and it applies to the extent a valid will does not. As the "every-person" estate plan, ready-made and off-the-rack, anyone may employ it by doing nothing to overcome it (i.e., by dying without a will).

### *Property Subject to Intestate Succession*

Only a decedent's net *probate* property passes by intestate succession under the governing jurisdiction's statute of descent and distribution. See Chapter 1. Nonprobate property is not subject to intestate succession, and the distributable probate estate is reduced by such items as taxes, debts, administration expenses, funeral expenses, and any family allowances. See Chapter 10. To illustrate, assume that D died intestate. At death D owned an insurance policy on D's life, the death benefit of which was $100,000, and an interest in a retirement plan, the value of which was $200,000. The beneficiary D designated for each was D's surviving spouse (S). D also owned investment assets of $150,000, and had debts of $20,000. The administration expenses for D's estate were $5,000, and the cost of D's funeral was another $10,000. S's family allowance was $15,000. D's net probate estate that will pass by intestacy is $100,000, the difference between probate property of $150,000 of investment assets and the sum of D's debts, the administration and funeral expenses, and the family allowance ($20,000 + 5,000 + 10,000 + 15,000 = $50,000).

### *Governing Law*

A state statute of descent and distribution is applicable to all intestate personalty of a deceased resident of the state, no matter where that personalty is located, plus all the decedent's realty located in the state, no matter where the decedent was a resident. On occasion state law defers to the law of the decedent's domicile with respect to realty as well, but usually the law of the situs governs. As we study the rules governing intestacy (and a wide variety of other issues affecting wills, trusts, and estates), you will see that they differ from state to state, sometimes substantially and sometimes in very fine and hard to discern ways. This makes conflict of laws and plain old malpractice serious and omnipresent concerns.

### Surviving Spouse

The share of a surviving spouse of an intestate decedent varies significantly from state to state. In many jurisdictions, the spouse's share depends on who else survived the decedent. In general, the surviving spouse's intestate share under the Uniform Probate Code (the UPC) is greater than the share of a surviving spouse under most non-UPC intestate succession statutes. For example, UPC §2-102 gives a surviving spouse a fixed dollar amount (the exact amount is set by each state and the UPC only makes a recommendation), plus at least a fraction of any balance of the estate, notwithstanding any other potential beneficiaries (such as children) of the decedent's bounty. This off-the-top fixed amount effectively gives many small estates entirely to the surviving spouse, superseding all other rules announced in the statute.

The fixed dollar amount under the UPC reflects both a presumption of the decedent's intent plus a support theory that the surviving spouse will need a certain minimum amount to avoid becoming a ward of the state. Notice that the spouse is entitled to receive this amount regardless of the spouse's own resources and regardless of the amount of nonprobate property the spouse received as a result of the decedent's death. UPC §2-102 also gives the balance of the probate estate to the surviving spouse if (1) there is no surviving descendant or parent of the decedent, or (2) if all of the decedent's descendants also are descendants of the spouse *and* there are no descendants of the *spouse* who are not also descendants of the decedent. This last element reflects a presumption that such a spouse is not likely to divert the decedent's property to objects of the spouse's bounty who the decedent would not necessarily favor. This spousal entitlement is a significant departure from traditional intestate succession law under which the surviving spouse shares the decedent's intestate estate with the decedent's descendants.

UPC §2-102 limits the entitlement of a surviving spouse if there are living descendants of the decedent, or of the spouse, by another relationship. The fixed dollar amount if the decedent had descendants from a prior marriage would be the first $100,000. Curiously, if the spouse has descendants from a prior marriage (and all of the decedent's descendants also were descendants of the spouse), the spouse's recommended share would be the first $150,000. In either case the spouse also receives ½ of the balance. Further, if the decedent is survived by a spouse but by no descendants, the spouse receives the entire estate unless the decedent was survived by one or both parents. In that case the spouse's UPC share is the first $200,000, plus ¾ of the balance.

These UPC provisions for a surviving spouse are more generous than the statutes of most non-UPC states, many of which limit the spouse's share to ⅓ or ½ of the decedent's net probate estate. Further, if the decedent was not survived by any descendants, some states would give the entire estate to the surviving spouse but many others do not alter the spouse's share. If there are no children by a former marriage, most decedents probably would want the surviving spouse to take the entire estate. So you can see that the non-UPC intestacy laws may be antiquated or out of sync with the intent of the average decedent. They are not very quick to change.

### *Nonprobate Property Ignored*

The intestate share of the surviving spouse and other heirs is limited to the probate estate. The surviving spouse also may receive nonprobate property that passes under contract provisions or a right of survivorship. See Chapter 1. This means that a surviving spouse may benefit to a much greater extent than the intestate statute anticipates. This especially is true in this age, because nonprobate property (e.g., life insurance, annuities, and joint tenancy) is so common.

The decedent would effectively disinherit the surviving spouse to the extent the decedent owned little or no probate property, and most or all of the nonprobate property was arranged to pass to persons other than the surviving spouse. This possibility raises the subject of the spousal elective share, which is discussed in Chapter 10. Although the surviving spouse's intestate share might be reduced, in most jurisdictions such a plan of casual disinheritance will not work. Other planning may, however, be effective to minimize a surviving spouse's share.

### Survivorship

The question necessarily arises here (and with respect to testate decedents and nonprobate property passing by will substitute) whether an heir, devisee, or designated beneficiary *survived* the decedent. *Janus v. Tarasewicz*, 482 N.E.2d 418 (Ill. App. Ct. 1985), is illustrative. Stanley and Theresa (spouses) died after having taken cyanide-laced Tylenol. Stanley was pronounced dead that evening but Theresa was placed on life support and was not pronounced dead until two days later. A policy of insurance on Stanley's life named Theresa as the primary beneficiary and his mother as the contingent beneficiary. The insurance company paid the proceeds to Theresa's estate and through it they passed to Theresa's father. After a close review of the medical evidence the court agreed that Theresa survived Stanley and that her father was the proper ultimate beneficiary.

Unless the decedent's will contains an explicit survivorship condition, in most jurisdictions (including Illinois, the law applied in *Janus*) the question of survivorship is determined under the Uniform Simultaneous Death Act. The prospective recipient of property is treated as having predeceased the property owner if there is no sufficient evidence as to the order of their deaths. But the Act does not apply if (as in *Janus*) there is adequate evidence of survivorship.

To avoid litigation over the order of deaths in cases like *Janus*, UPC §2-104 requires an heir to survive an intestate decedent by 120 hours. UPC §2-702 imposes a similar condition that a beneficiary survive the property owner by 120 hours when the gift is made under a will or other dispositive instrument that does not address the survivorship issue. Given the state of medical care and issues surrounding removal of life support, 120 hours may be too short and many thoughtful estate planners affirmatively require survivorship by 30 days or more.

As illustrated, survivorship provisions should be used to plan for the possibility of multiple deaths that occur in rapid succession. Too often, however, the planning is in the form of a "common disaster" clause that creates problems. For example, in *Ogle v. Fuiten*, 466 N.E.2d 224 (Ill. 1984), the wills of spouses left the estate of the first to die to the other, if the other survived by 30 days, and provided that the estate was to be divided equally between two nephews if the spouses died in a common disaster. The husband died from a stroke; the wife died 15 days later from cancer. Because the wife did not survive the husband by 30 days *and* because they did not die in a common disaster, their estates passed by intestacy to their respective heirs, who were not the nephews. Predictably, the nephews sued the drafting attorney, who unsuccessfully defended (on lack of privity grounds).

## Descendants: Representation

The portion of an intestate decedent's estate that does not pass to a surviving spouse typically passes to the decedent's descendants, to the exclusion of other relatives (such as parents and siblings). For the discussion below on how the share for the decedent's descendants is divided among them, we assume application of a basic rule giving half of an intestate decedent's estate to a surviving spouse, and the other half to the decedent's descendants. (For this example, and all others in these materials, persons represented in parentheses are deceased; all others are living.)

$$(D) \text{---} SS \quad \tfrac{1}{2}$$
$$|$$
$$C \quad \tfrac{1}{2}$$

Here, if decedent D were survived by a spouse, SS, and one child, C, the division would be half and half between them.

$$(D) \text{---} SS \quad \tfrac{1}{2}$$
$$|$$
$$(C)$$
$$|$$
$$GC \quad \tfrac{1}{2}$$

Alternatively, if C were deceased but survived by a descendant, GC, the half C would have received if living would descend by representation to GC. This illustrates the "right of representation" by which C's descendants stand in C's shoes—represent C—to take what C would have received if living.

$$(D) \text{---} SS \quad \tfrac{1}{2}$$
$$\tfrac{1}{4} \; C_1 \quad\quad C_2 \; \tfrac{1}{4}$$

As you would predict, two children would share equally whatever the surviving spouse did not receive. And if there were three children they would split the half equally among them, one-sixth each. No surprises yet.

$$(D) \text{---} SS \quad \tfrac{1}{2}$$
$$|$$
$$(C)$$
$$\tfrac{1}{4} \; GC_1 \quad\quad GC_2 \; \tfrac{1}{4}$$

Equality applies at every level, in this case among the grandchildren who represent the deceased child.

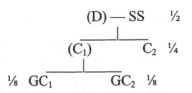

Different here is the combination of equality at the child level—division as if both children were alive—with the concept of representation among the children of $C_1$ (with equality among them as well).

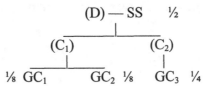

Here, the notion of equality appears to be violated, because three grandchildren are sharing in unequal amounts. The logic of this approach (sometimes referred to as "classic" or "strict" per stirpes) is that division occurred at the child level as if both children were alive, and their respective shares then pass to their respective representatives, with equality within each blood line. So, $C_1$'s ¼ goes in equal shares to the two representatives of $C_1$, and $C_2$'s ¼ goes entirely to the one representative of $C_2$. This is equality with representation as opposed to some form of equal distribution. Notice the most important factor is division into equal shares at the child level, regardless of whether any children are living.

Notice also that, under this approach, each child's blood line will receive the same aggregate share of D's estate regardless of whether a child survived D and subsequently left that share to descendants, or predeceased D and it went to those descendants by the right of representation.

$$(D) \text{ — } SS \quad \tfrac{1}{2}$$

|        $(C_1)$        |          $(C_2)$        |  $(C_3)$  |
| :---: | :---: | :---: |
| ⅛ $GC_1$     $GC_2$ ⅛ |     $GC_3$ ¼     |           |

This example just rounds out a notion only implied in the discussion above that no share is created for $C_3$ if $C_3$ is deceased and has no representatives who are alive. The distribution is exactly the same as in the prior illustration. This is true if $C_3$ never had descendants, or if all of $C_3$'s descendants also predeceased D.

With shocking frequency among poorly drafted documents you find the language "in equal shares, per stirpes." As the last two examples reveal, per stirpes distribution is not a system that necessarily produces equality. It is based on the two concepts of equal division and representation, but it does not guarantee equality among what appear to be similarly situated beneficiaries. What drafters of this language probably mean is "in equal shares, with the right of representation." But because per stirpes means more than just the principle of representation, the phrase "in equal shares, per stirpes" has led to all sorts of judicial interpretations trying to ferret out the decedent's intent (which is to say the intent of the drafter of the document, who usually was not the decedent).

To summarize, a traditional definition of "per stirpes" in its classic sense entails two concepts. One is division into equal shares at the level of the decedent's children, regardless of whether anyone is alive at that level. One share is created for each person at that level who is alive and one share for each person at that level who is deceased with descendants who are alive. The other concept is distribution with the right of representation.

### The 1969 UPC

The 1969 version of UPC §2-103(1) altered the classic per stirpes approach to give each of the three grandchildren in the last two examples $1/_6$ providing equality among the three grandchildren. This is a "per capita" division (sometimes referred to misleadingly as "modern per stirpes" or, more accurately, as "per capita with representation"). It was meant to guarantee equality at more remote levels of descent. It did not achieve equality in the sense that the drafters anticipated, and it was changed in the 1990 version of the UPC to what is known as "per capita at each generation." However, many states still have the old version of the UPC with its original per capita system. Let's start by understanding that approach.

The old UPC per capita approach divided the portion not passing to the spouse into equal shares at the first level below the decedent *at which someone was alive*, creating one share for each living descendant at that level and one share for each descendant at that level who is deceased but with descendants who are alive. Thus, the difference from classic per stirpes is at what level the stirps begin: under the old UPC per capita system it is at the first level at which you find a living descendant, while under classic per stirpes it is at the child generation, regardless of whether any of the decedent's children are alive. In the example above with both children deceased before D the result is equality at the grandchild level.

Notice, however, that the grandchildren can receive different sized shares under the per capita system, based on the "accident" of the order of deaths. To illustrate, consider again the last two examples, in which D died intestate, survived by surviving spouse (SS), who will receive ½. D also had two children ($C_1$ and $C_2$). $C_1$ had two children ($GC_1$ and $GC_2$); $C_2$ had one child ($GC_3$). If both $C_1$ and $C_2$ predeceased D, the per capita distribution would generate shares for the three grandchildren of $\frac{1}{6}$ each. But if $C_1$ survived D, even by only a short time, $C_1$'s share would be ¼ under the per capita system, while $GC_3$ would receive the other ¼. If $C_1$ then died intestate and $GC_1$ and $GC_2$ were $C_1$'s only heirs, they would receive ⅛ each. The point is that the order of death as between $C_1$ and D in this easy example can make a difference in the equality among grandchildren sought by the per capita approach.

We will see momentarily that the fortuitousness of the order of deaths also can affect the size of shares under the "per capita at each generation" approach of the 1990 UPC. Indeed, it is a problem in all but the classic per stirpes approach. This is important because surveys of lay individuals indicate that they want their grandchildren to share equally if the only takers are grandchildren, which supports the per capita result when a decedent is survived by grandchildren, but not by any children. The problem with those surveys is that they did not ask the respondents whether they would want different sized shares based on the fortuitousness of the order of deaths.

### Comparison of Classic Per Stirpes, Per Capita (1969 UPC), and Per Capita at Each Generation (1990 UPC)

In the next illustration the essential question is where the stirps begin. Under a classic per stirpes distribution they begin (i.e., the first division is made) at the child level, regardless of the fact that no children are living. The size of each share is illustrated, and again the lack of uniformity among ostensibly similarly situated beneficiaries is apparent.

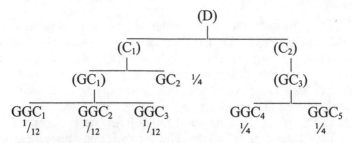

A per capita distribution like that provided for by the 1969 UPC starts the division at the first level at which a descendant is living, which is the grandchild level here. Under that approach, the division is into three shares at the grandchild level, one for each who is alive and one for each who is deceased with descendants who are alive. The curious thing is that, under per capita, the two shares created for representatives of deceased grandchildren in this example would pass by representation in the same manner as in the classic per stirpes distribution, meaning that the great grandchildren still receive unequal shares. To illustrate:

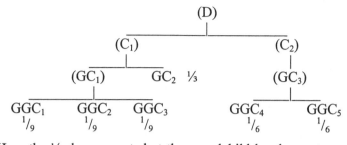

Here the ⅓ shares created at the grandchild level pass to representatives of deceased grandchildren just like in a classic per stirpes distribution, which produces inequality at the next generation down the ladder: equal shares among grandchildren, but not among great grandchildren. This is because the only change per capita made was in dividing the estate the first time: the stirps begin at the first level at which someone is alive, rather than at the first level below the decedent. But after making that one change, everything else remains the same. If the object is to treat similarly situated beneficiaries (i.e., the great grandchildren in this example) alike, this system does not accomplish that result.

The old (1969) UPC did contain a refinement over this per capita with representation approach, but it requires a change in facts to illustrate when it would operate and it failed to address the inequality shown above. The modification can be referred to as per capita with per capita representation and would be implicated in the prior example if we assume that $GGC_4$ and $GGC_5$—both descendants of $GC_3$—both are deceased and leave three children between them (not all the children of just one of them, however). In that case the ⅓ share that would have gone to $GC_3$ if living would be divided equally among these three great, great grandchildren in equal shares of $^1/_9$ each (rather than $^1/_6$ to one of them and $^1/_{12}$ to the other two) as a per capita distribution among $GC_3$'s grandchildren. If you're having a little trouble with all this, consider again those surveys of lay individuals that "informed" these statutory reforms: how reliable are they if the respondents did not consider all these permutations?

1990 UPC §2-106 adopted a system known as "per capita at each generation," which guarantees equal shares to those in equal degrees of relation to the decedent. To illustrate, again under the same example:

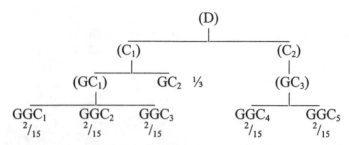

What happens here is that, as with the per capita approach of the 1969 UPC, the first division is made at the level at which someone is alive—the grandchild level here—with one share for each who is living and one for each who is deceased with descendants who are living. The difference is that the shares created for descendants of deceased grandchildren are distributed differently. Here their ⅔ of the estate is distributed in equal shares among the great grandchildren who stand in the shoes of deceased grandchildren (that is, any children of $GC_2$ are excluded), which creates five equal shares of the ⅔ that is available. Now you find equality within each generation.

Again, however, the intended equality is subject to the death lottery. In the example above, if $GC_3$ had survived D by as little as one moment (or by 120 hours, if a 120 hour survivorship requirement like UPC §2-104 applies), then ⅓ would have gone to $GC_3$ and only the remaining ⅓ would be distributed to the three great grandchildren representing $GC_1$, giving them each $^1/_9$ rather than $^2/_{15}$. Thus, the order of deaths still makes a difference. Only the classic per stirpes approach avoids that issue, and one more. That added issue reflects that per capita at each generation, like original per capita, rewards the more prolific blood lines. This is because the more children a deceased descendant leaves, the more that bloodline benefits.

To focus better on the difference between the two UPC per capita distribution systems (per capita [1969 UPC] versus per capita at each generation [1990 UPC]), consider another example. Because under both systems the stirps begin at the first level at which a descendant is living, we consider only the number of living grandchildren and grandchildren who are deceased with descendants who are alive. We exclude the child level because we assume all children are deceased.

(D)

| $GC_1$ | $(GC_3)$ | $(GC_4)$ | $GC_7$ | $GC_8$ | $GC_9$ |

$GGC_1$   $GGC_2$   $GGC_3$

In this example (which assumes $GC_2$, $GC_5$, and $GC_6$ predeceased D and that none of their descendants survived D), six equal shares would be created, four of which would be allocated to the living grandchildren. Under the per capita system of the old UPC the remaining two shares would pass by representation. $GGC_1$ would take one share as $GC_3$'s only child, and the other would pass in equal shares to the two children of $GC_4$. Thus, under the old UPC per capita with per capita representation, $GGC_1$'s share might be twice as large ($^1/_6$) as the shares of $GGC_2$ and $GGC_3$ ($^1/_{12}$ each). The new UPC per capita at each generation approach would take the two unallocated shares and divide the two $^1/_6$ shares of $GC_3$ and $GC_4$ equally among the great grandchildren who stand in their shoes, giving each of those three great grandchildren an equal $^1/_9$ share.

### Modified Per Stirpes

There is one other modification that deserves mention. If *all* the takers are in the *same* degree of relation (e.g., all are grandchildren, because no children are alive and because there are no great grandchildren representing deceased grandchildren) in some per stirpes states the traditional per stirpes division is abandoned and the takers receive equal shares. Usually this "modified per stirpes" approach does not apply if there is *any* taker who is not in the same degree as the rest, so it is not the same as either the 1969 UPC per capita or the 1990 UPC per capita at each generation approach. And because of the factual requisite, it also is not very likely to apply.

### Summary of Representation

In thinking through representation, the various options are easy to distinguish.

- Under the classic per stirpes system, each line of descendants receives, in the aggregate, an equal share of the intestate estate. Thus, if D had two children, A and B, and if D is survived by A or any descendant of A, and by B or any descendant of B, half of D's estate will pass to A or A's descendants and the other half will pass to B or B's descendants.

- The only difference between the classic per stirpes and traditional per capita systems is the determination of the level at which equality among the lines of descent occurs. Under classic per stirpes, equality occurs at the child level regardless of whether any children survive the decedent. Thus, if D's two children, A and B, both predeceased D (and each was survived by at least one descendant who survived D), A's descendants will share half of the estate and B's will receive the other half, regardless of how many descendants of each survive D. By contrast, under the traditional per capita system, the generational level at which lines of descent take equal shares is not necessarily the child level; rather, it is the level closest to the decedent at which there is a living descendant. After that determination is made, traditional per capita operates exactly like classic per stirpes. Thus, if D's two children, A and B, each predeceased D and if at least one grandchild of D survived D, the first division of D's estate under a per capita system would be at the grandchild level but the rest of the distribution would mirror classic per stirpes.

- Only the per capita at each generation system ensures that all members of each generation of descendants who are entitled to receive a share receive equal inheritances. Thus, under per capita at each generation all grandchildren who are heirs always receive equal shares of the estate, as will all great grandchildren, all great, great grandchildren, etc. That is not necessarily the case under the other systems. And blood line equality is not preserved.

### Ancestors and Collaterals

If an intestate decedent is survived by descendants, typically whatever does not pass to a surviving spouse will pass to the descendants (with the representation questions discussed above). If there are no descendants, in some states a surviving spouse will receive the entire estate. In others (e.g., under UPC §2-102(1)) the spouse takes all only if there also is not some other heir, such as a surviving parent. Otherwise any portion of the estate that does not pass to a surviving spouse is divided among ancestors and collaterals.

In most states, if there are no descendants the portion that does not pass to a surviving spouse passes to the parents in equal shares or, if only one parent is alive, then all to that parent. Under the law of several states a parent who abandoned the decedent is precluded from benefiting. For example, UPC §2-114(c) allows a parent to inherit from an intestate child only if the parent openly treated the decedent as a child and did not refuse to support the child.

If there is no living parent or descendants of the decedent, some jurisdictions (e.g., UPC §2-102(1)(i)) would leave the entire estate to the surviving spouse, while others would leave the share the parents would have received to descendants of the parents by representation under the per stirpes, per capita, or per capita at each generation system of that jurisdiction. If the decedent is not survived by a spouse, descendant, or parent, typically (e.g., UPC §2-103(3)) the estate will pass to descendants of the decedent's parents, again by whatever form of representation is embraced in that jurisdiction.

### More Remote Heirs: The Parentelic System

If there is no descendant and no parent or descendant of a parent alive to take, some states follow the "parentelic system" under which whatever property the spouse does not take goes up and back down the family tree again. The estate is given to the nearest living lineal ancestor or per stirpes to the living descendants of the nearest lineal ancestor of whom descendants are living. For example, if the decedent is survived by one or more grandparents or one or more descendants of deceased grandparents, the estate would be divided among them, with half to the maternal grandparents (or their descendants, with rights of representation, if neither maternal grandparent is living) and the other half to the paternal grandparents (or their descendants, with rights of representation, if neither is living). If the decedent is not survived by any descendant, parent, descendant of parents, grandparent, or descendant of grandparents, in states that follow the parentelic system the estate would be distributed to great grandparents, or their descendants by right of representation, and if none, to great, great grandparents, or their descendants by right of representation, and so on. This can entail pretty remote relatives (so-called laughing heirs) and some states preclude distribution beyond a certain degree. For example, the UPC does not recognize as heirs relatives who are more remote than grandparents and their descendants.

### More Remote Heirs: The Degree of Relationship System

Some states do not follow the parentelic system of determining the decedent's heirs by passing up and down the family tree. Instead, they abandon representation at some level (such as if there is no parent or descendant of parents) and distribute the portion not passing to a spouse (the entire estate if there is no surviving spouse) to more remote family members under a degree of relationship (consanguinity) system. Distribution typically is in equal shares to all who fall within the nearest degree of consanguinity, with no rights of representation. Degrees of consanguinity are determined by adding (1) the number of steps from the decedent up to the nearest common ancestor of the decedent and the relative to (2) the number of steps down from the common ancestor to the relative.

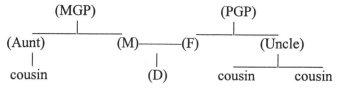

Under the degree of relationship method, the three cousins illustrated here all are in the fourth degree of consanguinity, determined by counting the number of steps up to the common ancestor (in each case a grandparent) and then down to the cousin. Here the three cousins would share the estate in equal ⅓ shares. The parentelic method would look for the nearest lineal ancestor of the decedent of whom any descendant is alive and distribute the property per stirpes to that ancestor's descendants. Here again, the three cousins would take, but the cousin on the maternal side would take half and those on the paternal side ¼ each because parentelic division is on a per stirpes basis.

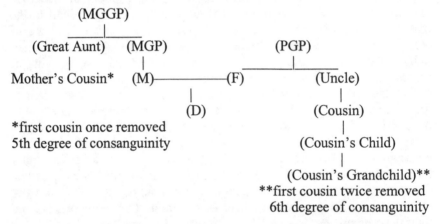

In this illustration, Mother's Cousin (a first cousin once removed, in the fifth degree) would take all under the degree of relationship method. But under the parentelic method, Cousin's Grandchild (a first cousin twice removed) is descended from the closer common ancestor with D and would take all.

### Escheat

Escheat would apply if there is no one alive to take the decedent's property (i.e., the decedent had no heirs) under the applicable intestate succession rules. In that case the estate would pass to the state. In some states, the statute of descent and distribution limits the extent to which ancestors and collaterals of remote degree are considered heirs (e.g., UPC §2-103 limits heirs to grandparents and their descendants). This laughing heir limitation is designed to preclude property passing to someone who is so removed from the decedent as not to be personally affected by the decedent's death. These states claim the property over those heirs who would laugh all the way to the bank if allowed to inherit.

### Summary

Intestate succession varies from state to state. In analyzing questions of intestate distribution:

- First determine the surviving spouse's share. The surviving spouse may receive the entire estate depending on which other relatives survive the decedent and the governing law.

- In most jurisdictions whatever the surviving spouse does not receive will pass to descendants. So, next consider the shares of the decedent's descendants and the representation issue.

- If no descendants survive the decedent, the governing statute may dictate that the entire estate pass to the surviving spouse. If not, or if there is no surviving spouse, usually the decedent's parents are next in line.

- If the decedent also is not survived by either parent (or if the surviving parent or parents do not take the entire estate), next in priority are descendants of the decedent's parents, by representation.

- If the decedent is not survived by a spouse, any descendant, any parent, or any descendant of a parent, the estate will pass to more remote family members, generally either under the parentelic or degree of relationship system.

- If there still are no takers, the estate will escheat. Remember that under the UPC a relative who is not a grandparent of the decedent, or a descendant of a grandparent of the decedent, cannot be an heir.

### Partial Intestacy

A decedent may die partially intestate (with a will that does not effectively dispose of the entire estate). For example, assume that D's will left $1,000 to the Red Cross and the residue of D's estate to a friend, F. D's will would be valid even though it did not provide an alternative devisee in the event F died before D, in which case the Red Cross still would receive $1,000. But the residue of the estate would pass to D's heirs under the jurisdiction's intestate succession statute. The devise to F is said to "lapse," or fail. It would not pass to F's successors. In many states, "antilapse" statutes prevent devises from lapsing, and instead result in the property passing to the deceased devisee's descendants, by representation. But antilapse statutes usually only apply to devises to specified relatives. We will study this in Chapter 8.

Now assume that D's will left half of the estate to friend A, and the other half to friend B, and that A predeceased D but B survived. The old "no residue of the residue" common law rule was that the half left to A would pass to the testator's heirs by intestacy. In the majority of states today the entire estate would go to B. See UPC §2-604(b).

## Negative Wills

Assume that a testator expressly disinherits a family member (let's say a child) with language in the will stating that the child will take nothing under the will or by intestacy. If the testator dies partially intestate the child would be an heir of the testator's estate, in most states despite the will (sometimes referred to as a "negative will" with respect to the child) specifically disinheriting the child. The theory is that the property undisposed of by the will passes outside of its terms to the decedent's heirs as determined solely by the jurisdiction's intestacy statute. UPC §2-101(b) is nearly unique in allowing the testator to override application of the intestate succession statute by use of a negative will. If the testator then dies partially intestate, the part of the estate that otherwise would have passed to the disinherited heir passes as if the heir had disclaimed the intestate share. See page 45 with respect to disclaimers.

## Questions of Definition and Status

Difficult questions may arise whether a person is related to the decedent within the meaning of the jurisdiction's intestate succession statute.

### Spouse

In all states the spouse of a decedent is an intestate taker and most observers equate this with being an heir. Yet relation by affinity (versus consanguinity) is not otherwise adequate, and there are cases in which a spouse does not enjoy true "heir" status. See, e.g., advancements treatment, as discussed at page 41. So the status of a spouse is a tad confused.

Marital status is critical for a variety of reasons in addition to intestate distribution. The most immediate involves a surviving spouse's right to receive an elective share, homestead, and a family allowance. See Chapter 10. Marital status also matters with respect to rights under a will, insurance policy, or retirement plan that designates the decedent's "spouse" as a beneficiary. A former spouse will not be treated as a spouse for intestate succession purposes if the decedent divorced the spouse prior to death, but this treatment is not universal. See Chapter 4 for a discussion of the effect of divorce on provisions for a former spouse in a will, trust agreement, or other dispositive instrument. A similar result may obtain if a marriage is annulled. See, e.g., UPC §2-802(a).

A married couple will not be treated as divorced if they enter into a decree of separation that does not terminate their relationship as husband and wife. Upon the death of one the other will be treated as a surviving spouse. This might change if an order was issued purporting to terminate all marital property rights. UPC §§2-802(a) and (b)(3), and 2-213(d). Moreover, desertion or adultery generally will not affect the marital status of the parties, or otherwise bar the offending party from exercising rights as a surviving spouse on the other's death.

In a minority of jurisdictions persons who live together as husband and wife and hold themselves out to the public as such (a "common law" marriage) will be treated as being married to each other even if they have not participated in a formal marriage ceremony. Finally, a surviving partner presumably will enjoy spouse status in jurisdictions that recognize civil unions or marriages between same sex partners for state law property purposes, including intestate succession.

### Posthumous Heirs

A posthumous child is one who was conceived before, but who is born after, the decedent's death. Usually such a child can take as an heir of the parent, because posthumous children are treated as born at conception if they subsequently are born alive. Depending on state law this may apply only to children of the decedent and not with respect to other representatives. The question of status as a child has taken on a new significance with respect to children of aided conception. For example, a biological child can be conceived after the death of the DNA provider. The issue is whether state law will follow the Uniform Status of Children of Assisted Conception Act or the Uniform Parentage Act and treat those whose birth is engineered (e.g., artificial insemination with the frozen sperm of a long deceased "father") as not the children of the gamete providers. Case law to date appears to favor these children, meaning that these advances have altered traditional estate planning concepts. We return to this concept at page 37 because effective estate plans probably do not want to leave this issue to chance or to litigation.

### Half-Bloods and Step-Siblings

As we will see, most states no longer discriminate against adopteds or nonmarital children, but some still provide different shares for half-bloods (meaning relatives who share only one common ancestor):

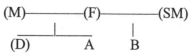

A is a full-blooded sibling of D but B is a sibling of the half-blood. In most jurisdictions (e.g., UPC §2-107) A and B would share equally in D's estate. In a few states half-bloods receive half the share received by a whole-blooded relative, or the whole-blooded relative is favored to the total exclusion of a half-blood. To illustrate, assume that Child A and children B and C are half-bloods, related through a common mother but with different fathers. C's estate is passing.

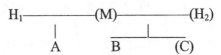

If C's estate were passing to M's descendants, it would go in equal shares to A and B in most states. UPC §§2-103(3) and 2-107. In states that provide the half-blood with only half the share of a whole-blood, C's full sibling B would take ⅔ and half-sibling A would take ⅓ of C's estate. *Beware* the math: some observers would say that B takes ½ and, because A should receive half of that amount, they would say only ¼ goes to A. That leaves the final ¼ undistributed, which is wrong. The easy way to figure this out is to count noses: two shares for B and one share for A makes three shares into which the estate is to be divided, with allocation of two to B and one to A, which will dispose of all of C's property.

With half-bloods, compare *step*-siblings who share no common blood.

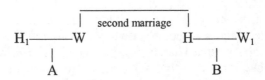

A and B have parents (H and W) who are married, but A and B have no common ancestors between them. Although most states do not discriminate between siblings of the whole and the half-blood, few states would regard step-siblings as related at all. This requires added vigilance in planning for blended families, such as if H and W are raising A and B as if they were biologically related to both H and W.

### Aliens

Most modern statutes have no discrimination against aliens (non-U.S. citizens). See, e.g., UPC §2-111. Although the nature of the special treatment varies, in some states aliens are discriminated against. In some states they may inherit only a certain number of acres of land, in others the limit is on the value of what may be held, and in still others they may inherit an unlimited amount but may not hold it for longer than a specified period. Federal law contains its own brand of discrimination in Internal Revenue Code §2056(d), which denies the estate tax marital deduction if the surviving spouse is not a citizen of the United States unless a special §2056A "qualified domestic trust" is used.

### *Adoption*

Adoption statutes enacted since the 1950s generally treat adopted children as natural born in most jurisdictions. Under the common law adopteds inherited *from* both their natural and adoptive parents, but only inherited *through* their natural parents. Adopteds did not inherit *through* their adoptive parents due to the "stranger to the adoption" rule, which basically assumed that the adoptive parents' decision to adopt could bind those parents but not their relatives, whose estates might later devolve through the adoptive parents. Over the last several decades, this rule has been rejected in most states. In Vermont, for example, a statute implementing it was held to violate the state constitution in *MacCallum v. Seymour*, 686 A.2d 935 (Vt. 1996).

Most jurisdictions now sever the natural parent-child relationship when a child is adopted away (except, as discussed below, in the step-parent adoption context) and the adopting parents take the natural parents' place for all purposes. This makes the adopted child the same as a natural born to the adopting parents for all purposes, even to inherit through the adopting parents from the adopting parents' relatives. See, e.g., UPC §2-114. The following chart compares the effect of adoption on the right to inherit by intestate succession under the common law and under most modern statutes. Notice the last line: don't forget to consider the *child's* death and who may inherit up the family tree.

| **Common Law** | | | **Modern Statutes** | |
|---|---|---|---|---|
| *Natural* | *Adoptive* | | *Natural* | *Adoptive* |
| Yes | Yes | Adopted Inherit From? | No | Yes |
| Yes | No | Adopted Inherit Through? | No | Yes |
| Yes | No | Parents Inherit From/Through? | No | Yes |

In some jurisdictions there are additional statutory provisions, like UPC §2-113, directed at cases such as grandparent (or other relative) adoptions, in which the intent is to limit the beneficiary to only one share of a decedent's estate. For example, imagine that child (C) bears a child (G) and then dies, leaving G to be raised by C's parents, who adopt G. The question is whether G should inherit from the adopting parents (1) as a child, (2) as a grandchild representing C, or (3) as both. Adoption statutes typically would cause G to inherit only as a child of the adopting parents. (This is not universal, however: the generation-skipping transfer tax would continue to consider G to be a grandchild for tax purposes (although a proposed regulation specifies that adoption of G while under age 18 will be respected as it is for state law purposes). Inheritance rights would not be affected, but the tax consequences of that inheritance may not be altered by the adoption.)

Typically a special rule also applies if a natural parent is married to an adopting parent. See, e.g., UPC §2-114(b). Were it not for this rule, adoption by such a step-parent would cut a child off from inheriting from relatives of a deceased natural parent. See, e.g., *Hall v. Vallandingham*, 540 A.2d 1162 (Md. Ct. Spec. App. 1988). Many of the most thoughtful statutes therefore provide that adoption by the spouse of a natural parent (a step-parent) does not cut the child off from either natural parent (or their relatives). These statutes allow the child to "triple-dip," in the sense that the child could inherit from and through both natural parents and the adopting step-parent as well.

UPC §2-114 follows this approach of allowing a child adopted by a step-parent to inherit from and through both natural parents and the adopting parent. With respect to the *converse* situation, however, the parent/child relationship is terminated with respect to the natural parent who is not married to the adopting parent. This precludes that natural parent, and his or her relatives, from inheriting from or through the child. In addition, the UPC more broadly breaks the natural parent connection for inheriting from or through the child unless the natural parent has openly treated the child as his or her own and has not refused to support the child.

To illustrate this, imagine that Father and Mother, natural parents of Child, divorce. Mother remarries and her new husband, H, adopts Child. Under most state adoption laws, such an adoption effectively terminates the parent/child relationship between Father and Child and could only occur if Child is an adult who consents to the adoption, Father already is deceased, or Father either consents to the adoption or has his parental rights terminated (such as for refusal to pay child support). Under state law Child may remain a child of Father for purposes of inheriting from or through Father, but whether Father may inherit from or through Child may depend on Father's on going treatment of Child. Under the UPC, Child—and Child's descendants—may inherit from and through Father, but neither Father nor his relatives may inherit from or through Child.

Application of these rules can yield inappropriate and inequitable results if an adoption followed the death of a natural parent. For example, after Father and Mother died in an automobile accident Mother's sibling adopted Child. The unfortunate reality is that, in many states (and under UPC §2-114(b)), this will cut off the child from Father's family and they from the child, which probably is an unintended result and thoroughly inappropriate. Further, had the adoption been by someone not related to Mother, in most states (including those that have adopted the UPC) the child would be cut off from *both* natural lines and they from the child.

Most of the adoption issues discussed above address inheritance involving adopteds in the intestacy context. Absent a provision to the contrary, those rules also may determine whether a person qualifies as a member of a class to whom a gift is made under a will, trust agreement, or other dispositive instrument. For example, if a will gives $10,000 to each of the testator's nieces and nephews, will an adopted child of a sibling of the testator take? The answer would be "no" under the old "stranger to the adoption" rule, while under the law of many states and the UPC the answer would be "yes." UPC §2-705(a). The question is whether state law applies to more than just the probate code or to more than just intestate distribution.

## Virtual Adoption

Virtual (or equitable) adoption is a doctrine under which someone who has not been formally adopted may be treated for inheritance purposes as having been adopted. As an equitable doctrine it is designed to protect a child against the consequences of reliance on an adoption that was not (properly) performed. The concept is that a child should not be punished just because a purported parent never formally or properly accomplished the purported adoption. Georgia pioneered the concept and under Georgia case law a person is virtually adopted despite there having been no formal adoption if (1) there was an agreement for adoption between the person's natural and adopting parents, (2) the natural parents gave up custody, (3) the child lived with the adopting parents, and (4) the adopting parents treated the child as a natural child.

The concept is not universally recognized and it may not be totally effective even where it is. For example, in *O'Neal v. Wilkes*, 439 S.E.2d 490 (Ga. 1994), the child was not acknowledged by her natural father, her mother died, and she was placed by another family member with a couple who raised her as their natural child. When the putative adoptive father died intestate the child claimed an intestate share as an equitably adopted child. The court denied virtual adoption because no one with authority to consent to the adoption did so. The dissent argued that this turns equity and the object of the virtual adoption rule on their head, because it certainly was not the child's fault that this authorization never existed.

Reminding us that status questions can apply to inheritance up or down the family tree, *Estate of Riggs*, 440 N.Y.S.2d 450 (1981), properly held that equitable adoption does not apply to let the alleged adopting parents or their relatives inherit from or through a deceased "virtually adopted" child. *Riggs* makes it clear that virtual adoption is a one-way street: the child may rely on what should have been done but the parents and those claiming through them cannot. Whether a virtually adopted child may inherit *through* the putative parent is an unresolved question because cases go both ways.

## Common Adoption Issues

Two major issues involving wills and trust agreements exist under most adoption statutes. One is whether adopteds are treated as natural born under documents that were in existence or in effect before a statute treating adopteds as natural born was enacted (e.g., a testator died before enactment, with a will that created a trust as to which it is necessary to determine if an adopted descendant is a beneficiary of the trust). Many statutes did not provide for retroactive application to pre-existing documents and typically the law in effect when a trust becomes irrevocable (or at a decedent's death) will govern for all purposes in the future construction and interpretation of the trust (or that decedent's will). Thus, in many instances the old stranger to the adoption rule would apply. Some statutes, however, have been amended to allow full retroactivity.

In addition, many statutes appear on their face to apply only to intestate distribution, leaving open the second question of their effect on a class gift (such as to "grandchildren" or "nieces and nephews") made in a will or inter vivos trust. UPC §2-705 covers all three situations, but many statutes are silent regarding applications other than under intestacy. The predictable result is that courts will search for a way to apply the intestacy adoption statute in cases involving dispositive instruments, because the common law stranger to the adoption rule is not favored even without a statute. Unfortunately, the failure of such a statute to address such circumstances can be seen as an indication that the state legislature did not so intend, which makes it difficult for courts to decide these cases.

### *Nonmarital Children*

Nonmarital (also known as out of wedlock, illegitimate, or bastard) children were filius nullius (the "child of nobody") at common law: they simply did not exist and had no inheritance rights or other status under the law. The scope of the issue of how nonmarital children are treated should not be underestimated in America today. In recent years, of total births, over thirty percent are nonmarital and, of the total American population under the age of 18, more than a quarter are nonmarital. Furthermore, these issues cut across all racial and economic lines.

The typical intestacy statute today allows a nonmarital child to inherit from its mother and vice versa. Although nonmaritals also may inherit *through* their mother (and vice versa) in most states, in a few states they may not. *Trimble v. Gordon*, 430 U.S. 762 (1977), held unconstitutional under the Equal Protection Clause of the Fourteenth Amendment an Illinois statute prohibiting a nonmarital child from inheriting from her father who died intestate and whose paternity had been established in a paternity suit during the father's life. The Court held that only legitimate state interests may be effected by statutes that discriminate against the rights of nonmarital children.

For example, states may address concerns regarding the orderly administration of estates and subsequent proof of title by a nonmarital child who claims parentage after the purported parent no longer is alive and able to defend against the charge. Thus, a year after its decision in *Trimble*, the Supreme Court held valid a New York statute that precluded a nonmarital child from inheriting from an intestate father unless the father had married the mother or his paternity had been established in a proceeding during his life. *Lalli v. Lalli*, 439 U.S. 259 (1978). States may treat nonmarital children differently than marital children, if done in a rational way to further a legitimate state interest, such as efficient administration of estates and protecting against unfounded paternity claims.

Thus, the focus of statutes dealing with the rights of nonmarital children is how paternity is established. Statutes usually include any of the following as acceptable means: (1) litigation resulting in a judicial determination of paternity; (2) subsequent marriage by a man to the child's mother—sometimes with the additional requisite of acknowledgement of the child or failure to reject the child (notice that in many states there is a conclusive presumption that a man is the child's father if he is married to the mother when the child is born, even if it can be proved that he is not); (3) simple acknowledgement, although what constitutes an adequate acknowledgement that the child is the person's child will vary from state to state; and (4) a determination of paternity made after the father's death during the probate administration of his estate, such as by DNA evidence.

Remember that these issues can work in reverse. UPC §2-114(c) addresses the question of a parent inheriting from a nonmarital child, with only proof of abandonment (i.e., failure to openly treat the child as his or her own or refusal to support the child) serving to preclude the parent from benefiting from the child's death.

### *Children of the New Biology*

*Gillett-Netting v. Commissioner of Social Security*, 231 F. Supp.2d 961 (D. Ariz. 2002), rev'd, 371 F.3d 593 (9th Cir. 2004), *Woodward v. Commissioner of Social Security*, 760 N.E.2d 257 (Mass. 2002), and *In re Estate of Kolacy*, 753 A.2d 1257 (N.J. Super. 2000), are illustrative of cases that will arise with increasing frequency because of the growing use of artificial insemination, embryo and gamete transplants, and surrogate motherhood, often without benefit of formal adoption, filiation, or (in some cases) knowledge or a record of what has occurred. Such cases raise the question whether a child conceived after the death of a sperm donor can inherit as an heir of the donor, and the difficulties such a result could pose to the timely administration and distribution of the donor's estate. The Uniform Status of Children of Assisted Conception Act and the newer Uniform Parentage Act provide that the donor in this kind of situation will not be treated as the parent of a child conceived after the donor's death, but all three cases held to the contrary.

Some jurisdictions have adopted statutes under which an artificially conceived birth is treated as natural, and the husband of the mother is treated as the natural father, even if there is positive proof that his paternity is a biological impossibility. Consider that these cases, which have traditionally involved deceased sperm donors, can work in biological reverse, with the provider of eggs being the alleged mother notwithstanding that another woman was the birth mother. With respect to such surrogate motherhood, the wife of the natural father may not be regarded as the mother without a formal adoption, and the law must wrestle with the historical notion that motherhood is the easy side of most questions of status (because, at least in "the old days," the natural mother typically could prove the parent-child relationship). Historically it was the natural father that was uncertain of proof, and that issue has not been made any easier in cases of assisted conception involving implants or transplants of embryos. But today the risk of multiple "mothers" exists and raises questions of status that historically were reserved for fathers.

## Limitations on Inheritance

### *Homicide*

Homicide is a pervasive bar to inheritance rights, whether by intestate succession, under a will, or by any other dispositive instrument. Based on the equitable maxim that "no one may profit by a wrong committed," the majority of jurisdictions have statutes addressing the subject. The more difficult cases arise in states in which there is no governing statute. For example, *In re Estate of Mahoney*, 220 A.2d 475 (Vt. 1966), presented the question of what to do about a wife who killed her husband (who died intestate). She was convicted of manslaughter and was entitled to his entire estate under Vermont's intestate succession statute. In holding that legal title to estate assets descend to the wife by intestacy, the court also declared that she received those assets in constructive trust for the decedent's other heirs if the killing was intentional. See Chapter 11. The *Mahoney* court rejected the argument that the slayer should take without restriction because disqualification would be an improper added form of punishment. It also eschewed treating her as having predeceased the victim.

The need to wrestle with such questions is addressed by most state statutes, which prohibit most killers from inheriting. But there is great disparity among state law approaches, and there are many glitches in these state statutes. For example, if A kills D and is barred from sharing in D's estate, the issue is who should receive the part of D's estate that A would have received (either as an heir of D if D died intestate, or as a devisee if D died with a will that devised property to A). There are at least three approaches that states take to this issue. First, some statutes (e.g., UPC §2-803) provide that the slayer's share passes as if the slayer had disclaimed it. Second, in some states the slayer's share passes as if the slayer predeceased the victim. As illustrated below, that approach will not always yield the same result as the disclaimer alternative. Third, some statutes provide that property that would have gone to the slayer passes to the victim's other heirs.

Difficult policy questions also arise if, for example, P leaves property to C if living, otherwise to C's descendants who survive P, and C kills P; should C's descendants profit from the wrong committed by C, or should they also be punished along with C? To illustrate a more refined application of the same essential question, assume a slayer statute provides for the decedent's property that would have passed to the slayer to go instead to the decedent's other heirs. How would such a statute be applied in the following case, if B murdered P and P's will left P's estate to B?

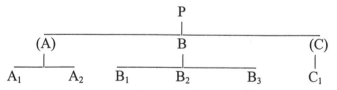

B cannot take P's estate, so P's heirs will receive all of it, meaning $A_1$, $A_2$, $B_1$, $B_2$, $B_3$, and $C_1$. The issue here is whether a per stirpes or per capita distribution is applicable and, if the latter, whether B is treated as predeceased for purposes of determining the size of the shares to be distributed or only for purposes of preventing B from taking anything. If a per capita distribution is applicable and B is treated as actually having predeceased P, then $B_1$, $B_2$, and $B_3$, as well as $A_1$, $A_2$, and $C_1$, each would receive $1/6$ of P's estate. If instead B is treated as having predeceased P only for purposes of preventing B from taking, then $B_1$, $B_2$, and $B_3$ share just $1/3$ of the $1/3$ intestate share B would have received, meaning equal shares of $1/9$ each.

To avoid this kind of question, an enlightened statute would specify that B is not treated as predeceased for purposes of distributing P's estate among P's heirs but, rather, as having disclaimed the intestate share to which B otherwise would be entitled. See UPC §2-803. Here B cannot take the entire estate so we're only dealing with what B would take as an heir of P, and $B_1$, $B_2$, and $B_3$ each would receive $^1/_9$, $A_1$ and $A_2$ each would receive $^1/_6$, and $C_1$ would receive ⅓ under either a per stirpes or a per capita approach. Under a per capita at each generation system, the only difference would be that $A_1$, $A_2$, and $C_1$ each would receive ⅓ of the ⅔ that would not go to B, meaning they would each receive equal shares of $^2/_9$. Meanwhile, $B_1$, $B_2$, and $B_3$ share the ⅓ B would have received, meaning $^1/_9$ to each of them.

In the above illustration, what would happen if P's will left ⅓ of P's estate to B (or if P died intestate)? If the governing statute provides that the share the slayer would have received passes by intestacy as if the slayer had predeceased the victim, now the question is whether B's descendants share the portion B would have received with $A_1$, $A_2$, and $C_1$, or would $A_1$, $A_2$, and $C_1$ take it all. *Misenheimer v. Misenheimer*, 325 S.E.2d 195 (N.C. 1985), held the descendants of B took all of B's bequest. In doing so, the court stated: "While it may be true that 'the gods visit the sins of the fathers upon the innocent children,'. . . this Court will not do so." These are curiously difficult questions for a statute to leave for court interpretation, but they are not unique. Let's consider a few other issues.

Typically, only felonious and intentional killings trigger application of a slayer statute. Thus, a successful insanity defense will prevent operation of most statutory bars, as may conviction of an offense that does not establish intent (such as involuntary homicide). Moreover, many statutes require a conviction before the slayer must forfeit an inheritance, meaning that the slayer's death before adjudication of guilt may prevent operation of the bar. This most often arises in a murder-suicide situation. If there is no conviction, some more enlightened statutes (e.g., UPC §2-803(g)) permit the probate court to adjudicate the question of guilt as if it was a criminal proceeding and some statutes also permit determination of "guilt" in this case (or if the slayer was found not guilty in a criminal case) by applying a lower threshold than beyond a reasonable doubt.

Yet another set of issues arise because the purpose of slayer statutes is to prevent a slayer from profiting from the crime, rather than to impose an additional punishment in the form of a forfeiture. Thus, no statute should divest the slayer's own property interests. For example, assume that the slayer is a remainder beneficiary following a life estate in the victim. One way to address the slayer bar issue is for the life estate to be sequestered (paid to the victim's estate or beneficiaries), but to allow the slayer to take the remainder when the victim's life expectancy would have expired, if the slayer still is living. Alternatively, the discounted present value of the life estate could be computed and paid to the victim's estate or beneficiaries (it would be "commuted") with the remaining property (the value of the remainder) to belong to the slayer immediately.

Similarly, assume that the slayer was a joint tenant with the victim, with the right of survivorship. The Restatement of Restitution §188(b) (Restatement (Third) of Restitution and Unjust Enrichment §45) position is that the slayer is deemed to have died first (at the end of the slayer's life expectancy); the slayer therefore is entitled to receive only half of the income for the balance of the slayer's natural life. UPC §2-803(c)(2) instead treats the killing as a severance of the property and a transformation of the interests of the decedent and killer into tenancies in common. According to *Estate of Garland*, 928 P.2d 928 (Mont. 1996), the estate's tenancy in common interest in the property would be greater than fifty percent if the victim's estate could prove the victim made more than half of the contributions towards acquisition of the property. Under both approaches, the policy result is that improvement of the slayer's position is precluded by statute, but the slayer is not punished by a relinquishment of property already owned by the slayer.

Some slayer statutes also specifically bar a slayer who is the designated beneficiary from receiving the proceeds of an insurance policy on the victim's life, and insurance contracts typically are more comprehensive than state law, precluding any beneficiary from benefiting if that person caused the insured loss in any way. But other forms of nonprobate property (consider deferred compensation with a beneficiary designation) may not be addressed by state law *or* a provision in the governing document.

### Disqualification for Other Misconduct

Although relatively rare, in limited circumstances other than homicide a person who engages in wrongful conduct will be precluded from receiving a share of a decedent's estate. Marital misconduct (adultery or desertion) typically will *not* bar inheritance. But refusal to support or to openly acknowledge a child may preclude a parent from inheriting from the child. See, e.g., UPC §2-114(c). This too is not common outside the UPC states.

### Advancements

If P gives child C $10,000, and P then dies intestate, the question is whether the $10,000 gift counts against C's intestate share of P's estate. Known as the concept of advancements, the question generally applies only to *fully* intestate estates. UPC §2-109 applies the concept to partially intestate estates as well, but the logic behind inapplicability to a testate estate is a presumption that a testator would state any intent regarding the effect of prior transfers on dispositions under a subsequently executed will. Similarly, we presume that the testator was aware of the provisions in an existing will when a gift was made, and determined to make the gift anyway. The concept of ademption by satisfaction under a will may serve the same purpose for a testate estate as advancement treatment in an intestate estate, as we will see in Chapter 9.

Historically, advancement treatment also was applicable only for transfers to children, based on an assumption that an intestate decedent would want to treat all children equally. That assumption was not thought to apply in other situations. Nevertheless, many advancement statutes now apply to all descendants, or even to all heirs, but frequently *not* to a spouse (UPC §2-109 is unusual in that it *does* apply to a spouse). Notice that this is an illustration of the occasional circumstance in which the law sometimes creates ambiguity regarding whether a spouse is an "heir" or simply enjoys a special status that is not quite the same. This could be important in an express gift "to A if living, otherwise to A's heirs," the question being whether A's surviving spouse would share in that alternative gift.

Also at issue for advancements purposes is whether descendants of a donee who received an inter vivos gift and then predeceased the decedent are charged with those advancements and, conversely, whether an ancestor should be charged with advancements made to the ancestor's descendants. For example, assume that P made an advancement to P's child C, who predeceased P leaving one child, GC, surviving. Should GC's entitlement as C's representative be reduced by the advancement to C? Conversely, if P gave the advance to GC but C survived to take, would C's share be adjusted because of the gift to GC? The UPC does not charge advancements down to representatives of an advanced party unless the decedent indicated an intent to do so (§2-109(c)) and fails to even consider charging advancements up to ancestors of recipients. Most statutes are silent on both questions.

Lifetime gifts to children were presumed to be advancements at common law. Statutes in most states have reversed this presumption and now require some proof of intent to treat a gift as an advancement. This reveals that the doctrine of advancements is not favored, especially with respect to small amounts (think of the administrative difficulties of proving the amounts of gifts made by a parent to several children over a lifetime and who died intestate at, say, age 80). To prove intent to advance usually requires a contemporaneous written declaration by the decedent or an acknowledgement by the donee that the transfer counts against the donee's ultimate distributive share of the transferor's estate. See UPC §2-109. The declaration must be contemporaneous with the transfer if (as under the UPC) the intent that the gift constitute an advancement must exist at the time of the transfer. A subsequent change of heart cannot convert an outright gift into an advancement, although an intent to advance can later be abandoned, making the transfer a gift that will not be charged against the donee's intestate share. Which is to say, a donor can become more generous in the future, but not more parsimonious. Therefore, a donor who after the fact wants to convert an outright gift into an advancement must do so by executing a will that takes the gift into account.

The mechanism by which advancements are charged against the recipient's ultimate distributive share is known as "hotchpot." To illustrate, assume that: (1) Decedent's probate estate is $100x; (2) inter vivos advancements (all declared in contemporaneous writings by Decedent) included an outright transfer of $40x to Child A, placement of $60x in joint tenancy with Child B, and an insurance beneficiary designation of Child C that will pay proceeds of $80x; and (3) Child D received nothing. Computation of any advancement is at the fair market value when the transfer was made, computed without interest. Note the unfairness in that approach: the recipient receives (but is not charged in the hotchpot process for) the use of the money from the time of the gift to the decedent's death, along with any income earned and appreciation generated. So, in this illustration, if all the recipients of lifetime transfers participate in hotchpot (which we will see they likely will not all do in this case), each child's share of the probate estate would be determined as follows:

| Probate estate at death | | $100x |
|---|---|---|
| Add advancements: | | |
| to Child A | | $40x |
| to Child B | | $60x |
| to Child C | | $80x |
| | Total | $280x |

divided by four would give each child $70x, which would be reduced by their respective advancements.

One issue we've begged here is whether advancement applies to insurance. If it does, would we count the insurance as an advancement at the value of the policy at the time of the beneficiary designation, or at the higher face amount of the proceeds payable at death? For now, let's assume state law is clear and that the latter is the case. Another issue we're glossing over is whether the joint tenancy with B should count as a gift of only half the value of the property. For now let's assume not. On the basis of these two assumptions, C cannot benefit from P's probate estate (because C already received $80x, which is more than C's $70x share under hotchpot) so C probably will "opt out" of hotchpot—no one can be forced to participate. With C and C's advancement out of the picture, the hotchpot would be recomputed at only $200x, and it would be divided by three to give each of the other three children $66,666x. To reflect amounts that A and B already received, the distribution of P's probate estate then would be made as follows:

Child A receives $66.66x  − $40x =     $26.66x
Child B receives $66.66x  − $60x =      $6.66x
Child D receives $66.66x  −  $0x =     $66.66x
                Total distributions =     $99.98x

If C's insurance is not charged as an advancement at all, the hotchpot would be:

Probate estate at death          $100x
Add advancements:
   to Child A                      $40x
   to Child B                      $60x
              Total    $200x

divided by four, would give each child $50x. Now B likely would opt out because B's $60x advancement is greater than the $50x B would receive under hotchpot, leaving:

Probate estate at death          $100x
Add advancements:
   to Child A                      $40x
              Total    $140x

$140x divided by 3  = $46.66x each

Thus, A would receive $6.66x and both C and D would receive $46.66x, for a total of $99.98x.

Make note of the fact that the hotchpot calculation can be a useful technique in other affirmative drafting situations. This is learning you should not compartmentalize solely under advancements and intestate succession.

### *Release and Assignment*

The doctrines of release and assignment relate to the concept of advancements. Assume that single parent P has two living children, A and B, who are *potential* heirs of P. Although A and B have no property rights in P's assets yet, they each are said to have an "expectancy" with respect to P's assets in that, if P dies intestate, A and B may share in P's estate.

A release is an agreement between a potential heir and the property owner, sometimes called a "liquidated" or "negotiated" advancement. In effect, A could ask for early distribution of A's share of P's estate in exchange for a release of A's expectancy. If A dies after the release and before P, and P is survived by children of A, those grandchildren of P will be barred by A's release so that B will take the entire estate. An exception to this general rule may apply, however, if B also predeceases P, in which case some jurisdictions will allow A's children to share in P's estate.

An assignment is the transfer for consideration of an expectancy by a potential heir, in this case to a third party. Assignment is not common in the United States because the assignee receives only what the assignor is entitled to receive, which is zero if the assignor is disinherited by or predeceases the decedent. Because a prospective assignee of an expectancy has no way to protect the "right" to benefit from the expectancy when the prospective decedent dies, an assignee generally will not be willing to pay much for the assignment (unless the prospective decedent becomes involved in the transaction and contracts or otherwise commits not to take any action that would defeat the assignee's expectancy). Furthermore, although a release usually will bind descendants of the releasing potential heir, an assignment will not. It is easy to find fault with the distinction, but it is said to be based on the fact that a release is an agreement with the decedent (a "negotiated" disinheritance) while an assignment is a contract with a third party to which neither the decedent nor the assignor's representatives were parties.

As a general rule, both releases and assignments are honored only if supported by full and adequate consideration, meaning that what the beneficiary receives is a fair reflection of what he or she would receive at the decedent's death. If that consideration is found to be inadequate most cases will then regard it as an advancement.

### Disclaimers

A disclaimer, sometimes called a renunciation, is a refusal to accept an inheritance or other property interest. Disclaimers of intestate property were not recognized at common law, but statutes typically now permit them. So, for example, assume that P is not married and has one child, C, who also has one child, GC. If C disclaimed any inheritance, under the typical state law (e.g., UPC §2-1106(a)(3)(A), which also is the free standing Uniform Disclaimer of Property Interests Act—UDPIA) the disclaimed interest would pass as if C predeceased P. Thus, if P died intestate, the estate would descend to GC, as C's representative. If P died testate any will provision directing that any property disclaimed by C should go to an alternate taker would control. But the devise to C would pass under the terms of P's will as if C had predeceased P if P died testate and the will did not address the possibility of a disclaimer. Thus, a disclaimer by C again would result in GC receiving the property if P's will or state law provided that the devise to C would go to GC if C died before P (as usually would be the case).

Typically most people disclaim either for federal tax reasons or to preclude their creditors from reaching the disclaimed property. In the example above, the disclaimer is not regarded as a gift by C to GC if it is "qualified" under the rules of Internal Revenue Code §2518. Rather, the property disclaimed would be treated for tax purposes as having passed directly from P to GC, meaning that C would have no adverse gift tax consequences (and a generation-skipping transfer tax might be imposed).

Similarly, disclaimers generally are effective to pre-empt most creditors of the disclaimant from reaching the disclaimed property. *Drye v. United States,* 528 U.S. 49 (1999), held that disclaimer did *not* preclude attachment of a federal tax lien, however. And courts differ on whether disclaimer pre-empts a state's claim for reimbursement of a disclaimant's nursing home expenses paid by Medicaid. The court in *Troy v. Hart,* 697 A.2d 113 (Md. App. 1997), held that it is "ludicrous, if not repugnant, to public policy" for a Medicaid recipient to be able to disclaim an inheritance that would allow the disclaimant to become financially self-sufficient. By contrast, *In re Estate of Kirk,* 591 N.W.2d 630 (Iowa 1999), held that public policy did not allow the state to reach disclaimed assets to satisfy its claim for reimbursement of Medicaid-paid nursing home expenses. But aside from these special cases, in the main a disclaimant can protect property from creditor claims by disclaimer.

Under Internal Revenue Code §2518 there are a number of technical requirements that must be met for the disclaimer to be qualified for tax purposes. The most important aspect of making a qualified disclaimer is being timely, usually meaning that the disclaimer must be made within nine months of the transfer by which the disclaimant becomes entitled to the property. (An exception allows a minor nine months after reaching age 21, if later.) In addition, for the disclaimer to be qualified the disclaimant cannot accept any benefits from the disclaimed property prior to making the disclaimer. Thus, to some extent the nine month period within which to decide whether to disclaim is misleading, particularly for nonprobate property that passes directly to the recipient as a result of the decedent's death (such as life insurance, retirement plan interests, and joint tenancies with the right of survivorship).

In UPC states that have not amended their rules to reflect the UDPIA also beware the fact that the UPC §2-801(b) nine month timing requirement for disclaimers differs from the federal Internal Revenue Code requirement. Unlike the UDPIA, which imposes no time limit, the UPC nine month period is measured from vesting or the event determining the taker, whereas federal law measures it from the transfer that created the interest (even though it may not be clear who will take the property until many years later when all elements requisite to vesting occur). To illustrate the difference, consider an agreement for a trust created in Year 1, which provided "to A for life, then to B, if B survives

A, otherwise to C." If B died in Year 20, survived by A and C, the UPC would allow C nine months from the date of B's death in Year 20 to disclaim. A disclaimer by C generally would not be qualified under the Internal Revenue Code unless it were made within nine months after creation of the trust in Year 1. A disclaimer under the UDPIA would have no time restriction.

Both UPC §2-801(d) and newer §2-1106(b) provide that only the "disclaimed interest" passes as if the disclaimant had predeceased the decedent. Most statutes provide for the decedent's entire estate to pass under that presumption. The rationale for this carefully drafted UPC modification is to be certain that a disclaimer under the UPC per capita system of representation does not alter the size of other shares of the estate. For example, assume A disclaims in the following hypothetical:

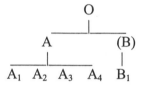

The UPC dictates that A's half interest would pass to A's descendants as if A predeceased O, and *not* that the entire estate would pass as if A (as well as B) predeceased (in which case $B_1$ would receive $^1/_5$ rather than $^1/_2$ of the estate, and A would be able to increase the share of A's descendants from $^1/_2$ to $^4/_5$).

The 1990 version of UPC §2-801(a) also makes clear what the prior UPC and many state statutes do not, that a disclaimer is permissible by a personal representative on behalf of a deceased beneficiary. This is important because often the decision to disclaim occurs when the taker dies quickly after the decedent whose estate is passing and an analysis of the tax consequences reveals that a disclaimer will reduce taxes. Although it is clear that the federal estate tax liability may be reduced in such a manner, state law in many jurisdictions remains unresolved as to whether other creditors may be disfranchised by disclaimers made by personal representatives for deceased beneficiaries. For example, *In re Estate of Heater*, 640 N.E.2d 654 (Ill. App. Ct. 1994), disallowed such a disclaimer because a personal representative for the disclaimant must act for the benefit of all parties interested in the disclaimant's estate, including creditors.

### Survivorship

The UPC imposes a 120 hour survivorship condition on the ability of an heir to inherit from an intestate decedent (and on the ability of a devisee under a will or a beneficiary under another dispositive instrument to take, if the will or other instrument does not address the survivorship issue). Thus, under the UPC, C will not share in P's estate if P dies intestate, survived by C, who dies within 120 hours after P's death. But what if P and C in this example owned Blackacre as joint tenants with the right of survivorship, and they died within 120 hours of each other? If they died "simultaneously" (meaning that there was insufficient evidence to determine who died first), the result under the Uniform Simultaneous Death Act would be to treat each as having predeceased the other as to half of the property. Thus, the property would pass as if it had been owned by them as equal tenants in common, with each treated as having survived the other. The original Uniform Simultaneous Death Act would not apply if one clearly died after the other, but within 120 hours. Thus, the survivor would take the entire property, and it would then pass to the survivor's heirs (if the survivor died intestate) or devisees (if the survivor died testate). By contrast, under the most current UPC §2-702 120 hour survivorship rule the same result would be reached as if they died simultaneously, even if one clearly died after (but within 120 hours of) the death of the other. And the most recent version of the Uniform Simultaneous Death Act also would produce that result (because it is the free standing version of the newest UPC rules).

CHAPTER 3

# WILL EXECUTION FORMALITIES
# AND CONTEST

This Chapter addresses will validity issues: whether execution complied with required formalities, and whether the will is invalid due to lack of capacity, undue influence, fraud, duress, or mistake. Also covered are several related topics: the doctrines of (1) integration (multiple pages constitute the decedent's will, even if only the last of them was executed); (2) incorporation by reference (documents outside the will but referred to in it may be treated as part of the will even though they were not executed as a will); (3) independent legal significance (matters extraneous to the will are considered in interpreting the will because they have significance independent from the testator's testamentary wishes); and (4) republication by codicil (an earlier revoked or invalid will or codicil is revived or made valid for the first time by execution of an amendment to the will).

## Testamentary Capacity

Historically several classes of persons lacked capacity to execute wills. In some jurisdictions married women, aliens, and certain convicted criminals were denied the opportunity to convey property by will. Today, anyone who is of the requisite age and mentality may execute a will. Thus, lack of testamentary capacity can be of two types: the testator is too young or lacks mental capacity. Most capacity issues involve the latter.

The former is easy. A minimum age to execute a will is a statutory requisite in all states. The required minimum age typically is 18, but variations exist. For example, the minimum age requirement is waived in some states for married testators.

On the other hand, the test of mental capacity is much more subjective. The requisite mentality usually is articulated as something like "of sound mind." Usually this is presumed to exist if the will properly was executed and attested by witnesses.

Attestation provisions usually say something like "we the witnesses whose signatures are affixed below swear that we saw X sign the will and believed X to be over the age of * and of sound mind and memory. . . ." With this affirmation the testator is regarded as competent until proven otherwise. On this score, most statutes do not address the mentality necessary to meet the statutory requisite; this is determined by case law. Generally, courts hold that being of sound mind means that the testator had the ability to understand: (1) the nature and extent of the testator's property; (2) the natural objects of the testator's bounty (i.e., those persons—usually family members—who the testator "ought" to have in mind when deciding to whom to leave property); (3) the disposition being made; and (4) how these three interact with each other.

It is not necessary that the testator *actually* understood these things; it only is necessary that the testator had the *capacity* (i.e., the ability) to understand them. Nor does the capacity to understand the disposition the testator is making require an appreciation of all the technical aspects of the plan. The testator only needs to be able to comprehend the general pattern of the dispositive provisions. Boilerplate, technical tax jargon, drafting formalities, and such need not be within the ken of the average individual.

In addition, a testator can know and understand the natural objects of the testator's bounty without providing for them. The key is whether the testator knew that any unnatural dispositive provisions were out of the ordinary (such as leaving the estate to a friend or caretaker, instead of to children, or leaving the entire estate to one child to the exclusion of others). On the other hand, that the dispositive provisions are "normal" will not prove capacity, nor is capacity belied by an unjust or unnatural disposition. A person with capacity may make as eccentric, injudicious, and unjust a will as caprice, frivolity, or revenge may dictate. Eccentricities, peculiarities, exaggerated personality traits, religious beliefs, or beliefs in the supernatural typically will not invalidate a will on grounds of insanity.

Finally, the testator need not know with any precision the property the testator owns. The testator needs only the ability to understand the kinds and values of property owned. Thus, it may be that a marginally competent testator would have the requisite mental capacity to dispose of a small or simple estate, but lack the capacity to dispose of a large or complex one.

Although cases sometimes refer to a testator's ability to perform other tasks as indicative of testamentary capacity, it is not determinative whether a testator could contract, transact normal business, or manage the normal affairs of living. Indeed, a greater level of capacity generally is required to enter into a contract or to conduct normal business affairs than to execute a will. Curiously, in some jurisdictions (but not under the new Uniform Trust Code, if the trust is revocable; see UTC §601), the capacity to enter into a trust relationship (which could transfer all of a person's property) is higher than to execute a will. Thus, a marginal case may create problems if both a will and a trust are involved. Also curious is that being declared incompetent or having a guardian or conservator appointed will not prove incapacity to execute a will, especially if a guardian or conservator was appointed to ease the burdens of property administration for a testator who was late in life, ill, or just did not want to be bothered.

Capacity is tested at the moment of execution; losing it thereafter, or lacking it before execution, will not affect validity. Incapacity may be fleeting; the impairment may be temporary (a chronic alcoholic may execute a valid will while sober) or testators with serious mental impairments may enjoy a "lucid interval." As a consequence, the most important testimony truly is from witnesses to the execution.

### Lack of Mental Capacity

Two forms of mental incapacity can affect the validity of a will: (1) Deficient capability, meaning that the testator simply was unable to understand the four items just discussed that are required for a proper execution. In those cases the entire will is invalid. (2) Derangement, which may be paranoia, general dementia, or a delusion, each of which generally affects the validity of only those portions of the will that are the product of the derangement. Either results in a lack of capacity. A person lacks testamentary capacity if there is either derangement that affects any part of the will or deficient capability, or both.

Evidence of mental derangement also may show that the testator had deficient capability. For example, *In re Hargrove's Will*, 28 N.Y.S.2d 571 (1941), involved a decedent who allegedly suffered from an insane delusion that two children born to his wife during their marriage were not his, and that he therefore had deficient capability because he was not able to know the natural objects of his bounty. And *In re Strittmater*, 53 A.2d 205 (N.J. 1947), illustrates that derangement cases are unpredictable. The testator left her entire estate to the National Women's Party, for which she worked as a volunteer and of which she was a member. In holding the will invalid, the court noted that the decedent's doctor diagnosed her as suffering from paranoia and considered, among other things, that the decedent wrote that her "father was a corrupt, vicious, and unintelligent savage, a typical specimen of the majority of his sex." According to the court, the evidence showed "incontrovertably her morbid aversion to men," and that "[s]he regarded men as a class with an insane hatred." For all we know, the decedent in *Strittmater* may have been raped, sexually abused by her father, or subjected to discrimination that would inform her judgment. Although some might regard the testator's reaction to be too severe, the degree of her response to factors that we all understand is not relevant. Quaere whether this will would fail today, or would it have failed when *Strittmater* was decided in 1947 if the facts were a man leaving property to an all-male group, a racial activist to the NAACP, or a white supremacist to the Ku Klux Klan.

### Insane Delusions

An insane delusion is a belief to which the testator adhered without knowledge or evidence that a sane person would believe. An *insane* delusion must affect the disposition(s) under the will, *and* the conclusion(s) the testator drew from the delusion must be such that no rational person would draw. Some states also require that the falsity of the testator's conclusions were pointed out and the testator continued to believe them nevertheless. Thus, it is not an insane delusion if the testator's belief is based on evidence a rational person could believe, from which a rational person might draw the same conclusion.

*In re Honigman,* 168 N.E.2d 676 (N.Y. 1960), illustrates that the equities of a particular case may influence the application of these rules. The decedent substantially disinherited his wife of many years, notwithstanding that she had participated in the business from which the decedent's wealth was accumulated. He did so because he believed that she was philandering. Her challenge of the will for lack of mentality was successful, despite evidence that the decedent allegedly hid outside his home and saw the other man enter the home while his wife was inside. If the evidence was believable, then the conclusions he drew might be different or more paranoid than those that might be drawn by others. The decedent's conclusions, however, would not have been based on a lack of evidence and probably would not have been such that no rational person could draw. So, if the evidence was believable, a finding of insane delusion sufficient to invalidate the will probably would have been improper. Trial was to a jury, however, and the appellate court viewed their verdict as demonstrating that the jury simply did not believe the evidence.

A person may have basic mental capacity but still lack the mentality to execute a will. In *Strittmater* and *Honigman*, for instance, the question was not whether the testators had the ability to understand the nature and extent of their property, the objects of their bounty, the disposition they were making of their property, and the relationship among these three. Rather, the questions were whether they suffered from a derangement and whether any part of their wills was a product of that derangement.

### Testamentary Intent

To be a valid will the decedent must execute it with the intent that it be a will. Lack of testamentary intent is unusual because it may serve as a will contest ground or a ground to deny probate to a will. Contest grounds usually are not adequate to deny probate of a will. The usual remedy if there are grounds to contest a will is to admit the will to probate and then challenge its validity in a contest action. Recall also that proper execution of a will raises a presumption that the testator knew the contents of the will and understandingly executed it with the requisite capacity and intent. The burden in this regard is on the contestant to rebut the presumption of testamentary intent raised by proper execution.

One common source of a challenge based on lack of testamentary intent is a client letter to an attorney asking for the preparation of a will, spelling out the client's testamentary objectives. This letter cannot constitute a will even if it otherwise meets the statutory requisites for execution of a will, because the client did not intend the *letter* to constitute a *will*. The client clearly knew the difference between them and intended only that the letter result in the production of a will.

Occasionally a decedent's duly executed will is challenged on the ground that it was executed to accomplish a purpose other than disposition of the testator's property and thus was invalid due to a lack of testamentary intent. For example, in *Lister v. Smith*, 164 Eng. Rep. 1282 (1863), the decedent's codicil was invalid for lack of testamentary intent because the testator did not intend it to have testamentary effect: it revoked a bequest to a family member to induce the family member's mother to move out of a house she was occupying. Note, though, that some courts will not admit extrinsic evidence to make such an argument. See Chapter 7.

## Undue Influence

Undue influence probably is the most frequent contest ground, particularly if lack of capacity cannot be proven. Frequently contestants attack a will on both grounds and, in some cases, the same evidence (e.g., a weak and feeble minded testator) may be relevant to both claims. Also note that undue influence often is confused with fraud because both terms sometimes are used to describe what is in fact undue influence. Fraud as a separate will contest ground is discussed below.

A will beneficiary can exert influence on a testator that affects the testator's dispositive provisions without that influence being *undue*. For influence to be undue, it generally must satisfy three requisites. First, the influence must be directly connected with execution: required is a causal connection between the influence and the will, operating at the time of execution (although the influencer need not be present at the time of execution). Thus, general influence unrelated to execution of the will is not undue influence.

For example, assume that Child A and Child B do not speak or otherwise communicate with or see each other. Child A prevails upon Parent to cut Child B out of Parent's life. There is no undue influence if Parent later executes a will that leaves nothing to Child B, *if* Child A had nothing to do with creation or execution of that will. Note in this regard that influence directed at dispossessing someone else is not undue influence, although it might be actionable fraud, deceit, or tortious interference with an expectancy. So, the second requisite is that the influence must be directed toward procurement of a disposition in favor of the influencer or someone the influencer wishes to favor. For example, *In re Estate of Maheras*, 897 P.2d 268 (Okla. 1995), involved a testamentary gift to the testator's church that was found to be the product of undue influence by the testator's pastor. Alternatively, assume T's will left ¼ of T's estate to a nephew. There is no undue influence if T's child prevails upon T to instead leave the nephew's share to T's alma mater, to which T's child had no connection.

The third, and perhaps most important, requirement for activity to be undue influence is that the influence must destroy the testator's free will and result in a will that reflects the wishes of the influencer instead of the testator. The testator's independence must be overcome such as to leave the testator unable or unwilling to resist the influence. Thus, in many jurisdictions a factor bearing on the question whether influence was undue is the susceptibility of the testator to influence. As a result, undue influence claims (which are difficult to prove in any case) are most likely to succeed with respect to elderly, dependent, and weak-willed testators. To prove undue influence it is necessary to show what *this* testator thought and whether *this* testator was influenced. It will not suffice to show what the *average* individual in the testator's circumstances would have done or thought in the face of an alleged influence.

Undue influence frequently is said to involve an element of coercion. The influencer so overcomes the will of the testator as to coerce the testator into executing a will that reflects the influencer's wishes rather than the testator's. Duress is not common as a will contest ground, but it relates to undue influence because a will executed by a testator under duress may not reflect the testator's testamentary desires. Holding a gun to the testator's head during the signing makes the will invalid because it was signed under duress. Moreover, a threat need not be unlawful to constitute duress. See, e.g., *In re Sickles' Will*, 50 A. 577 (N.J. Prerog. Ct. 1901), in which a threat to abandon a paralyzed elderly testator was held to be undue influence.

Unjust or unnatural provisions in a will may *support* (but will not *prove*) a case that the testator was prevailed upon to do something that otherwise would not have been done, and that this influence was undue. In addition, some courts improperly state that influence is not undue if it does not result in an injustice. That conclusion is wrong, although it might be hard to make the case and it depends on what the court would consider an "injustice." To illustrate, consider a will leaving an equal share to a child who exerted undue influence to overcome the testator's antipathy toward the child that resulted in a previous will that cut the child out completely.

### Proving Undue Influence

The initial burden of proof with respect to undue influence is on the contestant. This burden requires evidence of the testator's subjugation to the will of the influencer, which could be next to impossible to produce: because the influence usually occurs in private, proof of undue influence usually is scant, often only circumstantial and lacking in verifiability. Consequently, in many jurisdictions proof of three elements suffices to shift the burden of proof from the contestant to the proponent of the will. As a practical matter, it typically is the burden shifting that is most important to winning an undue influence case. To shift the burden of proof, typically it is necessary to show three things: (1) that the testator's condition or state of mind made the testator susceptible to undue influence (the more feeble minded the testator, the easier will be the proof of this element). (2) that the influencer had the opportunity to exercise control over the testator, with special scrutiny if the alleged influence came from the testator's attorney or other advisor. (3) that the alleged influencer was disposed to exercise control over the testator (i.e., there was a motive). Proof of actual activity exercising control, or of advantage to be obtained by the influencer, usually will suffice and frequently is shown by a testamentary gift to the influencer (or someone the influencer wanted to favor) in an amount that is greater than would have passed without the alleged influence.

Proof that will not establish undue influence is argument, persuasion, advice, assistance, affection, kindness, or solicitude. Normally, to be undue influence this activity must rise to the level of violence, abuse, litigation, or abandonment. To illustrate, assume that T's child, C, cares for T in T's home. C threatens to move T to a nursing home and files litigation to declare T incompetent and have C appointed as T's conservator, all with the intent of procuring a will that leaves all of T's estate to C (to the exclusion of T's other children). Any new will that T executes in exchange for C abandoning the litigation and allowing T to remain in C's care is infected by undue influence.

The level of persuasion is very important given the nature of the proof required and the elements that must be proven. Typically only a preponderance of the evidence is required, although clear and convincing evidence is the standard applied in some jurisdictions. Furthermore, in many jurisdictions in two circumstances a presumption of undue influence will shift the burden of proof to the proponent. One such circumstance is if the will benefits the drafter of the will or a natural object of the drafter's bounty. That drafter is presumed to have exerted undue influence over the testator. For a case in which the presumption was not applied (we think improperly), see *Lipper v. Weslow*, 369 S.W.2d 698 (Tex. Civ. App. 1963), in which an attorney child of the testator drafted a will that left her estate equally to her two children by her second marriage, with no provision for children of a deceased child by her first marriage. Had the burden shifted, the child who was the proponent of the will would have been required to prove that the will was not the product of undue influence.

More common is the presumption of undue influence arising if there is a confidential or fiduciary relation with the testator, if the dominant party in that relation participated in procurement of the will. In this case the relation is not enough; there must be proof of participation in preparation of the will. Relations that allow application of this presumption include clergy, attorney, physician, nurse, trustee, conservator, or close business partner. A questionable case in this regard is *In re Kaufmann's Will*, 247 N.Y.S.2d 664 (1964), aff'd, 205 N.E.2d 864 (N.Y. 1965), involving a nontraditional relationship between a wealthy testator and his same sex partner in which undue influence was found. The relationship lasted for approximately 10 years prior to the testator's death. Over the last eight of those years the testator executed numerous wills benefiting his partner. The court effectively struck all of those wills by a finding that undue influence was exerted when the first of them was executed. We question the legitimacy of that decision, particularly in this day and age.

Usually insufficient to raise undue influence presumptions would be relation as a parent, spouse, or child (although a child who cares for and manages the finances of an aged parent may be held to occupy a confidential relationship with the parent). If, however, the drafter/beneficiary also is the testator's attorney (as was the case in *Lipper*), the presumption of undue influence would arise both because the will drafter was a beneficiary and because of the confidential attorney-client relationship.

So, in an undue influence case, first determine what constitutes undue influence (conduct by the influencer that is directly connected with execution of the will, that is designed to produce a provision benefiting the influencer or someone the influencer wishes to favor, and that so overcomes the free will of the testator as to substitute for it the desires of the influencer). Then consider whether the burden of proving undue influence shifts from the contestant to the proponent (e.g., depending on the jurisdiction, because of (1) susceptibility, opportunity, and disposition or motive, or (2) a confidential relationship and participation in procurement of the will). A presumption of undue influence can be overcome in some jurisdictions by a showing that the testator received independent legal advice (which is unlikely if the testator's attorney also represents the influencer); that showing also might negate that the testator's free will was overcome by the influencer. The will proponent also can introduce direct evidence tending to negate that the testator's free will was overcome by the influencer. For example, a testator may be elderly, infirm, and dependent on others for physical care, but still be strong willed, with an independent mind and a free spirit that is not malleable to the influence of the will's proponent.

### *Effect of Undue Influence*

A finding of undue influence will vitiate only the affected parts of the will. The entire plan will fail only if the remaining portions cannot stand alone, or if the court concludes that entire invalidity is required to best implement the testator's intent. Notice also that an allegedly revoked will can be admitted to probate if the testator revoked it pursuant to undue influence.

### *Bequests to Attorneys*

A presumption of undue influence arises if a testator's will includes a gift to the drafting attorney, or to objects of the attorney's bounty. The same may be true if the attorney did not actually draft the will but participated in its preparation in some other way. A "natural" bequest no larger than if another drafter were involved *may* be permissible, without contest concerns (e.g., if a single testator with two children and no descendants of deceased children leaves half of the estate to one child who is the attorney/drafter). Nevertheless, a bequest to the drafter in a will always raises eyebrows and presents the potential for a contest. See page 54 as to the possibility of undue influence even if there is not an "unnatural" disposition.

In addition to concerns about validity of the will itself, there are ethics issues to address. Rule 1.8(c) of the Model Rules of Professional Conduct provides that a gift to the drafting attorney (or a close relative of the drafting attorney) is copacetic only if the testator and the attorney are "related." The question of how closely they must be related is addressed loosely (in a manner, for example, that may allow a drafting lawyer who is part of a same sex couple to be a beneficiary), which might be desirable in some cases but yields less precise guidance in others. In addition, a gift to an unrelated drafting attorney is permissible under Rule 1.8(c) if it is not "substantial." Although the rule seems to indicate that the gift must be nominal in value, *In re Tonken*, 642 P.2d 660 (Or. 1982), held that a $75,000 gift to the drafting attorney from a decedent who had a $6 million estate did not warrant disciplinary action. And a parent/child relationship between the testator and the drafting attorney might avoid both the will contest and the ethics issues. Even so, the time, expense, and hassle the family suffered because of the son's involvement in drafting the will in *Lipper* could have been avoided. In that regard, consider whether the drafter's sister could have recovered litigation expenses from him.

*In re Will of Moses*, 227 So. 2d 829 (Miss. 1969), illustrates the lengths to which some courts will go to prevent attorneys from being beneficiaries under their clients' wills. In *Moses*, the testator was a widow who was sexually involved with her attorney, to whom she devised the bulk of her estate. The attorney/beneficiary did not draft the document, however, and apparently did not participate in the decedent obtaining other counsel to do so. Nevertheless, the court held that the attorney-client relationship between the beneficiary and the testator when the will was executed, and their sexual relationship, gave rise to a presumption of undue influence, even though the attorney/beneficiary apparently played no role in preparation of the will. In another questionable part of the opinion, the court held that the drafter did not provide any "meaningful independent advice" relating to the testator's decision to leave her estate to her attorney rather than to her blood relatives. The court essentially rejected the drafter's independence, notwithstanding that this attorney met with the testator, ascertained that she was not married and had no children, discussed her property with her to consider possible tax issues, learned from her what she wanted done with her property at her death, and then drafted her will accordingly. Still, the presumption of undue influence was held not to be overcome and the will was held invalid.

A will nominating the drafting attorney as personal representative, or as attorney for the personal representative, does not create the same kinds of problems as a will devising property to the drafting attorney (because the nominations are not binding, and an attorney who serves in one or both of those capacities will provide services for which compensation will be received, rather than receiving a gift under the will). Neither is the attorney signing the will as a witness a will contest or ethics problem. But overreaching or solicitation in obtaining an appointment is an ethics concern, and writing the drafter's name into a document for any purpose always raises questions of propriety. See Chapter 21. Even so, for an attorney to serve as a fiduciary for an estate or trust of a client is not necessarily unethical and should not raise serious will contest concerns if proper precautions are taken.

## Fraud

Generally speaking, fraud as a ground for a will contest is a trick, device, or deception, typically involving a misrepresentation to the testator. To be a contest ground it must be intended to deceive the testator and to induce execution of a will or codicil that benefits the perpetrator of the fraud. It also may be fraud to prevent revocation of a prior will, or to prevent execution of a new will (although these are not nearly as common). For example, in *Latham v. Father Divine*, 85 N.E.2d 168 (N.Y. 1949), the plaintiffs alleged that the defendants used misrepresentations, undue influence, physical force, and murder to prevent the testator from revoking her will and executing a new one in the plaintiffs' favor. In agreeing with the plaintiffs that the allegations stated a cause of action, the court held that the defendants (who would then be devisees under a will that was not revoked, due to their wrongful conduct) would hold the estate in constructive trust for the plaintiffs, if the allegations were proven.

Fraud usually takes either of two forms: fraud in the execution or fraud in the inducement. Fraud in the execution is a deception as to the provisions of the document the testator intended to sign, or as to the character of the document itself. It is more likely with someone who is unable to read (poor eyesight, illiteracy, or the testator knew only a foreign language and was relying on a true translation). For example, imagine that the testator is told by X that the will the testator is about to sign leaves the entire estate to a church, which the testator intends, but the instrument actually leaves the estate to X; or the testator is asked to sign a document that is presented as a lease agreement for the testator's apartment, but is in fact a will.

Fraud in the inducement occurs when the testator knowingly executed the document, with provisions that the testator intended to include, but the will or its provisions resulted from a deception worked upon the testator in forming that intent. Six elements must be proven to establish fraud in the inducement: (1) false statements or material omissions of fact that prevented the testator from recognizing the truth (e.g.: "Dad, brother Billy is bankrupt—a spendthrift"); (2) if false statements are involved, they were made with knowledge that they were false; (3) the statements or omissions were made with the intent to deceive; innocent misrepresentations or omissions are not actionable; (4) the statements or omissions were material; (5) the statements or omissions actually deceived; and (6) causation, being a link between the misrepresentation or omission and production or execution of the will or the affected provision. The tests applied to determine causation vary, including a "but for" approach (requiring only that fraud was a link in the chain resulting in a given provision), a "sole motive" test (requiring that fraud was the operative reason for the provision), and a "would have made" standard (requiring proof that the testator would have done something different had the truth been known).

If fraud is established, the remedy will depend on the circumstances. As illustrated by *Father Divine*, fraud after execution that prevents the revocation of a will results in the imposition of a constructive trust (discussed in Chapter 11). The proper remedy is not denial of admission of the will to probate or invalidation of the will in a contest. If the entire will is the product of fraud, however, then the entire will fails. Thus, testamentary intent will be lacking if fraud in the execution occurs and the testator did not know that the instrument signed was a will. In that case the will can be denied admission to probate or it can be successfully attacked in its entirety in a contest. Similarly, if X fraudulently induced the testator to leave the entire estate to X, the entire will may be challenged successfully in a contest.

On the other hand, if fraud taints only some provisions of the will, then only those provisions will be invalidated. The entire will does not fail unless the entire will was the product of the fraud or it is impossible to separate the portions of the will procured by fraud from the others. Consider the following: By fraud, Child persuaded the testator to provide a life estate to Child, with a remainder to charity. Absent the fraud the charity would have received the estate immediately. The remedy will be to invalidate the life estate and accelerate the remainder so the charity takes the estate immediately. If the will had failed entirely, the estate may have passed by intestacy, maybe even to Child and certainly not to the charity. As an alternative example, if the facts were that Child would have received the entire estate had it not been for a fraud committed by the charity, invalidation of only the charitable remainder would cause the remainder to pass by intestacy following Child's life estate. That might be acceptable if Child is the testator's sole heir who will receive the remainder by intestacy. Indeed, the rest of the will remaining valid might be a preferable result if, for example, the will contains other provisions for innocent beneficiaries, such as a preresiduary gift to a beneficiary who would not be an intestate heir, or because the life estate is in a spendthrift trust that protects Child. See Chapter 13. All this is academic, however, if Child is not the sole heir, in which case a more aggressive remedy would be required to accomplish the testator's intent absent the fraud.

### Practicalities

States differ on how the burdens of proof are allocated between proponents and contestants of a will. In many states, the *proponent* of the will is required to prove the will was validly executed (i.e., in accordance with the jurisdiction's required formalities) and the fact of the testator's death. See, e.g., UPC §3-407. Assuming those proofs are made, the *contestants* then have the burden of proving lack of testamentary intent or capacity, or undue influence, fraud, duress, mistake, or revocation. Although this division of the burden of proof is fairly common even among non-UPC states, in some jurisdictions the proponent also bears the burden of proving testamentary capacity, rather than the contestant having to establish a lack of such capacity.

Although the distinction is blurred in many jurisdictions, issues related to proper execution generally affect whether the will is *admitted to probate* (i.e., determined by the probate court to have been executed in accordance with the required formalities), while issues related to capacity, undue influence, and so forth are addressed in *will contest* proceedings. In some jurisdictions probate and contest proceedings are separate, while they are combined in others. Lack of testamentary intent often may be raised in either context.

A person generally has standing to contest a will if that person has an interest or right that will be adversely affected if the will is allowed to control disposition of the testator's estate. For example, an heir who receives nothing under the will clearly has standing to contest it. On the other hand, an heir who receives at least as much under the will as if the will fails cannot contest it. Similarly, a person who is a devisee under two wills may not contest the later one unless it leaves that person less than did the prior one. Curiously, the cases are divided on whether a creditor of a potential beneficiary of a decedent's estate may contest a will. For example, if A is a devisee under Will 1, but not under subsequent Will 2, or if A is an heir of a testator whose will disinherits A, in some jurisdictions a general, unsecured creditor of A may not bring the contest, but a secured creditor may. Similar uncertainty applies if Will 1 appoints B as personal representative of T's estate, and then T executes Will 2, which appoints someone else. B may have standing to contest Will 2, but the cases are divided.

It is predictable that most will challenges will fail because will contests typically are brought after the will has been admitted to probate (because there often is no question as to proper execution of the will) and admission usually raises a presumption of validity. The prevailing presumption favoring validity is consistent with the court's determination (in admitting the will to probate) that the will is the final, properly executed expression of the testator's intent.

### Predicting and Planning in Anticipation of Contest

Common circumstances under which it is likely that a will contest might result include a testator who (1) has children by a prior marriage and intends to favor a surviving spouse who is not their other parent, (2) treats similarly situated descendants differently, (3) has no close relatives who might be inclined to accept an unfavorable will rather than to contest it, because they don't want to tarnish the testator's reputation with a will contest action, or (4) enjoyed an "alternative" lifestyle or made an "unusual" disposition (e.g., a dedicated Hare Krishna, an open homosexual, or a donor to an "extremist" organization). In any of these circumstances affirmative planning that minimizes the risk or effect of a successful contest may be wise. A variety of steps can be taken.

The most effective would be for the testator to contract with a potential contestant not to contest the will. Estoppel also may bar a person from challenging a will if that potential contestant accepts benefits under the will. So, if the client anticipates a challenge from a particular individual, a second approach is to include a bequest in the will to that individual that is sufficiently attractive that the contest will be discouraged. This may dissuade a contest because the contestant's bequest is defeated if the contest is successful.

In essence this is the root of an effective no-contest clause (also often referred to as an *in terrorem* provision). A no-contest clause typically provides that a devisee who contests a will forfeits any devise under the will. The provision eliminates the bequest for a contestant under the challenged will, but only if the contest fails and the will is upheld. As a result, the contestant must decide whether to accept the sure thing of a devise under the will, or to challenge the will and lose all if the contest fails.

If the contest *succeeds*, however, the will itself fails and with it the *in terrorem* clause also fails. If the contestant takes enough more in that case, the *in terrorem* clause may not be an adequate dissuasion unless the contestant is sufficiently risk averse. In addition, even if a contest fails and the will is upheld, some courts regard an *in terrorem* provision as valid only to the extent the contest was frivolous, vexatious, not in good faith, or based on no reasonable grounds. If the contest was deemed to be in good faith (even if unsuccessful), many courts will not allow the *in terrorem* provision to apply. For example, UPC §§2-517 and 3-905 provide that a no-contest clause will not be enforced in the case of an unsuccessful contest for which there was probable cause. As a result the no-contest clause is not a sure thing for premortem planning against a likely contest.

A court that is reluctant to enforce a forfeiture against an unsuccessful contestant may avoid the *in terrorem* result (depending on the language of the no-contest clause and the form of the plaintiff's claim) by construing the action brought by the "contestant" as other than a "contest." As a result, "contestants" of wills that include devises to them and no-contest clauses frequently make claims in forms other than traditional will contests. For example, a claimant might bring an action to construe the will more favorably to the contestant, or to be treated as a pretermitted heir (see Chapter 10), or to have a subsequent instrument with more favorable provisions admitted as the decedent's last will, or to have the devise to the claimant be free from estate taxes, etc.

A small number of jurisdictions authorize the premortem validation of a will, allowing the testator to appear while alive to be interviewed by the court to determine whether any contest grounds are valid. Short of such an authorized procedure, often the answer to the question of how to avoid contests is to use inter vivos trusts, which substantially reduce the likelihood of a contest being brought or of it being a success. There are a number of reasons why this may be the case. For example, a third party trustee who knew the testator can vouch for competence. In addition, the plan was effected while the testator was alive and could alter it, indicating that it was not the product of undue influence. Although it may not make a great deal of sense, trusts are not frequently challenged and are even less often defeated. Consistent with this use as will substitutes (see Chapter 6), the Uniform Trust Code permits challenges to the validity of inter vivos trusts on will contest grounds and the limitation period for such actions runs from the settlor's death, not from creation of the trust. See UTC §§402(a)(1), 601, 406, and 604.

### Tortious Interference with Inheritance

Closely related to a will contest is an action in tort for intentional interference with inheritance. It is a separate cause of action, not a will contest ground or a ground for denying admission of a will to probate. And note, a will contest action may preclude the tort action if the outcomes of each would be essentially the same. *Keith v. Dooley*, 802 N.E.2d 54 (Ind. Ct. App. 2004). The elements of the tort cause of action are: (1) the plaintiff had an expectancy; (2) conduct by the defendant interfered with it; (3) the defendant intended to interfere with it; (4) the defendant's conduct was tortious, such as fraud, duress, or undue influence; (5) but for defendant's interference, the plaintiff would have received the inheritance; and (6) damages. By way of example, *Commerce Bank v. Blasdel*, 141 S.W.3d 434, 452 (Mo. Ct. App. 2004), regarded the tort action to be an effective remedy "to preclude . . . 'bounty hunters' . . . who enter into sham adult . . . adoptions" to garner a portion of a decedent's estate.

A successful will contestant shares in the decedent's estate, whereas a successful tort action results in a judgment against the tortfeasor. For that reason, if an estate has few assets a tort action may be preferable. In addition, a will contest cannot be brought until after the decedent's death. A tortious interference with inheritance might be actionable prior to the property owner's death, when the property owner as well as others may testify. See, e.g., *Plimpton v. Gerrard*, 668 A.2d 882 (Me. 1995). In *Brown v. Kirkham*, 926 S.W.2d 197 (Mo. Ct. App. 1996), however, the court held a tort claim filed before the decedent died was premature because the plaintiff had no vested interest, only an expectancy, and thus had no damages yet.

### Attestation and Execution Formalities

To validly execute a will typically requires strict compliance with a variety of very specific rules (*formalities*). Although some of the traditional formalities remain in place in most states, in many states they have been relaxed considerably and the trend is further in that direction. The most clear example of this trend is the so-called "dispensing power" of UPC §2-503. Adopted in 1990, it provides that a document not executed in compliance with the execution formalities required for a traditionally valid attested or holographic will nevertheless may be treated as valid if the proponent establishes by clear and convincing evidence that the testator intended the document to be a will. See the discussion on page 76.

In many cases the clearly expressed intent of the testator has been thwarted by non-compliance with technical execution (or revocation) formalities. The trend towards liberalizing will execution formalities recognizes the fact that the foremost objective should be to effect the testator's expressed intentions if they can be ascertained reliably. Will execution formalities have been a part of the law for centuries; the relatively recent changes liberalizing them are the product of careful and deliberate consideration and a study of empirical evidence regarding the abuses to which the formalities were directed. Among the questions raised are why the execution formalities arose in the first place, and why they have persisted for so long. In this vein, four functions of execution requirements can be articulated:

- The ritual function. The issue is whether the property owner really meant it. To illustrate, assume D writes a letter to A stating: "When I die, I want you to have Blackacre." The law needs a relatively high degree of certainty that the decedent really intended that a transfer be made because the devolution of a decedent's property to successors is a significant event about which the decedent no longer is able to speak. The various execution formalities make it unlikely that a document not intended by the testator to have testamentary effect will do so, and that a will not be casually considered.

- The evidentiary function. We need to know that a writing or other communication offered after a decedent's death is in fact the decedent's will. To take an extreme example, think of the difficulties and uncertainties that arise in trying to prove the existence and terms of oral wills, which are allowed in only a few jurisdictions, and only in very limited circumstances. See page 80. The same kinds of issues are not as pronounced for writings, but the many cases dealing with the question whether an offered document is the decedent's will demonstrate that they do arise even for writings. Presumably there would be even more of those cases without will execution formalities. Thus, compliance with execution formalities results in documents that courts and persons interested in decedents' estates can rely on with some confidence.

- The protective function. To be valid it is necessary that execution of a will be the free act of the testator, and not the result of undue influence, fraud, or duress. The execution formalities (e.g., requiring the will to be witnessed by two disinterested witnesses) reduce to some extent the possibility of a will being executed under those kinds of circumstances.

- The channeling function. The will execution formalities contribute to wills providing testators with a routine, accepted, and thus fairly reliable means of validly and effectively disposing of property.

### Essential Requirements

Essential requirements for the valid execution of a will are statutory and are virtually identical everywhere. The will must be written (unless, as discussed on page 80, a nuncupative will statute is applicable, which today is quite uncommon). Almost anything readable will satisfy the writing requirement. Valid wills have been written on the fuselage of an aircraft that crashed, or on the wall of a flop house, or in the drawer of a dresser, on postcards, in books. In ink, chalk, blood, with a knife blade, awl, ice pick, you name it. The will must be signed by the testator unless it is nuncupative. Witnesses, if any (i.e., the will is not holographic), must attest (under most statutes, in the testator's presence, and often in each other's presence too).

Testing the validity of an execution usually follows the maxim that "valid anywhere is valid everywhere," meaning that courts look for reasons to apply the law of a state that provides an execution procedure under which the will is valid. Generally, a will is valid if it was valid when executed under the law of the jurisdiction in which it was executed. Similarly, it is valid if it was valid under the laws of the jurisdiction in which the testator was domiciled at death, either under those laws at the time of execution or at the time of the testator's death, and even if it was physically signed someplace else.

### Signed by the Testator

Numerous issues have arisen involving the seemingly straightforward requirement that a valid will (other than a nuncupative one) be signed by its testator. Generally, the testator signs immediately after the *testimonium clause* of the will (e.g., "In witness whereof, I have signed this will on the ____ day of _____, 200*, at Hometown, Anystate.") Execution statutes usually require the testator to sign the will (or acknowledge the testator's signature) in the presence of witnesses (unless it is holographic, in which case witnesses are unnecessary and actually may be harmful). This "presence" requirement is discussed further below because it is a source of numerous failed executions. If signing in their presence is not required, then in most states the will may be valid if the testator *acknowledges* to the witnesses that the signature on the will is the testator's (or, in some jurisdictions, merely that the will is the testator's, which is deemed to include an implicit acknowledgement of the signature by the testator; see, e.g., UPC §2-502(a)(3)).

Almost any form of signature or mark (e.g., "X") will suffice, if it is the full act intended for validation of the will by the testator. There are cases in which a thumbprint or similar mark was accepted as the testator's intended signature. And, if that is not simple enough, assistance is permissible if the testator cannot complete the full act intended. In most states no request for assistance is required. So there are plenty of cases allowing an observer to seize the testator's hand or arm and "help complete the act" if the testator starts to get the vapors during execution and literally runs out of energy before the full signature is completed.

Extraordinary amounts of assistance have been held to be permissible. For example, there are cases in which someone wrote the testator's name with the testator merely touching the top of the pen, or the assistor guided the testator's hand in making the signature or mark. No doubt, there is contrary authority as well. See, e.g., *In re Estate of Dethorne*, 471 N.W.2d 780 (Wis. Ct. App. 1991) (grasping the dying testator's hand and making the signature was rejected). The key in *Dethorne* was that the testator never requested the assistance. Unusual about the case is that in most states a request is not required. It is essential, though, that the testator intend to execute the will, and in *Dethorne* concern about a lack of such intent may have influenced the result.

It can be important to distinguish between signature with assistance (the testator is signing but needs help) and signature by proxy, in which someone else signs for a testator who does not physically participate in the signing. To illustrate, if Professor Newman signed Professor Pennell's will for him, the signature would be by proxy and might be: "J. Pennell, by A. Newman" (the way you often see a letter signed by the writer's secretary). Here the testator must request the proxy to sign for the testator, and the proxy must make that signature in the testator's presence.

A few states require all this signature business at the *physical* end of the document. Presumably the notion is that it is too easy for forged additions to the will to be made after the signature. But questions may arise with respect to where the "end" of the will is. For example, to avoid invalidating wills, several cases have held that the "end" of the will is the "logical" end, which is not necessarily the physical end. So, imagine a will written on foolscap (like a greeting card), in which the cover is written first, then the right hand inside page facing you when you open it, then the inside page that is the backside of the cover, and finally the back cover. If the will did not need the back page and thus ended on the inside page that is the backside of the cover, courts in some jurisdictions would uphold the will because—even though it was not signed at the physical end—it was signed at the logical end of the document.

If signature at the end is required and there are provisions after the testator's signature, the first question is whether the offending provisions were there when the will was executed or were added after execution. If the latter, the additional provisions likely constitute an unexecuted and thus invalid attempted codicil to the will that will not affect its validity. If the former, the consequence of having provisions after the testator's signature may depend on the nature of the provision. Nondispositive provisions (e.g., a provision naming a personal representative) typically would be ignored, without affecting the validity of the will. Dispositive provisions may cause the purported will to be invalid. Alternatively, if the provisions of the will that appear before the signature can be interpreted and make sense, they may be allowed to stand on their own. The document will not be given effect as the testator's will only if the provisions appearing before the signature do not produce a comprehensible dispositive scheme for the testator's estate.

### Publication

Publication is a declaration by the testator at execution that the document is the testator's will. It is required in a decreasing number of jurisdictions. Publication seeks to impress all parties involved in the execution with the nature and import of the act of execution. The preferred method of satisfying a publication requirement is simply for the testator to state to the witnesses that the instrument before them "is my will," either expressly or by answering "yes" to a question to that effect posed by the person who is supervising the execution. There are, however, many cases to the effect that the testator can publish the will other than verbally, such as by conduct that clearly indicates the testator's understanding that the document being executed is a will.

### Attestation and Acknowledgement by Witnesses

Only two witnesses are required to attested wills in virtually all American jurisdictions. Even so, use of a third is common, and good practice to protect against one witness being unavailable at probate (e.g., has died, is disqualified by interest [discussed below], is incompetent, or cannot be located). In most jurisdictions, qualification to be a witness to a will requires only that the person be competent to understand and relate events (i.e., is able to "attest"); in others, witnesses must have attained a minimum age.

A significant witness issue involves persons who are "interested" in the estate. At common law, a person interested in the estate simply could not serve as a witness; the will was not validly executed if there were an insufficient number of disinterested witnesses. The approach in most jurisdictions today is to allow the interested witness to serve as a competent witness to the will. In such a case the question is not whether the will is valid; instead it is the effect, if any, the witness' interest will have on the devise to the witness.

An interested witness is one who takes more under the will than without it. Absence of interest usually does *not* require that the witness not be a devisee under the will. Rather, it usually means the person takes at least as much under a prior valid will or by intestacy. The minority view is that a person is interested simply by virtue of being a beneficiary under the will, regardless of what would have passed to them from the testator's estate under a prior will or by intestacy.

For example, in most jurisdictions A can serve as a witness to a new will without being an interested witness if T has a valid will leaving A one third of T's estate and then T executes the new will that leaves A no more than one third of T's estate. The result is the same if A is an heir of T, who executes a will, witnessed by A, that leaves A no more than A's intestate share.

In some states a devisee's spouse is an interested party (the devisee's interest taints the spouse, as if the spouse and the beneficiary were a single individual) but the potential heirs of a devisee usually are not themselves tainted.

Purification of interest by renunciation of any benefit to the witness typically is not permitted. For example, in *Estate of Parsons*, 163 Cal. Rptr. 70 (1980), the decedent's will was witnessed by Nielson, who was left $100 under the will; Gower, who was left certain real property; and Warda, who also served as notary and who was not a devisee under the will. California's disinterested witness statute voided gifts under the will to interested witnesses in excess of what they would have received without the will, unless the will was witnessed by two other disinterested witnesses. Nielson, who would not have taken anything in the absence of the will, disclaimed the $100 gift to her. The court nevertheless held that this did not purge her interest, stating that the purpose of the statute is to protect the testator from fraud and undue influence and the interest determination therefore occurs at the time of execution. The result was that Gower, who also would not have taken anything without the will, was unable to take the real property.

If the logic of *Parsons* is sound, then we must confess that purge statutes are unreliable. If the witness might lie at execution to validate a will that benefits the witness, that inclination is no more reversed at the time of execution by the purge statute operating at death than it was by Nielson's ineffective disclaimer operating at death.

Devises that do *not* constitute interest include a bequest to a church; the minister is permissible as a witness. Similarly, it is not an interested witness problem if the will names the drafting attorney as personal representative and the attorney witnesses the will. If the attorney serves as personal representative of the estate, the benefit the attorney receives will be compensation for services and not a gift. Note, however, that being a witness usually is a bad idea, because if called to testify the attorney cannot also represent the estate. Better that the attorney serve as the notary public and not otherwise.

The approach taken in some states is to treat a devise to a witness as creating a presumption of undue influence by the witness. Unless the witness can rebut the presumption the devise is forfeited (or at least the portion of the devise in excess of what the witness would receive in the absence of the will). Still another approach is to consider interest in judging credibility and to purge the interest by statute, but only if the witness is needed to testify to admit the will. If required, the witness is forced to testify and is left with only that amount (if any) the witness would have received if the will were not admitted.

Do you wonder why purge is appropriate to protect against fabrications but disclaimer/renunciation is not? Perhaps it is because other beneficiaries of the will might pay a witness to disclaim or renounce so that the remaining beneficiaries could take under the will, so there remains the opportunity and even an incentive to lie. The purge statute operates automatically, so the thought may be that there is not the same risk of skullduggery. Further reflection suggests that this may be a distinction with no significance, and UPC §2-505(b) goes further. It is representative of state laws that avoid the problem altogether, without purge, by simply declaring that interest is not a disqualification. Thus, a devisee can serve as a witness in a state that has adopted UPC §2-505(b) without affecting either the devise to the witness or the validity of the will (except to the extent, if any, that the devisee being a witness is a factor leading to a finding of undue influence).

So, consider T, who is eccentric and hermetic; the only people T will allow to be near enough to act as witnesses are interested because they all are devisees under T's will. To validly attest the will witnesses A and B attest will number 1, in which they are not beneficiaries. Then will number 2 is executed, attested by witnesses C and D, who take no more under will number 2 than they do under will number 1. Will number 2 may include witnesses A, B, C, and D as devisees, as T intended. It should be valid because will number 1 is valid and C and D who witness will number 2 are not interested.

Note also that allowing the proponents of a will to count the notary as a witness (as was done in *Parsons*) is not common but it also is not unique. See 1 Casner & Pennell, ESTATE PLANNING §3.1.1 n.24 (6th ed. 1995) as supplemented, showing a growing number of such cases. Further note that a minority of statutes require the testator to ask the witnesses to attest the will. As with the publication requirement, this should not be an impediment because usually it can be satisfied either by conduct or by words of the testator.

### *Presence*

Discussed at page 65 is the requirement that the testator sign the will in the presence of the witnesses (or, if not, that the testator acknowledge the will or the signature on the will in the presence of the witnesses). Many statutes also require the witnesses to sign in the presence of the testator, and some in the presence of the other witnesses as well. Further, a proxy typically may sign for a testator, but must do so in the testator's presence. The presence requirement in each of these contexts has generated considerable unnecessary litigation. For example, *In re Groffman*, 2 All E.R. 108 (1969), involved a testator who signed his will outside the presence of the witnesses, before asking them to witness it. The testator acknowledged his signature on the will to each of them separately. The will was denied probate because the governing statute required the testator to sign or acknowledge the will in the presence of two or more witnesses (which he did) and that both witnesses be "present at the same time" (which was lacking). Most regrettable was that the court admitted that the will reflected the testator's intent. The intestate beneficiary was the testator's widow (who was a second spouse, and there were children from a prior marriage) who received the entire estate, rather than a life estate in the testator's property as left to her under the will. Perhaps the court was engineering a result that it thought was more equitable.

The reason for the requirement that the witnesses be present together when the testator signs or acknowledges the will is that, if the validity of the will is challenged, the witnesses will testify with respect to what happened, and the testator's capacity, at the same time. Without this requirement a testator could sign or acknowledge the signature in the presence of witness A, and then wait years to acknowledge the signature to witness B. Because the benefits of this requirement are marginal at best, most states and the UPC have done away with the present-at-the-same-time requirement.

Although many statutes do not require witnesses to sign in their collective presence, most require that each witness sign in the testator's presence. The UPC, however, requires only that each witness sign within a "reasonable time" after witnessing the testator's execution of the will or acknowledgement of the signature or the will. UPC §2-502(a)(3). *Estate of Sauressig*, 19 Cal. Rptr. 3d 262 (Cal. Ct. App. 2004), allowed postmortem attestation by a second witness, who observed the testator acknowledge the will to a notary public (who was accepted as the first witness) because state law was modeled after the UPC reasonable time standard. But *In re Estate of Royal*, 826 P.2d 1236 (Colo. 1992), refused to allow the witnesses to sign after the testator's death even though it was impossible (or nearly so) for the witnesses to sign before the testator died. The UPC "reasonable time" within which to sign was deemed to end with the testator's death. By contrast, *In re Estate of Peters*, 526 A.2d 1005 (N.J. 1987), indicated that the witnesses might be able to sign after the testator's death in a proper case, but did not allow it in that case because the witnesses did not sign until 15 months after the testator's execution of the will, which the court held was too long. See cases collected in 1 Casner & Pennell, ESTATE PLANNING §3.1.1 n.22 (6th ed. 1995).

Historically, the presence requirement itself was justified because it assured the testator that everyone did the requisite acts to make the will valid. Given that this knowledge had to be provided in a different way if the testator was blind, alternative tests for presence developed, and that development ultimately relaxed the requirement in general. Today, there are two tests for compliance with the presence requirement: the line of sight test and the conscious presence test. The more strict line of sight test requires proof that the testator either did or could have (without great physical effort) seen the witnesses sign (and, if needed, that they could have seen each other sign). You wouldn't believe some of the case law that developed under this approach, with testimony from experts about where the testator was lying and how much contortion would have been required to view the witnesses signing at a table in the next room, or over in the corner or behind a privacy curtain, and such.

For example, T, who is very ill, executes a will while in bed; the witnesses are in the same room and attest while sitting at a table in a corner of the room. In a strict line of sight jurisdiction, the witnesses would not be deemed to have attested the will in T's presence if the evidence was that T could not see the witnesses without moving, and could not move (or could move only with great difficulty or danger). Similarly, the court in at least one old case held that the presence requirement was not satisfied if the testator could see only the backs of the witnesses, and not their hands and the will itself. *Graham v. Graham*, 32 N.C. 219 (N.C. 1849).

The more liberal conscious presence test, which is followed by the UPC, requires only that the testator had a conscious awareness that the witnesses were attesting, that the testator was capable of understanding what they were doing, and (unless blind) could have seen the attestation if the testator had wanted (either by moving or requesting the witnesses to move). To illustrate, if the testator is in a bedroom next to the kitchen, and the witnesses attest the will at the kitchen table while carrying on a conversation with the testator, the line of sight test would inquire into whether the door between the rooms was open (unless the door was glass or otherwise could be seen through), whether the testator's position in the bedroom was such that the kitchen table could be seen, and so forth. By contrast, it would be sufficient under the conscious presence test that the testator could hear the witnesses and was generally aware that they were signing the will—better yet that they promptly returned with the fully executed will to show the testator that all was in order.

As thus revealed, in a will execution situation it may be necessary to consider whether a presence issue exists under the applicable jurisdiction's governing law in one or more of the following contexts:

- If the testator's signature was made by a proxy for the testator, many statutes require that the testator request the proxy to sign for the testator, and that the proxy do so in the testator's presence.

- Many execution statutes require that the testator sign, or acknowledge a pre-existing signature, in the presence of the witnesses. Notice that UPC §2-502(a)(3) does not expressly require that the testator sign or acknowledge in the witnesses' presence, but instead requires that the witnesses must have "witnessed" the testator's signing the will or the testator's acknowledgement of the signature or the will. To "witness" a signature or an acknowledgement, however, the witness must be in the testator's presence.

- As illustrated by *Groffman*, some statutes require that the testator sign or acknowledge in the collective presence of the witnesses (i.e., that the witnesses be in the presence of each other when the testator signs or acknowledges).

- Most execution statutes require that the witnesses sign in the presence of the testator. UPC §2-502(a)(3) does not. It only requires the witnesses to sign within a reasonable time after they witnessed the testator sign or acknowledge.

In jurisdictions that impose the latter requirement, a witness cannot sign the will outside of the testator's presence and then acknowledge the witness' signature to the testator (although you have to wonder why not). Proxy signature or the witness signing by mark or with assistance ought to be permissible, but this is not clear in most states either. (Quaere: if an able person is available to serve as proxy or to assist another who has trouble writing, why would you ask the person who has trouble writing to attest instead of simply having the person who is able to write to act as witness? The answer likely is in the interested witness statutes.)

Is the will validly executed if the witnesses sign before the testator? How can a witness who signs first be attesting to the testator's signature (or acknowledgement)? Notwithstanding the risk of a will being held invalid if signed by one or more witnesses before the testator, there is ample authority upholding such wills when the testator and witnesses were all together when they signed. The order of signing is not critical if execution was an integrated ceremony all done in one sitting, as for example at a conference room table around which all the papers were circulated for signing. See, e.g., *Waldrep v. Goodwin*, 195 S.E.2d 432 (Ga. 1973).

### *Effect of Attestation*

Attestation is the witness' certification that the testator signed the will. Technically, "attestation" is bearing witness to the proper execution of the will by the testator; "subscription" occurs when the witness signs the will, which serves as a certification by the witness that the will was executed by the testator. Although some execution statutes require witnesses to both attest and subscribe, the term "attestation" in many jurisdictions generally is understood to include both bearing witness and signing. The witness' signature is regarded as proof that the testator signed (and declared, if necessary), or acknowledged after having signed earlier, in the witness' presence, and that the witness signed in the testator's presence and at the testator's request (if necessary), and so forth.

It is good practice to include an *attestation clause* in a will, reciting compliance with required execution formalities. As an example:

We, the undersigned persons, of lawful age, have on this day, at the request of T, witnessed T's signature to this instrument, which T declared to be T's will in the presence of each of us, and we have, at the same time in T's presence and in the presence of each other, subscribed our names hereto as attesting witnesses, and we each declare that we believe T to be of sound mind and memory.

If the witnesses cannot remember the will execution, or are unavailable, an attestation clause along with the witnesses' signatures provides prima facie evidence of due execution. *Young v. Young*, 313 N.E.2d 593 (Ill. App. Ct. 1974), held that a will could not be admitted to probate if the will did not contain an attestation clause and the witnesses could not remember enough to establish compliance with execution formalities. The important point is that generally a witness cannot recant, by later alleging that the attestation is not true, unless the witness proves that attestation was made without the required intent to validate the will (or worse, that it was produced under duress).

### Self-Proving Affidavits

Most states now permit self-proving affidavits for attested wills. These affidavits are signed by the testator and the witnesses and state that the requisites for valid execution in the jurisdiction were followed. Good drafters regard a self-proving affidavit as a necessary part of the execution process (because it facilitates the admission to probate of an uncontested will), but it is not essential to a valid will. Essentially the self-proving affidavit is a deposition: in most cases the witnesses need not appear at probate to certify that the signatures that appear are theirs and that they really saw the testator sign, etc. Instead, if the will is not contested, the affidavit affirms all the things to which the witnesses would testify and may be admitted in lieu of their personal appearances. The UPC goes a step further. According to the comment to UPC §2-504, a self-proved will may not be contested as to signature requirements.

### Procedure for Validly Executing a Will

The following recommended procedure from 1 Casner & Pennell, ESTATE PLANNING §3.1.1 (6th ed. 1995), should result in a valid will execution in any American jurisdiction.

- First, the testator should examine the entire will and understand all its substantive provisions.
- The testator, three observers who will witness the will (and who are not "interested," as discussed beginning on page 68), the person conducting the execution, and a notary public (if required with respect to a self-proving affidavit and the person conducting the execution does not meet this requirement) should be in a room from which all others are excluded and from which no one will depart until the execution is completed.
- The person supervising the execution should ask the testator: "Is this your will? Do you understand it? Does it express your wishes regarding disposition of your property after your death? Do you request these observers to witness your execution of it?" The testator's affirmative responses should be audible to the three observers.

- The observers should witness the testator date and then sign the testimonium, which should appear at the end of the will. In addition, it is desirable to have the testator initial or sign each prior page of the will.
- The person conducting the execution should instruct the three observers that, "your signature as witness attests that (1) [the testator] declared to each of you that the document is [his/her] will, (2) [he/she] dated and signed the will in your presence, and (3) [he/she] asked you to witness the execution. You are attesting that you signed in the presence of [the testator] and the other witnesses, believing [the testator] to be of sound mind and memory." If the observers agree, then in the presence of the testator and of each other, they should witness the will by signing the attestation provision and writing their addresses for future identification. If there is a self proving affidavit they also should sign it and the notary should perform the notarial function.

### Mistake in Execution

*In re Pavlinko's Estate*, 148 A.2d 528 (Pa. 1959), is representative of a classic execution mistake. All the requisite execution formalities were met, but each spouse in a married couple signed the will intended for the other. Acknowledging that the result dictated by the applicable Wills Act—failure of the will because it was not signed by the testator identified as such in the document—was "very unfortunate," the court followed the traditional approach of refusing to correct mistakes in the execution of a will and denied probate of the will. Oddly, the law will correct *wrong*doing (fraud, undue influence, etc.) that occurs in the will production and execution process, but the black letter law is that there is no remedy when an innocent mistake is involved.

In a case like *Pavlinko* there is no uncertainty about the mistake, or the intent of the decedent. Nevertheless, a majority of courts would deny relief. Most of the mistake cases in which relief is denied cannot be explained by some notion of a lack of intent or issues of credibility (fraud, forgery, and such). There simply is an historical "aversion" to correcting mistakes that take the form in these kinds of cases of requiring strict compliance with the formalities for execution.

According to the opinion in *Pavlinko*, if courts ignore the requirements of the jurisdiction's will execution statute "to accomplish equity and justice in that particular case, the Wills Act will become a meaningless . . . scrap of paper, and the door will be opened wide to countless fraudulent claims which the Act successfully bars." *Pavlinko* is an older case and the modern trend (but not yet a majority approach) is otherwise.

For example, *In re Snide*, 418 N.E.2d 656 (N.Y. 1981), involved similar facts as *Pavlinko*, and thus presented the same issue. Unlike the *Pavlinko* court, however, the *Snide* court admitted the will to probate that purported to be the will of the decedent's spouse but that was signed by the decedent, relying on the fact that the instruments contained identical dispositive provisions and were executed at the same time, all in compliance with the required formalities. The court found there was no risk of fraud; thus, to deny probate of the will would "unnecessarily expand formalism" and produce an "unjust result." For a similar holding in a case involving wills of sisters, see *Guardian, Trust & Executors Co. v. Inwood*, [1946] N.A.L.R. 614.

### Substantial Compliance

*In re Will of Ranney*, 589 A.2d 1339 (N.J. 1991), adopted a "substantial compliance" approach to rectify or ignore the defective execution of a decedent's will. In *Ranney*, the witnesses signed the self-proving affidavit that was attached to the will, but failed to sign the will itself. Other cases with similar facts have held such signatures to be adequate by regarding the affidavit as part of the will proper. The *Ranney* court correctly held that the affidavit is not part of the will, and may be the first court to hold that close is good enough when the requisite intent is apparent and there are no facts indicating a potential abuse or impropriety.

### UPC Dispensing Power

A 1990 amendment to the UPC goes even further than the substantial compliance approach to dealing with execution mistakes. UPC §2-503, referred to as a "dispensing power," allows an instrument to be probated as a decedent's will regardless of noncompliance with execution formalities if the proponent establishes with clear and convincing evidence that the testator intended the instrument to be a will. The comment to UPC §2-503 states an expectation that it will be applied most often when (1) a will is not properly witnessed and (2) a testator attempts to change a previously executed will with, for example, an interlineation that is not executed in compliance with required formalities.

UPC §2-503 applies to "a document or writing added upon a document." Oral wills and, arguably, videotaped or electronic wills therefore should not be validated by the dispensing power. The document or writing need not be signed, and it is clear that an addition or change to a previously executed will may be valid under the dispensing power even though the addition or change is not signed. If the decedent never signed the instrument offered as a will, however, it likely will be very difficult to establish by clear and convincing evidence that the decedent intended the instrument to be a will. UPC §2-503 by its terms also applies to an instrument offered as (1) an addition to or change of a will, (2) a partial or complete revocation of a will, and (3) a partial or complete revival of a formerly revoked will. See Chapter 4. But note, the UPC dispensing power only cures defects in execution. It does not cure other kinds of problems, such as a defective revocation by physical act (again see Chapter 4), the execution of a will by a testator who lacks testamentary intent, or a testator validly executing an instrument under a mistake of fact or law.

In many jurisdictions the will proponent bears the burden of proof as to due execution. A presumption of capacity arises after that burden is met and the burden to disprove that requisite shifts to the contestant. In *Estate of Brooks*, 927 P.2d 1024 (Mont. 1996), the court held that no such presumption exists when the proponent seeks to have an instrument that does not comply with the execution formalities admitted under the UPC dispensing power. Rather, the proponent bears the burden of proving testamentary capacity as a part of the burden of proving that the testator intended the instrument to be a will. So, you need to be careful here, as the law develops and creates ancillary changes.

### The Consequences of Strict Execution Requisites

A case that demonstrates the serious consequences of requiring strict compliance with will execution formalities is *In re Estate of Peters*, briefly discussed on page 71. In *Peters* a wife left all her property to her husband, who died 126 hours after she did. He left all of their collective property to her son, which clearly was consistent with her intent. His will, however, was invalidly executed and the court refused to relax the requirements, notwithstanding that the decedent's intent also was clear. There was no suggestion of impropriety, but strict imposition of the requirements resulted in *escheat* of the property. Formalities often provide grist for the litigation mill. Many cases find ways to admit wills that lack formalities, to work the appropriate equities, and the movement towards relaxing the execution requirements shows that courts and legislatures are troubled by these realities—and by the frustration of testators' intentions. Further changes are likely, as more states adopt the UPC dispensing power or otherwise embrace, directly or indirectly, the substantial compliance doctrine. To date there does not appear to be any negative backlash or fallout consequence to this development.

## Holographic Wills

About half the states recognize holographs: a will that is handwritten by the testator and valid without attestation by witnesses. See, e.g., UPC §2-502(b). Most states that recognize holographs require them to be *entirely* in the testator's handwriting. Under the surplusage theory followed in some jurisdictions, a will that contains some material not in the testator's handwriting may be a valid holograph if the nonholographic provisions can be ignored and the balance of the will administered without them. By contrast, under an intent theory only those nonholographic items that are not intended to be an operative part of the will are ignored; substantive nonholographic material invalidates the will.

The UPC requirement for a valid holograph is only that the "material portions" (and the signature) be in the testator's handwriting. That approach should allow more valid holographs than does even the surplusage theory, but questions will arise as to whether the handwritten portions constitute the "material portions." For example, *In re Estate of Johnson*, 630 P.2d 1039 (Ariz. 1981), involved a preprinted will form with only the fill-in-the-blanks portion of the will being in the testator's handwriting. In holding that the handwritten portions did not establish the necessary testamentary intent, and thus that the material portions of the instrument were not in the testator's handwriting, the court found inadequate to establish the decedent's testamentary intent the handwritten words "To John M. Johnson $^1/_8$ of my Estate," with a handwritten list of other devisees and fractions. *In re Alleged Will of Ferree*, 848 A.2d 81 (N.J. Super. 2004), is to the same effect notwithstanding the substantial compliance rule in New Jersey (which the court said should not apply to holographs because they already constitute a relaxation or deviation from traditional will execution formalities). UPC §2-502(c) addresses the *Johnson* problem and provides that portions of a holographic will that are not in the testator's handwriting may be considered to establish testamentary intent.

Many states (but not the UPC) require a holographic will to be dated, even though most do not require an *attested* will to be dated. Presumably, the different treatment is attributable to an expectation that the witnesses to an attested will can testify as to the execution date. Holographs have no witnesses to provide that information.

The state law signature requirement also may differ for a holograph. Typically a testator may sign a holograph by mark or with assistance, but usually not by proxy. This might be relevant if the will was written (but not signed) before the testator became ill or lost the ability to make a signature. Remember that a will need not be prepared all at one time. Indeed, many holographs give the appearance that they were prepared over a period of time, perhaps in multiple sessions. So the ability to write may wane and the inability to sign is not necessarily inconsistent with the fundamental notion of a holograph.

Testamentary intent questions most often arise with respect to holographs. For example, *In re Kimmel's Estate*, 123 A. 405 (Pa. 1924), involved a letter from a father to two sons that was held to be a holograph. Language in it essentially stated that the father might come to visit the sons. If he did, he said he would bring some valuable papers he wanted the sons to keep for him so that, if anything happened to him, various listed assets would go to named persons. He wrote that the sons should keep the letter because it might help them out, and the court found this was adequate to constitute a will. Do you agree? The other common occurrence is the handwritten letter to an attorney requesting preparation of a will that was not drafted or signed before the intended testator died. Because the letter anticipates creation of a will it is easy to see that it was not itself intended to be a will, which usually squelches any effort to probate the letter.

### Conditional Wills

As just noted, a valid will requires testamentary intent. The issue that arises if the will states a condition that did not occur is whether the will nevertheless was intended by the testator to be an all-events disposition. Generally, that depends on whether the statement was intended by the testator to be a true condition, or whether it was instead merely a statement of what induced the testator to make the will. Examples of language raising the issue are: "if anything happens to me," "if I do not return from my trip," or "if I do not recover from surgery." The favored construction is that the statements were merely a gratuitous expression of the inducement for writing a will that would apply under all circumstances, thus allowing a finding of intent to make the will and for it to be applicable in all events.

The question arises throughout the law of wills whether extrinsic (meaning outside the will itself) evidence of facts or circumstances can be considered to explain what a testator meant by a provision in a will. See Chapter 7. With respect to conditional wills, the question is whether extrinsic evidence should be admissible to show that the statement in the will was a mere statement of inducement and not a statement of true condition. Recall that such evidence is rejected in other cases involving pure mistake in execution. In addition, extrinsic evidence almost certainly would be rejected if offered to show that a will that is absolute on its face actually was meant to be conditional.

The extrinsic evidence issue is one of the least definable in the entire law of wills. Historically, extrinsic evidence has been admitted only with respect to "latent" ambiguities (those that are not apparent on the face of the will). Extrinsic evidence has not been permitted with patent ambiguities (those in which it is clear from the provisions of the will that something is not clear or complete) to explain what the will meant. See Chapter 7. Because the condition in a conditional will is apparent from the face of the will, consideration of extrinsic evidence is fundamentally inconsistent with this historical position. So these battles continue.

## Nuncupative (Oral) Wills

In narrowly defined circumstances, testators may make their wills orally in some jurisdictions. Generally, such wills are valid only if the testator was in the military, or in a last illness, and typically can pass only a small amount of personal property. They are rarely used.

A question that comes up occasionally is whether oral instructions given to an attorney can be a valid will if the document is not prepared and executed before the intended testator dies. The answer is that the oral instructions were not meant to be a will (remember the testamentary intent issue, even with a letter written to the attorney) and therefore intent is lacking because a written will was intended.

## Integration

Wills typically consist of many pages that may not be prepared all at once. Thus, there must be proof of which pages were present at execution and were intended to be included (i.e., "integrated") in the will. Only those can be given testamentary effect and constitute the testator's will.

### *Additional, Revised, or Retyped Pages*

Pages that are added, changed, or even retyped after execution cannot be a valid part of the will unless the formalities for execution of a valid codicil (an amendment to a will) are met. Pages that were not present at execution of the will in its final form are not integrated into the validly executed will. If those changes are not validly executed (in that regard, perhaps the UPC §2-503 dispensing power is available), the original, unaltered page *might* remain a valid part of the will, if it still is identifiable. See dependent relative revocation, discussed in Chapter 4.

If the original, unaltered page does *not* remain a valid part of the will, however, then the question may be whether removal or substitution of even one page invalidates the entire will. The will may be able to stand on its own without either the original or the invalid page if the pages are separable (not physically, but in substance, because the provisions on the pages are sufficiently independent of each other). The whole will may be invalidated, however, if the revision, addition, or replacement shows indications of fraud or forgery in the execution, a lack of testamentary intent at the time of execution, or an implied revocation of the whole will.

For example, imagine that page 2 of T's holographic will contains a single provision that leaves $10,000 to X. T destroyed the original page 2 after the holograph was executed and inserted a new one providing for the $10,000 to go to Y. New page 2 was not validly executed, however. The balance of the will can stand on its own as valid. The $10,000 is not devised to anyone, but will instead pass with the residue of the estate to the residuary beneficiaries. In contrast, if page 2 also left the residue of T's estate to Z (and the new page 2 attempted to do the same), the pages would not be separable and the will would fail unless saved by the doctrine of dependent relative revocation.

### *Two Versions of a Page at Execution*

If there were two versions of a certain page at the time of execution (e.g., because the decedent had not decided which to include), only the one proven that the decedent intended at that time to be part of the will can be valid. That might be neither, but if one of the two pages is inserted in the proper order in the will, and the pages of the will were stapled or clipped together, that page presumably was the one intended by the testator. On the other hand, if both versions of the page were kept together with the other pages of the will it may not be possible to prove which the testator intended. In that case, neither is valid and the will can stand only if that page is separable. Alternatively, this might be analyzed as a patent ambiguity, as to which extrinsic evidence might be admissible. See Chapter 7. The problem with that notion is that the "ambiguity" does not involve the usual interpretation issue but rather which of the two pages was intended to be part of the will.

### *Integration Proof*

In the suggested procedure for execution of an attested will at page 74, the witnesses were not asked to examine the will or count its pages. (In many states it is not even necessary that the witnesses know the document is a will, to say nothing of seeing what is written on any page or how many pages there are.) Some drafters intentionally place the attestation clause (after which the witnesses sign) on a separate page to prevent the witnesses from seeing any of the will provisions. Therefore integration is an issue, as it often is for holographs, because typically there are no witnesses. So, usually the only way to prove that all the pages were present at the time of execution is a presumption, in this case that the condition of the document at death was its condition when it was signed. In that regard physical attachment of the pages at death implies that all pages were together at the time of execution. Addition of initials or the testator's full signature on each page is only as reliable as the handwriting analysis procedures employed. *In re Estate of Beale*, 113 N.W.2d 380 (Wis. 1962), shows that this can be flawed, because the decedent's initials appeared on pages of his will that clearly were typed after he died.

An internal connection or flow of the provisions one to another (e.g., page 4 ends in the middle of a sentence that continues on page 5) also is taken as indicative of presence and intent at execution, but modern word processing equipment can make this appear to be the case even if a page was revised after execution. Fortunately, extrinsic evidence typically is admissible to show any facts and circumstances at execution that might indicate the presence of all pages at that time. But statements relating to the substance of any provision or the intent of the decedent regarding the presence of any particular page or provision typically would not be admissible.

### Multiple Wills

Wills that lawyers draft typically include clauses expressly revoking all prior wills. Persons who prepare their own wills (often holographs) may die with more than one will, none of which expressly revokes any of the others. Multiple wills that each are valid documents standing on their own all are entitled to probate. In such a case judicial integration applies to the extent the wills are not inconsistent. Each document is considered alone to determine whether all its pages were present at the time of its execution. To the extent each is separately valid, then the several valid documents are considered in terms of their effect on each other. To the extent they are not inconsistent, the multiple valid documents are integrated to form a single dispositive plan. Only to the extent the documents are irreconcilably inconsistent will any provision be regarded as ineffective: the last of the inconsistent wills to be executed prevails. In this regard see Chapter 4, which challenges the meaning of "inconsistent." As an appetizer, consider what a court would rule if there are multiple inconsistent holographs and no evidence which was executed later in time, one leaving the entire estate to the Red Cross and the other to the Salvation Army. Intestacy would be intention defeating and giving everything to one charity or the other cannot be informed by any evidence. The theory under which the two charities each would take half is that the two wills are not inconsistent—they should be integrated and read as if one document gave the entire estate to the Red Cross and the Salvation Army.

## Incorporation by Reference

Incorporation by reference probably serves only two planned functions. Most common is to facilitate laziness. Second, in jurisdictions in which the incorporated document is not made part of the public record in probate, incorporation may allow an added degree of privacy. If this were the concern, however, the more appropriate alternative usually is to use a form of transfer that is not a public record in the first instance, such as a trust.

Incorporation by reference says "treat this other writing as if it were a part of the will," even though it is not—and usually was not physically present at execution (and was not signed or witnessed). Nevertheless, the other writing may be treated as if it was physically part of the will. The basic requisites for incorporation by reference are:

- Intent to incorporate the other writing into the will, which must be apparent from the face of the will.

- Existence of the incorporated document before execution of the will. Handwritten lists disposing of tangible personal property (e.g., mementos, furniture, jewelry, and the like) often fail to be validly incorporated on this ground. As a result, UPC §2-513 authorizes such a list, which need not be handwritten, without regard to its existence at the time the will is executed, if the list is signed by the testator as if it were a valid holograph. Under the UPC, the only kind of tangible personal property that cannot be disposed of by such a list is money. See page 88 regarding the UPC provision, and see *Hanson v. Estate of Bjerke*, 95 P.3d 704 (Mont. 2004), regarding the notion that cash usually is not regarded as "personal property" in the context of such a tangible personal property provision.

- Third, the will must refer to the incorporated document as being in existence. The cases that deny incorporation on this ground may just be situations in which the court believed (but could not be sure) that the document to be incorporated was not in existence when the will was executed and therefore failed the prior requirement. For example, words of futurity (e.g., "I give my ABC Co. stock to my children and grandchildren as set forth on a list that I *will* prepare") can disqualify what otherwise might be a valid incorporation.

- Fourth, the will must describe the incorporated document with reasonable certainty. Required is a clear, definite, explicit, and unambiguous reference, to make clear which document is being incorporated and avoid concerns of fraud.

- Fifth, the incorporated document must be identifiable as the document described in the will. Any alteration to the incorporated document after the will is executed precludes incorporation of the new provisions and might prevent incorporation of the original provisions as well. Parol evidence may be admissible to prove that the document produced conforms to the description in the will, but as with other uses of extrinsic evidence this is unpredictable.

*Johnson v. Johnson*, 279 P.2d 928 (Okla. 1954), illustrates use of incorporation by reference as a fall back argument, rather than an affirmative estate planning tool, to validate a will that was not executed in the usual fashion. The decedent was a lawyer who had prepared many valid wills for clients. He died leaving a single, unsigned typewritten sheet of paper stating that it was his will and providing for various devises. At the bottom of the page, in his handwriting and signed by him, were the words: "To my brother James I give ten dollars only. This will shall be complete unless hereafter altered, changed, or rewritten." The court admitted the will to probate, saying that the typed portion was a "will" (even though it was not validly executed), and the bottom portion was a validly executed holographic codicil to the will that republished it. See page 88. Did the testator intend the typewritten page to be his will and the handwriting at the bottom of the page to be a codicil or, as the dissent persuasively argued, did the testator intend the entire document to be his will? Not all jurisdictions allow a validly executed codicil to republish a will that was not validly executed. Compare *Hogan v. Sillers*, 151 So. 2d 411 (Miss. 1963), and *Everett v. Everett*, 309 S.W.2d 893 (Tex. Ct. App. 1958), with *In re Brown's Will*, 160 N.Y.S.2d 761 (1957).

More important, could the handwritten portion constitute a holographic will—not a codicil—that incorporated the typed portion into it by reference? If the testator intended the entire page—the typed and handwritten portion—to be his will it could not be valid as a holograph because not even the material portions were handwritten, and it clearly was not executed in compliance with the formalities required for attested wills. Even if somehow the entire document was valid as a holograph, in many jurisdictions the non-handwritten portion would be excised as surplus (which it clearly wasn't, as substantially all of the dispositive provisions were contained in the typed portion). If, however, the handwritten portion was a holographic will, did it adequately refer to the typed portion to incorporate it by reference (assuming there was an intent to incorporate)? The only possible reference to the typed portion in the handwritten portion was the "This will . . ." sentence; arguably that reference, along with the placement of the handwriting on the bottom of the typed portion, adequately identified the typed portion to satisfy that requirement for application of incorporation by reference. That sentence, however, seems to indicate that the testator viewed both portions of the page as a single will, rather than that the typed portion was to be incorporated into the "separate" handwritten holograph.

In a state that allows holographs, arguably a holograph should not be permitted to incorporate a typewritten document by reference, because the verification function of a holograph (written in the testator's handwriting) is lacking with respect to the typewriting. On the other hand, the verification function of an attested will is the attestation by witnesses, which also is lacking for typed documents that are incorporated by reference into the fully attested will and incorporation routinely is allowed for them. Even if the typed document is treated as being incorporated into the holograph, it should invalidate the holograph (because it is not in the testator's handwriting), or at least be excised from the holograph as surplusage. Nevertheless, some courts allow holographs to incorporate typed documents. And, as we hope you can sense, incorporation by reference is a messy concept.

### The Doctrine of Independent Legal Significance

Like insurance, if we didn't already have this concept, we would need to invent it. Independent legal significance is the doctrine underlying the pour over will, which is an absolute mainstay in estate planning, and it is how wise estate planners avoid the messiness of incorporation by reference. The doctrine allows a testator to describe property, or identify persons who will be beneficiaries under a will, by reference to acts, circumstances, or documents that are extraneous to the will. All that is required is that the referenced acts, circumstances, or documents have a "substantial significance apart from their impact on the will."

For example, to "my mother-and-father-in-law" or "my spouse" or "my employees at the time of my death" all are valid dispositions because marriage and employment have significance independent from the will. As a consequence, if your will gave $10,000 to every employee of yours at the time of your death, an individual could be added as a beneficiary merely by putting them on the payroll rather than by amending the will. Similarly, disposition of "my car" or "my household furnishings" or "the contents of my safety deposit box at ABC Bank" or "the contents of my top desk drawer" all would be valid, and a larger or smaller bequest could be effected by buying or selling, adding to or deleting from, and such. Although a person might marry/divorce, hire/fire, or move assets around, we assume those acts would not be done solely for testamentary disposition. They presumably have a significance apart from their testamentary effects.

Also notice that the act, circumstance, or document that has independent legal significance need not be subject to the testator's control. For example, "to the person married to X at my death" or "to each grandchild of mine who survives me" or "to each grandchild who is married at my death" all would be valid, even though the will gives X or each child or each grandchild the power to alter the testator's bequest. Similarly, "to the persons named as beneficiaries in the will of X as in effect at my death" also would be valid notwithstanding that X may name beneficiaries with no significance independent from X's testamentary objective. The point is that naming beneficiaries in X's will *does* have significance (the disposition of X's property) independent from the *testator's* testamentary purpose.

Invalid under independent significance is a gift to the "persons listed on the paper to be found with my will" because this has the sole objective of a testamentary disposition and therefore has no independent legal significance. Such a disposition might be valid, however, under incorporation by reference or, for tangible personal property, under UPC §2-513, discussed at page 88.

### Pour Over to Trust

Most importantly, the doctrine of independent legal significance makes valid a gift "of the residue of my estate to the acting trustee of the trust executed by me on [date], to be added to and administered as a part of the trust estate held under that trust as in effect at my death." This is what a typical pour over will would provide, pouring the residue of the decedent's estate into the trust and allowing the trust document to govern its disposition. A valid pour over relies on the doctrine of independent legal significance, which is essential because it permits the trust to be altered after execution of the will.

Historically some states required that the trust instrument be executed prior to execution of the testator's will. The UPC and the Uniform Testamentary Additions to Trusts Act only require that the trust be in existence and able to accept the pour over when the testator dies. This could include a trust created under the will of someone else, provided that the pouring over testator dies second.

Pour over wills typically do not rely on incorporation by reference unless the drafter was inept, and would not qualify in many cases as an incorporation by reference because frequently the trust is amended after execution of the will, making the independent legal significance doctrine critical to this common planning approach. Thus, unlike incorporation by reference, (1) the pour over concept does not require republication of the will each time the trust is amended, and the trust amendments will govern if the pour over will does not provide otherwise, (2) the trust is not made testamentary (meaning that it need not be executed in accordance with will formalities to be valid), nor is it subject to probate, and (3) the trust is not treated as part of the estate or made subject to creditors' claims or the claims of a spouse under the statutory share concept addressed in Chapter 10 (although quite independent of the pour over the trust assets may be subject to claims of both creditors—see Chapter 6—and a surviving spouse).

UPC §2-511, which also is the freestanding Uniform Testamentary Additions to Trusts Act, permits pour overs to trusts that have not been funded during the decedent's life. Under traditional trust law there cannot be a trust without trust property. See Chapter 12. Nevertheless, UPC §2-511 permits a pour over to a trust initially funded by the devise itself. Because substantially all of the ultimate dispositive provisions for the testator's property usually are in the trust instrument, this result really turns fundamental notions of wills (and their effect) on their head. Yet the Uniform Testamentary Additions to Trusts Act has been adopted in all states, either as part of the UPC proper or as a freestanding enactment. This is contrary to much traditional wills doctrine, and it has contributed to the modern trend of courts moving toward greater flexibility in their interpretation of the formalities for execution.

In addition, under UPC §2-511 (1) the trust terms may be contained in an instrument executed before, after, or concurrently with execution of the will, (2) the pour over is permissible if the terms of the trust permit the devised property to be administered in accordance with the terms of the trust as amended after the testator's death (provided that the will does not specifically provide against such postmortem changes), and (3) the testator's will may provide that the devise does not lapse even if the trust is revoked or terminated prior to the testator's death. See Chapter 8. This may occur by incorporating by reference the terms of the trust as a part of the pour over will if the trust is not in existence to accept the pour over—which might be useful if the pour over is to the trust of someone else and they might revoke it without the testator's knowledge or at a time when the testator lacks the ability to change the testator's will.

### Dispositions of Tangible Personal Property

Disputes often arise over the disposition of a decedent's tangible personal property. Under traditional wills doctrine, this property is subject to the same rules as apply to the testamentary disposition of other kinds of property. Thus, a writing separate from a will purporting to dispose of tangible personal property would not be valid unless it was executed and attested in compliance with required will formalities (or it satisfies the requirements for a holographic will or codicil, or is valid under incorporation by reference, the doctrine of substantial compliance, or the dispensing power of UPC §2-503).

UPC §2-513 provides a special dispensation because it is so common for testators to attempt to dispose of tangible personal property by writings separate from their wills, because such property typically is not of substantial value, and because such attempted dispositions so often were invalid under traditional wills doctrine. A will can refer to a list or other statement to dispose of any item of tangible personal property other than money. The list or statement need not be valid as a holograph (e.g., it can be typed), and it need not comply with incorporation by reference requirements (e.g., it can be prepared or revised after the will is executed).

In some respects, UPC §2-513 is a special application of the doctrine of independent legal significance, deeming the written statement or list to have a sufficient independent existence from the testator's testamentary disposition to validate it. This is truly a fiction, but it is allowed because usually (although not always, and it does not matter) the amounts involved are de minimis and the havoc wreaked by invalidating this common disposition outweighs the damage that purists regard as done to traditional wills doctrine. Note, however, that UPC §2-513 requires that the list or statement be in writing, that it be signed by the testator, and that it be referred to by the will. Problems likely will continue to be encountered in this area even in jurisdictions that adopt UPC §2-513 because, for example, many homemade attempts to dispose of tangible personal property in writings separate from wills probably are not signed.

## Republication by Codicil

A codicil is a document executed with all the formalities of a will (either a traditional attested will or, if the jurisdiction permits them, a holographic will) that changes provisions in a will referred to in the codicil. It may supplement, explain, modify, add to, subtract from, qualify, alter, restrain, or revoke provisions in the will. Important here is that, in some circumstances, a codicil may in the first instance validate an otherwise invalid will, or may revive a once valid will that subsequently was revoked.

To illustrate, T executed a will in Year 1 under undue influence (or when T lacked testamentary capacity), and the will therefore was not valid. T validly executed a codicil to the will in Year 2 when T was no longer under undue influence or incapacitated. The codicil is said to "republish" the will, meaning that for many purposes the will is treated as having been re-executed on the date the codicil is executed, making the will valid. As another example, assume T executed in Year 1 a document intended to be a will, but it was not valid as a holograph (material portions were typed), it was not properly attested, and the jurisdiction had not adopted the UPC dispensing power or the substantial compliance doctrine. If T validly executed a codicil in Year 2, it may republish and thus validate the will. Finally, imagine that T executed Will 1 in Year 1. T executed Will 2 in Year 2, expressly revoking Will 1. In Year 3, T executed a codicil to Will 1, specifically referring to Will 1 and making no mention of Will 2. The codicil republishes, and thus validates (i.e., "*revives*"), Will 1. (Note: assuming both wills dispose of T's entire estate, the republication of Will 1 by the codicil may operate as a revocation by inconsistency of Will 2. See Chapter 4.)

It may help you to understand the concept of republication to think about it as if, in effect, a codicil incorporates the underlying will by reference. But be careful, because in republication analysis we don't technically follow the incorporation by reference approach, all the formalities of incorporation by reference are not required, and timing issues and interpretation of the documents may differ from what you might expect under traditional incorporation doctrine. More importantly, republication may apply in states that do not recognize incorporation by reference.

The requisites for republication by codicil (and thus validation of a will) include:

- Just as the incorporated document must be in existence when a will incorporating it is executed, a validated or revived will must be physically in existence when the codicil republishing it is executed. Physical revocation of the will (such as by burning it) precludes its republication by codicil.
- Intent to validate or revive.
- A sufficient description of the will to be validated or revived. Physical attachment to the codicil probably will suffice. Finding both together in the same physical location (an envelope, box, or drawer, for example) may suffice if the codicil refers to "my will" and no other will is found.

The effect of validation through republication is restoration of the underlying will, plus (1) all prior valid codicils to that will that are not inconsistent with the reviving codicil (even if those codicils are not specifically identified in the reviving codicil), and (2) all invalid or inconsistent codicils that are specifically identified by the reviving codicil. The general rule is that "republication comprehends republication of all codicils." So look for an expansive interpretation of the effect of a valid codicil.

The general treatment of a codicil as republishing a will (and other codicils) on the date of execution of the codicil raises a number of questions. Should we look to circumstances at original execution of the will or prior codicil, or those on the later date of validation/revival by codicil if circumstances at execution are relevant for interpretation of a will or earlier codicil? Typically changes in circumstances between execution of the will and execution of the codicil become part of the parol evidence available for interpretation. And for purposes of statutes that refer to the date of execution, would that be the date of original execution of the will or the date of republication of the will by the codicil? Frequently it will be the date of original execution of the will, although this is not certain. See *Azcunce v. Estate of Azcunce*, 586 So. 2d 1216 (Fla. Dist. Ct. App. 1991), and its discussion in Chapter 10 for an example dealing with a pretermitted heir statute when the date of the republishing codicil was used, yielding an unfortunate and inequitable result.

# CHAPTER 4

# REVOCATION

Wills may be revoked by physical act, by subsequent written instrument, or by operation of law. Revocation by physical act requires an act done with the intent to revoke. Revocation by subsequent instrument can be by express provision or by inconsistency. Revocation by operation of law generally constitutes only a partial revocation and occurs if the testator's circumstances have changed in a major way, such as by divorce resulting in revocation of provisions in favor of the former spouse.

Certain wills that were revoked can be "revived" (for example, if Will 1 was revoked by Will 2, which then was revoked by physical act). And revocation of a will may be ineffective under the doctrine of dependent relative revocation because it was conditioned on the existence of facts or law that were not as the testator thought. All of these concepts are the focus of this Chapter.

## Revocation by Physical Act

Physical revocations normally take either of two forms: mutilation of the paper on which the will is written, or obliteration or cancellation of the words on the paper.

Mutilation includes tearing, cutting, burning, or other forms of destroying the paper. Unlike revocations by obliteration or cancellation, mutilation — acts like tearing, burning, cutting, or otherwise — need not touch the words on the paper of the will. But the mutilation must affect the will proper and not just a backing, a self-proving affidavit, or a cover. Total destruction is not required, but if the will is only partially mutilated the issue will arise whether the testator intended a partial or complete revocation. If partial revocation by physical act is not valid in the jurisdiction, then the question is how much of an act is needed to constitute a total revocation (vice none at all). With partial mutilations, there always are questions of fact about what the testator intended.

For example, assume the pages were singed rather than the entire will being destroyed by fire. A court might assume that the testator had a change of mind and pulled the will out of a fire, intending not to revoke. Or the court might assume that the testator acted under an assumption that holding a match to the pages was enough to revoke the will, or ran out of matches before one caught the will on fire and burned it up.

Physical act revocations should destroy the entire will to avoid such uncertainties with respect to intent.

The second form of physical revocation is a physical act done to the printed words on the paper. Obliteration renders the words unintelligible (for example, if T tapes strips of paper over or completely blacks out words of the will). Cancellation involves writing over or marking through words. Under the traditional view, writing only in the blank spaces, margins, or on a cover will not suffice. By contrast, UPC §2-507(a)(2) expressly provides that a cancellation need not touch *any* words to revoke the will. Thus, in *Thompson v. Royal*, 175 S.E. 748 (Va. 1934), the attempted revocation was made by the testator's lawyer writing on the back of the will's cover that it was null and void. The statement was dated and the testator signed it. When the testator died, the will was admitted to probate over objections that it had been revoked, because the writing on the back cover did not touch the words of the will. Had UPC §2-507(a)(2) been in effect, the revocation would have been valid. The attempted revocation also was not effective as a revocation by subsequent instrument because the writing was not attested and it was not in the testator's handwriting, so it was not made in compliance with the formalities for an attested or a holographic will.

Writing "canceled" or "revoked" across the printed page is a cancellation by physical act (and *may* be a revocation by subsequent instrument as well). Similarly, making an "X" over one or more provisions of a will is a cancellation. Among the questions raised by such an act are: (1) did the testator intend to revoke the will in whole or in part (or perhaps not at all); (2) if a partial revocation was intended, are partial revocations by physical act valid in the jurisdiction; (3) if a partial revocation was intended and respected, which provisions were revoked; and (4) if a partial revocation occurred, will it increase devises to others and, if not, with what result? See page 94.

### *Act and Intent Required*

Any physical revocation will be unsuccessful lacking either the proper act or intent to revoke. Thus, physical acts do not revoke if they were done by mistake, to the wrong document, or if the testator's intent changed before the full intended act was completed. A physical act also will not suffice if the testator was incapable of forming the requisite intent, or if it was not done by the testator (unless it was a valid proxy revocation).

*Thompson v. Royal*, discussed above, is representative of cases that require strict compliance with specific statutory provisions for revoking wills. By contrast, the dispensing power in UPC §2-503 validates instruments that attempt to revoke wills but that are not duly executed, if the intent to revoke is established by clear and convincing evidence.

### Presumption of Revocation by Physical Act

There is a presumption of destruction by the testator with the intent to revoke if a will cannot be found, or is produced in a mutilated, obliterated, or cancelled condition, provided that (1) the testator was the last person to have possession of the will, (2) possession was not available to others, and (3) if the will is lost, there was a diligent search for it. The presumption of revocation may be rebutted if someone who would benefit if the lost will was revoked had access to the place where the testator kept the will. Compare *Estate of Travers*, 589 P.2d 1314 (Ariz. 1991), with *Lonergan v. Estate of Budahazi*, 669 So. 2d 1062 (Fla. Dist. Ct. App. 1996). In such a case, if the presumption of revocation is rebutted, admission is possible by proof of the will. For example, in most jurisdictions, an unexecuted or conformed copy will suffice. ("Conformed" means that an unexecuted will is made to show by typewritten entries what appears in handwriting on the signature and date lines of the original. For example, a document with a signature line that appears like "*/s/ John Doe 1/1/96*" means that John Doe signed and dated the original in his handwriting.)

*Harrison v. Bird*, 621 So. 2d 972 (Ala. 1993), involved an intended revocation that was effective because of the presumption of destruction with intent to revoke. The testator had executed duplicate original wills, one kept by the drafting attorney and the other by the named beneficiary/personal representative. When the testator decided to revoke the will, she called the attorney who tore it up (or had his secretary do so) and advised the testator in a letter that he had revoked the will for her and was sending her the pieces. The pieces of the will, however, were not found after the testator's death. The duplicate original of the will was denied probate, notwithstanding that the governing statute imposed a common requirement that a proxy physical revocation must be performed in the testator's presence. Thus, the act of tearing up the will did not revoke it. But the presumption that the testator destroyed the will with the intent to revoke it applied and was not rebutted because the pieces of the will had been sent to the testator and were not found following her death.

The will might have been valid if the testator in *Harrison* had thrown the pieces of the will in a trash basket by her desk and the pieces were recovered after her death. This is because the testator did not tear, burn, cut, obliterate, or mutilate the will, nor was it subjected to such an act by her proxy in her presence. If the governing statute allows physical revocation by "destruction," perhaps the testator's disposal of the pieces in the trash constituted a "destruction" of the will. UPC §2-507(a)(2) allows a will to be revoked by a "revocatory act" to the will, which is defined to include burning, tearing, canceling, obliterating, or destroying it. The UPC philosophy of relaxing technical wills-related requirements in favor of giving effect to the testator's intent arguably would result in the term "revocatory act" being held to include the act of throwing the will away. But if this is not true, and if merely throwing the will away did not constitute a "destruction" of it, then the will likely would not have been revoked.

### *Extrinsic Evidence*

Extrinsic evidence usually is admissible to prove lack of possession by the testator (and thus that a physical act may not have been done by the testator and therefore is invalid as a revocation), declarations by the testator regarding intent (which might explain the significance of a physical act), and circumstances showing reasons (or the lack thereof) for the testator to revoke (which might help understand the testator's intent or ascertain the consequences of a revocation).

### *Partial Revocation by Physical Act*

Some jurisdictions permit partial revocation by physical act if less than all of a will is torn, burned, obliterated, cancelled, or made subject to another act that can revoke it. Many others do not, however. If partial revocation by physical act is not allowed, and the testator performs a revocatory act on only a part of the will, the presumption is that none of the will was revoked, as opposed to the attempted partial revocation resulting in a revocation of the entire will. The partial revocation necessarily will be effective, however, if the attempted partial revocation obliterates provisions of the will such that they cannot be read (and there is no extrinsic evidence, such as a copy of the will, that can prove what the obliterated language said).

If partial revocation by physical act *is* allowed, the next issue is what becomes of the property that was subject to the revoked provision? That property necessarily passes to someone else. The question is whether the partial revocation is effective to make a new bequest. The issue is really one of formalities for a *change* as opposed to an effective revocation. In some jurisdictions a partial revocation results in the property passing by intestacy. In others, a partial revocation may increase a residuary gift (but not a preresiduary gift).

For example, T's will provided: "I give Blackacre to A, B, C, and D. I give the residue of my estate to E." Under a law that allows partial revocations by physical act, T crosses out "B" in the devise of Blackacre and also revokes the residuary provision. The residue will pass to T's heirs as intestate property. The attempted partial revocation of B's share of Blackacre might not increase the gifts to A, C, and D even though most observers probably assume that was the intent and should be the result. Instead it might cause ¼ of Blackacre to become part of the residue, or it might be wholly ineffective. But if D's will provided: "I give Blackacre to X; I give the residue of my estate to A," and if D crossed out the gift of Blackacre, the effect would change the beneficiary of Blackacre from X to A. The rationale for this result is that A already was entitled to the residue, and the residue of any estate always is subject to change. Indeed, A probably would take Blackacre notwithstanding this change if X simply did not survive the testator (unless an antilapse statute were applicable, as discussed in Chapter 8).

### *Proxy Revocation by Physical Act*

Most states permit proxy revocations by physical act, but typically only if the proxy performed the act in the presence of the testator, at the testator's direction and, in some states, in the presence of witnesses. The same presence issues discussed for execution apply to proxy revocation. See Chapter 3. As such, proxy revocation under UPC §2-507 must be in the testator's conscious presence and at the testator's direction, but does not require witnesses. Furthermore, a will should be admitted to probate if the presence requirement is not met but the will was destroyed by a proxy. The difficult aspect is proof of the provisions of the will, again resolved if state law has a "lost" will provision.

### *Multiple Documents*

When revocation is by physical act the intent of the testator may not be clear, as it normally would be if revocation was by a writing (which presumably states or reveals the testator's intent). This can raise problems if there are multiple documents that make up the estate plan. For example, assume there is a will and several codicils to it. If the revocation is by physical act to the will the presumption is that the act also revokes all codicils to that will. Revocation of a codicil, however, is not regarded as a revocation of the underlying will, or of other codicils to it. This rule is not necessarily intuitive, given that a codicil must be executed with all the formalities for execution of a valid will, meaning that a codicil really is a freestanding document that could be probated as a will. Such a codicil, however, probably would not dispose of the entire estate, and may not make sense without reference to the underlying (and now revoked) will.

Even in a state that does not recognize partial revocations by physical act, revocation of just a codicil and not the underlying will or other valid codicils is not regarded as an invalid partial revocation.

## Stapled Wills

Most wills consist of multiple pages held together with a staple. The problems that can arise when a staple is removed are illustrated by *Estate of Goldey*, 545 N.Y.S.2d 464 (1989), in which a probate petition was filed to remove the staple in a final will to permit separation and inspection of the pages, all to explain the fact that there were excess holes in the pages that could be seen (on the top and bottom of the stack). Suspected in a case like *Goldey* is that some pages in the middle have only one set of holes, indicating that they were not part of the original will and therefore were added after execution of the will. *Estate of Weston*, 833 A.2d 490 (D.C. Ct. App. 2003), was even more clearly a case of tampering, with two pages that did not match the other three in terms of staple holes, paper quality, formatting, and printer. Those pages not present for the execution are not valid and the pages they replaced (or, indeed, in some cases the entire will) may have been revoked by the physical act of their removal and disposal. In this regard see the discussion of integration in Chapter 3.

## Duplicate Original Wills

Duplicate executed originals are neither necessary nor advisable. Notwithstanding extensive misconceptions on this score, revocation of one duplicate executed original typically (although not always) revokes all. To illustrate, assume that T executed duplicate originals at the recommendation of an attorney, who explained that it would reduce the likelihood of "inadvertent" revocation by destruction of the will. One copy was left with the attorney for safekeeping; T took the other home. At death, T's copy cannot be found, and extrinsic evidence supports a motive for revocation. The general rule is that all originals must be produced to avoid a presumption that destruction of one that was in T's possession was a revocation of that one, and that revocation of the one is a revocation of all. This presumption of revocation is weak or nonexistent, however, if the testator possessed multiple copies and retained at least one executed copy of the will. The notion is that, if revocation was intended, all copies in the testator's possession would have been destroyed. That is the key: if all copies in the testator's control are missing the existence of other copies in someone else's possession is not adequate to frustrate the testator's intent to revoke. That being the case, there is no sense in using duplicate original executed wills.

### Revocation by Subsequent Instrument

The second way to revoke a will is by a will, a codicil, *or any other instrument* executed with the formalities of a will. For example, T wrote a note to the custodian of T's will, requesting destruction of the will by the custodian. Two witnesses attested the note. At T's death, the will had not been destroyed and the note does not constitute a sufficient subsequent instrument to revoke the will. Often these letters are not attested and state law does not recognize a holograph, but here that is not the problem. Instead, a more important impediment is the same as regards letters requesting the production of a will. See Chapter 3. This is the fact that there was no intent to revoke by the letter; the intent was to solicit a physical revocation by proxy, not to accomplish a revocation by subsequent instrument. Thus, the dispensing power of UPC §2-503, which can cure execution defects, would not save the "revocation." Also significant is the reality that, if the custodian had complied with the request, in most states the resulting "revocation" would fail as a physical revocation (because the presence requirement for a proxy revocation would be unmet). That being true, it seems sensible to argue that the naked request should not suffice if the act requested itself would not. See *In re McGill*, 128 N.E. 194 (N.Y. 1920). Note, however, that some states by statute *do* permit proxy revocation pursuant to a written request, even if not done in T's presence. See, e.g., Ohio Rev. Code 2107.33(A)(3). But lacking such a rule, this case is dramatic on what it reveals about revocation and frustrated intent.

Let's carry further with things that are not as they appear. Writing on a will may act as a revocation by subsequent instrument even though at first blush it looks to be a revocation by the physical act of writing on the document (i.e., a cancellation). The point is that a subsequent instrument need not be on a separate piece of paper (although usually it is). To illustrate, intending to revoke it, T writes across the middle of the first page of T's will "This will is void." T then dates and signs the writing. The writing constitutes a revocation by subsequent instrument if the jurisdiction recognizes holographs. It also constitutes a revocation by the physical act of cancellation. Note that in a jurisdiction that required a touching for a cancellation the intended revocation would be ineffective as a physical act if the writing was in the margin and did not touch the words of the will, and it would fail as a revocation by subsequent instrument if holographs were not recognized in that state.

### *Revocation by Inconsistent Subsequent Instrument*

A subsequent instrument can revoke a prior one even if it does not say it is doing so, because revocation by subsequent instrument may be by inconsistency rather than by an express provision. In some cases the inconsistency is such that there is little question that the testator intended the subsequent instrument to revoke the prior one. In other cases, the subsequent instrument raises difficult questions as to whether the testator intended it to revoke any part of a prior will.

If the subsequent instrument is a codicil, the presumption is that the testator did not intend to revoke the underlying will, because codicils normally operate to amend wills, not revoke them. As a result, in the revocation by inconsistency context a codicil generally is presumed to be only a partial revocation of the will, if a revocation at all, meaning that the issues would be whether and to what extent an inconsistency exists. So, assume a will left the testator's property all to X and a subsequent codicil devised Blackacre to Y. The presumption is that the codicil overrides the will only with respect to Blackacre. Y therefore takes Blackacre but X takes the residue of the testator's estate.

Hard cases can arise when a subsequent will does not include an express statement of revocation. The issue would be moot if the later will effectively disposed of all assets in an inconsistent manner. Integration of the two documents would honor the last in time first, trumping all inconsistent prior documents, and it effectively would override — and thus revoke — all earlier documents. Thus, if Will 1 gave all the testator's property to X and Will 2 devises Blackacre to Y, Greenacre to Z, and the residue to A, Will 1 would be totally revoked by inconsistency. If the multiple documents are not so clearly inconsistent, however, integration may work unintended results.

To illustrate this notion, consider a series of alternative situations, all without express indications of intent.

| **Will** | **Codicil** |
|:---:|:---:|
| *"100 shares of IBM stock to A"* | *"Blackacre to A"* |

These gifts will cumulate. That A is the beneficiary in each document creates no inference that the later gift is meant to replace the former.

| **Will** | **Codicil** |
|:---:|:---:|
| *"100 shares of IBM stock to A"* | *"50 shares of IBM stock to B"* |

These would cumulate, because there is no reason on the face of the documents to suggest inconsistency. These might be deemed inconsistent if the testator owned less than 150 shares, or the estate might just acquire more shares. It might matter if the gifts were of *"my* shares of IBM stock" as opposed to any shares available for purchase in the open market. It also might matter that at no time did the testator own more than 100 shares, although extrinsic evidence of this type might not be admitted. The point here is that there is no reason to read these documents as creating an inconsistency at all, and therefore no reason to regard the codicil as a revocation of the will, unless there are added facts and a court finds them to be relevant and admissible. At most, this may raise an abatement issue of what to do when the testator is more generous than the estate can accommodate. See Chapter 9.

| **Will** | **Codicil** |
|----------|-------------|
| *"100 shares of IBM stock to A"* | *"50 shares of IBM stock to A"* |

This is not as easy a case as the prior two, but the same result ought to obtain. There simply is no more reason to suspect that the gift in the codicil (absent some express admissible statement otherwise) was meant to substitute for the disposition in the will rather than cumulate with it.

| **Will** | **Codicil** |
|----------|-------------|
| *"100 shares of IBM stock to A"* | *"100 shares of IBM stock to B"* |

Although this might look more like a substitution because the gifts otherwise are identical, in fact this is an even easier case than the last, with the same nonrevocation result. The testator has made a total gift of 200 shares.

| **Will** | **Codicil** |
|----------|-------------|
| *"Blackacre to A"* | *"Blackacre to B"* |

Unlike IBM stock, Blackacre is not fungible, which most courts would assume to mean that the codicil supersedes the will. It could be that A and B should take as tenants in common, just as the gifts of stock cumulate and both A and B would take. We think that most courts would regard this last case as an inconsistency and regard the codicil as superseding the will, so that B would take Blackacre to the total exclusion of A. As the progression in examples is meant to indicate, however, this is not necessarily intuitive.

Note that some opinions suggest that it might make a difference in each of the prior examples if the second document were called a will instead of a codicil, because of a presumption that a codicil amends while a will replaces a prior will. We suggest that you not succumb to such overbroad formulations.

## Revocation by Operation of Law

Certain changes in a testator's circumstances can result in a partial (or, less frequently, complete) revocation of the testator's will by operation of law. In most states, only divorce (with or without a property settlement) or annulment still operates to revoke a will (in whole or in part, as discussed below) by operation of law.

In a few states marriage also revokes an earlier will, or results in the surviving spouse being entitled to an intestate share of the decedent's estate, unless the will contemplated the marriage (e.g., by bequeathing something to the testator's intended spouse, who was identified as an intended) or the testator provided for the spouse to receive nonprobate assets in lieu of a testamentary gift. See, e.g., UPC §2-301, discussed in Chapter 10. If marriage does not revoke a prior will the surviving spouse typically is protected by elective share statutes or by community property regimes. See again Chapter 10.

In at least one state (Georgia) the birth of a child revokes a will. More states do not regard births as a revocation because their pretermitted heir statutes protect children born after execution of a parent's will. Yet again see Chapter 10.

### *Revocation by Divorce*

Various statutes provide for divorce in different ways. For example, some statutes treat the former spouse as predeceased, or as having disclaimed any bequest under the will. See Chapter 2 for a discussion of the difference between these two approaches. In these states, the will is not actually revoked. Rather, the will is valid and may be admitted to probate, but the former spouse cannot take. Other state statutes reach a similar result by deeming all provisions in favor of the former spouse as having been revoked but the rest of the will remains valid. Finally, some state statutes still regard the entire will as revoked.

A variety of problems may be encountered with revocation by divorce statutes. For example, if the testator remarries the former spouse, UPC §2-804(e) revalidates the will provisions for the spouse. Most non-UPC states do not address the issue. In addition, treating a former spouse as predeceased or as having disclaimed, or revoking all provisions in favor of the former spouse, may work unintended results. For example, if the testator's will provided for the former spouse for life, remainder to the spouse's child by a prior marriage, or bequeathed property to the former spouse if living, otherwise to a child of the former spouse by a prior marriage, exclusion of the spouse may merely move the former spouse's child into immediate possession. In many cases it is likely that the testator would have preferred other contingent beneficiaries under the will, or that the estate be intestate, rather than having anything pass to the former spouse's family. But this is not universal or predictable.

In some cases courts have ruled that the former spouse's child is entitled to the interest only if the child actually survives the former spouse (rather than being alive when the former spouse is treated as having predeceased the testator). Thus, if the former spouse survives the testator, the child of the former spouse cannot take because the condition has not yet occurred. Clearly, courts sometimes work equity as they see it. UPC §2-804 addresses the problem by providing that divorce results in both the former spouse and relatives of the former spouse being treated as if they disclaimed all devises to them under the will.

Although this Chapter does not address will substitutes, these revocation by operation of law situations also impact nonprobate property, such as a beneficiary designation under a life insurance policy or employee benefit annuity contract. See Chapter 6. The only real solution is legislation — such as UPC §2-804 — that applies the revocation by divorce statute to all wealth transfer situations. Outside the UPC jurisdictions that result is uncommon, although some state statutes apply the revocation by divorce concept to specified will substitutes, such as life insurance policies or revocable trusts.

## Revival

A will that is revoked may be made valid again without a new execution. If Will 1 is revoked by Will 2, which itself is later revoked, the revocation of Will 2 might restore (i.e., "revive") Will 1. Some states do not treat Will 1 as revived. The rationale for the no-revival result is that Will 2 revoked Will 1 immediately upon execution of Will 2. As a consequence, revocation of Will 2 could not revive Will 1. By contrast, the theory underlying the revival result is that wills are ambulatory, meaning that Will 2 had no legal effect until the testator's death. Thus, revocation of Will 2 prevented it from revoking Will 1 because Will 2 had no legal effect during the testator's life.

Note that redrafting and execution of a new will is a virtual necessity if Will 1 also was physically destroyed. The later revocation of Will 2 cannot revive a Will 1 that is not physically in existence.

Some courts purport to decide the revival question based on their perception of the testator's intent. Unless there is some evidence of an intent otherwise it probably is fair to say that the prevailing assumption is that Will 2 immediately revokes Will 1, so that a later revocation of Will 2 does not revive Will 1.

If Will 2 revoked Will 1 only by inconsistency ("to make room" for the Will 2 provisions), some cases hold that Will 1 is revived by revocation of Will 2 because there was no explicit expression of intent in Will 2 that Will 1 be revoked. Under this approach, a codicil would revoke only by inconsistency, if at all. Thus, a subsequent revocation of the codicil likely would revive those provisions of the will that the codicil had revoked. But if Will 2 revoked Will 1 expressly, the intent is clear that Will 2 should be deemed to be an immediate revocation of Will 1, with the result that Will 1 cannot be revived by the subsequent revocation of Will 2.

UPC §2-509 abandons all of this express/inconsistency distinction. Under it, the effect on Will 1 of a revocation of Will 2 depends on whether Will 2 was a total or only a partial revocation of Will 1. If Will 2 is *physically* revoked (1) UPC §2-509(b) presumes revival if the revocation of Will 1 by Will 2 was partial, but (2) UPC §2-509(a) presumes against revival if Will 2 completely revoked Will 1. By contrast, if Will 2 is revoked by Will 3, Will 1 is revived only if that intent is shown in Will 3. Confused? The bottom line is that for planning you should not ever rely on revival. Do a new will that is identical to Will 1 if that is T's intent.

### Dependent Relative Revocation

Dependent relative revocation addresses a revocation that was brought about by mistake of fact or law. Dependent relative revocation ignores the revocation of Will 1 if, for example, Will 1 was physically revoked in connection with the execution of Will 2 and it turns out that Will 2 was not validly executed. Unlike revival, if dependent relative revocation is applicable the prior will need not be physically in existence. Dependent relative revocation does not restore the purportedly revoked will. Instead, we say its revocation never occurred. Dependent relative revocation is a "never revoked" concept and the fact that the will is not *physically* present is not an impediment (if its terms can be proven).

"Dependent relative" revocation means that revocation implicitly was dependent — conditioned — on the existence of certain facts or legal results to which the revocation related. Thus, if the facts or the law were not as the testator thought, the revocation that was conditioned on them is deemed not to have occurred. Dependent relative revocation most often is applied when a testator revokes a will or codicil in connection with an alternative disposition that fails. It also can apply if the revoking instrument recites the mistake. For example, "I revoke the $50,000 devise to B because B just won $1,000,000 in the lottery," when in fact B won only $100 in a $1,000,000 lottery. Dependent relative revocation is broadly applicable any time a revocation is made because of a mistake of fact or law that can be established by clear and convincing evidence. Thus, if the testator lined through B's $50,000 bequest with the intent to revoke it, but clear and convincing evidence shows that the revocation was made because of the mistaken belief regarding B's lottery winnings, the revocation would be denied effect even without a recital of the mistake in the instrument making the revocation.

Dependent relative revocation is a doctrine of presumed intent. If the testator revokes Will 1 in connection with executing Will 2, which for whatever reason is invalid, it is presumed that the testator would have preferred that Will 1 remain in effect rather than be intestate. Dependent relative revocation will not apply if that presumption can be rebutted. *Carter v. First United Methodist Church*, 271 S.E.2d 493 (Ga. 1980), illustrates the role of the presumption in dependent relative revocation. The decedent's 1963 will was found with pencil marks through the dispositive provisions, folded with a 1978 handwritten but unsigned document that was labeled her will and that included dispositive provisions different from those in the 1963 will. Because the two documents were found folded together, the purported revocation of the 1963 will was deemed conditioned on the unsigned 1978 document taking effect as her will. Dependent relative revocation was applied because the 1978 document was not valid, raising a presumption that the testator would not have wanted the 1963 will revoked if the 1978 document was not effective. The presumption might be rebutted with evidence that intestacy would come closer to accomplishing the testamentary objectives of the 1978 document than would the 1963 will. In such a case it would be more likely that the testator wanted the 1963 will revoked regardless of whether the 1978 document was effective.

The usual factual context for application of dependent relative revocation is illustrated by *Carter*: a revocation of Will 1 in connection with an ineffective making of Will 2. *Estate of Alburn*, 118 N.W.2d 919 (Wis. 1963), was functionally the exact opposite, because Will 2 was revoked in the mistaken belief that Will 1 would be revived. Because that belief proved to be wrong, the revocation of Will 2 was ignored by dependent relative revocation. Ignoring the revocation prevented the perceived injustice of intestate takers receiving the estate. And we say that we know the testator would have preferred Will 2 over intestacy because the beneficiaries under Will 1, which the testator wanted to revive, were very similar to the beneficiaries under Will 2, and both were very different from the intestate heirs.

Dependent relative revocation cures mistakes notwithstanding statements that "there is no remedy for mistake" in the law of wills. One explanation for the dissonance in result is that dependent relative revocation returns the testator to a previously valid will, which differs from curing a mistake — that typically prevented validity of a will in the first instance. Seen in this light, all we're witnessing is that the law with respect to substantial compliance and harmless error in execution has taken longer to develop than in revocation.

A frequent application of dependent relative revocation involves a testator who tried to make a change by physical alteration without the benefit of proper execution. To illustrate, assume that T's will included a bequest of $1,000 to B, and that T crossed out the "$1,000" and wrote above it "$1,500." If that increase is not effective, because it was not accompanied by the formalities required to execute a codicil, dependent relative revocation should cause the act of physically revoking the $1,000 gift to be ignored, because the testator clearly would want a bequest of $1,000 if $1,500 could not pass. If the change was from $1,000 to $500, however, it is impossible to predict with confidence how a court would rule. Given that the attempted change to $500 cannot be given effect, the only options are for B to receive the original $1,000, if dependent relative revocation is applied, or nothing, if the revocation stands. Note that the dispensing power of UPC §2-503 may apply if the proponent can establish by clear and convincing evidence that the change was made by the testator with testamentary intent. In that case the $1,500 bequest would be honored and dependent relative revocation would not be relevant.

### *Other Doctrines May Apply*

Dependent relative revocation often is considered in contexts in which other doctrines also would produce the same result. For example, a prior revocation may not be effective if it was performed by mistake and the requisite intent was lacking (if extrinsic evidence to prove the mistake is admissible). In addition, Will 2 might be invalid because the testator lacked either the intent or the capacity to execute a new will. There would be no revocation of Will 1 at all if Will 1 was not physically revoked, but was instead "revoked" only by Will 2. In such a case there need be no reliance on dependent relative revocation.

Finally, the revocation of Will 1 may have been expressly conditional such that failure to meet the condition causes the revocation to be a nullity, again without regard to dependent relative revocation.

CHAPTER 5

# WILL CONTRACTS

Individuals may contract for any of them to make a will, to not make a will, to revoke a will, or to not revoke a will. This Chapter addresses whether a will contract exists and, if so, the effects of a breach of the contract. We will see that contractual wills are the same as any other wills, and that a breach of contract spawns contract remedies but does not affect the will or intestacy. Indeed, we will learn why contracts to make a will (or not to make a will, which is much less common) or to revoke (or, more likely, not to revoke) a will are litigation breeders, which is why knowledgeable estate planners eschew their use.

## Terminology

Remember that a will is revocable during the testator's life and that it is ambulatory, meaning that it has no legal effect until the testator dies. In that environment, a little terminology is important.

- A *joint will* is one document that is executed by more than one testator. It is the separate will of each and is entitled to probate on each testator's death. The will cannot deny probate at the first death and defer it until the death of the survivor. However, often the testators of joint wills own everything in joint tenancy, meaning that their will often is not and need not be produced until the survivor's death.

- A *mutual will* is the separate will of one person, containing provisions that mirror or that are the reciprocal of those in the will of another person. Reciprocal typically means each person leaves everything to the other testator(s). Mirror image means that each will does the same thing on the death of the last to die. For example, Husband leaves his estate to Wife if she survives, Wife leaves her estate to Husband if he survives, and each leaves everything to their children in equal shares on the death of the survivor of the two of them. These mutual wills are reciprocal (he to her and she to him) and mirror image (to the children on the second death in each document).

- A *joint and mutual will* is one document signed by more than one testator (most commonly spouses) with reciprocal provisions and a single residuary provision operating on the death of the last to die. The phrase often is used with reference to a joint will with reciprocal and mirror image provisions made pursuant to a contract between spouses under which each spouse agrees not to revoke the will during their joint lives without the other's consent and not to revoke it at all after the first of their deaths. A joint will that also is a mutual will usually is not referred to as a "joint and mutual will" unless it is contractual. To illustrate, Husband and Wife, each of whom has children from a prior marriage, agree to execute, and not revoke, a joint and mutual will under which, on the first of their deaths, the decedent's estate will pass to the survivor and, on the survivor's death, his or her estate will pass to their children equally as if their respective separate children were common to the marriage.

Neither joint wills nor mutual wills are necessarily contractual. Indeed, mutual wills — at least those that are not also joint wills — usually are not. In some states, however, execution of a joint will gives rise to a presumption that it is contractual and cannot be revoked unilaterally without breaching the contract. Under UPC §2-514 no such presumption is created by the execution of either a joint will or mutual wills.

### Proving a Will Contract

In the last example, no recourse would be available if the survivor died after changing the will to cut out the step-children unless they could prove the existence of the contract not to revoke the will. Mere similarity of dispositive provisions does not make wills contractual. Nor does the existence of either reciprocal or mirror image provisions, or both, suffice to prove a contract not to revoke. Similarly, in most states the existence of a joint will, even one with reciprocal or mirror image provisions, does not necessarily mean the will is contractual. Only a few states *presume* that a joint will is contractual.

Thus, there ought to be written evidence of any contract. UPC §2-514 deals exclusively with the issue of proof, not with questions of validity or enforceability of these contracts. Under it the contract may be proven *only* by a writing in one of the following forms: (1) the will itself states the terms of the contract, (2) the will expressly refers to the contract and the terms of the contract are proved by extrinsic evidence, or (3) a written contract is signed by the decedent.

Even in a jurisdiction without a statute like UPC §2-514, proof of an agreement is made difficult by application of the Statute of Frauds, which typically requires that contracts to sell land be in writing, and which also has been held applicable to contracts to dispose of land by will. So, imagine that Testator orally promised to devise Blackacre to Caregiver, but Testator's will leaves Blackacre to someone else. Whether Caregiver can enforce the contract depends on whether it is excepted from the Statute of Frauds, and several exceptions relative to oral contracts to make wills disposing of realty do exist. One is part performance. Caregiver's performance of services for Testator may constitute part performance sufficient to avoid the Statute of Frauds. Similarly, in the mutual wills context, death of the first to die with a will that complies with the agreement constitutes a part performance that avoids application of the Statute of Frauds. The other exception is estoppel, which may bar reliance on the Statute of Frauds by someone who has accepted benefits under the mutual will of the first mutual testator to die. Thus, if Wife dies first and her mutual will leaves property to Husband, which he accepts, he and those claiming through him may be estopped from relying on the Statute of Frauds to defend against a subsequent breach of the contract.

Because proof is a severe issue for contractual wills, an estate planner who chooses to draft contractual wills should avoid the Statute of Frauds problem by documenting the agreement. And there are better alternatives if the estate planner is going to engage in that added labor.

## Avoiding Will Contracts

The difficult problem of proving there was a will contract can be solved by documenting the agreement. But will contracts typically present other substantial problems, so wise planners typically solve the issue that informs the use of a contractual will with some other mechanism and avoid the will contract altogether. This particularly is true because the contract obligation can cause reduction of the federal estate tax marital deduction, so contractual mutual wills are not a wise plan for spouses whose estates are large enough to make marital deduction planning important. Using a so-called Qualified Terminable Interest Property (QTIP) trust is far easier and more certain.

Spouses are far and away the most likely suspects for use of a contractual will, but consider another illustration. Two siblings, neither of whom has descendants, inherit property from their parent. Each wants the other to have the property on the first of their deaths, and for it to go to another designated family member on the second death. Contractual mutual wills are not a good idea in this situation because questions of what the surviving mutual testator may do with the property abound. For example, assume one sibling survives the other by 15 years. During that period, may the survivor consume the principal as well as the income from the property? If so, for what purposes? May the survivor make gifts of either portion of the property? Or give away the survivor's own assets and consume the inherited portion of the property for the survivor's own uses? Sell it and reinvest the proceeds? Must the survivor provide accountings to the designated family member? And does the survivor have any obligations to that family member with respect to maintenance of the property? With regard to all of these questions a trust would serve the client's objectives better.

In the example above, the siblings could place the property they inherit from their parent into a single trust during their joint lives, with the trust to become irrevocable on the first of their deaths. Such trusts may involve a gift tax on the death of the first settlor to die, difficulties in the event of divorce (if the two settlors are spouses), and questions concerning management and use of the property during their joint lives. So, if prohibiting disposition of the property is not their objective, an even better approach yet is for each individual to create their own trust for the benefit of the survivor for life, with the remainder passing in the agreed manner. If control is important, however, you can see that a certain price is paid for that restriction.

The circumstance in which control seems to be most important often involves spouses. For example, a "widow's election" estate plan typically provides for a surviving spouse for life, but only if the surviving spouse agrees to leave property to designated beneficiaries on the second death. For a number of tax and other reasons, these are not common outside the community property jurisdictions and may not be good planning in taxable situations even there. Again, the preferable approach is a trust.

Finally, will contracts are used — and often create serious problems that lead to litigation — in a variety of situations in which mutual wills are not involved. For example, Testator is elderly and in need of care. As an inducement, Testator promises to leave half of Testator's estate to Caregiver if Caregiver will live with and care for Testator for the rest of Testator's life. What happens if Testator is not satisfied with Caregiver's care or Caregiver dies or becomes incapacitated before Testator? If Caregiver satisfactorily cares for Testator until Testator's death, should Caregiver receive the same property regardless of whether Testator lives one or twenty years? And are any limits placed on Testator's use of the property by entering into the contract? When you begin to think about these agreements you realize that they are much more involved than the typical will contract might suggest, which is just one of the reasons why they are litigation-breeders.

### Remedies

Even if a valid contract is proven and its terms are clear, any party may alter or revoke the will that is envisioned, even if it is a joint will. Thus, imagine that A agreed to make (and not revoke) a will devising A's property to B. Also assume that A made such a will and the contract for the will was valid. Nevertheless, A later revoked the will and executed Will 2 devising A's property to C. The revocation of Will 1 and the execution of Will 2 are unaffected by the contract. Will 1 is revoked and Will 2 will be admitted to probate. B has no remedy in probate. Instead, B's only remedy is for breach of contract.

Similarly, a contract to make a will is not the same as the will it anticipates, meaning that there can be no probate of the contract if the promised will is not executed, nor can the promised will be treated as if it was executed. There is no specific performance available in this context. Instead, the only available remedy when a promisor fails to make a promised will or revokes or alters a will that the promisor agreed not to revoke or alter is for breach of the contract, with typical contract law requirements relating to consideration, ascertainability of provisions, and so forth. For example, some property, dollar amount, fractional share, or other identifiable portion of a decedent's estate that is subject to the contract must be spelled out in a manner that would allow a court to enforce the contract. Lacking some specific promise, however, at best the recovery will be for something like quantum meruit. Thus, assume that Testator's promise to Caregiver was: "If you care for me for the balance of my life, I *will take care of you* under my will." If Testator's will does not provide for Caregiver, or leaves an "inadequate" amount, the likely remedy (if any) is only for the fair value of the services rendered.

Consideration is critical as it is in any contract enforcement case, and it exists in mutual will cases once the first to die has complied with that testator's end of the bargain by dying with the anticipated mutual will. Otherwise, consideration often takes one of the following forms:

- Services. Caring for the testator, living with the testator, or supporting the testator (assuming there was no family law obligation to do so and that services provided were not provided gratuitously). Close family members are presumed to provide care for free, and one spouse may have a legal obligation to care for the other spouse, meaning that this care may not qualify as consideration for an alleged contract relating to a will.
- Marriage to the testator (or, conceivably, to someone else, like a child, who the testator wanted to be married). Thus, a promise in a premarital agreement to devise $X to a spouse-to-be who survives the promisor is supported by consideration (assuming the marriage takes place).
- Property transfer. Conveyance of property to a third party, or payment of an annuity or similar amounts to the testator for life.
- Forbearance of suit or of a contest of another will.

Consideration likely will not support litigation for breach if the object of the agreement was to perform acts that violate public policy or that are illegal or immoral (e.g., divorce someone, commit adultery, or commit a crime at the decedent's request).

It may become known that a will contract promisor breached the contract prior to death. If so, one or more of the following remedies may be available for the anticipatory breach: (1) recovery of any consideration already given to the breaching promisor; (2) restitution for property conveyed in reliance on the contract; (3) maybe an injunction against a threatened conveyance to a third party of property subject to the contract; or (4) a constructive trust imposed on the transferee if property promised under the contract is conveyed to a third party (unless, perhaps, the third party is a bona fide purchaser for value). An injunction against revocation or specific performance ordering execution of a promised will are out of the question, however.

To illustrate, assume that Testator does not have sufficient liquid funds to pay ongoing living expenses and is unable to continue managing Blackacre. Testator agrees to leave half of Blackacre to Manager, if Manager will pay to Testator $X per month, and manage Blackacre, for the rest of Testator's life. Then, in breach of their contract, Testator gives Blackacre to Child after Manager has complied with the contract for two years. Manager may bring an action during Testator's life for breach of the contract. If Manager wants to continue with the contract, an available remedy might be the imposition of a constructive trust on half of Blackacre. If Manager does *not* want to continue the contract, it should be possible to recover amounts paid to Testator under the contract and probably the fair value of prior services in managing Blackacre for the two year period. On the other hand, Manager has no actionable claim if Testator continues to own it but simply does not execute the promised will, or after having done so revokes it. Only after Testator dies without the promised will may Caregiver seek a remedy for breach.

Also note that any action to recover for breach of the contract at the death of the contracting party is not in probate. Again, a promised will cannot be restored after the decedent revoked it and cannot be regarded as executed if the contracting party never signed it. Entitlement probably will be limited to damages, specific performance in the form of a constructive trust, restitution, or quantum meruit, all in the local court that decides contract actions. So, picture Husband and Wife, each of whom has one child from a prior marriage. They execute a joint and mutual will under which each agrees to leave his or her property to the other spouse, or equally to the two children if the other spouse is not living. Husband dies and leaves his estate to Wife, and Wife later changes her will to leave her entire estate to her child alone. Although the omitted child has no actionable claim prior to Wife's death, upon Wife's death the omitted child could assert a claim for a constructive trust to be imposed on half of the property left by Wife to the other child.

## Contractual Wills and the Surviving Spouse's Elective Share

The spouses in *Via v. Putnam*, 626 So. 2d 460 (Fla. 1995), executed contractual mutual wills providing for the estate of the first to die to pass to the survivor, and for the survivor's estate to pass to their children. Joann died first, after which Edgar married Rachel. When Edgar died Rachel claimed a pretermitted spouse's ½ share of Edgar's estate. See Chapter 10. The court held that the children's claim under the contractual wills lacked priority over Rachel's claim. The same issue arises when a surviving spouse in Rachel's position asserts a claim to an elective share, and cases go both ways. *Putnam* held for Rachel on the basis of the strong public policy in favor of a surviving spouse's pretermitted heir status.

We question whether that is the right result. Consider that, at least in some cases involving contractual mutual wills between spouses, the first spouse to die would have left less to the second to die were it not for the contract. Thus, without the contract, the second of the spouses to die would have less property. If that surviving spouse subsequently remarries, denial to the new spouse of a share of property subject to the contract in such cases is not inequitable. Indeed, the decedent's net worth is greater just because of the life estate received in the property of the first spouse to die. In such a case, equity doesn't favor a claim by the new spouse against property subject to the contract. But you never know how a court might rule in such a case.

And let's not forget breach in the other direction. For example, if D and S, spouses, enter into a contract to execute and not revoke wills leaving property of the first to die to the other, and property of the survivor to named beneficiaries, the survivor may renounce the will and elect to receive a statutory share of the decedent's estate unburdened by the contract. Again see Chapter 10, and *Bauer v. Piercy*, 912 S.W.2d 457 (Ky. Ct. App. 1995) (the contract precluded a revocation by the survivor, but not a renunciation). Do you get the picture that contractual wills are problematic? One last example may help.

Assume that T entered into a contract with A under which T agreed to leave A half of T's estate if A would serve for the rest of T's life as the president of a company T owned. T executed the required will. Later, A breached the agreement and terminated A's employment relationship with the company. A is entitled to half of T's estate if T dies without having revoked the will. A's breach of the agreement does not cause a partial or complete revocation of T's will (although T or the company may have separate breach of contract claims against A). Similarly, if T executed a will devising T's entire estate to someone else, the will would control the disposition of T's estate even if A had complied with the contract. T's breach of the contract would not affect the validity of the will; A's remedy would be a breach of contract claim against T's estate, or perhaps a claim for a constructive trust to be imposed on ½ of T's estate left to the devisees under the will, or maybe just a quantum meruit claim against the company. No one is likely to be pleased with any of those alternatives (except, perhaps, all the lawyers who get involved *other than* the hapless planner who put this ill-fated contract into operation).

CHAPTER 6

# WILL SUBSTITUTES

A substantial part of this book involves the law of intestacy, wills, and decedents' estates. However, much of a typical decedent's property may not pass under either the terms of a will *or* by intestacy. Rather, it is "nonprobate property" and passes pursuant to the terms of the particular instrument or rules — sometimes called "will substitutes" — that govern it. Common forms of nonprobate property include joint tenancies, life insurance, retirement plans, annuities, and trusts. A common theme addressed in this Chapter is the extent to which the law of wills governs or informs the rules that apply to will substitutes.

Even the most "perfect" will has no effect on the disposition of nonprobate property. To wit: your client is a single mother with one small child. You work through all of the questions she must answer for you to draft her will with a testamentary trust for the child: who should be trustee, how long should the property stay in trust, may the trustee expend trust funds for the child, what if the child dies before the trust terminates, etc. You draft the will, your client executes it, and she dies in a car accident. The value of her probate estate — net of debts — is $25,000; she also had a $500,000 face value life insurance policy on her life, the beneficiary of which was her child and it pays double indemnity due to the accidental death. The $25,000 net probate estate passes under the terms of the will into the trust for the child; the $1 million of insurance proceeds are paid to a court appointed guardian for the child, to be distributed outright to the child at age 18, subject to cumbersome and expensive court supervision until then. The estate plan failed because the life insurance beneficiary designation was not coordinated with the will.

If you will think about most wealth in America today, it is in nonprobate form. See Chapter 1. Even with improvements that facilitate probate administration, several common purposes for using will substitutes explain their popularity. The most popular is avoiding probate. Some states still lack independent (i.e., not subject to court supervision) probate administration, making avoidance of the cost, publicity, and delay of probate important. Another is tax planning. Minimizing wealth transfer and income taxation is possible (but not common) through lifetime gifts that "mature" at death, such as gifts made to an irrevocable life insurance trust. Third, planning for incapacity may utilize lifetime management and protection of the assets with a trust.

For more information, see Chapter 16. Fourth, life insurance (the instant estate) is used to provide liquidity to pay death taxes and debts, and to augment the estate. With proper planning, the insurance proceeds can be received free of federal income and estate tax. Finally, some transfers are employed to minimize the rights of predators, such as creditors and surviving spouses who may exercise elective share rights. See Chapter 10.

### Validity of Will Substitutes

Nonprobate transfers are subject to challenge to the extent they look like testamentary dispositions but lack the formalities of a will. Litigants who make such challenges include surviving spouses, creditors, and an occasional disappointed heir, all seeking to reach nonprobate property through a claim against an estate that they hope to augment. Those with claims against the probate estate benefit to the extent the nonprobate transfer fails and the property that would have been subject to it instead becomes a part of the probate estate. The clear trend, coincident with the increased use of will substitutes, is to uphold these transfers. See, e.g., UPC §6-101. Still, two conflicting factors sometimes create chaos in this arena. First, some courts appear to decide these cases with at least one eye on the equities involved (claimant through the estate versus potential beneficiary of the nonprobate disposition). Second, courts seem to uphold the more common nonprobate transfers more often than they uphold the more unusual.

Among the few identifiable generally applicable principles in this area, consider the following three. First, wills are both ambulatory (they have no legal effect until the testator's death) and revocable during the testator's life. The challenger of a will substitute should at least be able to establish a similarity based on the notion that the will substitute also constituted no irrevocable transfer during the decedent's life. Second, another way to look at the same concept is that a valid will substitute should operate during the decedent's life to create some interest in a beneficiary. Enjoyment of the interest may be deferred, provided that the interest is created presently. It is adequate that the interest is contingent, provided that an interest actually is created in a third party presently. Third, showing that a will substitute is ambulatory and revocable (that no interest was created in any beneficiary of the will substitute until the decedent's death) does not guarantee a successful challenge. Several of the most common will substitutes (e.g., life insurance) look testamentary under these standards but they still are treated as valid. Indeed, the most common are so prevalent and well accepted that they rarely are challenged.

## Life Insurance, Annuities, and Retirement Benefits

Insurance on a decedent's life is most notable among the nonprobate transfers that look testamentary because it does nothing until the decedent's death. In the typical case people own insurance on their own life for which they have designated a beneficiary to receive the proceeds at death. That arrangement typically is both ambulatory and revocable. No interest in the policy is created by the beneficiary designation. Unless you really stretch, the beneficiary designation does not create an expectancy that counts under state law as an interest in the policy. No fiduciary or other duties are owed by the policyholder to the beneficiary, and a beneficiary has no more of an interest in the policy than a devisee under a will has in the property of a living testator. Thus, life insurance would seem to be a good candidate for a successful attack as being a testamentary arrangement that is invalid because it typically does not comply with required will formalities. Nevertheless, life insurance is clearly and consistently regarded as not being invalid or testamentary in nature.

As such, insurance proceeds traditionally are not controlled by the insured's will unless a mistake occurred. *Cook v. Equitable Life Assurance Society,* 428 N.E.2d 110 (Ind. Ct. App. 1981), illustrates this corollary to insurance being nontestamentary. The insured's will has no effect on disposition of the proceeds if a beneficiary of the policy is named. In *Cook,* the insured named his wife as beneficiary before they were divorced. Without changing the beneficiary designation, the insured executed a will that purported to leave the proceeds of the policy to a new spouse and child. At the insured's death, the court awarded the proceeds to the ex-spouse. (Unlike the traditional approach followed in *Cook,* Restatement (Third) of Property (Wills and Other Donative Transfers) §7.2 allows an insured to change the beneficiary by will, while protecting an insurer that pays the designated beneficiary without notice of the change by will.) *Cook* is a dramatic example that some rules that apply with respect to wills would be useful with respect to will substitutes (in this case, the Probate Code rule causing a revocation by operation of law of the will or a bequest under a will in favor of a former spouse; see Chapter 4). Indeed, many states have addressed the *Cook* problem with statutes that revoke insurance beneficiary designations naming the insured's ex-spouse. See, e.g., UPC §2-804.

In limited circumstances the will of an insured policyholder may control the disposition of life insurance proceeds on the insured's death. For example, if the beneficiary of the policy is the insured's estate, the proceeds will be payable to the estate for disposition with the rest of the insured's probate estate under the terms of the insured's will (or the jurisdiction's intestacy statutes, if the insured died intestate). However, for reasons discussed at page 125, it generally is not a good idea to name the insured's estate as the beneficiary of a life insurance policy. Rather, it is preferable to coordinate the disposition of the insurance proceeds with the disposition of the rest of the insured's estate in another manner. So payment to the estate usually is a default result that applies only if a beneficiary designation fails or, worse, never was made.

Also very common these days are annuities. In their purest form, annuities pay a person a fixed amount per month for life. At death, there are no further rights under the annuity arrangement to pass on to others, and the question of validity as a will substitute does not arise. Annuities with refund or survivorship features, however, provide benefits to others after the annuitant's death, typically by beneficiary designation as a nonprobate transfer by will substitute. Although such annuities, like life insurance, are revocable and ambulatory and thus would appear to be vulnerable to attack for lack of compliance with will formalities, they are enough like life insurance that they also are not regarded as testamentary. Similarly, IRAs and retirement benefit plans payable postmortem to designated beneficiaries generally are not regarded as invalid will substitutes, again without regard to their looking testamentary in nature or failure to create any premortem interest in any beneficiary.

### Payable on Death Contracts

Payable on death (POD) contracts include a wide variety of arrangements under which one party's death causes benefits to be payable to one or more designated beneficiaries. These contracts apply without regard to the terms of the decedent's will or the jurisdiction's intestacy statutes. Theoretically, POD contracts include life insurance, annuities, and deferred compensation plans. But the term more commonly is used to refer to bank accounts owned by one person and payable on death to another, stock ownership arrangements (sometimes referred to as transfer on death (TOD) accounts), and other contracts such as employment agreements, partnership agreements, depository agreements, and so forth. For example, many banks respect accounts that are owned in the name of one person, payable on death to another. These are pure will substitutes: the depositor has unrestricted ownership, and the payee-to-be has no interest in the funds until the depositor's death. Consequently, POD accounts are vulnerable to attack as testamentary because they also lack compliance with will execution formalities. Statutes in a majority of states, however, authorize such accounts. See page 122 for a discussion of the very similar Totten trust bank account form of will substitute.

The more common POD arrangements routinely are viewed as immune to challenge for failure to comply with will formalities, notwithstanding their testamentary characteristics. As shown by *Wilhoit v. Peoples Life Insurance Co.*, 218 F.2d 887 (7th Cir. 1955) (life insurance proceeds deposited with the insurance company under a settlement arrangement), some less common POD contracts have been held unenforceable but UPC §6-101 broadly authorizes POD arrangements in all contracts, as well as in a variety of other instruments that are not usually viewed as contracts, such as promissory notes, bonds, conveyances, deeds of gift, and trusts. In modern times most states have followed the UPC approach.

## Joint Tenancy

Each joint tenant is treated as owning the entire fee simple, subject to equal rights of the other joint tenants. Thus, if A owns Blackacre and transfers ownership to A and B as joint tenants with the right of survivorship, A is treated as having made a gift of an interest in Blackacre to B. The issue is when that gift is complete, and joint tenancy bank accounts are different in this regard than joint tenancy in realty. Generally each tenant has full access to the funds in the account during their joint lives, and the survivor becomes the sole owner on the death of the other tenants. In the event of a dispute, however, most jurisdictions treat the funds as owned in proportion to the respective depositors' net contributions to the account. See, e.g., UPC §6-211. This means that no gift from one to the other occurs until a tenant withdraws more than that tenant contributed. The same rule *may* apply under state law with respect to a stock brokerage account or other forms of intangible financial accounts. But beware that a joint tenancy safety deposit box is only that; it does not make the *contents* of the box joint tenancy property.

An important glitch in many state laws relates to joint tenancy between spouses and the effect of divorce. Although state statutes revoke provisions in a will in favor of an ex-spouse, many do not apply to nonprobate assets. See Chapter 4 and the discussion of life insurance at page 115 in this Chapter. Thus, a surviving ex-spouse joint tenant would be the sole owner of property owned in joint tenancy with the right of survivorship if no change was made incident to a divorce. By contrast, UPC §2-804 would sever the joint tenancy upon divorce and convert it to a tenancy in common.

The survivorship feature in a joint tenancy is not regarded as testamentary, even if all tenants have a unilateral right to terminate the tenancy until death. This result is more defensible than the nontestamentary treatment afforded life insurance, annuities, retirement benefit plan interests, and many POD or TOD contracts because each joint tenant is viewed as owning the whole property, subject to similar ownership rights of every other tenant, from inception of their concurrent ownership. Thus, something *does* occur inter vivos when this nonprobate device is created. However, a joint tenancy created solely for convenience can be treated as not constituting a conveyance at all. Such cases typically arise with respect to bank accounts. For example, *Franklin v. Anna National Bank*, 488 N.E.2d 1117 (Ill. App. Ct. 1986), involved an individual who established a joint tenancy bank account with his sister-in-law when she began caring for him. When he changed caregivers he unsuccessfully attempted to substitute his new caregiver as the other joint tenant on the account. At his death, the personal representative of his estate and the sister-in-law both claimed the funds. Based on the facts, the presumption that the depositor intended a "true" joint tenancy with survivorship was successfully rebutted and the funds in the account were deemed part of the decedent's probate estate because no gift was intended and no true joint tenancy with right of survivorship was created.

Although *Franklin* may yield the "right" result, the presumption of a true joint tenancy with ownership rights often means that the surviving joint tenant takes in cases in which that result seems questionable. Thus, *Franklin* illustrates a danger with such accounts: without intending the right of survivorship, many people create them for convenience or to solve a property management problem to which an inter vivos trust or a durable power of attorney would be better answers. See Chapter 16.

Without going into detail, joint tenancies produce adverse tax results in various cases. See the discussion of Internal Revenue Code §2040 in Chapter 19.

### Deeds

Labeling an instrument as a deed, and using language usually found in deeds ("I grant, bargain, sell, and convey . . ."), will not ensure that a purported conveyance is effective. To illustrate, assume that Grantor executed a deed that conveyed Blackacre to Grantee with the proviso: "this deed to be effective only at Grantor's death." The deed might be regarded as testamentary and invalid if it did not and was not intended to convey an interest until the grantor's death. See *Butler v. Sherwood*, 188 N.Y.S. 242 (1921) (the deed was invalid even though it was delivered to the grantee). On the other hand, there are cases that hold such a deed to be nontestamentary and valid, with the grantor viewed as having conveyed a vested remainder subject to a retained life estate. Also recall your property law training: no completed gift is made if an instrument on its face is an unconditional conveyance but it was not delivered until after the grantor's death. Actual or constructive delivery is required. There is no lifetime conveyance of an interest absent delivery, and the instrument does not pass the property at the grantor's death if it was not executed with Wills Act formalities. Such a deed *might* be valid to effect a conveyance of the property at death under the UPC §2-503 dispensing power discussed in Chapter 3. The grantee's burden would be to show by clear and convincing evidence that the deed was intended to operate as a will at the grantor's death.

## Revocable Trusts

A trust is an arrangement by which one or more trustees hold legal title to property for the benefit of one or more beneficiaries. See Chapter 11. The settlor may revoke a trust that is not irrevocable, in which case the trust property is transferred back to the settlor (or to a designee). Settlors usually create revocable inter vivos trusts for their own benefit. The settlor often is the sole beneficiary until death, after which the trust property is administered for and ultimately distributed to beneficiaries named by the settlor in the trust instrument. In substance, this resembles probate property owned and enjoyed by a decedent until death and that is administered and distributed to devisees under the testator's will (or to heirs at law to the extent the decedent died intestate). Nevertheless, these are valid will substitutes.

Revocable trusts are extremely common for a variety of reasons: To minimize the rights of a creditor or spouse (a goal that may fail; see *State Street Bank* at page 121); to prepare for the settlor's incapacity (which can be accomplished more simply by use of a durable power of attorney); to secure management assistance (although a durable power of attorney also can accomplish that efficiently); to avoid a will contest; and to avoid probate. None of these objectives entails giving up ultimate control over the trust assets. Indeed, in addition to being the sole beneficiary of the trust for life, often the settlor serves as its sole trustee or, if a third party is named as trustee, the settlor typically reserves a right to remove and replace the trustee.

If there is a present declaration of trust and a transfer of property to it, a revocable trust is a valid will substitute without regard to execution formalities. (Florida is an exception to this rule: the testamentary features of revocable trusts are not valid there unless executed with certain formalities.) Usually validity turns on whether the trust is valid and not on whether it is a will substitute. See Chapter 12. Validity merely requires the trustee to presently become the owner of some trust assets. Almost anything will do, and many trusts are created with a de minimis amount (e.g., $10). A "self-trusteed declaration of trust" requires no physical delivery or transfer of property, because the settlor is the trustee and need not deliver assets to own them as trustee. This makes it look like there has been no real change in ownership, which then supports the charge that the trust is testamentary because it is revocable and has not accomplished anything prior to the settlor's death. The common solution to this is to cause assets that are represented by a document of title (such as the deed to realty, certificate or book entry ownership of securities, or the title to a car) to be reregistered to show trust ownership. With respect to any asset that lacks a document of title, we merely use a bill of sale to prove delivery: "I, X, hereby sell to X as trustee of the X trust dated _____ all of my tangible personal property, including all household goods and furniture, clothing, and articles of personal use. . . ."

A transfer funding an inter vivos trust usually is effective if the settlor does all that is required to make the conveyance, even if the trustee has not yet received the property. For example, imagine that the settlor signed stock powers (which are instruments for the transfer of stock) and placed them and the underlying certificates (which typically would be mailed in a separate envelope for security purposes) in the mail, but died before the trustee received them. The black letter rule is that the settlor's acts are regarded as causing the stock to be a part of the trust corpus already, notwithstanding that delivery was not immediate because of incomplete administrative steps that were beyond the settlor's control.

Assuming a trust is valid under state law, the real issue then is whether it is testamentary in nature. Lifetime retention by the settlor of enjoyment and control is normal and permissible, and may include (1) rights to receive income and principal, (2) powers of appointment (see Chapter 14), (3) powers over investment and administration, (4) even powers as trustee, and (5) powers to amend or revoke the trust. Such a revocable trust is deemed not testamentary for two fundamental, interrelated reasons. One is fiduciary duties. The fiduciary relation between the trustee and the beneficiaries creates fiduciary duties, and exposure for breach, that are not present with respect to property the settlor owns outright. That makes the ownership of property under a trust indenture different from holding assets that will be subject to probate and the Wills Act. This is true even under UTC §603, which extends the duties of a trustee of a revocable trust only to the settlor, unless or until the settlor dies or becomes incapacitated.

In addition, creation of equitable interests in a third party (in a revocable trust, typically a remainder beneficiary) validates the trust and constitutes something more than a purely ambulatory will would accomplish during the testator's life. Their existence impairs alienability at least to some extent and allows enforceability of the trust even if those beneficial interests are contingent, defeasible, or remote. Unlike a will, which has no legal effect until the testator's death (i.e., it is ambulatory), present rights in others are created by even the most naked trust.

*Farkas v. Williams*, 125 N.E.2d 600 (Ill. 1955), is a wonderful case to showcase these elements. The settlor named himself as trustee, retaining a life estate and a power to amend or revoke the trust. The trust provided for the assets to be distributed at the settlor's death to a named beneficiary. The court relied on both the elements of impaired alienability and fiduciary responsibility and found the trust to be a valid will substitute. Essentially the court determined that the settlor accomplished something during life that was sufficient to distinguish the trust from a purely testamentary disposition. A revocable trust might be vulnerable to a testamentary attack if the settlor is trustee and sole lifetime beneficiary, and if the only remainder beneficiary is the settlor's estate, but it is difficult to envision why a settlor might so provide, and how a challenge might result. Otherwise, trust validity is not a serious issue with respect to the use of revocable trusts as will substitutes.

If the validity of a revocable trust is at issue, we have seen that we should consider the following:

- Did the settlor lack the requisite capacity to create a trust? The capacity required under UTC §601 to create a revocable trust is the same as that required to execute a valid will. See Chapter 3. Similarly, undue influence, fraud, and duress also are grounds for attacking the validity of a trust.

- There can be no trust without trust property. An exception to this rule applies if the unfunded "trust" is the devisee under the settlor's pour over will, because the Uniform Testamentary Additions to Trusts Act validates the trust — and the pour over to it — without regard to whether the trust otherwise had a corpus.

- The most likely circumstance for a successful testamentary challenge is if the settlor is the sole beneficiary for the settlor's life and serves as the sole trustee. Even then, however, if there is a remainder beneficiary a testamentary attack will fail because the trust creates present rights in the remainder beneficiary; the trustee has fiduciary duties to the remainder beneficiary and the settlor's ability to alienate the trust property has been impaired.

A revocable trust issue that frequently arises is the proper effect of the settlor's subsequently executed will that purports to dispose of trust assets. UTC §602(c) permits such a will (or codicil) to revoke or amend the trust if (1) the trust does not provide that another specified means is the exclusive method, and (2) the later will or codicil either expressly refers to the trust or specifically devises property that otherwise would have passed under the trust.

UTC §602(e) also permits an agent of the settlor acting under a power of attorney to exercise the settlor's rights with respect to the revocable trust, but only to the extent expressly authorized by either the terms of the trust or the power of attorney.

*State Street Bank and Trust Co. v. Reiser,* 389 N.E.2d 768 (Mass. App. Ct. 1979), illustrates the nature of an inter vivos revocable trust vis-a-vis the outside world. The court held that a creditor of the settlor could reach trust assets after the settlor's death. Its rationale was that the creditor could have reached the trust assets during the settlor's life. See

Chapter 13. Furthermore, if there had been no trust and the settlor had owned the assets at death, they would have become part of the probate estate and the creditor could have reached them there. The court concluded on policy grounds that the creditor could reach trust assets after the settlor's death, as it could estate assets, because of the settlor's retained powers over the trust assets. Although that holding was not necessarily "wrong," it is contrary to Restatement (Second) of Trusts §330, which was applicable at the time and provided that creditors usually could not reach trust assets postmortem, in the absence of fraud (which did not exist in *Reiser*). Today see UTC §505(a)(3), which is consistent with *Reiser*.

Notice also, however, that the coordination of trust and estate law is not always followed. For example, *In re Estate and Trust of Pilafas*, 836 P.2d 420 (Ariz. Ct. App. 1992), involved a settlor's alleged revocation of an inter vivos trust that authorized the settlor (who also served as trustee) to revoke by a written instrument delivered to the trustee. The original trust was in the settlor's possession but was not found following the settlor's death. In this case the court refused to apply the presumption of revocation by destruction that applied to the settlor's will (the original of which also could not be found). See Chapter 4. This was because the trust specified the means of revocation, which did not include physical destruction of the trust instrument, even if the settlor performed that act. *Pilafas* thus illustrates that trusts are valid will substitutes and that will principles generally do not apply to trusts. But even this general conclusion is subject to limitations.

To illustrate, many banks permit customers to open savings accounts in the name of the settlor "as trustee" for the settlor for life, remainder to another. Called "Totten trusts" (after *In re Totten,* 71 N.E. 748 (N.Y. 1904), which held them valid), these "savings account trusts" are only barely legitimate trusts, created simply by signing the appropriate signature card when opening a bank account, usually with absolutely no formalities that anyone could even argue rise to the same level of protection as the Wills Act. Totten trusts were developed as a will substitute for bank accounts before the advent of POD accounts and are valid in most states, either by court decision or, more commonly, by statute. See, e.g., UPC §6-201 et. seq., which treats them the same as POD accounts. This is the case even though (1) they have virtually no terms or formalities, (2) fiduciary obligations are nonexistent, and (3) beneficial interests are tentative during the settlor's life. Absent an indication that the settlor intended otherwise, during the settlor's life the account belongs to the settlor as trustee, who may spend or give away the funds for any purpose the trustee chooses. Nevertheless, Totten trusts have routinely been regarded as subject both to creditors and spousal claims at death because they are such a thin will substitute device. See

Chapter 10. Consistent with the settlor's almost complete and unrestricted control over funds in a Totten trust, creditors (and usually a surviving spouse) simply cannot be disfranchised by creation of such an account. See Restatement (Third) of Trusts §26 comment *d*.

The general trust rule is that a trust is irrevocable unless expressly made revocable by the creating instrument. This rule will change in states that adopt Uniform Trust Code §602(a), but elsewhere a final point is that Totten trusts are treated differently. Delivery of the passbook or giving notice of creation to the beneficiary may (but will not necessarily) make a Totten trust irrevocable. That is a question of the settlor's intent. Otherwise, normally Totten trusts are revocable, absent an indication that the settlor intended otherwise. Partial revocations (by withdrawal) are possible and any funds remaining in the account on the settlor's death belong to the beneficiary only to the extent the settlor's will does not provide otherwise. That is, unlike most will substitutes, the beneficiary of a Totten trust traditionally can be changed by the settlor's will. There is a presumption against a will acting as a revocation, and UPC §6-213(b) (applicable to Totten trusts, POD accounts, and joint bank accounts) provides that the right of survivorship under any of these accounts cannot be changed by the depositor's will. Even with that change, however, Totten trusts will remain on the edge of the division between wills and valid will substitutes and show that, depending on the issue involved, the dividing line is not straight or unwavering.

### "Blockbuster" Wills

The blockbuster will concept suggests that a will *should* be adequate to alter any beneficiary designation with respect to any property — nonprobate as well as probate — held during life and passing at death, including insurance proceeds, employee benefits, or POD contracts and accounts (excluding joint tenancies). But under the law today usually a will provision is *not* effective to alter a trust (other than a Totten trust) or other beneficiary designation. So, for example, assume Settlor created a revocable trust, retaining rights to income and principal for life and providing for distribution of the trust assets to Trust Beneficiary on Settlor's death. The trust instrument provides that any revocation must be written and delivered to the trustee during life. Settlor's will leaves the trust assets to Will Beneficiary. On Settlor's death, both Trust Beneficiary and Will Beneficiary claim the trust assets. If a third party served as trustee, the revocation provision in the trust would preclude any argument that the will constitutes an effective revocation of the trust (unless the UTC applies and the trust did not specify the exclusive means of revocation). But if the settlor was serving as trustee when the will was executed, *perhaps* the settlor as trustee could be deemed to have received the will, which arguably constitutes a revocation or amendment of the trust. This would be an unlikely result and the blockbuster will concept would alter that notion.

In a broader view, sometimes it is unfortunate that the law is not better coordinated with respect to wills and various will substitutes. For example, the law of wills has developed responses to issues that are not addressed by the rules applicable to various forms of nonprobate property. The good news is that the UPC (which does not recognize the blockbuster will concept per se) extrapolates to nonprobate assets many of its concepts that traditionally have applied only to wills and probate property. But most states do not so provide. Among the rules that apply to a decedent's will and probate estate but often fail to apply to nonprobate transfers are those that address divorce, adoption, pretermission, survivorship, lapse, tax apportionment, and creditors' rights. Chapter 10 addresses the rights of a surviving spouse with respect to nonprobate transfers and we will see that many state statutes do a remarkably poor job in this respect, which again argues for an integrated approach to all of a decedent's wealth transfers. We think that is the developing trend, and that you will continue to see evidence of it and inroads on the traditional separation (and jealousy) between will and will substitute law. But for now it is sporadic and at times frustrating and unpredictable.

### Equitable Election

This issue assumes a decedent who created certain rights in a beneficiary by a will provision but also attempted to dispose of that beneficiary's interest in nonprobate property (such as the proceeds of insurance on the decedent's life) by another provision in the will. For example, D and X own Blackacre in joint tenancy with right of survivorship but D's will gives Blackacre to Z while devising Greenacre to X. As we have just seen, normally a will cannot control the disposition of nonprobate property. But the rightful owner of nonprobate property can be put to an election either to take under the will and allow the will to operate in all respects (i.e., to dispose of the nonprobate property), or to deny the effect of the will on the nonprobate asset and, in the process, relinquish all beneficial interests under the will. So here X can allow Blackacre to go to Z and can take the devise of Greenacre, *or* X can deny the will's effort to control Blackacre but in the process must forego the will provisions in favor of X.

Equitable election is particularly common with both life insurance and joint tenancy because decedents often do not know that a will cannot control the devolution of those assets, so they put the beneficiary to an unintended election. Typically, there is no remedy for mistake under the law of wills. This means that the beneficiary cannot argue that a will provision attempting to dispose of nonprobate property is invalid but not the balance of the will. Thus, the will either applies in toto, due to the election, or it fails with respect to the nonprobate assets, and the beneficiary who was put to the election loses any right to probate property bequeathed under the will. Reformation is not customarily available as a remedy.

Because of the possibility that a testator will devise property to a beneficiary and also attempt to devise nonprobate property to others without knowing that the testator could not do so, some jurisdictions apply the doctrine of equitable election only if the testator expresses an affirmative intention to put a devisee to an election. In *Williamson v. Williamson,* 657 N.E.2d 651 (Ill. App. Ct. 1995), for example, the testator and a son owned real property in joint tenancy. The testator's will devised ⅔ of the property to five other children and the residue of his estate to all six children. The son accepted a distribution from the residue and his siblings claimed he therefore was required to convey to the father's estate ⅔ of the joint tenancy property. The court held for the son, refusing to apply the equitable election doctrine to joint tenancy property without an express indication that the testator so intended.

An effective, binding election by a beneficiary requires acceptance of benefits under the will, with knowledge that the effect of doing so is relinquishment of the beneficiary's interest in the nonprobate property. If the election is not made, and the rightful taker of the nonprobate asset retains its ownership, then the disappointed taker under the will might be compensated with the rightful taker's designated interest under the will (although this kind of equitable rearrangement is not predictable). So, for example, imagine that T's will leaves Blackacre to A and Whiteacre to B. T owns Blackacre outright but T and A own Whiteacre in joint tenancy with the right of survivorship. A must elect either to accept Blackacre and allow Whiteacre to pass to B, or to keep Whiteacre and give up the bequest of Blackacre. If A decides to keep Whiteacre, part or all of Blackacre may go to B as compensation.

### Insurance Trusts

It often is advisable (for a variety of both nontax and tax reasons) to place insurance proceeds in trust on the death of an insured. For example, the insurance may provide for minor beneficiaries, or for a surviving spouse for life, with remainder to children, in each case to insulate the proceeds from estate tax. The insured could name the insured's estate as beneficiary under the policy, with the proceeds being distributed to devisees under the will (including a testamentary trust). But this rarely is advisable. For example, naming the estate as beneficiary subjects the proceeds to claims of the decedent's creditors. By contrast, in most states insurance proceeds paid to a trust as the designated beneficiary are not subject to that risk. Also, the proceeds are part of the probate administration if the estate is the beneficiary, which means added delay and expense. And the proceeds will be subject to federal estate tax (if the estate is taxable) and probably any state transfer tax as well.

In many states it is possible for the proceeds to be paid to the trustee of a testamentary trust without subjecting them to creditor claims. That approach also should exclude the proceeds from probate administration. It will, however, cause some delay in the beneficiaries' access to the proceeds (because the will creating the trust must be admitted to probate before the trust can be put into operation and then claim the proceeds) and the proceeds will be subject to estate tax. In addition, a surviving spouse's elective share rights may extend to a testamentary trust and, if the insured wants to change the terms of the trust, a validly executed codicil is required, as opposed to a simple trust amendment. Finally, testamentary trusts are subject to supervision by the probate court in some jurisdictions for the duration of the trust. As a result, this alternative, although preferable to naming the estate as beneficiary, also is not advisable.

The preferred alternatives are funded or unfunded, revocable or irrevocable, insurance trusts. Funded insurance trusts are not common, and most unfunded trusts are revocable. Unless part of a divorce property settlement or an estate tax minimization plan, both funded and irrevocable insurance trusts normally are unattractive because of a loss of control and because any transfer of the policy or other funds to the trust may generate a gift tax. Ongoing premium payments must be considered and they also increase the gift tax exposure. Problems also exist in using insurance proceeds from irrevocable trusts to provide estates with liquidity to pay estate taxes and other obligations. In addition, trustee fees during the insured's life (if a third party acts as trustee) often discourage creation of a funded insurance trust.

All things considered, therefore, most clients use the unfunded revocable insurance trust, in which there will be little or no cost during the insured's life because there are no trust assets. Further, there are no taxable gifts because there are no transfers to the trust. And the trust is revocable, so flexibility is maintained through the ability to change the beneficiary of the policy and the terms of the trust. And full liquidity may exist at death because there was no effort to keep the proceeds out of the insured's taxable estate. Given these results, however, an unfunded revocable insurance trust is more vulnerable to challenge as being testamentary. The argument is not usually based on the control retained by the settlor, nor on the lack of terms during the insured's life. Instead, if the trust is only named as beneficiary of the policy but is not funded and does not own the policy, the concern is lack of a corpus during the insured's life. (A trust usually fails if it lacks a corpus. See Chapter 12.)

Validity nevertheless usually is justified on at least two grounds. First, the trust is no more testamentary than the insurance policy itself. Insurance policies are not treated as testamentary, and the unfunded revocable insurance trust merely provides for administration of the proceeds following the insured's death and therefore is not regarded as different. Second, an unfunded revocable insurance trust as the designated beneficiary of insurance possesses either a vested right with respect to the insurance (subject to divestment on change of beneficiary), or an expectancy. The vested right constitutes a sufficient corpus to validate the trust, and some courts say that the expectancy means the trustee has made a promise to create a trust of the proceeds when received, which is supported by consideration (being made beneficiary of the policy) that makes it enforceable. Restatement (Third) of Trusts §40 comment *b* simply says the trustee's interest is adequate to constitute the corpus of a trust, which makes the trust valid, and typically this resolves any controversy. Furthermore, an unfunded revocable insurance trust that is named as the devisee of the settlor's pour over will is valid under the Uniform Testamentary Additions to Trusts Act. See Chapter 12.

## Pour Over Wills

A *pour over* will leaves the residue of a decedent's estate to a trust in existence at the testator's death. Pour overs are valid under state statutes or the doctrine of independent legal significance. See Chapter 3. Most states have adopted the Uniform Testamentary Additions to Trusts Act, which relies on the doctrine of independent legal significance to permit a pour over to either an inter vivos or a testamentary trust. Under that Act the trust need not be in existence when the will is executed. Rather, the Uniform Act requires only that the trust be in existence and able to receive the assets when the pour over occurs. Further, under the Act amendments to the trust instrument after execution of the will are valid. If the trust was created by another person, for example, or otherwise is subject to amendment, it can be changed after the testator's death. The most common use of pour over wills is with revocable trusts that are used to avoid probate and provide for incapacity. These trusts typically prohibit amendment after the testator's death. But the pour over may be to a trust that can be amended by a third party after the testator's death, which creates problems only if the pour over will did not anticipate and authorize those changes.

Under the Act, the pour over is permitted even to a trust that was not funded by the settlor during life. In the absence of the Act, the failure to fund the trust would result in there being no trust into which the decedent's assets could pass. See Chapter 12. The Act finesses this issue by regarding the pour over itself as the funding required to validate the trust that then can be the pour over receptacle. The recipient trust is not made testamentary by virtue of the pour over, nor is it subject to probate court control or local law restrictions on who may be trustee under a testamentary trust. Especially important is that the pour over is not an incorporation by reference, notwithstanding erroneous statements to that effect in *Miller v. First National Bank & Trust Co.,* 637 P.2d 75 (Okla. 1981). *Miller* involved a decedent who had divorced his spouse, but who had not substituted another beneficiary for her under a revocable trust that was the beneficiary of insurance on his life. A state statute provided that divorce revoked provisions in a will in favor of a former spouse but the statute did not apply to trusts. The court held that the will incorporated the insurance trust by reference by virtue of the pour over provision, which was aberrational and almost certainly equity driven.

If you are troubled by the conclusion in *Miller,* compare that result to the available alternatives. For example, the former spouse would be excluded if the proceeds were payable to the decedent's estate and the decedent's will left them to the former spouse. But if the former spouse were directly named as beneficiary under the policy she would have taken. Which result is more appropriate? Like UPC §2-804, state law should cover the effect of divorce in all these cases, but many state statutes are not that sophisticated.

*Clymer v. Mayo,* 473 N.E.2d 1084 (Mass. 1985), illustrates a different approach that courts have taken when a decedent's revocable trust named a spouse as beneficiary, the spouses divorce, the trust is not amended after the divorce, and the state divorce/revocation statute applies only to wills. In *Clymer,* the court held that the divorce terminated the ex-spouse's interest in the trust, not because the trust was incorporated by reference, but because the statute was deemed to reflect or presume the settlor's intent to revoke the trust. The trust was unfunded and therefore was viewed as operating similarly to a will. According to the court, the wills/divorce statute was indicative of the intent of the average citizen with respect to this kind of trust, as well as to a will. And of course the result was pure legal bootstrapping. The court may not have applied the wills revocation by divorce statute if the trust had been funded, or the court might have applied the statute only to property passing to the trust under the pour over will.

A blockbuster will concept could avoid many similar controversies, but absent any of these cures the estate plan simply needs to be updated upon such "life events." The fact that we have the will statute to address the issue just confirms that many people fail to follow through as they should. Some trusts finesse these issues by defining beneficiaries (such as "the spouse to whom I was married at my death") but that is not the most gratifying approach to either a client (or to the client's now happily married spouse).

As illustrated in this Chapter, will substitutes raise a variety of issues. One is who takes. For example, generally, proceeds of insurance pass to the designated beneficiary, as does a decedent's interest in a retirement plan or IRA, without regard to the terms of the decedent's will. A joint tenancy bank account will pass to the surviving tenant(s) unless it is established that the account was an agency account that was made joint only for the owner's convenience, such as to allow the other tenant(s) to pay bills for the owner if the owner was unable to do so.

Another issue is whether the will substitute is testamentary. If so, it fails unless will execution formalities were met. Revocable trusts generally are not testamentary if there is a remainder beneficiary following the settlor's death, even if the settlor was the sole trustee and the sole beneficiary for life. POD bank accounts and Totten trust savings account trusts also are allowed by statute or judicial decision in most states.

If capacity is at issue, a third surprising reality is that a higher standard of capacity may be imposed for a will substitute than for a will. This is not the case for revocable trusts under UTC §601, which is an improvement on the law elsewhere.

Finally, do the subsidiary rules of the law of wills apply? For example: (1) if the person named to receive the nonprobate property on the decedent's death dies before the decedent, does that person's estate or descendant take? See lapse, discussed in Chapter 8. (2) If the named beneficiary is the decedent's ex-spouse, does the spouse nevertheless take? See Chapter 4. (3) May creditors of the decedent reach the nonprobate property? See and compare Chapter 13. (4) Does a slayer statute apply if the named beneficiary killed the decedent? See Chapter 2. (5) May the decedent by will change the recipient of nonprobate property? (6) May mistakes be corrected? See Chapter 7. (7) Does a surviving spouse's election against the will reach nonprobate property? See Chapter 10. There are many more questions, which will continue to unfold as you study further.

# CHAPTER 7

# INTERPRETATION:
# WHAT THE DECEDENT INTENDED

Interpretation is searching for the "plain meaning" of the language used from within the "four corners" of a document. Absent an ambiguity, evidence extrinsic (outside the terms of the document) to a will or trust typically is inadmissible in this search for the testator or settlor's intent. On the other hand, most courts today admit extrinsic evidence to interpret an ambiguous will, without regard to the kind of ambiguity. Some jurisdictions treat patent and latent ambiguities differently (so we will study the difference between them), and some courts will not admit extrinsic evidence in the form of the testator's declarations in any case. Notwithstanding these relatively easy to state rules, much difficulty flows from the fact that courts use a variety of ways to avoid harsh and inequitable results attributable to the traditional rejection of extrinsic evidence offered to correct alleged "mistakes." And, curiously, extrinsic evidence is admitted in many jurisdictions to correct mistakes made in will substitutes. In large part the reluctance to consider extrinsic evidence with respect to wills is historically a function of the Wills Act, and that reluctance is changing. Unfortunately, perhaps the hardest question in all of wills and trusts law is when will a court admit extrinsic evidence, because the answers are so unpredictable under current jurisprudence.

## Interpreting Wills and Trusts

Some folks call "interpretation" reading the lines, and "construction" reading *between* the lines. We will see examples of this in Chapters 8 and 9. Interpretation determines what the testator or settlor (for ease we will just say "decedent," because we usually could just *ask* what was meant by the settlor of a trust who still is living) meant by the words used. Construction is closer to ascertaining what the decedent *meant* to say and supplies rules to resolve questions raised by gaps in the document if there is no indication of what the decedent actually intended. These distinctions, however, are not always observed. Some courts refer to interpretation and construction interchangeably and the line between the two is not always clear.

When we "interpret" a will or trust, we say that we are attempting to determine what the decedent meant by the words used in the instrument. Often interpretation is a search for the "plain meaning" of a word, phrase, or entire provision from within the "four corners" of the document. Typically evidence extrinsic to the will or trust is inadmissible in this search of the document for the decedent's intent. As discussed below, however, extrinsic evidence may be admitted to resolve the ambiguity and ascertain the decedent's intent if the document is ambiguous, or if the document is not ambiguous on its face but an ambiguity arises in attempting to apply the document to the facts existing outside of the will or trust. And let's be honest: often the decedent had *no* intent, because the issue that arose never was anticipated or addressed. So to a large extent we are dealing here with fiction, a search in some cases for what the decedent *would* have intended (and all the while courts tell us that we don't do such things as supply intent when there was none stated; don't believe it!)

### *Interpretation Methodologies*

Interpretation in the classic four corners sense limits itself to methodologies that do not involve the admission of extrinsic evidence, such as (1) viewing the pattern and logic of the gifts made, in toto, as providing meaning about the decedent's overall intent; (2) comparing other uses of the same or related terms elsewhere in the document to understand terminology used that may be unclear or inconsistent with other indications of intent; (3) considering special usage — nicknames, abbreviations, slang, or even concepts used in nontraditional or informal ways — when it appears that the decedent did not intend a common or technical meaning to apply (e.g., using the term "heirs" in a context that reveals that the intent was "children" or "lineal descendants"); and (4) perhaps considering facts and circumstances known to the decedent at the time of execution — probably meaning when signed, and not at a later date if a will was republished (see Chapter 3) — to assist in determining what the document says. Notice, however, that even this little deviation from the four corners approach is a relaxation of the traditional no-extrinsic-evidence rule.

Interpretation is not an effort to determine what a decedent *should* have said, or what the average person *would* have meant by the words used, although courts often do just this, notwithstanding protestations otherwise. Rather, the effort is to determine what *this* decedent meant by the words used. Nevertheless, consider the difficulty of interpretation without reliance on what you personally mean by language, or your experience or expectations based on what the average individual would mean by certain language.

For example, imagine that T's will provides: "I leave all my personal property to A." Do you regard "personal" as juxtaposed with "real" property or as expressing some sense of personal ownership? Is it all of T's property other than T's real property, or is it all property owned by T, including real property (that T considers "mine personally" as opposed to shared or jointly owned)? If you answered the former, what would you have thought before enrolling in a law school property course? The presence of other provisions in the will may affect our interpretation of "personal." For example, if the will included another provision leaving "everything else" to B, that may mean T intended for B to receive only real property and for A to receive all the tangible and intangible personal property. Perhaps T meant for A to receive only assets such as jewelry and clothing (personal effects), with B to receive such "impersonal" assets as cash, stocks, bonds, and real property. This is what interpretation tries to determine.

Try another one: If T's will left $1,000 to "my sister-in-law," would T mean a brother's wife, a spouse's sister, or the wife of a brother-in-law? Most people would answer "all three," but by now you know that your brother-in-law's wife is not *your* sister-in-law — she is your spouse's sister-in-law, but is nothing to you, notwithstanding common usage of the term. The will or trust interpretation question, however, is what T meant, not what most people would have meant and not what *you* know to be correct. If nothing within the four corners of the instrument indicates what T meant, the particular language generally will be given its usual, "plain meaning," without regard to any meaning that extrinsic evidence might show that T may have intended.

### *Gaps or Omissions*

If there clearly is a gap or omission in the document — a paragraph or a disposition missing or a contingency not addressed — interpretation is not supposed to be a process by which a court may insert what it thinks the decedent would have wanted to provide. Implied gifts that fill such gaps is a difficult concept to characterize then because it normally is regarded as "interpretation," because it is premised on a notion that it is clear from what is said in the document that the decedent intended the gift that the court implies. In that sense construction fills in gaps based on fixed rules only if there is no indication of intent, and interpretation determines what this particular decedent intended, based on other indications or clues in the instrument (or extrinsic evidence if there is an ambiguity and the court will allow it).

Notwithstanding efforts to distinguish these concepts and draw boundaries around their proper application, beware a court "interpreting" a document based on an "implied" intent generated under rules of construction. For example, *Engle v. Siegel*, 377 A.2d 892 (N.J. 1977), involved wills of spouses who provided that each of their mothers would take half of their respective estates if the spouses and their children died in a common disaster. The husband's mother died after the wills were written. The spouses and children later died in a common disaster. The issue was whether the wife's mother would receive all of both estates, or whether other blood relatives of the husband (siblings, in that case) should receive the half that the husband's mother would have received if living. By statute, the surviving residuary beneficiaries took the entire residue if a testator's will provided for multiple residuary beneficiaries, at least one of whom died before the testator (and if the antilapse statute does not apply — see Chapter 8 — as it did not in *Engle*). Application of that statute would have excluded the husband's family. Extrinsic evidence (testimony of the drafter), however, made it clear that this was not the testators' intent. So the court applied a "doctrine of probable intent" to imply a provision that did what the antilapse statute would have done if it were applicable and that effected the "obvious" intent of the testators. As a result, half of each estate was distributed to the husband's siblings. *Engle* was not copacetic interpretation jurisprudence, although the result was equitable. This was *reformation*, without admitting it.

The *Engle* court considered extrinsic evidence in interpreting the testators' wills. Doing so also was a departure from the tradition of not considering extrinsic evidence in interpretation except to reveal special usage or circumstances at the time of execution, or to resolve ambiguities. So be aware that courts don't always recognize or follow the rules stated in this Chapter. And that may be acceptable, because construction cases seek to determine not what the decedent meant by what was said, but what the decedent meant to say. Oh, and we *do* fill gaps, based on notions of whether we believe the decedent considered the issue and formulated an intent. Again see Chapters 8 and 9. In that regard, sometimes the only error in a case is a court saying it is "interpreting" when in fact it is "construing" or "reforming."

## Mistake

Issues of interpretation typically arise in the context of ambiguities or mistakes and involve questions of whether and to what extent extrinsic evidence is admissible. Two general rules commonly are professed about ambiguities and mistakes in wills (as we will see, trusts and will substitutes traditionally have been treated differently). One is that a court cannot use extrinsic evidence to alter, limit, or extend unambiguous provisions in a will that can be applied without problem to the facts and circumstances existing outside of the will. The other is that there is no remedy for mistake. These rules can produce harsh and inequitable results, and many courts use a variety of techniques to avoid them.

The traditional approach is illustrated by *Mahoney v. Grainger*, 186 N.E. 86 (Mass. 1933). The decedent left the residue of her estate to her "heirs at law . . . to be divided among them equally, share and share alike . . . ." Recall that "heir" refers to someone who is entitled to receive the estate of an intestate decedent. Although the decedent had several dozen first cousins, her sole heir was an aunt. Extrinsic evidence showed that the testator's lawyer asked her who were her nearest relatives and who she wanted to receive the residue of her estate, and the testator responded that she wanted 25 of her first cousins to split the residue of her estate. This evidence was admitted, however, only to establish the circumstances that existed when the will was executed. It was not admissible to contradict the plain meaning of the residuary clause of the testator's will and establish a contrary intent for disposition of the residue of her estate. According to the court, if the will was ambiguous, when applied to the facts existing at the testator's death (i.e., if there had been a *latent* ambiguity in the will), extrinsic evidence of the testator's intent would have been admissible to resolve the ambiguity. But the court held there was no ambiguity. Accordingly, the aunt received the residue. The result would have differed if the will had contained language indicating that the testator meant her cousins when she used the term "heirs." There was no basis for such a finding, however, because the will contained no such language, so the extrinsic evidence was not admissible to that effect because the court determined that the will was not ambiguous.

Mistakes that affect wills raise interpretation and extrinsic evidence issues and come in many forms. For example, thinking that only one witness is needed, that "heirs" means children, or (in *Mahoney*) that heirs meant the testator's cousins, all are examples of mistakes *of law*. Generally, extrinsic evidence to prove and correct such a mistake is not admissible. See *Estate of Taff*, at page 142, for an exception. Mistakes *in the inducement* occur under various circumstances. These innocent misrepresentations or self-induced mistakes also generally cannot be proven by extrinsic evidence. For example, the testator may have included a provision based on misinformation innocently provided by others. Or the testator may have been mistaken about such things as whether prior loans, gifts, or advances were made; the extent of a beneficiary's poverty or property; or a person's relation to the testator (e.g., a reference to "my first cousin once removed" when the person is really a second cousin, or a reference to "my sister-in-law" when the person is the wife of the testator's brother-in-law).

Mistakes of *omission* or of *fact* are those that courts seem most willing to correct. For example, cases involving execution of the wrong mutual will now might be rectified, as discussed in Chapter 3, and courts in cases involving typos may be willing to include or excise material that was improperly omitted or included by stenographic mistake, assuming there is clear proof of the original intent and of the mistake. *Wilson v. First Florida Bank*, 498 So. 2d 1289 (Fla. Ct. App. 1986), illustrates gaps or omissions caused by errors of drafting attorneys. The will made several specific devises, after which appeared language "[t]o the University of Georgia" in trust for a scholarship fund. The will did not state what property was left to that trust. The heirs argued that the residue passed to them by intestacy because the will otherwise did not contain an effective residuary clause. The court found the will to be ambiguous, admitted extrinsic evidence, and determined on the basis of it that the testator intended the residue to pass to the trust. It corrected the mistake, essentially by inserting the omitted but intended language into the will. Cases like *Wilson* that involve mistakes in documents caused by the drafter's error seem to be more likely candidates for relief than cases involving other kinds of mistakes. But many courts apply the same rules to cases of mistakes caused by a scrivener as they do to other mistakes. Mistaken revocation of a testamentary instrument also may be a mistake of fact that may be proven by extrinsic evidence and corrected under the doctrine of dependent relative revocation. The kind of mistake is not determinative if it is resolved in *that* context. See Chapter 4.

### Lack of Intent to Execute a Will

This Chapter is mostly about extrinsic evidence used to determine what a decedent intended by the words used in a document. Occasionally a contestant will argue that a document that appears to be a will and that was executed in accordance with required execution formalities nevertheless should not be admitted to probate. The argument is that the maker did not intend for it to make a testamentary disposition and instead executed it to serve another purpose. Such a challenge necessarily relies on extrinsic evidence of the "testator's" intent. The question is whether extrinsic evidence of that intent is admissible. *Fleming v. Morrison*, 72 N.E. 499 (Mass. 1904), admitted extrinsic evidence that the testator executed a will leaving his estate to Mary Fleming, not because he intended to make a testamentary disposition of his estate, but only to induce her to sleep with him. The will was denied probate on the basis of that evidence because the testator lacked the requisite testamentary intent. Although extrinsic evidence would not be admissible to interpret the document, it was admitted to show that the document was not valid. *Lister v. Smith*, 164 Eng. Rep. 1282 (1863), discussed in Chapter 3, similarly admitted extrinsic evidence to show lack of testamentary intent of the maker of a document purporting to be a will. By comparison, in *Estate of Duemeland*, 528 N.W.2d 369 (N.D. 1995), the testator's two children were involved in a business dispute. With the testator's encouragement, his son made a settlement offer to his daughter. The testator threatened to disinherit the daughter when she refused to accept the offer, and he then executed a new will that did disinherit her. The testator died less than three months later and the daughter claimed the will was invalid because it lacked testamentary intent. She offered extrinsic evidence that the testator was "merely bluffing," that he executed the will not to dispose of property but to encourage settlement of the dispute. The court refused to allow the evidence and, based on that ruling, admitted the will to probate.

## Ambiguities and Inaccuracies

The most common illustrations of courts admitting extrinsic evidence involve ambiguities or inaccuracies, traditionally classified as either patent or latent, with the classification historically dictating whether extrinsic evidence was admissible. Patent ambiguities involve errors that appear on the face of the document. For example, T's will provides: "I leave my IBM stock to my friend John Doe, my AT&T stock to my partner John Smith, and my Coca-Cola stock to John." This is a patent ambiguity because we know from reading the document that we don't know which John is to receive the Coca-Cola stock. *Historically*, courts professed that no extrinsic evidence was allowable to alter the meaning of the written provisions to clarify patent ambiguities. An exception was made for evidence of the facts and circumstances at execution and that exception has grown such that today most courts admit any extrinsic evidence to resolve patent ambiguities.

Latent ambiguities are those that appear only when the document is applied to the facts at hand. Typically extrinsic evidence is allowed in these cases, although sometimes declarations of the decedent are not admitted. The professed logic behind the historic inconsistent treatment of patent and latent ambiguities was that extrinsic evidence is required in the latent ambiguity case just to discover that an ambiguity exists. That is, the ambiguity is not apparent from the face of the document, it only becomes obvious when we apply the will to the facts that exist outside the will. And, once the door to extrinsic evidence is open, the courts may as well admit extrinsic evidence of all sorts for all purposes, including resolution of the ambiguity. But in the patent ambiguity situation, because the glitch is apparent on the face of the document and no extrinsic evidence is needed to raise the issue, courts historically said that the door should be kept shut.

*Mahoney v. Grainger*, discussed at page 134, illustrates the traditional approach. The testator's sole heir was her aunt but her will left the residue of her estate to her "heirs at law . . . to be divided among them equally, share and share alike. . . ." Was "heirs" (in the plural) a latent ambiguity or just good drafting (because the testator likely would have multiple heirs if the aunt died first)? The court held there was no latent ambiguity and refused to consider extrinsic evidence of an intent to benefit her cousins.

*Estate of Russell*, 444 P.2d 353 (Cal. 1968), discarded the distinction between patent and latent ambiguities and reflects the modern trend that allows extrinsic evidence to resolve any form of ambiguity. There the decedent's holographic will included specific bequests to her sole heir and left the residue of her estate to "Chester H. Quinn and Roxy Russell." Chester was a friend of the testator. Roxy was the testator's dog. Because dogs may not own property, the issue was whether Chester received the entire residue or whether half of the residue passed by intestacy to the sole heir.

The lower court in *Russell* admitted extrinsic evidence that the testator and Chester had discussed his caring for Roxy after the testator's death and that the testator did not want her heir to receive more than the specific bequests the will left her. On that basis the lower court held that the testator intended Chester to receive the entire residue. According to the lower court, including Roxy in the residuary clause was only to express the testator's desire—a precatory wish not intended to be legally enforceable—that Chester care for Roxy. The Supreme Court confirmed the holding that extrinsic evidence is admissible to resolve ambiguities without regard to whether they are patent or latent. But before using such evidence, it said that it is necessary to determine if there *is* an ambiguity. Considering the extrinsic evidence, the question is whether the language is reasonably susceptible to more than one meaning. If so, extrinsic evidence is considered to determine the testator's intent. If not, the evidence is not admissible to controvert the only reasonable meaning of the language in the will. In a questionable decision, the court then held that the language of the residuary clause (even interpreted in light of the extrinsic evidence that Roxy was a dog) was not reasonably susceptible to the interpretation that Chester was to take the entire residue, *or* that the provision for Roxy was precatory. Rather, the court held the language "to Chester H. Quinn and Roxy Russell" could only be interpreted to mean that Chester and Roxy were intended by the testator to share the estate equally. The devise to Roxy failed, and the heir took Roxy's half.

Note here as an aside that *Russell* involved the common law rule that a failed portion of a residuary devise passes by intestacy. In jurisdictions that have adopted UPC §2-604(b), or a similar statute, the failed portion of a residuary devise passes to the other residuary devisees. There is no intestate property unless there are no other residuary devisees. See Chapter 8. Had the UPC rule applied, Chester would have received the entire residue without regard to whether the testator intended a flawed gift of half of the residue to her dog.

### Three Types of Latent Ambiguities

All three of the following types of ambiguity are apparent only when applying a seemingly clear provision to the facts. In a moment we will explain why the differences between them are important.

- Equivocations are language that is *accurate* with respect to more than one person or asset. For example, "my antique car to X." Testator owned several. Or, "my car to my cousin Jim." Testator has two cousins named Jim. (Note: it is not uncommon for a single family to have multiple individuals with the same name.)

- Misdescriptions involve language that is *inaccurate* with respect to more than one person or asset. For example, "my antique Lincoln automobile to X." The testator had an antique Ford and a new Lincoln. Or a gift "to my cousin John" when the testator has only one cousin, named Jim, but also has a nephew whose name is John. And "to Erma's daughter, Irene" would be a misdescription if Erma has two daughters, one Aileen and the other Arleen.

- Inaccuracies involve language that is *inaccurate* but arguably applicable only to one person or asset. For example "my house in Atlanta on Decatur Street." Testator's house is on Atlanta Street in Decatur (the names were transposed) or on Decatur Street but across the city line in the next suburb of Stone Mountain. Or, "to Erma's daughter, Irene." Erma's only daughter is Aileen.

Admission of extrinsic evidence in cases of latent ambiguities traditionally involves two steps. First, in attempting to apply the will to the facts existing at the testator's death, the court would examine proffered extrinsic evidence to determine whether an ambiguity exists. Second, if a latent ambiguity is found, the court then would determine whether to consider the same extrinsic evidence (and perhaps more, if there is any) to resolve the ambiguity. Quaere how a court performs the second step objectively, or how it objectively resolves the case if it sees the evidence, determines there is no ambiguity, and thus chooses to decide the controversy without admitting it.

To illustrate, the testator's will includes a devise of "my house in Atlanta on Decatur Street." A court might conclude that an ademption by extinction should result (see Chapter 9) if the extrinsic evidence shows that the decedent once owned a house on Decatur Street in Atlanta when an earlier will was executed, but sold it before executing a later will. This might be true even if the decedent replaced the Atlanta house with one on Atlanta Street in Decatur and either the testator or the drafter was confused in drafting the decedent's final will.

Cases in this arena are difficult to predict because many courts appear to be willing to consider the equities in cases involving mistake. So it is easy to find results that clearly are not informed by the stated rules regarding interpretation, the four-corners approach, or traditional limitations on the admission of extrinsic evidence. See, for example, *Engle*, discussed at page 133, and *Gibbs*, discussed at page 142.

### *Resolving Ambiguities*

After admitting extrinsic evidence to identify an ambiguity and to determine the testator's intent, courts often will either ignore or excise the offending language in a will if doing so will resolve the ambiguity in a manner consistent with what the court determines (with the help of extrinsic evidence) to be the testator's intent. This is most common with a latent ambiguity in the form of an inaccuracy (only one person or asset arguably meets the disposition). Courts are prone to use this "fictional eraser" method as a relatively easy and non-invasive method of resolving the ambiguity without "rewriting" the decedent's will by inserting clarifying language. So, in the examples of inaccuracies at page 139, a court might use a fictional eraser to eliminate the bracketed language: "My house [in Atlanta] on Decatur Street" if the testator's house was on Decatur Street in Stone Mountain, or "My house in [Atlanta on] Decatur [Street]" if the testator's house was on Atlanta Street in Decatur. Or "To Erma's daughter [Irene]" if Erma had only the one daughter.

Some courts will follow the same fictional eraser tactic to excise language creating a misdescription (more than one person or asset that could be referred to by the disposition) if doing so will resolve the ambiguity in a manner consistent with what the court determines is the testator's intent. Thus, if the misdescription was "My [antique] [Lincoln] automobile to X" and the testator owned an antique Ford and a new Lincoln, the ambiguity could be remedied by erasing either "antique" or "Lincoln," depending on what the extrinsic evidence showed to be the testator's intent. Similarly, if the bequest was "to [my cousin] [John]" when the testator had only one cousin, named Jim, and a nephew named John, the ambiguity could be resolved by striking either "my cousin" or "John," depending on the testator's intent.

*Ihl v. Oetting*, 682 S.W.2d 865 (Mo. Ct. App. 1984), illustrates that the fictional erasure technique won't work in many misdescription cases. The testator left property to "Mr. and Mrs. Wendell Richard Hess, or the survivor of them, presently residing at No. 17 Barbara Circle." Wendell was married to Glenda when the will was executed, and they resided at No. 17 Barbara Circle. Before the testator died, however, Wendell and Glenda divorced, No. 17 Barbara Circle was sold, and Wendell married Verna. The issue was whether Glenda or Verna should receive the property. There was an ambiguity because wills are deemed to speak at death even though they are written and executed only with knowledge of facts and circumstances at an earlier time. At the testator's death, Glenda was not "Mrs. Wendell Richard Hess," and Verna was not residing (and never did) at 17 Barbara Circle. The result was a latent ambiguity of the misdescription type. Extrinsic evidence was admitted to determine that the will was ambiguous and that the testator intended to benefit Glenda. But the fictional eraser approach to resolve the ambiguity was not appropriate, because using it (to erase "No. 17 Barbara Circle") would have given the devise to Verna as the only Mrs. Hess at the testator's death. As a result, the court "resolved" the ambiguity by simply holding that Glenda was to receive the devise. That was a much greater deviation from traditional principles.

Similarly, in the devise "to Erma's daughter, Irene" when Erma had two daughters, Aileen and Arleen, the erasure approach would not work because eliminating "Irene" would leave two persons who could claim and an unanswered question of intent. However, a court might engage the tactic anyway because "Irene" does not identify either daughter. With the name removed, the fictional erasure would create an equivocation and extrinsic evidence most often is admitted to resolve these cases. Indeed, latent ambiguity cases involving equivocations (e.g., "my antique car to Fred" when the testator owned several, or "my car to my cousin Jim" when the testator had two cousins named Jim) were among the first in which courts admitted extrinsic evidence to determine a testator's intent to resolve an ambiguity. Such cases frequently result in admission of all relevant extrinsic evidence, including oral declarations by the testator, in search of the true intent. And you can understand why: the will is *accurate* in the sense that someone or something meets the description found. The problem is that more than one is discovered, but little or no change to the will itself is entailed in these cases.

To illustrate, assume the testator had eight houses in DeKalb County and the will provision read "My seven houses in DeKalb County to A." The quoted language is not ambiguous until it is applied in the context of the extrinsic evidence that, at the time of the testator's death (when the will speaks), the testator owned eight houses in DeKalb County. The result is a latent ambiguity. Extrinsic evidence would be admissible to determine whether the testator intended A to receive all eight houses, or only seven houses (and which of the eight to exclude). In the absence of extrinsic evidence that the testator intended A to receive only seven houses, a court likely would resolve the ambiguity by striking "seven," resulting in a devise of "my houses in DeKalb County to A." Doing so would allow all eight to pass, and spare the court from trying to figure out which was not meant to be given. It is unclear how a court would resolve the issue if there was extrinsic evidence that the testator intended A to receive only seven houses, but no evidence of which seven houses. If the testator owned only seven houses at execution, perhaps that would be sufficient extrinsic evidence to indicate an intention that A was to receive only those seven. (Although the will speaks at the testator's death, most courts consider facts and circumstances existing at the time of execution in interpreting the will.) Alternatively, that evidence might convince the court that the testator intended A to receive all of the testator's houses, now totaling eight.

## Correcting Mistakes Absent an Ambiguity

A few courts have been persuaded to abandon the traditional rule that extrinsic evidence is not admissible to correct mistakes in wills absent an ambiguity. *In re Gibbs*, 111 N.W.2d 413 (Wis. 1961), is illustrative. The wills of the decedents (spouses) included a bequest "to Robert *J.* Krause, now of 4708 North 46th Street, Milwaukee." There was a Robert J. Krause who lived at that address. Although he did not know the testators, he speculated that he had been named in their wills because he was a taxi driver and an elderly woman passenger (who he assumed to be one of the testators) had expressed sympathy and asked his name when he told her of his wife's illness and his need to take a second job. Nevertheless, if allowed, extrinsic evidence would show that a Robert *W.* Krause was an employee of one of the testators (and a friend of both of them), that he lived quite close to the address of Robert *J.* Krause, and that he had been named a devisee in earlier wills of the testators.

This testators' wills were not ambiguous: this was an accurate description of one person. It just happened to be a mistake. (Interestingly, however, Restatement (Third) of Property — Wills and Other Donative Transfers §11.2 comment j characterizes *Gibbs* as involving a latent ambiguity, because applying the wills to the facts would yield a gift to someone the testators did not know.) The lesson for drafters is that someone — the drafter, a legal assistant, or maybe the testators themselves — apparently looked up "Robert Krause" in the telephone book and found a listing for one in the general neighborhood as the intended Robert Krause. *Gibbs* involved a mistake, not an ambiguity, and the traditional law of wills is not to correct mistakes (except, in the context of revocation, under the doctrine of dependent relative revocation; see Chapter 4). The judge acknowledged that there was no ambiguity but still ruled in favor of Robert W. Krause and against the Robert J. Krause named in the will. According to the court, identifying details, such as street addresses and middle initials, are particularly subject to error and should not frustrate the "clearly demonstrable intent" of the testator "when the proof establishes to the highest degree of certainty that a mistake was, in fact, made." The court essentially reformed the will to correct the mistake.

The court in *Gibbs* candidly acknowledged that there was no ambiguity in the testator's will. It granted relief anyway by carving out an exception for cases involving details of identification from the usual rule denying the admission of extrinsic evidence in the absence of an ambiguity. In *Estate of Taff*, 133 Cal. Rptr. 737 (1976), the court was not so forthright. The *Taff* will left the residue of the decedent's estate to her sister and provided that, if her sister did not survive her, the residue was to be distributed to the testator's heirs under the California intestate succession statute. The testator's sister predeceased her and the residue of the estate should have been distributed under California intestacy law half to the testator's blood relatives and half to blood relatives of the testator's deceased husband. The court nevertheless admitted extrinsic evidence to show that the testator misunderstood California law because she intended only her own blood relatives to take. The court therefore held that her relatives were entitled to the entire residue of the estate, to the exclusion of her husband's relatives. According to the court, the evidence was admissible to create an ambiguity and then to resolve the ambiguity so created. In essence, the court admitted extrinsic evidence to prove a mistake that it then corrected by implicitly reforming the will, even though there was neither a patent nor a latent ambiguity.

A few courts also have relaxed the traditional rule to admit extrinsic evidence to correct mistakes attributable to scrivener error. To illustrate, the testator in *Erickson v. Erickson*, 716 A.2d 92 (Conn. 1998), executed his will two days before his marriage and devised his estate to his bride-to-be. Because it did not expressly provide for the contingency of his marriage, however, the testator's children claimed that the will was revoked by Connecticut's pretermitted spouse statute. See Chapter 10. The court remanded the case for a new trial, at which the surviving spouse would be permitted to introduce extrinsic evidence that, if clear and convincing, could be used to establish and correct the mistake.

Consistent with the rules applicable to will substitutes, discussed next, Restatement (Third) of Property—Wills and Other Donative Transfers §12.1 provides that *any* mistake in any donative transfer (including a will) may be corrected, without regard to whether there is an ambiguity, if the mistake and what the testator or donor intended are proven by clear and convincing evidence. This abandonment of the common law plain meaning rule for interpreting wills was rejected in *Flannery v. McNamara*, 738 N.E.2d 739 (Mass. 2000), in which T's will devised T's estate to T's spouse but did not name a contingent beneficiary in case the spouse died first, which occurred. Relying in part on Restatement §12.1, the spouse's siblings offered extrinsic evidence that T intended them to be the contingent devisees. In holding that the estate instead passed by intestacy to distant relatives of T, the court stated that "the reformation of a will, which would dispose of estate property based on unattested testamentary language, would violate the Statute of Wills. (Citation omitted.) Strong policy reasons also militate against the requested reformation. To allow for reformation in this case would open the floodgates of litigation and lead to untold confusion in the probate of wills. It would essentially invite disgruntled individuals excluded from a will to demonstrate extrinsic evidence of the decedent's 'intent' to exclude them."

## Will Substitutes: Reformation and Extrinsic Evidence

The rules in many jurisdictions prohibiting the admission of extrinsic evidence in the absence of an ambiguity, and the refusal to correct mistakes when there is no ambiguity, apply only to wills and not to will substitutes such as trusts, life insurance beneficiary designations, and so forth. In these jurisdictions mistakes in an unambiguous will substitute can be proven by extrinsic evidence and the document may be reformed to effectuate the decedent's intent and to prevent an unintended beneficiary of a mistake from being unjustly enriched. If simple reformation of the document cannot correct the mistake, then a constructive trust may be imposed on the recipient of the property, obligating that beneficiary to convey legal title to the intended beneficiary.

Wills may have been treated differently historically because the issue of mistake in a will typically only arises after the testator's death, when the testator is unable to address whether a mistake was made. Precluding admission of extrinsic evidence was viewed as the best means of ensuring that the testator's intent is carried out rather than subverted by fabricated or mistaken evidence that the testator intended something other than what the will specified. Thus, unless there is intentionally wrongful or fraudulent conduct, constructive trusts typically are *not* imposed in will cases to remedy mistakes when there is no ambiguity.

In at least one case, however, a court imposed a constructive trust to correct a mistake involving a will when there was no intentionally wrongful conduct. *In re Estate of Tolin*, 622 So. 2d 988 (Fla. 1993), involved a testator who wanted to revoke a codicil to his will. He mistakenly thought a photocopy of the codicil was the original. He showed the copy to a lawyer, who also thought it was the original. The lawyer told him he could revoke the codicil by tearing it up. Intending to revoke the codicil, the testator tore up the copy, believing it to be the original. At his death, the original was offered for probate. The court held that revocation of a copy of a testamentary document is not a valid revocation and admitted the codicil to probate. Because of the mistake, however, the court imposed a constructive trust on the beneficiary under the codicil in favor of the person who would have received the property if the codicil had been revoked properly.

The substantial use of will substitutes, combined with the increasing acceptance of the UPC philosophy to unify the law of probate and nonprobate transfers and to subordinate strict compliance with formalities to effectuate the testator's intent, all may lead to a further relaxation of the traditional no extrinsic evidence and no reformation rules of the law of wills. See, e.g., the dispensing power in UPC §2-503, discussed in Chapter 3. To illustrate, imagine that T's will left $50,000 to each of two grandchildren, A and B, and nothing to a third grandchild, C. About the same time T executed the will, T bought a $100,000 insurance policy on her life, and named A and B as the sole beneficiaries. T died later that year. Extrinsic evidence would show that T believed that C was wealthy as a result of the success of a business that C owned, and that T's belief of C's business success was the only reason T did not treat C the same as A and B. In fact, C's business was insolvent throughout the year in which T executed the will and bought the insurance policy, and C's financial condition was no better than A or B. If C attempts to share on an equal basis with A and B, the extrinsic evidence might be admitted in connection with the insurance policy but not the will, and C has a better chance to receive a third of the insurance proceeds than to receive any of the property passing under T's will. This disparate treatment is difficult to justify and the probate result might gravitate toward the nonprobate result in appropriate cases.

Mistake in the inducement (occasioned by someone's innocent misrepresentation or by the testator's own misconception) is sometimes regarded as a special case in which relief may be given from the no-extrinsic-evidence or no reformation rules applicable to wills. Generally, however, that is not the case and the usual rules apply: no extrinsic evidence will be admitted if there is only a mistake in the inducement and no ambiguity. An exception may permit extrinsic evidence to be admitted to correct a mistake in the inducement in the rare case in which the will itself reveals both the mistake and what the testator would have done if the truth had been known. See, e.g., *Gifford v. Dyer*, 2 R.I. 99 (1852) (dicta). For example, T's will leaves $100,000 to T's alma mater, City University. A codicil to the will provides, "I revoke my $100,000 bequest because City University has been left $10 million by A. Phil Anthropist." In fact, Anthropist left the $10 million to City *College*, not City *University*. Extrinsic evidence would be admissible to correct the mistake and reinstate the $100,000 bequest to City University under the *Gifford v. Dyer* dictum. Although the codicil does not expressly state what T would have done if T had known City University did not receive the $10 million bequest from Anthropist, it implicitly does and that likely would be sufficient to correct the mistake.

Consider another example: T's will provides, "because my son is dead, I leave my estate entirely to my daughter." In fact, T's son was not dead and actually survived T. Extrinsic evidence that T's son is not dead may be admissible notwithstanding that the *Gifford v. Dyer* exception is not directly applicable (because the will does not state what T would have done had T known that the son was living). It may not be necessary that the will state what the other disposition would be in a case such as this, in which a will states that nothing is left to a child because of a mistaken belief that the child is dead. Absent evidence that the testator would have cut out the son anyway (that was the situation in *Gifford v. Dyer*) the son and daughter likely would share the estate equally because the law generally presumes an intent to treat all children equally. Such a result would be reached in a jurisdiction that has adopted UPC §2-302(c), under which a child who is not provided for in a testator's will solely because the testator believes the child is not living may receive a share of the estate as an after-born or after-adopted pretermitted heir. See Chapter 10.

Let's summarize the rules that we have seen on this topic:

- If the document involved is a will substitute, extrinsic evidence may be admissible to correct a mistake by reforming the document without regard to whether there is an ambiguity.

- If the document is a will and there is a patent ambiguity the traditional approach was not to admit extrinsic evidence, but most courts today will allow extrinsic evidence without regard to the type of ambiguity.

- If the document is a will that is not ambiguous on its face, but the ambiguity arises in trying to apply the terms of the will (a latent ambiguity), extrinsic evidence probably is admissible to determine the existence of and then resolve this latent ambiguity. In some jurisdictions, however, declarations of the deceased testator will not be admitted, except perhaps in the case of an equivocation (an accurate description of more than one asset or person).

- An ambiguity may be resolved by use of the fictional eraser method. If not, the court still may resolve the ambiguity and order the estate distributed in accordance with what the court determines to be the testator's intent, based on extrinsic evidence admitted to establish the ambiguity and what the testator intended.

- If there is neither a patent nor a latent ambiguity, at best there is a mistake. Generally, absent an ambiguity, if a will is involved extrinsic evidence is not admissible to prove the testator meant something different than what was said in the will (i.e., unambiguous wills are given their plain meaning and mistakes in them usually go uncorrected).

- Courts have created a variety of exceptions to avoid the harsh results of not correcting will mistakes when there is no ambiguity. First, the mistake may be corrected if the mistake is apparent from the will itself, and the will states what the testator would have done if there had been no mistake. Second, if the mistake involves a detail of identification (such as a street address or a middle initial), some courts may admit extrinsic evidence to correct the mistake. Third, in rare cases the court may admit extrinsic evidence to create an ambiguity when none otherwise existed, and then resolve it. And if the mistake resulted in a revocation of a will or codicil, dependent relative revocation may be available to correct it. See Chapter 4. It remains to be seen whether courts will follow Restatement (Third) of Property — Wills and Other Donative Transfers §12.1 in providing for correction of mistakes in unambiguous wills if the mistake and what was intended can be proven with clear and convincing evidence.

## Implied Gifts

Implied gifts are a legal fiction, employed to provide what a court perceives to be the decedent's intent in cases in which the document is incomplete or ineffective to dispose of the decedent's assets. Interpretation may determine that the decedent intended gifts that must be implied because the language of the instrument (and extrinsic evidence) show that their omission was inadvertent. They are supplied as needed to effect the decedent's intent.

*Engle v. Siegel*, discussed at page 133, illustrates the operation of this totally unpredictable theory. Recall that there was no ambiguity in *Engle*. There was not even a gap in the dispositive plan that would have caused part of the estates to pass by intestacy. Rather, not allowing the wife's mother to receive the entire residue and implying a gift to the husband's family to effect probable intent amounted to a reformation of the will. The court acted to correct a mistake in the form of an unanticipated (and thus unplanned for) contingency that actually occurred. *Engle* shows how far the court was willing to go to give effect to the testators' probable intent, which it determined from extrinsic evidence. It is not representative of the law in this area, however, because in most cases extrinsic evidence would not be admissible to contradict the intent of the testators as evidenced by unambiguous terms in their wills. Thus, under the usual rules, the wife's mother would have taken the entire residue of their estates, which was the wrong result based on the extrinsic evidence.

The "rule" of implied gifts for unanticipated contingencies (if it can be elevated to that status) in a case like *Engle* is that a court will provide for an *un*anticipated contingency that *did* occur the same way the testator provided for an *anticipated* contingency that did *not* occur. Absent other evidence addressing the issue in the document or otherwise, the assumption is that the decedent would want the same result under either contingency. But this remedy clearly is a deviation from the traditional rule that says there is no relief for mistakes in wills, even if the glitch was the failure to anticipate all possible contingencies.

### *Implied Gifts on Incomplete Dispositions*

Failure of a dispositive provision (for example, due to violation of the Rule Against Perpetuities, renunciation, or lapse) may create a gap in the distribution plan for the decedent's estate. The question is how to cure this dispositive gap. Implied gifts are more likely in this kind of situation than in a case like *Engle,* in which the will was not ambiguous and it disposed of the entire estate. For example, assume that a trust provided for X for life, remainder to X's descendants by representation, and that X renounced the life estate or otherwise is precluded from enjoying it (e.g., because X killed the decedent and the slayer statute is applicable, see Chapter 2, or because X was a surviving spouse who renounced the plan in favor of an elective share of the decedent's estate, see Chapter 10). In either case X would be deemed to have predeceased the decedent. How should the balance of the plan be implemented? Is X's life estate eliminated so that X's then living descendants take the property, by representation, immediately? If not, what happens to X's life estate during X's remaining life?

If X is precluded from taking the life estate and another beneficiary is adversely affected, some cases will sequester X's life estate for the benefit of that disappointed beneficiary. For example, if X were to take ⅓ of the residue of the decedent's estate under a forced share election, the residuary beneficiaries who suffer that invasion of "their" residue might receive the life estate X otherwise would have received. More common is acceleration of the remainder, as if X in our example were deceased, unless there is an obvious reason to delay distribution. For example, if X renounced the life estate and the remainder goes to X's then living descendants immediately, there is a possibility of afterborns of X who would be cut out if the remainder is accelerated. In such a situation, the life estate might be sequestered. That would not be the case if the gift were to X for life, remainder to Y's descendants who survive X, and Y already is deceased. In such a case acceleration to Y's descendants would be the likely result. See the discussion of the *Gilbert* case in Chapter 15. If these approaches do not solve the dilemma, we will soon learn that gaps are filled with a reversion to the decedent.

Assume that a trust provides for its "income to be equally divided between A and B until the death of the survivor of them." If A dies first, the question unanswered by the quoted language is what should be done with A's equal share of the income after A's death, pending the death of B. Should we assume that B is to receive all the income during this period, should it go to the remainder beneficiaries, or should it pass to A's estate? There are cases reaching each result.

Implied gifts most often are used to fill a gap if the intent of the testator is clear. To illustrate, imagine that T's testamentary trust provided separate shares of the residuary estate for T's children, A and B, with distribution on a child's death to that child's living descendants by representation or, if none, then to the child's sibling. Child A died survived by descendants who took A's share. Child B then dies with no descendants. To whom does B's share pass? A is not alive and no provision gives B's share to A's descendants. Our choices are A's estate, A's descendants, a reversion to the testator's estate to pass by intestacy, or B's other siblings, if any. Note that the takers of A's estate (A's heirs, if A died intestate, or A's devisees, if A died testate) may be different than A's descendants. Also note that T may have other children.

Did A need to survive B to take B's share? Traditional future interests law discussed in Chapter 15 does not impute a survivorship requirement in such a gift, in which case A's estate would receive B's share. Allowing A's estate to take may not be the "right" result if (as likely is true) the testator intended A's descendants to take under these facts. This especially is true if A's estate does not pass to A's descendants. (UPC §2-707, discussed in Chapter 15, changes the traditional future interests rule that survivorship is not required. Under it, A's estate would not take under this example.) In this case, some courts likely would find the testator's intention clear that A's descendants should take B's share, and imply a gift to A's descendants to reach that result. A third approach would be to treat the right to receive B's share as retained by the testator (i.e., a reversion). Because disposition of that reversion would not be provided for under the will, it would pass by intestacy. The law normally abhors an intestacy in a testate estate, so this would not be our first choice. It might, however, be the preferred approach if it generates the same result (all to A's descendants, because A and B *were* T's only children and T was not survived by a spouse) without resort to the implied gift remedy.

### *Implied Gifts to Avoid Unintended Results*

Likewise, if a gap results in a disposition that the testator obviously did not intend, a court likely will imply a gift that appears consistent with the testator's intent and that avoids the unanticipated and unintended consequence. For example, T's will specifically disinherits T's child, C, who is T's only heir, and leaves T's estate: "To my grandson, GS, if he graduates from college before he reaches age 25 with a grade point average of 2.5 or better on a 4.0 scale. If GS does not graduate from college with a grade point average of 2.5 or better on a 4.0 scale, I give my estate to my granddaughter, GD." T dies. GS subsequently graduated from college with a 2.6 grade point average, but he was 27 years old. To whom should T's estate be distributed? The choices: (1) GS, even though he did not graduate from college before he reached age 25, and thus did not satisfy the clearly expressed condition for taking. (2) GD, even though GS did not graduate from college with a grade point average of less than 2.5, and thus the clearly expressed condition for GD to take also was not satisfied. (3) C, as T's heir, because T did not make an effective disposition of T's estate (assume that the jurisdiction has not passed a "negative will" statute like UPC §2-101(b), as discussed in Chapter 2). It is not likely that GS would take. He was the primary residuary beneficiary, but his devise was expressly conditioned on graduating from college before he reached age 25, which he did not do. It appears that the testator intended GD to take the estate if GS did not satisfy the condition to receive it. Expressing GD's gift as subject only to the condition that GS graduate with a GPA of less than 2.5, rather than also being payable to GD if GS did not graduate before reaching age 25, appears to be an oversight by the drafter. An implied gift to GD under that condition is a likely alternative to allowing the property to pass by intestacy to T's disinherited child, C.

### Implied Gifts to Avoid Multiple Generations of Income Beneficiaries

An implied gift also may be useful to keep multiple generations from being income beneficiaries at the same time. For example, if a testamentary trust provided "to H and W for life, and on their deaths to their descendants," the question is what happens on the death of the first of H and W to die. Does the survivor continue to enjoy all the income, or do their descendants share income with the survivor, which is not likely the intent of most donors? Many courts would imply a gift to the survivor of all the income after the first death. But if the gift was income to siblings A and B rather than to spouses, with half the remainder to each of their descendants, the implied gift of half the income on the first sibling's death might be to that sibling's descendants.

### Implied Gifts for Similar Contingencies

Finally, if two similar contingencies are possible, and one is provided for but the other occurs, the presumption is that the same result is intended under each. For example, "To W for life, then to A and B in equal shares. If A dies without descendants, to B, and if B dies with descendants, to those descendants." What if A dies and B already is dead: do B's descendants take A's share the same as they took B's original share? And what if A dies with descendants? Should A's descendants take as provided with respect to B and B's descendants, or does A have a vested share that passes through A's estate if A does not die without descendants? Absent evidence that the testator for some reason intended otherwise (which might not be admissible, because the document really is not ambiguous), the likely result is that a gift would be implied to A's descendants, if any, and if there were none, that B's descendants would take the share.

This last example illustrates the importance of distinguishing between cases involving ambiguities or mistakes and cases in which a gift may be implied. Ambiguity cases are those in which the decedent provided a devise in an unclear way (e.g., "$100 to my cousin Jim" when the decedent had two cousins named "Jim"—a latent ambiguity—or "$100 to John Smith, $100 to John Jones, and Blackacre to John"—a patent ambiguity). Implied gift cases involve a gap in the dispositive scheme. The court's alternative usually is to fill the gap with a reversion to the settlor's estate, in the case of a trust, or with the property falling into the residue, in the case of a gap in a preresiduary testamentary gift, or with the property passing by intestacy, in the case of a gap in a residuary testamentary gift. In the right circumstances some courts will imply a gift to avoid these alternatives. In one sense a "mistake" occurs if there is an ambiguity or the need to imply a gift, but the pure mistake cases involving wills or will substitutes occur when there is no ambiguity and no gap to be filled. Rather, the allegation is that the gift of the specific property to the specific beneficiary was made by mistake and does not reflect what the decedent really intended.

# CHAPTER 8

# CONSTRUCTION: LAPSE AND CLASS GIFTS

Rules of construction are needed when a document does not provide for the disposition of property under a contingency that occurs. This can occur in numerous situations but two are especially common. One is "lapse," which occurs when a devisee predeceases the decedent. The devise fails unless the document addresses that contingency or an antilapse statute applies to send the devise to the devisee's descendants. The other involves gifts made to members of a class (e.g., "to my children" or "to my siblings"). Among the many issues that arise for class gifts are whether the gift *is* a class gift or a gift to individuals, how the lapse and antilapse rules apply, and when the class closes to exclude afterborn or afteradopted persons as members of the class.

It is not uncommon for a decedent's will to lack answers to some questions that arise about how the decedent's property is to be distributed. We saw in Chapter 7 that interpretation involving the decedent's intent is the process of answering those questions from the language of the document. We only resort to a rule of "construction" to resolve questions that must be answered for which there is no indication of the decedent's intent. Various rules of construction apply only because the document does not address an issue. There is no opportunity or option to resort to a rule of construction if the instrument does not create a gap in the disposition, or if interpretation can answer the question. Thus, the decedent's intent (either expressed or determined through interpretation) controls. Rules of construction are called upon to provide answers only if there is no clearly expressed or discernible answer.

In a few circumstances, even the clearly expressed intent of a decedent will not be given effect. Rather, issues raised in these circumstances are governed by rules of law. The Rule Against Perpetuities is an example. If the common law rule is applicable in the jurisdiction and a dispositive instrument violates it, the offending devise fails without regard to the decedent's intent. See Chapter 17 for further information.

## Lapse

If a gift lapses, it fails. Lapse applies if a named devisee predeceases the testator. If T's will leaves property to A, and A dies before T, the bequest to A is said to lapse.

## Implied Condition of Survivorship

Lapse results even if survivorship is not a stated condition, because the common law implies a condition of survivorship on a devisee taking a bequest under a will. The devisee must survive the transferor. This survivorship requirement exists even if the document is silent regarding the need for the devisee to be alive to inherit. Thus, if the testator's will provides "Blackacre to A," without specifying whether A must survive the testator to take, the common law interprets the will as if it read "Blackacre to A if living at my death" or "Blackacre to A if A survives me," and not as if it read "Blackacre to A, or to A's heirs, estate, or devisees if A does not survive me." The gift lapses if A does not survive. In a well drafted will the alternative usually is to give the gift to A if living and if not to A's descendants, by representation, or to an alternate devisee.

In a lapse case failure of the gift to a devisee who predeceases the testator raises the question whether the gift passes to someone else or as a part of the decedent's residuary or intestate estate. A well drafted document always specifies whether survivorship is required and, if so, what happens if the devisee does not survive. If survivorship is not required, the will may preclude lapse and provide that the interest passes to a predeceased devisee's estate and through it to the devisee's own heirs or devisees. Most wills expressly require survivorship, however, and direct disposition of the devise if the devisee predeceases. Indeed, you should never expressly address survivorship and then fail to provide what happens otherwise.

The lapse rules are provided by the law to address cases of bad drafting. These rules of construction apply only if the instrument does not adequately address the contingency of a devisee predeceasing the testator. Especially under the Uniform Probate Code, the adequacy of a provision addressing the lapse issue is not easy to predict. But in any situation involving the death of a devisee before the testator, the initial consideration should be whether the instrument provides an alternative disposition to a devisee who survives the testator. If so, that provision controls. If not, the lapse rules then may apply to resolve the issue.

### Common Law Lapse Rules

The normal common law implied condition of survivorship and lapse rules do not provide an alternative distribution, meaning that a lapsed gift simply fails. Thus, if a devise is to A and A dies before the testator, under the common law the gifted property does not pass to A's estate or to A's descendants. Instead, the devise fails and the property remains a part of the testator's estate. If the disposition precedes the residue (is preresiduary), the traditional rule is that the lapsed gift falls into the residue. Thus, if T willed "Blackacre to A, residue to B," and A dies before T, Blackacre would be distributed to B as a part of the residue. The property becomes intestate, however, if the lapsed gift is part of the residue. Thus, if T's will read "I leave my entire estate to A," and A died before T, under the common law T's estate would pass by intestacy to T's heirs. This is a result (intestacy) that the law traditionally abhors for a testate decedent.

The harder issue arises if T willed "the residue of my estate to A and B in equal shares," and A died before T. Under the common law A's half would pass by intestacy to T's heirs, not to B. See the discussion of *Russell* in Chapter 7 for an application of this "no residue of the residue" rule. Most state statutes, including UPC §2-604, have reversed that rule. Thus, now if A predeceased T (and if an antilapse statute did not apply) in most jurisdictions B would take the entire residue.

### *Antilapse Statutes*

Today most states have "antilapse" statutes to prevent failure of gifts and the disfavored intestacy that can follow. If applicable, they dispose of a lapsed gift, usually to the predeceased devisee's descendants by representation. In addition, many antilapse statutes expressly apply to void dispositions as well as to lapse. The difference is that, at common law, a devise to someone who was not living when the will was executed was "void." Technically such a gift did not lapse (although it too failed). Lapse occurs only if the devisee was alive when the will was executed but died before the testator. So void and lapsed gifts are different. But the issue of what to do is the same and lapse statutes (uniformly referred to as "antilapse" statutes) usually address both cases without added or special reference to void dispositions. So their application is easy: regardless of whether the devisee died before or after execution of the will, the antilapse statute will apply if all the conditions of the statute are satisfied.

### Application to Will Substitutes

Typical antilapse statutes do not apply to transfers under will substitutes, even if distribution occurs at the testator's death. This is subject to exceptions, the most notable being UPC §§2-706 and 2-707, which generally treat will substitutes the same as wills for antilapse purposes. For example, antilapse statutes typically apply to testamentary trusts. Thus, the antilapse statute may apply if T's will provides for T's estate to be held in trust for A and A dies before T. A's descendants would be substituted for A as beneficiaries of the testamentary trust if the will does not address the contingency and the other conditions for application of the antilapse statute (discussed below) are met. The reason this makes sense is because the trust is created by T's will and therefore is subject to the Wills Act and the antilapse statute. An inter vivos trust, however, would be a different story unless state law is like the UPC in its reach.

There is a certain logic in all this. The common law implied condition that the devisee must survive the decedent (and the rule that the gift lapses if the devisee does not) typically also does not apply to gifts made by will substitute. Thus, there is no lapse upon which an antilapse statute could operate and the deceased devisee's estate is entitled to the property. To illustrate, imagine that the AB Partnership agreement provides that D's interest in the partnership passes to D's spouse, S, when D dies. S dies a year before D's death. Assuming the arrangement does not fail as being testamentary and not executed in compliance with the will execution formalities (see Chapter 6), in many jurisdictions D's partnership interest will pass as a part of S's estate to S's heirs or devisees if the contingency of S dying before D is not addressed. No condition of survivorship is implied or imposed on S, there is no lapse, and there is no need for or application of an antilapse statute.

### Required Relationship

Another important limitation on the application of antilapse statutes is that the predeceased devisee must be within a designated group — typically relatives of the testator, sometimes lineal descendants. UPC §2-603 is broader than most antilapse statutes. It applies to beneficiaries who are grandparents or descendants of grandparents of the testator. It even includes step-children. Most antilapse statutes (including the UPC) do *not* apply to spouses (yet another illustration of the uneasy difference between spouses and blood relatives). And most antilapse statutes do not apply to persons who are not related to the testator at all. Thus, the implied condition of survivorship still applies for gifts to predeceased beneficiaries  and the gift will fail unless the will provides otherwise (which would be unusual). For example, assume T's will leaves $10,000 to a sibling, S, $20,000 to a child, A, and the residue ¼ to a friend, F, ¼ to charity, and ½ to child B. S, A, F, and B all predecease T. S's descendants who survive T will take the $10,000 by representation if the applicable antilapse statute includes a testator's sibling. Otherwise, or if no descendants of S survive T, the $10,000 will fall into the residue. The $20,000 left to A will pass under every antilapse statute to any of A's descendants who survive T, by representation. Only if there are none will the $20,000 fall into the residue. (Note that, either way, the $20,000 will not pass as a part of A's estate to A's heirs or devisees.) Any descendants of B who survive T will take B's share of the residue by representation, but the ¼ of the residue left to F probably will lapse because most antilapse statutes do not apply to gifts to non-relatives. If the jurisdiction follows the approach of UPC §2-604 (rather than the common law no-residue-of-the-residue rule discussed at page 155), F's ¼ would simply remain a part of the residue to be divided pro rata between B's descendants and the charity. Thus, if any of B's descendants survive T, the residue will be divided ⅔ to B's descendants and ⅓ to the charity. If no descendant of B survives T, the charity will receive the entire residue. On the other hand, if local law still adheres to the no-residue-of-the-residue rule, F's ¼ would become intestate property in T's estate and pass to T's heirs. T's will could provide for the possibility of one or more of the named beneficiaries not surviving T, in which case the will would govern and the antilapse statute would not apply.

In this last regard, remember that antilapse statutes dictate default results that apply only if the testator's will does not say what happens to a gift to a devisee who is not alive. There is no lapsed gift on which the statute can operate if the will addresses that possibility with a gift over to another devisee. Thus, if T's will provides: "$10,000 to A if living, otherwise to A's spouse, B, if living, and if neither A nor B survive me, to charity C," the antilapse statute will not apply regardless of whether A or B survives T. The existence of C might also be addressed by the will because no antilapse statute is likely to reach that far.

## Requirement of Survivorship

An antilapse statute may not apply if the will makes a gift to a predeceased devisee who is covered by the antilapse statute and the will expressly requires the devisee to survive. This nonapplication of the statute may result even if the will does not expressly provide an alternative disposition if the devisee does not survive. For example, assume T's will provides "Blackacre to my Child, C, if C survives me, residue to X," and that C dies before T, survived by a descendant of C who survives T. The will expressly conditioned the gift to C on survivorship. Because C did not survive, the condition is not satisfied and there is no bequest on which the antilapse statute may apply. The same would be true with respect to the residuary gift to X if T required X to survive and even if there was no gift over if X did not. Thus, traditionally a condition of survivorship overrides (or negates the need for) the antilapse statute. Put another way, antilapse statutes can apply only if a testator devises property to a devisee who predeceases the testator and the will does not provide for that possibility. In most states, an express survivorship condition is an adequate provision to negate application of the antilapse statute. In such states, the devise to C above would fail by its own terms and not by virtue of the lapse rule, the antilapse statute would not apply, and Blackacre would pass as a part of the residue of T's estate. And if X was expressly required to survive but did not, the residue would pass by intestacy.

*Allen v. Talley*, 949 S.W.2d 59 (Tex. Ct. App. 1997), illustrates that sometimes it is difficult to determine whether a will states an intent that an antilapse statute should not apply. The testator's will left her estate to "my living brothers and sisters: John . . . , Claude . . . , Lewis . . . , Lera . . . , and Juanita . . . share and share alike." John, Lewis, and Juanita were living when the testator executed the will but predeceased the testator. Their descendants claimed their parents' shares. The court instead held that Claude and Lera received the entire estate because the quoted language was deemed to impose a condition of survivorship, thereby expressing the testator's intent that the antilapse statute not apply.

Consider another example: T's will bequeathed her estate "to my siblings, A and B, share and share alike, or all to the survivor of them." A died, then B died, and then T died. One child of A and two children of B survived T, who also was survived by another sibling, C. T died unmarried, survived by no other relatives. The alternatives for distribution of T's estate are (1) half to A's child and the other half in equal shares to B's children, under the antilapse statute, (2) the entire estate in equal shares to B's children by virtue of the antilapse statute, leaving the entire estate to B's descendants because B survived A, or (3) by intestacy, with the relative shares of C and the descendants of A and B depending on the jurisdiction's system of representation. See Chapter 2. The antilapse issue is the same as in *Allen*: does the survivorship language in T's will reflect T's intent that the antilapse statute not apply?

Because the survivorship condition expressly applies only if one of A or B survives T, the will states no intent with respect to the contingency of both A and B predeceasing T. Accordingly, and because of the presumption against intestacy, the antilapse statute probably would apply. Further, the will speaks at death, at which time the testator's survivors are determined, and there is no indication that T would prefer the descendants of B over the descendants of A. As a result, it seems most likely that all the children of A and B would share under the antilapse statute without regard to B having survived A. Note, however, that the antilapse statute would not have applied if B had survived A and T, in which case B would have taken the entire estate. And from B the descendants of B likely would have succeeded to it all, so our judgment on this may be all wrong. Note also that the antilapse statute gives A's child half of the residue while B's children, who are similarly situated (all being nieces or nephews of T), split the other half. Even under the UPC antilapse statute, the share of a named devisee who predeceases a testator passes to the devisee's descendants, by representation, and there is no per capita at each generation system for property distributed under antilapse statutes to descendants of multiple predeceased beneficiaries, as there is under the UPC for intestate property. No reason is articulated in the UPC for this inconsistent treatment. For a case with facts similar to those of this example, see *Early v. Bowen*, 447 S.E.2d 167 (N.C. Ct. App. 1994).

Different results may be reached under UPC §2-603(b)(3), which specifies that a survivorship condition alone does not override the antilapse statute, absent additional sufficient indications of a contrary intent (such as an alternative disposition in the event of a devisee not surviving the testator, or extrinsic evidence — such as testimony of the drafter — that the testator did not intend the devisee's descendants to take the devisee's share). Thus, assume that T's will leaves "$1,000 to A if A survives me," that the will does not otherwise address the possibility of A dying before T, that A does not survive T, and that there is no extrinsic evidence that T would not want the antilapse statute to apply. Despite the survivorship condition, the UPC antilapse statute will apply if A is within the required relation to T and A's surviving descendants will take the $1,000 by representation. That is the most controversial application of the UPC, because good drafters believe the intent is clear without needing to say that A's gift *should* fail and fall into the residue because A did not survive T. Because this provision is so controversial, you should ascertain whether the legislature adopted this rule, even in a UPC jurisdiction.

### Substituted Gifts

Before application of an antilapse statute the first question to consider if a devisee dies before the testator is whether the will provides for an alternative taker for the gift. If so, the alternative taker receives the devise, there is no lapse, and the antilapse statute is not an issue. On occasion courts stretch to find an alternative taker under a will if the antilapse statute would not apply to save a gift, because failure to do so would cause the devise to lapse.

For example, in *Jackson v. Schultz*, 151 A.2d 284 (Del. Ch. 1959), the testator's will provided, "I give . . . to my beloved wife, Bessie . . . all my property . . . to her and her heirs and assigns forever." Bessie predeceased the testator. Three of Bessie's children from a prior relationship survived the testator, who had not adopted the children (although he had helped raise and support them). The testator died without heirs and his property would have escheated if it did not pass to Bessie's children under his will. Finding that the testator intended that his estate would pass to Bessie's heirs if she predeceased him, the court held for Bessie's children even though the antilapse statute did not apply to gifts to spouses. This construction avoided both intestacy and escheat to the state.

This raises a very troubling distinction between "To A *or* her heirs" and "To A *and* her heirs." If the gift had been to "Bessie *or* her heirs and assigns," the result the court wanted to reach would have been easy — a gift over to the children if Bessie predeceased. In *Jackson*, however, the gift was to "Bessie *and* her heirs and assigns." This language generally is construed to mean only that the devisee receives a fee, not that heirs and assigns take an alternative gift if the devisee predeceases the testator. (This sometimes is described as the words of "limitation v. purchase" distinction — the fee simple is limitation and the alternative gift is purchase.) Nevertheless, the court held that "and" can be read as "or" if, as in this case, doing so will carry out the testator's intent. By comparison, in *Hofing v. Willis*, 201 N.E.2d 852 (Ill. 1964), language similar to that employed in *Jackson* was used — "to A *and* her heirs and assigns" — and the same argument was made that "and" should be read as "or" to allow the heirs of A (who predeceased the testator) to take. The court held that construction to be unreasonable because it would allow A to assign the right to receive the devise to whomever A chose. The *Hofing* analysis probably is preferable to the construction in *Jackson*, although *Jackson* is revealing in how ardent the law is about avoiding a lapse, especially when it would cause property to pass by intestacy, or worse (in *Jackson*) to the state by escheat.

### Survivorship

Lapse occurs if a devisee predeceases the testator and the will does not name an alternative taker. There is no lapse if the devisee or the alternate survives the testator. In some circumstances (e.g., an automobile crash in which the testator and the devisee are killed) it may not be possible to determine if a devisee actually survived the testator. Further, the devisee may be treated as having predeceased by statute or by the will even if it is clear that the devisee actually survived the testator. See, e.g., UPC §2-702 (the 120 hour survival requirement).

A provision in the governing instrument controls if it addresses the question whether a devisee named in the instrument survived another person, such as the testator or another devisee. So, assume T's will leaves $10,000 to T's friend, F, if F survives T. The will also defines "survives" to require survival by at least 30 days. T dies. Twenty days later F dies. Despite having actually survived T, F will not take under T's will. If the will does not provide an alternative taker the devise will lapse (unless the governing antilapse statute applies to non-relatives, which is not likely) and fail.

Survivorship that is not addressed by the governing instrument is resolved by statute in most cases. The original Uniform Simultaneous Death Act (USDA) applied if deaths occurred under such circumstances that it was not possible to prove the order of deaths. Because of litigation that avoided application of the original USDA by proving the order of deaths, such as *Janus v. Tarasewicz*, discussed in Chapter 2, the USDA and the UPC were revised to require a devisee to survive a decedent by 120 hours to be treated as a survivor. Although this (or any other) statutory survivorship requirement will not apply if the document addresses the survivorship issue, the document must override the statute explicitly.

In that regard, a comment to both the revised USDA and the UPC includes the following example. G's will leaves her estate to her husband, H, and provides that, "in the event he dies before I do, at the same time that I do, or under circumstances as to make it doubtful who died first," G's estate goes to her brother, Melvin. G dies. H dies about 38 hours later. Under the USDA and the UPC, the comment says that Melvin takes G's estate. Although G's will addressed survivorship, the provision used is not operable because G and H did not die at the same time or under circumstances that make it doubtful who died first. Further, G's will did not explicitly override the 120 hour statutory survivorship requirement. Accordingly, it applies. H is thus treated as having predeceased G because H did not survive G by that 120 hour period. And thus alternative devisee Melvin receives G's estate. Quaere whether that reflects G's actual intent.

The USDA, and UPC §§2-104 and 2-702, provide rules for the disposition of property on the death of a decedent when a devisee does not survive the decedent by at least 120 hours. As between two individuals whose wills benefit each other, the rule is that each is treated as the survivor with respect to his or her own property, thus preventing double administration of any of their property. With respect to a life insurance beneficiary designation, if the statute applies the insured is treated as surviving the designated beneficiary. And if the statute applies to joint tenancy with the right of survivorship, each joint tenant is treated as the owner of an equal share of the property and is regarded as surviving for purposes of disposing of his or her share. But not addressed by statute in most states is the order of deaths between beneficiaries, neither of whom is the transferor (e.g., "to Child for life, remainder to Grandchild" and Child and Grandchild die under circumstances such that the order of their deaths cannot be proven). In some states that do address this subject the oldest is deemed to die first.

Survivorship conditions in a document (and the survivorship provisions of the USDA and the UPC) serve two purposes when two persons die within a relatively short time. First, they cause each decedent's property to pass to the decedent's designees (usually relatives), rather than the devisee's designees (usually the devisee's relatives). For example, G's will leaves her estate to her husband, H, but if he predeceases her, to her brother. G's property will pass to her brother if H fails to survive G by the requisite period, instead of to H's estate, from which it might pass to H's relatives. Second, survivorship conditions prevent double administration costs because property does not pass from one estate to another. The point here is that either state law or, preferably, the document should properly articulate the decisions of the donor and attention must be devoted to whether either the document or statute works the right result under a variety of otherwise unexpected circumstances.

### Lapse and Class Gifts

In the context of lapse, class gifts raise two issues. Is a particular gift a "class gift" and, if so, how do the lapse and antilapse rules apply, if at all? The second question is easier. For example, "to my children in equal shares" is a class gift. The issue is what happens if one or more of the children predecease the donor.

The common law provided no protection to the descendants of a member of a class gift who predeceased the testator. For example, assume that (1) T's will devises property to children, equally, making no provision for the possibility of a child predeceasing; (2) T's child A predeceases T; and (3) A's only child GC survives T. At common law GC would not take the share of the class gift that A would have received if living. Rather, the common law rule is that the remaining class members take the entire class gift. Indeed, there is no share for a predeceased class member and, thus, nothing for antilapse to salvage from failure. Only if no child survived T would the gift fail, meaning that the property would become residuary (if the class gift was preresiduary) or intestate (if the class gift was the residuary provision).

Most antilapse statutes apply to class gifts. Accordingly, a deceased class member's descendants take the share the deceased class member would have received if living if (1) the gift is a class gift, (2) a member of the class died before the testator, (3) the instrument does not include an alternative gift over, and (4) the antilapse statute is applicable (because the predeceased class member is within the proper relation to the testator). As in any antilapse situation, the descendants take directly from the testator, not through the deceased class member's estate. In every respect, it is as if they were members of the class, meaning that the deceased class member's creditors and surviving spouse have no claim against the descendants' share.

There are a number of rules that could apply in any given case, necessitating a rank ordering of the rules if a will contains a gift to a class and a member of the class fails to survive the testator. Here is their priority:

- **Survivorship condition.** Any survivorship condition — either expressly stated in the document or under an applicable statute regarding survivorship (such as the UPC 120 hour rule) —

applies first. A class member who does not survive by the requisite period has no entitlement and neither do that person's representatives, unless an antilapse statute then kicks in.

- **Alternative gift.** A gift over specified in the document in the event of nonsurvival applies. (E.g., "to my siblings, but if any does not survive me, his or her share to the Red Cross.")

- **Antilapse statute.** If there is no alternative disposition or if it is not effective (e.g., "to my children, equally; if any do not survive me, to his or her spouse who survives me," and the testator's child predeceases with no surviving spouse), then an antilapse statute that applies to class gifts may apply to cause the deceased class member's descendants to take the share. An antilapse statute would not solve the problem, however, if the deceased class member is not within the required relationship to the testator or if no descendant of the deceased class member survives the testator.

- **Survivorship within the class.** If an antilapse statute does not salvage the situation, then the deceased class member's "share" crosses over to the other class members, if any. This means that the surviving class members take everything.

- **Lapse.** Finally, if a cross-over within the class cannot apply (e.g., because no class member survives) and the gift is not caught by any of the prior rules, then the gift lapses and falls into the residue or, if it *is* the residue, it passes by intestacy.

To illustrate all this, assume that T's will leaves $60,000 to "my nephews who survive me by 30 days." T is survived by 30 days by two nephews, A and B. T had a third nephew, C, who predeceased T. C's only child, X, survived T by 30 days. In most states, the survivorship condition would negate application of the antilapse statute (even if nephews are within the category of devisees to whom the antilapse statute otherwise would apply), in which case A and B each would take $30,000. Under the UPC the survivorship language (absent other sufficient evidence of the testator's intent) would not negate application of the antilapse statute that applies to devises to descendants of the testator's grandparents. Thus, A, B, and X each would receive $20,000 under the UPC.

Let's look at another one. T's will left the residuary estate to "my first cousins, equally, and if any of them are not living, to their spouses." Assume T had four first cousins (A, B, C, and D). A and B survived T. C and D predeceased T. C was survived by a spouse (S) who also survived T. D was unmarried at death but left an only child (X) who survived T. S will take C's share without regard to the jurisdiction's antilapse statute because the will included a gift over to the spouse of a first cousin who predeceased T. D's share may pass to X if the applicable antilapse statute applies to class gifts and if first cousins are within its reach. Otherwise there will be no share for D. In the latter case the entire residue will be divided equally among A, B, and S. If the UPC were in effect, X would take ¼ of the residue (as would each of A, B, and S), because the UPC antilapse statute applies to class gifts (as do most) and because it applies to devises to descendants of the testator's grandparents, which includes first cousins.

### What Is a Class Gift?

The second class gift/lapse issue is whether the gift is to a class in the first place. Usually this question should be addressed first (we deferred it only because it is the more elaborate concept to digest). A "class gift" is one to takers who are defined by one or more common characteristics. For example: to my "children," "grandchildren," "employees," "former spouses," "siblings," "nieces and nephews," "first cousins," or such. When the recipients of a gift are identified as a group, the assumption is that the donor was "group minded" and intended the gift to be shared by those persons who were members of the group at the appropriate time (more on that shortly). Thus, a fundamental characteristic of a class gift is that the number of persons who are to receive it can increase or decrease, as changes in composition of the class occur.

In a class gift the size of each member's share is subject to change as the number of shares changes (the number increasing while the class is "open" and decreasing *if* a member dies and survivorship is required). The important point is that the number of takers and the size of their respective shares are uncertain until a determination is made at some definite time as to who is included in the class. For example, a devise in equal shares to grandchildren who survive the testator may fluctuate as grandchildren are born or die between the time the will is executed and the time the testator dies. Thus, in *Dawson v. Yucus*, 239 N.E.2d 305 (Ill. App. Ct. 1968), the testator's will left an interest in a farm half to Stewart and half to Gene, both of whom were nephews of her predeceased husband. Gene died before the testator and Stewart claimed that the devise of the farm was a class gift, in which case he would take the entire interest as the only survivor of the class. (Note, the antilapse statute did not apply to Gene, who was related to the testator only by marriage and not by blood.) The court held that the devise was not a class gift because the devisees were designated by name and the size of their shares was fixed at half each. As a result, Gene's gift lapsed. Because it was a preresiduary gift, it fell into the residue and passed to the residuary beneficiaries.

For a devise like in *Dawson* to be a class gift the will would have said something like "in equal shares to such members of the class consisting of (in *Dawson*, my husband's nephews, Stewart and Gene) as survive me." There can be a class that is as small as two potential takers, and all persons who could qualify as class members need not be included in the class (e.g., the quoted language would constitute a class gift even if there were additional excluded nephews of the testator's husband who survived her, which was the case).

For example, assume that T's will includes a gift of "the residue of my estate ⅓ to A, ⅓ to B, and ⅓ to C." The gift is not a class gift, even if A, B, and C share a common characteristic that would allow them to be described as a class (e.g., if they were siblings). This would be the case even if C predeceases T, the antilapse statute is not applicable and, in the absence of class gift treatment, C's ⅓ would pass by intestacy. (Note that intestacy would result if the jurisdiction follows the traditional no-residue-of-the-residue rule, rather than the approach of UPC §2-604, under which A and B would share C's ⅓ even without class gift treatment.) In *Sullivan v. Sullivan*, 529 N.E.2d 890 (Mass. App. Ct. 1988), the court improperly deemed such a disposition to be a class gift, presumably to avoid intestacy. The preferable means of achieving class gift treatment in such a situation would be for the will to say something like "to my siblings who survive me" or (if there were more siblings than A, B, and C but only those three were meant to benefit) "to such members of a class consisting of my siblings A, B, and C as survive me."

*In re Moss*, 1899 2 Ch. 314 (Eng. C.A.), illustrates the question whether a gift — in *Moss*, of a remainder — "to A and the children of B" is a single class gift, or an individual gift of a part of the property to A and a class gift of the balance of the property to the class of B's children. The cases are divided. The *Moss* court held the gift to be a single class gift. Perhaps that was because otherwise the gift to A would have lapsed, which would have caused part of the remainder to pass to the life tenant, whom the testator clearly intended to receive only a life estate. But in most cases there is said to be a slight presumption in favor of the gift being to individuals rather than to a class if the issue whether there is a class gift is in doubt. Thus, drafters cannot be too explicit in describing a gift as to a class if that is the intent.

As just illustrated, class gifts raise various construction issues, in addition to the threshold question whether a class gift has been created and the lapse and antilapse problems. These issues arise only if a contrary intent is not clearly expressed. Resort to the class gift rules of construction is not necessary if all of the various contingencies concerning class membership, the deaths of class members, and distributions are clearly addressed in the document.

## Composition of the Class

Central to class gift issues is the question of who comprises the class and thus who shares in the gift to the class. The key questions are when is membership in the class determined and under what conditions may someone who shares the common characteristic for class membership nevertheless be excluded from the class. These questions require an understanding of open and closed classes. An "open" class means that it can get larger. For example, if the class is your grandchildren, and your children are still alive, the class is open (unless treated as closed under the rules described below) because your children can have more children who will be your grandchildren.

"Closing" a class means that no one born or adopted or otherwise made to qualify for class membership (e.g., by marriage) after the class has closed can become a member of the class, even if they otherwise share the class characteristics. Afterborns in gestation are deemed to be alive when conceived. Thus, a child conceived before a class closes, but born after, is a member of the class. But being alive but not yet adopted will not suffice — the adoption does not relate back to birth for class closing purposes. The class closes no later than when it is physiologically impossible for a person to be born into a class. For example, if T left Blackacre in trust for A for life, remainder to B's children, the class will close no later than on B's death during A's life. Some classes close even sooner than that, as we will see.

## Survivorship

A different question is whether survivorship of a future event, such as the death of a person, is required to become a class member in the first instance, or to share in a distribution of the class gift after the death of the class member. The interest of the class member is an asset that passes through the class member's estate (to the member's heirs if intestate, or to devisees if testate) if survivorship is not required and the class member dies before distribution occurs.

To illustrate: T's will left Blackacre in trust, with income to be paid to A for life, remainder to B's children. A and two children of B, C and D, each survive T but C predeceased A. At A's death, what disposition is to be made of Blackacre? At common law, and in most jurisdictions today, the remainder beneficiary is not required to survive the life tenant, and C's remainder interest in Blackacre vested when C survived T. Thus, at A's death, half of Blackacre passes to D and the other half to C's estate to be distributed to C's heirs or devisees. Notice that this rule, with respect to *future* interests and survival of the prior life estate interest, differs from the common law rule that a devisee must survive the testator to avoid a lapse. Although it might seem that a consistent survival rule should apply, we will see that these two cases are very different at common law. (As discussed in Chapter 15, a recent change in the UPC reverses this traditional treatment, requires that C survive A to take, and injects an antilapse concept into future interest law, all of which is a major change in the law of future interests.)

On the other hand, if survivorship is required the interest of a class member who predeceases the specified event fails. Thus, for example, assume T's will left Blackacre to T's children, equally. T had three children, A, B, and C. A predeceased T but B and C survive T. At common law, the gift to A would fail. Class membership for an immediate gift at the death of the testator is determined at the testator's death and the common law implied survival requirement at T's death is applicable even in this class gift. Because A did not survive T, A was not a member of the class and had no interest in Blackacre. Thus, at T's death A's estate would not share in the gift of Blackacre. In most jurisdictions antilapse statutes apply to class gifts, and gifts to children are covered by antilapse statutes. As a result, in most states any descendants of A who survive T will stand in A's shoes to take the share of Blackacre that A would have received if living. Blackacre would pass to B and C, the members of the class who survived T, if no descendant of A survives T or if the gift was to a class whose members are not covered by the applicable antilapse statute, or if the applicable antilapse statute does not apply to class gifts.

### General Principles

If a gift to a class is intended, three general principles or presumptions, and one basic rule modifying them, are found in most cases (although they may conflict):

- **Include as many members as possible.** The first assumption is that the donor wants to benefit as many members as possible (subject to the rule of convenience, discussed below).

- **Avoid failure or lapse.** The second presumption is that the donor wants to avoid lapse. Although delayed determination of class membership is not favored, neither is closing the class *before necessary* if the effect might be to exclude possible members.

- **Early distribution.** The third presumption is that the donor wants an early distribution.

Consider two examples of these principles:

T's will left Blackacre in trust, income to A for life, remainder to B's children. T died, survived by A, B, and a child of B (X). At common law, X's interest vests at T's death even if X dies before A (in which case X's share passes when A dies, through X's estate to X's heirs or devisees). The class of B's children does not close at T's death, however, because distribution of Blackacre is not required until A dies. Thus, if another child of B is born or adopted after T's death but before A dies, that child also will have a vested share in the gift of Blackacre. Blackacre will be distributed at A's death and the class therefore closes then *even if B is then living.* A child of B born thereafter would not share in the gift.

T's will left $30,000 to A's children who reach the age of 30 years. T died, survived by A and by two children of A, W (age 10) and X (age 6). The class closes when A's oldest living child reaches the age of 30 years. The presumption is that T intended distribution to A's children as they reach the age of 30, not at a later date when we would know with certainty how many children of A actually will reach the age of 30. If X is living when W reaches the age of 30, along with a third child of A who was born after T's death, W will receive $10,000, and the remaining $20,000 will be held for X and the third child until they reach the age of 30. If X dies before reaching the age of 30, half of X's share will be distributed to W and the other half will remain as part of the share being held for the third child (unless an antilapse statute were applicable in this order of death situation, in which case X's descendants would be substituted, by representation, for X as members of the class). Any additional children of A born or adopted after W reaches the age of 30 years are excluded from the class because it closed when W reached the age of 30. This was to facilitate an early distribution.

The Rule of Convenience is a basic rule that modifies the three general principles. A gift of a fixed dollar amount (or quantity of other property) to each member of a class sometimes is referred to as a *per capita gift* and requires, under the rule of convenience, closing the class when the fund must be established (the time of "funding"). Thus, if T gave a specified amount to each member of a class, the class closes at the testator's death regardless of whether distribution of the gift is to be made at the testator's death or thereafter, or whether any members of the class survive the testator. To illustrate why, consider the issues that arise if T's will left $1,000 to each grandchild who survived T. T is survived by two grandchildren, GC1 and GC2, and by three children. The class closes at T's death. GC1 and GC2 each receive $1,000. Any grandchildren born after T's death (unless in gestation when T died, in which case $1,000 also is set aside for each of them) are excluded from the gift. If T's will had provided for $1,000 to be distributed to each grandchild who survived T, each to receive the $1,000 when they reach age 30, the class still would close at T's death, even if GC1 and GC2 both were under 30 at T's death. Grandchildren born after T's death would be excluded from the gift regardless of whether they were born before or after either or both of GC1 and GC2 reached age 30. All of this is because we want to set aside the money required for this gift and distribute the balance of T's estate. It is not convenient to keep T's estate open while we wait to know how many $1,000 gifts must be set aside for additional grandchildren who are born or adopted after T's death.

An exception to the rule of convenience would apply if T had no grandchildren at T's death and the gift is a per capita affair. In that case some states might leave the class open to admit someone born or adopted thereafter, to avoid total failure of the gift. And because this violates the principle of the rule of convenience, those states would leave the class open until all of T's children are dead because, after all, now that convenience is lost we may as well be equitable. But most courts would close the class at T's death and the gift would fail (assuming an antilapse statute was not applicable).

Per capita gifts are treated differently for class closing purposes than gifts of a fixed total sum or specified property, to be divided among members of a class, because the gifted property that is the subject of a per capita gift cannot be calculated and set aside for later division when distribution is required. With a per capita gift there is no way to know how much to set aside to fund the per capita gifts, so the rule of convenience closes the class to make early distribution of T's estate possible. If per capita gifts are *not* involved, then under the rule of convenience the class remains open until the first mandatory distribution of principal to a class member is required. For example, if a trust were created for T's grandchildren and the trustee could distribute income or principal to them in its discretion but must distribute corpus only when each grandchild reaches age 35, the class would remain open until the first living grandchild actually reaches age 35, at which time a distribution must be made to that grandchild of an equal share of the trust corpus. The class closes then, so the trustee can determine how large a share to distribute.

### Immediate Gifts

If T's will leaves Blackacre to X's children, the rule of convenience dictates that the class closes at T's death, at which time distribution is to be made to the children of X who survive T (and, if an antilapse statute is applicable, to descendants of any deceased child of X), without regard to X also having survived T and thus without regard to the possibility of there being additional children of X. To do otherwise would be unworkable. To hold the gift in T's estate until X's death would delay the distribution to children of X who survive T, and it would delay closing T's estate for what could be many years. To distribute part of Blackacre to X's children who survive T and withhold the balance for future born children entails the same ongoing estate administration problem and presents the possibility of X having more or fewer children than anticipated. Finally, to distribute Blackacre to the children of X who survive T, subject to an obligation that they convey interests in Blackacre to any children of X subsequently born or adopted raises questions of enforceability, administration, title, and such.

### Postponed Gifts

On the other hand, if a fixed sum or gift of specified property is not to be distributed until a future date, the rule of convenience closes the class when the first mandatory distribution of principal is required, even though that occurs well after the testator's death. For example, assume T's will devised Blackacre to A for life, remainder to B's children. B had two children, V and W, both of whom were living when T executed this will. V died first, followed by T, who was survived by A, B, and W. B had another child, Y, during A's life, but after T's death, and then W died. A then died, survived by Y, after which B had yet another child, Z. Distribution is not required until the death of the life tenant, A. Accordingly, the class did not close until then. Z is not a member of the class and does not share in the distribution of Blackacre because Z was born after the class closed. Y is a member of the class and shares in the distribution because Y was born before A's death. V is not treated as a member of the class (although V's descendants may be substituted for V as class members if an antilapse statute applies) because V did not survive T. Finally, note the rule regarding survivorship for this future interest class gift. W survived T but died before A. In most jurisdictions W's remainder vested at T's death because there is no requirement that W survive A, so W's share would pass to W's estate to be distributed to W's heirs (if W died intestate) or devisees (if W died testate). Under UPC §2-707, however, W's interest would fail, unless saved for W's descendants by an antilapse statute. See Chapter 15.

Circumstances *may* dictate that the distribution of a gift be accelerated if a testator provides for a postponed gift to a class and the class closes on its own. For example, T's will left $25,000 "to A's children, to be paid to them when they reach age 30." T died, survived by A and A's only child, X, who was age 10. X died two years after T and A died three years after X. The interest of X in the fund vested at T's death. (Note that the gift is to A's children, "*to be paid to them* when they reach age 30," not "to A's children *who reach* age 30." See the discussion of *Clobberie's Case* in Chapter 15.) Probably no portion of the fund was distributed to X's heirs or devisees at X's death, however, because A was still living and could have additional children before X would have reached 30. In other words, the class was going to remain open after X's death at least until X would have reached age 30, and any children of A born or adopted before that date would become class members. The class closed physically upon A's death, even before X would have reached 30. At that time there is no further reason to withhold distribution of the fund to X's heirs or devisees, and the distribution of their share likely would be accelerated. Note too that we are ignoring the new biology and the possibility of more DNA offspring of A many years after A's death. The law just has not confronted that issue yet.

Assume now that T's gift was to A for life, remainder to A's children and that T died survived by A and by A's only child, X. If A disclaims, the class is not physiologically closed, because A could have additional children, but UPC §2-801(d)(1) provides that a future interest (the remainder to A's children) that becomes possessory after the termination of a disclaimed current interest (A's life estate) takes effect as if the disclaimant predeceased the decedent. In this example, A would be treated as having died before T and the class would close at T's death. This means that any children of A born or adopted thereafter would be excluded from the gift. That result was reached under the UPC in *Pate v. Ford*, 376 S.E.2d 775 (S.C. 1989), even though (1) the disclaimer was by a sibling who had five children, (2) another sibling had none but could have had children in the future who would have been beneficiaries, and (3) the disclaimer resulted in the disclaimant's five children taking to the exclusion of any of their afterborn or afteradopted first cousins. That seems unfair but the class closing rules reflect certain presumptions that can apply at cross purposes.

Another set of criteria is illustrated by *Lux v. Lux*, 288 A.2d 701 (R.I. 1972), in which a grandmother's will left the residue of her estate to her grandchildren, but further provided that any realty in the residue was to be maintained for the grandchildren and not sold until the youngest reached age 21. The first question was whether the realty passed outright to the grandchildren at their grandmother's death, in which case the class would have closed then, or whether the gift was made in trust, in which case the class would not close until the youngest grandchild reached age 21. Recognizing the income producing nature of the real property and the young ages of her grandchildren, and providing for the realty to be maintained for them and not to be sold until a future date, the court held that the grandmother intended to create a trust with principal distributions to the grandchildren delayed until a future date. Thus, the class did not close at her death. Instead, the court considered four possible dates for closing the class: (1) when the youngest grandchild living when the will was executed reached 21, (2) when the youngest grandchild living when the grandmother died reached 21 (one of the five grandchildren who were living when she died was born after the will was executed), (3) when the youngest of all grandchildren living at any time reached 21, or (4) when the youngest grandchild whenever born reached 21, even if that grandchild might be born or adopted after all others were over the age of 21 years. (The testator's only son, the father of the five grandchildren, informed the court that he and his wife planned to have more children.)

The first of the alternatives would exclude the one grandchild living at the testator's death but born after execution of the will. The second alternative would exclude grandchildren born after the testator's death but before the youngest of the grandchildren who survived the testator reached age 21. These alternatives each were rejected, presumably because they would exclude grandchildren born before any distribution of principal was required. The fourth alternative would require delaying distribution until the son's death, when the class would close physiologically, even if all of the living grandchildren had long since reached age 21. The court also rejected that construction and adopted the third alternative, which it viewed as representing the average testator's intent. It also is the alternative recommended in such a situation by the Restatement (Third) of Property—Wills and Other Donative Transfers §15.1 comment *o*.

### Exceptions to the Rule of Convenience

There are two minor exceptions to the rule of convenience. The first was stated above: afterborns in gestation are deemed to be alive when conceived. The other is if no class members exist when distribution is required and it is not a per capita gift. Failure is prevented by admitting *all* afterborns and afteradopteds. The class does not close until no more may be born or adopted. For example, the class would not close until all the children die if distribution is to grandchildren when the testator dies, the testator's children are alive at that time, but there are no grandchildren yet.

Remember that the class closing rules are rules of construction, designed in significant part to carry out the presumed intent of the testator. If T's will provides for an immediate gift at T's death to grandchildren and at least one grandchild is then living, the assumption is that T wanted distribution to occur at T's death. Closing the class at that time accomplishes that result, as well as avoiding the administrative problems of keeping the class open until the death of the last of T's children. Afterborns or afteradopteds are excluded if there is anyone alive in the class to take at the testator's death. But if there are no grandchildren living at T's death (and an antilapse statute does not apply to substitute as class members descendants of a predeceased grandchild), the class cannot close at that time without defeating the gift altogether. The implicit assumptions underlying this exception to the rule of convenience are that T did not want the gift to fail, that T knew no grandchildren were living at T's death, and that T therefore must have wanted the class to remain open to benefit all members of the class whenever born or adopted. In this case T's estate probably will be kept open to hold the property until the death of T's last child. It had to be kept open beyond T's death in any event. Once it is kept open beyond

T's death, it is not closed at the birth or adoption of any grandchild. Instead, it is kept open as long as additional class members might be born or adopted.

### Class Gifts of Income

Finally, special rules apply to class gifts of income from a fund. Assume that A survived T and that T's will left property in trust, with income to be paid annually to A's children and the remainder to be paid to B at the death of the last of A's children to die. The class will not close at T's death. Rather, income is distributable each year to those children of A who are alive at the time of each income distribution. As a result, if one child of A (X) survives T and A has a second child (Y) five years after T's death, the trust income for the first five years will be paid to X only. Income for subsequent years will be shared by X and Y until one of them dies (in which case, assuming no antilapse statute is applicable, income would thereafter be paid to the survivor), or until additional children of A are born (in which case they too would share in future income distributions). In a sense, each income distribution is treated as a separate gift as to which the class closing rules apply.

To illustrate, imagine T's will devised property in trust, with the principal to be distributed to the children of A who reach age 30 and with the income to be distributed to them currently, as it is earned. T died, survived by A and by two children of A, W (age 15) and X (age 10). A had another child, Y, before W reached age 30, A had a fourth child, Z, after W reached age 30. Here, income will be distributed to A's children who will receive distributions of principal upon reaching age 30. Under the class closing rules for postponed gifts, the class will close when the oldest of A's children, W, reaches age 30. Because Z was born after that, Z is excluded from the class and will not share in either income or principal. W will receive ⅓ of the principal when W reaches age 30. X will receive ½ of the remaining principal when X reaches age 30, and Y will receive all of the remaining principal when Y reaches age 30. Meanwhile income will be distributed equally to the current class members. Thus, W and X will share the income from T's death until the birth of Y. Income will be distributed in equal thirds among W, X, and Y from the birth of Y until W reaches age 30. X and Y will share the income from W's 30th birthday until X reaches age 30. All income will be distributed to Y after X reaches age 30.

In all of this class gift complication, also remember that the class gift rules are rules of construction. As such, they give way to a contrary intent stated in the instrument. In most cases, the preferable course is to avoid the class gift rules of construction by specifically addressing each of the various contingencies that can arise with a class gift.

# CHAPTER 9

# CONSTRUCTION: ADEMPTION, ABATEMENT, ACCESSIONS, AND EXONERATION

Interpretation and construction focus primarily on problems of identifying the property being devised or the devisees to receive it. This Chapter addresses other more structural issues affecting the distribution of a decedent's property that often are not resolved by the testator's will: ademption, abatement, accessions, and exoneration. *Ademption* involves a will that devises property that the testator did not still own at death. *Abatement* occurs if the will devises more property than the decedent owned at death. It often arises because the will did not adequately address how taxes and administration expenses would be paid, or because of other unexpected changes. *Accessions* issues include whether beneficiaries are entitled to receive dividends, interest, rent, or other income earned by the estate on assets specifically bequeathed, or interest on general pecuniary bequests. *Exoneration* is relevant if the testator devised encumbered property, the issue being whether the devisee takes the property subject to the debt or must the estate repay the debt so the devisee takes the property unencumbered.

### Classification of Dispositions

Most topics in this Chapter are affected by the type of disposition (specific, general, demonstrative, or residuary) involved, which makes *classification* of a disposition critical. Recall from Chapter 1 that a "devise" is a gift of land, a "bequest" is a gift of personal property, and a "legacy" is a gift of money. The UPC refers to all three as "devises." Sometimes we use the traditional terms but mostly we follow the UPC approach. For purposes of this Chapter some new terms are important.

*Specific* devises are gifts of particular assets or gifts payable from specified sources.

*Demonstrative* devises are specific gifts that may be satisfied from general funds if the specified funds or particular assets are exhausted. These gifts are treated as specific first but, if the asset or fund is inadequate, general estate assets are used to fund the balance of the gift. The notion that the testator intended such a result often is a fiction to avoid ademption of a specific devise or to delay abatement of a general devise.

*General* devises are neither specific nor demonstrative. They are gifts that are made to the devisee, but not of particular assets nor from a specific fund. General devises are satisfied out of any available assets or funds.

***Residuary*** gifts are what remains after all specific, demonstrative, and general devises have been satisfied.

Here are some examples:

- "My living room furniture" is a specific bequest.
- "The money that X owes me" is a specific legacy.
- "100 shares of X company stock" is a general bequest, maybe demonstrative if the testator owned X stock but, if there were not enough shares of X stock in the estate, the personal representative would acquire additional shares.
- "$100 worth of my X company stock" probably is a specific bequest (because of the use of the word "*my*": it is not just *any* shares of X stock being given).
- "$100, to be satisfied with my X company stock" is specific and probably a pecuniary legacy, although it may be a specific bequest of stock. This distinction — between a gift of money or a gift of stock — probably does not matter except for income tax purposes (which are addressed in Chapter 20). What would the decedent want if there is not enough X stock at death? Should cash or other assets be used to make up the difference? Because of the word "my" the estate presumably cannot just buy additional shares to satisfy this gift.
- "The greater of money and property of the value of $1 million or one-third of my estate" is a general legacy or a residuary bequest, depending on which is greater.
- "$100 from my account at the X bank" is a specific legacy, arguably demonstrative (which would be easier to argue if a comma appeared before "from") if the account is inadequate to satisfy the legacy and other funds are available.
- "The residue of my property" is residuary.

The next two examples illustrate how clarity may be elusive notwithstanding a simple, common disposition.

- "All the rest of my land" probably is a residuary devise (although "*my*" may make it specific).
- "All my personal property" might be a general bequest, residuary, or specific (because of "*my*").

Note that courts trifle with the classification rules (because they often dictate resolution of the issues addressed in this Chapter) to serve their sense of equity or justice in a given case. As such it is critical to know that classifications are not absolute and may differ, depending on the substantive issue at stake and who the court wants to protect or disfranchise. (This explains why the plaintiff in *Wasserman v. Cohen,* discussed next below, was complaining about the court's decision to classify the gift before determining whether it adeemed.) For example, a disposition may be regarded as general for ademption by extinction purposes but specific for abatement or ademption by satisfaction reasons. Both (inconsistent) classifications would protect the beneficiary of the gift, as we will see. So be careful with caselaw that classifies a disposition — the holding may reflect the reason why the classification was being done.

### Ademption by Extinction

The concept of ademption by extinction (often called just ademption) is applicable only to specifics, the subject of which is no longer in the estate at death. Unless the will provides otherwise (such as by making an alternative gift), generally the gift will simply fail due to extinction of the gifted property. This concept cannot apply to general, demonstrative, or residuary dispositions because, in all three of those categories, there is no gift of a particular identified item that can be exhausted or adeemed. Notice, however, that general, demonstrative, and residuary gifts can abate to exhaust those forms of gifts.

### *Theory of the Doctrine*

Ademption by extinction is based on an assumption that a testator who intended to preserve a gift to a devisee after extinction of the subject of the specific devise would have changed the will to do so. In most states, failure to alter the will to preserve the gift is taken as conclusive proof of an intent to adeem. These states follow an "identity" theory: the gift fails if the specifically devised property is not owned by the testator at death, without regard to what the testator's actual intent may have been. For example, in *Wasserman v. Cohen,* 606 N.E.2d 901 (Mass. 1993), the settlor provided for a specific gift of an apartment building to a beneficiary. The gift adeemed when the settlor sold the building prior to death and did not amend the trust to provide an alternative gift. The court refused to consider the question whether the settlor *actually* intended the gift to adeem.

Notice that the *Wasserman* court applied the traditional wills doctrine of ademption to a revocable inter vivos trust. According to the court, "a trust, particularly when executed as part of a comprehensive estate plan, should be construed according to the same rules traditionally applied to wills." See Chapter 6. In addition, the *Wasserman* gift adeemed because the settlor voluntarily sold the property. Ademption by extinction traditionally applies even if the property was extinguished *without* the testator's consent. Thus, at common law and in many states today, it is not necessary to find (or even presume) that extinction of the item was voluntary.

Note in this regard that some states depart from traditional ademption doctrine in an involuntary extinction case. Those states give the devisee any insurance proceeds (in case of a loss of the specifically devised property by casualty or theft), or the proceeds from condemnation (limited in each case to amounts that are unpaid at the testator's death). Further, if a personal representative of an incompetent or disabled individual sells specifically devised property, in many states the devisee will be entitled to the proceeds of the sale, including proceeds received before the testator's death. See, e.g., UPC §2-606. But case law allowing the devisee of an extinguished specific devise to receive other property in its stead are in the minority. And they will not apply if there is actual proof of a positive intent to adeem. Also, in some states the beneficiary may need to identify the proceeds from a particular disposition to avoid ademption. On the other hand, among the most liberal statutes is UPC §2-606(a)(6), which prevents ademption if there is proof that ademption would be inconsistent with the decedent's intent, and under which tracing is *not* required. In the face of proof of an intent not to adeem, the devisee of the extinguished item simply receives the value of the specifically devised property, paid from other assets in the estate.

### *Inability to Change the Will*

Ademption by extinction is based on a presumption that the testator would have changed the will to substitute other property if ademption was not the intent. As such, the doctrine should require that the testator had the ability to alter the will after extinction of the item. Thus, the doctrine should not apply if extinction of the item occurred after the testator's death, incapacity, or if there were time or space limitations that prevented alteration of the will. For example, even without a state statute to dictate this exception, the intended beneficiary should receive any insurance proceeds representing or replacing a destroyed asset if the property was destroyed in a fire or wreck in which the testator died. UPC §2-606(b) goes further, applicable to any disposition of specifically devised property during the testator's life by an agent acting under a durable power of attorney (or other personal representative, such as a guardian). The disappointed devisee receives an amount equal to the proceeds from the disposition, payable from other assets of the estate, which also is quite unusual.

Probably more representative of the majority approach, *In re Estate of Hegel*, 668 N.E.2d 474 (Ohio 1996), strictly followed ademption doctrine despite the testator's inability to change her will after a sale of specifically devised property. In *Hegel*, an agent under a durable power of attorney sold property of an incapacitated testator shortly before the testator's death. The agent did not realize that she personally was the specific devisee of the property under the testator's will. Ohio's ademption statute protected specific devisees from sales made by guardians, but not from sales made by attorneys-in-fact for incapacitated principals. So the Ohio Supreme Court held the devise adeemed. This is a tough result, but unfortunately not so uncommon.

### *Partial Ademption*

Pro tanto ademption is possible in the case of a disposition or destruction of a portion of the specific devise. To illustrate, assume T's will devised an 80 acre tract of land to A. Subsequently, T sold 20 of the 80 acres to a third party. In an identity theory jurisdiction the gift is adeemed to the extent of the 20 acres, and A will receive only the remaining 60 acres. In an intent theory or UPC jurisdiction, A would receive the 60 acres plus the value of the 20 acres sold, unless it is established that T intended the gift of the 20 acres to adeem.

### *Avoiding Ademption*

In addition to drafting to provide an alternative gift if specifically devised property is adeemed, ademption by extinction may be avoided in any of three other ways.

First, the specific gift may be interpreted to apply to after-acquired items matching the item that was extinguished. The new property will pass in place of the asset originally owned. For example, if the will said "I give my home" to X, whatever home was owned at death would pass, even if it is different from the one that was owned when the will was executed.

Second, ademption does not apply if the gift is construed to be demonstrative or general. For example, assume that T's will devises "100 shares of IBM stock to each of A, B, and C." When the will was executed, T owned 300 shares of IBM stock. Subsequently, however, T sold the IBM stock and died owning none. If the gifts are specific, they might adeem (because, as a specific, additional shares cannot be bought). If they are general they do not. To avoid failure of the gifts, many courts would classify them as general (thus requiring the personal representative to purchase 300 shares to satisfy the gifts). But if the devise had been "100 shares of *my* IBM stock to each of A, B, and C," the gifts likely would be classified as specific, and adeem by virtue of the sale and that classification.

Third, changes only in form do not cause ademption. For example, T's will devised "my 100 shares of ABC stock to A." ABC merged into XYZ after execution of the will, and T received 200 shares of XYZ stock in exchange for the ABC stock. A will receive the 200 shares of XYZ stock if T died owning the XYZ stock and did not change the bequest.

To illustrate that this theory may not be so easy to apply, imagine that T owned two pearl necklaces and executed a will bequeathing "my larger string of pearls" to A and "my other string of pearls" to B. Subsequently T had the pearls restrung and combined them into one string. If the combination is regarded as a mere change of form, A and B would take as tenants in common, probably with their fractions of ownership depending on the relative values of the two strands. But that result seems sufficiently odd that we're not sanguine that a court would produce it, and we don't know whether B's gift alone would adeem or they both might.

UPC §2-606(a)(5) expands and codifies this change-in-form exception. Property acquired as a "replacement" for specifically devised property passes to the specific devisee. According to a comment to the UPC, this provision does not introduce tracing into the law of ademption, but is intended to be a "mere change in form" principle. For example, T's will devised Blackacre to A. After execution T sold Blackacre for $100,000. Three months after the sale, T bought Whiteacre for $150,000. Shortly thereafter, T died. In a UPC §2-606(a)(5) jurisdiction the devise to A is not adeemed if Whiteacre was acquired as a "replacement" for Blackacre. For example, the gift would not adeem if both were principal personal residences of T. By contrast, the devise of Blackacre probably would adeem if Blackacre was T's principal residence and, after selling it, T moved into a rented apartment and Whiteacre was commercial realty. If Whiteacre was a duplex and T lived on one side and rented out the other, perhaps A would take the duplex as replacement property for Blackacre. If Whiteacre cost $400,000 and was a triplex or a four-plex, and T lived in one unit, perhaps A would take an undivided interest in Whiteacre (½ if Whiteacre is a duplex, ⅓ if it is a triplex, or ¼ if it is a four-plex). We don't think UPC §2-606(a)(5) would apply if Blackacre was farmland and Whiteacre was a convenience store. And if Blackacre were T's personal residence and T sold it and used the proceeds to buy investment securities, we think A would not take the new investment because it would not be replacement property for the personal residence. We don't know if that also would be true if Blackacre was investment real estate and its sale proceeds were reinvested in securities. Ademption is a slippery concept, particularly with some of the modern variations meant to ameliorate its application.

Note that uncertainty under the UPC is not so critical. The devisee will take the actual replacement property if the change-in-form, replacement property exception applies. Otherwise the devisee will take the value of the specifically devised property if the change-in-form exception does not apply and there is not a showing that the testator intended the devise to adeem. In either event, under the UPC the devisee's gift will not adeem. But the replacement issue would be important if the property subsequently acquired is significantly more valuable than the property specifically devised that the testator no longer owned.

## Ademption by Satisfaction

If you remember advancement, this is the testate equivalent. The doctrine of ademption by satisfaction may apply if the testator makes lifetime gifts to will beneficiaries after execution of a will. Generally, it applies only if the testator made lifetime gifts to beneficiaries of general bequests under the will, but occasionally it applies to lifetime gifts to residuary, demonstrative, and even specific devisees. When it applies, ademption by satisfaction (often referred to as just "satisfaction," to distinguish it from ademption by extinction, which often is referred to as just "ademption") is the testator taking care of or accelerating the testamentary transfer by making a gift during life.

For example, if T's will gave $25,000 to a hospital, and T subsequently gave the hospital $25,000 before death, the hospital will not receive another $25,000 from T's estate at death if the doctrine of satisfaction applies. Be sure to carefully distinguish terminology: this is *not* "advancement," which only applies in completely intestate estates. See Chapter 2. But the concepts operate in essentially the same manner, and the logic and effects can be quite similar.

Also note that satisfaction usually does not apply to specifics, because the testamentary gift usually would adeem by extinction rather than by satisfaction if the specifically devised property is transferred during life. The net effect, however, is the same. The gift under the will fails. Satisfaction *could* apply to a specific, however, if it were shown that a gift of asset A was meant to satisfy a specific bequest of asset B. Similarly, a gift of "50 of *my* shares of IBM" (a specific bequest because of the word "my") could adeem by satisfaction if 50 shares were given during life and another 50 shares remain in the estate at the testator's death (meaning that ademption by extinction could not apply and only satisfaction would generate the "right" result of preventing the beneficiary from receiving another 50 shares).

To adeem a demonstrative gift would require both satisfaction and ademption by extinction because a demonstrative has the characteristics of both a specific and a general. That is, in theory, an ademption by satisfaction would only affect the general bequest. To affect the specific bequest in a demonstrative would require an ademption by extinction. To illustrate, if a bequest was of "$50,000, to be satisfied first from my bank account at ABC Bank," and a lifetime gift of $50,000 was made, the general bequest might be said to be adeemed by satisfaction regardless of whether there was $50,000 (or more) in the account at T's death. But if the bequest was of "1,000 shares of *my* IBM stock, to be satisfied first from shares acquired in 2001 from X," the argument might be made that an inter vivos gift of *any* shares of IBM stock do not adeem by satisfaction or extinction the specific gift of those shares the testator acquired in 2001. Fortunately, demonstratives are not common and probably amount to a legal fiction in terms of what the testator intended. It would be very hard to argue that ademption was not intended in either circumstance. Our study of abatement will show why demonstrative is regarded as a useful theory notwithstanding its fictional nature. But remember that it probably is just theory when it comes to the real world.

It is easier to say that satisfaction of a residuary gift will not apply if there is a single residuary beneficiary, because that residuary devisee presumably was intended to receive whatever constitutes the residue of the estate, without regard to amounts of lifetime gifts. A finding that a lifetime gift satisfied the residuary gift to the sole residuary devisee would result in partial or complete intestacy and there is a relatively strong presumption against intestacy. But there could be a satisfaction of part or all of some of the residuary devises if the residue was left to two or more devisees and lifetime gifts were made to some but not all of them, or were made to all of them in different proportions than the gift of the residue. Furthermore, satisfaction is not customarily applicable to gifts of land, because they usually are specific and because satisfaction is a form of partial revocation as to which the Statute of Frauds would apply, requiring a writing.

Just like advancements, satisfaction may be pro tanto (with a presumption against total satisfaction by receipt of a lesser amount unless the beneficiary consents to a total satisfaction). Modest gifts, however, usually are not regarded as a satisfaction, even if they are great in the aggregate or over a long period of time. Also like advancements, satisfaction usually applies only if a gift made by the testator was intended to be in partial or complete satisfaction of a devise under the will. In most cases the biggest stumbling block is proving intent to satisfy. At common law, no proof was required because intent to satisfy was presumed. UPC §2-609 reverses this and, similar to the treatment of the advancement issue by UPC §2-109, requires a statement in the will or a contemporaneous written declaration by the testator or acknowledgment by the devisee when the satisfaction gift occurs. Compare advancements in Chapter 2. The presumption of intent to satisfy in non-UPC cases most frequently applies if the testator and beneficiary are parent and child (in loco parentis), because the law presumes that a parent wants to treat all children equally. If a gift inter vivos disrupts that presumed testamentary equality, in some non-UPC jurisdictions the intent required for ademption by satisfaction likely would be presumed. In other non-UPC cases, parol evidence (including the testator's own declarations) may be admitted to prove the intent to adeem by satisfaction.

## Abatement

Someone must be disappointed if there are more obligations of an estate ("obligations" includes to devisees, creditors, and the government) than assets available to satisfy them. An estate may not have enough assets to satisfy all (or any) devises under the will for such reasons as: (1) depletion (either before death or after death and before final distribution of the estate to its beneficiaries), (2) debts, expenses, or taxes (especially when the probate estate is exhausted to pay those that relate to nonprobate assets), (3) a forced heir or spousal share entitlement, as discussed in Chapter 10, or (4) the testator has provided testamentary gifts with a higher priority that simply exhaust the testator's wealth. The abatement issue is which dispositions are preferred and which abate (i.e., are reduced or eliminated) if necessary to satisfy true obligations (e.g., debts of the decedent, administration and funeral expenses, and taxes), forced heir claims, and dispositions that are preferred.

The standard abatement priority, often statutory, is: (1) intestate assets abate first, (2) then any fund specified for payment, (3) then the residue (in some cases debts, expenses, taxes, and prior testamentary gifts would exhaust the estate and there would *be* no residue), (4) then generals, (5) next, demonstratives, and (6) finally, specifics. Remember in considering the abatement of demonstratives that this category is a fiction that straddles the fence between generals and specifics. To illustrate the significance of this, consider this hypothetical: T's will leaves "$50,000 to A, to be satisfied first from my account at ABC Bank." If this was a general bequest it would *abate* with all the other general bequests, meaning that A might receive less than the amount T had in mind. As a specific bequest it might *adeem* by extinction if the ABC Bank no longer exists or if T's account in that bank was insufficient. As a demonstrative, the gift would abate with the specifics and adeem as a general, meaning that it is favored under both concepts.

Within each class, abatement usually is pro rata and no longer gives any preference to devises (i.e., in the olden days, a general devise of land [e.g., an undivided ¼ of all the testator's farmland] would abate only after all generals of personalty [e.g., cash of $25,000]). So, let's try a couple of examples:

T's will gave Blackacre to A, a painting to B, $20,000 of XYZ stock (a publicly held company in which T did not own stock when the will was executed or at T's death) to C, $50,000 to D, and the residue of the estate to E. It provides for T's debts, funeral and administration expenses, and taxes to be paid from the residue of the estate. At T's death, the estate included Blackacre (with a value of $60,000), the painting (with a value of $10,000), and other assets (with a value of $50,000). T had debts of $60,000, funeral expenses of $5,000, and estate administration expenses of $15,000. As near as we can tell there are no wealth transfer or income tax issues. How is T's estate distributed?

The total value of T's estate is $120,000 and the total of the debts, funeral costs, and administration expenses is $80,000, leaving net distributable assets of $40,000. T's will purported to make gifts of assets with aggregate date of death values of $140,000 to A, B, C, and D (with any residue going to E). Accordingly, a total of $100,000 of gifts will abate. There is no intestate property from which debts and expenses can be paid, and the fund designated for their payment — the residue — is nonexistent because the value of the general and specific devises under the will ($140,000) exceeds the value of the assets in the estate ($120,000). The next gifts to abate are general devises. Here there are two: the $20,000 gift of XYZ stock to C and the $50,000 gift to D. Both will be wiped out by abatement and another $30,000 of the specific gifts (Blackacre to A, with a value of $60,000, and the painting to B, with a value of $10,000) also must abate. That abatement will be pro rata between them, meaning that $6/7$ of the $30,000 shortfall (approximately $25,715) will be charged against the gift of Blackacre to A and the other $1/7$ (approximately $4,285) against the gift of the painting to B. The hard question then is how to partially abate assets like this.

One method would be for the personal representative to borrow $25,715, secured by a mortgage on Blackacre, and $4,285 secured by the painting, and then to distribute Blackacre and the painting as so encumbered. Another would be for A and B to use their own assets to pay their shares of the shortfall. A third would be for the personal representative to sell Blackacre and the painting to raise the remaining necessary funds and to distribute the balance of the sales proceeds to A and B in the appropriate ratio. And either A or B could be the purchasers of these assets if they so choose.

The standard order of abatement is subject to modification by statute (such as for estate taxes, as discussed next), by a specific direction in the will (usually in the form of a provision directing the payment of taxes and expenses from a specified source), or by an overall intent as shown by the scheme of distribution or circumstances at execution that illustrate a desire to protect certain beneficiaries.

### Tax Payment

The way federal and state estate and inheritance taxes are borne by the beneficiaries of a decedent's probate and nonprobate assets has a significant effect on the distribution of the decedent's wealth. The apportionment of these taxes (particularly the federal estate tax, which might exceed forty five percent of the decedent's taxable estate) among beneficiaries usually is governed by special rules. On the other hand, state "inheritance" taxes (as opposed to state "estate" taxes) often are an obligation of the recipient of property from the estate, although it is customary for a tax clause in a will to shift this obligation back to the probate estate. Under federal law, estate taxes on nonprobate and probate assets alike befall the residue of the probate estate, and the personal representative potentially is personally liable to the extent these taxes are not paid. This burden-on-the-residue rule may be altered by the terms of the decedent's will, and several notable exceptions exist under the tax law itself. For example, six Internal Revenue Code apportionment provisions impose the tax attributable to certain nonprobate assets on the recipients of those assets (e.g., life insurance proceeds). Couched in terms of "discretion" to seek reimbursement from those nonprobate takers of the estate taxes paid on such assets, a testator may waive these rights of reimbursement, meaning the taker of the nonprobate assets receives them unburdened by federal estate taxes. Without a waiver the fiduciary obligation imposed on the personal representative effectively makes discretionary reimbursement a mandate to the extent ultimate distributions to probate estate beneficiaries will be affected.

In addition, most states have adopted the Uniform Estate Tax Apportionment Act, or something similar, which governs estate tax apportionment unless the will provides otherwise. This legislation requires that each taker of property included in the decedent's taxable estate (whether probate or nonprobate) pay a pro rata share of the estate taxes based on the value of property received by the taker relative to the value of property received by all takers. In making this calculation, property passing tax-free (such as to a spouse or charity) generally is excluded. This exclusion is referred to as "equitable apportionment" and is illustrated by the following example.

T's will gave $800,000 to C, a child from T's first marriage, $400,000 to T's brother, B, $100,000 to charity, and the residue to T's surviving spouse, S. In addition, C was the beneficiary of a $1 million insurance policy T owned on T's life. T's will did not provide for the apportionment of estate taxes. Under federal law, the devises to charity and to S are not subject to federal estate tax because of the unlimited charitable and marital deductions. Accordingly, T's taxable estate will consist of the $2.2 million of probate and nonprobate assets passing to C and B. Because C will receive 81.8 percent of the $2.2 million and B

18.2 percent, under an equitable apportionment approach the estate tax liability will be borne by them in the same 4.5 to 1 ratio.

The common law burden-on-the-residue rule imposes inequitable and unintended results. For instance, in the example the residue passing to S would bear the estate taxes for the property passing to C and B even though the devise to S generated no tax itself (because of the marital deduction). The taxes owed on the property passing to C and B might exhaust the residue so that S receives nothing. A tax clause in the will or trust may change the applicable rules and may be essential to effect the decedent's intent, as well as to minimize the tax itself (by avoiding loss of the marital deduction).

### *Spousal Elective and Pretermitted Heir Shares*

A surviving spouse may have a right to elect against the will of the decedent to take a statutory forced heir share of the estate, and certain heirs of a decedent who were omitted from the decedent's will also may have rights to take pretermitted heir shares of the estate as defined by statute. See Chapter 10. In these cases the claims of the surviving spouse or pretermitted heirs may be so large that they disrupt the estate plan and require abatement of other gifts to fund them. Most elective share statutes force a surviving spouse who elects a forced heir share to forgo other rights under the will. In other states the first property used to satisfy this elective share is property devised to the spouse under the will. Usually that property will not be enough to satisfy the full elective share, however, and the normal abatement rules (first intestate assets, then the residue, next generals, demonstratives, and finally specifics) typically apply in satisfaction of the shortfall. As with other abatement issues, however, the instrument can override these rules and control to the extent it effectively addresses the possibility of a spouse's election against the will and the resulting abatement issue. In this regard, UPC §2-209(b) and (c) alter the traditional rules for abating devises to satisfy an elective share. Under them, abatement is pro rata among all probate and nonprobate beneficiaries alike.

To illustrate, consider that T's will is silent regarding priority and abatement. It directs the following dispositions: (1) summer home to brother, (2) specific bequests and legacies that total $100,000 to persons other than the surviving spouse, (3) a formula bequest to the surviving spouse (designed to accomplish estate tax minimization) of "the smallest amount needed to reduce my estate taxes to the lowest possible amount," (4) $200,000 to charity, and (5) "$200,000 plus the residue" to a trust for children. Also assume that the estate consists of $800,000: (1) the summer home, worth $50,000, (2) a residence (in joint tenancy with the surviving spouse), worth \$150,000,[1] (3) life insurance (payable to the spouse) of \$200,000, and (4) liquid probate assets of \$400,000. The only probate assets are the summer home and the \$400,000 of liquid probate assets.

The amount of property passing to the spouse under the formula marital bequest is zero due to the tax situation here. The charitable bequest and the nonprobate property passing to the surviving spouse are fully deductible and will reduce the taxable estate to well below the amount at which no federal estate taxes need be paid. So there is no need for an additional marital bequest to zero out the taxes, and the formula bequest will therefore give the spouse nothing. The nonprobate property that passes automatically to the spouse will not be affected here, so the only issue is who will take which dispositions from the probate estate, who will pay taxes (if any), and who will suffer abatement if available assets are insufficient. In this case the brother will receive the specific devise of the summer home, and the other specifics of \$100,000 have the same first priority. After taking them out of the estate, only \$300,000 remains in the probate estate, and there are two general claims against that amount: the \$200,000 to charity and the \$200,000 to the children's trust, totaling \$400,000. This means that there will be no residue and the children's trust and the charity both will abate pro rata, each receiving only \$150,000 instead of the \$200,000 specified in the will.

If you want a challenge, add a zero to every number and go through this problem again. Note that the formula marital bequest is a general and will abate with the charity and the children, and that its size will depend on the applicable exclusion amount for federal estate tax purposes at any given date of death. Also consider that as it and the charity abate, taxes will be increased and add to the complexity. No document should leave to conjecture what should happen in such a case!

## Accessions

The accessions issue is whether a gift under a will or trust instrument bears interest or receives income (such as dividends or rent) that accrue or are paid (either before or after death) before final distribution. For

---

1. Notice that, under IRC §2040(b), only half of the value of the joint tenancy with the surviving spouse would be includible in the decedent's gross estate for federal estate tax purposes. Nevertheless, we are reporting it here at its full value for two reasons. One is that, whatever the value, it all qualifies automatically for the marital deduction so the amount includible also is deductible, making the valuation irrelevant for federal estate tax purposes. Second, for those of you who have not studied tax and do not care to, it simply is easier to understand what is going on by looking at the real value of the property and not the limited amount that the tax law considers.

example, if T's will gave Blackacre to A and it is leased during estate administration for $10,000, with rental expenses of $2,000, does A receive the $8,000 of net rental income in addition to Blackacre? Careful drafters address such questions in the instrument because the state law rules that otherwise govern may be inadequate, unclear, or inconsistent with the testator's intent.

### *Premortem*

If the accession occurs before death, the issue applies only to specifics. Interest, dividends, rent, and other accessions received before death on assets not specifically devised become a part of the general estate available to satisfy obligations and general, demonstrative, and residuary devises. As to premortem accessions attributable to assets specifically devised, by the general rules an accession that is paid before death and is separated from the underlying asset does *not* pass to the recipient of the underlying asset. Interest, rent, or cash dividends received before death typically are separated from the underlying asset (i.e., the specifically devised interest bearing asset, cash dividend paying stock, or rent generating asset) and thus do not pass with the property that produced these accessions. Imagine a cash rent paid on Blackacre, rather than rent paid in kind in the form of an improvement (such as a new fence or building). Thinking on this rule, consider a stock-on-stock dividend, declared in the payor's own stock. The dividend shares do not alter the percentage ownership of the corporation held by the estate (there are just more pieces of paper representing the same investment). So the percentage ownership of the company will be reduced (and control may be lost) if the dividend shares do not pass with the specific bequest of the investment. Nevertheless, the majority rule is that the dividend shares do not pass with the underlying bequest. There are courts that are changing this rule, as does UPC §2-605. In appropriate cases you can draft around it.

For example, assume there are 1,000 shares of stock of XYZ Corp. outstanding. T owns ten percent of them — 100 shares — and T's will gives "*my* 100 shares of XYZ Corp. stock" to A. After execution of T's will but before T's death, XYZ Corp. pays a fifteen percent dividend in its own stock, which means that T receives an additional 15 shares. At T's death, the estate owns 115 shares (still ten percent of XYZ's outstanding stock, which now consists of 1,150 shares). Under the majority rule, A receives only 100 shares and not also the dividend shares. Under the UPC/minority rule, A receives 115 shares. A different result would obtain even in a majority rule jurisdiction if the bequest were something like "All my shares of" XYZ Corp. stock, instead of something specific like "My 100 shares." A would receive the 115 shares in that case. And if this had been 501 shares of XYZ and some other shareholder had the remaining 499 shares, a failure to give the dividend shares to A would mean a loss of control shareholder status, which could be a very important issue.

*In re Tase*, NYLJ, May 31, 1990, at 31, involved a decedent who made a specific bequest of "all my American Telephone and Telegraph stock" and then provided for six named legatees to receive 30 shares each. When the will was executed the decedent owned 180 shares of AT&T stock. At death the decedent owned 621 shares of AT&T and 1,178 shares of the seven regional holding companies (the "Baby Bells") that were spun-off by AT&T for antitrust purposes. The questions presented were whether the bequest disposed of all of the decedent's AT&T shares or only 180 of them, and whether the will addressed *any* of the regional holding company shares. The court held that the reference to "all my" stock meant the entire holding at death should pass under the specific bequest. Also, the court held that all of the regional holding company shares were bequeathed under the same bequest. We think these are proper results and probably reflect the decedent's intent, but they are not predictable under the common law rule. The drafter definitely should have provided for these accessions.

A stock split is very similar to a large stock-on-stock dividend and occurs when a company issues, say, one or two new shares of stock for each outstanding share (if one new share is issued, the split is referred to as a 2-for-1 split, because the shareholder now has two shares for every share held before the split). Unlike stock dividends, stock split shares usually *do* pass to the named taker, which is inconsistent with the stock-on-stock dividend rule. This also is the right result, and the stock-on-stock dividend rule is changing to match it. Better drafters do not, however, rely on either rule or state law to get the result "right." Instead, they address this accessions issue in the bequest itself.

### *Postmortem*

All beneficiaries of specific devises are entitled to accessions paid after they become entitled to the gifted property. With a specific devise, the beneficiary is entitled to the property as of the moment of death (subject to abatement), meaning that all receipts from the property after death pass with the property, even if the accession was earned (but not paid) before death. This rule is consistent with the premortem rules noted above. If the accession is still attached to the property, it passes with the property and not to the estate.

For example, assume T's will gave Blackacre to A. As of death there are rents that accrued before death that had not yet been paid to the decedent premortem. Although the rent accrued before T's death, it was not paid until after death. In most states A gets these rent payments made postmortem, in addition to Blackacre itself. Notice that in many commercial rental situations the rent is prepaid (think about the typical apartment or house lease), so this problem would not be common. In agricultural rentals the rent often is payable after the harvest, so this example could be very common. And some commercial retail rents are based on sales or profits and may be payable after the term rather than before, also making the example relevant. If the rent is paid annually in advance (e.g., on December 31 for the next year) and the testator dies after the rent is paid (e.g., on January 1), the prepaid rent belongs to the estate, not to the specific devisee, even though it is rent for a postmortem period, and even if the new owner needs the rent to service a debt that encumbers the property. See Exoneration, discussed at page 191.

The taker receives nothing (other than the specifically devised property itself) if no income or other accession is paid after the testator's death (but before distribution) on the subject of a *specific* devise. This is true even if distribution is delayed during administration. But general and demonstrative devises differ. Because the taker is not entitled to specific assets, the taker is not entitled to actual accessions on the property actually distributed. Instead, interest usually is payable at a statutory rate from a statutory date of entitlement, which usually is one year after death.

So, assume T's will gave Investmentacre to A and $100,000 to B. There are no receipts attributable to Investmentacre between T's death and the date it is distributed to A. Thus, because this is a specific devise, A receives Investmentacre but is not entitled to interest on its value, regardless of the length of time between T's death and the date Investmentacre is distributed. Assume also that the personal representative has authority (under the will or applicable state law) to satisfy B's $100,000 entitlement in kind (rather than in cash) and selects for distribution Farmacre, which has a fair market value of $1 million but is subject to mortgage indebtedness of $900,000. The crop grown on Farmacre was harvested just before T's death, but the debt service is due at year end, just around the corner. Assume the decedent died on January 1 and that the personal representative distributes Farmacre before the following December 31, to avoid paying the debt service. B would receive no interest (because in most states a beneficiary of a general devise is not entitled to interest on it unless distribution is delayed more than one year after death) or other income but would incur the debt service. The impending debt service obligation might alter the fair market value of the property for purposes of determining whether B receives the full $100,000 bequest to which B is entitled. Regardless of how much more property B might be entitled to receive, these rules produce a serious cash flow issue to B.

To round out the picture, the residuary takers receive whatever is left in the estate after the payment of all specifics, generals, and demonstratives, and after the payment of accessions on the specifics and interest on the generals and demonstratives. This is just a function of the definition of a residuary entitlement. Although residuary takers are not entitled to interest, or specific accessions, they do benefit from any income earned by the estate (it remains a part of the residue) to the extent it is not paid to the takers of specifics (if, for example, an interest bearing investment was specifically devised), generals, or demonstratives. Thus, the residue bears the risk that interest on general and demonstrative dispositions will exceed actual earnings on estate assets not specifically devised, but the residue also benefits from investment performance in excess of statutory interest requirements on generals and demonstratives.

Note that, in all these rules on accessions, demonstratives are governed by the rules applicable to specifics to the extent of the specified fund or asset, and by the rules applicable to generals to the extent the entitlement is satisfied from general funds because the specific is inadequate. Thus, no special rules are needed for demonstratives.

## Exoneration

Our final issue is whether a devisee of property that secures a debt takes the property subject to the debt or whether the estate must repay the debt so that the devisee takes the property free of encumbrances. Unless changed by statute (as has been done in many jurisdictions), the common law requires that debts, even though not yet due, be paid out of the estate as a whole. This applies only if three requirements are met. First, the debt was a personal obligation of the decedent (i.e., not just nonrecourse purchase money debt). Recourse debt or personal obligation means that, in the event of a default, the lender could have sued the testator and collected from other property rather than being limited to foreclosing on the property. Second, the debt must encumber realty or specifically devised personal property. (Notice that this is the converse of satisfaction, which typically does not apply to any gift of realty or specifics of personalty.) Third, the will must not have expressed a contrary intent. In some jurisdictions, an implied intent not to exonerate can be shown by surrounding circumstances.

If exoneration is required, payment comes from the residue or from intestate personalty, if there is any (perhaps also from personalty that otherwise would be used to satisfy general bequests). Because exoneration applies to realty and specifics, these classes of gifts are *not* used to finance exoneration. The theory is that one set of specific beneficiaries or takers of realty should not be burdened to benefit another set. To illustrate, assume T's will gave Blackacre to A, Whiteacre to B, a valuable painting to C, and the residue to D. At T's death Blackacre was worth $60,000, but it was encumbered by $50,000 of mortgage indebtedness on which T was personally liable. Whiteacre was worth $100,000. The painting was worth $10,000. And the residue, which consisted of cash, was worth $20,000, net of administration and funeral expenses and other debts of T. At common law, the indebtedness on Blackacre is to be exonerated, but the only asset available to do the job is the $20,000 of cash. Thus, A receives Blackacre burdened by $30,000 of the mortgage debt. B and C receive Whiteacre and the painting, respectively, unencumbered. And D receives nothing.

As illustrated, this is a bizarre result, informed by the common law assumption that the loan creating the debt somehow benefited the personal estate (e.g., that T borrowed $50,000 against Blackacre and put the funds in the bank). That rationale is not necessarily accurate today (consider a home mortgage that finances purchase of the dwelling, and a second mortgage or home equity line of credit that financed lifestyle purchases), and UPC §2-607 reverses the common law rule. Reversing the common law exoneration rule is appropriate if the testator does not distinguish personalty from realty in terms of benefits or burdens. And exoneration probably should be waived if the secured debt was purchase money debt, meaning that the debt benefited the taker of the encumbered asset, not other property of the estate. But a different approach may be wise to the extent of a second mortgage on the personal residences, which just shows that the drafter ought to address the issue with the testator and establish the proper result on a case-by-case basis.

Either the common law rule to exonerate or the UPC rule not to exonerate may be overcome by proof of a contrary intent. A standard debt payment clause (e.g., "I direct my Personal Representative to pay all of my just debts") typically won't prove intent because it usually applies only to debts that are currently due. To overcome the common law rule, language should specify that property passes "subject to outstanding debts." Conversely, it would be wise to specify that exoneration is intended, if that is the case, by stating that a gift of property is "free from all outstanding debts, which shall be paid from (a specified source)."

# CHAPTER 10

# RESTRICTIONS ON DISINHERITANCE: PRETERMISSION, ELECTIVE SHARES, AND COMMUNITY PROPERTY

Marital property rights at the death of the first spouse to die come in two forms. In a community property jurisdiction the surviving spouse owns half of the couple's community property, even if title is in the deceased spouse's name. In all noncommunity property jurisdictions except Georgia, the surviving spouse is entitled to receive a statutory share of the deceased spouse's probate estate (and, in many cases, nonprobate assets as well). Both rules tend to restrict a deceased spouse's ability to favor third parties and effectively disfavor or disinherit the surviving spouse. In addition to these spousal restrictions, protection is afforded to certain pretermitted heirs who are omitted from a testator's will, including a surviving spouse (if the testator's will was executed before the marriage), children, and sometimes more remote descendants. Each pretermission entitlement assumes that the testator "forgot" to include the heir in the will and evidence that the omission was intentional will preclude a successful claim under these rules. In that respect the pretermission rules are less restrictive than the spousal protections but all are avoidable and need to be considered.

## Status as a Spouse

Spousal rights are available only to a survivor who was a spouse at the decedent's death. In America in 2005 approximately ¼ of the states still recognized non-ceremonial, common law marriages in which a couple lives together and holds themselves out as spouses. At the same time, same sex marriages were not yet recognized in the vast majority of states, although Vermont permitted civil unions, Massachusetts allowed marriages, California and Hawaii extended benefits to certain couples, and turmoil, constitutional initiatives, litigation, and such were the order of the day. Time will tell where this ends up. It does not alter *our* inquiry, which is the rights of someone who *is* regarded as a spouse.

## Additional Marital Rights

A surviving spouse typically has a variety of rights in addition to the elective share or community property. For example, homestead is an entitlement that usually is free from creditor claims (claims that are secured by a mortgage would be an exception to homestead rights in the mortgaged property,) and cannot be defeated by the decedent's will (although it may be waived in a marital property agreement). In some states it is a dollar amount (e.g., $15,000 under UPC §2-402). In others it is a right to occupy the family home for life without regard to its value. Exempt tangible personal property (e.g., automobiles, household furniture, appliances, and personal effects) of the decedent also may be protected from creditors' claims and cannot be defeated by the decedent's will (although it too may be waived). Most states limit exempt personal property in value (e.g., the UPC §2-403 limit is $10,000). And family allowances provide support during administration. In some states it is fixed (e.g., $40,000 in Ohio). In others it is set by the probate court in an amount that is "appropriate" (e.g., known as "year's support" in Georgia, the amount needed for one year). Again, this protection generally is exempt from creditors' claims and may not be defeated by the decedent's will (but generally it may be waived), although a larger bequest might be made "in lieu of" the allowance.

A federal form of protection of the surviving spouse is the spousal annuity requirements under Internal Revenue Code §401(a)(11) (which is part of what commonly is referred to as ERISA — the Employee Retirement Income Security Act — which involves retirement benefits). A surviving spouse is entitled to an annuity following the death of the plan participant in retirement benefit plans subject to these rules. A spouse (but *not* a fiancée) can waive the entitlement and must do so if the participant wants to make any beneficiary designation other than the spousal annuity — even to provide a more favorable disposition to the spouse (such as a lump sum distribution at the participant's death). Social Security also provides survivor's benefits that belong to the spouse and, therefore, are not subject to claims of the decedent's creditors, may not be defeated by the decedent's will, and may not be waived. And a few states still recognize the common law dower (generally provided to a widow, it is a life estate in ⅓ of her deceased husband's real estate) and curtesy (provided to a widower, it is a life estate in all of his wife's real estate, but only if there were children of the marriage).

## Community Property

Community property protects spouses in Louisiana, Texas, New Mexico, Arizona, California, Washington, Idaho, and Nevada — and the very similar statutory community property under the Uniform Marital Property Act (UMPA) does the same in Wisconsin. "Voluntary" community property was enacted in Alaska as a tax dodge and no one yet knows what its impact or respect might be. In every noncommunity property jurisdiction (except Georgia) a surviving spouse may elect a statutory share of the decedent's probate estate (and in some jurisdictions nonprobate assets as well) regardless of the terms of the decedent's will (and, in some states, notwithstanding the terms of instruments governing nonprobate property). This forced heir share generally is a poor substitute for the more effective system of community property, by which each spouse owns half of the couple's community property from the time it is acquired, regardless of how title to the property is held. Generally, community property consists of all property acquired by onerous activity by either spouse during the marriage. Property acquired by gratuity — by gift, devise, bequest, or inheritance — is not community property, nor is property brought to the marriage. That all is separate property in which a surviving spouse has no mandatory entitlement (but usually does have intestate succession rights). In some states (e.g., Texas and under UMPA) the income from separate property (other than mineral interests in Texas) also is community property, and there are other quirks and differences among the community property states.

To illustrate community property, consider Young Lawyer, who is single, successful, and engaged. When Young Lawyer and Spouse marry, Young Lawyer has assets (net of debts) of $100,000 and Spouse has $50,000 of net assets. During the marriage, Young Lawyer accumulates an additional $300,000 from earned income from practicing law and Spouse accumulates another $150,000 from earnings. Also during the marriage Young Lawyer receives a gift of $75,000 and Spouse receives a $200,000 inheritance. The $100,000 of assets Young Lawyer brought to the marriage and the $75,000 gift are separate property, as are the $50,000 of assets Spouse owned when they married and the $200,000 inheritance received during the marriage. The $450,000 they accumulated from their earnings during the marriage is community property — each is treated as the owner of half of it regardless of the fact that Young Lawyer earned and accumulated twice as much as Spouse, and regardless of how they hold title to the $450,000. This is the "economic partnership" concept of marriage.

Noncommunity property lawyers need to know about community property for several reasons. First, for conflict of laws purposes, real estate located in a community property state may be governed by the community property laws. Second, with the migratory nature of clients, many couples will possess some community property because they lived and accumulated earnings in a community property state at some time during the marriage. Generally, "once property is community property, it always is community property," unless they "partition" the property to destroy its community nature. Plus, UMPA may be the wave of the future (although there has been little interest in it for quite some time).

Typically, a community property surviving spouse has no statutory forced heir rights in the decedent's separate property (or in the decedent's share of the community property). Thus, if there is little or no community property when a spouse dies, a survivor who owns little or no separate property may be left with little or nothing — if the decedent does not provide for the survivor — regardless of the amount of separate property the decedent owned. For example, assume D and S lived their entire married life in a community property jurisdiction. They owned little property when they married. During the first part of their marriage they each worked, but they accumulated little in the way of assets — they spent what they earned and assets they acquired were bought with borrowed funds and little equity. D then received a substantial inheritance, after which D and S "retired" and began enjoying the good life. When D died, the inheritance was intact (they had managed to live off its income) but they had little or no community property. Regardless of the length of their marriage and the value of D's inherited separate property, S will have no claim to any of D's separate property and will be left with only half of their meager community property (and any homestead, exempt personal property, and family allowance provided by law).

Some states (California, Idaho, Louisiana, and Washington) have a "quasi" community property system that may treat some of a deceased spouse's separate property as if it was community property. For example, imagine Spouses D and S, who lived their entire working lives in Illinois, a noncommunity property state, and then retired to Arizona, a community property state that does not embrace quasi-community property. All their wealth was acquired during their marriage from their earnings, and all their wealth is titled in the name of D, who dies first. S will receive nothing from D's separate property under Arizona law, meaning that S will receive only whatever modest amount constitutes S's share of their community property from earnings received while they lived in Arizona prior to D's death. If, however, they had moved to California, which recognizes quasi-community property, D's separate property would be deemed half owned by S to the extent it represented earnings received while they were married. Quasi-community property treats as community property earnings that would have been community property had the spouses lived in the quasi-community property state when the property was earned.

Although the notion of quasi-community property generally is to treat separate property the same as if it was community property, some quasi-community property states (e.g., Arizona, New Mexico, and Texas) apply the concept for divorce only and not at death. And excepting homestead, exempt personal property, and a family allowance, there is no other spousal entitlement guaranteed under state law in a community property state, and no election against the decedent's estate plan is provided if the decedent chooses to exclude the surviving spouse.

Sophisticated estate planning in community property states (and, less frequently, even in noncommunity property states — sometimes less accurately referred to as the "common law" property states) may take advantage of a "forced election" plan that basically says to the surviving spouse: "If you agree to subject your separate and community property to the provisions of my trust, I will give you a life estate in my separate and community property, and in your separate and community property, all held in the same trust." The object of the plan is for the decedent to control devolution of all the couple's property after the surviving spouse's death. There are income and wealth transfer tax consequences of the exchange by the surviving spouse of the remainder interest in the spouse's property for a life estate in the decedent's property, and the plan is not nearly as common today as it was before adoption in 1981 of the QTIP marital trust provisions in Internal Revenue Code §2056(b)(7). We don't need to plumb those depths here.

## The Elective Share

The other significant spousal entitlement is the statutory forced heir share (sometimes referred to as an "elective" share, because the spouse must elect to receive the forced share) found in all noncommunity property states except Georgia. The size of the spouse's forced heir share varies considerably among the states. Frequently it is ⅓ of the decedent's probate estate (or of the decedent's "augmented" probate estate, which includes nonprobate property), sometimes increased to half if the decedent was not survived by any descendant or was survived by only one line of descendants. In some states the forced share is the same share the spouse would receive if the decedent died intestate, which may be the entire estate. See Chapter 2. Almost without exception the surviving spouse's intestate share will be at least as large, and often it is larger, than the forced share. For example, under the UPC the intestate share never is less than the first $100,000 plus half the balance, but the forced share is half at a maximum (unless the supplemental elective share amount is larger, which would occur only in a very small estate) and may be much less.

The difference may be more subtle. For example, Illinois differs on equitable apportionment of estate taxes for intestate or forced shares, as discussed below. Note, however, that the intestate share is limited to the decedent's probate estate. The UPC forced share applies to the augmented estate, which includes most nonprobate assets and may be significantly larger than the probate estate. Thus, for intestate decedents who own substantial amounts of nonprobate property and who die in a UPC augmented estate jurisdiction, the forced share may be greater than the intestate share even though the fraction or percentage designated is smaller. Other refinements noted below also impact the respective entitlements in even less predictable ways.

To illustrate, assume that D and S were married 20 years when D died intestate with a net probate estate of $100,000. D had a child, C, from a prior marriage. D and C owned real property with an aggregate value at D's death of $400,000 as joint tenants with the right of survivorship (D provided all the consideration to acquire this property). The jurisdiction has adopted the UPC. Accordingly, S's intestate share of the probate estate is the entire $100,000. See Chapter 2. Because D's augmented probate estate includes D's half of the joint tenancy real property ($200,000), S's elective share under the UPC (assuming S had no probate or nonprobate property) would be $150,000 (half of D's augmented probate estate of $300,000). The entire $400,000 would be included in D's augmented probate estate and S's elective share would have been $250,000 (half of D's augmented probate estate of $500,000) if the $400,000 joint tenancy property had been a bank account and D had provided all the funds in the account.

The surviving spouse's elective share claim commonly is referred to as a right to elect against the decedent's will. Don't let that concept lull you into not considering an elective share claim in the case of an intestate decedent. As shown, if the decedent has substantial nonprobate assets, the elective share may be greater than an intestate share. In the absence of nonprobate assets, the intestate share usually, if not always, will equal or exceed the elective share. But both should be analyzed.

### *Effect of Election on Spouse's Other Rights*

An electing spouse is allowed simply to reject the decedent's estate plan in favor of an affirmative election to take a statutorily defined share of the decedent's probate (or augmented) estate. Typically, "equitable election" will apply when the forced share election is made, meaning that the spouse may take under the will of the decedent or may elect against the estate, but not both. In some jurisdictions the same result is reached by statute, because the spouse who elects a statutory share is treated as predeceased with respect to all provisions for the spouse under the will. Also, in some jurisdictions (e.g., UPC §2-209) the share of an electing spouse is satisfied first from property left to the spouse under the decedent's will or passing to the spouse by will substitute. Usually the spouse is entitled to share in any intestate property, as when a will gives away less than the decedent owned. A spouse who elects against the will, however, also elects against taking any share of intestate property, meaning that this really is an election against the estate, not just against the decedent's will.

In many states (e.g., UPC §2-202(c)) the homestead allowance, exempt personal property, and family allowance are in addition to the statutory forced heir share, because these rights often are directed toward maintenance of the surviving spouse during administration of the estate and are not part of the equitable division of the marital wealth. And, as we will discuss shortly, the election does not normally disfranchise the spouse's interest in nonprobate property. The prime exception to this is under the UPC augmented probate estate concept.

### *Estate Taxes*

Equitable apportionment as described in Chapter 9 is a significant issue with respect to the elective share. Does the spouse receive the statutory share before or after payment of estate taxes? Or, stated differently, does the spouse share in the gross estate (before tax) or the net estate (after tax)? The same issue may arise under intestacy, and the answer may differ. For example, in Illinois the intestate share and the forced heir share are the same fraction but the intestate share is computed as a fraction of the gross estate (before tax) but the forced heir share is a fraction of the net estate (after tax). In that state, if the estate is large enough to generate an estate tax liability, a spouse therefore would be better off challenging and defeating a will in a will contest action to cause intestacy than to just reject the will and take the elective share (all other factors being equal).

Under the UPC, the elective share is calculated before estate taxes. That is regarded as the equitable result because the spouse's share qualifies for the estate tax marital deduction and therefore generates no tax. Equitable apportionment provides that only the taxable shares should pay the tax. Moreover, an interrelated computation is required if the forced share is calculated after tax, because the tax cannot be calculated without knowing the spouse's share (because a marital deduction is allowed for it) and the spouse's share cannot be calculated without knowing the amount of tax (because it is a fraction of the after-tax estate). So a before tax division is easier and more equitable.

### *Incompetent or Deceased Surviving Spouse*

A second question is whether a personal representative for an incompetent or later deceased surviving spouse may elect on behalf of the spouse. Not all states allow the personal representative of a subsequently deceased surviving spouse to elect. See, e.g., UPC §2-212(a). Most allow the personal representative of an incapacitated spouse to make the election, but the conditions under which an election can be made differ. Remember too that a spouse only will have a right to elect to take a statutory share of the decedent's estate if the spouse survives the decedent. As discussed in Chapter 2, the Uniform Simultaneous Death Act and the UPC require a person to survive by at least 120 hours to be treated as having survived. Consequently, if the USDA or the UPC is in effect, a spouse who survives by less than 120 hours will not be treated as having survived for elective share purposes and it will be irrelevant whether the jurisdiction otherwise allows the personal representative of a now deceased surviving spouse to make the election.

In some states the personal representative of an incapacitated surviving spouse may not make the election absent a showing of need. *In re Estate of Cross*, 664 N.E.2d 905 (Ohio 1996), involved such a statute and a disinherited surviving spouse who was living in a nursing home, the expenses of which were being paid by Medicaid. An election on the spouse's behalf was upheld because failure to make the election would have jeopardized the surviving spouse's continued qualification for Medicaid. In other states, the election can be made on behalf of an incapacitated surviving spouse if doing so would be in the spouse's best interests. *In re Estate of Clarkson*, 226 N.W.2d 334 (Neb. 1975), and *Spencer v. Williams*, 569 A.2d 1194, 1198 (D.C. Ct. App. 1990), held that "best interests" means simply that the election should be made if the monetary value of what the spouse receives is greater under the elective share than under the will. Consistent with *Clarkson* and *Spencer*, some commentators feel the personal representative of an incapacitated or subsequently deceased surviving spouse has a fiduciary obligation to elect against the will if doing so will maximize the spouse's estate, even if this is not what the spouse would have done and even though it may bastardize the decedent's estate plan.

We will study shortly that, under the UPC, provisions made for a surviving spouse under the decedent's will count toward the elective share entitlement. Thus, if the will leaves the spouse $100,000 and the elective share amount is $250,000, the $100,000 bequest will be credited against the $250,000, leaving the spouse with a net elective share claim of $150,000. How to treat a surviving spouse's lifetime interest in a trust has been a controversial issue under the UPC, and it also may speak to the issue of need of an incapacitated surviving spouse in those jurisdictions that look to need as a threshold qualification for a personal representative to elect for the surviving spouse.

To illustrate, assume that the surviving spouse's elective share is $250,000, and that the decedent's will provides for $500,000 to be left in trust, with the surviving spouse entitled to all income from the trust for life. Assume also that the actuarial value of the spouse's interest in the trust (determined by current interest rates and the spouse's life expectancy) is $250,000. The question is whether the spouse may be forced to accept the trust interest (by counting it as part of the elective share), or whether the spouse may disclaim it and instead take the elective share outright. Until 1993 the UPC position was the former. Now it is the latter. This issue is significant because the decedent can control the disposition of the assets remaining at the spouse's death if the spouse effectively can be forced to accept a life interest in a trust in lieu of an outright elective share.

## Impact on Other Beneficiaries

Other estate beneficiaries usually will receive less than they otherwise would if a spouse elects to receive a forced share. As a result, abatement typically is required to accommodate the spousal election. Under UPC §2-209(b) and (c) the obligation is a claim that is allocated pro rata among the other takers of both the decedent's probate and nonprobate assets, but in many states it is charged according to traditional abatement rules. See Chapter 9. The electing spouse is treated as predeceased for the balance of the decedent's testamentary estate plan, but often not for purposes of any nonprobate transfers. This may accelerate any remainder interest under the will as drafted, which could create unfairness. It also could provide the spouse with a windfall if nonprobate transfers that benefit the spouse are plentiful or generous.

For example, assume that D's will devised $200,000 to a preresiduary trust of which the surviving spouse (S) is the income beneficiary for life, remainder to Z. The residue of D's estate totals $400,000 and it is left to X. S elects against the estate plan and state law provides a ⅓ ($200,000) elective share of the $600,000 estate, to be satisfied out of the residue according to normal abatement principles. Z would receive the $200,000 trust corpus early, because the election would cause S to be treated as predeceasing D, which accelerates the remainder. Meanwhile the residuary beneficiaries suffer for having satisfied the $200,000 elective share. The appropriate remedy is to sequester S's life estate to compensate the residuary beneficiaries for this inequity (i.e., continue the trust for S's remaining life, paying the income to the residuary beneficiaries). In some cases the court will "commute" the value of that life estate (i.e., determine its discounted present value) and distribute that value to the residuary beneficiaries and then the remainder of the trust to Z at D's death, instead of continuing the trust until S actually dies.

## Effect of Nonprobate Transfers

Nonprobate assets (such as transfers in trust, property that passes by beneficiary designation, joint tenancy, or payable on death and Totten trust accounts) may benefit the spouse or they may pass to other takers, with the potential effect of reducing the property subject to the surviving spouse's election. Whether nonprobate assets are considered in determining and then in satisfying the elective share is a question upon which courts have gone in every possible direction. To illustrate, picture D, who owned $600,000 of assets. The elective share is ⅓ of a deceased spouse's estate. If D died with the $600,000 as probate property, the elective share of the surviving spouse (S) would be $200,000. But S gets nothing if D transfers the $600,000 to a revocable trust and the elective share is strictly limited to the probate estate (and S is not a beneficiary of the trust at D's death). Alternatively, if D places $300,000 of the $600,000 in joint tenancy with S, with the right of survivorship, S will keep the $300,000 of joint tenancy property and may elect against the will to take ⅓ of the $300,000 probate estate. Legislatures and courts have resolved these kinds of questions in a wide variety of ways.

For example, *Snodgrass v. Lyndon State Bank*, 811 P.2d 58 (Kan. Ct. App. 1991), held that the surviving spouse could not reach a POD bank account. Apparently a state statute shielded the account from claims. Since *Snodgrass* was decided, however, Kansas adopted the 1990 UPC elective share provisions, discussed below, under which POD accounts are part of the decedent's augmented estate and subject to the spouse's elective share. UPC §2-205(1)(iii). Further, other courts employing an illusory transfer test, also discussed below, might subject POD accounts to the spouse's elective share because the deceased owner of such an account typically retained complete and unrestricted control over it until death, and the payee has no interest in or rights over the account until the decedent's death. Similar to *Snodgrass*, *Dalia v. Lawrence*, 627 A.2d 392 (Conn. 1993), held that a surviving spouse could not reach Totten trusts, joint tenancy real estate transferred with a retained life estate, or joint tenancy bank accounts. UPC §§2-205(1) and 2-205(2)(i) would allow the survivor's elective share claim to reach all of these assets.

*Snodgrass* and *Dalia* illustrate that an elective share can be defeated by nonprobate transfers to beneficiaries other than the spouse in many non-UPC states. By contrast, lifetime gifts and nonprobate transfers *to* the spouse in a non-UPC state may cause the surviving spouse to receive *more* than the elective share percentage of the decedent's assets, because the spouse is entitled to a statutory forced heir share of the decedent's probate estate *in addition to* receiving the gifts or nonprobate transfers. A classic illustration is *King v. King*, 613 N.E.2d 251 (Ohio App. 1992), in which the decedent made a deathbed gift of real property to the surviving spouse (to avoid it going through probate) and the spouse also received the full elective share from the remaining probate estate. Although lifetime gifts and nonprobate transfers to the spouse effectively may increase the spouse's entitlement in a non-UPC jurisdiction, in some states complete (no strings attached) gifts to third parties, even if made close to death, generally are effective to disfranchise the spouse, as is placing property in joint tenancy with third parties. We will see that UPC §2-205(3) may bring back into the augmented estate even completed gifts made to others within two years of the decedent's death, but not in every case. And what you should begin to realize is that state law regarding the elective share is a crazy patchwork from state to state.

## Revocable Trusts

Depending on the jurisdiction, a settlor may transfer assets to an inter vivos trust for the settlor's own benefit and disfranchise a surviving spouse at death, particularly if the settlor retained no more enjoyment and control than a life estate and a power of revocation. *Seifert v. Southern National Bank*, 409 S.E.2d 337 (S.C. 1991), disregarded a change in South Carolina's elective share statute that expressly limited the forced share to the decedent's *probate* estate, which was specifically defined as property passing under the will (or by intestacy), and allowed a surviving spouse's elective share claim to reach assets held in the decedent's revocable inter vivos trust. The decision illustrates the strength of the elective share policy in some states, protecting a surviving spouse from disinheritance.

But *Johnson v. La Grange State Bank*, 383 N.E.2d 185 (Ill. 1978), shows that a trust may be used to disfranchise a surviving spouse in other states. This consolidated case involved an inter vivos revocable trust created by the decedent for her own lifetime benefit (she was trustee and retained the income for life, along with a power to revoke), and then for the benefit of several relatives (including the surviving spouse) and various charities. A second case involved joint tenancy savings accounts created by the decedent in which the surviving spouse had no interest. Not so unusual about each case was that the plaintiffs lost in their bids to invalidate nonprobate transfers and claim a share of the assets involved as part of the statutory forced heir share. Not so common in each case was that the plaintiff was a surviving husband. The Illinois court went out of its way to hold against the surviving spouse and courts today would not limit such a decision to cases involving deceased wives disinheriting their surviving husbands.

Non-UPC elective share statutes are the law in many states. They typically limit the elective share to assets in the decedent's probate estate. As we will see in the elective share calculation, the UPC augmented probate estate concept includes some nonprobate assets, including those held in inter vivos revocable trusts. Without the UPC augmented probate estate concept, the alternative for an elective share claim to reach inter vivos trust and other nonprobate asset transfers is to find them invalid or illusory as against a challenge by the surviving spouse. The question involving a trust is the degree of enjoyment and control that a settlor may retain without subjecting the trust to the surviving spouse's elective share. *Seifert* did not answer that question but *Johnson* did, illustrating how easy it is, at least in Illinois, to disfranchise a surviving spouse. On the issue of the degree of control that may be retained without making a trust subject to a spouse's forced share, *Johnson* said that retention of no more than a life estate and power to revoke will make the trust immune to challenge. Quaere why that is the proper test. After all, hardly any power is more important than the power of revocation, which (because the assets are returned to the settlor on revocation of the trust) gives the settlor the ability to exercise unrestricted control over the assets at will.

If a trust is subject to the elective share of a surviving spouse, the remedy also may differ depending on the jurisdiction. One approach, exemplified by *Seifert*, is to hold the trust invalid in its entirety. As a result of *Seifert*, however, the South Carolina legislature amended state law to clarify that the trust is only invalid for purposes of computing and funding the statutory share. That is, if the effort to use a trust to disfranchise the spouse is not effective, trust assets may be counted in determining the elective share and an invasion of the trust (or other nonprobate property) may be necessary if probate property is not adequate to satisfy that share. But the trust should not be invalidated otherwise. Similarly, the UPC augmented estate concept does not treat Totten trusts as invalid, but includes the trust assets in computing the size of the spouse's share. Total invalidation in those states with a more blunt approach to the issue presents a number of problems: (1) it unnecessarily subjects all the property to probate; (2) it may alter the disposition of assets not passing to the spouse; (3) it will defeat a pour over estate plan; and (4) it creates title problems for real estate held in revocable trusts. So please be aware that even this aspect of the law is a mess in many states.

### Testing Nonprobate Transfers

In some states (e.g., Connecticut and Ohio), revocable trusts are not subject to a surviving spouse's elective share because the forced share statutes make the election applicable only to probate assets, and the courts view it as the legislature's prerogative whether to expand the election to nonprobate assets. Many other states, however, subject nonprobate assets (including revocable trusts) to the spouse's elective share. The crucial question in those states is the proper test for reaching trust assets. Historically, a variety of tests have been used to determine the validity of a trust against a spouse's challenge. And they often have been confused. The primary reason for this is due to a misuse of terminology (e.g., "fraud" is used interchangeably in cases involving will contests, secret transfers, intent to defeat spousal rights, illusory trusts, or absence of donative intent, notwithstanding that it means different things under each). Confusion also results because in some cases courts say they are doing one thing when in fact they are responding to equities without admitting this added factor.

The oldest approach is the intent or motive test, which asks whether the establishment of the trust was a "fraud" on the surviving spouse's marital rights. It is imprecise and may be difficult to prove, but may be favored by some courts because it allows the court to weigh various equities: (1) proximity of the transfer to death; (2) extent of the decedent's retained enjoyment and control; (3) the relative size of conveyances to and away from the surviving spouse; (4) the relative wealth of the various parties; (5) the moral standing of the surviving spouse; and (6) identifiable motives of the settlor (e.g., in *Johnson* the decedent's motive was to protect the surviving spouse as well as the decedent's mother and other relatives, and not to disfranchise the surviving spouse).

The illusory trust or retention of control test, used by the South Carolina court in *Seifert*, is the most predictable because the diversity of enjoyment or control that may be retained is not great. The sole inquiry is whether the alleged transfer into trust was "real." Essentially a court asks whether the settlor took back as much control or enjoyment as was given and whether the settlor lost any meaningful entitlement. (As indicated above, however, a problem with this test is that, if the settlor retains only the power to revoke, essentially the settlor has retained complete control even if no other controls or beneficial interests are retained.)

*Johnson* adopted the present donative intent test. It is just the opposite of the retention of control test. This third approach asks whether anything was given up presently rather than whether too much was retained. As we saw in *Farkas v. Williams* in Chapter 6, the same test was applied in Illinois to determine that an inter vivos trust is a valid will substitute.

A fourth test, adopted prospectively for Massachusetts in *Sullivan v. Burkin*, 460 N.E.2d 571 (Mass. 1984), subjects trust assets to the spouse's elective share if the settlor alone had a general power to appoint the trust, exercisable during life or at death. This would be a power to direct the assets for the settlor's own benefit, as explained in Chapter 14. Because the power to revoke a trust is such a general power of appointment, this test results in all revocable trusts being subjected to spousal elections (but only, apparently, if the power is exercisable by the settlor alone, and not if the power is exercisable only with a third person, such as a child of the settlor). Because *Johnson* and *Sullivan* are virtually identical on their facts, the difference in result (or at least the result the *Sullivan* court announced it would reach in such cases in the future) is just a function of the test used.

## The UPC

The spousal elective share augmented probate estate concept of the UPC is designed to deal with the issue whether nonprobate transfers (by the decedent to the surviving spouse or others, or *by* the surviving spouse) will affect the surviving spouse's entitlement. Under the UPC, the surviving spouse's elective share is a percentage of the augmented probate estate and not just of the decedent's probate estate. As we will see, property passing to the surviving spouse (probate and nonprobate alike) is included in the augmented probate estate and is applied against the elective share to satisfy or partially satisfy the spouse's claim. This alone is a major improvement over the law of other noncommunity property states and makes the elective share much more fair.

Here is an example of how the UPC works. The decedent's revocable trust had $400,000 of assets at the decedent's death, all of which were to be distributed to the decedent's child from a prior marriage. The decedent had $500,000 of investment securities titled in the name of the decedent, TOD to the decedent's spouse. And the decedent had $100,000 of probate assets. Under the UPC, the spouse's elective share claim is against the decedent's augmented estate, not the probate estate, which includes both the revocable trust assets and the securities as well as the traditional probate estate ($1 million total). In addition, the $500,000 of securities received by the surviving spouse will be credited against the elective share claim. If there were no other assets in the augmented estate, the result is that the spouse's elective share claim would be no more than half of the $1 million augmented estate, or $500,000. (As discussed below, the size of the spouse's elective share under the UPC depends on the length of the marriage, and except for the so-called "supplemental" elective share in small estates, it cannot exceed half.) Because the spouse already received $500,000 of securities, there would be no net elective share entitlement.

Inter vivos transfers away from the spouse in excess of $10,000 per donee per year, made within two years of death, and nonprobate transfers to others that essentially are not effective until death, are "brought back" into the "augmented probate estate" to compute the spousal entitlement. Thus, under the UPC a decedent's augmented probate estate generally will include the probate estate, nonprobate assets (such as the decedent's equal share of any joint tenancies, plus revocable trusts, POD accounts, and Totten trusts), and even gifts exceeding $10,000 per donee per year made within two years of death. Until 1990, the UPC did not include the proceeds of insurance on the decedent's life in the augmented probate estate, even if the decedent owned the policy. Now those proceeds are included in the augmented estate. The insurance industry really dislikes this change and has lobbied extensively, successfully in some states, for insurance to retain its protected status, not subject to the augmented estate calculation or satisfaction of an elective share. So be sure to carefully study state law. Most importantly, nonprobate transfers *to* the spouse (which are included in the augmented estate against which the elective share is calculated) are counted against the augmented estate entitlement. In most non-UPC states nothing transferred *to* the spouse counts, *either* in determining the elective share *or* in satisfying it.

Prior to the 1990 changes discussed below, the surviving spouse's elective share under the UPC was ⅓ of the decedent's augmented estate, which included (in addition to the decedent's probate estate and most of the decedent's nonprobate assets) assets the decedent transferred to the spouse during life. The surviving spouse's net elective share claim was the difference, if any, between that product and the lifetime and other transfers at death to the surviving spouse. To illustrate, assume D transferred $50,000 to S during life. At D's death, D's net probate estate was $200,000, half of which D left to S and the balance to D's child (C). D also had a revocable trust with assets of $250,000, all of which were left to C. Finally, D had a POD account of $100,000, payable to C. D's augmented estate is $600,000. S's ⅓ share is $200,000. Credited against that entitlement is the $50,000 lifetime gift and the $100,000 gift from the probate estate, leaving S with a net elective share claim of $50,000.

In 1990 this UPC elective share system was completely redesigned. Unique about the new spousal share is that the spouse's own property (including property the surviving spouse effectively owns in nonprobate form, such as a revocable trust), also is included in the augmented probate estate computation, regardless of how the spouse acquired that property. This reveals an economic partnership theory of marriage under which (as with community property) all the property they both accumulate during their marriage is considered, regardless of how title to their property is held. As we will see, the 1990 UPC sneaks community property concepts into the adopting states without saying that is the effect. Indeed, it is community property on steroids because, unlike true community property, the 1990 UPC system is not based on classifying the spouses' property as marital or separate, and it applies to property brought to the marriage as well as acquired during the marriage. Pay attention to how this works out. Also pay attention to an important policy underlying traditional elective share systems, which was to ensure support for a surviving spouse to protect against the spouse becoming a drain on the social welfare system. The new UPC reflects this support theory for the elective share in only a limited fashion by providing the surviving spouse with a "supplemental" elective share amount. This added entitlement is designed to ensure that, following a decedent's death, the surviving spouse will have at least $50,000 of assets (including the spouse's own property as well as property received from the decedent), excluding any homestead, exempt personal property, and family allowance — all of which are in addition to the spouse's elective share and supplemental elective share amounts.

The principal object of the redesigned UPC elective share system is to incorporate a partnership theory of marriage. The idea is that the survivor is entitled to a share of all property the couple accumulated during their marriage from both of their earnings. That is a pseudo community property concept. It is accomplished not by trying to identify and divide their marital property (while ignoring their separate property), as is necessary in community property states, but by approximating how much property the couple acquired during the marriage. Rather than by tracing or other accounting methods, this approximation is conclusively determined by the length of the marriage. Thus, for a marriage of less than a year, the assumption is that none of the couple's property is marital. As a result, the surviving spouse of such a short marriage has no elective share (unless a supplemental elective share is available, to provide the survivor with a total of no more than $50,000). But all of their property implicitly is treated by the UPC approximation system as marital in a marriage of 15 years or more. As a result, for marriages of that duration the survivor's elective share essentially is that amount of the decedent's property needed to leave the surviving spouse with half of the combined total of *all* of their property.

An increasing percentage of the couple's property is treated as marital for marriages of between one and fifteen years. For example, for a marriage of between 10 and 11 years, sixty percent of the couple's aggregate property is assumed to be marital and the surviving spouse is entitled to half. As actually implemented, the augmented estate concept for a marriage of between 10 and 11 years gives the spouse thirty percent of the augmented estate. Thus, if D died with a $500,000 net estate, if there were no nonprobate assets, and if S had no other property, $300,000 of D's assets would be regarded as marital property and S's elective share would be half of that, or $150,000. The UPC accomplishes this by giving S thirty percent of D's $500,000 augmented estate. This is convoluted and the UPC architect has written an article suggesting that the concept has been around long enough for states now to just embrace a true community property scheme. Until they do, however, here is an illustration that will help you understand the community property approximation approach of the current UPC.

The decedent's probate estate, all left to C (a child from a prior marriage) is $100,000. Joint tenancy property (all consideration provided by the decedent) with the surviving spouse was worth $150,000, insurance payable to X (a third party) totals $75,000, a Totten trust with Y (a third party) holds $100,000, and an inter vivos trust for Z (a third party) is worth $125,000. The amount the surviving spouse receives under the UPC depends on how long they were married, and how much property the surviving spouse owns. Let's assume the marriage was for more than 15 years and that the survivor owned no other property.

| | |
|---|---|
| $100,000 | probate estate to C |
| 150,000 | joint tenancy with S |
| 75,000 | insurance to X |
| 100,000 | Totten trust to Y |
| 125,000 | inter vivos trust to Z |
| $550,000 | Augmented probate estate |

The spousal share of the augmented probate estate is half (because the marriage was for at least 15 years), or $275,000. Because S already owns the joint tenancy of $150,000, S will receive only $125,000 more under the UPC. (This $125,000 would come from the probate estate, insurance, Totten trust, and inter vivos trust pro rata.)

If S had owned $300,000 of assets, that amount would have been included in the augmented probate estate calculation, increasing it to $850,000. S's elective share would be half, or $425,000. Credited against that would be the $150,000 of joint tenancy property and S's own $300,000, for a total of $450,000. Thus, there would be no elective share (although S would not need to "pay back" the $25,000 overage). The no-elective-share result would be the same even if S could prove that S's $300,000 was inherited from a third party and that all of the rest of D's augmented estate was marital property.

Notice that in a non-UPC state, S would take the joint tenancy $150,000 plus a statutory share (usually ⅓ or half) of the probate estate, the Totten trust (which would not withstand challenge in most states, despite the holding in *Dalia*, discussed above, because it is such a thin will substitute), and maybe the inter vivos trust. Nothing received by S outside probate (e.g., the $150,000 joint tenancy), or owned by S before D died would count against the elective share.

As seen, therefore, the 1990 UPC elective share system addresses several shortcomings with other systems. For example, a surviving spouse of a short term, late in life marriage no longer will be entitled to ⅓ (or ½) of a decedent's property. Indeed, if the marriage lasted less than a year, the survivor will not be entitled to an elective share at all (unless the estate is small and the spouse is entitled to a supplemental elective share to ensure that the spouse will have at least $50,000 of assets, which might be 100 percent of the small estate). Similarly, consistent with the partnership theory of marriage, in a long-term (15+ year) marriage, the survivor's elective share is for half of the decedent's assets, not ⅓. But in some cases, the new system also will yield inequitable results. For example, in a long-term late in life marriage, all of a decedent's assets may be subject to an elective share claim by a surviving spouse even if all of those assets are separate property that, under the partnership theory of marriage, ought not be subject to a spouse's elective share claim. No system shy of community property is consistently equitable.

## Problems Created by Migratory Clients

The rule is that once property is community property, it always is community property. Thus, there is a tracing problem in identifying community property held by a decedent dying in a noncommunity property state. Similarly, there is a need to identify separate and quasi-community property of a decedent dying in a community property state. The surviving spouse may receive *more* from a forced share than is equitable if the spouses accumulated community property while living in a community property state and then moved to a noncommunity property state before the decedent died. But the surviving spouse may receive *less* than is equitable if the decedent died in a community property state owning property accumulated from the decedent's earnings while the couple lived in a noncommunity property state. Two examples illustrate these opposite results.

(1) Decedent died in a noncommunity property jurisdiction with $90,000 of community property and $60,000 of separate property. The statutory share is ⅓. The initial reaction that the surviving spouse will receive $50,000 (⅓ of the aggregate wealth of $150,000) is not correct. Instead, the spouse already owns half of the community property ($45,000) and is entitled to ⅓ of the decedent's separate property (another $20,000). Depending on state law, the spouse also may receive ⅓ of the decedent's share of the community property (another $15,000), for a total of $80,000. Notice that, at the most, the spouse's share would have been ⅓ of $150,000 if this all was the decedent's separate property. The disparity is produced because the community property share is half *and* state law does not cut the spouse out of the decedent's separate property and may not cut the spouse out of the decedent's share of the community property.

(2) Decedent died in a community property jurisdiction that does not recognize quasi-community property, with $140,000 of separate property and $10,000 of community property. Because community property states do not have elective shares, the surviving spouse receives $5,000 only, as half of the community, because there is no quasi-community property entitlement. Were this a jurisdiction that applies the quasi-community property concept at death, the surviving spouse would receive half of the $140,000 as well (if it all was earned during the marriage) as if it were true community property. Quaere whether this $75,000 aggregate result is more appropriate than the $80,000 result in the prior example.

## Is There a Better Way?

Commentators argue about whether there is a better way to address marital property rights than the existing elective share systems. One approach would mimic the federal estate tax gross estate as the decedent's true wealth (the UPC augmented estate comes close), and then base the elective share on that. Uncle Sam does not let much escape that system and the inclusion rules are pretty clear. Another avenue is to look to what the surviving spouse would have received under state law had the parties divorced just prior to the decedent's death. Arguably more equitable results would result, but at the cost of delay and less predictability. A third approach would be to convert to community property, recognizing quasi-community property at death as well as at divorce, and abolish the elective share altogether. A fourth would be to include only the couple's marital property in the augmented estate and establish the spouse's elective share without regard to the length of the marriage, excluding their separate property from the computation. The result arguably would be more equitable, but at a cost of having to classify the couple's property as marital or separate at the first of their deaths.

### Pre- and Postnuptial Agreements

Particularly for subsequent marriages if there are children from prior marriages, it is not uncommon for spouses to modify or waive marital rights they otherwise would enjoy, using a pre- or occasionally a postnuptial agreement. (Prenuptial agreements often are referred to as "antenuptial" agreements. Some people hear ante-nuptial as if it was anti-nuptial, however, so we use "prenuptial" instead.) Pre- and postnuptial agreements essentially are contracts regarding entitlement at death or divorce. Historically, in many jurisdictions these agreements were subject to special rules and close scrutiny in determining their validity. For example, in some jurisdictions a prenuptial agreement was not valid unless executed more than a specified number of days (such as 10) before the wedding. Today, in many jurisdictions the validity of these agreements is measured as in any contract, looking to sufficiency of consideration, fraud, duress, and overreaching. In others, however, the nature of the relationship between prospective spouses continues to subject prenuptial agreements to special scrutiny. A sufficient degree of inequality between the parties can result in the proponent having the burden of proving that the agreement was not procured by fraud or overreaching. See, e.g., *In re Grieff*, 703 N.E.2d 752 (N.Y. 1998). And in some states (e.g., Oklahoma, Iowa, and Ohio) elective share rights may not be waived in postnuptial agreements.

Otherwise, there is a growing trend in favor of upholding pre- and postnuptial agreements if (1) the agreement is based on full disclosure of the spouses' resources *or* each spouse freely signed and either did have or could have had knowledge of the other spouse's holdings, and (2) the provisions for the complaining spouse are fair and reasonable. For example, *In re Estate of Garbade*, 633 N.Y.S.2d 878 (N.Y. App. Div.

1995), upheld a prenuptial agreement limiting the surviving spouse's rights against the $2.5 million estate of her deceased husband to the proceeds of a $100,000 insurance policy (she apparently received another $240,000 of assets at her husband's death by other means) because there was no showing of fraud and the husband made a full disclosure of his assets. There is a presumption of inadequate disclosure if the amounts provided for the complaining spouse are disproportionately small, but that presumption is rebuttable with (1) proof of knowledge by the complaining spouse of the other spouse's resources (or, perhaps, lack of concealment by the other spouse), or (2) independent representation of the complaining spouse (this part is key because, in the absence of fraud, it virtually negates a successful challenge).

*In re Burgess' Estate*, 646 P.2d 623 (Okla. Ct. App. 1982), illustrates the new attitude towards marital agreements. In *Burgess*, the premarital agreement waived elective share rights and made no provision for the surviving spouse. The agreement was upheld despite conflicting evidence of whether there had been full and fair disclosure of the husband's assets, because the court found that the wife had a generally accurate knowledge of the husband's property. In so holding, the court stated:

[C]ourts have tended to be rather more exacting of such contracts than of other contracts. At the root of this tendency seems to lie an attitude of paternalism toward women. For example, [one] court labeled an antenuptial contract "a wicked device to evade the laws applicable to marriage relations, property rights and divorces," which was "clearly against public policy and decency," and an attempt by the husband to "legalize prostitution, under the name of marriage."

*          *          *

Well-intentioned though this chivalrous attitude may have been in the past, times have changed. It will no longer do for courts to look on women who are about to be married as if they were insensible ninnies, pathetically vulnerable to overreaching by their fiancés and in need of special judicial protection.

Moreover, there are today many policy reasons favoring the enforcement of ante-nuptial agreements. These contracts can be seen as fostering marriage since some couples, especially older ones who typically already have families and property of their own, might choose not to marry absent assurance that they will still be free to order their affairs as they wish.

The Uniform Pre-Marital Agreements Act is the same as UPC §2-213 and presupposes validity of a pre- or postnuptial agreement unless (1) the agreement was involuntary, *or* (2) there was (a) no disclosure to the complaining party of the other's financial condition, (b) no knowledge by the complaining party of the other's financial condition, (c) no reasonable basis for the complaining party to acquire such knowledge, (d) no waiver by the complaining party of such disclosure, *and* (e) the agreement was unconscionable (which is a subjective determination, to be made by the court as a matter of law) when executed. These are tough standards to meet and probably impossible, in the absence of fraud, if the complaining party had independent counsel.

### Pretermitted Heirs

We focus now on all the natural objects of a decedent's bounty. Most states have pretermitted (i.e., omitted) heir statutes under which heirs who are not provided for under a decedent's will *may* be entitled to share in the estate. Heirs who may benefit from these statutes usually include children and sometimes more remote descendants or the decedent's spouse. The theories alleged to support statutes that protect a spouse or child (or other descendant) who is not provided for in a will vary. For example, some courts would say that there is a postmortem support obligation. Others would say that there is an inheritance entitlement. If either rationale was correct it should not be possible to overcome the pretermitted heir statute with a showing of the decedent's positive intent to disinherit, and yet we will see that pretermission can be effected by an appropriate will provision. A third stated rationale is protection against mistake or inadvertence, which likely is the only logical explanation for this form of enforced heirship. A decedent might not get around to revising a will, but quaere how often it actually occurs that the decedent "just forgot."

### *Pretermitted Spouses*

Statutes providing protection to surviving spouses, if applicable, allow a spouse to reject a will that was executed before the marriage and take an intestate share. In noncommunity property jurisdictions other than Georgia (which does not provide the spouse with an elective share entitlement), the spouse may choose whether to take an elective share or as a pretermitted spouse. This election to take as a pretermitted spouse is based on an assumption that, after the wedding, the decedent forgot to amend (or intended but did not get around to amending) the will to include the new spouse as a beneficiary. The failure to provide for the surviving spouse is presumed to be inadvertent, not intentional.

Generally, a pretermitted spouse statute will not apply if the failure to provide for the spouse was intentional. The question is how to determine whether that was the case. *Estate of Shannon*, 274 Cal. Rptr.

338 (1990), involved a testator's will that left the entire estate to a child and included a boilerplate provision that the testator "intentionally omitted all other living persons and relatives." The testator's surviving spouse nevertheless took a share of the estate under a pretermitted spouse statute because the will (executed some 12 years prior to the testator's marriage to the spouse) did not show a specific intent to exclude the spouse. Extrinsic evidence in the form of testimony by the testator's attorney that the testator stated that the surviving spouse had more property than the testator and that the testator wanted the child to receive the entire estate did not affect the result. The controlling statute required a testator's intention not to provide for a spouse to be shown from the will itself.

The pretermitted spouse's share under the UPC is an intestate share, not of the entire estate, but only of that portion of the estate left to beneficiaries who are not descendants of the decedent born prior to the marriage. Under the UPC, a pretermitted heir entitlement is *not* available to a surviving spouse to the extent the decedent left the estate to descendants born prior to the marriage who are not descendants of the spouse, because the assumption that the decedent forgot to revise the will to provide for a new spouse is regarded as not sufficient to overcome the decedent's other testamentary objectives regarding those descendants. In such a case the omitted surviving spouse would need to elect against the will and take the elective share of the augmented estate.

Note that in some cases the elective share will be much smaller than an intestate share. Moreover, under the UPC, an omitted spouse will receive no pretermitted heir share (and will be left only with an elective share remedy) if the testator's failure to provide for the spouse was intentional, as shown by (1) evidence that the will was executed in contemplation of the marriage, (2) a provision in the will stating that it is to be effective notwithstanding a subsequent marriage, or (3) the decedent having provided for the spouse by will substitute, with evidence that the provision was in lieu of a testamentary gift.

As an example, imagine that T, a single person, executed a will that gave the entire estate to two favorite nephews and made no reference to the possibility of a subsequent marriage. Several years later, T, who had no descendants, married S. T died 13 months after the marriage without having changed the will or providing for S by will substitute. Under UPC §2-301, S is a pretermitted spouse entitled to receive an intestate share of T's entire estate (because no part of it passed to descendants of T). Because T had no descendants, S's intestate share will be the entire estate if T also was not survived by a parent, or the first $200,000 of the estate, plus ¾ of the balance, if T was survived by a parent. See Chapter 2. By contrast, S could not take as a pretermitted spouse if T's will had stated that it was to be given effect without regard to a subsequent marriage by T. S would be relegated to an elective share instead. For this one year marriage the spouse's elective share percentage under the new UPC forced share system would be only three percent of the decedent's augmented estate. If T's will made no reference to the possibility of a subsequent marriage and devised the estate half to a child and half to beneficiaries who are not descendants, S's share under UPC §2-301 would be an intestate share of the half left to nondescendants.

The augmented estate concept is missing from the UPC pretermitted spouse rule. Thus, in the preceding example, if T had arranged for property to pass to the two nephews by will substitute, S's pretermitted spouse share would not reach those assets. If all of T's property passed by will substitute, S would take nothing as a pretermitted spouse and again would be left only with an elective share. On the other hand, as a pretermitted spouse S is entitled to an intestate share of probate property left to nondescendants (assuming T's failure to provide for S was not intentional), even if S has more assets than T and therefore would not be entitled to an elective share. S also is entitled to a pretermitted spouse share even if T provides for S by will substitute, unless the proof shows that these transfers were meant to be in lieu of a testamentary provision. As you can see, the failure to coordinate the policies behind pretermission and the elective share can create a significant evaluation problem in deciding which to pursue on behalf of a disappointed surviving spouse.

### Pretermitted Descendants

The foregoing may be too much ado about nothing because there aren't many pretermitted spouse statutes and even fewer claims. But pretermitted descendant statutes are found in most states and they can be important. Some (e.g., UPC §2-302) protect only children. Others also protect more remote descendants. Generally, these statutes fall into two categories. Most protect only children (or more remote descendants) born or adopted after execution of the will. Some protect any child (or more remote descendant) not provided for in the will, whenever born or adopted.

The share of a pretermitted child (or more remote descendant) also varies from state to state. The typical entitlement is the share the child (or descendant) would have received had the estate been intestate (less any advancements). Notice that this may be substantially more or less than what other descendants in the same relationship to the decedent receive under the will. Protection under the UPC is afforded only to children, not to more remote descendants. The share of a pretermitted child depends on whether any children of the decedent were living when the will was executed, and often will not be as large as an intestate share. If no children of the testator were living when the will was executed, a pretermitted child will receive an intestate share, unless the will devises substantially all of the estate to the other parent of the omitted child. In that case, the pretermitted child takes nothing. If the testator had one or more children living when the will was executed, a pretermitted child will share pro rata with the other children all property devised to those children (or in trust for their benefit).

Except in Louisiana, a parent may disinherit children (and more remote descendants). Pretermitted descendant statutes do not provide forced share rights like those provided to spouses in noncommunity property elective share states. Rather, pretermitted heir statutes only protect from *inadvertent* disinheritance, meaning that proof of an intent to omit will preclude a claim. For example, *In re Estate of Laura*, 690 A.2d 1011 (N.H. 1997), involved a pretermitted heir statute that provided protection only to children and descendants of deceased children who were not "referred to" in the will. The court held that a provision expressly disinheriting a grandson, but not expressly referring to his descendants, nevertheless "referred to" the grandson's descendants for purposes of the pretermitted heir statute, and thus barred them from taking.

A significant difference among the statutes is where the burden of proof lies on the issue whether the failure to provide for a child (or other descendant) was intentional. In some jurisdictions the omitted individual must prove the disinheritance was unintentional. Typically extrinsic evidence is allowed because this chore (proving the negative — lack of intent) is so great. In other jurisdictions the proponents of the will must prove that disinheritance was intentional. Typically no extrinsic evidence is allowed in this endeavor (i.e., the intent to disinherit must be evident from the will itself).

### Negative Wills

A "negative" will (as discussed in Chapter 2) states an intent to disinherit a person who is a potential heir (remember, "heir" is a term of art, meaning those persons who take by statute from an intestate decedent) of the testator. Usually a will must dispose of the entire estate to effectively disinherit. In most states an heir's entitlement to intestate property cannot be prevented by a will that states only the decedent's negative intent regarding the heir. There also must be a valid alternative disposition. Exceptions are found in some states (e.g., New York and under UPC §2-302(b)(1)), which permit a will to state that some potential heirs are to receive nothing even from any intestate portion of the estate.

### Alternatives to Pretermitted Heir Status

If a decedent dies with a premarital will and a surviving spouse is precluded from receiving a pretermitted heir share, the spouse nevertheless may elect against the estate. By contrast, if a pretermitted heir statute is no help to an omitted child (or more remote descendant), the only other alternative is to bring a will contest action to defeat the will entirely. This alternative also is available to a surviving spouse, but as we saw in Chapter 3, it is not a very good alternative because success under contest actions is so unpredictable.

Also, as discussed in Chapter 3, a codicil normally operates to republish a will as of the date of the codicil. Pretermitted heir statutes often apply only if the testator was married after execution of the will, or protect only descendants born or adopted after execution of the will. As a result, the execution of a codicil can bar pretermitted heir status if a marriage, birth, or adoption occurs after execution of the will but before execution of the codicil, because the later codicil execution becomes the date of the will for pretermitted heir status. To illustrate, *Azcunce v. Estate of Azcunce*, 586 So. 2d 1216 (Fla. Dist. Ct. App. 1991), involved a father's 1983 will that devised property in trust for his wife and his three then living children. No provision was made for afterborns. A fourth child was born in 1984. Her status as a pretermitted heir was defeated by the father's execution of a codicil (which expressly republished the terms of the will) in 1986. There was evidence that the father did not intend to disinherit her (he had asked his attorney to revise his will to include her) but the controlling Florida statute protected only children born or adopted after execution of the will.

CHAPTER 11

# INTRODUCTION TO TRUSTS

This Chapter reviews the background, varieties, and purposes of trusts. Basically trusts facilitate creative estate planning and may be established during life or at death, may be revocable or irrevocable, and may be intentional or implied by operation of law (resulting or constructive trusts). Trusts are property management arrangements that bifurcate title between two parties, a fiduciary—the trustee—which holds legal title to the trust property for the benefit of one or more others—the beneficiaries—who hold the equitable or beneficial title to the trust property. For example, a parent might provide by will for estate assets to pass in trust for the benefit of a child until the child reaches a specified age, meanwhile providing management of the trust property for the child's benefit.

Trusts originated in the 1400s when they were known as a "use." Active uses, the forerunner to the modern trust, provided actual management of property. Passive uses, as to which the trustee had no management responsibilities, were used to avoid feudal duties, circumvent property ownership and transfer limits, evade creditors, or minimize dower rights. A passive use or trust is not effective (with the exception of "land trusts," which are recognized in a few states, in which the trustee's only "duty" is to hold legal title to land). A trust will be "executed" if the trustee has no duties to perform (other than not to interfere with the beneficiary's enjoyment of the trust property). This means that legal title passes to the beneficiaries on demand and thereby merges with their equitable title, causing the trust to terminate and the beneficiaries to have full fee simple ownership. Similarly, a "dry trust" is one that owns no property and thus fails for lack of a trust corpus. Active trusts do not become passive trusts because active trusts automatically terminate on fulfillment of their stated purposes.

Trust law essentially is equitable and judicial in origin, arising in the Chancery court and still lodged there. Most local trust statutes are merely piecemeal codifications of existing common law. The Uniform Trust Code (UTC), promulgated in 2000 and amended several times since, is the first comprehensive widespread trust law codification. It was adopted in modified form in ten jurisdictions by 2005 and was under consideration in many others. The UTC contains a number of innovations to the common law of trusts, and answers several issues that typically are not addressed or settled by local law.

Trusts are created by a *settlor* (or *grantor* or—very uncommonly—a *trustor*) who transfers property (the trust *corpus, principal,* or—also uncommon—*res*) to the *trustee* (a fiduciary) for the use or benefit of *beneficiaries* (present or future interest holders). Typically there is only one trust settlor, but there can be more. For beneficiaries it is the opposite. Typically trusts have multiple beneficiaries, although it is not unusual for there to be only one current beneficiary at any given time. Many trusts have one trustee. Some have multiple cotrustees. Each of the three roles may be held by a different person, or one person may serve in two or even all three of them. For example, in a revocable trust the settlor often will serve as the original trustee and be the sole current beneficiary. See Chapter 6. There also must be at least one remainder beneficiary (some person or entity other than the settlor's estate) to avoid the merger of title and failure of the trust that would occur if the sole trustee also were the sole beneficiary. Because that almost universally is the case, this requirement is of little practical significance. See Chapter 12.

## Distinguishing Trusts

Although trusts exhibit characteristics of contracts, agencies, deeds, wills, co-ownership (such as joint tenancy or a life estate followed by a remainder interest), and life insurance, they are unlike all other legal entities in three essential respects. One is bifurcation of title. Legal title is held by the trustee. The beneficiaries hold equitable title or the beneficial interest. This separation of title has made trusts unacceptable under many non-Anglo systems of law. Fiduciary duty is the second unique aspect of trusts. Imposed on the trustee is the fiduciary duty of undivided loyalty to the beneficiaries, which ensures the protection of the beneficial interest. The duty of a fiduciary is the highest recognized at common law. By it the trustee is barred from acting for its own benefit or from engaging in any activity that is not for the exclusive benefit of the trust and its beneficiaries. Even the appearance of impropriety, such as self-dealing (even if the terms are entirely fair), may result in discharge, surcharge, or other liability to the trustee. See Chapter 18. When you contemplate the bifurcation of title you will realize that a trust could not exist in the absence of this extreme fiduciary obligation.

Enforceability is the third element that distinguishes trusts. Unlike other relations in which any party may sue for enforcement, only the beneficiaries of a trust may engage the trustee in litigation to enforce the trust. Except to challenge its validity, or perhaps on contract grounds, no person who is not a beneficiary (not even the settlor, who has transferred full title and ownership) may enforce a trust. (An exception under UTC §405(c) permits enforcement by the settlor of a charitable trust.) As a result, trust litigation most often involves either drafting glitches (i.e., construction suits) or the allegation of breach and falls into relatively few categories. One is beneficiaries suing to enforce the trust, to rectify any breach of fiduciary duty, or for accountings to assess whether there has been any breach. A second is the trustee suing to have its accounts approved (protecting the trustee from liability for any act revealed in the account), to have the document construed when unclear or subject to conflicting claims (often due to deficiencies that may generate malpractice exposure to the drafting attorney), or to resign (a right that does not otherwise exist at common law unless granted by the trust document, but that UTC §705(a) grants without the need for court approval following proper notice to interested parties). Finally, outsiders may sue to invalidate the trust, asserting defects in creation or continued existence (such as a creditor who wants to reach the trust corpus to satisfy its claim) or on policy grounds (such as a surviving spouse who seeks to reach trust assets for elective share purposes. See Chapter 10).

It is helpful to remember that the trustee of a trust is charged with administering the trust to carry out the intent of the settlor as evidenced by the terms of the trust, but the rights and interests in a trust in which the settlor has not retained a beneficial interest belong solely to the beneficiaries. Accordingly, except as provided under the UTC for charitable trusts, a settlor who is not also a beneficiary may not sue the trustee to enforce the trust, nor for damages for breach of trust. Nevertheless, a settlor may play a role in the administration of the trust in a variety of ways. For example, generally a trust may not be terminated early by the beneficiaries and the trustee without the settlor's consent (but the settlor and *all* of the beneficiaries may terminate the trust without the trustee's consent. See, e.g., UTC §411(a)). Similarly, the settlor may provide input concerning construction and intent because the relevant intent is the settlor's, at creation of the trust, not at a later time during its administration.

Finally, the trust may authorize the settlor to participate in administration of the trust, such as by replacing the trustee in the event of a vacancy, or removing and replacing a trustee. (Indeed, under UTC §706(a) the settlor may sue to have the trustee removed even without express authorization in the trust.)

## Types of Trusts

There are various types of trusts and motives for their creation. Estate planners typically are not concerned with business and public trusts and, because of the complexity required to qualify for exempt status under the federal income tax law, our treatment of charitable express trusts is limited. See Chapter 13.

Most important for purposes of this study are private express trusts. Within this category, the common forms are:

- **Inter vivos trusts** (also called living or revocable trusts) typically holding most of a settlor's assets during life, along with the special type of living trust known as a "self-trusteed declaration of trust" in which the settlor also is the initial trustee (and, usually, the initial beneficiary too). Literally, an "inter vivos trust" is a trust created by a settlor during the settlor's life and may include a variety of different kinds of trusts, such as revocable and irrevocable insurance trusts and trusts for the education of the beneficiaries (typically irrevocable). The most common inter vivos trust is revocable and designed for more active purposes than receiving life insurance proceeds in the future. Among other purposes, inter vivos trusts can avoid probate, provide management of the settlor's property, and preserve privacy. See Chapter 6. Generally, inter vivos trusts become irrevocable at the settlor's death, at which time the assets may be distributed outright to the beneficiaries, after postmortem administration of the trust is completed. Alternatively, the trust may become irrevocable and continue for the beneficiaries, similar in operation to testamentary trusts (except that in some states testamentary trusts are subject to ongoing judicial supervision while the inter vivos trust is not).

- **Testamentary trusts** are created by a testator's will and are irrevocable (because the settlor is deceased) and funded (usually by the residue of the testator's estate). The will creates the trust, which does not come into existence and has no legal significance until the testator's death.

- **Insurance trusts** are created to receive proceeds from life insurance policies that typically insure the settlor's life. In some cases insurance trusts own the policy itself and these almost always are irrevocable and are part of a plan to avoid subjecting the proceeds to federal estate tax when the insured/settlor dies. Alternatively, insurance trusts often are revocable and "unfunded," in the sense that the only "property" owned by the trustee is the designation of the trust as beneficiary of an insurance policy, typically owned by and on the life of the settlor.

- **Other.** Divorce trusts usually are used to better guarantee the settlor's obligations under a decree. Tort settlement or damage trusts usually are created by court order and are held for the benefit of an injured party, often because that person is unable to manage the settlement and, perhaps, because the court does not trust their guardian or next friend with the money. Employee benefit trusts are the repositories of vast amounts of American wealth and (even more so than charitable trusts) are subject to complex tax qualification requirements and regulation. Notice that most other trusts are not subject to oversight by government agencies. Courts may have jurisdiction to settle disputes if they arise, and federal and state banking and trust company examiners regulate corporate trustees (and thus indirectly the trusts they manage), but private express trusts generally are self-executing and self-governing.

The third general category of trusts is implied trusts. These stand in juxtaposition to express trusts and come in two flavors: resulting trusts and constructive trusts. Both arise by operation of law, not by actions taken by a settlor who intends to create an express trust. The trustee of a resulting or constructive trust is not charged with managing property on behalf of trust beneficiaries over time, but instead is required to convey the trust property to a rightful owner. Until that conveyance is made, the trustee's duty is to hold title to the property and preserve it for that beneficiary.

Resulting trusts are created for the benefit of the settlor (or any successors in interest) in two different kinds of situations: (1) when an express trust fails in whole or in part or (2) when the purchase price for property is paid by one person and legal title to the property is transferred to another. In the first category, a resulting trust may arise if a private express trust fails, is invalid in whole or in part, or to the extent the trust exceeds its original purpose and there is no disposition of the balance of the trust property. In each case the law presumes that the settlor did not intend to benefit the trustee, so a resulting trust is created in favor of the settlor or the settlor's assignees, devisees under the settlor's will, or the settlor's heirs at law.

The second category, purchase money resulting trusts, arise in a purchase money transaction. For example, if A gave money to B to purchase Blackacre for the benefit of C (or for A, for that matter), and B completes the purchase and takes title in B's name, there may be a resulting purchase money trust, even if the agreement between A and B was oral and therefore violates the Statute of Frauds.

Many purchase money trusts are oral or secret because the purpose is illegal, such as to encourage immoral or illegal acts, to defraud a spouse or creditor, or to evade alien land laws. In such cases a resulting trust likely will not be established to assist in the conduct because the resulting trust concept is equitable. Unjust enrichment to the transferee is outweighed by a policy against providing relief to anyone who enters into an illegal transaction. Thus, a trustee who refuses to perform the illegal purpose may be allowed to keep the property.

In no event does a resulting trust violate the Statute of Frauds, because the "trust" is not really a trust at all. It merely is a legal fiction to cover what is, in reality in many cases, the absence of a trust, as where an express trust has failed or is incomplete. Moreover, in the purchase money situation a transfer of money, not of land, was involved, making the Statute of Frauds inapplicable. In each case, Section 8 of the original English Statute of Frauds exempted these trusts from its scope.

Constructive trusts are a fiction created by equity to avoid unjust enrichment. Unlike resulting trusts that arise on the basis of assumptions of a settlor's or payor's intent, constructive trusts are remedial. They may arise in the wake of wrongful conduct or mistake, such as a transfer that was induced by fraud, undue influence, mistake, or duress. Note, however, that if the transfer was by will, mistake alone usually is not a sufficient ground for relief, including imposition of a constructive trust. See Chapter 7. They also may arise following breach of a confidential relation. Or they may be required simply because retention of property would be unjust in any other case. Examples include succession to property by operation of law if the successor committed a homicide that led to the succession. See Chapter 2. Or it could be wrongful interference with testation that led to the succession. See the discussion of *Latham v. Father Divine* in Chapter 3. Constructive trusts are imposed on wrongdoers and innocent parties who would benefit from the wrongdoing alike, in each case to prevent their unjust enrichment at the expense of the person with a rightful claim to the property.

To illustrate, assume that A, the owner of Blackacre, borrowed $10,000 from B. To secure the loan, A conveyed title to Blackacre to B, although there was no documentation for the loan or for the "mortgage." B would hold Blackacre as constructive trustee for A if A repaid B but B refused to reconvey legal title to Blackacre.

Constructive trusts are not common or easy to create or impose. The necessary elements for imposition usually include (1) an express promise or an equitably implied agreement to hold the property in trust, (2) reliance or other detriment by the injured party, (3) unjust enrichment if the holder is allowed to retain the property, and (4) a superior entitlement in the claimant to possession, even if that person never was legally entitled to the property.

## Trust Purposes

The reasons to create express private trusts are even more varied than the types of trusts that may be created. Common motives fall into tax and nontax oriented categories. Fortunately, the tax oriented reasons for using trusts are beyond the scope of this text, but they generally entail minimizing the settlor's and beneficiaries' estate, gift, and generation-skipping transfer taxes, and minimizing income taxes (trusts are separate income tax paying entities that permit some income shifting).

The nontax objectives for using trusts are far more numerous than the tax objectives, and even more likely to endure as tax laws ebb and flow. For example, trusts allow imposition of dead hand controls over future use of property, allowing the settlor to do such things as defer beneficiaries' enjoyment of property, establish transmission that ensures accomplishment (or avoidance) of certain uses, or reward or punish certain conduct. Coupled with judicious use of powers of appointment and trustee discretion, flexibility also is inherent in trust dispositions but lacking in outright gifts. See Chapters 14 and 13, respectively.

Perhaps most important, trusts make possible a sharing or bifurcation of enjoyment of property in myriad contexts. For example, a trust for a child might be designed to defer the child's control over the property until the child reaches a specified age, but to have the assets managed by someone else and available for the child's benefit in the meantime. Along this second line, a single fund of assets may be made available for a group, such as for children until all have received an education, followed by any remaining funds being distributed in equal shares. And a trust may provide benefits to one beneficiary for life, with ultimate distribution of remaining trust property to other beneficiaries. For example, trusts sometimes are used to provide for a surviving spouse for life, but guaranteeing ultimate receipt by the settlor's descendants, such as children of a former marriage. Similarly, it is possible to use a trust to provide for a son- or daughter-in-law after a child's death, while preserving principal for ultimate distribution within the blood line.

Another common use of trusts is to provide enjoyment of benefits by successive generations without fear of dissipation through profligacy, improvidence, or inexperience. In part this is because trusts present advantages over other property management alternatives. For example, consider the hassles of co-ownership of property by several intended beneficiaries (in investing, operating, renting, selling, or mortgaging the underlying property, for example) as compared to having a single trustee hold title to the property for the benefit of these same beneficiaries. Assuming proper selection of the trustee, trust administration ensures better management if the beneficiary lacks the desire, experience, or ability to manage property given outright, or is immature or improvident and, therefore, cannot (yet) be trusted to manage the property. Furthermore, trusts permit greater flexibility and less supervision than agencies (which terminate with death in all cases, and on incapacity of the principal unless created as a "durable" power of attorney), conservatorships or guardianships, or custodianships under statutory arrangements such as the Uniform Transfers to Minors Act (which either involve court supervision or cannot be altered to fit certain needs or adapt to certain assets).

A increasingly attractive attribute of trusts is that they can provide funds for the use of beneficiaries without subjecting those funds to the claims of most creditors of the beneficiaries. See Chapter 13. Finally, several additional advantages are available with respect to inter vivos trusts or declarations of trust. Most common is avoiding the inherent delay and publicity that are common in states with no form of independent probate administration, and avoiding any interruption in management attendant to the public probate process in virtually all cases. In addition, although an inter vivos trust may be invalidated or reformed on the same grounds as may other lifetime gratuitous property transfers (fraud, duress, undue influence, or mistake), as a practical matter successful trust contest is much less likely than the contestability of wills. Further, trustee fees often are lower than personal representative fees for performing the same functions related to death of the settlor (such as filing federal and state estate and fiduciary income tax returns, paying creditors, and distributing assets), all due to the lack of court supervision and the attendant time drain involved in probate in many jurisdictions.

Even if probate administration would be an easy matter, avoiding ancillary administration of out-of-state realty is desirable because it seldom is advantageous to conduct more than one probate administration. Trusts can serve this purpose. Many astute planners also recognize that insurance and receptacle trusts are an expeditious device for the receipt of employee benefits or insurance proceeds at death, permitting collection and investment before probate may begin. And as we saw in Chapter 10, a living trust might not disfranchise the settlor's creditors but in some jurisdictions it is possible to disinherit a surviving spouse through creation of an inter vivos trust. Finally, trusts are easier to execute and amend than wills (there are virtually *no* formalities in most states), permitting the use of inter vivos trusts as the primary estate planning document (coupled with a simple pour over will) to avoid the formalities of wills.

Trusts may be created for any legal purpose. Assuming that no lack of capacity is evidenced by arbitrary, illogical, or capricious provisions, anything a settlor could do by an outright transfer may be done in the guise of a trust. Invalid purposes usually involve attempts to do what the settlor could not do outright, such as violate limits on trust duration imposed by the Rule Against Perpetuities, encourage or reward crime, torts, or immorality, or defraud creditors. In this last regard, property owners may create trusts that allow beneficiaries to enjoy the property free from the claims of most creditors, but settlors usually cannot create trusts of their own property for their own benefit that will withstand attack by their own creditors. See Chapter 13.

Trusts also may be invalid to the extent they offend public policy. For example, a trust may not interfere with familial relations, such as by (1) denying custody of a child (e.g., S creates a trust that will benefit P only after P agrees to grant custody of their child to S), (2) encouraging abandonment of child support (e.g., S creates a trust that will benefit P only after P agrees to give up P's practice of paying child support to P's nonmarital child), or (3) encouraging divorce (e.g., S creates a trust that will benefit S's child only if the child divorces a current spouse). And a trust may not call for destruction or waste of trust corpus. Thus, a direction to destroy trust assets would not be enforceable over the beneficiary's objection (the trustee also has standing to challenge the direction on its own motion).

Unreasonable restraints on marriage also are invalid trust purposes. The key is *"unreasonable"* restraints. The breadth and duration cannot be excessive, but some restriction is permissible. For example, a court likely would uphold a trust provision that conditioned a right to receive trust distributions on a beneficiary not being married younger than a reasonable age (e.g., 25) and a court might not invalidate a provision terminating trust benefits to a beneficiary who married outside a given faith (provided that sufficient opportunities to marry within the faith exist). See Chapter 1. In this, encouraging divorce might be viewed differently from providing a safety net in case thereof, the latter being valid even if the former is not. Even a skilled and careful drafter would have trouble walking the dividing line between these two objectives, and the apparent intent of the settlor likely would be significant. For example, a bequest "if X divorces Y" likely would be viewed differently from "to provide for X in the event of divorce and its effect on X's income or lifestyle." The former would fail. The latter might be valid.

Encouraging marriage or discouraging divorce almost certainly is copacetic, although a marriage might be abusive and the trust constitutes a financial handcuff preventing the beneficiary from breaking free, in which case it might be invalid. Restraints on *re*marriage ("in trust for S for life or until S's earlier remarriage") usually are permissible, because the trust presumably was created to support the beneficiary only while unmarried, and because there seems to be a "gigolo or gold digger" notion that the settlor should not be required to provide support to a surviving spouse (and, indirectly, a new spouse) who has found a replacement.

Finally, a trust conditioning enjoyment on a beneficiary changing a religious affiliation likely would be an invalid restraint on religious freedom.

The effect of an invalid trust or provision might be any of (1) a resulting trust for the settlor or successors in interest to the settlor, (2) segregation of the invalid condition from the valid provisions to deem it met or as if it did not exist, and (3) application of a clean hands doctrine that denies relief to anyone seeking to enforce the provision, as a way to deter future trusts of a similar variety or to punish culpability.

# CHAPTER 12

# TRUST CREATION

Among the more significant requirements for the creation of a valid trust are that the settlor intended to create a trust and the trust has a corpus. In addition, as a general rule trusts for realty (but not personalty) must be in writing, but the exceptions to that rule are sufficient to question it. More reliable is the requirement that enforceable duties must be created, which means that precatory language (e.g., hope or request) usually fails to create a trust and the transferee instead takes the property free of trust. Furthermore, because enforcement of the trust is essential to its existence, all trusts generally must have at least one beneficiary who is ascertainable and able to enforce the trustee's fiduciary obligations. Exceptions routinely exist for charitable trusts, which are enforceable by the state Attorney General, and under UTC §§408 and 409 (but not most other laws), which recognize trusts for the care of an animal or other noncharitable purposes.

The most common ways to create trusts are by testamentary devise (a testamentary trust), inter vivos transfer (an inter vivos or living trust), and the self-trusteed declaration of trust by which a property owner declares the intent to hold property as trustee. However it is created, a valid trust must have a *legal purpose*, it must clearly manifest the settlor's *intent*, it must impose *active* (versus passive) *duties* on the trustee, generally in favor of ascertainable *beneficiaries*, and it must have an ascertainable trust *corpus* (which requires a settlor with the requisite *capacity* to convey property to fund the trust).

Generally, testamentary trusts and trusts to hold realty require a *written instrument*, but aside from this limited writing requirement there are virtually no formalities for the creation of a trust other than those requirements that property law imposes on the transfer of the trust corpus. The trust document may create additional requirements to amend or revoke the trust, but these are after the fact issues and merely underscore how very different the trust creation rules are from the law of wills (e.g., witnesses generally are not required for the creation of a trust). In addition, we will see that a valid trust may be created without a trustee, because normally a court will appoint a trustee to fill a vacancy, nor is consideration or notice to or acceptance by the trustee or the beneficiaries required.

## Intent and Capacity

A trust cannot be created unless there is a proper manifestation of intent by a competent settlor. For testamentary trusts, the manifestation of intent appears in a valid will. For inter vivos trusts of land, the Statute of Frauds usually requires a written instrument. For other inter vivos trusts, the settlor's intent to create a trust relationship may be manifested orally, in writing, or by conduct.

The capacity required to create a valid trust depends on the nature of the trust created. For example, the settlor must have the capacity to execute a will to create a valid testamentary trust. See Chapter 3. Thus, a testator who had the requisite capacity to execute a valid will has the capacity to create a testamentary trust under that will, absent unusual circumstances (like a derangement that affects a testamentary trust but not the remainder of the will). Surprisingly, there is not much law on what capacity is required to create a valid revocable trust. UTC §601 requires a settlor to possess only testamentary capacity, but inter vivos trusts require a transfer of property. See the discussion of *Farkas v. Williams* in Chapter 6. Accordingly, the somewhat higher capacity necessary to make a valid conveyance of property by inter vivos gift free of trust is required in many non-UTC jurisdictions.

The issue whether a trust was meant to be imposed seldom arises unless the trust was poorly drafted or an alleged trust is oral or secret or both. The important element is that trusts are relationships under which trustees with fiduciary duties hold legal title to property to manage it on behalf of beneficiaries. The requisite intent is to create that relationship. Words like "trustee" or "trust" do not alone create a trust but their presence in a document may indicate an intent to create a trust. Their absence is indicative of nothing. For example, in *Jimenez v. Lee*, 547 P.2d 126 (Or. 1976), a father as a trustee was accountable to his daughter because gifts for the daughter's education, made shortly after her birth, were deemed to be in trust. There were no trust instruments nor any express mention made of the creation of a trust. Trusts nevertheless were created because the transfers were made with the intent that the gifts be held for the benefit of the daughter.

In addition, a valid lifetime gift requires actual, constructive, or symbolic delivery. Most courts will not recharacterize a donor's conduct as a declaration that the donor holds property as trustee for the benefit of a donee if the donor expressed an intent to make a gift but never made a delivery. See, e.g., *The Hebrew University Ass'n v. Nye*, 169 A.2d 641 (Conn. 1961), in which a donor's public declaration that she gave a collection of undelivered rare books to a university did not constitute a declaration of trust because there was no indication that the donor intended to create a trust relationship by assuming fiduciary duties before the books actually were delivered to the university.

### *Precatory Language*

The question is whether a "request" was meant to bind a transferee if a transferor conveys property with a *request* that the transferee use the property in a specified manner. If so (and the other requirements of a valid trust are met) the transferee holds the property as trustee with fiduciary duties to do as "requested." If not, the transferee takes the property as a donee, free of restrictions. Whether precatory language (e.g., desire, hope, wish, recommend, or suggest) in the dispositive provisions of a will or trust is binding creates perhaps the most uncertainty with respect to the intent requirement for the creation of a trust.

Consider several examples.

- "I give the contents of my home to my daughter, with the hope and expectation that she will share them with her brother and sister." This might be meant to create a trust (it is likely the testator intended the daughter to divide the contents among the three), but it likely would be held to be a transfer to the daughter free of trust. This form of disposition illustrates another method some testators use to accomplish the results authorized by the list of tangible personal property that UPC §2-513 addresses, as discussed in Chapter 3.

- "I give $X to my son and request that he pay my sister-in-law $208.33 per month until her death." Notwithstanding the "request," a court might read this as a "polite command" creating a trust and, given the specificity involved, it is sufficiently detailed to be enforceable. (Notice that this language also raises a question of what disposition is to be made of any funds remaining from the original gift after the sister-in-law's death. Likely they belong to the son.)

- "I give Blackacre to my wife, to be her absolute estate forever. I request that she leave the property to my siblings." This hard case probably is not a trust. The gift is absolute, in fee simple. The alleged obligation is in precatory words, and the notion might be that the spouses had discussed how things probably would go when they both were dead. As such, this statement probably just reflects those discussions, leaving it up to the survivor to do what he or she thought was best, given any changes in circumstances between the dates of their deaths. If it were regarded as a trust, however, the surviving spouse would be both trustee and beneficiary for life and would have full power to consume the property for reasonable needs and purposes during life and would be obliged to transfer only the amount that remained at the survivor's death.

In interpreting devises accompanied by precatory language, the usual inference is that the testator left the property to the devisee, unencumbered by a trust, with the intention that the devisee decide whether to follow the suggestion. Factors that may indicate an intent to instead create a trust include:

**(1) Identity of transferee.** Presumably there is an intent to create a trust if the precatory language is directed to an unrelated person. Directing precatory language to a natural object of a decedent's bounty presumably is a gift with no strings attached. However, the same direction to a close relative may be regarded as a polite command, with the possible imposition of a trust.

**(2) Relative size of the purported trust.** Small amounts given to natural objects of the decedent's bounty likely are outright gifts. Large amounts, especially if transferred to someone other than a natural object of the transferor's bounty, more likely are trusts.

**(3) Lifetime gifts.** The precatory language may extend a lifetime pattern of gratuitous transfers.

**(4) Relative financial positions.** The net worth of the purported trustee and beneficiary may indicate a trust if the former is well set and the latter is needy.

**(5) Specificity of language.** The intent to create a trust is more likely to be found if the language is specific enough to enforce as a trust (e.g., there are identifiable beneficiaries, specific terms, and a clearly defined property meant to be held). If not, finding the requisite intent probably will just result in an unenforceable semi-secret trust with a resulting trust back to the settlor's estate. Semi-secret trusts are discussed at page 248.

**(6) The equities.** The presumption against an intent to create a trust when precatory language is used may yield to equitable persuasions. To illustrate, consider that D supported an elderly and needy sibling (X) for several years before D's death. D's will devised the estate to D's spouse (S), with the "request that S continue to provide for X, as S thinks appropriate." D's estate is more than adequate to support S and to provide for X's continued care, particularly because S has significantly more resources than may reasonably be needed for S's future support. Despite the use of the word "request," which usually is deemed to be precatory and therefore not binding, S probably takes D's estate in trust for the combined support of S and X, with a duty to make reasonable provision for X's care.

The precatory language issue is whether the transferor intended to create a trust. Also important is whether an intended trust has terms sufficiently specific to be enforceable. For example, T's will provides: "I give all my personal effects to A, to be distributed as A deems would be my wish." X's will provides: "I give all my personal effects to A, to be disposed of according to the terms of a letter to be found with this will" (and no letter exists). Each potential trust would fail for lack of enforceable terms, even if an intent to create a trust is deemed to exist. Notice, however, that the trustee would not be allowed to keep the property if an intent to create a trust is found. A resulting trust would be imposed if the language is not regarded as precatory, requiring distribution to the residuary beneficiaries of the testator's estate.

## The Trustee

Trusts may have one or more trustees, who may be individuals or entities (such as a corporation). The requisite capacity to act as trustee is only the capacity needed to hold legal title to property. Generally anyone who can hold legal title may be a trustee (which is not, however, to say that just anyone is skillful enough to do the job properly and avoid liability for their inabilities). Note, however, that a minor or mental incompetent can hold legal title and thus *could* serve as trustee, but each also could be removed because of an inability to perform their duties, either permanently or until capacity is gained or restored (depending on the circumstances).

Usually an entity such as a corporation may not serve as a trustee unless it has received a charter or other permission to do so from the appropriate governmental agency. Foreign corporations and similar entities may have problems holding title to property as trustee due to local law limitations on ownership of land by an alien (which, for this purpose, refers to anyone not from within that jurisdiction). Thus, corporate (or similar entity) trustees from one state might not be able to serve in another. Many states have reciprocity statutes under which an out-of-state trustee may serve within the state if their trustees may serve in the other state. Other states may prohibit out-of-state trustees unless there is a resident agent for service of process (which is an easy condition to satisfy).

The settlor may serve as a trustee (e.g., in a self-trusteed declaration of trust), which is very popular with people who want to avoid probate and therefore find a trust attractive during life, but who do not want to relinquish control or incur trustee fees before they become unable to manage their own property. Similarly, a beneficiary may serve as a trustee, although the sole beneficiary of a trust may not serve as its sole trustee (because the legal and beneficial titles would merge and the trust would be extinguished) and tax issues may arise in any case of a beneficially interested trustee.

There is an odd dissonance in trust law that a trust must have a trustee, yet "no trust will fail for lack of a trustee." This might arise if no trustee is named but it is clear that a trust was intended, or if the named trustee is unable or unwilling to act or continue to act. Unless it is absolutely clear that the named trustee was meant to be the one and only (which would be quite rare) a court will appoint a successor trustee if the instrument does not provide for one. UTC §704(c) permits all of the current and first line remainder beneficiaries to appoint a successor trustee without court involvement, but a well drafted trust will provide for succession of trustees or a mechanism to identify and appoint successors. Nevertheless, a court will appoint a successor if a vacancy occurs, either because (1) there is no appointment process designated in the document (or it failed in some respect), (2) the named successors are unable or unwilling to act, (3) those who were designated to select a successor no longer are available to act, (4) the requisite beneficiaries acting under the UTC cannot agree on a successor, and so forth. Thus, "no trust will fail" simply reflects that a court will step in to resolve the lack of trustee issue, except in extraordinary circumstances.

But a trust *must* have a trustee. Property does not care who owns it, but it must *have* an owner, and that is no different with a trust. Someone must own the legal title to trust assets at all times. At a minimum that someone must have a duty to convey it to the next proper trustee or outright owner. Thus, if there is a complete vacancy in the office of trustee, a court must guarantee that the trust assets have an owner. For this reason, typically any resignation of a sole trustee (a voluntary act and not an unavoidable vacancy) is effective only upon conveyance of legal title of the trust assets to a successor trustee. If that is not possible (for example, because a vacancy was not avoidable or voluntary), a constructive trust may be imposed on the last predecessor trustee or successors in interest, to convey the trust corpus to the next trustee once one is appointed. Alternatively, if the trust terminated, a resulting trust would be imposed pending conveyance of the trust property to the proper remainder beneficiary.

Multiple trustees generally must act unanimously to bind the trust, although the instrument may provide otherwise and statutes in some jurisdictions allow a majority to act on behalf of the trust. See UTC §703(a). The remaining trustee(s) continue to hold title to all the trust assets if one of several trustees fails to become or ceases to act, but at common law a successor trustee is required and will be appointed unless the trust expresses a contrary intent by indicating that no successor needs to be named. UTC §704(b) reverses this rule by providing that a successor need not be appointed unless the instrument so requires. In all cases a replacement is required if there is *no* remaining trustee.

Substantial fiduciary duties expose trustees to significant liabilities. As a result, no one can be forced to serve as trustee, and a named trustee need not act. Rather, a designated trustee can decline to serve by timely filing a declination to act, which would be effective to avoid ever putting on the fiduciary mantle. The UTC actually provides that a designated trustee who knows of the designation but does not affirmatively accept the trusteeship within a reasonable time is deemed to have declined to serve. UTC §701(b). A trustee that does not timely or impliedly decline may resign only if authority to resign is granted in the document, a court expressly grants the power to resign, or state law provides authority to resign. For example, UTC §705(a)(1) permits the trustee to resign upon 30 days' notice to the current and first line remainder beneficiaries, the settlor (if living), and all cotrustees. In a non-UTC jurisdiction, this is no small matter because, once undertaken, the fiduciary duty is not easily thrown off.

Removal of trustees for cause is one of several options available to a court in the wake of fiduciary malfeasance or incompetence. Others include reducing or eliminating the trustee's fees or surcharging (imposing damages on) the trustee. Unless the instrument provides otherwise, a trustee generally cannot be removed without a showing of cause, and often, cause sufficient to warrant removal is difficult or impossible to prove. Generally, cause exists if the trustee's service creates a serious risk of loss to the beneficiaries. Among grounds that have been held sufficient to remove a trustee for cause are a material breach of fiduciary duty, conviction of a crime involving dishonesty, and incapacity. Many documents also give someone (a beneficiary or a "trust protector") authority to remove and replace trustees, often based on a list of factors such as too frequent turn-over in the trust officer, takeover of the trustee by another institution, excessive fees, inadequate investment performance, drug addiction or other personal problems of the fiduciary, a move out of state by the beneficiary, and so forth.

UTC §706 permits removal and replacement of a trustee if lack of cooperation among cotrustees substantially impairs administration of the trust. More important, a court may remove a trustee if there has been a substantial change of circumstances, or removal is requested by all of the current and first line remainder beneficiaries. In either case the court must determine that removal best serves the interests of all of the beneficiaries, that removal is not inconsistent with a material purpose of the trust, and that a suitable cotrustee or successor trustee is available.

Unless the document provides otherwise (which it often does, particularly with respect to successor trustee liabilities), cotrustee liabilities are joint and several. This explains why each cotrustee (if they understand their exposure) will charge a full fee (and maybe more), rather than split one fee. Each is fully responsible. Indeed each is responsible for the other's mistakes too — this is joint and several instead of shared responsibility. In this regard UTC §703(f) and (g) reverse the traditional rules by providing that a trustee is not liable for a cotrustee's mistakes unless (1) the trustee participated in the mistake, (2) the trustee failed to exercise reasonable care to prevent the cotrustee from committing a serious breach, or (3) the trustee failed to redress a serious breach that already was committed.

Moreover, successor trustee liabilities exist for any failure to redress improper acts of a predecessor trustee. This explains why a successor will charge a fee for accepting a trust. The successor must inspect the accounts of the predecessor to be sure it receives all it should or sues for any losses, mismanagement, etc. attributable to the predecessor. UTC §812 also relaxes these rules by making a successor trustee responsible only for breaches that the successor knows a former trustee committed.

The doctrine of merger applies if the sole beneficiary is sole trustee. A trustee cannot sue itself to enforce the trust, meaning the trust fails. Legal and equitable title become one ("merge") and the trust automatically ceases to exist. A self-trusteed declaration of trust is one in which the settlor, trustee, and beneficiary are all the same at inception, which would suggest that the trust should fail or collapse due to merger. It will not, however, *if* there is at least one other beneficiary, as there almost always will be (because the trust names persons to take upon the settlor's death, hence its status as a "will substitute"). The interest of even a contingent future interest beneficiary at the settlor's death is enough to preclude merger and failure. Furthermore, a sole beneficiary may be one of several cotrustees because trustees hold title as joint tenants, meaning that a total merger cannot occur even if a trustee is the only beneficiary. In addition, although the legal justification is a bit hazy, a cobeneficiary may be a sole trustee because, absent a partition, the cobeneficiaries cannot purport to possess any appropriate fraction of the equitable title, so there will be no merger even with respect to an undivided fraction of the trust. Finally, cobeneficiaries may act as cotrustees because their titles as trustee (joint tenants) and beneficiary (tenants in common) differ and therefore cannot merge.

Adverse tax consequences may result from a settlor or a beneficiary serving as a trustee, depending on the powers they possess as trustee. Worse, these consequences cannot be avoided by naming a third party as trustee, if the settlor or beneficiary may remove the third party and name him or her self as successor trustee. Indeed, for tax purposes the power to succeed to the trustee's power will be treated as exercised already if there is no impediment to its exercise.

## Trust Property

The essence of the trust relationship is that title to property is bifurcated. The trustee holds the legal title, subject to a fiduciary obligation to manage it on behalf of the beneficiary, who holds the equitable or beneficial title. Accordingly, generally there must be an ascertainable corpus or principal to have a valid trust. A trust can exist (temporarily) with no trustee and with beneficiaries to be identified in the future, but generally there cannot be a dry trust (one with no property).

In addition, a trust becomes a passive trust once it has completed its purpose and no longer has a function to serve. It must distribute its property and then cease to exist by virtue of becoming a dry trust. For example, D devised property to T, in trust, to provide for the education of A and B. At termination the trust is distributable equally between them. B completed law school, after which A completed medical school. The purpose of the trust has been accomplished if A and B have completed their educations. T has no further duties to perform (meaning that the trust is passive), the assets will be distributed equally to A and B, and the trust will become dry and thereby terminate.

The ascertainable corpus requirement can be a slippery concept. The existence of a corpus must be ascertainable, but neither the value, duration, nor the extent of the property need be. The trustee must own something to prevent existence of a totally dry trust, which would terminate, but that something does not need to be much. A viable trust property interest may be a present or a future interest, with vested or contingent title, legal or equitable ownership (a trust can be the beneficiary of another trust), in real or personal property. So this corpus hurdle is not particularly high. Nevertheless, the settlor's expectation of owning property in the future cannot constitute the corpus of a trust. Thus, for example, there is no trust corpus and no valid trust if child C executes a trust instrument under which C purports to hold in trust for the benefit of a third party part or all of the property C expects to inherit from a living parent. Upon the death of C's parent, however, any rights of C to a share of the parent's estate may become a trust asset and validate the trust at that time.

To further illustrate, assume that Author intends to write a book but has no contract with a publisher to do so. If there were such a contract, Author's rights under it could constitute the corpus of a trust. Nevertheless, Author agrees to hold in trust any royalties from the sale in the future of the book that has not been written. The expectation of receiving royalties in the future cannot be trust property. But any future royalties may become trust assets when they spring into existence if the trust otherwise is valid, and if it is funded with something (e.g., $1) to support it between the time Author executes the trust and the time Author actually earns a royalty. This further requires that (1) a valid contract right exists, supported by consideration, between Author and the trust (which is not likely), or (2) a reaffirmation of intent to entrust the royalties occurs when they come into existence. Often inaction will suffice if the trustee treats the asset as belonging to the trust and no one objects. To reaffirm, Author probably would need to endorse the royalty check and then hold the proceeds in a trust capacity (e.g., in a separate bank account titled in the name of the trust).

For example, *In re Estate of Brenner*, 547 P.2d 938 (Colo. Ct. App. 1976), involved a declaration of trust by a settlor, of real property that the settlor did not own at the time of the declaration. The property, however, was acquired shortly after the declaration, with title being taken in the name of the settlor, as trustee. In rejecting a challenge to the trust, the court held that acquisition of the property in the name of the trust validated the trust: "Where, as here, an individual manifests an intention to create a trust in property to be acquired in the future, and thereafter confirms this intent by taking the steps necessary to transfer the property to the trust, the property so transferred becomes subject to the terms of the trust."

*Brainard v. Commissioner*, 91 F.2d 880 (7th Cir. 1937), an income tax case, is consistent with *Brenner*. In *Brainard* the taxpayer orally declared a trust of any stock trading profits he might earn in the next year. Profits were earned the next year and they were reported for income tax purposes by the trust beneficiaries. The issue whether the taxpayer, instead, was taxable on the income turned on whether unearned profits expected from future stock trading could be held in trust on behalf of the taxpayer's family members. According to the court, an interest that has not come into existence cannot be held in trust. The declaration to do so for the unearned stock trading profits amounted to no more than an unenforceable (for lack of consideration) promise to create a trust in the future. The profits thus belonged to the taxpayer when earned and were taxable to him. The trust, however, did not fail. Rather, as the profits were earned, the taxpayer credited them on his books to accounts for the beneficiaries, which was a sufficient manifestation of intent to cause the profits to become trust assets at that time. But the timing precluded the taxpayer's effort to shift the tax liability for those profits to the trust.

The trust clearly would have been valid before the sales if the taxpayer in *Brainard* had declared that he held the stock itself, and not just the profits he expected to earn from the stock, in trust for others for a specified term. The stock would have constituted the corpus and the tax objective of taxing the profits to the trust would have been achieved. (Also note that *Brainard* was a 1937 case. Such a course of action might not succeed under current tax law to shift the income earned during the trust term to the trust or its beneficiaries for income tax purposes.)

Let's try another example. A orally declares that A is the trustee for B of a percentage of the royalties A expects to earn on a book A is writing. A writes the book, sells it, and begins receiving royalties, but refuses to hold any of them in trust for B. If there is no delivery of a written assignment, the oral statement likely would be viewed as one of intent to make a gift in the future and not a valid trust creation. Usually there is no delivery requirement for declarations of trust. If A declares to hold a painting in trust for B, a valid trust is created. But when the subject of the gift in trust is property not yet in existence, a delivery requirement (in the form of a writing) may be imposed. At a minimum, there should be a valid trust if A sufficiently manifests a reaffirmation of the intent to hold a percentage of the royalties in trust for B after the book is written and there are royalties. But there probably is no trust without such a manifestation of intent, made after the royalties come into existence.

One of the more difficult issues in this area involves an unfunded life insurance trust (i.e., a trust is created today. No assets are transferred to it, but it is named as the beneficiary of a life insurance policy). Is that trust supportable under the trust property requirement? Most courts would regard an unfunded life insurance trust as valid because the beneficiary designation under the policy is deemed adequate to create a present interest (subject to defeasance on change of the beneficiary designation or lapse of the policy) sufficient to constitute the trust corpus. The Comments to UPC §2-511 and UTC §401 note that the contract right to the proceeds of the policy on the insured's death is the trust corpus. The UPC Comment opines that the term "unfunded life insurance trust" is a misnomer: "the term 'unfunded life-insurance trust' does not refer to an unfunded trust, but to a funded trust that has not received *additional* funding." Nevertheless, just to be safe, many lawyers will fund an insurance trust with a Series EE U.S. Government savings bond (or its $25 purchase price) to guarantee that there is a corpus. It is a prudent investment and requires no investment management or other active administration. You just hold the bond until it matures (and thereafter if you want), earning interest that accrues and requires no action, so no fee and no liability is incurred during the interim, waiting for the insurance to mature and pay proceeds to the trust.

An exception to the requirement that a trust must have a corpus is found in the Uniform Testamentary Additions to Trust Act. A trust named as the devisee under the settlor's will is valid, as is the actual pour over from the settlor's estate under the will, all without regard to whether the trust is funded with any assets prior to the settlor's death. See Chapter 6.

Of real practical import is a rule that a trustee cannot hold its own debt obligation without special authorization. For example, assume S executes a trust instrument naming T as trustee for B, funded with

Blackacre. Later, T sells Blackacre to S for its fair market value, S paying with S's promissory note, payable two years later. This is no problem because S's debt obligation is property that T can enforce. But if T ceased to serve as trustee and S became the successor trustee, S's note no longer could be trust property because S cannot sue S to enforce it. Instead, the debt is said to be extinguished by merger because a trustee cannot sue itself to collect on its own obligation. This would result in an obvious unjust enrichment to the trustee (S, in this example), which would generate a resulting trust with a court appointed "trustee to collect" charged with the duty to force S to pay the debt. Corporate trustees would encounter this problem regularly with respect to deposits they make of uninvested trust cash in their own banking department were it not for authority granted by a Comptroller of the Currency regulation. Required is a security deposit by the trustee of its own marketable securities or U.S. government bonds equal to the amount of the cash deposit (reduced by the amount of any deposits that are FDIC insured). Merger technically occurs, but the trust has a right to an equitable remedy in the form of the security interest, and this prevents extinguishment by merger.

## Necessity of a Trust Beneficiary

The beneficiaries are the persons or entities for whose benefit property is held in trust. Although a trust may have just one beneficiary (as long as that beneficiary is not the sole trustee), the great majority of trusts have multiple beneficiaries, often seriatim. A trust beneficiary may have a present interest in the trust (e.g., "income to A for life") or a future interest (e.g., "remainder to B"), and the interest may be vested or contingent (e.g., "but if B does not survive A, remainder to C").

Anyone with capacity to hold title (the equitable interest) may be a trust beneficiary, including minors, incompetents, entities like charities, corporations, and partnerships and, depending on their status under state law, foreign corporations and individual aliens. The most significant trust beneficiary issue is whether a trust *has* at least one ascertainable beneficiary, able to enforce the trust. Without at least one beneficiary there can be no bifurcation of title and no one to whom the trustee's duties run. For example, in *Clark v. Campbell*, 133 A. 166 (N.H. 1926), the testator devised various items of tangible personal property to his "trustees" to be distributed by them to "such of my friends as they, my trustees, shall select." The trust failed and the gift was ineffective because the beneficiaries of the trust were not objectively ascertainable. UTC §402(c) rejects the traditional *Clark* rule and instead permits the settlor to grant power to the trustee to select the beneficiaries from an indefinite class. The trust fails if the trustee fails to exercise the power within a reasonable time, in which case the property "passes to the persons who would have taken the property had the power not been conferred."

It is not necessary to specifically identify each beneficiary of a trust. Beneficiaries often are described by class (e.g., "my children") and may include future-borns as well as living persons. Unless a statute such as UTC §402(c) is in effect, a problem arises if a class of beneficiaries is named but it is not possible to determine objectively any members of the class. Granting discretion to a trustee to select beneficiaries from a class of members who are not objectively ascertainable is not objectionable because the trustee has discretion. Instead, it is problematic if the discretion is too broad to be enforced. Sufficiently narrow classes of potential beneficiaries include descendants, employees (at a certain time), and heirs (if the designated ancestor is deceased). "Relatives" is problematic. It may be construed to mean heirs, in which case it might be an ascertainable class (but remember that there are no heirs to the living), but if it is construed to mean anyone related to the settlor, no matter how remotely, the trust likely would fail for indefiniteness of beneficiaries absent a statute such as UTC §402(c).

Consider also how "family," "friends," "anyone the trustee may wish to select," or "those the trustee knows the settlor would have wanted" would be enforced if the designated trustee is unable or unwilling to serve and a replacement is required to exercise this discretion. And how would a court review the exercise even by the original trustee if other individuals claim that they should have been selected? For these reasons, such classes should not be used. They invite disputes and, as in *Clark*, likely would result in trust failure in a non-UTC jurisdiction. There is no problem if the trustee selects (and no one objects). The issue arises if the trustee refuses to select the beneficiaries (typically coupled with a claim that the trustee is entitled to retain the "trust" property), or if the settlor's successors in interest (those who would take the property if the trust fails) challenge its validity. A major trust law principle is that a court will not exercise discretion on behalf of a trustee. Instead, the court only will judge whether the trustee properly exercised the discretion granted. Therefore, required are sufficient guidelines or standards for a court to exercise its review (in this context, for the selection of beneficiaries). Because UTC §402(c) runs counter to this traditional doctrine, presumably a court will be very deferential in reviewing the appropriateness of any exercise if a trustee's selection of a beneficiary from an indefinite class is challenged.

Trustee discretion to select beneficiaries is in some respects not different in function from a power of appointment in a beneficiary or fiduciary powers to distribute income or corpus. See Chapter 14. The difficulty is that these similar powers need not be exercised, but the selection of beneficiaries is imperative. Also, if a fiduciary power to distribute income or corpus is involved, the beneficiaries to whom distributions may be made may enforce the trustee's obligation to exercise the discretion reasonably and in good faith. By contrast, there is no one to enforce the trust if the discretion is to select the beneficiaries in the first place. UTC §402(c) avoids this problem by granting standing to enforce exercise or relinquishment of the power to those who would have received the property if the power had not been conferred.

To illustrate, assume that D devised property to T, in trust, for Spouse (S) and Child (C) for S's life. The instrument directed T to distribute income to S and authorized T to make discretionary distributions of principal to S and C to provide for their best interests. D's will also granted S a testamentary power to appoint the takers of the property remaining in the trust at S's death. Property as to which S did not exercise the power is distributable to D's then living descendants, by representation. T is not required to exercise the discretionary power to invade principal. Failure to do so simply results in the principal being preserved for distribution at S's death. Similarly, S is not required to exercise the testamentary power of appointment. Failure to do so results in the property passing at S's death to D's descendants. But if D's will had devised the property to T, in trust, with distribution at S's death to those persons T believes D would have wanted to benefit, T would be required to select the beneficiaries and there would be no way for a court objectively to determine who the beneficiaries should be and thus who could enforce the trust. Accordingly, in a non-UTC jurisdiction the remainder interest in that trust would fail.

The trustees in *Clark* argued unsuccessfully that their power to select the takers of the testator's tangible personal property should be valid as a power of appointment. The court regarded the trustees as holding an imperative power to select beneficiaries. This is a "power coupled with a trust," which is unlike a simple power of appointment because it *must* be exercised. As a result, the trust principle that there must be an ascertainable beneficiary applied and the trust/imperative power failed. With a simple power of appointment, not coupled with a trust, a failure to appoint simply causes trust corpus to pass to "default" beneficiaries designated by the creator of the power in the document or provided by court order, through a resulting trust. See Chapter 14. In any case (including under UTC §402(c)) the trustee would not be allowed to keep the trust property.

Similar to UTC §402(c), ascertainable beneficiaries are not required by the Restatement (Third) of Trusts, which provides that a trust for an indefinite class of beneficiaries is valid if the trustee chooses to act, its acts are not outside the scope of its discretion, and the class is sufficiently definite to ascertain whether any person falls within it. But this is not yet the majority position and the standard rule is that there must be an enforceable identification of the beneficiaries. Furthermore, even under the Restatement, a court will order a resulting trust for the testator's residuary beneficiaries if the trustee is not willing to act, or attempts to use the trust funds for other purposes. Thus, in a non-UTC jurisdiction the effect if no ascertainable beneficiaries are named is a failure of the trust and a resulting trust for the settlor or his or her successors in interest. The property is returned, the sole obligation under the resulting trust being distribution of the trust corpus to the settlor or to the settlor's successors in interest.

An exception of sorts to all of this is a charitable trust, which does not need ascertainable beneficiaries. This is because the public is considered the beneficiary of a charitable trust, with its rights enforceable by the state Attorney General. See Chapter 13. At the other end of the spectrum are honorary trusts (e.g., for the care of a pet or a grave site or for the erection of a monument, the trust being "honorary" because the trustee is on its honor to comply, there being no human who can enforce the trust). Because their purposes are viewed as worthy of protection, these trusts also are an exception to the rule requiring an ascertainable beneficiary. But the theory is that the trust is valid only *if* the trustee chooses to comply. Silly as all this may seem, this is not a minor problem. Many people attempt to create mechanisms to provide for their surviving pets (their legal dependents, if any, having grown up and become self-supporting). Indeed, this is so common that there are state and federal inheritance and income tax rulings involving these trusts.

To illustrate, *In re Searight's Estate*, 95 N.E.2d 779 (Ohio Ct. App. 1950), involved two gifts by a testator—one of his dog, Trixie, to Florence, and a second of $1,000 in trust, from which Florence was to be paid $0.75 per day for Trixie's care. This trust was upheld by the court. It was not an honorary trust because Trixie was given to a person who was made the trust beneficiary and who therefore could sue to enforce the trust. That is the key. An added advantage would exist if the trustee was directed to oversee the individual's care of the pet and to place the pet with a different individual (who then would become the trust beneficiary) if necessary.

UTC §§408 and 409 permit settlors to create trusts with no ascertainable beneficiaries (for the care of pets and for other noncharitable purposes). Enforcement is addressed by allowing the settlor (or a court if necessary) to appoint someone to enforce the trust. Trusts for the care of animals may be validly created only for pets alive during the settlor's life, and only for the life of the pets. Trusts without ascertainable beneficiaries for other noncharitable purposes may be enforced for up to 21 years.

Another exception to the rule that a trust will fail without an ascertainable beneficiary exists if the trust is for unborns and a possibility of birth or adoption exists that would solve the lack of beneficiary problem. A resulting trust (enforceable by the settlor or the settlor's successors) would be maintained pending the birth or adoption of a child, probably to accumulate income while awaiting the existence of a beneficiary. Once beneficiaries are born or adopted, the trust is then held for those beneficiaries, according to the trust terms. The resulting trust would terminate by distribution to the settlor or his or her successors in interest if the possibility for births or adoptions expires without a beneficiary having been generated (e.g., if the trust is for the settlor's grandchildren and there are none, then on the death of the last of the settlor's children).

A final exception may apply to the rare case in which no beneficiaries are named because the trustee refuses to exercise its authority to select, but a definite and reasonably small class of potential beneficiaries exists, in which case an implied default or power in trust may cause the class from which the trustee could select to be given equal shares. See Chapter 14.

## Notice or Acceptance

The following is subject to the reality that someone must know something about a purported trust or the notice and acceptance issues never will surface. A trust can be validly created without prior notice to any trustee. A court will appoint a trustee if necessary. Similarly, validity is not dependent on a beneficiary having notice of the trust or accepting benefits under it. If the settlor also is the trustee, however, the failure to notify any beneficiary of the trust may evidence the settlor's lack of intent to create a present trust. Moreover, if a named trust beneficiary refuses to accept the beneficial interest, usually by disclaiming it, the interest will pass according to the terms of the instrument that created the trust, if it addresses that possibility, or under applicable state law if it does not. See Chapter 2. Ultimately a resulting trust for the settlor or the settlor's successors in interest would arise if no beneficiary accepts the beneficial interest.

## Oral Trusts

The great majority of trusts are created by written instrument. In some circumstances, however, a writing is not required to create a valid trust. The Statute of Wills prohibits use of extrinsic evidence to alter or establish a testamentary trust of *either* realty or personalty. As a result, a testamentary trust may be validly created only by the terms of a validly executed will. But the Statute of Frauds only prohibits use of extrinsic evidence to establish or prove an oral trust of *realty*. Thus, an inter vivos trust of personalty may be created orally.

Under either the Statute of Wills (to create a valid testamentary trust), or the Statute of Frauds (to create a valid trust of realty), the only requirement is a signed writing identifying the trust property, purposes, and beneficiaries. Absent fraud, duress, undue influence, mistake, or similar grounds, extrinsic evidence is admissible only to the extent it does not contradict any express terms of a testamentary trust. Otherwise extrinsic evidence cannot be used to vary the expressly stated intent. Unlike the case with a will, however, extrinsic evidence generally is admissible to prove a mistake in a trust and to reform the document to correct it. See Chapter 7.

Extrinsic evidence of fraud, duress, or undue influence also is admissible. A trust may fail if it is proven that it was created under any of those circumstances. Alternatively, depending on the circumstances, a court may choose to enforce such a trust even without a writing that otherwise would be required. Note that a court may review extrinsic evidence offered to establish whether there was a fraud or another basis for enforcing the oral trust, but then ignore the offered evidence if the court determines that there was not. But consider how well a court that has heard the evidence for the one purpose then puts it out of mind for purposes of the balance of a case.

Finally, as with wills, extrinsic evidence also is admissible to resolve latent ambiguities in trust instruments, and usually is admissible to resolve patent ambiguities as well. See Chapter 7.

There are exceptions to the general Statute of Frauds rule that a trust of realty will not be enforced without a writing. In *Hieble v. Hieble*, 316 A.2d 777 (Conn. 1972), for example, a mother who had recently undergone surgery and believed she might be terminally ill transferred real estate to her son and daughter as joint tenants subject to an oral agreement that she would remain in control of the property, and that if her condition improved they would reconvey the property to her at her request. When requested to reconvey, the daughter complied but the son refused. In upholding the trust, the court avoided the Statute of Frauds by creating a constructive trust, to prevent the son's overreaching and unjust enrichment, based on the confidential relationship between the settlor and her son. See Chapter 11 for a discussion of constructive trusts. But compare *Pappas v. Pappas,* 320 A.2d 809 (Conn. 1973), in which a father conveyed realty to his son in anticipation of the father's divorce from a second spouse. In the divorce proceedings the father testified that the conveyance to the son was for consideration. The son originally agreed to reconvey after the divorce but refused to comply. The father's subsequent suit to recover the property was unsuccessful because he had unclean hands as a result of his misrepresentation to the divorce court of the nature of the transfer to his son. The court merely refused to grant the equitable remedy of a constructive trust.

In several other circumstances an oral trust of realty may be valid despite the Statute of Frauds and the Statute of Wills. For example, the absence of a writing does not invalidate the purported trust if the trustee chooses to comply, because only the holder of legal title (the trustee) may assert the defense of the Statute of Wills or of the Statute of Frauds. So, if O conveys Blackacre to T, subject to an oral agreement that T will hold it in trust for B, the trust is valid if T agrees to do so. T may decline to assert the Statute of Frauds. Note, however, that the trust would fail if the gift had been in the form of a devise under O's will, with no mention made in the will of the trust for B. See the discussion of secret trusts at page 247.

A legal titleholder also may be estopped to assert the defense of the Statute of Frauds or the Statute of Wills if a beneficiary acts in reliance on the purported trust. And in all cases any waiver of the defense must occur while the legal titleholder still has the title. To illustrate, in the last example, T could not assert the defense of the Statute of Frauds as a bar to B's suit if T sold the property to X for its fair market value and B then sued T for breach. Nor could T defeat the sale to X by later asserting that T could not sell because T was only a trustee or that T did not have title because the purported trust was invalid due to the Statute of Frauds.

There also may be a dodge to the oral trust issue if there was an agreement by the trustee to convert realty into other trust investments. This is not because a promised conversion will upgrade an otherwise voidable trust. Instead, it is because the promise to convert on its own may be enforceable in contract and that promise could be the valid corpus of an enforceable trust.

Grounds for imposition of a constructive trust in favor of intended beneficiaries include fraud, duress, misrepresentation, undue influence, constructive fraud, etc. In these cases the Statute of Frauds is no bar and extrinsic evidence is admissible if a settlor attempts to create orally a trust of realty and the trustee refuses to comply. In other cases, a resulting trust in favor of the settlor or successors in interest may be the relief available if it is clear that a trust was intended. Sometimes, however, a resulting trust is not the remedy of choice, because the trustee is an heir of the decedent who benefits by refusing to perform the trust, or because the heirs paid the trustee to refuse to perform the trust. Cases like these are messy and produce inconsistent results, all of them equity driven.

To illustrate, assume that S has no descendants and that S's sole heir is N. S creates an inter vivos trust into which S transfers Blackacre, and executes a pour over will under which S's probate assets, if any, are devised to the trust. S serves as the sole trustee, but the instrument designates N as successor trustee. The trust instrument further provides that, at S's death, the trust corpus is distributable to N. Extrinsic evidence shows that S intended that Blackacre be held in trust for the benefit of third parties and that S discussed that trust with N. A constructive trust likely would be imposed if the extrinsic evidence also shows that the trust was not properly set out in the instrument due to N's fraud, misrepresentation, undue influence, or duress. The likely remedy would be a resulting trust in favor of S's estate if there was no wrongful conduct by N, who instead simply refused to comply with the oral trust. The problem with that result is that Blackacre would pass to N as S's heir. Note that, for these purposes, a trustee's refusal to comply with an oral trust is not fraud. Nevertheless, a court would likely impose a constructive trust for the intended third parties, given the enrichment to N that otherwise would result from N's refusal to enforce the trust S intended.

If a trustee refuses to comply with an oral trust of realty, a third alternative is for the trustee to keep the property in an individual capacity. This would be quite unusual. For example, assume that S conveys Greyacre (commercial real estate) in fee simple absolute to T, with an oral agreement that T will hold it in trust for B and lease it to X. Unbeknownst to T, the plan of S, X, and B is for Greyacre to be used for the conduct of criminal activities. T refuses to comply with the oral trust when T learns of the criminal activity being conducted on the premises, and terminates the lease to X. T may be allowed to retain title to Greyacre, individually, because of the unclean hands of S and B.

## Secret and Semi-Secret Trusts

"Secret" trusts arise when a devise that appears on its face to be outright to one person is made subject to a separate (usually oral) agreement that the recipient will hold it for the benefit of another. By contrast, with a "semi-secret" trust it is clear from the devise itself that the taker is to receive it in trust, but the beneficiaries of the trust or its other terms are not stated. These cases often also involve elements of unenforceable discretion. For example, D's will devised Blackacre to T. Before death D secured T's promise to hold Blackacre for B's benefit until a serious problem with B's creditors was resolved and then to distribute Blackacre to B. The trust would be secret if there was no mention of a trust in D's will. The trust would be semi-secret if D's will devised Blackacre to T, "to keep until it is safe to deliver it to the person T knows I want to have it." In that case we would know from the devise that it is meant to be in trust, rather than to T outright, but the will does not name the beneficiary of the trust or the terms for its administration.

Recall the discussion in Chapter 7 of the distinction between patent and latent ambiguities. The analogy is to a latent ambiguity in a secret trust. Extrinsic evidence may be allowed to prove the alleged settlor's intent to establish a trust (and preclude the recipient from being unjustly enriched). Once this door is open, all other extrinsic evidence needed to prove the terms and beneficiaries then may be admitted. By contrast, the analogy is to a patent ambiguity in a semi-secret trust. The intent to create a trust is clear and there is no need to consider any extrinsic evidence to prove that intent or to prevent the recipient from being unjustly enriched. Because the extrinsic evidence door is not opened, no other extrinsic evidence would be admitted either. Thus, for example, in *Olliffe v. Wells*, 130 Mass. 221 (1881), the testator's will devised the residue of her estate to Reverend Wells "to distribute the same in such manner as in his discretion shall appear best calculated to carry out wishes which I have expressed to him or may express to him." The intent to entrust is clear but not the purpose or any of the specifics regarding trust beneficiaries or operation. The result was a semi-secret trust that failed and the residue simply passed back to the decedent's heirs by resulting trust.

It may be necessary to distinguish between semi-secret trusts and outright gifts in which precatory language is used. With the former, the testator's intent is to create a trust, which fails (not because of a lack of intent) because of a lack of specified terms (usually including the identity of the beneficiaries, as was the case in *Clark v. Campbell*, discussed at page 240). With the latter, the testator's intent is to make an outright gift. The "terms" the testator wants the recipient to follow may be set forth in the instrument, but the intent is for those terms to be only a request, not an enforceable trust.

In any secret or semi-secret trust, the corpus must be disposed of. To prevent unjust enrichment, clearly a court should not allow the intended trustee to keep it. There are two options: a resulting trust for the settlor or the settlor's successors in interest, or a constructive trust for the intended beneficiaries. Secret trusts often are enforced by way of a constructive trust for the intended beneficiaries because extrinsic evidence is necessarily admissible in the first instance to prove that a trust was intended rather than an outright gift and to prevent the recipient from being unjustly enriched. Once extrinsic evidence is admitted for that purpose, it also is admitted to establish and allow enforcement of the terms of the intended trust. By contrast, extrinsic evidence is not needed to prevent unjust enrichment if the trust is semi-secret. Instead, it is clear from the document itself that the gift was not outright and extrinsic evidence is not needed to establish that proposition, nor will it be admitted to prove the intended terms of the trust. Thus, there often will be a resulting trust in favor of the settlor or successors in interest with a semi-secret trust that fails.

Of the two options, Professor Scott argues that a resulting trust for the settlor or the settlor's successors in interest is more legitimate for *both* secret and semi-secret trusts. 5 Scott & Fratcher, The Law of Trusts §462.1 at 313 (4th ed. 1989):

Although the distinction between a constructive trust and an express trust is clear, it is more difficult to draw the line between constructive trusts and resulting trusts. It would seem, however, that a resulting trust arises where property is transferred under circumstances that raise an inference that the person who makes the transfer or causes it to be made does not intend the transferee to take the beneficial interest in the property. In the case of the resulting trust, as in the case of an express trust, the intention of the parties is of importance. But in the case of a resulting trust that intention is not so much an intention to create a trust as an intention not to give to another the beneficial interest, and it is an intention that appears from the character of the transfer rather than from direct evidence of the intention of the parties. On the other hand, a constructive trust is not based upon the intention of the parties but is imposed in order to prevent unjust enrichment.

The Restatement position is that constructive trusts for the intended beneficiaries should be imposed for semi-secret as well as secret trusts, and that extrinsic evidence be admissible in each case. As you might imagine from this disparity, state law is difficult to predict. As a practical matter, often the solution to the settlor's desire to accomplish an intent like that of the testator in *Olliffe* is to create powers of appointment. We will study these in Chapter 14. And, because we approach you as a future estate planner rather than a litigator in cases like this, the planning message of this secret and semi-secret trust segment is clear. Don't be shy about articulating the terms of the trusts your clients intend to create. After all, trusts are not the subject of public record when they are not part of the probate court's jurisdiction. Create the trust inter vivos and avoid the need for secrecy if a trust purpose is sensitive.

# CHAPTER 13

# TRUST OPERATION

Trust operational issues addressed in this Chapter include the rights of beneficiaries and creditors of beneficiaries in discretionary trusts, support trusts, spendthrift trusts, and Medicaid qualifying trusts. Also relevant are rules governing the modification or termination of trusts, and issues that are peculiar to charitable trusts.

## Discretionary Trusts

Most trusts provide for distributions of income, principal, or both, all in the trustee's discretion. The following example is typical:

> To T, in trust, to pay income and principal to A in T's sole discretion, adding any undistributed income to principal. After A has reached age 25 T shall pay the income to A and may distribute principal to A in T's discretion for A's health, education, maintenance, and support in reasonable comfort. A may withdraw any part of the trust after reaching age 35. If A dies before withdrawing the full corpus, any remaining trust assets shall be distributed at A's death as A directs by will pursuant to a nongeneral power of appointment, and any corpus not effectively appointed shall be distributed to A's then living descendants, or if none to the XYZ Charity.

This trust is discretionary with respect to both income and principal until A reaches age 25, after which it is mandatory with respect to income and discretionary with respect to principal. It would be mandatory with respect to principal if the trust required distributions to A when A attained a certain age. The trust is not as discretionary as it would be if the trustee's discretion was not tied to the objective standard (for health, education, maintenance, or support) or on any other triggering event.

A discretionary trust may have one or many beneficiaries, one or more trustees, or any combination of trustees and beneficiaries. Although not common, a trust may be discretionary with respect to one or more beneficiaries and mandatory with respect to others. For instance, in the example above, if the trust instrument also provided for a monthly distribution of $1,000 (indexed for inflation if desirable) to D's elderly dependent relative, the trust would be discretionary with respect to A and mandatory with respect to D's relative.

The example above does not illustrate a trust in which the trustee has complete discretion over distributions, with no standards to guide or limit the trustee's exercise of that discretion. Even that kind of discretion would be subject to a degree of judicial review, and most well-drafted trusts provide for discretionary distributions of income or principal or both for one or more specific purposes, such as for the beneficiary's best interests, health, education, maintenance, support, welfare, or similar constraints. Trustee discretion of whatever latitude must be exercised in good faith for the trust purposes and courts generally will review a trustee's exercise of discretion under a reasonableness standard unless otherwise expressly provided by the trust terms.

Although there was some doubt historically, it is well established today that trust beneficiaries own their equitable interests rather than merely having a chose in action to enforce them. In this respect the beneficial interest is like any other asset that a person can own, enjoy, or incur taxes on. Thus, subject to any spendthrift limitation, the beneficial interest is both assignable by the beneficiary and attachable by the beneficiary's creditors. If a beneficiary's interest survives the beneficiary's death (which usually is not the case) it passes to the beneficiary's heirs or devisees. And perhaps most important, the beneficiary's interest is entitled to protection against waste, fraudulent transfer, trustee malfeasance, and other harm or wrongdoing. Thus, although a trustee may have broad discretion over distributions to a beneficiary, it only appears that the beneficiary owns nothing that is capable of conveyance, taxation, or enforcement. In fact, the beneficial interest has more substance because trustee discretion is subject to certain constraints and cannot be excessive. For example, no amount of discretion given to a trustee exempts the trustee from judicial supervision.

A trust document may exonerate the trustee from surcharge liability, but it cannot relieve the trustee from acting consistent with its overall fiduciary obligation to exercise good faith for a proper purpose and without caprice or arbitrariness. As a result, a court *always* has the power to review a fiduciary's performance and, if appropriate, to impose sanctions or exact remedies for violation of the terms of the document and other fundamental fiduciary obligations. In *Briggs v. Crowley*, 224 N.E.2d 417 (Mass. 1967), for example, language in a trust purporting to relieve the trustees of the duty to account to anyone was invalid as against public policy. The trustees were required to faithfully perform their duties under the trust, which could not deprive the court of jurisdiction nor the beneficiaries of standing to enforce that obligation.

A court may remedy a breach of fiduciary duty by (1) directing the trustee to perform or desist from certain actions, (2) removing and replacing the trustee, (3) surcharging the fiduciary (assessing damages), or (4) denying the fiduciary's compensation (a lesser remedy). The remedies available to a court to redress fiduciary breaches may be limited by an exoneration or an exculpation provision in the trust. The former provides that the trustee will be repaid by the trust estate for any amounts assessed against it, and the latter essentially holds the trustee harmless for enumerated actions (or failures to act). Either protection usually will not be effective if the fiduciary is deemed to have breached its duties recklessly, in bad faith, or by dishonest acts. The Restatement (Second) of Trusts §222, comment d, lists factors that may be considered in determining the validity of an exoneration provision, particularly including whether the trustee drafted the trust provision (which is not uncommon with banks that promulgate their own trust forms) and whether the settlor was independently advised (which is not always the case, some banks helping settlors create trusts without the interference, input, or assistance of an attorney). See the similar approach in UTC §1008.

Somewhat difficult to reconcile with the rule that a trustee's conduct always is subject to judicial review is the principle that a court will not substitute its discretion for that of the trustee. The exercise of discretion in the administration of a trust is not a court's function, and the trustee presumably has special skills that made it appropriate for the settlor to repose discretion in the trustee. Nevertheless, although a court will not substitute its judgment for that of the trustee, a court may review what the trustee has done (or refrained from doing) and determine whether there has been an abuse of discretion that requires judicial action. That is, a court will not act affirmatively with respect to an exercise of the trustee's discretion in the first instance, but it *will* second guess the trustee in reviewing its exercise of discretion. Further, in reviewing a trustee's exercise of discretion over distributions, a court may conclude that the trustee acted too parsimoniously in the past. If so, the usual remedy is merely to require it to be less so in the future, rather than to order it to distribute amounts that it would have paid out if its discretion had been exercised properly. And the court is not likely to direct the trustee's discretion going forward (although it might note that a certain minimum distribution is required).

Thus seen, trustee discretion can be pretty close to a blank check, subject to little restraint or oversight. A settlor might grant broad discretion to a trustee because the settlor *trusts* the fiduciary to do what the settlor would do if still living. The discretionary trust provides flexibility, like an extension of the settlor's pocketbook. We will see a more protective reason when we study spendthrift trusts beginning at page 257. Discretionary trusts grant an interest that is too amorphous to be anticipated (i.e., sold or borrowed against by the beneficiary, or attached by a creditor), which imposes some degree of control over the beneficiaries and, more importantly, generally provides creditor protection.

In light of these realities and this ephemeral character of the discretionary trust beneficiary's interest, it is hard to pin down exactly what the beneficiary of a discretionary trust owns and how, if at all, it may be enforced. The easier case is one in which the trustee is given discretion to make distributions for stated purposes, such as the beneficiary's support, health, or education. In these cases the trustee is required to exercise discretion reasonably to provide for the specified needs or circumstances of the beneficiary. Courts opine that fiduciary good faith and the beneficiary's best interests always are implied standards that govern every relation, even if the trustee is granted "absolute," "unfettered," or "uncontrolled" discretion over distributions, or is simply authorized to distribute to the beneficiary such amounts as the trustee determines in its sole discretion. Although these are the broadest standards known to the law (meaning a fiduciary has the broadest latitude in doing its job), enforcement always is available as against the trustee's bad faith or capriciousness. Because absolute discretion subject to no court review would mean there is no trust (because there could be no enforcement of it), you can see that there *never* is unfettered discretion in a trustee, regardless of what the document says. If the settlor intended to create a trust extended discretion will be interpreted as subjecting the trustee to a minimum standard of acting in good faith and for proper purposes. See UTC §814(a).

Some fiduciaries prefer maximum discretion (i.e., no standards) because they believe it gives them maximum flexibility with minimum exposure to second guessing by beneficiaries or courts. By contrast, some fiduciaries *want* a standard, even if only "best interests" (the broadest standard known to trust law), to which they can point in asserting that their actions were above reproach. Further, because trustees always are required to act in a fiduciary capacity (in good faith and for proper purposes), the objective of maximum flexibility may be elusive and unavailable, even in a document that purports to give the trustee "absolute" discretion over distributions.

One classic tension that exists always is whether consideration of a beneficiary's other resources is proper in determining whether the trustee should exercise its discretion to make or withhold distributions to the beneficiary. From a planning perspective, allowing the trustee to consider the beneficiary's other resources may be advisable if the beneficiary has a taxable estate and undistributed trust assets will not be taxable in the beneficiary's estate at death. Considering the beneficiary's resources also is appropriate if the remainder beneficiaries (e.g., the settlor's descendants from a prior marriage) may differ from the persons the beneficiary will favor with his or her own assets at death. In this regard, absent a trust provision otherwise, normally the common law provides that a trustee may not consider other resources of the beneficiary in exercising its discretion. In theory, if the rule was otherwise the beneficiary might be inclined to maximize trust distributions by minimizing the beneficiary's other resources, by not working, which would encourage sloth while discouraging industry and prudence, saving, or being frugal. Restatement (Third) of Trusts §50, comment e, provides that the trustee *presumptively* should consider the beneficiary's other resources in exercising its discretion, which reflects the common law that the trustee may consider the beneficiary's ability to be gainful, along with the beneficiary's other family needs.

Unless provided otherwise (e.g., in a spendthrift clause, which we study beginning at page 257), a beneficiary may assign a beneficial interest and the beneficiary's creditors may attach it. Attachment is a spendthrift issue, so let's focus now on a beneficiary's transfer of the beneficial interest, either by an affirmative assignment or by renunciation or disclaimer (a rejection, which causes the interest to pass to someone else). See Chapter 2. With respect to the affirmative act, most trust spendthrift provisions preclude assignment, which is not always a good result, as we will study. Assuming that assignment is possible, however, questions of priority arise if several assignments of the same interest are made. It happens, sometimes because the beneficiary is not careful (or forgets), and sometimes because something not entirely proper is happening. Restatement (Third) of Trusts §54 specifies that the first assignment in time prevails, but the trustee is protected if it has no notice of an assignment and makes payment to a later assignee.

Notwithstanding a valid assignment, another question in a credit resolution context is whether a creditor or other assignee must exhaust the beneficiary's other assets before attaching trust interests. Because most discretionary trusts have other beneficiaries, most states permit the creditor to reach only the amount needed to satisfy an insufficiency in the assigning beneficiary's own assets, and then only to the extent of the beneficiary's interest in the trust and only when the beneficiary is entitled to receive it (meaning that there is no acceleration of the beneficiary's interest just because there is an assignment of it). Renunciation or disclaimer is regarded differently than an assignment, because the beneficiary is not directing to whom the interest passes. Instead, the beneficiary just refuses to accept it. Assuming that the renunciation or disclaimer satisfies applicable state law requirements, its effect is as if the beneficiary predeceased creation of the interest and, because there is no affirmative disposition of the trust interest by the beneficiary, a spendthrift clause is no restriction.

## Support Trusts

A classic support trust uses an enforceable standard that provides more of a guarantee to the beneficiary (and any creditors who provide support to the beneficiary) and less discretion to the fiduciary, to insure that a certain ascertainable level of support will be provided. Absent language in the instrument providing other guidance to the trustee, "support" generally is thought to mean the beneficiary's support (and perhaps that of the beneficiary's dependents) in an accustomed standard of living. Questions can arise, and should be addressed in the instrument, as to the time at which the beneficiary's accustomed standard of living is determined, because there is no general rule to resolve that question (other than that intent of the settlor controls). Thus, if the beneficiary's standard of living is modest and the transferor intends the trust to improve the beneficiary's standard of living, language to that effect should be included.

Support trusts often provide for distributions to the beneficiary for "health, education, maintenance, and support." These standards are said to be "ascertainable," meaning that the trustee's duty to make distributions to the beneficiary for these purposes can be objectively reviewed and enforced. For tax purposes it may be critical that the trustee's ability to make distributions to a beneficiary is limited by such an ascertainable standard. There are other terms that also may be ascertainable, but this particular standard is the most commonly recognized ascertainable standard because it is provided in the Treasury Regulations.

The line between support and discretionary trusts may not be clear. Indeed, it has been abolished by the UTC for purposes of determining the rights of beneficiaries' creditors. Transferors often provide for the trustee to make distributions to the beneficiary for support (or a combination of health, education, maintenance, and support), "in such amounts as the trustee in its absolute discretion determines," or similar language to that effect. Such trusts are a species of discretionary trust, with the trustee's discretion being significantly more limited than a trust that provides no standards to guide or restrict exercise of the trustee's discretion in making distributions for a number of reasons. It is not necessary to hobble a reliable fiduciary's discretion by creating a support trust and in many cases support trusts are inadvisable. This most notably is true because of the rights of third parties (such as the state) to obtain reimbursement for necessary services provided to the beneficiary or to disqualify a beneficiary from receiving public benefits, such as Medicaid.

## Creditors' Rights

Virtually all trusts today contain some form of provision that restricts or eliminates the ability of a beneficiary's creditor to reach the beneficiary's equitable interest in the trust to satisfy the creditor's claim. The term "spendthrift trust" often refers to a trust that expressly prohibits voluntary or involuntary alienation of the beneficiary's interest. But other trust provisions also can protect the beneficiary's interest from creditors and sometimes those also are referred to as "spendthrift" provisions. We will return to the question whether automatic insertion of a spendthrift provision is wise. The reality is that automatic insertion is the norm.

Trust protective (spendthrift) provisions come in a variety of formats. For example, traditionally a trust created to provide only support or education is immune to attachment or assignment for items unrelated to the beneficiary's support or education. That distinction is eliminated under UTC §501 if the trust does not include an express spendthrift provision. In any event, attachment in reimbursement of necessaries provided to the beneficiary is thought to be consistent with the intent of a settlor who created a trust for just the support or education of a beneficiary. For example, B is the beneficiary of a trust that T created to distribute income to B on an annual or more frequent basis. Bank loaned money to B for an investment, B defaulted, and Bank now attempts to be repaid from the trust. The trust is not a support trust with respect to trust income because B is entitled to receive current income without regard to support needs. Thus, Bank may attach B's trust income interest to satisfy its claim unless the trust contains a spendthrift clause. Rather than wait until trust income is payable to B, the Bank will want to accelerate the value of that interest by commutation, meaning that the trustee would determine the discounted present value of B's life estate and distribute corpus equal to the lesser of Bank's claim or that amount.

If, however, the trust provided for distributions of income and principal only for B's support, Bank would not be able to reach the trust assets (although the landlord of a personal residence that B rents could). UTC §501 allows Bank to attach the trustee's discretionary distributions, but it authorizes a court to limit the creditor's award in consideration of the support needs of the beneficiary and the beneficiary's family. Thus, a trust created only for the beneficiary's support may yield results like those under the traditional rules even under the UTC.

Forfeiture provisions are common in Great Britain but not in the United States, because they are a blunt form of protecting the trust from creditor attachment or beneficiary alienation. Any attempted assignment (and in some cases a third party's levy on or attachment of a beneficiary's interest) works a termination of the beneficiary's interest. This approach may protect the trust property, but not the beneficiary. In most cases, a better alternative to a pure forfeiture provision is a provision like that in *Scott v. Bank One Trust Co.*, 577 N.E.2d 1077 (Ohio 1991), which prohibited distributions to any beneficiary who was insolvent, filed a petition in bankruptcy, or would not personally enjoy the property. In any such case the beneficiary's interest became discretionary until the beneficiary's creditor problems were resolved, which raises a third form of protection.

Discretionary trusts have a spendthrift nature because there is nothing a creditor can attach or that the beneficiary can assign unless or until the trustee chooses to exercise its discretion. Thus, for example, *United States v. O'Shaughnessy*, 517 N.W.2d 574 (Minn. 1994), held that the beneficiary of a discretionary trust had neither "property" nor any "right to property" in undistributed trust principal or income that the United States could attach in a federal tax lien enforcement action. Short of suing to force an exercise of discretion based on a breach of fiduciary duty, there is little a claimant can do to squeeze money out of a discretionary trust. UTC §504 prohibits such a suit by any creditor other than a child, spouse, or former spouse with a judgment or court order for support or maintenance. Thus, in most jurisdictions, a creditor of a beneficiary of a discretionary trust must wait until the trustee has exercised its discretion and made a distribution to the beneficiary, and then attempt to collect from the beneficiary. In some jurisdictions, the creditor may obtain an order directing the trustee to pay to the creditor any amounts it otherwise would distribute to the beneficiary pursuant to an exercise of its discretion. The result is that, if the trustee properly chooses to make no distributions, neither the beneficiary nor the creditor can benefit from the trust property, which likely would lead to settlement of the claim.

State law regarding discretionary trusts varies, and the ability of a state to reach trust assets or to cut the beneficiary off from Medicaid benefits (e.g., the cost of living in a nursing home) while the trust has assets is a subject of constant change and extreme sensitivity. There is a severe tension between a settlor who wants the beneficiary to receive maximum state benefits while maintaining the trust as a safety net if state aid is insufficient, and the state that has limited resources and therefore wants to deny public funds to people who can afford to pay for their own care. The parameters of this intersection between spendthrift protection and public benefits law will continue to evolve and is too amorphous currently to define in a meaningful manner for the 51 American jurisdictions. This subject is discussed further below, subject to this inevitable uncertainty.

In-hand payment and pure spendthrift clauses require the trustee to make payments directly to the named beneficiary and not to any assignee or agent, or expressly deny any attachment or assignment. Together these are the most common American creditor protection approaches. Trusts including these provisions commonly are referred to as "spendthrift trusts" and, although controversial (because they allow beneficiaries to enjoy trust property that is not available to satisfy legitimate claims of the beneficiaries' creditors), spendthrift trusts are effective to varying degrees in the great majority of American jurisdictions. But there are some limitations.

### Creditors of the Settlor

A spendthrift provision in a trust in which the settlor also is a beneficiary normally does not insulate the trust from claims by the settlor's *own* creditors, even if the trust is irrevocable. As an initial matter, creditors of the settlor may reach the full trust if a transfer into trust was a fraud on creditors. Required is that the settlor was insolvent at the time of, or became insolvent by virtue of, the transfer. In such a case the settlor's creditors normally may reach the transferred assets even if the settlor is not a beneficiary. Even absent such a fraudulent transfer, however, creditors of the settlor still may reach the full amount the trustee *could* pay to the settlor as a beneficiary, regardless of whether anything actually is paid.

To illustrate, assume that S created a trust with T as trustee, providing "income and principal to S, as determined by T in its sole discretion, to provide for S's support. On S's death, remainder to S's descendants, per stirpes." The trust has a standard spendthrift provision preventing any beneficiary's interest from being alienated or attached voluntarily or involuntarily. Later, S defaults on a debt to C. Under the traditional rule, C may reach the full amount that T could distribute to S. C could reach all assets in the trust if creation of the trust was a fraudulent transfer or if T was authorized to distribute such amounts to S as T in its discretion determines. In this particular case C may not be able to attach enough trust assets to satisfy the claim in full, depending on factors such as the size of C's claim, S's age and life expectancy, and the amounts T could distribute to S for S's support without violating T's fiduciary duties to the remainder beneficiaries. Still, this trust is not immune to S's creditor claims.

Apparently in an effort to compete for trust business by becoming safe havens in cases such as this, several states—led by Alaska and Delaware, the list now includes Colorado, Maryland, Missouri, Nevada, Oklahoma, Rhode Island, South Dakota, and Utah—have enacted legislation under which a settlor may transfer assets in trust (provided the transfer is not in fraud of existing creditors) and retain the ability to receive distributions from the trust without the trust assets being reachable by the settlor's creditors. In effect, these laws have eliminated the special rule applicable only to self-settled trusts and regard all beneficiaries (settlors and third parties) alike.

Finally, assets subject to a settlor's retained general inter vivos power of appointment, as discussed in Chapter 14, also can be reached by the settlor's creditors, but a creditor usually cannot force exercise of a power to revoke a trust. The distinction that permits a creditor to force exercise of a general power of appointment but not a power to revoke makes no sense to us and it has been rejected by UTC §505(a)(1). So, for example, G created Trust 1 for D and D's descendants and Trust 2 for S and S's descendants. G is not a permissible beneficiary of the income or principal of either trust, but G retained a general inter vivos power of appointment over Trust 1, under which G could appoint the assets in the trust to anyone, including G personally. No such power was retained in Trust 2, but G reserved the power to revoke Trust 2, in which case the assets would be conveyed back to G. Assuming transfers to the trusts were not made in fraud of G's creditors, under the traditional rules a creditor of G could not reach the assets in Trust 2, either directly or by forcing an exercise by G of the power to revoke the trust. But G's creditor could reach the assets in Trust 1, regardless of whether the transfers to it were made in fraud of the creditor's rights and without regard to whether G chooses to exercise the power to appoint.

### *Any Other Beneficiary*

In most states most creditors of a beneficiary are precluded from reaching the beneficiary's interest in a spendthrift trust, if the beneficiary is *not* the settlor of the trust. Generally, spendthrift provisions work to protect trust assets from such a beneficiary's creditors. This protection extends only to the beneficiary's interest in the trust. Assets distributed to the beneficiary from the spendthrift trust lose their protection from creditors. As a practical matter, a beneficiary attempting to avoid paying creditors will try to spend distributed trust assets before creditors can attach them, but in many states (specifically excepting any that have adopted the UTC) knowledgeable creditors can simply garnish the trust (obtaining a court order requiring the trustee to make payment directly to the creditor). Many trust instruments contain facility of payment provisions that authorize distributions to the beneficiary directly or to third parties for the beneficiary's benefit. If the beneficiary is having creditor problems, the trustee of such a trust may make distributions for the beneficiary directly to third parties that the beneficiary designates (such as a landlord or the mortgagee of the beneficiary's home), but again only in the absence of a garnishment order.

In bankruptcy, the trustee of the bankrupt's estate succeeds to all the rights and interests of the bankrupt, but subject to the same limitations that apply to the beneficiary's interest, such as a spendthrift clause.

Accordingly, creditors of a beneficiary who cannot reach a trust interest directly because of a spendthrift clause also cannot do so in a bankruptcy proceeding.

This is extraordinary protection for inherited wealth and the policy underlying enforcement of spendthrift clauses is protection of the transferor's property rights. As stated by *Scott v. Bank One Trust Co.*, 577 N.E.2d at 1083: "[A]s a matter of policy, it is desirable for property owners to have, within reasonable bounds, the freedom to do as they choose with their own property. That freedom is not absolute . . . . But . . . in a society that values freedom as greatly as ours, this consideration is far from trivial." On the other hand, "[t]here are many who consider it contrary to their notions of right and wrong that a person should be permitted to live on income that he does not earn and yet that is not subject to the claims of his creditors." *Utley v. Graves*, 258 F. Supp. 959, 960 (D.D.C. 1966), rev'd, 382 F.2d 451 (D.C. Cir. 1967). Three other policy issues also affect the validity of spendthrift provisions.

One allegation is that disabling restraints such as spendthrift clauses take property out of commerce and thus adversely affect the economy. A response with respect to spendthrift provisions in trust is that the trustee has free alienability of trust assets. Only the beneficiary is restricted with respect to transfers of the equitable interest. A counter response is that entrepreneurial investments generally may not be made with spendthrift trust funds because of the investment limitations imposed on fiduciaries. This is not compelling, because that argument would apply to any trust, not just a spendthrift trust, and would not justify defeating any trust.

A second argument is that spendthrift provisions serve to improperly mislead creditors. A legitimate response is that voluntary creditors have no right to rely on the appearance of wealth and should not extend credit without verification of the nature and extent of the beneficial interest and the debtor's ability to pay. (A very compelling argument for an exception does exist, relative to involuntary tort creditors. It is discussed at page 262.) In any event, some argue that a transferor's property should not be subjected to the beneficiary's debts, whatever their origin.

A third policy argument against spendthrift protection is that spendthrift provisions tend to protect inherited wealth from creditors in ways that earned wealth cannot enjoy (at least in those states that prohibit self-settled spendthrift trusts), which seems improper. One legitimate response may be that, by protecting against improvidence, the spendthrift provision protects those beneficiaries who were left wealth *in trust* because they were unable to earn or manage wealth on their own. Further, tax qualified retirement plan interests represent a substantial portion of many persons' earned wealth, they generally are subject to the federal Employee Retirement Income Security Act (ERISA), and that law also protects participants' interests from their creditors.

In an effort to balance these conflicting concerns, some states recognize spendthrift provisions but limit their effectiveness in various ways (and a few states do not enforce them at all). The law on these issues varies significantly from state to state and increasingly is governed by statute. For example, as discussed at page 259, in virtually all states a spendthrift provision will not protect a settlor's retained interest as a beneficiary in a trust created and funded by the settlor. Generally, you cannot create a valid spendthrift trust for yourself. In addition, a spendthrift clause prohibiting attachment by creditors is valid only to the extent it also prohibits voluntary assignment by the beneficiary. A spendthrift clause that expressly prohibits attachment but is silent with respect to assignment may be construed to prohibit both.

A controversial issue is whether involuntary tort claimants may reach spendthrift trust assets held for the benefit of a tortfeasor beneficiary. The policy supporting an exception for *involuntary* tort judgment creditors is that they did not voluntarily extend credit on the appearance of wealth and should not be barred from collecting on their judgment while the tortfeasor enjoys wealth that is immune to creditors. See 2A Scott & Fratcher, The Law of Trusts §157.5 (4th ed. 1987), *In re Estate of Nagel,* 580 N.W.2d 810 (Iowa 1998), and *Sligh v. First National Bank,* 704 So. 2d 1020 (Miss. 1997). Although the policies supporting an exception are strong, most states that have considered the issue reject the exception. For example, the Mississippi legislature reversed *Sligh* shortly after it was decided. See also *Scheffel v. Krueger,* 782 A.2d 410 (N.H. 2001), *Duvall v. McGee,* 826 A.2d 416 (Md. Ct. App. 2003), and the UTC, which bars tort judgment claims notwithstanding the nature of the beneficiary's conduct.

Some states balance the equities by restricting the fund or the amount of income that can be protected. And most states preclude application of a spendthrift restriction against the provider of necessaries. The theory is that the trust presumably was created to ensure support without dissipation by a profligate. The necessities exception is thought to be consistent with that overriding intent of the settlor. Under such a theory, the amount available to the furnisher of necessaries should be limited to a reasonable, fair value, not any higher contracted price agreed to by a profligate beneficiary.

Most states also preclude reliance on a spendthrift clause to prevent collection of governmental claims (e.g., a state may count the trust interest in determining eligibility for public benefits or attach the trust to reimburse it for benefits already paid (usually as an estate recovery claim after the recipient's death and not as against a properly drafted trust. See page 263 regarding the effect on Medicaid qualification of a trust beneficial interest.) Generally, a beneficiary's interest in a spendthrift trust also may be reached to satisfy the claims of both federal and state taxing authorities against the beneficiary. And finally, cases are divided on whether alimony and child support claimants may reach a beneficiary's interest in a spendthrift trust. The majority rule probably is that claims for child support may be successfully asserted while alimony claims often cannot. UTC §503 permits a spouse, a former spouse, and children all to reach the trust for support and alimony and is a controversial element, particularly with respect to alimony claims by former spouses.

Note that a trust may provide protection from creditor claims both by making the beneficiary's interest subject to the discretion of the trustee, and by including a spendthrift clause. For example, in *Shelley v. Shelley*, 354 P.2d 282 (Or. 1960), the trust beneficiary (Grant) was entitled to receive current distributions of income, but principal only in the trustee's discretion, and the trust included a spendthrift clause. The court said that alimony and child support claimants could reach Grant's interests in the trust despite the spendthrift clause but it did *not* in fact violate the spendthrift nature of the trust. Those claimants only received income that Grant was entitled to, when he was entitled to it, and could not reach principal unless and until the trustee exercised its discretion. So you need to be careful in reading authority too. Sometimes a court acts as if it was making an inroad on established policy when in fact it did not. Also note regarding *Shelley* that a trust in which a beneficiary is entitled to receive current distributions of all trust income ordinarily should have little or no accumulated income. If a trustee nevertheless accumulates income rather than distribute it to the beneficiary, the accumulated income should be viewed as the beneficiary's property and it should be subject to the claims of *any* creditors of the beneficiary, without regard to a spendthrift clause or the nature of the creditor's claim. See, e.g., UTC §506, which applies if the trustee does not make a mandatory distribution within an undefined "reasonable time."

### *Qualification for Public Benefits*

Qualification and reimbursement for government assistance raises significant issues for trust beneficiaries or for applicants who have made transfers of their assets within a relatively short period prior to applying for assistance. There are more elderly persons in the United States than ever and they are living longer than ever. Many are unable to care for themselves and the costs of institutional care are high. Persons who require institutional care may qualify to have these costs paid by Medicaid, which is a joint federal-state program that is the primary government program providing funds for institutional care of the elderly. To qualify for Medicaid assistance, a person must have nonexempt resources and income of less than specified amounts (exempt resources may include, among others, part or all of the value of a residence, household goods and personal effects, an automobile, and a burial fund). Although the disqualification amounts vary from state to state, they are uniformly very low. A prospective Medicaid recipient whose nonexempt assets exceed the resource threshold must "spend down" before qualifying. For married couples, complicated rules consider the assets and income of both spouses in determining the eligibility of either, but make provision for one spouse to be institutionalized and qualify for Medicaid without the other having to be totally impoverished.

For some who can afford to pay for nursing home care, the idea of government assistance is offensive to their personal values and their desire not to be, in effect, "middle class welfare recipients." Many others (and often their children) are offended by the prospect of their life savings being dissipated in the last years of their lives to pay for nursing home care. Sometimes their view is that they have paid taxes all of their lives and that there is nothing wrong with doing everything possible to preserve assets for their families by letting the government pay for their end of life care. Also difficult to confront is the desire of parents of disabled children who want to provide care that is not funded by the government without having funds they set aside for that purpose disqualify their children from receiving basic government support.

Various rules and exceptions establish whether the assets and income of a self-settled trust (including trusts created by a guardian, conservator, attorney-in-fact, or even by a court out of the proceeds of a judgment or settlement award obtained on the settlor's behalf) will be counted in determining eligibility for Medicaid. Generally, consistent with the normal spendthrift rules for self-settled trusts, the maximum amount a trustee *could* distribute to the settlor from such a trust will be counted as an available resource unless an exception applies. And termination of a settlor's trust interest at the time of institutionalization is treated as a transfer by the settlor that triggers application of the look-back rules discussed at page 265, resulting in a period of ineligibility for Medicaid. In certain limited circumstances a settlor's "pay-back" trust will not be counted in determining Medicaid eligibility. These trusts provide that the state be repaid for assistance it provided, using any assets remaining in the trust at the settlor's death.

The Medicaid rules are much more lenient if a trust was established for a beneficiary by a third party (not the beneficiary, the beneficiary's spouse, a representative of the beneficiary, or a court acting on the beneficiary's behalf). "Supplemental needs" or "special needs" trusts (SNTs) are created by settlors who want to provide benefits to a beneficiary over and above the basic support that the state provides. Done properly, these SNTs are not counted as available resources of the beneficiary and will not jeopardize that assistance. Support trust or mandatory distribution trust assets *are* counted, making the distinction important. In *Myers v. Department of Social and Rehabilitation Services*, 866 P.2d 1052 (Kan. 1994), a testamentary trust provided that the trustee "shall hold, manage, invest and reinvest, collect the income [therefrom and] pay over so much or all the net income and principal to my son as my trustee deems advisable for his care, support, maintenance, emergencies and welfare." The court held this was a discretionary trust because the trustee was required to pay only amounts it deemed advisable. Neither the beneficiary nor any creditor could compel the trustee to pay trust income or principal to the beneficiary (although the beneficiary could have compelled distributions if the trustee had abused its discretion in refusing to provide funds). In contrast, *Corcoran v. Department of Social Services*, 859 A.2d 533 (Conn. 2004), held that discretionary support trust assets were available for the beneficiary's support, thus disqualifying the beneficiary from Medicaid and illustrating the unpredictability of these cases.

A person who has too much property to qualify for Medicaid but who needs institutionalized care, may transfer assets to a third party (for example, a child) and then qualify. To succeed, however, the transferor must wait long enough after the transfer to apply for benefits. That is, assets transferred within a "look-back" period are considered in determining eligibility for benefits. The look-back period is 36 months for outright transfers and 60 months if a trust is involved.

Under the look-back rule asset transfers may cause the transferor to become disqualified for a period of time (not the 36 or 60 month look back period) determined by a formula. For example, assume that $160,000 was transferred during the look-back period and that the state's monthly cost of nursing home care is $4,000. The formula is the amount transferred during the 36 or 60 month look-back period, divided by the monthly cost, so the transferor would be disqualified for 40 months from the date of the transfer. Because the look-back period is only 36 months, the transferor in this example would have been better off to simply wait 36 months after the transfer to apply, because no part of an outright transfer made outside the look-back period would be considered in determining the period of ineligibility. To succeed, however, the transferor would need to retain enough wealth to survive during the look back disqualification period.

Exceptions apply to the asset transfer, ineligibility, look-back rules. For example, transfers to trusts for the benefit of the transferor are not subject to the 60 month look-back period rules. Rather, these assets are counted as resources of the transferor for eligibility purposes (unless the trust is excepted). Further, residences transferred to certain family members are excepted, as are all transfers to a spouse (because each spouse's assets are considered in determining either spouse's eligibility). In addition, transfers to or in trust for the benefit of a blind or disabled child are exempt, as are transfers in trust for the benefit of a disabled person under 65 years of age. These rules are constantly changing, so be sure to verify them in their current iteration before making any transfer or any application.

A related question to Medicaid eligibility is whether a state may be reimbursed from a trust for costs the state pays for the care of a beneficiary. If the beneficiary was the settlor the usual rule allowing creditors to reach as much of the trust assets as the trustee could have distributed to the beneficiary applies. If the trust settlor was a third party, the state's claim for Medicaid reimbursement generally does not arise until the recipient's death and is an "estate recovery" claim that cannot be asserted against the third-party created trust. With respect to any other state reimbursement claims, the state can reach third-party created discretionary trust assets only if and to the extent the trustee exercises its discretion to make distributions. If the trust is a support trust, however, the state may reach it for any support the state provided.

These rules for qualifying for public assistance, a state's ability to successfully seek reimbursement for assistance provided, and the issue of asset transfers are complex. They derive from federal and state statutes and regulations, they involve sensitive questions of public policy with significant budget implications, and they seem to be in an almost constant state of change. And there can be difficult ethical and malpractice issues. To illustrate, imagine that an elderly parent transferred assets to a child to qualify for assistance at termination of the look-back period. The oral and perhaps unenforceable understanding is that the child will use the transferred assets for the parent's benefit, if needed, or return the assets to the parent if requested. Even after expiration of the 36 month look-back period, there is a question whether the oral agreement means the parent cannot apply for Medicaid without committing fraud. Moreover, it probably is not possible for the parent to force the child to comply with their understanding if the parent requests that the child return the assets and the child refuses. If that is true, the parent may attempt to hold a lawyer who was involved with the planning responsible.

If spendthrift clauses are given effect in the jurisdiction, an obvious effect of including a spendthrift clause in a trust instrument (or providing that distributions to the beneficiary are subject to the trustee's discretion) is that it will be difficult or impossible for the beneficiary to borrow against the interest or for a creditor to reach it, both of which are desirable consequences for some transferors. But no boilerplate should be used without thought and, on occasion (for tax purposes especially), an assignment that could *not* be made if there *is* a spendthrift provision may be very useful. Although a renunciation or disclaimer is not precluded by a spendthrift clause, the taker in the event of a disclaimer might not be the person in whose favor an assignment would be best. So in some cases spendthrift provisions that preclude an affirmative assignment to a particular recipient can be harmful. Further, because they also may preclude trust termination under the *Claflin* (unfulfilled purposes) doctrine discussed on page 270, in many added cases spendthrift provisions may be harmful. For this and other reasons, a spendthrift clause coupled with a power of appointment may be a more acceptable method to preserve flexibility if creditor protection is needed, as we will see in Chapter 14.

## Modification and Termination

For a variety of reasons, the settlor or one or more trust beneficiaries may want to modify the trust terms or terminate it early.

### *Modification and Termination by the Settlor*

Consider a hypothetical: Settlor was scheduled to receive a substantial sum of money at age 18 (perhaps from a Uniform Transfer to Minors Act account or a trust created by an ancestor). Settlor's parent, trust officer, and their attorney recommended that Settlor create an irrevocable trust to receive the sum, over which Settlor retained generous lifetime enjoyment, with provision for a life estate for Settlor's surviving spouse (if any) for the spouse's overlife, and payment of the remainder per stirpes to Settlor's descendants who survive the survivor of Settlor and the spouse. Among the issues raised are whether the attorney had a conflict of interest in this representation, why this trust would be irrevocable, and under what circumstances Settlor later may revoke the trust.

Certainly the attorney had a conflict of interest because the parent and trust officer were the attorney's clients and they were pushing the irrevocable trust. Indeed, if the attorney prepared the trust instrument, it would be difficult (if not impossible) to argue that the attorney was not also representing Settlor, regardless of whether the parent paid the attorney's fee. Was it in Settlor's best interests and who did the attorney represent with respect to the trust? That conflict may be compounded by the fact that Settlor arguably was unable to give an informed and voluntary consent by virtue of the same defects of age, character, and experience that prompted the parent and trust officer to recommend this rollover trust. Unless it is clear that the attorney represented Settlor alone — which the facts almost certainly do not support — there has been a real ethical breach here and the attorney also potentially is liable for malpractice.

Why would this trust be irrevocable? There is no tax advantage (Settlor's retained enjoyment will cause the trust to be taxable when Settlor dies). We also know from the spendthrift provision material that there is no protection from creditors to the extent the trustee may pay income and principal to Settlor. There are some potential reasons for the trust to be irrevocable, but none are likely to apply in this case. And that raises the question whether Settlor may revoke the trust.

Revocation of an "irrevocable" trust is available at common law only if one of the following applies:

- An express power to revoke was reserved. If the instrument is silent on the settlor's power to revoke, in most jurisdictions the trust is irrevocable. Uniform Trust Code §602(a) reverses this rule.

- The settlor was the sole beneficiary. The ability to revoke under this exception is relatively rare, because even if the settlor is the sole lifetime beneficiary, most trusts provide for remainder beneficiaries (as opposed to the trust assets being distributed to the settlor's estate at the settlor's death).

- The consent of all beneficiaries is obtained, which often is difficult or impossible because of, among other things, minor, unborn, and contingent or unascertainable beneficiaries. For example, the trust may name the settlor's surviving spouse as a contingent beneficiary and we have no idea who would be married to and survive the settlor in our example.

- The trust was invalid due to incapacity, duress, undue influence, or fraud, which might exist in our example, although it is more likely that simple ignorance was exploited.

- The power to revoke was meant to be included but was inadvertently omitted (assuming this could be proven, based on extrinsic evidence such as the testimony of the drafter).

Note that a mistake of law usually will not suffice to make the trust revocable (e.g., the settlor or drafter thought the trust was revocable if it was not expressly made irrevocable). A mistake of fact also might suffice (e.g., the settlor was confused about what document was involved), but again it could be hard to prove.

In the hypothetical, Settlor probably could not revoke, because there are unborns and an unknown (perhaps unborn too?) spouse who cannot consent, and arguably none of the other exceptions to irrevocability apply. In addition, the doctrine of virtual representation (under which an unrepresented beneficiary's interest is deemed adequately represented by a similarly situated beneficiary who *is* a party) will not apply here because there is no one who virtually represents Settlor's unborn children or potential future spouse. Sometimes a guardian ad litem can be appointed to give the requisite consent, but it is not likely in this case that a consent would be given because it clearly is not in the best interests of those unborns who would be affected by a revocation.

As the hypothetical illustrates, irrevocability means that the terms of the instrument limit the beneficiaries' access to the trust assets, which are controlled by a trustee to whom fees must be paid, and there may be other administrative costs (e.g., accounting and legal fees). In short, irrevocability is serious business. It may be appropriate for such purposes as tax planning, creditor protection (effective in most cases only to the extent the settlor is not a beneficiary), or resolution of a dispute (e.g., a divorce), but a trust never should be made irrevocable without careful deliberation. Although some of the adverse consequences of irrevocability can be mitigated through the use, for example, of powers of appointment, adequately drafting for unexpected changes in the future is difficult. See Chapter 14.

Note that some state statutes (e.g., in California, Iowa, Montana, Oklahoma, Texas, and jurisdictions that have adopted the UTC) change the default rule to provide that a trust is revocable unless expressly made irrevocable, and the Restatement (Third) of Trusts makes the same change. Reliance on them is foolish, however, because of the conflict of laws principles that may apply and the significant time it will take for the Restatement position to become the law (if it ever does) or for the Uniform Trust Code to be more widely adopted.

Under the common law, creditors cannot force a settlor to exercise a power of revocation (although a creditor might set aside a trust that was created with a fraudulent transfer). On the other hand, a settlor's trustee in bankruptcy may exercise all the settlor's powers, including any retained power to revoke. As we will see in Chapter 14, a settlor's creditors may reach a retained general power of appointment and force its exercise to the extent the settlor as the power holder is insolvent. The curious aspect of these rules is that, for all practical purposes, a power to revoke and a general inter vivos power to appoint don't differ. Yet the power to revoke is favored here. We are unable to give a good justification for the disparity in treatment. UTC §505(a)(2) rejects it by simply providing that revocable trust assets may be reached by the settlor's creditors.

### *Modification and Termination by Trustee*

Trustees generally have no power to modify or terminate a trust absent express authority granted in the instrument. For example, an express power to revoke often is granted in the form of a provision granting the trustee the authority to terminate a trust if it becomes too small to justify its continuance. (Caution is needed in such "small trust termination" provisions, however, because an individual trustee who also is a beneficiary may have a taxable ownership interest in the trust if, upon termination, any portion of the trust corpus passes to the trustee as beneficiary.) Even without express authority in the trust instrument, UTC §414(a) permits a trustee to terminate a trust early if it has less than $50,000 of assets. An implicit power to terminate a trust also exists in the form of a trustee's power to distribute "so much or all of the principal of the trust as the trustee deems appropriate . . . ," or as the trustee deems appropriate for certain designated purposes. Termination may occur to the extent the trustee's exercise of the granted discretion is proper under the applicable standard, because the trust becomes "dry," due to distribution of all the trust assets to any one or more of the beneficiaries.

A difficult question exists whether a trustee may terminate a trust purely for tax purposes (e.g., because the income tax rate on undistributed trust income is so much higher than it is for individuals). Most courts hold that the trustee may not, because the remainder beneficiaries' interests deserve protection notwithstanding what may be a significant diminution in wealth due to taxes if termination is not permitted. Further, investment alternatives usually are available to reduce adverse income tax consequences. The UTC does not generally permit a trustee to terminate a trust for tax purposes, but §416 authorizes a court to modify trust terms to achieve the settlor's tax objectives, provided that modification does not contravene the settlor's probable intention.

As does authority expressly granted by many well drafted trust instruments, UTC §417 allows a trustee to combine multiple trusts into a single trust, or to divide a trust into multiple separate trusts, provided that no beneficiary's interest is impaired and no trust purpose is adversely affected. Division most frequently is desired for tax purposes, especially in generation-skipping transfer tax planning.

### *Modification and Termination by Beneficiaries*

Surprisingly, perhaps, this is an extremely limited opportunity. The beneficiaries acting without the settlor's consent may modify or terminate a trust early (even without the trustee's consent) only if two requirements are met. First, all interested parties must consent. Required is that all interested parties be in existence or represented, and sui juris (i.e., competent adults or represented by guardians). "Interested parties" does *not* include the settlor, even if living, unless the settlor also is a beneficiary, nor is the trustee interested. Second, any unfulfilled purpose of the trust will preclude termination. This is the *Claflin* doctrine, named after an 1889 Massachusetts case and is as old and important a concept in trust law as any. Unfulfilled purposes include protection of the trust corpus from the beneficiary's improvidence or creditors, as evidenced by inclusion of a spendthrift clause; postponement of possession, as evidenced by a provision delaying distribution until a beneficiary is a certain age to protect against the beneficiary's improvidence or immaturity; and more generalized objectives, such as providing management, support, bifurcation of title (providing for multiple beneficiaries seriatim), or protection against dissipation (e.g., a life estate with a testamentary power of appointment but no opportunity for a beneficiary to invade or withdraw).

Fulfillment of one or more trust purposes will not allow early termination by all beneficiaries if other trust purposes remain unfulfilled. For example, *In re Estate of Brown*, 528 A.2d 752 (Vt. 1987), involved an education trust that continued for the life of a nephew and his wife. After the education aspect was accomplished the court rejected a petition to terminate the trust because, in addition to educating the beneficiaries, a material purpose was to provide for the nephew and his wife for their lives, to allow them to live in their accustomed standard of living. That purpose would have been defeated if the trust had been terminated.

UTC §411(b) permits termination in a case like *Brown* only if all the beneficiaries agreed and no *material* unfulfilled purpose exists. This modest shift of emphasis codifies the *Claflin* doctrine with the refinement that not just *any* unfulfilled purpose will bar termination, but guidance will be required before it is clear what purposes are not "material" for this purpose.

The general policy in this country with respect to trust termination and modification is to respect and protect the settlor's intent, which translates into denial of any proposed early termination or modification that is inconsistent with the settlor's intent. A few exceptions do exist, however, including:

- **Perpetuities limits.** We only allow the settlor's dead hand to control for the applicable period of the Rule Against Perpetuities (if any) in the state. See Chapter 17.

- **Annuities.** If the document provides for acquisition of an annuity that can be resold, the rule is that the beneficiary can ask for the cash that would be used to purchase the annuity or, if it already was purchased, can demand for acceleration (by sale of the annuity and distribution of the proceeds). With a resalable annuity, the rationale here is that there is no reason to incur the costs of purchase and then resale if the beneficiary doesn't want the annuity in the first place. And because it *is* an annuity, there is no remainder beneficiary to consider.

- **Distribution of sale proceeds.** Directions to sell land and distribute the cash proceeds can be overridden by the beneficiary's request that the property itself be distributed in kind. This exception is based on notions that land is nonfungible and having the sale proceeds that could be used to purchase other property is not the functional equivalent of having the original property instead.

- **Termination by merger.** A termination may be produced by merger, if it is possible for a sole beneficiary to become the owner of both the life estate and the remainder, which then would yield the power to terminate the trust. This is not easy to accomplish, however, especially because most trusts have a spendthrift provision that would preclude transfers to or acquisition of the life estate and remainder interest by the same person.

So how can a beneficiary avoid the unfulfilled purpose bar? Consent of the settlor would be an estoppel to the bar of an unfulfilled purpose, but in most cases the settlor won't be alive to consent. If the settlor *is* available, that fact alone in some cases creates a problem because additional potential beneficiaries can be born or adopted by the settlor, meaning it may be difficult or impossible to obtain the consent required from all potential beneficiaries. In addition to the presumption of the fertile octogenarian (anyone at any age can parent a child), there always is the possibility of adoption (and the new biology). Appointment of a guardian ad litem (GAL) often is suggested as the answer to needing the consent of all potential beneficiaries when some are not available. For any one of several reasons, however, that often will not suffice. For example, a GAL may not be able to consent for the ward under the law of your state; some courts are reluctant to appoint GALs; in courts that are not reluctant, costs, delays, and fraud (yes, some of the abuses that occur in this realm would curl your toenails) all may be involved in an appointment; or consent may prove to be not in the ward's best interests, meaning that the GAL should not consent.

Applicable rules of construction also may eliminate an interest that stands in the way of consent. Unfortunately the Rule in Shelley's Case (remainder to the heirs of a named beneficiary is instead a remainder in the named beneficiary) and the Doctrine of Worthier Title (remainder to the settlor's heirs instead is a remainder in the settlor, known by the name "reversion") are in disfavor. Alternatively, conveyance of a quid pro quo may produce consent. That is, if ascertained but nonconsensual beneficiaries are reluctant, perhaps they can be bought off.

Short of these options, in most cases virtual representation is the only answer. Under this doctrine (which is codified with other representation provisions in UTC Article 3) beneficiaries who are similarly situated to unascertainable or unascertained (and therefore nonconsensual) beneficiaries may represent all beneficiaries whose interests are similar. This is based on a theory that what is good for some is good for all and that the consent of those few should suffice. Given that assumption, the doctrine is not available to the extent there is a conflict of interest between the representative and the represented person. It is not unheard of, but it probably is fair to say that a trustee or other court appointed representative should not be allowed to virtually represent an unascertained beneficiary. And if a court appointment is being used, it usually will be a GAL, raising the problems noted above.

A general inter vivos power of appointment might be regarded as tantamount to making the powerholder the sole beneficiary, in which case a termination by merger could occur. This is not a truly copacetic notion unless there are no takers in default of an effective exercise of the power, which is unusual. See Chapter 14. Further, even if this general inter vivos power of appointment solution is viable, a general *testamentary* power or any *nongeneral* power will not suffice, so the opportunity of a beneficiary/powerholder to terminate is limited (if useful at all). Indeed, any takers in default of exercise also are beneficiaries who must consent (although permissible appointees probably are not). Again see Chapter 14.

The most fruitful source of an exception to the unfulfilled purpose bar to modification or termination is the trustee's participation in a termination, made with the consent of all beneficiaries. See UTC §1009, which provides that a trustee's conduct that normally would constitute an actionable breach (such as consent to early termination) is not actionable by any beneficiary who consented to or ratified that conduct, or who released the trustee with respect to it. The only exception to this estoppel is if the consent, release, or ratification was induced by the trustee's improper conduct or the beneficiary did not know the beneficiary's rights or any material facts relating to the breach. Thus, the trustee and all beneficiaries may agree to conduct that is inconsistent with the settlor's intent. A willing trustee simply goes along with a proposal and is estopped to object by virtue of its participation.

So, for example, assume a trust provides for income to A for life, remainder to a charity. A, the charity, and the trustee agree to terminate the trust and to distribute the discounted present value of each interest. Some courts hold that the settlor's assurance of income to A for life or preservation of an unreduced corpus for the charity is a purpose that should prevent termination. Nevertheless, termination in cases like this occurs often, frequently because the trust fails to qualify for the federal estate tax charitable deduction as drafted but the deduction can be salvaged by an immediate termination and distribution. 4 Scott & Fratcher, The Law of Trusts §337.6 (4th ed. 1989), says this is a legitimate action if it is designed to preserve the settlor's overall intent (which may include qualification for the deduction) as opposed to being part of a scheme to defeat the settlor's intent. If all the beneficiaries consent and the trustee does not object, an unfulfilled purpose does not act as a bar. So why might a trustee object to termination?

Contrary to your first suspicion, in most cases involving a professional trustee it is not to preserve its fee. Often a knowledgeable trustee will resign if possible if the beneficiaries are dissatisfied, because the beneficiaries are more trouble than they are worth. Indeed, many trustees make money by termination because they charge a termination fee that can run in the neighborhood of several percentage points of the trust value. Nevertheless, a trustee might object to modification or termination for several reasons.

One is because the state Attorney General in most jurisdictions oversees all trusts involving charities. So there could be legal problems emanating from the Attorney General. Another might be that the trustee shares a philosophy with the settlor about the beneficiaries' abilities to handle the assets responsibly and the right time to distribute the wealth. In addition, conservative or prudence concerns may preclude a trustee's consent, there being exposure if not all beneficiaries (e.g., unascertained or unborn beneficiaries) have given a competent consent. And finally, professional trustees have their reputations to protect. The fiduciary obligation is to object to premature termination, and other potential settlors won't likely hire a trustee that is known to be a pushover.

### Judicial Power to Modify a Trust

Traditionally, judicial restraints on modification of trusts vary depending on whether the requested modification is with respect to an administrative or a distributive provision. Deviation from *administrative* provisions is the more commonplace request and, although administrative provisions may permit an indirect diversion from one beneficiary to another (e.g., reallocation of receipts or disbursements will shift some enjoyment between income and remainder beneficiaries), these changes don't normally alter substantive distributive rights. According to Restatement (Second) of Trusts §167, the general requirements to authorize an administrative deviation include: (1) it is necessitated by a change of circumstances that was unanticipated by the settlor (it probably needs to be one that the reasonable settlor *would* not have anticipated); (2) the change in circumstances is such that it would defeat or substantially impair the primary purpose(s) of the trust if deviation is not allowed; and (3) deviation must be the only means to correct the problem. Restatement (Third) of Trusts §66 greatly simplifies this standard by allowing changes "if because of circumstances not anticipated by the settlor the modification or deviation will further the purposes of the trust."

To illustrate an unanticipated event, consider an economic depression or other significant change in investment climate. Some trusts drafted just after the Great Depression (and many still are in existence) specifically deny the trustee power to invest in stocks. Today that prohibition would be quite unfortunate and a court might allow deviation from it. Similarly, but not very likely, a trust drafted during a bull stock market might command investment *only* in stocks, which might be unwise from a diversification perspective, and a court might allow deviation if unanticipated events showed that dictate also to be unwise. Less sudden than a depression or stock market crash but equally dramatic unanticipated changes (like run-away inflation) also might suffice to permit deviation from restrictive investment proscriptions for purposes of the changed circumstance requirement.

Most deviation cases involve provisions that prove to be unwise. The most common is requiring nontraditional investments or failing to consider the effects of inflation, or both. For example, *In re Pulitzer*, 249 N.Y.S. 87 (Surr. Ct. 1931), involved an express prohibition against sale "under any circumstances whatever." In the face of a downturn in the business the beneficiaries wanted to sell and the court allowed it. The settlor stated in the instrument that he sacrificed his health to maintain the business, and likely anticipated that it was tentative and might not succeed, which proved to be the case. The question therefore was whether the settlor's primary purpose for the trust was to preserve principal and maintain a fair income stream for the beneficiaries, or to preserve the business. The factor that probably justified the result in *Pulitzer* was the court's conclusion that the settlor's dead hand had controlled long enough. The court chose to protect what little remained for the living beneficiaries. The UTC addresses this sort of problem in a conventional manner by allowing administrative deviations (§412) and by requiring that all trusts and their terms be for the benefit of the beneficiaries (§§105(b)(3) and 404).

In some cases public policy grounds may favor deviation. For example, assume that a testator devised land in the heart of a city's business district in trust for a long period and directed that no building shall be erected on it that is more than three stories high. The provision may be so harmful to the community, as well as to the trust beneficiaries, as to be unenforceable as against public policy. Similarly, trust provisions to tear down or board up a house for 20 years or throw money into the sea would be unenforceable (e.g., they would violate the UTC "for the benefit of the beneficiaries" mandate).

Because the requirements for deviation are not easy to meet, good drafters consider and reflect the importance of drafting for flexibility to meet changing circumstances, and usually repose significant discretion in the trustee to adapt to changing circumstances rather than being locked into a fixed formula for investment, allocation of principal and income, situs for trust administration, or whatever.

A far more difficult consideration arises with respect to deviation from *distributive* provisions. The traditional rule is that a court may alter the time or manner of a beneficiary's enjoyment to meet the beneficiary's legitimate needs, but a court may not alter or deprive a beneficiary of an entitlement unless the trustee is able to secure the consent of the beneficiaries who are affected by it, which is not always possible. For example, *In re Trust of Stuchell*, 801 P.2d 852 (Or. Ct. App. 1990), involved an unsuccessful effort to modify a trust to prevent a required distribution from adversely affecting an incompetent beneficiary's receipt of public assistance. A guardian was not appointed to consent for the incompetent beneficiary, perhaps because such a consent arguably would not have been in the beneficiary's best interests and might have exposed the guardian to future personal liability. Further, virtual representation was not a viable solution because the other beneficiaries were not similarly situated (they were going to receive their shares as drafted). The result was a denial of deviation even though it might have made the trust more advantageous to the beneficiaries as a class and notwithstanding the virtual certainty that the settlor could not have anticipated this state of affairs and arguably would not have objected to the deviation if still alive.

Another UTC modification of the common law is §412, which expands the deviation doctrine to permit distributive modifications as well as administrative changes if (1) there are unanticipated circumstances, (2) the modification or termination will further the purposes of the trust and (3) not violate the settlor's probable intention. For example, if the trust provides for distribution of fixed periodic amounts a court may increase the entitlement if the settlor's intent was to provide for the beneficiary's support and that originally designated amount no longer is adequate due to inflation or the beneficiary's incapacity.

### Charitable Trusts

Charitable or "exempt" organizations may be formed as trusts or corporations. It matters whether a trust is a "charitable trust" for several reasons: (1) the Rule Against Perpetuities typically does not apply, (2) the state Attorney General has standing to enforce the trust, (3) favorable tax treatment (deductions for contributions and no trust income tax) may be available, and (4) cy pres may be available to reform the trust.

A "charitable" trust is administered for charitable purposes. Most jurisdictions favor charitable trust status and instruments purporting to create them usually are interpreted to do so, if reasonably possible.

Charitable purposes are those generally that relieve poverty, advance education, religion, health, or for governmental or municipal purposes, or other purposes that are beneficial to the community. See UTC §405(a). But a stated charitable purpose will not necessarily ensure charitable trust status. For example, in *Shenandoah Valley National Bank v. Taylor*, 63 S.E.2d 786 (Va. 1951), the testator's purpose was characterized as "benevolent" (motivated by "mere kindness, good will, or a disposition to do good") but not charitable. The difference is that a charitable trust is public in nature; a benevolent trust is private. Unspecified charitable purposes can support a charitable trust, without specifying the particular charitable purpose the trust serves. For example, in *Jordan's Estate*, 197 A. 150 (Pa. 1938), a trust simply for "charity" was upheld against a claim made by the testator's heirs that the gift was void for uncertainty. Similarly, a trust established for charitable purposes as selected by the trustee normally will be charitable. Some trusts further exclusively charitable purposes, but many others have mixed charitable and private purposes.

The beneficiary of a charitable trust must be the public at large, or a sufficiently large or indefinite class of the public to give the public a sufficient interest to enforce the trust. Thus, a trust to benefit named individuals likely would be characterized as private even if distributions were to be made only for their education, religious welfare, or to provide them relief from poverty. Further, a trust to provide only for needy relatives, or for their education, would not be a charitable trust regardless of the size of the transferor's family. On the other hand, a trust for education or for needy persons generally may be charitable even if the trustee is to prefer relatives of the transferor. Note also that a trust for charitable purposes with priority given to the transferor's relatives *might* be charitable for state law purposes, but it would not be for federal tax purposes. To avoid controversy, many charitable trusts limit their beneficiaries to organizations that are recognized as charitable by the Internal Revenue Service. Such trusts are much easier to create and administer as charitable trusts and to be recognized as such for tax purposes than are trusts formed to engage directly in charitable activities.

Generally, a trust to provide assistance to victims of catastrophes is charitable regardless of whether benefits are restricted to victims who are poor. The relief of suffering provides a benefit to the community as a whole. An exception may apply if the class of affected persons is sufficiently small. Such a trust might be characterized as private. The test under Restatement (Second) of Trusts §375 is that the class must be sufficiently large "so that the community is interested in the enforcement of the trust." For example, assume a building was bombed in an act of terrorism, killing and injuring several hundred people. A trust to provide assistance to the survivors and families of the victims for their medical needs, housing, and education would be charitable. But if the terrorist act killed only one and injured two others, a similar trust might not be.

It is not necessary that the number of persons who receive benefits is large, if the class of persons from whom the recipients are selected is sufficiently large. Thus, a trust to provide a single college scholarship to a student at a specified high school who is selected as deserving by the trustee likely would be charitable because the advancement of education is a charitable purpose in its own right, regardless of whether the recipient must be needy. But an exception might apply if the high school graduating classes are very, very small, even if the recipient must be needy.

Charitable trusts are enforced by the state Attorney General. An innovation under UTC §405(c) is to also permit enforcement by the settlor. Merely being a permissible beneficiary of a charitable trust does not confer standing to enforce it, but a person with a "special interest" in enforcing the trust may do so. To illustrate, imagine a trust for the benefit of the persons who serve from time to time as minister of a specified church. This is charitable because it is viewed as promoting religion. Moreover, the currently serving minister has a special interest in enforcement of the trust, and has standing to do so.

Cy pres means "as near as possible" and the doctrine permits a court to alter a charitable trust to substitute a purpose that approximates the settlor's intent, rather than allow the trust to fail if the stated charitable object of the trust is or becomes illegal, impracticable, or impossible to accomplish. There often is no difficulty in determining whether a specific charitable purpose is illegal or impossible to carry out. Rather, cy pres cases often turn on whether such a purpose has become "impracticable." A general charitable intent to devote the property to charitable purposes is required, and usually will be found if a specific charitable purpose fails. For example, *In re Neher*, 18 N.E.2d 625 (N.Y. 1939), involved a gift to a village as a memorial to the transferor's late husband, "with the direction . . . that said property be used as a hospital." Because it was impracticable for the village to do so, the court reformed the trust to allow the property to be used for an administration building that would be named after the testator's husband, all because the testator's paramount intent was to give the property to the village for a general charitable purpose.

Finding a general charitable purpose will not always salvage a charitable trust that is or becomes impossible, impracticable, or illegal. For example, in *Evans v. Newton*, 148 S.E.2d 329 (Ga. 1966), a trust created to accomplish an illegal purpose (to provide a park only for whites) failed because the sole purpose was impossible to achieve. The result was a reversion to the transferor's heirs, as upheld in *Evans v. Abney*, 396 U.S. 435 (1970).

In some circumstances a failure to identify a trust's charitable purpose causes cy pres to be unavailable. For example, a trust would fail if D devised property to T in trust "for the charitable purposes I communicated to T before my death" if, following D's death, it is established that D never communicated any charitable purposes to T. This semi-secret trust would be impossible to enforce and clearly should not benefit T, so a resulting trust for D's estate beneficiaries would be imposed.

UTC §413 makes several changes to traditional charitable trust rules: (1) Cy pres may be applied if a charitable purpose becomes wasteful, in addition to unlawful, impracticable, or impossible to achieve. (2) Cy pres also is not dependent on a finding that the settlor had a general charitable intent. (3) Trust terms passing trust assets to noncharitable beneficiaries in lieu of cy pres are respected only if the property reverts to a settlor who is then living, or less than 21 years have passed since the trust was created.

A variety of difficult constitutional and policy issues arise if a charitable trust calls for discrimination, such as by race or gender. The Fourteenth Amendment prohibits states, or their instrumentalities, from engaging in discrimination. "State action" exists and the discrimination is prohibited state action if public officials participate in the trust administration. In such a case the trust will fail and the trust property can revert to the settlor (or the settlor's successors) if an alternative disposition was not provided in the instrument. Alternatively, cy pres might be used to modify the trust to eliminate the impropriety. Or any participation by the state in administering the trust could be eliminated (the Fourteenth Amendment not prohibiting private discrimination) and the trust could continue as intended. As such, private charitable trusts that discriminate may be valid for state law purposes (even though they are invalid for federal tax purposes). However, if the trustee of a trust intended to be administered on a discriminatory basis does not comply with the discrimination mandate, it is unlikely that the state Attorney General or a court could act to enforce the discriminatory nature of the trust without violating the Fourteenth Amendment. Meaning there would be no relief for the unintended (or intended) violation of the trust purpose.

# CHAPTER 14

# POWERS OF APPOINTMENT

Powers of appointment add flexibility to an estate plan. With them the powerholder may decide how to distribute property subject to the power after considering changed circumstances. Thus, the primary rationale for using powers of appointment is to enable the powerholder to take a "second look" at the facts and circumstances as they develop over the life of a trust and alter the donor's plan accordingly. For example, if a trust were distributable to the settlor's descendants by representation, and one descendant developed significant needs, the powerholder could exercise the power to benefit that descendant to a greater degree than other objects. It is as if the settlor of the trust were still alive and able to respond to changing needs and circumstances. Within limits prescribed by the creator of the power a power of appointment permits the power holder to select who will receive the property subject to the power. A power of appointment may be granted over property not in trust to permit the powerholder to alter who will receive property that is subject to the power. More commonly, however, powers of appointment are used only with trust property. Thus, the more likely scenario would be a transfer by a property owner in trust for the benefit of one or more beneficiaries, one of whom also would be given a power to appoint the trust property to others, usually at death or termination of prior interests.

A second reason for the use of powers is suggested by the title to the classic song by Tina Turner: "You Better Be Good to Me." Or, as Professor Halbach says, a power to appoint is a power to *dis*appoint, meaning that the powerholder may impress on the class of permissible appointees the need to pay attention to the powerholder lest they be divested of their expectancy by effective exercise of the power in favor of others. Thus, any beneficiary who is not appropriately attentive to the powerholder may be excluded from the property by exercise of the power in favor of other descendants.

A third use of powers is in lieu of mandatory distribution to a beneficiary who has reached the age or other qualification for distribution. The more appropriate drafting approach is not to force distribution of the share to that person but to allow the beneficiary to withdraw the entitlement. That power to withdraw is a general inter vivos power of appointment, as we will see shortly.

Finally, powers of appointment are used to accomplish tax objectives. For example, it usually is possible to avoid present gift tax treatment on a transfer to a trust if the donor retains a testamentary power of appointment, because the transfer is not sufficiently complete to incur the gift tax. This may be desirable because, depending on the tax planning involved, a completed gift on an initial transfer of property to a trust may not be appropriate. Certain taxable powers also are used to qualify for the estate and gift tax marital deduction and the gift tax §2503(c) qualified minor's trust annual exclusion. Further, efficient use of nontaxable powers may defer the incidence of generation-skipping transfer taxation, and there is a "Delaware Tax Trap" (along with other highly refined uses) to select between estate tax and generation-skipping transfer tax, depending on which is cheaper. This last concept is relatively complex and therefore is deferred to Chapter 19.

### Terminology

A general power permits the powerholder to personally benefit. It is a taxable power for federal wealth transfer tax purposes. All other powers are nongeneral. The creator of a power may make it presently exercisable (during the holder's life), at the holder's death (testamentary), or both. The person who creates a power to appoint is known as the donor of the power, regardless of whether the power is created by inter vivos instrument or by will. The person who is authorized to exercise a power of appointment is known as the donee of the power, regardless of whether the powerholder may not personally benefit from it. Because this can be confusing, modern literature and the Restatement (Third) of Property — Wills and Other Donative Transfers instead refers to the donee as the *powerholder* and we do so also.

The persons in whose favor a power of appointment may be exercised are known as the objects or permissible appointees of the power. If the donor provided that a power could be exercised only in favor of the donor's descendants, all those descendants would be objects or permissible appointees.

The persons who take appointive property to the extent a power is not validly exercised are known as the takers in default of exercise or the default beneficiaries. Thus, if the donor authorized exercise in favor of the donor's descendants and provided in default of exercise that the powerholder's descendants would benefit, the powerholder's descendants would be the default beneficiaries and the donor's descendants would be the objects or permissible appointees.

Powers come in two flavors (general or nongeneral) and may be exercised inter vivos or at death (or the donor may permit both). These characteristics also yield definitions. Indeed, classification typically focuses on these two relevant characteristics: the time and scope of exercise.

To wit, an *inter vivos*, or *presently exercisable*, power of appointment is exercisable by the powerholder by deed or other written instrument delivered to the trustee during the powerholder's life. Many statutes regard an inter vivos power of appointment as also exercisable at death, but technically and without statutory authority otherwise, an inter vivos power that is not expressly also a testamentary power ends the nanosecond before death. A *testamentary* power of appointment is exercisable by the powerholder by a valid will or, in some cases, a document *other than* a will that is regarded as effective only at death. Many powers are expressly both inter vivos and testamentary, meaning the powerholder may exercise them at any time during life or by will, effective at death.

A *general* power of appointment is defined for tax purposes as one that is exercisable in favor of the powerholder, the powerholder's estate, or creditors of either. Any other permissible appointee is irrelevant to classification. The key is whether the powerholder can benefit personally, directly or indirectly. For example, a trust beneficiary with a power to withdraw trust assets for the beneficiary's own enjoyment has a general power of appointment. Similarly, a transferor may convey a life estate to a transferee and authorize the transferee to consume principal if necessary to meet the transferee's needs. Such a power of consumption also would be a general power of appointment. A *nongeneral* power of appointment for tax purposes is any other power, including *statutory powers* that are exercisable in favor of anyone in the world except the powerholder, the powerholder's estate, or creditors of either. The old property law definition of "special" or "limited" powers of appointment is being subsumed by the tax definition of a nongeneral power, and the Restatement (Third) of Property — Wills and Other Donative Transfers has abandoned the old terminology in favor of general and nongeneral powers, with tax definitions to control for property law purposes.

Here are several sample power of appointment provisions:

### GENERAL TESTAMENTARY POWER
(from a Marital Deduction Trust)

Upon the death of my spouse the principal and any accrued and undistributed income of the trust estate shall be held in trust hereunder or distributed to or in trust for such appointee or appointees (including the estate of my spouse), with such powers and in such manner and proportions as my spouse may appoint by will, making specific reference to this power of appointment. Upon the death of my spouse, any part of the principal and accrued and undistributed income of the trust estate not effectively appointed shall be distributed to . . . [insert default beneficiaries]

Notice that this is a general power because the spouse can appoint to the spouse's own estate. The second sentence is the "default" clause, which governs distribution of the appointive property to the extent the power is not effectively exercised. Note also that it is not limited in application to a situation in which the power is not exercised, because it also should apply if the power is exercised ineffectively. To avoid several problems noted below relating to inadvertent exercise by will this testamentary power of appointment also could require exercise by an instrument delivered during life, with no effect until the powerholder's death.

## STATUTORY TESTAMENTARY POWER
### (from a Child's postponement trust)

Upon the death of a child who survives me, the child's trust shall be held in trust hereunder or distributed to or in trust for such appointee or appointees other than the child, his or her estate, his or her creditors, or the creditors of his or her estate, with such powers and in such manner and proportions as the child may appoint by his or her will making specific reference to this power of appointment. Upon the death of a child, any part of his or her trust not effectively appointed shall be distributed per stirpes to his or her then living descendants or, if none, then per stirpes to my then living descendants.

This is a "statutory" power of appointment because exercise may be in favor of the broadest class of permissible appointees allowed by the tax statutory definition without being a general power. With only one exception, only general powers of appointment are taxable, so the distinction is significant.

## NONGENERAL INTER VIVOS POWER
### (from nonmarital trust for a surviving spouse)

My spouse may at any time or times during [his or her] life by instrument in writing delivered to the trustee appoint any part or all of the principal to or in trust for any one or more of my descendants and their respective spouses and charitable, scientific, or educational purposes as [she or he] directs, and the trustee shall reimburse [him or her] from the remaining principal, if any, for the amount of any gift taxes incurred thereby.

This inter vivos power of appointment is more limited than the statutory power because the donor has allowed exercise only in favor of a limited class of permissible appointees. Still, both powers are nongeneral.

Two added classifications exist for nongeneral powers. Exclusive or nonexclusive involves the question whether the powerholder may exclude any permissible appointee in exercising the power (an exclusive power) and, if not (a nonexclusive power), how much must be given to each permissible appointee. Under a nonexclusive power each member of the class must receive a share, so a very broad class of permissible appointees would be impossible to administer. Thus, a nonexclusive power would be an impossibility in a statutory power of appointment and many other nongeneral powers, because nonexclusivity requires a narrow class of permissible appointees and a clear intent to preclude exclusion. The nonexclusive label also is contrary to a fundamental objective of powers (being to add flexibility), so this classification is disfavored. As a result, the intent to create a nonexclusive power must be clear. Proof may include extrinsic evidence of the relation of the appointees to the donor or to the powerholder and the size of the class, and a four corners consideration of the pattern of the estate plan and the use of certain language ("to," "among," or "between" are said to imply a nonexclusive power. Addition of "such of" or "any of" is said to negate this implication).

Without a clear articulation of intent, however, exclusive versus nonexclusive power cases may turn upon poorly crafted provisions and easily can constitute a source of malpractice liability. Consider *Hargrove v. Rich*, 604 S.E.2d 475 (Ga. 2004), in which the powerholder was permitted to appoint "to her brothers *or* sisters *or* her nieces *and* nephews, *or* descendants of deceased nieces *and* nephews" (emphasis added). The powerholder attempted to appoint to just one niece, to the exclusion of other nieces and nephews, which the court held was improper because the power was nonexclusive as among nieces and nephews. Thus, appointment in favor of *any* required exercise in favor of *all*. This was primarily a function of the court's focus on the use of the conjunctive "and" in the phrase "nieces and nephews" as compared to the disjunctive "or" in describing siblings. As a matter of construction the court also reflected the presumption that the same terminology will be used if the same intent exists in two different provisions. Given the use of polar opposite terms ("and" in one place, "or" in the other), the powerholder may have been signaling a different intent as between the two classes of permissible appointees. Moreover, another power in the same document used the term "to or among" appointees, which more clearly informs an exclusive power. Absence of that term in the subject power was important evidence of intent. Attention to detail would have avoided the need to litigate, either by using "or" consistently, adding a "between" or "among" reference, or better stating a positive intent to require exercise of the power to benefit every member in the class, which raises a second bedeviling issue.

If a nonexclusive power exists, this second concern is whether exercise was illusory, essentially meaning that so little was provided to a particular permissible appointee that the exercise should not be respected at all. To avoid invalidity if a power of appointment is nonexclusive, required is an appointment to each permissible appointee of a substantial and fairly proportionate amount in relation to the total fund. Given that requirement, if a donor truly wants the power to be nonexclusive it would be better to bequeath a certain amount to each intended beneficiary and not create the power at all, or give an exclusive power over amounts in excess of the minimum amount that the donor wanted each appointee to receive.

The second classification for nongeneral powers is whether the power is a "power in trust" (also referred to as an "imperative" power). Such a characterization applies, if at all, only to nongeneral powers with a very narrow class of permissible appointees and *no* default provision. This is a highly disfavored theory that is applied because we don't know what to do with the appointive property on the powerholder's death if there is no effective exercise (because there are no takers in default of exercise). Normally the property would revert to the donor in the absence of an effective exercise or a default provision. The imperative label is applied to avoid that result when it is clear that a reversion is contrary to the wishes of the donor, regardless of the powerholder's failure to effectively exercise the power. Instead, the imperative power label causes the property to go to the permissible appointees.

If an imperative power exists the permissible appointees take equal shares in default of exercise, equality being the law's favor and a court not being willing to create different sized shares. The reversion that normally would apply if there is no default provision and the powerholder fails to completely and effectively exercise the power always will be the case for general powers (unless the doctrine of capture applies, as discussed at page 294). The power in trust, or imperative power, classification merely deals with the problem of what to do with property subject to a power that is not exercised and for which default beneficiaries were not named by the donor. It is applied if it appears that the donor would not favor a reversion.

If it is a nongeneral power with a class that is ascertainable and reasonably limited, it may be reasonable to imply a default to each member of the class of permissible appointees, typically in equal shares with the right of representation. For example, in *Loring v. Marshall*, 484 N.E.2d 1315 (Mass. 1985), the testator did not provide for takers in default under a contingency that occurred, the powerholder did not exercise the power, and the permissible appointees were the powerholder's descendants. The two sets of alternative recipients of the trust property were the testator's heirs (on the theory that the testator effectively retained a reversion by not providing for default takers under the contingency that occurred) or the powerholder's descendants (on the implied default theory that the testator intended to benefit the class of permissible appointees and a taker-in-default-of-exercise provision in their favor therefore should be implied). The court chose the implied gift in default of exercise to the permissible appointees in large part because intestacy is not favored.

Cases go both ways on the question whether a deceased permissible appointee has a share that can descend — a share that is vested (subject to divestment if the power is exercised) — or whether only living appointees can take as the default beneficiaries of an imperative power. For example, assume that D devised Blackacre to S "with a power to devise Blackacre to such of my children as S may choose." If a power of appointment is deemed to exist and is not effectively exercised when S dies, then the issue is whether S's failure to exercise the power, combined with the failure of D to designate default takers, causes there to be a reversion to D (which may go to the children as takers of D's estate) or whether S has a fee simple absolute and the property passes with the balance of S's estate (which may not go to D's children). Alternatively, the power could be classified as imperative, which would guarantee that the children would receive the appointive property in default of S's effective exercise of the power. If so, and if one of D's children predeceased S, the additional issue is whether that child's successors would take that share.

## Creditors' Rights

Another important issue is whether a powerholder's creditors may reach property subject to a power of appointment on a theory that a powerholder should not be generous to appointees before being equitable to creditors.

### *Donor as Powerholder*

If the donor is also the powerholder (a self-created power of appointment, which is not common but it is permissible), the general rule is that creditors of the donor may reach the appointive property, but only to the extent the donor is insolvent. This rule applies whether the power is general or nongeneral, exercised or not. Curiously, with respect to creditors' rights, a power to revoke is given better protection — creditors usually cannot force exercise of a power to revoke. We cannot justify this disparate treatment of what appear to be similar powers, but recall the discussion in Chapter 13 regarding the exalted status of powers to revoke with respect to spendthrift clauses in general and the discussion in Chapter 10 in the context of the rights of a surviving spouse as against a funded revocable inter vivos trust.

### Third Party as Powerholder

If the donor is not the powerholder, the rights of the powerholder's creditors may depend on whether the power is general or nongeneral. Property subject to a nongeneral power is immune to claims of the powerholder's creditors, even if the power is exercised, because the property subject to the power is not and never could be the powerholder's property. This result is fully consistent with a traditional view that the holder of a power of appointment is not the owner of the property but acts only as an agent for the donor in exercising the power. Under this vision any exercise of the power is deemed to relate back to creation of the power by the donor, and the property is viewed as having passed directly from the donor to the appointee, not from the donor through the powerholder to the appointee.

The traditional rule, still the law in most states, is that property subject to a general power created by a donor who is not the powerholder may be reached by the powerholder's creditors *only* to the extent the power is exercised *and* only to the extent the powerholder is insolvent. Which is to say that the powerholder's own property should be exhausted to pay creditors before appointive property is taken for that purpose. Illustrative is *Irwin Union Bank & Trust Co. v. Long*, 312 N.E.2d 908 (Ind. Ct. App. 1974), in which a debtor was the income beneficiary of a trust from which he also was given the right to withdraw up to four percent of the trust principal annually. The debtor's former spouse obtained a divorce related judgment against him and unsuccessfully attempted to reach the portion of the principal he could withdraw to satisfy the judgment. The debtor's right to withdraw principal from the trust was an inter vivos general power of appointment but the property subject to that power was not his and thus was reachable by his creditors only to the extent he exercised the power.

Some states allow creditors to reach assets subject to unexercised inter vivos general powers to the extent the powerholder is insolvent, the notion being that the living powerholder could at any time seize these assets and creditors should be able to reach them too. UTC §505(b)(1) allows a powerholder's creditors to reach the property subject to the power, whenever the power may be exercised, apparently without regard to the powerholder's solvency. The comment to §505 notes that property subject to the power may be reached by the powerholder's creditors if the powerholder's probate estate is insufficient, if the powerholder retains the power until death. No mention is made of a similar limitation during the power holder's life. Inter vivos general powers are not common, except in lieu of a mandatory distribution of a trust share (or in the form of a withdrawal right used in trusts for tax planning purposes), so this rule does not arise often except in cases in which we would regard the trust corpus as "belonging" to the powerholder anyway. The Federal

Bankruptcy Code produces this result because the trustee in bankruptcy may exercise all the debtor's powers.

In most states, a powerholder's surviving spouse may reach appointive assets to satisfy an elective share claim only to the extent the powerholder exercised a general power in favor of the powerholder's estate, or the concept known as "capture" applies, to which we turn shortly. See page 294. Also note that under UPC §2-205(1)(i) a surviving spouse's elective share may reach assets subject to an inter vivos general power that the decedent held immediately before death.

## Contracts Regarding Powers

Occasionally, a powerholder wants to commit in advance to exercise the power in a specified manner, or to not exercise the power at all. A contract regarding exercise is the donee's agreement with a third party — a permissible appointee or otherwise — to exercise (or not to exercise) a power of appointment in a particular manner. In most jurisdictions contracting to exercise an inter vivos power is permissible but a contract to exercise a testamentary power is not enforceable. The different treatment relates to the donor's intent. The contract to exercise a testamentary power violates the donor's second look objective by presently locking in an exercise that the donor wanted to be performed only in the future, at the powerholder's death.

The powerholder's voluntary exercise in compliance with the contract is valid but the disappointed promisee of an unenforceable contract to exercise a power of appointment is not entitled to specific performance, nor to damages. This is because a damage recovery would act as an incentive to exercise the power in compliance with the contract, which the law wants to discourage. Restitution will apply for any consideration given pursuant to the contract, but exercise simply cannot be compelled by enforcement of the contract in any manner.

The release of a power of appointment acts like a renunciation. The powerholder essentially announces that the power will never be exercised. A release of a power is permissible, even if the power is testamentary and even though the release violates the donor's second look objective for giving the power. A release is acceptable but a contract to exercise is not, because a release amounts to an exercise in favor of the default takers, and this frustration of the donor's second look objective is permitted because the donor selected the ultimate (default) beneficiaries of the appointive property. That is not the case when the powerholder exercises under a contract (unless the contract was to not exercise the power and allow the appointive property to pass by default, or it was to appoint the property in favor of the takers in default). So the law addressing the two concepts differs in the results it is willing to accept. An exception to the rule allowing powers to be released applies if there is no default provision. Recall that the absence of default takers also is the circumstance in which an imperative power *might* be deemed to exist (although the two concepts may not overlap, because other requirements for application of the imperative power rule may not exist, such as a sufficiently small class of permissible appointees).

*Seidel v. Werner*, 364 N.Y.S.2d 963 (N.Y. Sup. Ct. 1975), aff'd, 376 N.Y.S.2d 139 (N.Y. App. Div. 1975), illustrates the difference between a permitted release of a testamentary power and an impermissible contract to exercise that power. In *Seidel* the holder of a testamentary power agreed to exercise it in favor of two of his four children, but failed to do so. A claim was made that the contract was effectively a release of the power because by statute the contract to exercise the power was unenforceable. That argument failed because the parties did not intend the contract to be a release, and because the effect of the promised exercise was substantially different than a release (e.g., a release would have resulted in all four children taking as default beneficiaries, not just two of them and, unlike the result under the default provision, the contract called for property to be held in trust for the two children until they reached majority, with the property to revert to the powerholder if they did not).

### Fraudulent Exercise

A powerholder's attempt to benefit nonobjects of the power usually results either in invalidation of the improper provisions of the appointment and the balance of the exercise being allowed to stand or, if those provisions are inseparable, the entire exercise being deemed void. An exercise in fraud of the power also is void if it is clear that the powerholder would not have exercised the power if the invalid attempt failed. For example, imagine that Powerholder wants to benefit Surviving Spouse, but the power of appointment allows exercise only in favor of lineal descendants of Powerholder's grandparent (the donor who created the trust). So Powerholder elicits an agreement from a nephew — a permissible appointee — under which Powerholder will direct $150,000 to the nephew for his sole enjoyment and another $100,000 that the nephew will deliver to Surviving Spouse. A court might bifurcate the exercise, allowing the nephew to keep the $150,000 and invalidating the purported appointment of the other $100,000. More appropriately the court should invalidate the entire exercise, finding the provisions to be inseparable and tainted by the powerholder's motives and the nephew's participation in the fraud on the power. See *In re Carroll's Will*, 8 N.E.2d 864 (N.Y. 1937).

Note that, although there can be nonobjects of a limited class general power of appointment, this fraudulent exercise doctrine is applicable only to nongeneral powers because the holder of a general power could withdraw or appoint to the powerholder's own estate and then leave the appointive property to whomever the powerholder wanted. Also note that a powerholder's exercise in favor of a permissible appointee is valid without regard to the powerholder's motive for the exercise. Thus, a capricious or arbitrary exercise of a power of appointment is copacetic and the possibility of such an exercise should be considered by the donor in deciding whether to grant a power. The powerholder has the discretion to change the donor's plan to the extent the power is exercisable. Only a fraudulent exercise is not valid.

## Effective Exercise of Powers

The capacity of a powerholder and the formalities required to exercise a power are those applicable to the relevant medium for exercise. For example, testamentary capacity is required to exercise a testamentary power; the capacity to deed (which generally is a little higher than the capacity required to execute a will) is required to exercise an inter vivos power over land by written instrument. In addition, most states permit the donor to impose extra formalities, which most often is done by requiring the donee to make specific reference to the power to validly exercise it. For example, review again the sample powers at page 283. Each testamentary power of appointment contains a specific reference requirement, designed to prevent inadvertent or "blanket" exercise of unknown powers by a broad residuary clause employing language such as: "I leave all the residue of my estate, *including all property over which I may have any power of appointment, . . .*" Preventing this form of blind exercise is very important.

### *Blanket Residuary Clauses*

Many wills contain a blanket exercise provision that purports to exercise all powers over property that the testator may control, even if the power is unknown to the testator. By it, even without knowledge of a particular power, the powerholder's will seeks to serve as a conclusive (nonrebuttable) exercise, because the powerholder's intent to exercise is manifest on the face of the will. Such an exercise will not be effective, however, if the donor conditioned exercise of the power on the powerholder making a specific reference to the power in the powerholder's will.

There is a tension at work here. Without doubt, the intent of the average testator is to exercise all powers under either a statutory presumption applicable to a silent residuary clause or a blanket "exercise all powers" provision. We know that, if asked, a powerholder would desire that appointive assets pass to the objects of the powerholder's selection, rather than to those designated by the donor as takers in default of exercise or to the donor's successors if there is no default provision. Thus, assuming the groups of potential beneficiaries differ, exercise has the perceived advantage of substituting the powerholder's devisees for those who would receive in default of exercise of the power. It is precisely this blind desire to control the property that wise planners seek to prevent.

The unfortunate aspect of any blind or inadvertent blanket exercise is that frequently unknown powers would be better left unexercised. By way of example, assume Testator (T) is unaware of the existence of a testamentary power of appointment of which T is powerholder. Assume also that the default provision would dispose of appointive assets not effectively appointed to T's descendants living at T's death (which is a pretty common scenario) and that these descendants are the persons to whom T's estate passes by will. T's objectives might be equally well served in such a situation without exercise of the power. Yet, exercise could create some or all of the following problems.

First, if the power is a general power created before October 22, 1942, the assets subject to the power will be includible in the powerholder's gross estate for federal estate tax purposes only to the extent the power is exercised. Thus, unnecessary taxes will be avoided if the property is left to pass under the default provision. Although the incidence of such pre-1942 powers is dwindling, the older the power is, the more probable it is that the powerholder is unaware of its existence and that exercise therefore will be inadvertent. Second, as we saw earlier, under the common law creditors of the powerholder of a general power of appointment may reach appointive assets only to the extent the power is exercised and the powerholder is insolvent. This protection is lost through unanticipated exercise of unknown powers of appointment.

In addition, unintentional exercise of a power of appointment may cause the exercise to fail (e.g., the power of appointment may be nonexclusive or the donee may cause appointment in favor of impermissible appointees). Inadvertent exercise of a power also may run afoul of the Rule Against Perpetuities. This especially is true in light of the differing axioms governing when the period of the Rule commences with respect to powers of appointment. See Chapter 17 for further information. If unintended exercise violates the Rule, a state's *cy pres* statute may apply to reform the exercise. In such a case, however, litigation likely would be fostered, along with thorny administrative problems of segregation and marshaling of assets validly passing under the exercise to individuals whose interests do not violate the Rule. These complications are further compounded by the doctrine of capture, applicable to any attempted exercise of a general testamentary power that is incurably invalid. Both marshaling and capture are discussed next below. And further yet, all of these problems are exacerbated if the existence of a power of appointment is not discovered until some time after the powerholder's death, notwithstanding that the power was exercised unknowingly by the powerholder's will.

### *Marshaling*

If a power has been exercised inadvertently, of greater significance is the potential liability of a powerholder's personal representative attributable to the doctrine of marshaling. Applicable only with respect to testamentary powers of appointment, the doctrine of marshaling (sometimes referred to as "allocation") may govern if exercise of a power is valid in part. The doctrine applies only to a "blending" exercise that treats appointive assets and the powerholder's own assets as commingled prior to distribution pursuant to the powerholder's will. Under the doctrine, appointive assets will be used to fund those dispositions that are valid under the will, while the powerholder's own assets will be applied to dispositions that violate the power. The doctrine thus results in "saving" the exercise to the fullest extent possible.

If there is a blending exercise, it is incumbent upon a powerholder's personal representative to ascertain the extent to which appointive assets and the powerholder's own assets must be marshaled to the various interests created under the will, which is a virtual impossibility with respect to unidentified powers. To illustrate, assume that D devised D's entire estate to T in trust, income and principal being distributable in T's discretion to D's grandchild, GC, for life. GC also had a nongeneral testamentary power to appoint the trust assets in favor of D's descendants. When GC died, the trust was valued at $1 million and GC owned additional assets also valued at $1 million. GC devised "all property I own and have a power to appoint as follows: half to the Red Cross and half to my descendants, per stirpes." GC was survived by one child, C. Because the trust assets could not be appointed to the Red Cross, the personal representative of GC's estate (PR) is required under the doctrine of marshaling to allocate GC's own assets to the Red Cross and the appointive assets to C. If PR was unaware of GC's power of appointment over the trust assets, however (which might be the case if, for example, GC was not receiving distributions from the trust when GC died), PR might distribute $500,000 of the assets in S's probate estate to each of the Red Cross and C. What happens when it later is discovered that GC possessed and exercised the power? Because the Red Cross is not an object of the power, none of the appointive assets may be distributed to it. In that case C receives more, and the Red Cross receives less, than they should have received if marshaling had applied. The Red Cross may have a claim against either PR or C for the assets the Red Cross would have received if GC's own assets and the appointive assets properly had been marshaled. PR likely would escape liability only if PR neither knew nor reasonably could be expected to know of the trust and of GC's power.

### Capture

The doctrine of capture may apply to the extent a powerholder makes an invalid or ineffective effort to exercise a *general* power of appointment. An attempt to exercise a general power is taken as an intent to "capture" the appointive assets, taking them out of the donor's plan and allowing the powerholder to dispose of them, even if exercise fails. Under this doctrine, a powerholder is deemed to have made an exercise to the powerholder's own estate by virtue of a failed attempt to appoint to someone else. Thus, to the extent an exercise fails, capture applies, meaning that the appointive assets pass pursuant to the powerholder's estate plan, rather than under the power's default provision (or, in the absence of a default provision, to the donor's successors). Capture applies only to general powers because the powerholder of a nongeneral power could not have appointed the property to the powerholder's estate (i.e., could not have captured the property for disposition as a part of the powerholder's estate).

For example, D devised D's estate: "To T1, in trust, income to P for life, remainder to such person or persons, in trust or outright, as P appoints by will. To the extent P does not effectively exercise this power of appointment, remainder to the Red Cross." P's will provides: "I give the residue of my estate, and all property over which I have a power of appointment, to T2, in trust, . . ." Assume that the testamentary trust P attempted to create violated the Rule Against Perpetuities and failed (as discussed in Chapter 17, the perpetuities period for measuring the validity of P's exercise of the general testamentary power would begin to run at D's death, not at P's). The question is whether the trust assets should pass to the Red Cross, as the taker in default under D's will, or to P's heirs. Under the doctrine of capture, P's heirs take.

The exercise of a general power can fail and trigger application of the doctrine of capture because of a violation of the Rule, as illustrated in the example, or if the appointee predeceases the powerholder and antilapse does not apply (see the discussion of lapse at page 297), or if the exercise is to a trust that fails for a reason other than a violation of the Rule, such as indefinite beneficiaries. The powerholder's personal representative has the same fiduciary obligation to collect captured assets as with any other probate assets. Difficult as it is for the trustee of a power to know if the powerholder's will exercised a power (see the discussion above), there is no workable process by which the powerholder's personal representative may locate all powers the powerholder possessed and exercised. If the power was unknown to the powerholder, it presumably will be unknown to the personal representative as well (as it might be even if the powerholder knew of the power). Yet reasonable efforts must be made to identify any powers that may have been exercised.

Capture is applicable to either a blending exercise (as illustrated in the example above) or a nonblending exercise (e.g., "I leave the residue of my estate to A. I exercise any powers of appointment I may have as follows: . . . "). Also as illustrated by the example, the presence of a default clause will not preclude application of capture. The property will pass to the takers in default of exercise named by the donor only to the extent there is no attempted exercise. Capture will apply unless the powerholder of a general power fails to exercise or to attempt to exercise the power. There will be a reversion to the donor or the donor's successors only to the extent there was no default provision and no attempted exercise.

### *Exercise by Silent Residuary Clause*

Capture applies when a powerholder unsuccessfully attempts to exercise a general power (with a blanket or specific, blended, or nonblended exercise). The question we now consider is whether a *silent* residuary provision in the powerholder's will exercises powers held by the powerholder. As a general rule, a silent residuary provision that makes no reference to powers (e.g., "all the residue of my estate") typically does not serve as an exercise. But a residuary clause in the powerholder's will does exercise, even if it makes no reference to powers, if it can be established that the powerholder intended to exercise the power. For example, D's will devised Blackacre to T1, in trust, income to P for life, remainder as P appoints by will, otherwise to D's descendants, per stirpes, to the extent P does not effectively exercise the power. P's will provides: "I give my entire estate to T2 in trust for X for life." P's will also includes provisions granting powers and directing T2 in the administration of the trust. Among them is: "If X's child, C, desires to work on Blackacre, I request that T2 employ C to do so for as long as C desires." P's silent residuary clause would not exercise P's power under the general rule, but the reference to T2 employing C to work on Blackacre (the property subject to the power) indicates P's intent that the residuary clause exercise the power, and it would do so.

Proof of intent to exercise is allowable to rebut the presumption if the general rule (nonexercise) applies. Proof may include factors such as (1) the disposition under the powerholder's will if appointment occurs; (2) partial invalidity of the powerholder's plan if the power is not exercised (e.g., the powerholder's estate is $100,000; the trust assets over which the powerholder has a power are $500,000; the powerholder's will leaves $200,000 to X and the residue to Y; if the will does not exercise the power, X will get only $100,000 and Y will get nothing); and (3) factors showing that the powerholder could have meant to exercise, including knowledge of the power, lack of reason not to exercise, that the residuary taker was a natural object of the powerholder's bounty, that the amounts involved were not inappropriate for the situation, and mistake by the powerholder or the drafting attorney as to ownership of the appointive property or the necessity for express exercise.

An exception to the general rule (nonexercise) is recognized in some states for *general* powers because the powerholder/testator may think of the appointive property as if it belonged to the powerholder personally. Again, however, the question is one of the powerholder's intent, and a silent residuary clause will not be deemed to exercise the power if it is proven that the powerholder did not intend to exercise. In *Beals v. State Street Bank & Trust Co.*, 326 N.E.2d 896 (Mass. 1975), the powerholder had treated the appointive property as her own. This led the court to treat a power as having been exercised by a silent residuary clause. That power originally was a general power, but it had been cut back to a nongeneral power years earlier (probably for tax reasons). The jurisdiction treated silent residuary clauses as exercising general but not nongeneral powers and, for this purpose and under those unique circumstances, the court applied the general power of appointment rule notwithstanding the cutback. We think that probably was the wrong result in *Beals*, predominantly because the powerholder had another power of appointment that the powerholder expressly exercised, showing that the powerholder knew how to exercise when that was the intent.

Silent residuary clauses also exercise *nongeneral* powers in a few jurisdictions, *if* all the devisees of the residuary clause are permissible appointees of the power (and again unless an intention of the powerholder not to exercise the power is proven).

## Conflict of Laws

The question addressed here was at issue in *Beals*: which state's law governs exercise of a power if the donor died in state A and the trust is administered there, but the powerholder dies in state B? The traditional rule is to apply the law that governs the trust administration, which usually was the donor's domicile (state A in this case). But the logical approach to this issue would be to apply the law of the powerholder's domicile because exercise issues arise under the powerholder's will, because we are most interested in whether the powerholder intended to exercise the power, and because the powerholder (and any attorney who presumably assisted) planned with respect to the law of the powerholder's domicile. Although there is a modern trend to apply the law of state B in our example, and for very good reason, only a very small number of cases so far have deviated from the traditional rule.

To illustrate, assume that Donor died in New York, where Donor was a lifetime resident, and created a testamentary trust that grants Powerholder a nongeneral testamentary power to appoint the corpus of the trust. The trust now is administered by a California trustee for the benefit of beneficiaries located around the country. Powerholder's will, executed in Indiana where Powerholder was domiciled at death, fails to make any reference to the power, stating only that "the residue of my estate shall be distributed per stirpes to my descendants who survive me." Assuming for the sake of argument that Powerholder's descendants are all permissible appointees under Donor's power, the issue would be whether the New York rule that silent residuary clauses are effective to exercise nongeneral powers should apply. Also assume that Indiana follows the more traditional rule that a silent residuary provision does not exercise unspecified powers. Although it is possible that Powerholder (or Powerholder's attorney) was aware of the New York rule and therefore found it unnecessary to state the intent to exercise the power, it is far more likely that they were acting on the basis of their understanding of Indiana law that governed all other aspects of Powerholder's will. Indeed, it may be that Powerholder did not know that the power of appointment was available. Extrinsic evidence would be admissible to establish Powerholder's likely intent to exercise, but that endeavor would not be necessary if New York law applies to this case in the first instance, and New York law *would* apply under the traditional conflict of laws rule for this situation. Modern cases would apply the law of Indiana. No case would select California on the basis of the simple situs for administration. See, e.g., *White v. United States*, 680 F.2d 1156 (7th Cir. 1982) (applying Indiana law in the hypothetical facts); *Toledo Trust Co. v. Santa Barbara Foundation*, 512 N.E.2d 664 (Ohio 1987) (Ohio trust with a California powerholder, applying California law).

## Lapse Issues

We learned in Chapter 8 that a gift is said to lapse (i.e., fail) if a testator devises property to someone who dies before the testator, and does not provide for that possibility. Generally, antilapse statutes apply if the devisee and the testator were related in a specified manner. If so, the predeceased devisee's descendants receive the devise by representation under the antilapse statute. Does an antilapse statute apply if an appointee predeceases the powerholder of a testamentary power?

The lapse rules can be problematic in the context of powers of appointment, notwithstanding the fiction that a powerholder who exercises a power of appointment is an agent of the donor and that the exercise "relates back" (as if the exercise terms were written in the donor's trust all along). The general rule has been that antilapse statutes do not apply to powers of appointment because the statutory representatives of the appointee (typically, the appointee's descendants) may be individuals who are not within the class of permissible appointees. For example, D devised D's estate to T, in trust, to pay income to C for life, and gave C a testamentary power to appoint the trust assets at C's death among C's siblings. C's will exercises the power and appoints the property to C's sibling, S, who was living when C executed C's will but who died before C. S's descendants would take if the jurisdiction's antilapse statute applies, even though they were not permissible appointees. For that reason (and because antilapse statutes on their face often apply only to devises by will), the traditional rule has been that antilapse statutes are not applied to exercises of powers in favor of appointees who predecease the powerholder.

Some courts will apply an exception and invoke the jurisdiction's antilapse statute if the power is general. This is not necessarily copacetic if the class of permissible appointees of the general power is narrow (e.g., exercisable only in favor of siblings and creditors of the powerholder's estate, which makes it a general power, probably for tax purposes to avoid a generation-skipping transfer tax).

The modern rule is reflected in UPC §2-707(e) and Restatement (Third) of Property — Wills and Other Donative Transfers §18.6. They allow antilapse statutes to apply and permit descendants of deceased objects to take directly. Their theory is that the predeceased appointee, if alive, could have left the appointive property to those persons. A question that remains under such modern statutes may be whether the predeceased appointee is within the class of beneficiaries covered by the antilapse statute. In applying such a statute, it is necessary to determine whether the appointee must be a relative of the donor or of the powerholder. Consistent with the relation back theory applicable to powers, is it relation to the donor that counts? It should not be. The sensible rule is that relation to the powerholder should govern, but don't expect to find unanimity on this issue either.

### Analyzing Powers of Appointment

Consider the following approach in analyzing power of appointment questions. Because general and nongeneral powers are treated so differently for a variety of reasons, first determine whether the power is general or nongeneral.

o   If *general*, then consider the following:

- If inter vivos, in some jurisdictions the powerholder's creditors may reach property subject to the power, regardless of whether the power was exercised. In most, however, they may reach such property only to the extent the power was exercised. If testamentary, the powerholder's creditors may reach property subject to the power only to the extent it is exercised.

- If exercised in favor of an appointee who predeceased the powerholder, does the jurisdiction's antilapse statute apply to cause the appointee's descendants to take? If so, must they be related to the powerholder or to the donor?

- In a minority of jurisdictions, a silent residuary clause in the powerholder's will is presumed to exercise the power (unless the donor required the powerholder to make specific reference to the power to exercise it). If such a presumption arises, is there evidence to rebut it?

- If ineffectively exercised, consider application of the doctrine of capture, under which the property subject to the power would pass as a part of the powerholder's estate.

- If not exercised, are default beneficiaries named to take the property? If not exercised and default beneficiaries are not named, there is a reversion to the donor or the donor's successors.

o If nongeneral, consider the following:

- Creditors of the powerholder may not reach the property subject to the power regardless of whether it is exercised.

- Is the power exclusive or nonexclusive? The presumption is exclusive. Is there sufficient evidence of intent to the contrary? If a nonexclusive, nongeneral power is exercised, the question is whether a sufficient amount was appointed to each object to avoid allegations of an illusory exercise.

- If the power is exercised, are the appointees permissible appointees?

- To the extent the power was not effectively exercised, were default beneficiaries designated by the donor? If not, is the class sufficiently narrow to warrant characterizing the power as imperative, or is there an implied gift to the permissible appointees, in either case causing the property to be distributed equally among the permissible appointees? If so and if one or more of them predeceased the powerholder, does the jurisdiction allow successors of the deceased permissible appointee to take his or her share?

- The property will revert to the donor or the donor's successors if the power is not effectively exercised, default beneficiaries were not designated, and if imperative power classification and an implied default to the objects are not appropriate.

- Is the power exercised as part of a plan to indirectly benefit a nonobject, in which case the exercise may be invalid altogether under the fraud on a power doctrine?

o  Whether general or nongeneral, if the power is exercised by a blending clause in the powerholder's will, would part of the attempted exercise be invalid? If so, can marshaling be applied to save the exercise in whole or in part?

# CHAPTER 15

# FUTURE INTERESTS

Virtually all inter vivos or testamentary trusts create future interests. And virtually all future interest questions arise because the instrument did not clearly address a contingency that occurred. Rules of construction help to give effect to the presumed intent of the settlor. This Chapter addresses future interest classification and construction. Subjects covered include characteristics of future interests, distinguishing between vested and contingent future interests, whether the future interest holder must survive until the time of possession, and gifts conditioned on a beneficiary dying without issue or made to someone's heirs, descendants, issue, or children.

For many readers "future interests" connotes archaic rules of English law that have little or no relevance to the modern practice of law. In fact, future interests are fundamental to a modern trusts and estates practice because trusts are commonly used and routinely create future interests. Most trusts are created to permit enjoyment of trust income and principal by one beneficiary or group of beneficiaries, followed by distribution to a different beneficiary or group of beneficiaries (e.g., income to my spouse for life, remainder to my children). Fortunately, the future interests that we encounter are relatively straightforward and much of the confusion of future interest law is reserved for busted plans (not the kind that you will draft). Indeed, our endeavor in this Chapter is to highlight how to avoid common future interest drafting errors.

Future interests (and, for that matter, present interests) may be created with respect to the legal or equitable title to property. Historically, future interests typically were created for legal estates: e.g., a devise by D of "Blackacre to A for life, remainder to B." At D's death, A has a legal life estate in Blackacre (a present interest), and B has the legal remainder (a future interest). Today, the vast majority of future interests are created in trust: e.g., a devise by D of "Blackacre to T, in trust, for A for life, remainder to B." At D's death, A has an equitable life estate (again, a present interest), and B has an equitable remainder (a future interest). Our focus is on future interests in trust (equitable estates). The rules for future interests in legal estates *usually* are the same, but occasionally they differ. For example, the Doctrine of Destructibility of Contingent Remainders (discussed at page 316) only applies to legal estates. We will study it briefly only because it spawned rules that bleed over and affect future interests in trust.

On occasion we will distinguish rules of law versus rules of construction. A rule of law controls without regard to intent. For example, if D devised property in trust for a period equal to lives in being at D's death plus 22 years, the devise violates the Rule Against Perpetuities without regard to D's intent. By contrast, most of the rules we study in this Chapter are rules of construction that are needed because the controlling instrument was not properly drafted and did not address clearly the issue raised. In other words, if the instrument reflects the settlor's intent with respect to an issue about which a rule of construction applies, the settlor's intent and not the rule of construction controls. To a significant degree we are studying this material to know how not to draft certain provisions. As you proceed through this Chapter, consider how the issues you study could have been avoided by careful drafting.

It may help to keep in mind that a future interest is a presently existing property right or interest that may or will grant possession or enjoyment in the future. Enjoyment may be contingent. For example, consider a devise by D: "To A for life, remainder to B, but if B does not survive A, remainder to C." At D's death C has a future interest that may never vest in possession (if A and B still are alive). But the interest presently exists. It is transferable, enforceable, and protectable. In this regard, interests in unborns are supported by a relation back doctrine. Because the unborn cannot hold title to the future interest prior to birth, ownership is deemed to attach or fix at birth and relate back to creation of the interest. This explains the class opening and closing rules discussed in Chapter 8 — the interest fixing and relating back as if always there, as each member of the class is born (and, if survivorship is required, as each dies).

To illustrate, assume that T has two children: A and B. Only B has children. A does not, and is not expected to in the future. T wants to divide T's estate between A and B, but T wants what A does not use during A's life to be divided among B's children, if they reach age 25. Thus, T leaves the estate half outright to B and the other half in trust for A for life, remainder to B's children who reach age 25. T dies survived by A, B, and one child of B (C). The class of B's children who will share in the remainder does not close until A's death (if a child of B is at least 25 when A dies), or thereafter when a child of B reaches age 25 (if no child of B is at least 25 at A's death). If D is born to or adopted by B after T's death but before the class closes, D's interest fixes at D's birth or adoption and relates back to the date of T's death, as if D had a contingent remainder from that date.

## Classification

When a transferor conveys a present interest in property, the future interest that follows it may be retained by the transferor or it may be conveyed to one or more other transferees (or it may be conveyed in part and retained in part). In the chart below the interests that the transferor may retain are in the left hand column, of which there are three types, two that follow defeasible fees (a possibility of reverter and a power of termination) and one that does not (a reversion). The names of these interests remain even if the transferor at some later date conveys the retained interest to a third party. What counts here is that the transfer creating the present interest did not also convey the future interest. It was retained and later transferred.

If instead the entire fee simple absolute was conveyed by one instrument, with the present interest to one transferee and the future interest to another, then the labels in the right hand column apply. Note how the same "size" or "quality" of interest may be classified differently based on the side of this chart on which it appears. For example, if the present interest holder (in the center column) has a fee simple determinable, the future interest will be a possibility of reverter if it is held by the transferor. It will be a shifting executory interest if it was created in a third party by the same conveyance that created the present interest. As we proceed through the materials in this Chapter, note how such seemingly similar interests (except for the identity of the person holding the interest) may have different rights, attributes, and consequences.

| Future Interests Retained by Transferor (or Successors) | Present Interests | Future Interests Transferred to Another Person |
|---|---|---|
| None | Fee Simple | None |
| Possibility of Reverter | Fee Simple Determinable ("so long as" / "until") | Shifting Executory Interest |
| Power of Termination a/k/a Right of Entry for Condition Broken | Fee Simple Subject to Condition Subsequent ("but if" / "provided that") | Shifting Executory Interest |
| Reversion | Particular Estates (Life Estate / Term of Years) | Remainder |
| ∟———————>Reversion | | Springing Executory Interest |

In the right hand column, for most purposes there is no substantive difference between an executory interest and a remainder that is contingent. Each is created in transferees when the present interest is conveyed and in each case there is only a possibility that the future interest will become possessory. The contingent remainder or executory interest becomes possessory only if the required condition occurs. The difference in operation of the two estates is that (with one minor exception) an executory interest becomes possessory by divesting a preceding estate but a contingent remainder becomes possessory at the expiration of a preceding estate without "divesting" that estate.

For example, G devised an estate: "To T, in trust, for A for life, remainder to B, but if B does not survive A, then remainder to C." As discussed below, B's remainder is vested subject to divestment by a condition subsequent, and C's estate is an executory interest rather than a contingent remainder. By contrast, if G's devise was: "To T, in trust, for A for life, remainder to B if B survives A, otherwise to C," surviving A is a condition precedent to B's remainder. B's estate is a contingent remainder, which makes C's interest an alternative contingent remainder rather than an executory interest. In each case C's future interest will become possessory only if B predeceases A. The operational difference between the two is that, in the first example, C's interest becomes possessory by divesting B. In the second, B's death before A causes C's contingent remainder to become possessory without divesting B. Should you care? The truth for most every purpose is NOT AT ALL! So, don't obsess about these historical and picky distinctions unless you have a case in which they matter for some unforeseen reason.

Whether a transferee's future interest is a contingent remainder or an executory interest usually will not affect it becoming possessory (if the applicable condition precedent or subsequent occurs), but it may in limited circumstances. For example, the Rule in Shelley's Case, Doctrine of Worthier Title, and Rule of Destructibility of Contingent Remainders (each discussed below) exempt executory interests but not contingent remainders. To the very limited extent these arcane rules are still viable, they may allow extinction or merger of interests for modification or termination purposes, for different enforcement purposes, for marketability, and more.

For example, assume O conveyed property: "To T, in trust, to pay the income to A for life, remainder to B, but if B does not survive A, remainder to O's heirs." B's remainder is vested, subject to divestment. Therefore, O's heirs have an executory interest, not a contingent remainder. Accordingly, if the Doctrine of Worthier Title is still applicable in the jurisdiction (which is not likely) it would not apply to cause the gift to O's heirs to be treated as a reversion in O. (The Doctrine of Worthier Title is discussed at page 317.) Similarly, if O conveyed land: "To T, in trust, to pay the income to A for life, remainder to B, but if B does not survive A, remainder to A's heirs," A's heirs have an executory interest and the Rule in Shelley's Case (in the unlikely event that it still is applicable in the jurisdiction) therefore would not apply to cause the gift to A's heirs to be treated as a remainder in A. (The Rule in Shelley's Case is discussed at page 317.) Finally, assume O conveyed Blackacre (not in trust): "To A for life, remainder to B, but if B does not graduate from law school before reaching age 25, then to C if C graduates from law school before reaching age 25." Also assume that A dies survived by B (age 20), and by C (age 18). C has an executory interest, not a contingent remainder. As a result, the Rule of Destructibility of Contingent Remainders (if still applicable in the jurisdiction, which also is unlikely) would not apply to destroy C's estate at A's death.

Classification also is important because the Rule Against Perpetuities does not apply to vested interests and applies to contingent remainders and executory interests with different consequences. The Rule does not apply at all to any interest that the transferor retains, because they are not "transfers" that might "vest" outside the period of the Rule. Thus, the Rule does not apply to interests in the left column, retained when the present interest was created and later transferred to a third party by a separate document.

Vesting is very important because it affects entitlement, the class opening and closing rules, tax liability, and more. To illustrate, O conveyed Blackacre to T in trust for A for life, remainder to B. Assume B predeceased A. At A's death Blackacre belongs to B and will be distributed to B's estate and pass through it to B's heirs or devisees because B's remainder is vested (e.g., "to A for life, remainder to B," and UPC §2-707 is not applicable; see the discussion at page 323). O has retained a reversion if B's remainder is contingent (e.g., "to A for life, remainder to B *if B survives A*") and there is no alternative disposition. In such a case Blackacre will revert to O at A's death for disposition to O's successors. In the first case B's estate will include the value of the remainder for estate tax purposes. In the second case O's estate will include the value of the reversion.

As an illustration of how vesting can affect class opening and closing rules, consider the following. O's gift is "to B's children who reach age 25." B has two children, C (age 19) and D (age 10). C dies before reaching age 25. C has a contingent interest and C's death before age 25 causes the class to remain open until D reaches age 25. Thus, E will become a member of the class if E is born to B eight years after the gift is made (when D is 18). But if the gift had been "to B's children, payable at age 25," C's gift would be vested (see the discussion of *Clobberie's Case* on page 324) and the class would close no later than six years later when C would have reached age 25, regardless of whether C lives until then. As a result, E would be excluded from the class.

Transfer tax results may vary. The value of a transmissible interest (vested or contingent) is included in the holder's estate for estate tax purposes (but usually the contingency causes a contingent remainder or executory interest to have little or no value). On the contrary, a vested interest would be includible with a value that reflects only the delay attributable to deferred possession or enjoyment until the present interest ends. If the interest is not transmissible, it is not subject to estate tax at the owner's death, regardless of whether it is vested or contingent. For example, O conveyed Blackacre in trust, "income to A for life, remainder to B, but if B does not survive A, then to C." C has a transmissible executory interest because C need not survive A or B to take. If C predeceases A, C's executory interest passes to C's heirs or devisees and its value is includible in C's estate (although the value of C's executory interest would be a small fraction of the value of Blackacre if A is elderly and in poor health and B is young and in excellent health at C's death). But B's interest (which is vested, subject to divestment) terminates if B dies before A. In this event there is nothing for B to transmit to B's heirs or devisees and nothing to be included in B's estate for estate tax purposes. If the gift had been "income to A for life, remainder to B if living, otherwise to C," B's contingent remainder would have no value at B's death before A. For estate tax purposes, zero would be includible in B's estate.

In addition, vesting may affect state law rights to accountings and enforceability and the ability to enjoin actions or waste by the present interest holder. Thus, a vested remainder is entitled to more effective current protection than a contingent one. As a result of these differences courts sometimes trifle with classifications, to distinguish unwanted precedent. As such, future interests is either a "wonderful calculus" or "a particularly low sort of cunning," sometimes all in the same case! And care is required in every case in which the classification rules are applied, to be sure the precedent is from a case that is similar in its inquiry (e.g., a case looking to avoid application of the antiquated Rule in Shelley's Case isn't likely to be persuasive in a current tax dispute). Also be sure the precedent is not skewed by the application of rules that were developed in response to doctrines no longer in force (e.g., the preference for early vesting or for vested over contingent remainders to avoid the Doctrine of Destructibility of Contingent Remainders, which no longer exists and never applied to equitable interests in trust).

### Future Interests of the Transferor

Consult again the chart at page 303. The future interests the transferor retained (in the left column) when the present interest was conveyed are:

- **Possibility of Reverter**, retained when a transferor conveys a fee simple determinable and does not provide for a third party to take if the fee is terminated. A fee simple determinable is a fee simple estate that is limited or defeasible. It often is identifiable by the use of words of duration, such as "so long as" or "until." For example, "To X so long as she remains in the Navy"; "to Y until zoning laws prohibit the current use"; "to Z so long as she does not remarry." Each of X, Y, and Z has a fee simple determinable. If the interest that follows theirs has not been conveyed, the transferor still owns it. As such, the transferor's interest is a possibility of reverter. If a year later the transferor died and it passed to A, it still would be regarded as a possibility of reverter. On the other hand, if the grant had provided an alternative disposition (e.g., "and if X leaves the Navy, to A") there would be no possibility of reverter. Instead, A would have the future interest in the right column, known as a shifting executory interest. Same interest, different name (and a few differences in result).

- **Power of Termination** (also known as a right of entry for condition broken) is retained when a transferor conveys a fee simple subject to a condition subsequent and does not provide for a third party to take if the fee is terminated. A fee simple subject to a condition subsequent also is a limited, defeasible fee. Words that imply the condition would look like: "but if" or "provided, however." For example, "To X, provided that she not leave the Navy"; "to Y, but only if the zoning laws do not change"; "to Z, but only if she does not remarry." If the transferor does not provide for disposition of the property to a third party if the condition subsequent occurs, the transferor has retained that interest (a power of termination or a right of entry for condition broken — same thing, different names). If the transferor had provided an alternative disposition (e.g., "but if X leaves the Navy, to A") there would be a shifting executory interest instead of a power of termination. Notice how the terminology in the right column does not distinguish the future interest following a fee simple determinable and the fee simple subject to condition subsequent, but in the left column different names apply. No wonder if you were confused in first year Property!

In this regard, then, are powers of termination/rights of entry and possibilities of reverter the same interest, except for the semantics? Not exactly. First, with a fee simple determinable, occurrence of the divesting condition that causes expiration of the present interest fee automatically makes the transferor's possibility of reverter possessory. By contrast, an affirmative act is required for the transferor to reacquire possession under a power of termination/right of entry. The transferor has an option to reacquire the property or choose not to. Second, at common law, the power of termination/right of entry could not be alienated and was destroyed if you tried. Not so with a possibility of reverter. On the right side of the chart, however, if creation of the defeasible fee was accompanied by the transferor's conveyance of the future interest to a third party as transferee (instead of the transferor retaining that future interest), the transferee's future interest is a shifting executory interest (regardless of whether the present interest is a fee simple determinable or a fee simple subject to condition subsequent), and these distinctions are meaningless.

Also note that each of a possibility of reverter and power of termination/right of entry can be used to accelerate a reversion. To illustrate, assume O conveys Blackacre "to A for life" and retains the balance of the fee. O has a reversion that will become possessory at A's death. If instead the grant by O is: "To A for life, but if A remarries, to O," now O also has a power of termination/right of entry incident to the reversion (as a condition cutting short A's life estate, which effectively accelerates the reversion). Similarly, a grant by O: "To A until the first to occur of A's death or remarriage," involves the retention by O of both a reversion and a possibility of reverter, with O's reversion accelerated by the possibility of reverter if A remarries.

- **Reversions** are much more common than possibilities of reverter and powers of termination, which seldom are encountered in estate planning and estate and trust administration. Well-drafted documents avoid reversions as well, but reversions fill gaps in title, usually caused by the drafter's inadvertent failure to convey the full fee, and sometimes this "just happens." A transferor who conveys less than what the transferor owned retains whatever remains. That interest is a reversion if it follows a present interest and if it cannot be a possibility of reverter or power of termination.

So, in the following examples, let's identify the reversion:

- "To A for life." This is a pure reversion when A dies.
- "To A for life, then to such of A's children as survive A." The reversion at A's death will be cut off if any child of A survives A. (As discussed below, reversions always are vested. As this example illustrates, however, they may never become possessory.)
- "To B for life, and one year after B's death to E." The transferor has a reversion for the one year after B's death. E has an interest

that will divest the transferor in actual possession and is known as a springing executory interest. In the chart at page 303 this is illustrated by the last line, showing the reversion for the year, now in possession in the middle column, and the springing executory interest in a third party in the right hand column.

- "To D for life, but if D remarries, to E." The transferor's reversion at D's death will be cut off if D remarries. Because the transferor will not be in possession at that time, E's interest is a shifting executory interest.

Springing or shifting, what's the difference? See page 303 and don't fret about it! The more important point is that reversions always are vested. Because reversions are retained and not transferred, the transferor is deemed to own a fully vested interest that is effective automatically, although it may be divested either before (e.g., the second and fourth examples above) or after (e.g., the third example above) it becomes possessory.

## Future Interests of Transferees

Most intentionally created future interests are created in transferees, rather than retained by the transferor. Transferees' future interests come in two forms: remainders (which may be vested or contingent) and executory interests (which may be shifting or springing). We have already alluded to executory interests, so let's begin with remainders (which are much more common). The most common future interest is the remainder because it follows the most common intervening present interest, which is the life estate. There are two easy tests to identify remainders. First, would it be a reversion if the transferor had retained it? If so, it is a remainder. Mind you, if it *was* a reversion because the transferor *did* retain it, the interest remains a reversion even if the transferor later conveys it to a third party (remember the last line of the chart at page 303). Second, does it follow a particular estate (life estate, term of years, or fee tail) rather than a fee simple determinable or a fee simple subject to a condition subsequent? If so, it usually is a remainder.

If you are a purist, there are four technical requirements that must be met for a future interest to qualify as a remainder: (1) it was created by the same instrument that created the present interest; (2) it was created in another person (not retained by the transferor); (3) it follows a particular estate (life estate, term of years, or fee tail — the first two of which are important but not the fee tail — see page 342); and (4) it becomes possessory immediately upon the natural expiration of the preceding particular estate. Let's illustrate with some "negative" examples:

O conveyed Blackacre to A for life. O conveyed O's reversion to B at a later date during A's life. B has a reversion, not a remainder.

Retention of a future interest, followed by a subsequent transfer, does not create a remainder: "once a reversion, always a reversion." Remainders are created when a present interest is retained while transferring a future interest (e.g., the transferor transfers Blackacre to A following a reserved life estate), or when present and future interests are transferred at once. So, G conveyed Whiteacre "to B for life, and one year thereafter to E." E's interest follows the reversion in G that fills the one year gap, rather than following the life estate in B. As a result, E's interest cannot be a remainder. Instead it is an executory interest. What result if the conveyance is "to B for life or until her prior remarriage, then to E"? Because remarriage is not regarded as a "natural" termination of B's particular estate, again E has an executory interest rather than a remainder.

Remainders may be vested or contingent. And just because a remainder is vested does not mean it will become possessory. For example, if D devised Blackacre: "To A for life, remainder to B, but if B dies before A, then to C," B has a vested remainder, but it is subject to divestment. If B dies before A, B's vested remainder terminates without ever having become possessory. Whether a remainder is vested or contingent has a variety of consequences: (1) The Rule of Destructibility of Contingent Remainders applies, if at all, only to contingent remainders. See page 316. (2) The Rule Against Perpetuities is concerned only with vesting (not possession): an interest that does not vest within the period of the Rule violates it. (3) As illustrated by the example at page 305, whether an interest is vested or contingent may determine who is entitled to the property. (4) Similarly, although whether an interest is subject to estate tax depends on whether it is transferable, rather than on whether it is vested, a vested interest is more likely to be subject to wealth transfer tax than is a contingent interest. See the example at page 306. (5) If a spendthrift clause does not preclude assignment or attachment, a vested interest has real value that creditors may seek to attach and beneficiaries may try to alienate. (6) A future interest holder's ability to enjoin waste or other harmful activity by a present interest holder or by the trustee and to recover damages is partially a function of the likelihood of the interest becoming possessory, which also is partially a function of whether it is vested or contingent.

A remainder is vested if its holder is an ascertained person (e.g., an unborn cannot have a vested remainder, although an interest may attach at birth and relate back to original creation) and if the only condition precedent to it becoming possessory is the termination of one or more preceding estates. Vested remainders come in three flavors:

- **Indefeasibly vested.** "To A for life, remainder to B." The traditional rule for future interests is that no condition of survivorship is implied if none is expressed, meaning that B's estate will take at A's death even if B does not survive A. (Compare the treatment of such a gift made in trust, under UPC §2-707, which requires B to survive A unless the document makes it clear that survivorship is not required, and provides antilapse protection if B does not. See page 323. That provision is a huge departure from traditional common law.)

- **Vested subject to open or to close.** "To A for life, remainder to A's children." This vests as a class gift when A has a child, subject to open (meaning the class of takers will increase if A has additional children), and subject to close if survivorship is required. As stated, a condition of survivorship is not implied for future interests except under UPC §2-707 for gifts in trust (and unlike the common law implied condition of survivorship for testamentary gifts of present interests at the testator's death). For example, O devised property: "To T, in trust, for A for life, remainder to A's children." At O's death A had two living children (B and C). B then died, after which a third child, D, was born to A. Unless UPC §2-707 applies, A's children are not required to survive A to take. Their remainder as a class is vested at O's death, subject to open but not to close. Thus, at O's death B and C received vested remainders, subject to partial divestment, which occurs as a result of D's birth. At A's subsequent death, the property will be distributed ⅓ through B's estate to B's heirs or devisees, ⅓ to C, and ⅓ to D.

- **Vested subject to divestment.** "To A for life, then to B, but if A remarries, to C." B's remainder is vested, but it is divested if the specified condition subsequent occurs. Similarly, if D created a revocable inter vivos trust for D for life, remainder to D's child, A, the equitable remainder in A is vested, subject to divestment, because D may revoke or amend the trust to divest A. The same characterization would apply if the transfer were by O "to A for life, remainder as A appoints by will, in default of appointment to B." A's exercise of the power might divest B's vested remainder.

A remainder that becomes possessory subject to a condition precedent is a contingent remainder. Whether a condition is precedent or subsequent may be purely a function of the language used in expressing the condition. For example, "to A for life, remainder to B if B survives A; if not to C" contains a condition precedent and creates a contingent remainder in B. But a gift "to A for life, remainder to B. Contrariwise, if B does not survive A, then to C" creates in B a vested remainder subject to divestment by a condition subsequent. Doesn't this seem silly?

Perhaps the most common form of contingent remainder is a gift to the surviving descendants of a life tenant: "To A for life, remainder per stirpes to A's descendants who survive A." The interest of a descendant of A will become possessory, if at all, only if the precedent condition of surviving A is satisfied. Further, the interest of any grandchild of A is subject to the condition precedent that the grandchild survive A, and that the grandchild's parent who is a child of A must predecease A.

In the gift "To A for life, remainder to A's heirs," the remainder is contingent (assuming A is living when the transfer is made) because, by definition, a prospective heir must survive A to be an heir of A. Recall our discussion in Chapter 2 that living persons do not have heirs. Difficult questions arise if the gift of the remainder is to the heirs of someone other than the life tenant. See page 335.

If the gift is "to A for life, remainder to A's children" and A does not have children yet, the remainder is contingent until A has a child, at which time the remainder vests in the class. The first child's remainder is vested, subject to open (partial divestment) if additional children are born. Finally, consider a gift "to A for life, remainder to B unless B is not living, in which case to C if living." (There is a reversion if neither B nor C is living at A's death). Do B and C each have contingent remainders or is B's remainder vested, in which case C has an executory interest? There is a preference for vested interests over contingent ones, but also a preference for remainders over executory interests. Arguably the vested remainder/executory interest construction is preferable because it provides better protection and avoids potential Rule Against Perpetuities issues. For your purposes, although legal commentators dance with the angels on this pinhead, it really doesn't matter and most casual observers would say that B and C have alternative contingent remainders.

Now, let's go back to the top of the right column of the chart at page 303. Any future interest that is created in a transferee by the same document that created the prior present interest and that is not a remainder is an executory interest. As a matter of constructional preference, an interest is not executory if it could be a remainder. Moreover, as a rule, executory interests become possessory by divesting a prior vested estate. For example, "to A for life, remainder to B, but if B does not survive A, then to C." B's remainder is vested, subject to divestment if B does not survive A. C's executory interest becomes possessory by divesting B. The one exception to this rule is an executory interest following a fee simple determinable that expires on its own, without being divested. For example, "Blackacre to the City until it no longer is used as a park; then to X." X's executory interest becomes possessory when the City's estate expires through discontinuation of use of the property as a park.

Generally, a future interest that may or will divest the transferor as the possessory interest holder is a springing executory interest. It is a shifting executory interest if it may or will divest a third party transferee in possession. An exception applies if the transferor retains a reversion and later conveys it away. It remains a reversion in the hands of the subsequent transferee and any future interest that divests it from the subsequent transferee is still a springing executory interest. To illustrate, "To B for life, and one year after B's death, to E." The transferor has a reversion that will become possessory at B's death. A year later, the transferor's reversion is divested by E's springing executory interest. This terminology will not change if the transferor gives the one year reversion to X and E divests X. "To D for life, but if D remarries, to E," is a little trickier. The transferor has a reversion, conditioned on D dying without having remarried. If D remarries, the transferor's reversion is divested, which would indicate that E's estate is a springing executory interest. E, however, has a shifting executory interest because, although it divests the reversion, it actually snatches possession away from D. (E's interest would be a power of termination incident to a reversion if held by the transferor.)

The good news is that it does not matter whether an executory interest is shifting or springing for our purposes.

## Origin and Characteristics

The rules and constructional preferences for future interests originated in medieval English land law, when all land was viewed as being held by or through the king; when land was the predominant source of power, wealth, and social status; and when military protection and feudal duties were determined by land use. A legitimate question today is, given the change of context, which of these rules and constructional preferences still are justified. For example, we need to question the by-products of rules like the Destructibility of Contingent Remainders, the Rule in Shelley's Case, the Doctrine of Worthier Title, and the Statute of Uses, which all are of little or no currency. As we will see, some of the ancient rules and constructional preferences have gone by the wayside, others are alive and well, and still others are alive but their ongoing viability is in doubt.

Future interests are used regularly in modern estate planning, almost always in trust. Their characteristics and the rules of construction that apply when the transferor's intent is not stated or clear have continuing significance for us. Absent spendthrift prohibitions, as discussed in Chapter 13, vested and contingent future interests are transferable during life and at death. (Vested future interests always have been alienable. Contingent remainders and executory interests were not alienable under old English law, but are alienable in a substantial majority of jurisdictions today.) Thus, future interests are descendible (i.e., to heirs by intestacy) and devisable (i.e., to devisees of a testate decedent), but only to the extent they survive the holder's death. And during the holder's life future interests generally are alienable by the holder and attachable by creditors to the extent there is no spendthrift prohibition.

So, for example, if G conveyed "to A for life, remainder to B, but if B does not survive A, then to C," B's vested remainder is transferable during B's life. If B dies before A, however, B's remainder is terminated by occurrence of the condition subsequent (B's death before A) that divests B. Thus, there is nothing for B to transfer if B dies before A. In most jurisdictions, C's contingent remainder also is alienable, even during the joint lives of A and B. If C conveys the remainder to D and then B survives A, B takes the fee and the contingent remainder terminates. If B dies before A, however, C's remainder would vest and also would be descendible, devisable, alienable, and attachable.

There may be an exception in your state for the possibility of reverter and the power of termination. At common law, these were not alienable, but they were attachable by creditors. Further, although not freely alienable, an attempt to do so might have been protected by estoppel, equitable assignment, or release. Today, possibilities of reverter and powers of termination are alienable in many jurisdictions but they are rarely seen in trusts or for estate planning purposes.

Future interests normally become possessory upon the natural expiration of one or more prior estates or the occurrence of a required condition precedent or subsequent. But in several circumstances a future interest may be accelerated into possession by other events. For example, in most jurisdictions, a devisee of a life estate who disclaims is treated as having predeceased the testator. See, e.g., UPC §2-801(d)(1) and Chapter 2. This operates to accelerate the remainder, which can eliminate a contingent remainder of the life tenant's descendants. For example, *In re Estate of Gilbert*, 592 N.Y.S.2d 224 (1992), involved a son's renunciation of his life interests in trusts created by his father's will. The will provided for the remainder of the son's trusts at his death to be payable to his descendants, but the son had no descendants when he renounced. As a result, the other remainder beneficiaries took as if the son had predeceased his father, thus eliminating the contingent remainder in the son's descendants. As a practical matter, if the remainder had not accelerated, but the trusts instead were held intact until the son died, it would have been necessary to decide what to do with income during the son's remaining life (accumulate it, revert it to the father's estate, or distribute it to the presumptive next takers). The court properly avoided this issue with the acceleration result.

The same issue can arise in the context of a beneficiary being barred from inheriting by slaying the transferor. For example, assume that G's will devised Blackacre "to S for life, remainder to S's descendants, provided that if no descendant of S survives S, then to R," and S murdered G. Under UPC §2-803, R takes if S is barred from taking and S has no descendant. This cuts off future descendants of S, because G's estate passes as if S disclaimed S's interest (in which case S would be treated as having predeceased G and the contingent remainder in R would be accelerated). Further, the acceleration issue also can arise in connection with the exercise by a surviving spouse of the right to elect against the estate plan of a deceased spouse. See Chapter 10.

### *Protection*

Future interests are entitled to protection. When the future interest is equitable (i.e., in trust), the beneficiary's remedies usually relate to the trustee's fiduciary duties, and are a matter of trust law. See Chapter 18. The following is a brief summary of protections available to holders of future interests.

- **Reinvestment**. Sale and investment of the proceeds may be appropriate or necessary to preserve future interests.

- **Waste**. Generally, the holder of a present interest in property is entitled to its reasonable use and income. The future interest holder is entitled to possession and enjoyment only after termination of all prior interests. A trustee or prior interest holders may be committing waste if they commit acts (or fail to take actions) that adversely affect the value of the corpus, all of which may be enjoined or potentially actionable in damages. The nature and extent of the available remedy may depend on the nature of the future interest held. For example, the holder of an indefeasibly vested future interest may enjoin threatened waste or immediately recover damages for committed waste. The owner of a reversion or remainder, even if contingent or defeasibly vested, may enjoin threatened waste, but a successful suit for damages may result in the recovery being impounded pending resolution of the various contingencies. Typically injunction and recovery are allowed for executory interests, possibilities of reverter, and powers of termination only if the alleged wrongdoing is a wanton, unconscionable, or imprudent use, and there is a reasonable probability of the future interest becoming possessory.

- **Security**. Generally, the owner of a future interest in land may not require the present interest owner to provide security. Along with the remedies of injunction and damages for waste, the land itself is viewed as protection enough. The same would be true about personalty held in trust (although the trustee may be required to post a security bond). But if personal property is subject to a legal life estate, security in the form of a bond may be available to protect the remainder beneficiary against invasions or exhaustion of the corpus.

Having rights to protection and being able to exercise them effectively may be two different things. For example, notice and accountings may not be available to the future interest holder and, thus, it may not be possible to know what is happening. Further, unborn or unascertained beneficiaries may be only "virtually represented," meaning that they are not protected at all. Instead, their interests are deemed adequately represented because another person whose interest is similar to that of the unborn or unascertained beneficiary is a party and protecting their own interest is deemed to protect the unborn or unascertained beneficiary as well.

## Three Ancient Doctrines

The three doctrines discussed here have limited ongoing relevance.

### *Destructibility of Contingent Remainders*

At common law, a contingent legal (not in trust) remainder in land would be destroyed by operation of law (i.e., this is not a rule of construction) if it did not vest at or prior to termination of the preceding estate. To illustrate: "To A for life, remainder to B's heirs." A and B are living. A has a life estate, B's heirs (who are unascertained because a living person cannot have heirs) have a contingent remainder, and the transferor has a reversion (which will become possessory if A predeceases B, because we cannot know who B's heirs are until B's subsequent death). If this was a legal interest in realty (the rule did not apply to personalty or to interests in trust, nor to any executory interest), vesting of the reversion in possession (because B is alive when A dies) would destroy the contingent remainder.

This rule has been abolished in most (and perhaps all) jurisdictions, being replaced with a construction of a life estate, a reversion in the transferor that is subject to divestment, and a springing executory interest. Historically, the rule had several collateral consequences, which is the only reason why it is important to us today. For example, it contributed to the early development of the preference for remainders over executory interests at a time when the rule was in favor and destruction was desired so the property would revert and then pass through the transferor's estate, subject to feudal duties. The doctrine also spurred development of the Rule in Shelley's Case and the Doctrine of Worthier Title as alternative means of destroying remainders that the rule of destructibility did not reach. Later, when destructibility had fallen from favor, it contributed to the counterbalancing preference for vested over contingent remainders and the preference for early vesting.

### The Rule in Shelley's Case

The second ancient property law doctrine with limited current applicability is the Rule in Shelley's Case. If the Shelley rule is applicable, a remainder purportedly given to the heirs of a life tenant is deemed to be a remainder in the life tenant rather than in those heirs. Then, not by the Rule in Shelley's Case itself, but made possible by it, there may occur a merger of the life estate and the remainder, yielding a fee in the holder of the life estate. The merger could be prevented by an intervening interest or a remainder made contingent for reasons other than being held by heirs of a living person. To illustrate, consider "To A for life, remainder to A's heirs." Under Shelley, the remainder is in A, not A's heirs. A merger then would occur because A would have the life estate and the remainder, leaving A with the fee. But B's life estate would prevent a merger if the grant were: "To A for life, then to B for life, remainder to A's heirs." The rule itself, however, still would apply, the remainder would be in A, rather than in A's heirs. Compare "to A for life, remainder to A's heirs if A dies before reaching age 25." The contingency that A's heirs take only if A dies before age 25 avoids the merger because it avoids application of the rule altogether. Thus, A's heirs will take assuming A dies before reaching age 25.

There are five requirements for application of the Rule in Shelley's Case: (1) the conveyance must be of realty; (2) the transferee must have received a life estate (or a fee tail; see page 342); (3) the conveyance must be a remainder to the heirs of the life tenant; (4) the life estate and the remainder must have been created by the same instrument (typically, a will, trust instrument, or deed); and (5) both the life estate and the remainder must be legal or both must be equitable. Like the destructibility rule, if it applies at all, the Rule in Shelley's Case is a rule of law, not of construction. Thus, it applies notwithstanding intent. But the Rule in Shelley's Case has been abolished in most states. If the grant "to A for life, remainder to A's heirs" were made in a state in which the Rule in Shelley's Case has been abolished, the interests created would be: (1) a life estate in A, (2) a contingent remainder in A's heirs, and (3) a reversion in the transferor or the transferor's successors (because there are no heirs of A until A's death). The rule is that the transferor has retained a reversion if a transferor conveys a life estate not followed by a vested remainder in fee.

### Worthier Title

The Doctrine of Worthier Title operates to convert what appears to be a remainder (or executory interest) in the transferor's heirs to a reversion in the transferor. Thus, if G conveyed "to A for life, remainder to G's heirs," G is treated as having retained a reversion rather than as having transferred a contingent remainder to G's heirs. The requirements for application of the Doctrine are similar to but not identical to the requirements for application of the Rule in Shelley's Case. The most significant difference between the two rules is that Worthier Title operates when a remainder (or executory interest) purportedly is conveyed to the transferor's heirs. The Rule in Shelley's Case applies when a remainder is purportedly conveyed to the present interest holder's heirs. Another difference is that, unlike the Shelley rule, the Doctrine of Worthier Title applies to personalty as well as realty, and applies if the present interest is a term of years or a defeasible fee, as well as if it is a life estate (or fee tail). Furthermore, unlike the Shelley rule, it does not matter whether the transferee's estate or the purported remainder in the transferor's heirs or both are equitable or legal. Moreover, the Rule in Shelley's Case can apply to testamentary and inter vivos transfers, but the Doctrine of Worthier Title applies only to inter vivos grants. Like the Shelley rule, worthier title applies only if the transferee's estate and the purported remainder in the transferor's heirs were created by the same instrument.

The Doctrine of Worthier Title is a rule of construction, not of law. Thus, the transferor's intent to create a remainder in the transferor's heirs will be given effect if it is established. Like the Rule in Shelley's Case, the Doctrine of Worthier Title is disfavored most everywhere and it expressly has been abolished in many jurisdictions. Perhaps because it is a doctrine of construction and not a rule of law, however, statutory abolition of it has not been as widespread as that of the Shelley rule.

### Construction Problems

Construction issues are avoidable. They arise because a governing instrument does not adequately address a question. To be a good estate planner requires that you draft thoroughly and carefully, cover all contingencies, and use your knowledge of construction issues to anticipate problems based on prior drafters' mistakes. In this segment it is wise always to think about how to draft to avoid the issues being addressed. Moreover, although construction is a necessary evil in estate planning and trust administration, try to keep it in perspective. Often we are filling in a gap with a solution to a question that the settlor never even considered, much less formed an intent about. We should be careful not to manufacture intent when a provision should just fail and the property should pass by reversion and, if necessary, by intestacy. Moreover, using cases to construe similar language is often like using nonsense to construe nonsense. Like rules of construction, we need to keep precedent in perspective too. Finally, the entire area is uncertain. Black and white exist most often only in the treatises, not the actual decisions. You should not be distraught if it is hard to pin rules down and if you find that courts do equity while bending the rules to produce the result they want.

## *Vested or Contingent*

As discussed at page 310, whether an interest is vested or contingent is significant for a variety of reasons. In construing instruments under which vesting issues are raised, courts often employ preferences in favor of (1) early vesting, (2) vested rather than contingent interests, and (3) conditions subsequent rather than precedent. To illustrate, "To A for life, remainder to B if B attains age 30." While B is under age 30, B's future interest is a contingent remainder and the transferor has a reversion. Attaining age 30 is a condition precedent to B's remainder becoming vested or possessory, meaning that B will not receive the fee until A dies and then only if B reaches age 30. B's remainder will vest immediately if B is or attains age 30 during A's life, which will terminate the transferor's reversion. B's vested remainder will pass as a part of B's estate to B's heirs (if B dies intestate) or devisees (if B dies testate) if B dies after reaching age 30 but before A dies. B's successors will take the fee at A's death. If B is not yet age 30 when A dies, at common law the destructibility of contingent remainders rule would cause B's contingent remainder to be destroyed at A's death. Today, there would be a reversion to the transferor, with the property still subject to B's contingent remainder. If B reached age 30 thereafter, B would take from the transferor (or the transferor's successors). In essence, B's contingent remainder would then operate as a springing executory interest.

Let's try another one: "To X for life, remainder to Y, but if Y dies before X, to Z." Y's remainder is vested subject to divestment because it is subject to a condition subsequent. Z has a shifting executory interest because it will divest Y if it becomes possessory at all. Z need not survive to take. Z's estate will be entitled and Z's successors will take if Y predeceases X and Z is not living at X's death. By contrast, "To X for life, remainder to Y if living, and if not to Z," would give Y and Z alternative contingent remainders. Again, Z need not survive to take. Y's remainder is contingent on Y surviving X but Z's remainder is contingent only on Y not surviving X. There is no contingency that speaks to Z's survival of anyone.

## Twice Stated Age Contingencies

Let's compare two other grants before considering the following example that includes an age contingency that is stated twice. First: "To A for life, remainder to B if B attains age 30, and if B dies before then, to C." Probably B's remainder is contingent, subject as it is to the condition precedent that B attain age 30. In that case C has an alternative contingent remainder. By contrast, what if the language "if B attains age 30" was not included and the grant was: "To A for life, remainder to B, but if B dies before reaching age 30, to C"? Here, B's remainder is vested, subject to divestment. The condition on B taking that B reach age 30 is subsequent, not precedent. C has a shifting executory interest in that case because B's remainder is vested, subject to divestment.

Now, let's consider: "To A for life, remainder to B if B attains age 30, but in the event of B's death before age 30, to C." B's remainder is subject to an age condition that is stated twice, once precedent and once subsequent. Here we ignore the condition precedent and B receives a vested remainder subject to divestment. Why? One statement of the age condition is surplusage and we ignore the precedent condition at least in part because the law favors early vesting. Also, conditions subsequent are preferred over conditions precedent, which in the context of remainders is simply another way of saying vested remainders and their divesting executory interests are preferred over alternative contingent remainders.

The issue involved may affect the classification so it is important to know why the determination needs to be made. For example, we would expect a construction favoring early vesting to save the gift if the vested versus contingent remainder classification issue arises in connection with a Rule Against Perpetuities challenge. And a vested construction again would be expected, to save the gift, if the issue were possible application of the rule of destructible contingent remainders. But depending on how it viewed the equities, a court might reach a different result if the issue arose in connection with an attempt by a creditor of a beneficiary to reach the beneficiary's interest, if the creditor's ability to do so would be reduced if the beneficiary's remainder was contingent. The same might be true if tax valuation might be less if the beneficiary's remainder interest was contingent.

### Remainder to Life Tenant's Children

Poorly drafted language can raise a variety of construction issues if it attempts to leave property to one person for life, with the remainder to that person's children. For example, "To X for life, remainder to X's children, but if no child of X reaches age 30, to Y." If X has no children at the time of the grant, the remainder is contingent until a child of X is born. Then it is vested in that child, subject to open (i.e., subject to partial divestment), but not to close (i.e., neither survivorship nor reaching age 30 is required for any particular child of X, if at least one child of X reaches age 30). This means that, for example, if X was survived by two children, one age 32 and the other age 25, the 25 year old's interest is vested without regard to whether he or she reaches age 30. The remainder, however, is subject to divestment as a class, meaning that the remainder would be divested if no child of X reached age 30. Note the difference between there being no survivorship requirement (the successors of a child of X who does not reach age 30 will take that child's share if at least one other child of X reaches that age) and the requirement that at least one member of the class must reach age 30 before any child may take.

Compare: "To X for life, remainder to such of X's children as survive X, and if any child fails to do so, that child's share shall go to Y." As in the prior example, the remainder is contingent until a child of X is born if X has no children at the time of the grant. It also appears that a child of X who predeceased X cannot take. But how does a child who does not survive X have a share that can pass to Y if the children's remainders are contingent on survivorship? Arguably, therefore, the remainder is vested, subject to open (as additional children of X are born) and to divestment in favor of Y's shifting executory interest. Note that divestment is not the same as class closing. A child of X does not drop out of the class if that child dies before X. Rather, that child's remainder is divested in favor of Y's executory interest. In effect, Y is substituted as a class member for each child of X who predeceases X.

Finally, a remainder may be vested, but subject to divestment by exercise of a power of appointment. For example, "to A for life, remainder to such person or persons as A shall appoint; in default of appointment in equal shares to A's children who survive A." The remainder is contingent until a child of A is born, at which time the remainder is vested subject to open to admit afterborns or afteradopteds, subject to close to reflect the survivorship requirement, and subject to divestment by A's exercise of the power. The transferor has a reversion that will become possessory if A dies without having effectively exercised the power and is survived by no child.

### Survivorship

A future interest is a presently existing property right or interest that will or may grant possession or enjoyment in the future. The question here is whether the holder of a future interest must survive until some future date (such as the death of a life tenant) to be entitled to take. The first place to look for the answer to that question is the governing instrument. It controls if it expressly addresses the issue. If not, the issue is one of construction. Absent an express requirement of survivorship, the traditional rule is that the law will not imply a condition of survivorship with respect to a future interest. Thus, if G conveys a life estate to A, remainder to B, the remainder passes as an asset of B's estate to B's heirs or devisees if B predeceases A, because B's remainder was vested, not conditioned on B surviving A.

*Estate and Trust Planning*

This is the exact opposite of the common law implied condition of survivorship applicable to testamentary bequests at the testator's death. If T devises Blackacre to A without addressing the possibility of A dying before T, the gift will lapse and thus fail if A predeceases T. The only question is whether the devise is saved for A's descendants by an antilapse statute. See Chapter 8. No such remedy is needed if the holder of a vested future interest dies before becoming entitled to possession. The interest passes automatically to the future interest holder's successors because survivorship is not required (unless the settlor expressly required it). This difference in treatment is another illustration that using a revocable trust as the primary dispositive instrument in an estate plan may yield different results than using a will. *First National Bank v. Anthony*, 557 A.2d 957 (Me. 1989), is illustrative. The settlor of a revocable inter vivos trust retained a life estate in the trust corpus, with a portion of the remainder given to a son who predeceased the settlor. Had the gift of the remainder been made by will, it would have lapsed unless saved for the son's descendants by an antilapse statute. But because the son received a future interest upon creation of the trust, and because of the rule against implying a condition of survivorship when none is expressed, the son's remainder belonged to his estate for distribution to his heirs (if he died intestate) or devisees (if he died testate).

The lapse rules can apply in future interest cases but traditionally only in a testamentary trust and only if the future interest beneficiary predeceased the testator and not just predeceased the present interest holder. For example, D's will devised D's estate to T, in trust to pay the income to A for life, remainder to B. If B died before D, B's interest would lapse and might be saved by an antilapse statute. See Chapter 8. But if B survived D and died before A, neither lapse nor antilapse would apply under traditional principles. Rather, unless the instrument conditioned B's remainder on B surviving A, the traditional approach (now changed by UPC §2-707, discussed at page 323) is not to imply such a requirement, meaning that B's interest is vested and B's heirs or devisees take the fee at A's death. Apparently because revocable inter vivos trusts are so commonly used as will substitutes, a few courts (including the lower court in *Anthony*) have applied the lapse rule if a beneficiary of such a trust who is to receive a distribution at the transferor's death predeceases the transferor. If a lapse rule is applied in such a context, however, so also should the antilapse statute be applied.

There are several justifications for the rule that the future interest holder's interest is vested, rather than subject to an implied condition of survivorship, if the instrument is silent with respect to whether the holder must survive to the time of possession (i.e., be alive when all preceding estates terminate). Perhaps most important is the preference for early vesting, a relic of days when the doctrine of destructibility of contingent remainders was applicable but disfavored. In addition, if a gift of current income also is given to the remainder beneficiary, the "income vests principal" rule discussed at page 324 may support a finding that the interest vested without regard to survivorship at the time of possession.

Furthermore, it would be necessary to determine who would take (or the entire remainder would fail) if survivorship was required and all the named takers predeceased the present interest holder. Presumably there would be a reversion to the transferor and a significant possibility of the property then passing to the transferor's heirs by intestacy if survivorship was required and there was no gift over of the deceased taker's share (as often would be the case). The law abhors an intestacy that is avoidable, especially at some time in the future. Finally, the future interest holder's family would be excluded if survivorship was required. Notice that each of these concerns could be addressed by treating the holder's death before distribution as a lapse/antilapse issue, as the UPC does in §2-707, discussed next.

## UPC §2-707

Unlike the traditional common law rule that we have been illustrating, a condition of survivorship is implied under UPC §2-707 if a gift of a future interest is made in trust (to a specific beneficiary or to a class) and the instrument is silent with respect to whether the future interest holder must survive until possession. Further, an antilapse concept is applied if the beneficiary does not survive to possession. Any descendants of the future interest holder who survive to possession take by representation the share the holder would have received if living. Indeed, unlike the case when a testamentary gift lapses, the UPC §2-707 antilapse result is antilapse on steroids because it applies without regard to whether the holder of the future interest was related to the transferor.

The consequences of the change made by UPC §2-707 can be significant. Under it the future interest holder's descendants take. Only if there are none is there a reversion in the transferor. Under the traditional common law approach, the holder's heirs or devisees take and there could be no reversion. Moreover, the traditional approach results in the property passing to the future interest holder's heirs or devisees by going through the holder's probate estate. Under UPC §2-707 the property passes to the holder's descendants directly from the trust, which eliminates certain problems such as claims by predators or tax liability. This is because the traditional approach causes the future interest holder's interest in the trust to be includible in the holder's estate for estate tax purposes. Under UPC §2-707, the holder who does not survive to take has no interest in the trust, nothing is transmissible to others, and the value of the interest is not includible in the holder's estate for federal estate tax purposes. Note, however, that the estate tax consequence is more favorable under the UPC approach, but it may result in a generation-skipping transfer tax liability for a large estate. So, it is fair to say that these results differ but are not necessarily better or worse.

The traditional common law approach affords the future interest holder complete flexibility to direct disposition of the trust assets. The UPC directs the disposition to the holder's descendants, a result many transferors (but not the future interest holder) may prefer. A client who wants to give the holder flexibility to control the ultimate disposition of the trust assets (even if the holder dies before becoming entitled to possession) can simply give the holder a nongeneral power to appoint the future interest and thereby avoid inclusion of the interest in the holder's probate or taxable estate. See Chapter 14.

### Vested with Postponed Possession

The 17th century English decision, *Clobberie's Case*, 86 Eng. Rep. 476 (Ch. 1677), spawned a concept of vested ownership with postponed possession and several vested versus contingent rules of construction that survive to this day. There were three variations addressed in that decision.

- "To A *at age* . . ." If words of futurity are annexed to the substance of the gift (e.g., "to A at age 30"), the traditional approach (not universally followed) is to treat the recipient's interest as contingent. It requires survivorship to the specified age and vesting is postponed. Note that a gift "to A if A reaches age 30" would more clearly fail if A did not do so. Survivorship also is required under traditional rules if the gift was "to A *when* A reaches age 30" (although this construction also is not followed everywhere). In any of these cases A's interest would fail if A died before reaching the specified age. If the traditional construction (treating the interest as contingent) applies the interest would not pass to A's successors. Rather, it would pass to the transferor's successors by reversion.

- "To A, *to be paid* at age . . ." A gift is not conditioned on survivorship if words of futurity are "not annexed to the substance of the gift," but instead "are annexed to enjoyment" (e.g., "to A, to be paid at age 30" or, "to A, payable when A reaches age 30"). This is a vested gift, with possession postponed, and A's successors receive the property if A dies before reaching the specified age.

- "To A at age . . . , *to be paid with interest*." A hybrid exists if the words of futurity are annexed to the subject of the gift but the transferee also is given income from the gift (e.g., "to A, at age

30, to be paid with interest" or "income to A in the trustee's discretion, principal to A at age 30"). Although the dispositive provision looks like a gift for which vesting as well as possession is postponed, the income entitlement is said to vest the principal. Thus, A's successors will take even if A dies before age 30.

An exception to this result may apply if no single beneficiary is guaranteed sole current enjoyment of income and is not guaranteed distribution in the future of accumulated income. To illustrate, assume D's will devised the residue of D's estate to T, in trust, for distribution "half to A at age 30, the balance to B at age 30, with income to be distributed to them in T's discretion or accumulated and distributed with the principal." A and B each survived D, A died at age 28, and B later died at age 29. The income vests principal rule may not apply because A and B were not entitled to receive any portion of the income. In that case A's half would pass by intestacy to D's heirs as a result of D's reversion (probably at such time as A would have reached age 30 if A had lived, so that the fund would remain intact generating income for possible distribution to B). At B's subsequent death, D's heirs probably would take the remaining principal and accumulated income for the same reason they likely would take A's half. However, B's successors could argue that the "income vests principal" rule should apply to B after A's death, because any income not distributed currently to B would be accumulated for distribution to B at age 30. The problem with that argument is that it presupposes a different intent with respect to B than with A, and indeed a difference after A's death than before. As a result, we would not expect the argument to succeed, especially if no one could predict which of A or B would die first.

Assume a gift by D of $10,000 to A at age 30. The income probably was retained by D if the disposition does not direct what is to be done with the income from the $10,000 while waiting for A to reach age 30. Thus, the income would be payable to D or D's successors and would not vest the gift to A. If the gift instead was to A, *to be paid when* A reached age 30, the more likely construction would accumulate the income and treat it as passing with the underlying corpus when A reaches age 30, or to A's estate if A dies before reaching that age.

## Acceleration

Assume a beneficiary whose interest is vested dies before reaching the required distribution age. The next question is whether distribution should be made immediately to the beneficiary's successors, or whether it should be delayed until the beneficiary *would have* reached the age for distribution. If income from the fund was not distributable to the beneficiary, but was retained (expressly or implicitly) by the transferor, acceleration of the gift to the beneficiary's successors should not occur because doing so would defeat the transferor's retained interim income interest. If, however, income from the fund was distributable to the beneficiary, there is no reason to delay distribution until the beneficiary would have reached the specified age. Death eliminates the need to delay distribution when possession is deferred (usually for reasons relating to immaturity), and immediate termination would be favored.

Any interest that is not vested reverts to the transferor or her successors and the acceleration issue does not arise if a beneficiary dies before reaching the required distribution age. For example, a gift of $10,000 is made "to A at age 30." A is 20 at the time of the gift, but dies at age 23. The traditional construction (not followed in some jurisdictions) is that A's interest was contingent. A's premature death causes the interest to revert to the transferor or the transferor's successors. The absence of a provision for the income before A reaches age 30 probably means it was retained by the transferor in the form of a reversion, meaning that A would not be entitled to income even for the period before A's death.

Now assume the gift was of $10,000 "to A, payable at age 30." Again there is no provision for income but A's interest is vested and the income would be deemed vested with the underlying corpus in the absence of a provision for income earned on the $10,000 before A reached age 30. A's premature death should accelerate the gift to A's successors because this gift is about postponement of possession and there is no lingering reason to postpone distribution.

### Gifts of Future Interests to a Class

If a gift of a future interest is made to a class, the traditional rule (of construction only) is that the class is subject to open until distribution, but is not subject to close unless survivorship expressly is required (meaning there is no implied condition of survivorship). To illustrate, assume that D devised D's residuary estate to T, in trust, income to A for life, remainder to D's siblings. D died survived by A, by a brother (B), and by a sister (S). B predeceased A, survived by one child (N). B devised his estate to his widow (W). To whom is the trust estate distributable at A's death, survived by N, W, and S? S clearly will receive at least half of the trust assets. The question is whether B's death before A results in S taking the entire trust estate, or whether B's interest was vested so that B's successors take the share B would have received if B was alive. Generally, survivorship will not be implied in a future interest gift. As a result, B's remainder vested at D's death and passed through B's estate at B's death. Accordingly, W would receive B's half of the trust assets at A's death. (A different result would be reached under UPC §2-707, discussed at page 323.) Note that, if another sibling of D had been born or adopted after D's death but before A's death, the new sibling also would share in the class gift. On the other hand, any sibling born or adopted after A's death would be excluded from the class, which would close at A's death when distribution was required. See Chapter 8.

*Security Trust Co. v. Irvine*, 93 A.2d 528 (Del. Ch. 1953), is a good illustration of the application of this general rule. James devised his estate in trust for two of his sisters, Martha and Mary, for their lives. At the second of their deaths the remainder was to be "equally divided among my brothers and sisters, share and share alike . . . the issue of any deceased brother or sister to take his or her parent's share." James was survived by Mary, Martha, and three other siblings but Mary was the last to die of all the siblings. Of the five siblings, two were survived by descendants who also survived Mary's death. If survivorship until possession was required the descendants of these two siblings would take everything. Following the traditional rule, however (and the preference for early vesting upon which it is based), the court did not require survivorship. Rather, each of the five siblings had a share of the remainder that vested at James' death. Only the remainders belonging to the two siblings who did not survive Mary but who had descendants who did were divested in favor of those descendants. For the others the divesting gift over was not applicable because they did not leave surviving descendants.

The fortuitousness of the timing of death can generate inequity if survivorship until the time of possession is required in a class gift. The family of a class member who died one day before distribution would receive nothing but a class member who died one day after distribution could leave that share to anyone. Further, any class gift would fail altogether if survivorship until the time of possession was required and no member of the class survived. The early vesting rule (under which survivorship until the time of possession is not required) avoids that result. Note, however, that the lapse rule can apply if a future interest devisee under a testamentary trust dies before the testator. Any applicable antilapse statute may avoid this problem and UPC §2-707 avoids each problem by creating a lapse and antilapse regime for *all* future interests.

The general, no-implied-condition-of-survivorship rule applies to a future interest given to a class of single-generation members, but not to classes whose members are multigenerational. Thus, unless UPC §2-707 is in effect, survivorship typically is not required for gifts of future interests to children, first cousins, siblings, or nieces and nephews, but survivorship typically *is* required for future interest gifts to descendants, heirs, next of kin, or issue (if used properly to mean descendants). One explanation for this is definitional. How do descendants, issue, or heirs take other than by representation of deceased ancestors? Another is that the inequality posed by an implied survivorship condition in a single generation class does not exist in a multigenerational gift with the right of representation.

## Conditions Unrelated to Survivorship

A future interest may be conditioned on an event other than survivorship. For example, a gift: "To A for life, remainder to A's children, but if A dies with no surviving children, then to B" conditions B's interest on A dying without living children. Survivorship to possession is not also required, and it will not be implied as a condition *simply because the interest is otherwise conditional.* The majority view is that a remainder contingent on something other than survivorship is not also subject to an implied condition of survivorship. Thus, B's successors will take if A dies not survived by any child, even if B is not alive at that time.

The same result should obtain if the future interest is vested subject to divestment, such as by exercise of a power to revoke or to appoint, to distribute principal, or by occurrence of another condition subsequent. For example, if D created a revocable inter vivos trust, income to D for life, then income to S for life, then remainder to R, the remainder is vested in R from creation of the trust, subject to divestment if D revokes or amends the trust to reduce or eliminate R's interest. The fact that R's remainder is subject to divestment should not also imply a survivorship condition. Similarly, note that in *Security Trust* at page 327 the siblings' remainders were vested, subject to divestment if any died with issue before the last life tenant, but that did not mean that their interests also would be divested if they died without issue before the surviving life tenant.

The same reasons for not implying a condition of survivorship when no other conditions are involved, noted at page 322, also support not implying one when an interest is subject to another condition. In addition, the presumption when another condition is stated is that the absence of a condition of survivorship is intentional because the transferor knew how to impose a condition and did *not* impose a requirement of survivorship. Moreover, we presume that the transferor wanted to avoid failure of the disposition, so the absence of a gift over if the holder does not survive indicates that survivorship was not meant to be required.

## Time to Which Survivorship Condition Relates

"Surviving" is a relative term. If a future interest holder is required to survive, what or whom must that person survive? The usual rule is that a beneficiary whose interest is conditioned on the beneficiary "surviving" (without stating what or whom) must survive all prior interests, or until the time for distribution, if later. For example, G devised G's estate: "To T, in trust, income to my child (C) for life, remainder to C's surviving children." C had two children ($GC_1$ and $GC_2$) when G executed the will. C, $GC_1$, and $GC_2$ all survived G. $GC_3$ was born to C after G's death. $GC_2$ then died, after which C died. $GC_1$ and $GC_3$ survived C. In most jurisdictions the requirement that C's children be "surviving" to take means that $GC_2$'s remainder will fail because $GC_2$ did not survive C, the life tenant, after whose death distribution occurs. $GC_1$ and $GC_3$ each will take half of the trust estate. Note that a typical antilapse statute will not apply to save the gift because $GC_2$ survived the testator, G.

As discussed at page 323, UPC §2-707 implies a survivorship condition on gifts of future interests, and substitutes surviving descendants for any predeceased remainder beneficiary under an antilapse theory. As does the UPC in the context of lapse when a devisee predeceases a testator, UPC §2-707 also requires more to turn off this rule than merely limiting the takers to those who survive. Thus, in the hypothetical above, under UPC §2-707, $GC_2$'s descendants, if any, would take the share $GC_2$ would have taken if $GC_2$ had survived C (unless there was more affirmative evidence of G's intent to the contrary than just the term "*surviving* children"). That result also would have obtained under UPC §2-707 if the gift of the remainder had been to C's "then living children."

The future interest holder must survive all prior interests (or until the time for distribution, if later) if a survivorship condition is imposed without stating what or whom must be survived. Deviations from this rule may occur in several circumstances. For example, a gift of income will earlier vest the principal if the income beneficiary also is a remainder beneficiary (e.g., "income to my daughter A until she reaches age 23; remainder to my surviving children." If A dies at age 20, her right to income would have vested her share of the remainder without regard to her failure to survive to age 23). The general rule also may not apply if surviving the life tenant was too unlikely to have been the settlor's intent. For example, "to my surviving siblings at the death of all of my grandchildren." A sibling likely only needed to survive *creation* of the trust rather than death of the last of the grandchildren.

## Effect of Limited Survival Requirements

Consistent with the general rule that a survivorship condition will not be implied on a gift of a future interest, a limited condition of survivorship will be applied only as specified, and will not be treated as a general, broad, or global requirement. To illustrate, assume that G devised G's estate "to A for life, remainder to A's children, but if any child of A dies leaving descendants, that deceased child's share to those descendants." G was survived by A and A's three children (B, C, and D). B and C died before A. B was survived by one descendant (X), but C was survived by no descendant. D and X survived A. A's children owned vested remainders subject to divestment by dying before A leaving one or more descendants who survived A. That limited survivorship condition, however, did not create a survivorship requirement if a child of A died before A without descendants. Thus, C's remainder was vested and was not divested (because C did not leave descendants who survived A). It passes through C's estate to C's successors. X (as B's divesting surviving descendant) and D each share in the balance. We will explore whether X must survive A in the next example.

Let's try another one:

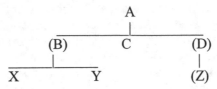

Here, assume again a gift from G "to A for life, remainder to A's children, but if any child of A dies leaving descendants, that deceased child's share to those descendants." Again, G was survived by A and by A's three children (B, C, and D) but assume that B and D died before A, that B was survived by two children (X and Y), both of whom survived A, and that D was survived by one child (Z), who predeceased A. The construction here is similar to that for a gift over if someone "dies without issue." See page 332. Thus, we determine whether a child of A "died leaving descendants" by whether a child of A died leaving descendants who survive A. B's vested remainder was divested by B's death before A, with B survived by descendants of B who survived A. Thus, X and Y take B's share. C also receives a share. D's vested remainder was not divested, because D was survived by Z but Z did not survive A. Thus, D's share would be distributed to D's successors. That probably is not what you would expect. Quaere whether this is what G intended.

A better way to express the most commonly misdrafted limited condition of survivorship is:

**To A for life, and on the death of A, remainder in equal shares to A's then living children, except that the then living descendants of a then deceased child of A shall take per stirpes the share the child would have received if living.**

or

To A for life and, on the death of A, remainder per stirpes to A's then living descendants.

Consider the following for analyzing survivorship issues. First, the instrument will control if it addresses the issue, such as by requiring survivorship to a specified time and providing for a gift over to an alternate taker if the first taker does not so survive. The following survivorship rules are rules of construction that apply only if the instrument is silent as to survivorship.

If the instrument making the gift is a will, issues of lapse and the applicability of the antilapse statute will be raised if (1) a devisee predeceased the testator, (2) the gift was to a class, a member of whom predeceased the testator, or (3) the gift was left to a testamentary trust, a beneficiary of which predeceased the testator. But what if a gift under a will was left to a testamentary trust, a beneficiary of which survived the testator but died before being entitled to possession? Here, the issue should not be lapse. If a survivorship condition was not expressly imposed, generally one will not be implied, even if the gift is subject to some other condition. Survivorship is required, however, if UPC §2-707 is in effect. Under it, if the beneficiary does not survive all prior interests, or to the time of distribution (if later), living descendants of the beneficiary, if any, will take under antilapse, regardless of the relationship of their predeceased ancestor to the testator.

If the instrument making the gift is an inter vivos trust instrument:

a. Lapse should not apply, even if the trust instrument is a revocable inter vivos trust that is being used as a will substitute. Such trusts typically will provide for the transferor to be a beneficiary for life (often the sole beneficiary). The beneficiaries designated to receive the trust estate at the transferor's death have future interests. If one of them dies before the transferor, the law of future interests should apply to determine who takes, not lapse or an antilapse statute. Some courts, however, have applied a lapse analysis in this circumstance, in which case the jurisdiction's antilapse statute should apply as well.

b. Assuming lapse and antilapse do not apply, the future interest survivorship analysis would be similar to that outlined above for a gift under a will. Thus, if the instrument addresses the survivorship issue, it will control. If it requires survivorship but does specify who or what must be survived, survivorship of all prior interests, or to the time of distribution (if later), normally will be required. If the instrument does not require survivorship, such a condition normally will not be implied, even if the future interest is subject to some other unrelated condition. But if UPC §2-707 is in effect, survivorship until the time of possession is required in that case. If the beneficiary does not survive, living descendants of the beneficiary, if any, will take under antilapse, regardless of the relationship of their predeceased ancestor to the transferor.

### Death "Without Issue"

A gift by G: "To H for life, remainder to A, but if A dies without issue, to X" raises three basic issues. But before looking at these, please note first that this is *not* a gift "to A, but if A dies without issue, to X." This is an important distinction because, as discussed below, the rules differ if the distribution is immediate and outright rather than involving a future interest. Also note that the term "issue" is a terrible one to use (because some folks assume it means children, when in fact it means descendants) but we use it here because this is how the legal question usually is framed. Please don't take this as an endorsement of that poor terminology. Finally, as you consider the possible constructions of this language, note that A's issue are not named takers. Rather, their only role is to affect whether A or X takes.

The first question is whether "if A dies without issue" means a "definite" or "indefinite" failure of A to have issue. That is, it could be read to mean: (1) X takes only if A never had issue; (2) X takes if A has no living issue at some definite time (definite failure of issue); or (3) X takes whenever the line of A's issue runs out (an indefinite failure of issue that is certain to occur sometime, however remote in the future). Definite failure is the favored construction. Indefinite failure may violate the Rule Against Perpetuities if followed by a remainder or executory interest. Never had issue simply is not what we know the average person would have intended.

Assuming the definite failure of issue construction is applicable, the second question is when does "dies without issue" mean? To determine whether X takes, what is the definite time at which we look to see if A has died and there are no issue of A living? The possibilities include the time of death of the settlor (G), the life tenant (H), the named taker (A), or anytime before the death of the alternative taker (X). This question is at the heart of this and numerous other construction questions. As discussed below, the preferred construction is that X takes if neither A nor any issue of A is living at the time of H's death.

The third question is the survivorship issue we examined above. If A does die without issue, must X be alive (or in existence, if X is not a natural person) to take? The general rule is that there is no implied condition of survivorship. If A dies without issue, X takes (actually X's heirs or devisees take) even if X is deceased. The exception we saw above may apply if the gift over is to a multigenerational class (e.g., if X is "descendants of Y"). Also, X must survive to take under UPC §2-707.

If X did not survive, X's descendants, if any, would take under the antilapse provisions of UPC §2-707.

The favored construction of the "dies without issue" hypothetical is: life estate to H, vested remainder in fee subject to divestment in A, shifting executory interest in X if neither A nor any issue of A is living at H's death. This favored approach keys taking to the time of termination of all prior interests and title is certain at H's death. A takes if A is then living. A still takes if A is not then living, but any issue of A is then living, meaning the remainder passes through A's estate to A's heirs or devisees. Only if neither A nor any issue of A is living at H's death does X take.

Consider why the other constructions do not make sense. First, a construction referring to death of the settlor is silly because distribution is not made until the end of H's life estate. It also is senseless to ask whether A dies without issue at any time before X's death. For example, nothing would support a construction that X should take if A survived H and then died survived by issue, but all of A's issue died before X.

Many (no, MOST) people want to read the hypothetical as saying that X takes if A is survived by no issue, whenever A dies. Thus, for example, they want X to take if A survived H and — on A's subsequent death — no issue of A survive A. These readers would say that the word "dies" in "dies without issue" obviously refers to the natural termination of A's physical life. Notice, however, that nothing ties the word to a "logical" application or interpretation and that this is only one of several possible meanings of when the word "dies" might apply. Moreover, the problem with this reading is that it gives A what is essentially a life estate with alternative contingent remainders to X or to whoever takes after A's death with issue surviving (which would be A's heirs or devisees, as if A had a testamentary power of appointment). More accurately, if A is survived by issue, A had a fee (albeit a defeasible one), and A could dispose of the property to whomever A chose. Moreover, we wouldn't say that A has a fee subject to a condition subsequent because A is sure to die and the divestment does not cut A short unnaturally. A divesting condition must cut short a prior interest unnaturally, and this does not. Thus, the proper construction is not to regard this as a fee in A subject to divestment by a condition subsequent. With a natural termination of A's interest at death "without issue," the future interest would be a remainder and the present interest in A therefore would be a life estate.

And that would create a conundrum. To construe this as a life estate in A creates a conflict when we consider that the settlor knew how to create a life estate. H has a life estate, by clear language. If the same were to be true for A, wouldn't the same language be used? For example, "to H for life, then to A for life, remainder . . . ." Notice that the law assumes that, if the same intent exists the same language will be used to create life estates in both H and then in A. The favored construction is sensible because it is the only one that does not have the foregoing problems *and* it accelerates determination of who ultimately takes. We know we must delay determination of the ultimate taker until the death of H, but the favored construction does not make us delay that determination further until the death of A. If your conclusion is that the favored construction does not make sense, then the lesson to be learned is that words and phrases don't always mean what you think they do, making the drafting of future interests a far more challenging chore than the casual observer or uninformed practitioner might expect.

What if G's devise to A had been an immediate one, instead of a future interest following another life estate: "To A, but if A dies without issue, to X"? Here, the majority rule is different than the favored construction when the gift involves a future interest. This preferred construction would be that A has a fee subject to divestment if no issue of A is living at A's death (before or after G). Thus, title is not certain until A's death. A's fee becomes indefeasible if A dies after G survived by issue. X (or X's successors if X is not then living) takes if A dies after G and no issue of A survive A. Quaere whether this is what the average testator would intend. Would they want A to take a fee simple absolute if A survives G, notwithstanding that A later dies without issue? And the more difficult questions are what happens if A predeceases G, either survived by issue or not?

What if A predeceases G with issue who survived A but who all also predecease G? A cannot take, because A predeceased G. The gift to A lapses (and because no issue of A survived G, A's gift cannot be saved by an antilapse statute, even if one otherwise would apply; see Chapter 8). A's issue also do not take, because they were not named as takers and they predeceased G anyway. X also may not take, because the condition on X taking was that A die without issue, which did not occur. X not taking in this circumstance, however, seems contrary to G's likely intent, which was that X take if A (or, perhaps, A's issue) did not. It would have been easy enough to say that, however, and G did not. The devise to X was not conditioned on A not taking; it was conditioned on A dying without issue. Perhaps, however, a court would imply a gift to X in this circumstance. See Chapter 7. If not, a reversion would occur and G's residuary beneficiaries would take, unless this is a gift of the residue, in which case G's heirs would take by intestacy. Was that G's intent?

Finally, assume again the same outright gift: "To A, but if A dies without issue, to X," but here assume that A predeceased G survived by issue who survived G. Who takes? A cannot, because A predeceased G and the gift to A lapsed under the implied condition of survivorship. A's issue arguably cannot take (directly, at least), because they were not named as takers. X cannot take because A did not die without issue. If the relationship between G and A is such that the jurisdiction's antilapse statute applies, A's issue should take under that statute. If not, perhaps a court would imply a gift to them, because it appears likely that G intended them to take in this circumstance. Otherwise, the property apparently will pass to G's residuary takers or, if this is a residuary gift, to G's heirs by intestacy. Again, what was G's intent? Obviously G's drafter did not do a very savvy job. And drafting properly is the important learning in all of this.

### *Gifts to Heirs*

A gift under a will or trust instrument to someone's "heirs" raises a number of construction issues. Consider a gift: "To A for life, remainder to B's heirs." Determining the "heirs" of B who will take at A's death requires answers to three questions. First, does "heirs" include the designated individual's spouse, or is it limited to blood relatives? If the spouse is not taking a statutory forced heir share, usually a surviving spouse is included as an heir. See, for example, UPC §2-711, which includes a surviving spouse who has not remarried before possession or enjoyment of the gift would occur. But we have seen that this is not a universal nor a predictable result. As with other construction issues, the drafter should anticipate this question, particularly because most people probably think "heirs" implies family (blood relatives or adopteds) and not relation by affinity.

Second, heirs are to be determined under the law of what jurisdiction, in effect at what time? If the subject of the gift is real estate, the law of the jurisdiction in which the real estate is located governs the determination of heirs. If not, the choices are the law of the testator's domicile, or the law of the domicile of the designated ancestor (i.e., the person whose heirs are being determined) at death. The cases go both ways. Further, if the intestacy law of State A governs, what if its intestate succession statutes have changed over time? Do we apply the law in effect at execution of the document? When the document became irrevocable? When the designated ancestor died? Or when distribution is to be made? The most likely candidates are the law in effect at the designated ancestor's death and the law in effect when the document became irrevocable (i.e., the transferor's death for a gift under a will or revocable inter vivos trust, or the date an irrevocable inter vivos trust was created). Quaere whether the normal individual would want to apply the law he or she knew or the law as the legislature amends it from time to time. The likely answer is the former, but that creates the problem of having to go back and ascertain the law at that time, which could have been decades ago.

Third, if the designated ancestor is not the beneficiary immediately before distribution, when do we determine the heirs? For example, in *Estate of Woodworth*, 22 Cal. Rptr. 2d 676 (Cal. Ct. App. 1993), Harold devised the residue of his estate in trust for his wife, Mamie, for life, remainder to his sister, Elizabeth, if living, otherwise to Elizabeth's heirs. Elizabeth died before Mamie. At Mamie's death, the question was whether Elizabeth's heirs were to be determined at the time of Elizabeth's death (in which case the successors of her husband, who survived her but predeceased Mamie, would receive a share) or at the time of Mamie's death (in which case Elizabeth's predeceased husband would not be her heir). The usual rule, followed in *Woodworth*, is to determine heirs when the designated ancestor dies, because "heirs" means those persons who inherit from an intestate decedent. But some or all of those people may be deceased by the time for distribution. This partially explains the different rule in UPC §2-711, which determines the designated ancestor's heirs at the time for distribution.

Consider again a gift: "To A for life, remainder to B's heirs." What if B survives A? At A's death, B has no heirs to take because a living person can have no heirs. See Chapter 2. The remainder in B's heirs would fail and the property would revert to the transferor (which might have disadvantageous transfer tax effects) if the destructibility of contingent remainders doctrine applied, which is unlikely (as discussed at page 316). If the destructibility rule is not in effect, another possibility would be for the property to revert only until B's death, at which time the remainder to B's heirs would kick in. Still another possibility would be to accelerate the determination of B's heirs to A's death by making the determination as if B had died at that time. Whichever way you look at it, this is poor drafting.

What if the gift of the remainder is to the transferor's heirs, and one of them is the life tenant? For example, assume a gift by G: "To A for life, remainder to G's heirs." G has four children, A, B, C, and D. Each of G's children has two children ($A_1$ and $A_2$; $B_1$ and $B_2$; $C_1$ and $C_2$; and $D_1$ and $D_2$). The order of deaths is D, then G, then B, then finally life tenant A. When A finally dies, A is survived by C and by all eight of the grandchildren. Who takes at A's death? Note that, if the Doctrine of Worthier Title (discussed at page 317) is applicable, there is a reversion in G rather than a remainder in G's heirs, meaning that G's devisees would take if G died testate. As that doctrine's ongoing validity is limited, we will assume it is not applicable for this example.

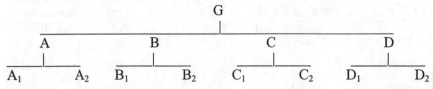

*Order of deaths*: Child D; Grantor G; Child B; Child/Life Tenant A. C still is alive.

Under the usual rule, G's heirs would be determined at G's death. Assuming no surviving spouse, that would mean A, B, and C each would have a vested remainder that would become possessory at A's death, and the other equal share would belong to $D_1$ and $D_2$, as representatives of D and heirs of G. Note the problems and questions this construction raises. For example, distribution is not made until A's later death. At that time B is not living. Must B's estate be reopened for this interest to pass through to B's successors? Also, at G's death A's remainder would become vested. Would it merge with A's life estate to give A a fee in ¼ of the property? Does it make sense that G would leave A both a life estate and a part of the remainder?

There are several alternatives to the usual rule of using G's date of death as the date for determining G's heirs in a case like our example above. One is to determine heirs at the time the instrument became irrevocable, which would be G's date of death if the gift is made under G's will and which would not address the problems discussed above if the gift is by inter vivos trust. Another is to determine heirs at the traditional time, but require survivorship to take. In our example, this would mean that any child of G who survived G but died before A would not take. This method would be unfair to those who do not survive the life tenant, and would raise the question of what to do if an heir of G who died before A (B in our example) was survived by descendants who survived A. In addition, this method creates the possibility of the gift failing altogether if no heirs determined at the traditional time (G's death) are alive at distribution (A's death). Yet a third possibility is to determine heirs at the traditional time (G's death) but simply exclude the life tenant (A) to prevent a merger problem. That, however, does not address the other problems, it is unfair to A's family, and it too may be contrary to G's intent. A fourth alternative would be to determine heirs at the traditional time but treat the life tenant (A) as having predeceased the determination (G's death). This still requires reopening B's estate.

Finally, we could determine heirs at the time for distribution (A's death) as if the designated ancestor (G) had died at that time. This is the sensible result adopted by UPC §2-711 because it avoids the merger problem and creating a share for any then deceased heir (as was necessary in *Woodworth* for Elizabeth's predeceased husband). Meanwhile, there is no delay while waiting for the designated ancestor (G) to die (e.g., if in our example the gift was inter vivos and A died before G, we would determine G's heirs at the time of A's death as if G had died then). Finally, no line of descent is cut out, nor is any line benefited if there is no one therein still alive to take. Despite its virtues, however, this approach is not the favored result. Death of the designated ancestor (G) would be the favored time for the determination.

Remember, however, that we are engaged in construction and rules of construction give way to a transferor's contrary intent. How would we show an intent of the transferor that the designated ancestor's heirs are to be determined at the life tenant's death rather than at the designated ancestor's death? There are several possibilities. One is if the life tenant is the sole heir at the time the gift is made, because it is likely the transferor did not intend for heirs to be determined until the life tenant's death. Under the *rule of incongruity*, in some jurisdictions heirs are not determined until the life tenant's death if the life tenant is an heir, even if not the sole heir, because it is presumed that the transferor would not have intended to give the life tenant both a life estate and any part of the remainder. If the life tenant is the sole heir, there is a greater likelihood that this rule would be followed.

If there are alternative contingent remainders, heirs arguably were not intended to be determined until we know which alternative is going to be met. For example, assume a gift by G "To A for life, remainder to B's heirs if A dies unmarried, or in equal shares to the heirs of A and the heirs of B if A was married at death." Here we have alternative contingent remainders in B's heirs, on the one hand, and A's and B's heirs, on the other. Arguably, G did not intend for B's heirs to be determined until A's death, when we know which of the contingent remainders will take. Note that, if B survives A, we have the added problem discussed at page 336.

Finally, the transferor arguably intended the determination to be made at the time of the distribution if the distribution is going to be made so long in the future that it is unlikely any heir determined in the traditional manner still would be alive. For example, F and G (age 80) are siblings. F's only descendant is a grandchild, GC (age 8), who is in good physical health but has diminished mental capacity. G has one child, age 60, two grandchildren, and two great-grandchildren. F's will leaves the residuary estate in trust for GC for life, remainder to G's heirs. G's life expectancy is relatively short. It is likely that G's only heir will be G's child, but it is unlikely that G's child will survive GC to take the remainder at GC's death. F probably intended for G's heirs to be determined at GC's death, in which case the usual rule of determining heirs at the death of the designated ancestor (here, G) should not apply.

Wills and revocable inter vivos trusts frequently provide for the testator's or settlor's property to pass to a surviving spouse. If there is no surviving spouse, such instruments commonly leave the probate or trust estate to or in trust for descendants. In such cases, a question is what disposition should be made if there are no descendants who survive the testator or settlor, or if property is left in trust for descendants and they all die before the trust terminates. (And, if other persons are named as beneficiaries, they also are not living.) The drafting solution is to provide for an ultimate contingent beneficiary to whom the property can be distributed. One choice is charity. Perhaps the more common one is the testator's or settlor's heirs. Consider the following provision:

SECTION *: If upon the death of the survivor of my spouse and me, or at any time thereafter but prior to complete distribution of the trust estate, there is no living descendant of mine, the trust property then held under this article and not vested or effectively appointed shall be distributed to my heirs at law determined according to the laws of the state of [**] as if I had died at that time.

Note that this provision establishes what law governs the determination of heirs and when the determination is to be made. Any well drafted provision should do as much.

### Gifts to Descendants, Issue, or Children

In Chapter 2 we studied the alternatives for distributing the portion of an intestate decedent's estate passing to descendants. Here, we consider how property left to "descendants," "issue," or "children" by a will or trust instrument is distributed.

#### To "Descendants" or "Issue"

Technically, "descendants" and "issue" are synonyms. "Issue," however, is not a good alternative for "descendants" because too many courts and drafters think it means only children. In *Security Trust*, discussed at page 327, for example, the will provided for "the issue of any deceased brother or sister to take his or her parent's share." The UPC once did but no longer uses "issue." Whichever term you use, a gift by will or trust instrument to a person's "descendants" (or "issue") raises at least three questions.

First, do grandchildren or more remote descendants share if an ancestor who also is a descendant of the designated ancestor survives? For example, if Grandparent devises Blackacre to "descendants," and Grandparent is survived by one child, A, and one grandchild, B (who is a child of A), does A receive Blackacre or do A and B receive it? Absent some indication of intent to the contrary, "descendants" are determined by representation. In this example, A alone would take.

Second, which of the three methods discussed in Chapter 2 of distributing an intestate decedent's estate among descendants (classic per stirpes, per capita, or per capita at each generation) is to be applied if the instrument does not specify how to make the distribution? In many jurisdictions property left to descendants (or issue) will be distributed among them in accordance with the method used for intestate succession. Under Restatement (Second) of Property — Donative Transfers §28.2, the distribution is to be made in accordance with the per stirpes method, even if that method is not used for intestacy, unless the gift provides otherwise. The UPC approach follows the jurisdiction's intestacy statutes unless the gift is to descendants or issue "per stirpes," in which case the classic per stirpes system controls. The best solution? Provide in the instrument how property left to descendants is to be divided among them.

Third, do adopted and nonmarital descendants take? Generally, a gift to "descendants," "issue," or "children" includes adopteds and nonmaritals under the same conditions as for intestacy. See Chapter 2. Historically, under the stranger-to-the-adoption rule an adopted child would not share in a class gift to "children," "descendants," or "issue" unless the transferor was the adopting parent. Statutes in most jurisdictions have rejected that rule. The significant issue that remains is whether such a statutory change applies to an instrument that became irrevocable before the statute was enacted. In some jurisdictions such legislation is not retroactive. As a result, the stranger-to-the-adoption rule may be followed for older instruments that were irrevocable before the statute reversing the rule was adopted.

In most jurisdictions a person adopted as an adult will share in a class gift to "descendants," "issue," or "children" in the same way as a person adopted as a child, regardless of the reason for the adoption. The minority view is that an adult who was adopted to create entitlement under another person's dispositive instrument will not be allowed to do so. For example, in *Minary v. Citizens Fidelity Bank & Trust Co.*, 419 S.W.2d 340 (Ky. Ct. App. 1967), a testator's son who had no descendants adopted his wife of 25 years in an effort to allow her to share in a trust his mother had established that was to be distributed to the mother's heirs at the son's death. Despite statutes allowing adults to be adopted and adopteds to inherit like natural borns, the court held that allowing the wife to take as an adopted adult would "be an act of subterfuge which in effect thwarts the intent of the ancestor whose property is being distributed and cheats the rightful heirs." Under UPC §2-705(c) adopted adults do not share in class gifts made by someone other than the adopting parent unless the adopted adult lived while a minor as a regular member of the adopting parent's household.

To illustrate, GP's will leaves GP's estate in trust for A for life, remainder to A's descendants. A married S, who had a child (C) who lived with A and S. A adopts C, but not until C is an adult. C will share in the distribution of the trust established by GP at A's death, if the UPC applies and C was a minor when C began living with A as a regular member of A's household. C would share in the trust distribution in all adoption situations in most non-UPC jurisdictions. In a jurisdiction following the *Minary* approach, C might not share if the adoption was made to confer on C trust beneficiary status. But even in such a jurisdiction, if C and A had developed a parent/child relationship, especially if they did so while C was a minor, C might share in the trust distribution without regard to whether A adopted C for the purpose of allowing C to do so.

In some jurisdictions the adoption of a person severs the parent/child relationship with the natural parent (and thus any status as a member of the natural parent's family), even if the adoption was made by a step-parent after the natural parent's death. The result can be to exclude the adopted child from membership in a class of "descendants" or "issue" of an ancestor of the deceased natural parent. In such a case, the adopted child is said to have been "adopted out" of the inheriting class. For example, GM's will leaves an estate in trust for GF, for life, remainder to GM's descendants by representation. C is GM's child who predeceased GF. A child of C (GC) survived C and C's surviving spouse (S) married SP, who adopted GC. The question is whether GC shares in the trust when GF dies. Under the UPC, the answer would be yes. This "adoption out" issue essentially is the same as we saw under intestacy. See Chapter 2. In non-UPC states, the answer might be no, which is not the result GM likely intended, nor is it the right result based on policy grounds.

In most jurisdictions today, nonmarital descendants share in class gifts made by will or trust instrument just as they share under intestacy. See Chapter 2.

### Gifts to "Children"

A question with gifts to "children" is whether the descendants of a deceased child will take their parent's share. For example, assume that G devised G's estate in trust for S for life, remainder to G's "surviving children." G was survived by two children, A and B, but B predeceased life tenant S. However, one child of B (GC) survived S. Will GC share in the distribution of the trust estate at S's death? Taken literally, "children" means just that, in which case A takes all and GC is excluded. Note that a traditional antilapse statute will not save the gift, because B did not predecease G. In addition, if this was not a testamentary trust the antilapse result could not apply in most jurisdictions. And in most jurisdictions the "surviving" condition makes the remainders of A and B contingent on surviving S. Because B did not do so, B's interest would fail and not pass to B's heirs or devisees. Did G intend that A should take to the exclusion of GC in this situation, or did the drafter of the instrument mistakenly use "children" when "descendants" is what G intended (or would have intended, if the question had been asked during the estate planning interview)? If the intent was to exclude grandchildren and more remote descendants, the way to avoid this issue is to say something like: "remainder to G's children who survive S, without regard to whether a predeceased child is survived by any descendant who survives S."

### Rule in Wild's Case

*Wild's Case*, decided in 1599, interpreted a devise by T "to A and A's children." Several interpretations are possible. The first resolution in *Wild's Case*: if there are no children of A at T's death, A would take a fee tail. The traditional method for the creation of a fee tail was a devise: "To A and the heirs of A's body," meaning that the property would pass to A and then descendants of A until A's line of descent ran out. Generally the fee tail estate is not recognized today. In many jurisdictions it is converted to a fee in A, although in some of these jurisdictions A is divested if A dies without descendants. In other jurisdictions A is treated as receiving a life estate, with a remainder in fee simple absolute in A's descendants. If a devise were made by T today: "To A and A's children," and A had no children at T's death, the likely result would be a fee in A, perhaps subject to partial divestment if A should have children.

The second resolution in *Wild's Case*, followed in some jurisdictions today: A and A's children alive at T's death take as equal tenants in common. Afterborn children of A are excluded because the class would close under the rule of convenience at T's death. This is what the Restatement (First) of Property — Donative Transfers said was the accepted approach. An alternative if A has children at T's death is the so-called Pennsylvania rule, also followed in some jurisdictions today: life estate in A, remainder in A's children with the class not closing until A's death. This probably is the better interpretation because afterborns are not cut out. The Restatement (Second) of Property — Donative Transfers favored this approach.

Still another alternative is to treat the gift as half to A and a class gift of the other half to A's children. Under this approach, A and A's children would take as tenants in common, with A's interest being half, and A's children dividing the other half equally among them.

The place this is most likely to arise involves drafting for a gift to a testator's spouse and children, or descendants. Alternatives would include:

- **Spouse and each child take equal shares; per capita among children:**

As many equal shares as necessary to distribute one share to each member of a class consisting of my spouse and my children who survive me, with no share for any class member or their descendants who do not survive me.

- **Half to spouse and half to children; per capita among children:**

Half to my spouse and half in equal shares to such of my children as survive me, with no share for any class member or their descendants who do not survive me.

- **Spouse and each child take equal shares; per stirpes distribution:**

Per stirpes to my then living descendants and, for purposes of division, treating my spouse as if [he or she] were a child of mine.

(This may be appropriate for a second marriage situation.)

"In Equal Shares to the Children of A and the Children of B"

The construction issue here is whether there is a single gift to a class consisting of the children of A and the children of B, or whether there is a class gift of half to the children of A and a second class gift of the other half to the children of B. For example, if A had one child and B had two, does each child receive ⅓, or does A's child receive half and each of B's children ¼? Is the most likely construction a single class gift that, in the example, would result in each of the children receiving ⅓, or do you perceive that the transferor intends what in effect is a per stirpes distribution? Clear drafting should resolve this issue.

# CHAPTER 16

# PLANNING FOR INCAPACITY

This Chapter deals with questions concerning management of an incapacitated client's property and making decisions with respect to the client's health care. A durable power of attorney for health care can appoint and authorize an agent to make health care decisions. A living will allows the client to direct that life sustaining treatment be withheld or withdrawn in certain circumstances (e.g., the client has a terminal condition or is in a persistent vegetative state). Alternatives for management of a client's property include revocable trusts and durable powers of attorney for property management.

The traditional estate planning focus is on transferring a client's property, usually at death. But estate planning clients also worry about the possibility of becoming mentally incapacitated. They fear that a court may appoint a guardian or conservator to manage their property and make health care decisions for them if they become mentally incapacitated without proper planning for that possibility. An incapacitated person may not want a court appointed representative who must serve under the ongoing supervision of the court, and that personal representative may not have the authority to do all the things the person wants or needs.

An incapacitated person for whom a court has appointed a representative is a "ward." In many states, a court-appointed fiduciary to manage a ward's property is a "guardian of the estate," and a representative charged with the care of the ward personally, including making health care decisions, is a "guardian of the person." The same person may serve as guardian of the estate and of the person. In some states, to avoid confusion, the fiduciary managing a ward's property is a "conservator," and the fiduciary responsible for the care of the person is a guardian. We usually just refer to the ward's "personal representative."

A judicial determination of incapacity is required if it is necessary to appoint a guardian to make health care decisions or to manage property. This determination can be painful and embarrassing to the ward personally and to their family. Worse, if a real need exists, it can be time consuming and expensive, in terms of out-of-pocket costs, missed opportunities, defaults that require correction, and perhaps even in medical terms due to the inability to act in a timely manner. In addition, most court appointed guardians are required to file annual or more frequent reports with the court that appointed them and to obtain the court's approval for all actions on behalf of the ward. In some cases supervision of the guardian is needed to protect the interests of the ward, but in many cases there is no concern about mismanagement or neglect and complying with guardianship requirements is an unnecessary burden and expense.

## Planning for Property Management

Clients may provide for the management of their property in the event of their incapacity in four ways.

### *Outright Transfers*

Usually poorly advised individuals reflect a concern about incapacity by transferring legal ownership of their assets to another, such as a spouse or adult child, with an understanding that the transferee will use the assets for the transferor's benefit. Medicaid rules address intentional efforts to diminish wealth to qualify for federal or state health care benefits, known as "spend down planning," and impose a period of ineligibility on a transferor if the transfer occurs within 3 years (5 years if a trust is involved) before an application is made for benefits. See Chapter 13. Outright transfers also raise a host of other problems, particularly if the transferee is not a spouse. Among them are loss of control while the transferor remains competent or after regaining capacity; uncertainties over whether the conveyances are completed gifts or transfers in trust and, if the latter, the terms of the trust; imposition of gift tax; income tax basis issues; the risk that creditors of the transferee will reach the transferred assets; and unenforceability of the implicit understanding that the transferee will provide for the transferor. As a result, outright transfers for dealing with potential incapacity usually are not advisable.

### *Transfers in Joint Tenancy*

In a desire to avoid legal arrangements that are perceived as more complicated, some clients who are concerned about their ongoing ability to manage property, pay bills, and so forth transfer title to some assets (particularly bank accounts) into joint tenancy with the right of survivorship with one or more trusted persons. Chapter 6 details several issues that often arise at the death of a joint tenant transferor. Other problems include the possibility that creditors of another joint tenant will reach the joint tenancy property and the inability of any joint tenant to unilaterally manage some kinds of assets that are held in joint tenancy, such as real estate. Unexpected adverse tax consequences also can result, and joint tenancy usually is a nightmare for effective tax planning. Consequently, joint tenancies generally are not advisable to deal with the prospect of incapacity, particularly if any other joint tenant is not a spouse or, if the tenants are spouses, if the size of their combined estates is large enough to incur federal or state estate tax.

### Revocable Trusts

Revocable inter vivos trusts often are considered in the context of probate avoidance, but in many circumstances probate no longer is a problem to be avoided. This particularly is true in UPC and many other states in which probate administration has been simplified and streamlined. In those cases trusts are more useful in providing for the management of trust assets in the event of the settlor's incapacity. See Chapter 6. Frequently the settlor will serve as the sole initial trustee of the trust. If the settlor becomes incapacitated the well drafted trust instrument appoints one or more successor trustees to serve and only if those nominees are unable or unwilling to act is a successor appointed by individuals or a court acting under the terms of the document. Either way, a guardianship is avoided without creating tax, creditor, or other issues that are present when outright conveyances or joint tenancies are used.

A court proceeding is not necessary to determine the settlor's incapacity if the trust instrument names the settlor as trustee and provides for a successor. A well planned trust provides for the settlor's incapacity to be determined by the settlor's physician(s), by a trusted family member or friend, or by a committee of several trusted persons (but not by the successor trustee, for fear that someone will allege that self interest informed a determination to take over). If medical personnel are involved the determination may require sharing information now protected by the Health Insurance Portability and Accountability Act of 1996 (HIPAA), so a procedure should be established in advance to guarantee the requisite consent to any anticipated disclosure.

### Durable Powers of Attorney

A power of attorney is an arrangement by which one person (the principal) appoints another (the attorney-in-fact or agent) to act on behalf of the principal with respect to matters (such as management of the principal's property) enumerated in the power. At common law, an agent's authority terminated automatically if the principal became incapacitated. That result is antithetical to the intended use in an estate planning context. Most principals give authority over their property to the agent only to provide for incapacity. As a result, statutes in every state now permit powers of attorney (called *durable* powers of attorney) to remain in effect after the principal becomes incapacitated, provided the power clearly expresses the intent that the power not lapse.

Under many state statutes, a durable power of attorney may empower the agent only if the principal becomes incapacitated, at which time the power "springs" into existence. As with self-trusteed revocable declarations of trust that provide for successor trustees in the event of the settlor's incapacity, the use of a springing power requires that the principal's incapacity be determined in a designated manner, and HIPAA concerns should be anticipated. Usually springing powers make little sense because (1) it can be difficult to determine the principal's incapacity (to trigger the power springing into effect) in a way that third parties will accept, (2) a competent principal always can repudiate an agent's actions, and (3) an agent who is not trustworthy should not be selected. Most planners advise immediately effective durable powers, but springing powers are popular because principals often don't want to relinquish control until they absolutely must.

Most durable powers of attorney broadly authorize the agent to deal with the principal's property the same as could the principal (e.g., to buy, sell, exchange, lease, mortgage, etc.). In most states, however, durable powers of attorney do not automatically authorize the agent to make gifts of the principal's property (because the agent's duty is to act in the principal's best interests), making a specific authorization to make gratuitous transfers important if the principal has a taxable estate and wants to empower the agent to make tax-wise gifts.

Two advantages recommend revocable trusts over durable powers for a client who wants to avoid a guardianship for managing property in the event of incapacity. Both advantages are attributable to the trustee holding legal title to the client's assets, in trust. One is that trustees generally may deal with third parties with respect to trust assets easier than can agents under durable powers of attorney. Third parties (e.g., banks, stock transfer agents, and insurance companies) are not as familiar with durable powers of attorney as they are with trusts. They may express concern that the durable power may have been revoked, a special worry if it is "stale" (was not executed recently) and they may ask to review the power of attorney to ascertain whether it authorizes the agent's action. The other advantage is unrelated to management of the client's property during life, but a revocable trust has the added benefit of avoiding probate of trust assets. This advantage can be significant, particularly in jurisdictions in which estate administration is fully court supervised, and for clients who own real property in more than one state (for which ancillary probate administration proceedings are required in states other than the state in which the client was domiciled at death). But sometimes probate is desirable, so don't be quick to prejudge this.

On the flip side of the durable power versus trust debate, a trustee has authority only over trust assets transferred to the trust. Transferring a client's assets to a revocable trust can be time consuming, involve expense, and raise questions that a durable power of attorney avoids, such as whether (1) a transfer of mortgaged real estate to a revocable trust triggers a due-on-sale clause, (2) the insurer of a car or home must be notified of the transfer and the trust added as an additional named insured under the policy, (3) the transfer of a home affects any available property tax exemptions such as homestead or an otherwise applicable Medicaid exemption, and (4) the transfer of a partnership interest or stock in a closely held business to a revocable trust is permitted by the governing partnership agreement or a shareholders' agreement for the corporation. Durable powers typically grant authority to deal with all of a client's assets with less complication inter vivos but do not avoid probate with respect to any of them.

## Planning for Health Care

Competent persons may use inter vivos trusts or property management powers of attorney because they don't want to manage their own property. For example, maybe they are going to be out of town for an extended period of time. By contrast, health care powers of attorney are used only when the principal is incapacitated (at least temporarily). The principal method of planning to avoid the need for a guardian of the incapacitated person is a durable health care power of attorney, which also is known as a "health care proxy" or an "advance directive for health care."

In many jurisdictions for many years the ability to delegate the authority to make health care decisions was not clear. Some early statutes authorizing durable powers of attorney did not specify whether the agent could make health care decisions for the principal. Today, even if a durable power of attorney statute is not specific about health care (and most are), the right of principals to direct the principal's medical treatment is recognized as a protected constitutional right that may be delegated to a surrogate if the principal is unable to exercise it personally. A health care durable power of attorney may broadly or narrowly authorize the agent to make health care decisions for the principal. Statutes in a number of states also specify that a health care durable power of attorney may authorize the agent to decide whether life-sustaining treatment should be withheld or withdrawn in circumstances in which the principal could make that decision if competent. Living wills remain useful in some states that do not address this use and for individuals who want to make that decision for themselves.

A living will, also known as an advance directive, directs that life-sustaining treatment be withheld or withdrawn in specified circumstances. Living wills are authorized by statute in most states, many of which prescribe with some specificity a form that can be used.

The circumstances under which they will be respected vary among the states, however, and these parameters are extraordinarily important because the document may not be effective to accomplish its intended purpose if the statutory requirements are not met. For example, under many statutes, a living will may authorize withholding or withdrawal of life-sustaining treatment if the patient is in a terminal condition or a vegetative state from which there is no realistic hope of recovery. In some states, however, a living will is not effective unless the maker is comatose or brain dead. In those states someone who is in a terminal condition but who is awake, although incompetent or severely handicapped, is not protected by an otherwise valid set of instructions under a living will. Some states also restrict when execution of the living will must occur. For example, the law may require the maker to be terminally ill (the notion being that, until then, you may not know what you want to do). In such a jurisdiction, a person who is competent until entering a permanent vegetative state, such as from an automobile or other accident, apparently cannot execute a binding living will.

In some states, a person's right to enforce living will directions is protected by a statutory requirement that an attending physician who is not willing to terminate or withhold treatment must refer the patient to another physician who will. In the absence of such a statute, however, enforceability of living wills also is a problem, because some medical professionals simply will not respect them (out of respect for human life, fear of litigation, or otherwise).

Consequently, in many jurisdictions the living will simply is not reliable. There are just too many ways it can fail its intended purpose. Although a client who does not want to be kept alive in a terminal condition or a persistent vegetative state should have a living will, a health care durable power of attorney may be more reliable and effective to accomplish the client's objectives. Further, living wills address only the issue whether life-sustaining treatment should be withheld or withdrawn. Durable health care powers of attorney can address all health care decisions that may arise if the principal becomes incapacitated from any cause, at any time, and with any level of debilitation, regardless of the expected duration of the incapacity (for example, if the principal is unconscious from an accident and needs surgery, an agent under a durable power can consent to the procedure from which, if successful, the principal will fully recover.) Thus, a health care power of attorney and a living will together are the appropriate planning package.

### *Organ Donation*

One final matter deserves mention. In many jurisdictions an organ donation designation routinely is made on a driver's license, rather than on a document prepared by a lawyer. In view of the shortage of organs for transplantation and the ability to save lives by donating organs, many estate planning lawyers use their unique role in counseling with clients to discuss organ donation and to assist them in becoming organ donors if they so choose, often with a separate document that clarifies their intent, explains to family members their objectives, and provides directions that check-the-box drivers' license designations do not provide.

# CHAPTER 17

# RULE AGAINST PERPETUITIES

Unlike the rules of construction for future interests we studied in Chapter 15, the common law Rule Against Perpetuities is a rule of law that applies to invalidate offending interests without regard to the transferor's clearly expressed intent to the contrary. Interests subject to invalidation under the Rule include contingent remainders and executory interests. Reversions and other interests retained by the transferor are not subject to the Rule because they are deemed to be vested. The Rule invalidates only those contingent future interests that are not certain to vest, or certain to fail to vest, within the perpetuities period. The perpetuities period begins when the contingent interest was irrevocably created and ends 21 years after the deaths of all persons who were living when the period began and who could affect its vesting.

A class gift will fail under the Rule as to all members of the class (even those whose interests are vested, subject to open, within the perpetuities period) unless the class is certain to close, and all conditions precedent are certain to be satisfied or fail, within the perpetuities period. Finally, application of the Rule to powers of appointment varies, depending on whether the power is (1) a presently exercisable general power, or (2) a testamentary general power or any nongeneral power. The Rule can operate to invalidate either the power itself or interests created by exercise of the power.

Because of the harshness of the Rule's operation, a variety of reforms and other devices have been used by legislatures, courts, and practitioners to avoid its application. All of this, and especially how to avoid the harshness of the Rule, are the focus of this Chapter.

Professor Gray's classic statement of the Rule was: "No interest is good unless it must vest, if at all, not later than twenty-one years after some life in being at the creation of the interest." This statement of the Rule requires a refinement with respect to contingent interests created under revocable trusts. Trust interests must vest, if at all, within 21 years after the death of some life in being when the trust becomes irrevocable, which is not necessarily when the trust and the contingent interest were created. In a revocable trust the perpetuities period usually begins at the settlor's death. In this respect, "creation" under Professor Gray's statement of the Rule means when the document creating the interest becomes irrevocable.

Fundamental to the historical development of the Rule Against Perpetuities were concerns about the alienability of land (yet the Rule applies to personalty as well as realty). In addition, the Rule reflects antipathy to eternal power of an individual to control wealth and its enjoyment by others after death. Because the Rule Against Perpetuities is a rule of law, not a rule of construction, it invalidates offending future interests despite the intention of the creator of the interest.

Note also that contingent *legal* interests (e.g., Blackacre to A for life, then to A's children for their lives, remainder to A's grandchildren) affect the marketability of property and are directly within the province of the Rule's fundamental underlying policies. But the Rule also applies even if property is held in a trust that allows free alienability by the trustee. Restrictions on the vesting of the beneficiaries' *equitable* interests in trusts hardly impact the alienability of property that is the trust corpus and therefore should not be subject to the first justification for the Rule. Today, for this reason (and increasingly as a sop to attract trust business, particularly to compete for generation-skipping trust business), many states have outright repealed the Rule, or allowed settlors to "opt out" of it, for interests held in trust if the trust assets are alienable by the trustee.

Although property held in trust may be freely alienated by the trustee, its use by the beneficiaries is restricted. In the majority of states that have not repealed the Rule with respect to beneficial interests in trust, another policy the Rule serves is to limit the "dead hand" control a transferor of property may exert over its future use by beneficiaries. This aspect remains viable with respect to all forms of property held in trust or outright and to legal and equitable interests alike.

### Operation of the Rule

Following a brief overview of the major components of the Rule we will look at each of them in more detail below. Keep in mind Professor Gray's shorthand statement of the Rule: "No interest is good unless it must vest, if at all, not later than twenty-one years after some life in being at the creation of the interest." The Rule applies only to contingent remainders and executory interests. It does not apply to vested remainders or any future interests retained by the transferor, even after the retained interest is later transferred to a third party. The period during which interests must vest to avoid violating the Rule is that period of time beginning when the contingent interest to be tested under it becomes effective irrevocably and ending 21 years after the deaths of certain persons who were alive ("lives in being") at that creation.

A contingent remainder or executory interest that might vest outside the period of the Rule is invalid from the time of its creation. Under the common law Rule, the interest is not invalidated only if it *actually* vests outside the period of the Rule. Rather, the Rule regards it as improperly created in the first instance if there is *any possibility* that it will do so, no matter how remote. To illustrate, assume that D devised the residue of D's estate in trust for a child, A, for life, then for A's children for their lives, remainder to A's grandchildren. A survived D. The contingent remainder to A's grandchildren violates the Rule and is invalid. A is a life in being at creation of the contingent remainder in A's grandchildren (when D died), but not all of A's children or grandchildren necessarily are lives in being at that time. Thus, the grandchildren's interest might not vest within 21 years after the deaths of A and all other lives in being when the trust was created. To appreciate why, assume that A has a child after D's death and that child of A has a child more than 21 years after all the lives in being die (at which time, but for the violation of the Rule, that grandchild's interest would vest). As proof, assume that D died in 2005, that A had a child (C) in 2007, that A and all other lives in being in 2005 die in 2008, and that C has a child (GC) in 2030. The remainder in GC would not vest until GC's birth (recall the discussion in Chapter 15 that a remainder cannot be vested in an unborn person), which is more than 21 years after the deaths of all lives in being. Note also that the result is the same even if A had a child, B, who was born before D's death and who survived D, and a grandchild, X, who was a child of B and who also survived D. The remainder in A's grandchildren is invalid because A could have an after born or adopted child, who could have a child more than 21 years after the deaths of A, B, X, and all other lives in being at D's death. We will return to a discussion of the Rule's applicability to class gifts at page 372.

The reach of the Rule is not limited to unusual, sophisticated, or complicated planning situations in which the intention is to tie up property for a long time. For example, assume your client, T, is 50, is single, has one child (C, age 25), and one grandchild (GC, age 2). T's plan is to leave T's estate to C, but T does not want C to receive the inheritance until C reaches age 30. If C dies before then, T wants the property to stay in trust for GC and any other grandchildren of T until they are age 30 and, if a grandchild dies before that age survived by any descendant, T wants the property to stay in trust for the grandchild's descendants until they reach age 30, and so on. If a descendant of T dies before the trust terminates and there are no other descendants of T then living, T wants the property distributed to T's heirs, as if T had died intestate at that time. An estate plan designed to accomplish T's very common objective would violate the Rule because the interests of grandchildren and more remote descendants, and the interest of T's heirs, *could* vest beyond the perpetuities period (which is all the Rule requires). It is common practice to prepare instruments creating such plans anyway, however, and to rely on a "saving clause," as discussed at page 381, to avoid a violation of the Rule. But under the traditional application of the Rule (that is, if a saving clause were not used or effective) T's plan would not be possible as T envisions it.

## Rule is in Disfavor

The Rule is today subject to various criticisms (which have resulted in its reform in most jurisdictions, as discussed beginning at page 383). For example, the Rule traps the uninitiated even though it is rather easily avoided by the well informed. Unfortunately, sometimes it also bites even well informed practitioners (which is why proper use of saving clauses is so common, to avoid that result). Further, most future interests today are created in trust, and the Rule is not needed to accomplish its traditional purpose (to protect the alienability of property) when the trust instrument allows the trustee to alienate the trust assets (as do the great majority of trust instruments). Thus, to a significant extent the Rule serves no legitimate purpose for trusts in which legal title to trust property is not restricted.

Another purpose of the Rule is to limit the ability of a transferor of property to control the use of the property or its proceeds by the beneficiaries. The effectiveness of the Rule to limit the dead hand is limited, however, by the fact that the Rule does not limit (at least not directly) controls over the possession of property. Rather, it only limits controls over vesting. So the dead hand can continue to govern long after an interest in trust has vested within the period of the Rule. To illustrate, assume that D devised D's estate "To T, in trust, to pay income to my descendants, per stirpes, until the date that is 21 years after the death of the last surviving descendant of mine who was living at my death, remainder to my descendants, per stirpes; provided that each remainder beneficiary's share shall be held by the trustee for the remainder beneficiary's benefit until his or her death, at which time it shall be distributed to his or her estate." This disposition satisfies the Rule, even though the remainder beneficiaries never will receive possession of their shares, and possession by the remainder beneficiaries' successors may be deferred for many decades after the interests vest. As discussed at page 385, however, after expiration of the perpetuities period the beneficiaries of the trust could force the distribution of income without regard to any intent by D to the contrary. Moreover, the beneficiaries also could choose to terminate the trust after expiration of the period, without regard to any remaining unfulfilled material purpose of the settlor. See Fratcher, 1 SCOTT ON TRUSTS §62.10 (4th ed. 1987).

Another powerful criticism of the Rule is that the period applied to determine whether an interest is valid makes no sense. Originally, the idea for the Rule was that it was reasonable for a property owner to tie up property for the rest of the lives of living persons the owner knew and wanted to benefit, plus a period of 21 years (time enough for the next generation to reach majority). Today, in most jurisdictions lives in being for validating a future interest under the Rule need not have any relationship to the property or to the transferor. Thus an oft quoted example of a valid disposition under the Rule is income to the descendants of the transferor, per stirpes, until 21 years after the death of the last to die of a dozen or more named healthy babies (unrelated to the settlor) born shortly before creation of the future interests, after which the remainder would be distributed to the then living descendants of the transferor, per stirpes. The number of specified measuring lives (the dozen healthy babies in this example) must be sufficiently limited so that it is not an unreasonable burden to ascertain when the last of them has died. Is descendants of Joseph Kennedy or the Queen of England living at inception of the interest sufficiently limited?

By careful selection of the measuring lives, vesting may be deferred without violating the Rule for 100 years or more (the remaining lifetime of the measuring lives plus 21 years). As illustrated by the example above, possession may be further delayed for many more years after vesting. By contrast, a disposition that may not delay vesting or possession for more than 21 years and a day could violate the Rule. For example, assume that D devised D's estate to a child, A, for life, remainder to A's descendants who reach age 22. The remainder violates the Rule because of the possibility that, after D's death, A will have an after born or adopted child, immediately after which A (and all other descendants of A) will die. Thus, the after born or adopted child's interest might not vest for more than 21 years after the deaths of all lives in being at D's death. Note that, as generally is the case in the law (whether of property, wills, trusts, estates, or otherwise), a person is treated for purposes of the Rule as in being from the date of conception if the person is born alive. Thus, the actual period of the Rule is lives in being, plus periods of gestation, plus 21 years. As a result, in this example the possibility of vesting outside the period of the Rule is a narrow one. The after born or adopted child of A would have to be conceived after D's death but reach age 22 more than 21 years after the deaths of A and all other descendants of A living at D's death.

Another oddity that generates criticism is that the Rule applies only to contingent interests in transferees (contingent remainders and executory interests), meaning interests on the right side of the chart in Chapter 15. Other future interests, such as vested remainders and all the future interests originally retained by the transferor, listed on the left side of that chart, are outside its reach. The Rule is thus easily avoided by structuring a remainder as one that is vested, subject to divestment, rather than one that is contingent. For example, a remainder to children of a life tenant who reach age 25 is a contingent interest that would violate the Rule. By contrast, a remainder to children of the life tenant, but if a child does not reach age 25 to the grantor's heirs, is a vested remainder subject to divestment, and would not violate. As a second example, the Rule would not apply if the transferor simply created the present interest life estate in one document and kept the reversion, and then conveyed away that reversion by a second document. Goofy, and properly criticized.

A final valid criticism of the Rule is that it sometimes relies on nonsense presumptions to invalidate a transferee's contingent future interest. Examples include the presumptions of the fertile octogenarian, precocious toddler, unborn widow, and administrative infinality, all as discussed beginning at page 366.

As you can begin to appreciate, good advice is to beware the Rule (we're only half kidding). It has been characterized by another of its authorities as a "technicality-ridden legal nightmare" and a "dangerous instrumentality in the hands of most members of the bar." W. Barton Leach, *Perpetuities Legislation, Massachusetts Style*, 67 Harv. L. Rev. 1349 (1954). Indeed, the complexity of the Rule is such that a California court held in a negligence action against an attorney who drafted an instrument creating a trust that was alleged to have violated the Rule that the alleged violation (based on the unrealistic administrative infinality presumption discussed at page 368) was "so remote and unlikely that an attorney of ordinary skill acting under the same circumstances might well have 'fallen into the net which the Rule spreads for the unwary' and failed to recognize the danger." Thus, there was no negligence. *Lucas v. Hamm*, 364 P.2d 685, 690 (Cal. 1961). In part because of the widespread use of saving clauses to avoid violations of the Rule today, it is far from clear that a drafting attorney who violates the Rule now would be let off so easily. See *Wright v. Williams*, 121 Cal. Rptr. 194, 199 n.2 (Cal. Ct. App. 1975).

If you find that you want more on the Rule than we provide in this Chapter, a good source for additional help is Featheringill, *Understanding the Rule Against Perpetuities: A Step-By-Step Approach*, 13 Cumb. L. Rev. 161 (1982). If instead you would like to cut to the chase, saving clauses are discussed at page 381 and modern reforms that may mitigate the inconvenience of the Rule in your jurisdiction are listed beginning at page 383. Next below is the gag-me in-depth version.

### The Essence of the Rule: Remote Vesting Prohibited

A contingent future interest created in a transferee (i.e., a contingent remainder or an executory interest) violates the Rule unless it is *certain* that the interest will vest, or fail to vest, within the period of the Rule. The interest is invalid if there is *any possibility*, no matter how remote or unrealistic, that the interest will vest after expiration of the period of the Rule.

## *The Perpetuities Period*

Determining the period of the Rule is critical for two reasons. First, the interest violates the Rule unless it must vest, or fail to vest, within that period. Second, the possibilities that must be considered to determine whether the Rule has been violated are those events that might occur in the future, given the facts existing when the period begins to run. A second look exception exists but only interests created by the exercise of any nongeneral or a testamentary general power of appointment allows consideration of facts existing at the time of exercise. See page 379.

When the period of the Rule begins to run (for class gifts as well as for gifts to individuals) depends on how the contingent interest being tested was created. Generally, the period begins when the transfer creating the interest becomes irrevocable. So, for example, the period runs from the testator's death if the interest was created by will. To illustrate, D devised D's estate by will "To T, in trust, to accumulate the income for the full life of my spouse, S, and on the death of S, to distribute the accumulated income and principal to the estate of S." D died first. The transfer by D was vested in S at D's death because S has full control over it. So the Rule begins anew with respect to S's disposition of the property. The perpetuities period for testing the validity of any contingent future interests created by S's estate plan will begin at S's death, because any contingent interests will be created by S's will and because any restrictions on alienability of the property and the dead hand control over it imposed by D terminated at S's death.

The period runs from the date of delivery if an interest is created by deed, because that is when the deed is effective. And, if the interest was created by irrevocable trust, the period runs from the date any property (as to which the future interest is being created) is transferred to the trust.

If the interest was created by revocable trust, the period begins to run when the power to revoke terminates. Until then the settlor can alienate the property freely (by revoking the trust). Usually the power to revoke a revocable trust terminates at the settlor's death, but the period would begin to run when the power was released if the settlor releases the power before then. Incapacity of the settlor is not treated for this purpose as a termination of the settlor's power to revoke because a guardian might be appointed who could exercise the settlor's power to revoke until the settlor dies.

For example, assume G created a trust, the dispositive terms of which are "Income to G's children for life, remainder to G's grandchildren who reach age 21." If the trust was a revocable inter vivos trust, the remainder is valid under the Rule because the perpetuities period does not begin to run until G's death (assuming G does not release the power of revocation during G's life). At G's death, all of G's children necessarily will be lives in being,[1] and the remainder in G's grandchildren will vest within 21 years after the death of the survivor of G's children. If it was an irrevocable inter vivos trust, the remainder is not valid. This is because the perpetuities period begins to run upon its creation. That results in a violation of the Rule because G could have another child, AB (for after born or adopted), after creation of the trust. All relevant lives in being when the trust was created (i.e., G and G's then living descendants) then could die, after which AB could have a child, GC, who would reach age 21 more than 21 years after the death of the last survivor of G and G's descendants living when the trust was created.

Please note special rules apply for determining when the period of the Rule begins to run when powers of appointment are involved. See page 376. Determining when the period of the Rule begins can be a challenge, but determining when it ends is even more difficult. As stated by Gray, it is 21 years after the death of "some life in being." The difficulty is determining what life or lives in being at the beginning of the period are to be considered.

The life in being we are searching for is one by whom we can prove that the transferees' contingent future interest(s) will vest within that person's life, plus periods of gestation, plus 21 years. If we find such a life, we refer to it as a *validating* life. The Rule is violated and the offending interest fails if we cannot find such a life, and cannot prove that the interest will fail within the perpetuities period. In searching for a validating life, consider only those persons who can affect the vesting of contingent interests under the instrument (such as by being born, having a child, or dying).

A person who is not a beneficiary of a trust can be a validating life for interests created under the trust. Thus, for a gift by D "To A's last child to reach age 21," A is the validating life regardless of whether A

---

1. Let's accept an important caveat, because the law has yet to address application of the new biology under the Rule. We simply must ignore the possibility that a child of G could be conceived and born alive many years after G's death. Cases holding that DNA offspring of G are G's children have been oblivious to the Rule Against Perpetuities implications, and it is anyone's guess what a court might do with this issue if or when it arises in the future. This is just one of several reasons why the Uniform Parentage Act takes a position that these DNA offspring are *not* the provider's children. But only time will tell what will happen in this arcane corner of such an important new development. Quaere whether a Rule as old as Perpetuities should have any role in the development of this emerging law.

also is a beneficiary. Assuming that A either is living when the gift is made, or is deceased at that time (i.e., as long as A cannot be born after the date of the gift), the contingent remainder is valid because it must vest, or fail to vest, within 21 years after A's death (again ignoring the new biology).

Further, the validating life need not be an identifiable individual, but may be a member of a class. Thus, a testamentary gift by D to D's children for their lives, remainder to D's grandchildren is valid under the Rule, the validating life being that of the survivor of D's children, including any yet to be born or adopted. The instrument may, but need not and usually does not, specify who are the validating lives. Rather, the validating lives, if any, are determinable from the terms of the instrument and knowledge of the extrinsic facts.

### *The Required Proof*

To be valid a transferee's contingent future interest must be certain to vest, or fail to vest, within the perpetuities period. If the interest is valid, the proof is in the form of a validating life by whom it can be shown that the interest will timely vest or fail. The test entails looking for any scenario under which the interest will not timely vest. For example, D's will devised Blackacre "To T, in trust, income to A for life, remainder to B's grandchildren who reach age 25." To know whether the remainder is valid or violates the Rule, we need to know whether, at D's death, B or any child of B is living. If so, the remainder is void under the Rule. If not, the remainder is valid.

For a test, assume that at D's death B is living. The remainder violates the Rule because, after D's death, B could have a child who could have a child who reaches age 25 more than 21 years after the deaths of all relevant lives in being at D's death (i.e., after the deaths of A, B, and all descendants of B living at D's death, those being the persons who can affect vesting of the remainder in B's grandchildren). Under that scenario the remainder could vest outside of the perpetuities period, and thus the remainder violates the Rule. To reiterate, D dies; then AB is born to B; then A, B, and all descendants of B other than AB die; then AB has a child, X; then X reaches age 25, which would occur more than 21 years after the deaths of all relevant lives in being at D's death. Similarly, assume that at D's death, C, a child of B, is living. The remainder violates the Rule because shortly after D's death A, B, and all descendants of B other than C could die; then AB could be born to C; then C could die before AB is age four; then AB could reach age 25, which would occur more than 21 years after the deaths of all lives in being at D's death. In each of these examples the Rule is violated.

The remainder would be valid, however, if D was survived by one or more grandchildren of B, but was not survived by B or by any children of B. The validating lives would be the grandchildren of B, all of whose interests necessarily would vest within their own lives and all of whom, by necessity, are lives in being at D's death. Assuming no more grandchildren can enter the class, the remainder is good. Similarly, if the remainder was given to B's grandchildren who reached age 21, rather than 25, it would be valid as long as B did not survive D. The validating lives in being are B's children, because the interests of B's grandchildren necessarily would vest within 21 years of the deaths of B's children (again ignoring the new biology).

As illustrated, although it is not always true, it frequently is the case that requiring the holder of a contingent remainder or an executory interest to reach an age over 21 for their interest to vest will cause violation of the Rule. This is common enough that we always are wary and carefully study a case when that is the fact.

There is no set number of validating lives who can be used to prove whether a contingent interest must vest within the perpetuities period. The number can be as low as one. For example, "To the first child of my child, C, who reaches age 21." C is the only life in being to consider in applying the Rule. This gift, by the way, would not violate the Rule, because any child of C necessarily will reach age 21 within 21 years of C's death — again ignoring the new biology. At the other extreme, the number of validating lives must be reasonable, and the death of the survivor of them must be determinable without unreasonable difficulty. For example, D's will devised D's estate "To T, in trust, income to my descendants, per stirpes, until 21 years after the death of the last survivor of all persons who were living at the time of my death, remainder to my then living descendants, per stirpes." This gift would not violate the Rule if everyone alive at the testator's death could be validating lives in being, but how would you determine when the survivor of that class died, which would be necessary to determine when, and to whom, to distribute the remainder? Clearly, this gift would be void, although probably for uncertainty, and not from having violated the Rule. See *In re Moore*, [1901] 1 Ch. 936.

What about a gift to the testator's descendants alive 20 years after the death of the survivor of all descendants of her Late Majesty Queen Victoria living at the testator's death? What if there were 120 or so of such descendants alive at the testator's death? Those were the facts of a relatively old English case, *In re Villar*, [1929] 1 Ch. 243 (Eng. C.A.), and the gift was upheld. Whether a similar result would be reached by an American court is doubtful. Restatement (Second) of Property §1.3 comment a, would hold such a gift invalid. As discussed at page 381, perpetuities saving clauses frequently use as the class of validating lives in being the transferor's descendants living at the effective date of the grant. Such a group should be regarded as reasonable in size.

The fundamental point is that validating lives must affect vesting. Let's illustrate several easy cases. If D devised D's estate "To A for life, then to A's children for their lives, remainder to A's grandchildren who reach age 25," whose lives can affect vesting? Clearly A can, because A could have additional children who could have children who would share in the remainder. Similarly, each of A's children living at D's death could have children who would share in the remainder. Finally, those grandchildren of A who are living at D's death also may share in the remainder, and thus affect its vesting. Now, can we find at least one person by whose life we can prove that the interests of A's grandchildren will vest (or fail to vest) within that person's remaining life plus 21 years? The answer is "no," and the proof is made by finding a possibility of the interest vesting more than 21 years after the deaths of all persons whose lives can affect vesting. A violative contingency would be: after D's death, A has an after born or adopted child, AB; A, A's other children, and A's grandchildren all then die; AB later has a child, X, who reaches age 25 more than 21 years after the deaths of all persons who were relevant lives in being. The result? The Rule is violated.

Note that all other lives in being could be assumed to die before AB reached age 4. Unrealistic? Unquestionably, but the common law Rule never has been particularly concerned with realities. If you are having trouble with the concept of validating lives, bear with us. It is fundamental to an understanding of the Rule and perhaps is best understood by working through examples. Here are two more.

D devised property "To T, in trust, income to A for life, remainder to B if B is elected to the United States Congress, otherwise to C." Here, B and C have alternative contingent remainders, each of which must be tested under the Rule. With respect to B's interest, it will vest only if B is elected to Congress, which necessarily will occur, if at all, during B's life. Thus, it is valid, B being the validating life (assuming B is living at D's death). Similarly, C's alternative contingent remainder will vest, if at all, at B's death if B had not been elected to Congress. Thus, it too is valid, B again being the validating life.

Assume the same devise except that the remainder is to B if any descendant of A is elected to Congress. Here, assuming that A or a descendant of A survives D, the contingent remainders of both B and C violate the Rule. A descendant of A might be elected to Congress more than 21 years after the deaths of all lives in being at D's death. On the other hand, B's contingent remainder never would vest if D was not survived by A or by any descendant of A, and we would know that right away. In that case C's remainder also would not violate the Rule, because it would vest at D's death, which also is within lives in being plus 21 years.

## More on Methodology

The difficult aspect of the Rule is learning to identify the person(s) who can serve either as a validating life or as proof that the interest will not timely vest. To illustrate, assume D devised D's estate "To T, in trust, income to my child for life, then income and principal for my child's children until no living child of my child is under age 21, at which time distribution is to be made per stirpes to my child's then living descendants." The entire interest of D's descendants is valid because the child is a life in being and vesting must occur no later than 21 years after the child's death. To see how we come to this conclusion, consider the following analysis: (1) determine when the period of the Rule begins; (2) identify all persons whose existence, death, or to whom the birth or adoption of a child is relevant to ultimate vesting under the terms of the trust; (3) give any of these people an after born or adopted child, and then assume all lives in being die. If the interest being tested must either vest or fail within 21 years the interest is valid.

In the hypothetical, the perpetuities period begins at D's death. The child is the person to whom we give an after born or adopted child, and then we assume all lives in being at D's death, including the child, immediately die. Still, the after born or adopted will reach age 21, and vesting will occur (or will die and vesting will not occur) no later than 21 years after those deaths (again ignoring the new biology). Consequently, the remainder does not violate the Rule. Obviously this method requires some unlikely assumptions, but the Rule requires this because the interests must be sure to vest or fail under all conceivable contingencies.

Now consider another hypothetical. This devise by D is "To T, in trust, income to child A for life, then income and principal to the children of B until no living child of B is under the age of 21 years, then distribute principal per stirpes to B's then living descendants." Here the person to whom we give an after born or adopted child is B, and again all interests are valid. For the proof, the period begins at D's death. Give B an after born or adopted child, then kill off all lives in being at D's death. The remainder in B's descendants is valid because the after born or adopted child will reach age 21 no more than 21 years later (again, we ignore the new biology). If the distribution to B's then living descendants was to occur when no living child of B is under age 22 the validity of the remainder would depend on whether B survived D. If so, the remainder violates the Rule (because a child of B born or adopted after D's death could reach 22 more than 21 years after the deaths of all relevant lives in being at D's death). If B is not alive, then the remainder is valid because no after born or adopted children are possible and the interests necessarily will vest during the lives of B's children, all of whom necessarily would be lives in being at D's death (ignoring the new biology).

As a general rule, look for cases in which a person could have a child who would take (or whose descendants would take). The interest is sure to fail if that person is not a life in being when the period begins, has not been conceived before the period begins, is not already deceased, and a delay exceeding 21 years is involved. To illustrate this notion, consider that D devised D's estate "To T, in trust, income to A for life, then to A's children for their lives, remainder to A's grandchildren." The remainder violates the Rule if A survives D. A is the person to whom we give an after born or adopted and then assume A and A's other descendants die. The after born or adopted child then could have a child who would take only when the after born or after adopted child dies, and that could be more than 21 years after all lives in being died. The interest of A's grandchildren violates the Rule because it will not necessarily vest (or fail to vest) within 21 years of those deaths. This is because children of A's after born or adopted child could have interests that do not vest until the after born or adopted child's death, which could be more than 21 years later.

Try another: G conveyed property to an inter vivos irrevocable trust with distributions to be made to G's descendants, per stirpes, when no living grandchild of G is under age 21. The person by whom we can prove that vesting will not be timely is G. Give G an after born or adopted who has an after born or adopted child and clearly the interest will violate the Rule. Note that this gift would be valid if it was made by G's will or revocable trust, because G could not have an after born or adopted child after the period of the Rule begins at G's death (ignoring the new biology). The interest of G's descendants would vest, at the latest, 21 years after the death of the survivor of G's children, all of whom necessarily would be lives in being at G's death.

### *Vesting v. Possession*

To satisfy the Rule, a transferee's future interest must vest in interest, not in possession. Thus, it frequently is said that the Rule is *not* a rule of *duration*. As illustrated beginning at page 356, this aspect of the Rule can result in a beneficiary of a trust not receiving control of trust assets for many years after the trust interest vests and the perpetuities period runs. Ultimately the Rule requires distribution of the vested interest either to the beneficiary in whom it vested or to that beneficiary's estate. Possession cannot be postponed forever, but an interest theoretically could be tied up in trust for 200 years or so if possession is delayed for the life of the beneficiary in whom the interest vested.

For example, D devised D's estate "To T, in trust, income to my descendants, per stirpes, until the date that is 21 years after the death of the last of my descendants who was living at my death, remainder to my descendants, per stirpes; provided that each remainder beneficiary's share shall be held by the trustee for his or her benefit, paying to the remainder beneficiary so much or all of the income or principal from his or her share as the trustee determines is appropriate for his or her health, maintenance, support, or education until the remainder beneficiary's death, at which time it shall be distributed to his or her estate." Assume that (1) D died in 2000, (2) D's youngest descendant living at D's death was a great-grandchild, GGC, who was age 1 at that time, (3) GGC dies at age 91, in 2090, (4) 21 years after GGC's death (in 2111), a descendant of D who has a vested share of the remainder is X, age 1, and (5) X dies at what then will be the young age of 90, in 2200. The interests created by D's will are valid under the Rule although possession of X's vested interest will not be received by X's successors under the trust instrument until 2200, 200 years after D's death.

Although the Rule does not directly limit the duration of trusts to the perpetuities period, continuation of a trust beyond the period of the Rule might be defeated by the beneficiaries. As discussed in Chapter 13, under the so-called "Claflin doctrine" beneficiaries of a trust generally may not terminate the trust if doing so would defeat a material unfulfilled purpose of the settlor in establishing the trust (unless the settlor is alive and consents). In some jurisdictions, however, beneficiaries may terminate a trust that would continue beyond the perpetuities period, notwithstanding any unfulfilled purpose.

### Any Possibility of Remote Vesting

Also note that the Rule is not one of probabilities. It can be almost certain that an interest will vest, or fail to vest, within the perpetuities period, but the interest violates the Rule if there is *any possibility* that it will not, no matter how remote. And it's worse than that. In determining whether there is any possibility of a violation of the Rule, we entertain a number of presumptions that may be illogical, or worse. One is the Fertile Octogenarian. In testing an interest under the Rule, we assume that any living person can have a child at any time, regardless of age or medical evidence. To illustrate, G (age 79) and S (age 89) were siblings. G devised G's estate "To T, in trust, income to S's children until the death of the survivor of them, remainder per stirpes to S's then living descendants." G died survived by S and several descendants of S. Under the common law Rule the contingent remainder in S's descendants is void because S is conclusively presumed to be able to have additional children. If S did, all lives in being at G's death then could die, after which the after born or adopted child could have descendants whose interests would not vest within 21 years because that after born or adopted child could live longer than that.

The fertile octogenarian presumption, ridiculous as it once seemed for natural born children, is made more germane by evidence of women bearing children after menopause and men of advanced age fathering children. The presumption is favored over a legal determination whether a person could still have children. Further, although not a consideration when the fertile octogenarian presumption was created in England in the 18th century (because there was no such thing then), today the possibility of adoption adds further rational basis for the presumption being applied even to persons who physiologically are unable to bear or produce children.

Still, some jurisdictions negate the fertile octogenarian presumption by statutes that specify the maximum age at which a person will be presumed fertile, or that allow introduction of medical evidence of infertility. Those statutes probably do not adequately address the new biology or issues raised by adoption. Another solution to problems like that illustrated by the example is for a court to construe the gift to the elderly person's children as referring only to existing children, and not to any children that person might have in the future. See, e.g., *Banker's Trust Co. v. Pearson*, 99 A.2d 224 (Conn. 1953). Today, however, the reach of the presumption seems quite unpredictable.

A corollary to the fertile octogenarian is a presumption of precocious toddlers, that young children are capable of parenting children, even before puberty. Some jurisdictions by statute establish that a minor below a certain age (e.g., age 14) is irrebuttably presumed incapable of having descendants. So far the new biology has not put the lie to these statutes.

Another often unrealistic presumption that can result in the Rule invalidating a contingent interest under the strict "any possibility" of remote vesting standard is the so-called unborn widow presumption. By it we presume that a person whose spouse can affect the vesting of a contingent interest might be survived by a spouse who was not alive when the perpetuities period began to run. Thus, a devise by D to "My child, C, for life, then to C's surviving spouse for life, remainder to C's descendants" violates the Rule because C's descendants who will take the remainder cannot be determined until the death of C's surviving spouse, and it is possible that C's spouse will be someone who was born after D's death. See *Dickerson v. Union National Bank*, 595 S.W.2d 677 (Ark. 1980), for a case in which the unborn widow presumption caused a violation of the Rule even though the testator's child was age 45 and married at the testator's death.

Notice that the example in the preceding paragraph involved a gift to a multi-generational class ("descendants") and violated the Rule in part because we imply a condition of survivorship on such gifts. See Chapter 15. As a result, the takers of the remainder cannot be determined, and thus it will not vest, until we know which of the testator's descendants survive C's surviving after born spouse. Compare that result with the result that would be reached if D's will provided "To my niece, N, for life, then to N's widower for life, remainder to N's children." Here, N could marry S, who was born after D's death, they could have after born or adopted children, N and all other lives in being at D's death could die, and S could live longer than 21 more years. The remainder in N's children nevertheless is valid if the general rule discussed in Chapter 15 that a condition of survivorship will not be implied governs this single generation class gift (to N's children). The interests of N's children vested for purposes of the Rule when N died (at which time we knew definitively how many members there would be in the class of N's children, if we ignore the new biology. See the discussion at page 372 of how class gifts are treated under the Rule). If UPC §2-707 applies, however, to impose a survivorship requirement, that "modern reform" would crash into the antiquated Rule Against Perpetuities. What irony!

"Administrative infinality" is yet another unrealistic presumption that has been applied to invalidate interests under the Rule. Under it, activities that almost certainly will be completed within the perpetuities period theoretically might last longer. Thus, a devise to descendants of T who are living when probate administration of T's estate is complete may be invalid because of the possibility that administration could extend beyond the perpetuities period. For example, after T's death, a child of T could have a child, AB, after which all lives in being at T's death could die. Because probate administration may not be completed within 21 years, the contingent interest in AB could vest outside the perpetuities period. See *Prime v. Hyne*, 67 Cal. Rptr. 170 (Cal. Ct. App. 1968). In *Belfield v. Booth*, 27 A. 585 (Conn. 1893), however, the court held valid such a devise on the strength of a finding that the personal representative's fiduciary duty to administer the estate expeditiously precludes a delay long enough to violate the Rule. This presumption also has been rejected legislatively in some states. A result like that reached in *Prime* also may be avoided if the language in the instrument can be construed to be a vested gift to T's descendants who survive T, with possession postponed until probate administration is completed.

*In re Wood*, [1894] 3 Ch. 381, involved a devise of a gravel pit, in trust, with directions that the trustee produce the gravel until the deposit was depleted and then distribute to the testator's then living descendants. This gift violated the Rule because of the possibility that the gravel pit might produce gravel beyond the perpetuities period. If the gift had been to those children of the testator living upon depletion of the pit the gift would have been valid, because the children's interests would vest or fail within their lives or at their deaths and they all are lives in being. But the gift was to descendants and not just to children. Further, a gift to the transferor's children by *inter vivos irrevocable trust*, instead of by will, also would be void. The settlor could have a child, AB, after the date of the gift in trust, then all persons who were lives in being on the date of the gift could die. If the pit was not exhausted until more than 21 years later, AB's interest would vest outside the perpetuities period. *Wood* is the reason the presumption of administrative infinality sometimes is known as the presumption of the magic gravel pit (that could produce and produce for longer than the period of the Rule Against Perpetuities).

## Effect of Violating the Rule

An offending interest is void if the Rule is violated. Nonoffending interests remain valid, except to the extent the doctrine of infectious invalidity is applicable. In either case, if an invalid interest was a contingent remainder, the gap caused by failure is filled with a reversion. Thus, consider a devise by D "To T, in trust, income to A for life, remainder to A's children who reach age 25." The contingent remainder in A's children violates the Rule if A survived T. The result is a valid life estate in A and a reversion in D. At A's death the property passes to D's residuary takers (or heirs if this is a devise of the residue).

On the other hand, if the failed interest was an executory interest, the prior interest is upgraded to a full fee. For example, consider a devise of Blackacre by D "To A as long as the property is not used for gambling, then to B." B's executory interest violates the Rule because Blackacre could be used for gambling well beyond the perpetuities period, at which time B's interest would vest. So A's interest is upgraded to a fee. Note that this does not mean that all executory interests following defeasible fees are invalid. If the devise had been "To A [a life in being] as long as A does not use the property for gambling, then to B," B's interest would vest, or fail to vest, during A's life and thus would be valid. Further, the Rule does not apply if both the present interest and the executory interest that otherwise would violate the Rule are held by charity. Thus, "To the City as long as the property is used for a park, then to the Red Cross," would not violate the Rule. This is simply because the Rule does not apply to purely charitable bequests. See page 384.

It would not be commonplace but a remainder in property that does not violate the Rule could be preceded by an interest in the same property that does violate the Rule. If so, the invalidity of the prior interest does not affect the validity of the other interests, including the remainder. Thus, consider D's devise "To T, in trust, income to A for life, then income to the children of A for their lives, then after the death of the last surviving child of A income to the grandchildren of A for their lives, and upon the death of the last surviving grandchild of A, remainder to the Red Cross." The life estate in A vests at D's death and the life estate in A's children vests at A's death (and A is a life in being) so both interests are valid, as is the remainder in the Red Cross, which vests at D's death. The life estate in A's grandchildren, however, violates the Rule and will be carved out of the gift, leaving the Red Cross with a vested remainder that will become possessory at the death of the last surviving child of A.

### *"Infectious Invalidity"*

Generally, the invalidity of a future interest under the Rule has no effect on valid interests created by the same instrument. The doctrine of infectious invalidity may defeat otherwise valid provisions, however, if a substantial inequity would result from application of the Rule and the grantor's intent would better be served by invalidation of otherwise valid interests. This doctrine is based on the presumed intent of the transferor and depends on the facts and circumstances. It is an equitable remedy designed to avoid the perceived inequity. To illustrate, D's devise was "Half to my child, A, outright; the other half to T, in trust, income to my child, B, for life, remainder to B's children who reach age 25." D was survived by A and B, who were D's only heirs. D's will conveys a contingent remainder to B's children that is void under the Rule (because B could have a child, AB, after D's death; A, B, and all other persons living at D's death could die before AB reaches age 4; AB's remainder could vest more than 21 years after the death of all relevant lives in being at D's death). D's estate has a reversion if the general rule on the effect of a violation of the Rule is applied. This would cause the remainder of B's half of the estate to pass half to A's side of the family and half to B's side. The result would be ¾ of the principal to A's side of the family and only ¼ to B's, which clearly was not D's intent. Application of infectious invalidity avoids that result by striking all dispositions under the will, causing the estate to pass outright in equal shares to A and B by intestacy.

### Alternative Contingencies

If the vesting of a future interest is subject to separately stated alternative contingencies, one of which is valid under the Rule and the other not, application of the alternative contingencies doctrine results in the interest being valid if the valid contingency occurs and invalid only if the other contingency applies. For example, D devised stock in trust for S and D's four children from a prior marriage. The trust was to terminate at S's death, if S survived D by at least 25 years; if S survived D but by less than 25 years, the trust was to continue for the children until the end of the 25 year period. At termination of the trust the assets were to be distributed equally to the four children, the "descendants of a deceased child to take their ancestor's share by right of representation." The share of a child who did not survive termination of the trust and had no descendants was to be divided among the child's siblings and their descendants. The analysis under the alternative contingencies doctrine is this: The remainder would vest either at S's death, if S died more than 25 years after D's death, or at the end of 25 years, if S survived D but died within 25 years after D's death. The first contingency is valid under the Rule (because vesting occurs at the death of S, a life in being at D's death). The second contingency violates the Rule (because S could die within four years after D, a child of D could have an after born or adopted child, then all relevant lives in being could die, and that after born or adopted child's interest then could vest more than 21 years later, beyond the perpetuities period). If the alternative contingencies doctrine is applied, we will wait until S's death to decide who takes. If S survives D by at least 25 years, D's descendants will take. If S dies within 25 years of D's death, the remainder fails, there is a reversion in D, and D's residuary devisees therefore would take. See *First Portland National Bank v. Rodrique*, 172 A.2d 107 (Me. 1961).

Discussed at page 383 is the wait and see doctrine under which courts do not automatically apply the Rule to invalidate an interest that might vest, or fail to vest, outside the perpetuities period. Instead of deciding the case on pure possibilities, we wait and see whether events unfold in such a way that vesting actually fails to occur within the period. The alternative contingency doctrine is different. To be valid under it, the expressly stated contingency under which there is no possibility of vesting beyond the perpetuities period must occur. If the other contingency (under which the interest might vest beyond the perpetuities period) occurs, the interest fails. This is true even if it actually vests, or fails, within the period. Thus, in the example above, if S died more than 4 but less than 25 years after D, the remainder would fail even though it would have vested within the permitted 21 years after the death of S, a life in being at D's death. This is torture, and easily reveals why there is so much reform and rejection of the traditional Rule Against Perpetuities.

Consider a devise by D "To A for life, remainder to A's children who reach age 25, but if A dies before any child of A reaches age 25, then to B." Under the alternative contingencies doctrine, B's remainder is valid if A dies without having had children but it is not valid if A has children who have not yet reached that age. What if D's devise instead had been more terse: "To A for life, remainder to A's children who reach age 25, and if none, to B"? Here, the contingency of A dying childless is not as clearly articulated but it still is implicit — if A did not have children, no child of A could reach age 25. The question is whether B's remainder can be saved if A survived D and did not yet have a child. If A ultimately dies childless the alternative contingencies doctrine would be effected if a court would separate the implicit, unstated alternative contingencies and treat the devise "To A for life, remainder to A's children who reach age 25, and if none, to B," as if it had been a devise "To A for life, remainder to A's children who reach age 25, but if A dies without having had a child or if no child of A reaches age 25, to B." Traditionally, the alternative contingencies doctrine was applied only if the testator or settlor separately stated the contingencies in the instrument. Recently courts have been more willing to separate implicit but unstated alternative contingencies, as illustrated.

## Class Gifts

For purposes of the Rule, a gift to a class is not regarded as vested until the number of members of the class and the size of their shares is fixed. The gift is not deemed vested for purposes of the Rule for any member of the class if the class is open, or if a condition precedent for the interest of any member of the class to vest has not been satisfied. See Chapter 8 for a discussion of the class closing rules. Moreover, the entire class gift fails if the interest of one member or potential member of the class can violate the Rule. All class members' interests must be certain to vest indefeasibly, or to fail, within the perpetuities period or the gift is invalid as to the entire class.

A common example of a class gift violating the Rule is a devise from D "To A for life, then to A's children for their lives, remainder to A's grandchildren." Assume that D dies survived by A, by a child of A (C), and by a child of C (GC). The interests of C and GC are vested, subject to partial divestment (vested subject to open) if additional children or grandchildren of A are born. That vesting is not sufficient for the Rule. At D's death it must be certain that the classes of children and grandchildren will close and all conditions precedent will be satisfied within the perpetuities period. Anything less is not considered vested under the Rule. In this case the class gift vests in A's children in time. A is a life in being at D's death and the interests of all of A's children will vest at A's death. This is because there can be no additional members of the class of A's children after A's death (remember that a child in gestation is treated for purposes of the Rule as alive at conception if subsequently born alive, and we're ignoring the new biology). And there are no conditions precedent to be satisfied by any of A's children. Thus, the class gift of the secondary life estate to A's children following A's life estate is valid under the Rule. That is true even though A could have children after D's death and the composition of the class of A's children who are entitled to income could get larger or smaller beyond the perpetuities period (e.g., after D's death, A could have several more children, then all the lives in being could die, and then more than 21 years later an after born or adopted child could die, which would change the size of the shares of A's children).

On the other hand, the class gift of the remainder to A's grandchildren is not valid. A could have a second child after the death of D. A and all other lives in being at D's death then could die, and the after born or adopted child could have a child more than 21 years later. This after born or adopted grandchild's interest would vest beyond the perpetuities period, making the entire class gift to A's grandchildren void. The remainder thus falls out and the trust reverts to D's successors. This is the case even with respect to GC, the grandchild who was a life in being and whose interest, under conventional property law principles, vested at D's death (subject to partial divestment), because vesting must be absolute. Subject to open is not good enough.

Now consider a devise by D to the life tenant's grandchildren that skips the life tenant's children: "To A for life, remainder to A's grandchildren," and assume again that D dies survived by A, by one child of A, and by one grandchild of A. Is the class gift to A's grandchildren valid? The test is whether the class must close, and all conditions precedent for all members of the class must be satisfied, within the perpetuities period. Here, under the rule of convenience discussed in Chapter 8, the class closes at A's death, because distribution is to be made to A's grandchildren at that time, even if children of A are living and additional grandchildren of A therefore are a possibility. Because there also are no conditions precedent to vesting the grandchildren's interests, the remainder vests in the class of A's grandchildren at the death of A, who is a life in being at D's death. Thus, the remainder is valid.

What this shows is a general rule that a class gift that vests after a life estate in someone who is *not* a life in being at the beginning of the perpetuities period will violate the Rule. But a class gift will not violate the Rule if it vests after a life estate in someone who *is* a life in being (and assuming there are no conditions precedent on the gift; see below as to age contingencies, for example). Thus, "To A for life, then to A's children for their lives, remainder to A's grandchildren," violates the Rule (A's potential after born or adopted children being the life tenants who are not lives in being), but "To A for life, remainder to A's grandchildren" does not (there being no life estate in a person who is not a life in being at the beginning of the period). The unborn widow cases also illustrate this general rule: "Income to my son, John, for life, then income to his widow for life, and on the death of the last to die of my son, his widow, and me, per stirpes to my son's then living descendants." The Rule is violated because of the possibility of an after born life tenant (the son's widow), with vesting of the class gift to occur after the widow's life estate.

## Age Contingencies

As stated, a class gift is not vested for purposes of the Rule unless the class has closed and all conditions precedent for all members of the class have been satisfied. The likelihood of a violation of the Rule is great (but not guaranteed) if a class gift is made contingent on class members reaching a stated age greater than 21. As an illustration, D's devise is "To A for life, remainder to A's children who reach age 25." The remainder violates the Rule if D is survived by A because A could have a child, AB, after D's death. All lives in being at D's death could die before AB reaches the age of 4 and AB's interest then could vest outside the period of the Rule. That is the result regardless of whether A has any children living at D's death, and regardless of their ages. For example, even if A has a child who is 30 at D's death, the class will not close under the rule of convenience until A's death. At that time, a child of A who was born or adopted after D's death may be under age 4, in which case the after born or adopted child's interest might not vest, or fail, within the perpetuities period. Also note that the remainder would be valid if A predeceased D, because (ignoring the new biology) all children of A necessarily would be lives in being at D's death (or also would have predeceased D), and all would reach age 25 or die within their own lifetimes.

Generally, the Rule will be violated if a gift of a remainder is made to a class following a life estate, with vesting to occur when class members reach an age exceeding 21. Thus, in a gift in trust for B for life, then for B's descendants until no living child of B is under age 22, then to B's then living descendants per stirpes, the remainder would violate the rule if B is alive when the perpetuities period begins. The exception to this general rule is if the class cannot include after born or adopted members, in which case the remainder will be valid without regard to the age of vesting. Thus, a gift "To my spouse for life, remainder to my children who reach age 50" is valid (unless the perpetuities period begins before the settlor's death, such as if the gift were made by an irrevocable inter vivos trust, or we consider the new biology).

*Ward v. Van der Loeff*, [1924] A.C. 653, illustrates application of the Rule to class gifts and the effect of the rule of convenience in two different circumstances. First was a gift in trust for D's spouse (S) for life, remainder to D's nephews and nieces who reached age 21. No niece or nephew of D already had reached age 21 when D died. If there had been such a niece or nephew the class would have closed at S's death under the rule of convenience (see Chapter 8), S was a life in being, and the gift would not have violated the Rule. Instead, the remainder was invalid because there was a possibility of a sibling of D being born or adopted after D's death, because D was survived by D's parents. Thus, all relevant lives in being could have died; after which an after born or adopted sibling could have produced their own child, who then would reach age 21 more than 21 years after the deaths of all relevant lives in being. Second was a gift in trust for S for life, remainder to D's nieces and nephews. Under the rule of convenience discussed in Chapter 8, the class of nieces and nephews entitled to share in the remainder closed at S's death, when distribution was required to be made. Because there were no conditions precedent on the gift of the remainder, vesting of the class gift for purposes of the Rule therefore would occur within the perpetuities period — at the death of S — and the gift was valid. Note that S was named and therefore was a life in being. This was not an unborn widow case.

### *Exceptions to the All-or-Nothing Rule*

Generally, a gift of a contingent future interest to a class will fail under the Rule as to all members of the class unless each class member's interest vests within the perpetuities period. There are two exceptions: gifts to subclasses and per capita class gifts.

The subclass exception is relevant if the grantor has not made a single class gift but instead has made more than one class gift to subclasses. The gift to one or more of the subclasses may be valid even if the gift to other subclasses fails. For example, consider a devise by D "To A for life, then to A's children for their lives, remainder on the death of A's last surviving child in equal shares to A's then living grandchildren." If A survives D this gift violates the Rule because A could have a child after D's death, who could have children whose interests would vest more than 21 years after the deaths of A and all descendants of A living at D's death. Here the Rule is violated because A's grandchildren constitute a single class. The share that any grandchild receives cannot be ascertained until the death of the last of A's children to die, an event that might occur beyond the perpetuities period (because of the possibility of A having a child after D's death).

Now consider a devise by D in trust to pay income to A for life, then income in equal shares to A's children for their lives, with a peel off distribution at the death of each child of A, giving a percentage of the remainder to that child's descendants. If D was survived by A and by two children of A (X and Y), and a third child of A (Z) was born or adopted after D's death, the class gifts to the descendants of X and Y are treated as separate from the gift to Z's descendants. The former are valid under the Rule. The latter is not. The following example illustrates why.

Assume the trust is $100,000. A will receive the income for life. After A's death, X and Y, and later Z, will share equally the trust income. If X is the first of A's children to die, at X's death ⅓ of the principal will be distributable to X's descendants. At Y's death half the balance would go to Y's descendants. Because X and Y were living at D's death, they are validating lives for the gifts of the remainders to their descendants; those gifts vest at the deaths of lives in being and are valid. By contrast, Z was not living at D's death. The gift to Z's descendants will not vest until Z dies, and that could occur more than 21 years after the deaths of A, X, and Y, the relevant lives in being at D's death. As a result, the gift to Z's descendants violates the Rule and is void. The principal of the balance from which Z was receiving income passes at Z's death to D's successors by reversion. Because that likely will benefit A, if A was D's heir, and may pass to X, Y, and Z through A's estate, we may have an infectious invalidity situation, in which case a court might invalidate all three subclass gifts to avoid that result. But notice that only Z's subclass gift actually violates the Rule. See *American Security & Trust Co. v. Creamer*, 175 F. Supp. 367 (D. D.C. 1959), for a similar case in which the subclass exception saved part of the remainder, but not the portion left to heirs of after born or adopted children of the life tenant. Infectious invalidity apparently was not argued.

Per capita class gifts are a second exception to the all-or-nothing perpetuities rule for class gifts. A per capita class gift is a gift of a fixed amount to each member of a class. Each such gift is analyzed separately under the Rule. Thus, assume that D's will included a gift of $10,000 to each of D's grandchildren who reach age 22, including any born or adopted after D's death. (The normal per capita class closing rule of construction discussed in Chapter 8 will not apply because of the language specifically including after born or adopted grandchildren in the gift.) Each per capita gift is tested separately under the Rule. The gifts to grandchildren who were living at D's death are valid because they are lives in being. The gifts to grandchildren born or adopted after D's death are void because they may vest after the perpetuities period. Again a question of infectious invalidity may arise, but again that is secondary to the finding of invalidity itself.

### Powers of Appointment and the Rule

The applicability of the Rule to powers of appointment raises two issues: the validity of the power itself and the validity of any exercise of the power. The rules governing these issues are different for presently exercisable general powers than for testamentary general powers and all nongeneral powers. Accordingly, we consider them separately.

## Presently Exercisable General Powers

The holder of a presently exercisable general power of appointment is treated for purposes of the Rule as the outright owner of the property subject to the power, because the holder may at any time unilaterally seize unrestricted ownership of the property by exercising the power in their own favor. With respect to the Rule, this treatment has two consequences, one related to the validity of the power and the other related to the validity of interests created by exercise of the power. Regarding validity of the power, it is sufficient if a presently exercisable general power becomes *available* for exercise during the perpetuities period. It is not necessary that it *must* be exercised before expiration of the period.

To illustrate, assume D's will created a trust, "income to A for life, then income to A's child (B) for life, remainder as B's first child to reach age 21 appoints by deed or will." B's first child to reach 21 may appoint to anyone, including that child, and the power is exercisable presently ("by deed" meaning it is exercisable inter vivos). Thus, to be valid under the Rule it is necessary only that during the perpetuities period the power must become available for exercise by B's first child to reach 21. Assuming B is living at T's death, B's first child to reach 21 necessarily will do so, if at all, within 21 years of B's death. Thus, the power itself is valid. The power would be invalid under the Rule if the power was exercisable by the first child of B to reach age 22 because B could have a child after D's death who could be the first child of B to reach the required age, all lives in being could die immediately after the child's birth or adoption, and reaching the requisite age could take more than 21 years. Thus, the power would not become exercisable within the perpetuities period.

With respect to the validity of any interests created by exercise of the power, for a presently exercisable general power the perpetuities period begins to run anew when the power is exercised, not when it was created. Thus, the validity of interests created by exercise of a presently exercisable general power is tested in the same way as are gifts of contingent future interests by the outright owner of property. To illustrate, consider a devise by D "To T, in trust, income to A for life; then income to B for life; remainder as B may appoint by deed or will." D died survived by A and B. After A dies B continued to receive the income from the property until B's death. By will, B exercised the power in favor of C for life, remainder to C's children who reach age 21. C was not living at D's death, but was living at B's death. The life estate in C and the remainder in C's children both are valid under the Rule because B's power is general and presently exercisable. As a consequence, the perpetuities period runs from B's exercise of the power, not from its creation (D's date of death). B exercised the power at B's death, at which time C was living. Accordingly, C's life estate is valid (C being the validating life) and, because the remainder in C's children will vest when they reach age 21 (which necessarily will occur within 21 years following the death of C, a life in being at B's death), the remainder also is valid (C again being the validating life).

### Testamentary General Powers and All Nongeneral Powers

Application of the Rule is governed by different rules with respect to general powers that are exercisable only at death, and to both testamentary and inter vivos nongeneral powers. Again we look both at the validity of the power itself and the validity of exercise.

It is not enough that testamentary general powers and both inter vivos and testamentary nongeneral powers might be exercised during the perpetuities period. Rather, these powers are void if it is possible that they *could* be exercised *beyond* the period of the Rule. Put another way, the power must become exercisable and must be exercised (if at all) within the period of the Rule. For this purpose the perpetuities period begins when the power is created. What this means is that the powerholder must be sure to die within the perpetuities period if the power is exercisable by the powerholder until or at death (which is the case with any testamentary power and most inter vivos powers as well). As a result, if the power is so exercisable, generally the holder must be living when the power is created. In other words, as a general rule this means that the power itself will be invalid if the holder of any power other than an inter vivos general power is not a life in being at the beginning of the perpetuities period. This circumstance is most likely to occur when the power is given to a grandchild for generation-skipping transfer tax purposes or was created by someone else's exercise of another power.

For example, D devised "To T, in trust, income to A for life, remainder to such persons as A appoints by will; to the extent A does not effectively exercise A's power, then after A's death income to A's children for their lives, remainder to such of my descendants as the last child of A to die appoints by deed or will." D died survived by A and by one child of A (C$_1$). Notice that there are two powers here. The one in A is a general testamentary power that must be exercised, if at all, at A's death. A's power is valid because A was living at D's death. By contrast, the power of the last child of A to die is void because it is a nongeneral power that is exercisable until and at the powerholder's death, and the powerholding child need not be a life in being at D's death, when the power was created. As a result, the power may be exercised beyond the perpetuities period, as measured from D's death. (E.g., after D dies, A has another child (C$_2$), then A and C$_1$ die, and C$_2$ dies more than 21 years later.) Note that the power would have been valid if D had limited exercise of the nongeneral power to the period ending 21 years after the death of the last to die of A and the last child of A living at D's death.

The rule governing the validity of interests created by exercise of a testamentary general power or a nongeneral power also differs from that applicable to interests created by exercise of general presently exercisable powers. This is because the perpetuities period begins when the power was created and no new perpetuity period begins with exercise. Unlike a general presently exercisable power of appointment, for testamentary general and all nongeneral powers, the holder is not treated as the outright owner of the property but is treated as an agent of the creator of the power. See Chapter 14. As a result, the exercise of a testamentary general power or any nongeneral power completes the transfer of property from the creator of the power to the appointee, not from the powerholder to the appointee. Accordingly, the validity of the appointed interest under the Rule is measured from the date the power was created and not from the date of exercise.

A special deviation from traditional Rule Against Perpetuities analysis allows facts existing at the time the power is exercised to be considered in determining the validity of the interests created by exercise of the power. This is known as the second look doctrine. Under it we consider facts existing at the time of exercise in determining the validity of all interests created by exercise of a testamentary general power or any nongeneral power. This is true even though validity of the appointed interests is determined based on a perpetuities period that began when the power was created. The reason for this second look approach is that it is impossible to know what interests will be created prior to exercise of the power. Because we must defer determining validity until exercise, when we know what interests have been created, it is sensible to consider facts and circumstances that exist at that time.

Any instrument creating a nongeneral or testamentary general power should (and usually does) provide for the default disposition of property subject to the power. Validity of the default interests is at issue if those persons are designated by class and the class is open, or if there are conditions precedent to the vesting of the interests of the takers in default. In a minority of states the second look doctrine applies even for testing the validity of *unexercised* powers. This represents nothing more than a wait and see approach, as discussed at page 383.

Let's consider an example. D's devise was "To T, in trust, income to A for life, remainder as A appoints by will." A appointed the property by will when A died after D "To B for life, then to B's children for their lives, remainder to B's grandchildren." A's general testamentary power of appointment was valid under the Rule because it had to be exercised, if at all, no later than A's death, and A was a life in being. The validity of the interests created by A's exercise of the power is determined as of the date of D's death, when the testamentary general power was created, but giving consideration to facts existing at A's death, when the power was exercised. A's exercise of the power is said to be "read back" into D's will, in which case the devise under D's will would have been "To T, in trust, income to A for life, then to B for life, then to B's children for their lives, remainder to B's grandchildren." Even if B was born or adopted after D's death, B's life estate is valid because B's life estate vested at the death of A, who was a life in being at D's death. But the interests in B's children and grandchildren would be void if B is not a life in being at D's death, because B could die long after all lives in being, and could have children, and they could have children, more than 21 years after the death of all lives in being. Thus, neither class would necessarily close within the period of the Rule.

If B was living at D's death, however, the remainder for life in B's children would be valid because it would vest at the death of B, a life in being at D's death. The remainder in B's grandchildren also could be valid, but only if B predeceased A, and B's children who survived A were lives in being at D's death. In that circumstance, the interests of B's grandchildren would vest at the death of the last to die of B's children, all of whom would have been lives in being at D's death. The fact that, at D's death, B *could have* had additional children who could have had children beyond the perpetuities period does not invalidate the grandchildren's remainder because, under the second look doctrine, we know that did not happen.

### Mitigating Application of the Rule to Powers

The doctrines of capture and marshalling discussed in Chapter 14 may mitigate the harsh result of the Rule invalidating the exercise of a power. Under the doctrine of capture, any attempt to exercise a general testamentary power is taken as an intent to dispose of the appointive assets, even if the exercise fails. Thus, notwithstanding a default clause in the instrument creating the power, the assets subject to an ineffectively exercised general testamentary power pass in the same manner as the powerholder's estate. If exercise was by a blending provision, as discussed in Chapter 14, the assets actually become a part of the powerholder's estate, subject to claims of the powerholder's creditors and spouse. Otherwise, the appointive assets pass *as if* they were part of the powerholder's estate. Either way, the unresolved issue is whether the appointive assets pass under the same perpetuities period as applies to the powerholder's own assets, or whether the period should begin when the power was created. In our view no new period should apply. Otherwise there is an end-run around the Rule. But you would struggle to find authority on this question.

The doctrine of marshaling also may mitigate application of the Rule. If portions of a blending exercise of a testamentary power would be valid and portions invalid, marshaling says to allocate the appointive assets to the valid portions to the maximum possible extent to save the exercise, and allocate the donee's own assets to those interests that would be valid only for nonappointive assets. Only to the extent marshaling does not save the exercise would capture apply in a case involving a general testamentary power, or result in total failure in a case involving any nongeneral power. For example, consider P's devise "To T, in trust, income to my child, C, for life, remainder as C may appoint by will; if C does not exercise this power, to the Red Cross." P died survived by C, but by no descendants of C. GC was born to C after P's death. The trust corpus was $100,000 at C's death and C's will provided "I give all of my property and all property over which I have a power of appointment as follows: $25,000 to my friend, X, and the rest to A, in trust, to be distributed to my now living descendants who are living 22 years after my death."

The perpetuities period for testing the validity of interests created under C's general testamentary power began at P's death. Accordingly, the appointive assets in the trust created by P's will cannot be validly appointed by C's will to the trust C created by exercise. Under the doctrine of marshaling, $25,000 of the assets in the trust created by P would be treated as having been appointed to X. Under the doctrine of capture, the remaining $75,000 of the trust assets would be captured into C's estate. If that results in a new perpetuities period for them, they would pass with C's own assets into the trust created by C's will, which we view as an improper result. If there is no new perpetuities period, the $75,000 of assets could not be added to the trust for C's descendants. In that case, the question is whether capture nevertheless would apply to cause the $75,000 to pass to C's heirs, or whether it would be distributed to the Red Cross as the taker in default under P's will. Our guess is that C's heirs would take.

## Saving Clauses

Perpetuities saving clauses always are used by experienced estate planners to avoid violations of the Rule in instruments that create future interests. Without regard to other dispositive provisions of the instrument, these clauses provide that all interests created under the instrument will vest just before expiration of the perpetuities period, if they have not vested sooner on their own terms. The following is an example of a Rule Against Perpetuities saving clause:

If not sooner terminated, the trustee shall terminate and forthwith distribute any trust created hereby, or by exercise of a power of appointment hereunder, one day prior to expiration of the permissible period under the relevant application of the Rule Against Perpetuities, if any. Distribution under this provision shall be made to the persons then entitled to receive or have the benefit of the income from the trust, in the proportions in which they are entitled thereto or, if their interests are indefinite, then in equal shares.

Note that this clause calls for the termination of all trusts and distribution of all trust assets one day before the perpetuities period ends. Also permissible would be a provision that simply called for vesting at that time, with distribution delayed until, for example, a beneficiary attained a specified age. Although the beneficiaries likely could cause the trust to terminate at expiration of the perpetuities period, as discussed at page 366, if they did not this approach would avoid distribution to a beneficiary at an age younger than desired by the transferor, and probably would preserve spendthrift protections until the later date.

Even experienced estate planners can inadvertently draft instruments that violate the common law Rule. If it is respected by the applicable governing law, a saving clause will avoid invalidation of the offending interest. In addition, and perhaps more importantly, estate planners often prepare instruments the dispositive terms of which make no attempt to comply with the Rule. Rather, saving clauses are relied on to avoid violations of the Rule. For example, assume D is single, has one child (C) who is age 18, and wants a will leaving D's entire estate to C. If C is under age 30 at D's death, however, D wants C's inheritance to be held in trust until C reaches age 30. If C dies before reaching age 30, D wants the assets to stay in trust for any children of C until they reach age 30, and a trust so created for a grandchild of D who dies before reaching age 30 should continue in trust for the grandchild's children, and so on. The dispositive terms of this common plan would violate the Rule were it not for a saving clause included in the instrument. Thus, if C is D's only surviving descendant the saving clause will dictate that all trusts terminate (or at least that all interests must vest) 21 years after C's death (unless persons other that D's descendants are defined as measuring lives in the saving clause, which would be unusual). This means that if C is age 22 at D's death, D is not survived by any other descendant, C has a child, GC, two years later, and C dies at age 26 survived by GC, who is then age 2, GC's interest will vest under the saving clause when GC is age 23, all without regard to the other dispositive provisions of the instrument that otherwise would delay the vesting of GC's interest until GC reached age 30. As a result, if GC died at age 25, survived by a child, GGC, the trust assets would pass as a part of GC's estate rather than being held in further trust for GGC.

## Modern Trends and Reforms

You can by now appreciate why the Rule is in disfavor these days. As a result, legislatures, courts, and practicing lawyers have devised a variety of ways to mitigate it. The most direct is the growing number of states that have legislatively abolished the Rule (or permitted transferors to "opt out" of its application by stating such an intent in the instrument) as it applies to most trusts. There appears to be a developing trend in that direction as states compete to become havens for generation-skipping perpetual "dynasty trusts." See Casner & Pennell, ESTATE PLANNING §11.2 n.3 (6th ed. 1999) for a comprehensive list. For states that have not gone to that extreme a variety of lesser changes mitigate the harshness of the Rule.

### *Wait and See*

One serious criticism of the common law Rule is that it often has been applied in a rigorous manner, based on unrealistic presumptions, to invalidate interests that in all likelihood would have vested, or failed, within the perpetuities period. In response, courts and legislatures have developed the "wait and see" doctrine. Under it, an interest is not invalid unless it does not in fact vest or fail within the period of the Rule. In its own right wait and see is criticized by some because it delays the certainty of title, especially if infectious invalidity may apply to invalidate otherwise valid interests, and it creates the possibility of administrative difficulties in recovering assets and making proper disposition upon failure of an interest, many years after it was created.

Many wait and see jurisdictions, however, do not invalidate an interest that time proves would have violated the Rule. Rather, an interest that has not vested or failed at expiration of the perpetuities period is judicially reformed to comply with the Rule, in a manner that will carry out the transferor's intention to the maximum extent possible. Known as *cy pres* statutes, these permit courts to reform instruments that create interests that violate the Rule, such as by reducing the age at which an interest vests. As with wait and see, reformations are accomplished in a way that carries out the transferor's intent to the fullest possible extent. Occasionally, reformation has been accomplished judicially, without benefit of an authorizing statute.

In addition, the Uniform Statutory Rule Against Perpetuities Act (USRAP) has been enacted in more than 20 states. It adopts a wait and see type approach under which contingent future interests are valid if they either satisfy the common law Rule or actually vest or fail to vest within 90 years after the perpetuities period began to run. An interest that would violate the common law Rule and that 90 years later has not yet vested or failed to vest is not invalid. Rather, as with wait and see generally, the instrument creating the interest is then reformed to comply with the Rule, with the reformation performed in such a way as to do as little damage as possible to the transferor's intent. Thus, the statute is both wait and see and cy pres all in one.

In a few jurisdictions, some of the more indefensible results made possible by the Rule have been addressed by statutes eliminating the fertile octogenarian, precocious toddler, unborn widow, and administrative infinality presumptions. Note, however, how adoption and the new biology are making some of those silly old presumptions prescient again. Time will tell whether any are restored in states that previously eliminated them.

Some jurisdictions also have applied special rules to powers of appointment, especially including application of the second look doctrine and use of the doctrines of marshaling and capture. Less common yet, as discussed at page 370, if vesting could occur under either of two alternative contingencies, one of which would be valid under the Rule and it occurs, the interest is deemed valid even if the other alternative would have violated the Rule. This is just a subset of the wait and see doctrine.

Still another approach to saving a gift from invalidation by the Rule is judicial construction of instruments. For example, a gift "To my son for life, then to my son's widow for life, then to my son's then living descendants" could be construed as providing a life estate only to the person the son was married to at the transferor's death, not to someone else not yet born at the transferor's death. This is a variety on repeal of the unborn widow presumption. And, finally, legislation in some states specifically authorizes the use of saving clauses to avoid potential violations of the Rule.

## Charities

Interests in an exclusively charitable trust are not subject to the Rule. Such a trust may continue in perpetuity. In addition, application of the Rule to interests held by charities depends on whether a preceding estate is held by a non-charity. If both the present and future interest are held by charities, the future interest is not subject to invalidation by the Rule. But the Rule is applied in the same way as if both interests were held by noncharities if a charity's contingent future interest follows a non-charity's present interest. For example, D devised Blackacre "To Religious Organization as long as the property is used for regular religious services. If the property is not used for religious services, to the Red Cross." The executory interest of the Red Cross might vest well beyond the perpetuities period, but it nevertheless is valid because it and the prior interest both are held by charities. By contrast, consider a devise of Blackacre by D "To my child, C, but if the property ever is used for a commercial purpose other than farming, then to the Red Cross." The executory interest of the Red Cross violates the Rule, because the nonagricultural commercial use might occur well beyond the perpetuities period. Because the invalidated interest of the Red Cross was an executory interest following a noncharitable interest it is not saved, and C's defeasible fee interest would be upgraded to a fee simple absolute.

## Accumulations of Income

Similar to but distinct from the Rule Against Perpetuities are rules against accumulating income. In most jurisdictions a direction to accumulate income for the perpetuities period is valid, but a direction to accumulate income beyond that period is not. In some jurisdictions no accumulation is allowed at all if the instrument provides for the accumulation of income for a period that may exceed the perpetuities period. In others, only accumulations beyond the perpetuities period are invalid. Income that is released by application of a rule against excessive accumulations may be distributed to the transferor's successors or in a manner determined to be consistent with the transferor's intent.

A common glitch in drafting is the failure to dispose of undistributed income. For example, D's devise was "To T, in trust, income and principal as needed for the care of my child, A, for life; after A's death, income to my child, B, for life; then principal to B's then living descendants." The issue regarding undistributed income arises if less than all of the trust income is required to provide for the care of A. In *Stempel v. Middletown Trust Co.*, 15 A.2d 305 (Conn. 1940), A was an incapacitated child, and B and B's descendants had serious financial needs. The court held that D died intestate with respect to income earned during A's life but not needed for A's care. Half of it (less a reasonable reserve) was deemed currently distributable to each of A's conservator and B. The income so distributable to A's conservator was to be considered by the trustee in exercising its discretion to make distributions in future years for A's care. The alternative to treating this undistributed income as intestate property is to accumulate it and add it to principal for distribution with the remainder. A well drafted document always includes such an "add to principal" provision.

# CHAPTER 18

# FIDUCIARY ADMINISTRATION

This Chapter addresses issues that arise in the administration of an estate or trust. Accordingly, the fiduciary relationships addressed primarily are those of trustee/trust beneficiary and personal representative/estate beneficiary. Much of the material in this Chapter, however, also is applicable to other fiduciary relationships, such as conservator or guardian/ward. Although there are some meaningful differences among the administration of estates, trusts, and other fiduciary entities, there are even more significant similarities than we study in this Chapter.

Among the most common differences among fiduciary relations is duration and thus focus. For example, the personal representative of an estate generally has a limited mission to wind up a decedent's affairs by collecting assets, paying creditors, and distributing property to estate beneficiaries, all in accordance with the terms of the decedent's estate plan and the law of the governing jurisdiction. Conservator or guardian involvement may be of longer duration, usually involves more management, and typically does not entail settlement and distribution. And a trustee usually has a long term, ongoing role in administration of trust assets over what may be many years, considering multiple beneficiaries and their varied and changing needs and circumstances, also in accordance with the terms of the governing instrument and controlling law. These fundamental differences in the purpose of various fiduciary administrations result in a number of differences in the duties and powers of personal representatives, guardians, conservators, and trustees, several of which are discussed in this Chapter.

On the other hand, the administration of estates (both for decedents and for living wards) and trusts occurs in a fiduciary context and the duties imposed by that common relationship in many respects are the same regardless of whether the administration is of an estate or a trust. Although the missions of a personal representative, guardian, conservator, or trustee may be qualitatively different, there are more similarities than differences in the standards by which fiduciary conduct is judged. UPC §7-302, for example, requires trustees to observe the standards in dealing with trust assets that would be observed by a prudent person in dealing with the property of another, taking into account any special skills of the trustee. Personal representatives are required by UPC §3-703(a) to observe the standards of care applicable to trustees, as are conservators under UPC §5-418. With the increased use of fully funded revocable inter vivos trusts to avoid probate or guardian and conservator administration, there are many cases in which there is no need for protective administration inter vivos or probate administration when a decedent dies. Rather, administration of the trust serves many of the same purposes as would administration of a ward's or a decedent's estate. In these situations courts tend to blur the distinctions between the duties and powers of various fiduciaries, even in non-UPC jurisdictions.

With many notable exceptions (unsupervised probate administration under the UPC, for example), estate administration during life or postmortem tends to be performed under court oversight. By contrast, in many states the administration of a trust is completely unsupervised (unless the trustee, a beneficiary, or another interested party initiates a judicial proceeding to, for example, construe an instrument, approve an accounting, or surcharge the trustee). In some jurisdictions, testamentary trusts — but not inter vivos trusts — are court supervised. The court's jurisdiction to oversee administration is viewed as a continuation of the probate administration of an estate. Even that, however, may be subject to waiver by an appropriate indication of intent in the governing document (in this case the will creating the trust).

## Duty of Loyalty

The foundation of any fiduciary relation is the fiduciary's absolute requirement of allegiance to the beneficiary. The fiduciary owes the ward or beneficiary an undivided duty of loyalty to administer the estate or trust for the sole benefit of the ward or beneficiary. Notable about this duty is that it is owed to the ward or beneficiary, *not* to the settlor or decedent. Arguably, the highest duty the common law imposes is the duty of a fiduciary to a beneficiary. The following famous quote from Judge Cardozo's opinion in *Meinhard v. Salmon*, 164 N.E. 545 (N.Y. 1928), should set the tone for your study of these materials. If you remember nothing else about the fiduciary obligation, and learn nothing more through your own independent study, keep *this* in mind (because courts do):

Many forms of conduct permissible in a workaday world for those acting at arm's length are forbidden to those bound by fiduciary ties. A trustee is held to something stricter than the morals of the market place. Not honesty alone, but the punctilio of an honor the most sensitive, is then the standard of behavior. As to this there has developed a tradition that is unbending and inveterate. Uncompromising rigidity has been the attitude of courts of equity when petitioned to undermine the rule of undivided loyalty by the "disintegrating erosion" of particular exceptions.

The fiduciary may not act either to profit personally (earning a fee for fiduciary services rendered is not such a profit) or to generate a detriment for the beneficiaries. Sharing a benefit, or directing a benefit to a third party, also would be improper.

For example, assume that T serves as trustee of the ABC Trust, the assets of which include Blackacre. For appropriate reasons, T decides to sell Blackacre. T is a licensed and accomplished real estate broker and sells Blackacre without using a third party broker. T may not charge the trust a commission for the sale absent a provision in the trust instrument authorizing it, court approval, or consent of the beneficiaries. Similarly, if T were a lawyer or accountant T could not hire T individually to provide legal or accounting services for compensation in addition to the trustee fee unless the trust instrument, the court, or the beneficiaries authorized it. Trustees often impose additional charges for unusual services, and it is not unusual for a lawyer to serve as personal representative of an estate and as attorney and collect a fee in both capacities, but this additional work and compensation must be authorized by the document or by state law. The fee of a fiduciary who performs services in addition to those normally required of a fiduciary may be increased to compensate the fiduciary for the additional services, depending on the jurisdiction, the document, and the circumstances, but never will the fiduciary be paid twice for the same service and never will the fiduciary properly be allowed to act in both roles without specific authority.

### *Self Dealing*

The most blatant examples of prohibited fiduciary conduct occur when a trustee or personal representative, acting in a fiduciary capacity, enters into a transaction with itself, individually. Such acts, referred to as *self dealing*, present the fiduciary with an obvious conflict of interest that is directly at odds with the duty to administer the trust or estate for the sole benefit of the beneficiaries. Examples include buying, selling, leasing, borrowing, or lending assets from or to the trust or estate. In *Hartman v. Hartle*, 122 A. 615 (N.J. Ch. 1923), the prohibition against self dealing properly was applied to a sale of estate realty by the executor to his wife, who shortly thereafter sold it to a third party at a considerable profit. But such obvious cases of abuse are not the only ones prohibited.

Except as described below, *all* acts of self dealing are prohibited and actionable. Confronted with such an act, a court will not inquire into the fairness of the transaction or the good faith of the fiduciary. Rather, the fiduciary will be liable for any losses incurred by the estate or trust, and must remit any profits made by the fiduciary, regardless of either fairness or good faith. Thus, in *Hartman* there would have been a breach of duty even if the executor and his wife had proven that she paid the estate more than the fair market value of the property (and then made a profit because of some special situation or change in the market).

A fiduciary can avoid liability for self dealing only if the act is permitted by virtue of court approval, either before or after the fact (but only after notice to the beneficiaries), beneficiary consent (again based on full disclosure), or exculpation under a statute or the governing instrument. In addition, a trustee of two trusts may sell assets from one to the other only if any such sales are fair to both accounts *and* are allowed by the instrument or by a statute (such as UTC §802(h)(3)). Similarly, only because federal law specifically allows it, a corporate trustee may deposit uninvested trust cash in the trustee's own commercial banking department (provided that the deposits are made to accounts bearing interest at market rates). Absent such special authority even such a simple act designed to make the trust productive would be regarded as improper. So bear in mind always that the transaction must be fair to the trust or estate for the fiduciary to avoid liability, even if the act of self dealing is authorized by the governing instrument or by statute, or if the beneficiaries have voluntarily consented to it after having received full disclosure of its terms.

### *Conflicts of Interest*

Transactions in which a fiduciary has a conflict of interest with the beneficiaries are qualitatively similar, but differ in degree, from those in which the fiduciary engages in self dealing. For example, the trustee has engaged in self dealing if the assets of a trust include Blackacre and the trustee buys it from the trust. The trustee has *not* engaged in self dealing if the trustee instead sells it to a buyer with whom the trustee has an ongoing business relationship (for example, an attorney who routinely steers additional fiduciary service business to the trustee). But the trustee *has* engaged in a prohibited transaction because it has a conflict of interest with the trust beneficiaries (e.g., sale to a buyer at a below market price or on favorable terms may benefit a business relationship with the buyer). *In re Rothko*, 401 N.Y.S.2d 449 (N.Y. 1977), is illustrative. The three fiduciaries of the estate of Mark Rothko, a famous abstract expressionist painter, arranged for the sale of paintings by the decedent to buyers with whom two of the fiduciaries had business dealings. Their conduct involved a conflict of interest, not self dealing.

A fiduciary who engages in a transaction for an estate or trust as to which the fiduciary's individual interests may be in conflict does not breach the fiduciary duty of loyalty if the transaction was fair to the trust or estate and entered into by the fiduciary in good faith. This differs from self dealing. The burden of proof with respect to fairness and good faith is on the fiduciary, however. In *Rothko*, the fiduciaries were unable to meet that burden. Thus, the two who had the conflict of interest were "guilty" of more than imprudent management and were held liable for the estate's losses calculated by reference to the market value of the paintings at the time of the sale, plus the appreciation in the paintings between sale and the time of trial.

A relatively common conflict of interest in fiduciary administration occurs if a corporate fiduciary (acting as trustee of a trust or personal representative of an estate) owns stock in the corporate fiduciary itself. The concern is that a corporation (usually a bank) serving as fiduciary of an estate or trust that owns stock in the fiduciary cannot manage that stock with the same objectivity that it applies to other assets. Rather, interests of the fiduciary's management and shareholders may influence decisions regarding the stock, in violation of the duty to act solely for the best interests of the beneficiaries. As a result, a corporate fiduciary normally may not invest in or retain its own stock (if the assets include that stock when the fiduciary begins to serve). Because of this general rule, however, transferors who own stock in a corporate fiduciary and who name the corporation as fiduciary (and who do not want the stock to be sold) must include in trust instruments waivers of this conflict to authorize retention of the stock.

For example, D's will named an individual, T, as trustee of a testamentary trust and authorized the trustee to retain assets that initially comprised the trust corpus. One such asset was stock in Bank, which later succeeded T as trustee of the trust. The retention authorization constitutes a waiver of the conflict of interest such that Bank may continue to hold the Bank stock as a trust asset. See *In re Heidenrich*, 378 N.Y.S.2d 982 (N.Y. Surr. Ct. 1976), which did not discuss whether the retention provision might have authorized only the retention of investments that otherwise would have been imprudent and thus impermissible. Note, however, that in any event authority to retain trust assets will never absolve a trustee from liability if the retention was reckless or not in good faith.

### Remedies for Breach of the Duty of Loyalty

A fiduciary that breaches the duty of loyalty may be held accountable to the aggrieved beneficiaries in a variety of ways. For example, the fiduciary may be held personally accountable ("surcharged") for any loss caused by the breach. In effect, breach of the duty of loyalty results in the fiduciary becoming an insurer to make good all affiliated losses. Remember, however, that a trustee will not be liable for breach if it engages in a transaction with respect to which there is a conflict of interest but that is fair to the trust and entered into in good faith.

As a second remedy, a constructive trust may be imposed to recover any profit made by the trustee. To illustrate, the trustee (T) of the Jones Family Trust sold Blackacre to a real estate partnership controlled by T. The fair market value of Blackacre at the time of the sale was $100,000; the purchase price was $125,000. The sale was not authorized by the trust, its beneficiaries, or the appropriate court. T's partnership developed Blackacre and made a profit of $50,000. Despite T's partnership having paid more than fair market value for Blackacre, the trust beneficiaries may recover the $50,000 profit from T, and T will be deemed to hold that profit as constructive trustee for the Jones Family Trust. The no-further-inquiry rule is designed to avoid a fiduciary from being tempted to put its own interests above those of the beneficiaries.

Further, because the duty of undivided loyalty is the cornerstone of the fiduciary relationship, in most circumstances it will be grounds for removal of the fiduciary unless the breach was immaterial. Plus, depending on the circumstances, the fiduciary may be denied compensation for services rendered to the estate or trust. This frequently is the least punishment imposed, but often the remedy is this *plus* any combination or all of the foregoing. Thus, depending on the circumstances, a denial of compensation, removal, and surcharge would not be unusual.

If the fiduciary purchased assets of the estate or trust without authority and still owns them (or has transferred them to someone who is not a bona fide purchaser — i.e., to a third party who did not pay fair market value for them or who took them with notice of the breach of trust), the beneficiaries may recover the assets under the so-called *trust pursuit rule*. Furthermore, if the trustee or non bona fide purchaser has exchanged trust property or disposed of it and acquired other property with the proceeds, the trust pursuit rule also allows the beneficiaries to pursue the proceeds into substituted assets. The fiduciary does not have the same option, however. To illustrate, if the value of the assets has declined, the fiduciary cannot return the assets to the trust or estate as a full repayment of the purchase price. Similarly, if the fiduciary sold assets to the trust or estate, the beneficiaries can compel the fiduciary to take them back in return for the purchase price, but the trustee may not force the beneficiaries to return them. Finally, the beneficiaries may enjoin a pending transaction that would constitute a breach of the fiduciary's duty of loyalty.

Because of the differing effects of a transaction being fair and made in good faith, it can be important to distinguish between fiduciary actions that constitute self dealing and those that involve a conflict of interest but not self dealing. Some cases are clear. A purchase by the fiduciary (or by a corporation or other entity in which the fiduciary has a substantial interest) of trust or estate assets is self dealing. A sale of such assets to a friend of the fiduciary involves a conflict of interest but not self dealing. The line is not always easily drawn, so UTC §802(c) presumes transactions between the trustee and close relatives (parents of the trustee and their descendants, and spouses of any of them) and business associates (an agent, attorney, or entity in which the trustee has a significant interest) as a conflict of interest but not as self-dealing. Otherwise, consider *Hartman* (discussed at page 389) in which a sale to the executor's wife was treated as self dealing, but what if the sale had been to the executor's child, parent, sibling, in-law, cousin, or business partner? Although we know of no bright line distinction between them outside of the UTC, the distinction can be critical. If there is self dealing the fiduciary is in breach without regard to good faith and fairness. If there is "only" a conflict of interest, there is no breach if the fiduciary can prove good faith and fairness. The distinction is of little or no significance if the transaction is not at market terms. It will make a difference only if the transaction arguably was fair to the trust or estate but it would be in the beneficiary's interest to avoid the sale or be able to surcharge the fiduciary because of other reasons (such as a substantial increase or decrease in the value of property involved in the transaction).

## Duty of Impartiality

Closely aligned with the duty of loyalty is the duty of impartiality. Absent a provision in the instrument to the contrary, the fiduciary's duty of loyalty is owed in equal measure to each current and remainder beneficiary. Administration of the entity in favor of one beneficiary at the expense of another is a breach of this duty unless disproportionate or discriminatory treatment is authorized by the governing instrument. As noted by the comment to UTC §803, "[t]he duty to act impartially does not mean that the trustee must treat the beneficiaries equally. Rather, the trustee must treat the beneficiaries equitably in light of the purposes and terms of the trust."

The context in which impartiality challenges most often arise is if a trust income or remainder beneficiary claims that the trustee favored the other. For example, the trustee breaches the duty of impartiality by administering the trust for the benefit of the remainder beneficiary at the expense of the income beneficiary if the trustee invests a material part of the trust assets in Blackacre, an undeveloped piece of property that is not leased or otherwise generating income but is expected to appreciate in value. By contrast, *Dennis v. Rhode Island Hospital Trust Co.*, 744 F.2d 893 (1st Cir. 1984), illustrates how a trustee can breach its duty of impartiality by favoring the income beneficiary. There, for 50 years or so the trustee held commercial buildings that produced a generous income, but that decreased in value because the trustee failed to properly maintain and update them or to establish an income reserve to protect the remainder beneficiaries from the buildings' depreciation.

Adopted in more than 30 states (and recently revised in response to, among other things, the relatively new prudent investor rule discussed at page 407), the Uniform Principal and Income Act provides rules for the allocation of receipts and disbursements between principal and income. Depending on the dispositive terms of the governing instrument, these allocations may have a material effect on beneficiaries' interests in the trust. To compare, one trust provides "Income to A for life, remainder to B." A second trust provides "Income and principal to A to provide for A's health, education, maintenance, and support. At A's death, remainder to B." A third trust provides "Income and principal to A to provide for A's health, education, maintenance, and support until A reaches age 30, at which time the remaining trust assets will be distributed to A; but if A dies before reaching age 30, to B." How receipts and disbursements are allocated between principal and income by the trustee of the first trust directly controls the amount of distributions A receives, and thus the value of the remainder B will receive at A's death. By contrast, A is to receive current distributions of income or principal from the other two trusts only as necessary for the stated purposes, and in the third trust it is likely that A will receive the remaining assets as well. For these trusts, the principal and income allocation issue is of less significance or, more accurately, it is of a different dimension with very different consequences.

Generally, the proceeds from the sale of trust assets are allocated to principal, regardless of whether the sale is made at a gain or a loss. Thus, if Blackacre and stock of ABC, Inc. became trust assets when they were worth $100,000 and $50,000, respectively, and if they subsequently were sold by the trustee for $120,000 and $40,000, respectively, the $160,000 of proceeds would be treated as trust principal. If, however, Blackacre was unproductive (i.e., if it had not been producing income) or underproductive (i.e., if it produced less than a certain amount of income), a part of the gain on its sale would be classified as income under most states' laws. As indicated by the discussion of *Dennis* at page 393, it also may be necessary for a trustee to establish a reserve for depreciation or depletion of trust assets (i.e., to treat as principal part of the receipts from the property that otherwise would be trust income) to protect the remainder beneficiary.

For example, imagine that a trust owns a producing oil well. The well will have little or no value when its oil reserves have been exhausted. There will be little or nothing left for the remainder beneficiary to receive on termination of the trust if all of its receipts are treated as trust income and distributed to the income beneficiary. Therefore, to protect the remainder beneficiary (and unless the document provides otherwise), the trustee must establish a depletion reserve (i.e., hold back from the income beneficiary a portion of the receipts from the property), which essentially would be treated as principal for ultimate distribution to the remainder beneficiary.

Generally, a trust's return on its investments consists of income earned (e.g., interest and dividends) and appreciation in the value of principal. If the terms of a trust provide for income to be distributed to A and the remainder to B, the duty of impartiality traditionally has required the trustee to invest in assets expected to earn a reasonable amount of income for A, and assets expected to at least maintain the value of the principal (perhaps adjusted for inflation) for B. As discussed at page 407, the Uniform Prudent Investor Act authorizes trustees to invest to maximize the trust's total return, regardless of its income and appreciation components. Such an investment program often benefits the remainder beneficiary because higher returns are available from investing in stocks that pay little income but offer significant appreciation potential. Uniform Principal and Income Act §104 authorizes the trustee to allocate principal gains to income (or vice versa) to adjust such investment returns consistent with the duty of impartiality.

## Duty to Collect Property

A trustee manages property for the benefit of the trust beneficiaries. A personal representative is charged with a variety of duties, including paying the ward or decedent's creditors and distributing estate assets to heirs or devisees. Necessary to the performance of a trustee or personal representative's duties is collection of the assets to be administered. Especially required of a probate estate's personal representative is a determination of what the decedent owned, and taking control of those assets. Similarly, the trustee of a testamentary trust is required to take control of estate assets from the personal representative when estate administration is complete and to monitor the personal representative's performance of its duties. Thus, if the personal representative allows the statute of limitation to run on the collection of amounts due the decedent, the trustee can be held accountable for the loss if the trustee does not pursue the trust's cause of action to make the personal representative account for the loss.

In many jurisdictions, a trustee who succeeds another trustee is responsible for the trust assets delivered to the successor by the prior trustee, *plus* the successor is liable for trust assets that would have been delivered had the trust been administered properly but that were lost because of a breach by the prior trustee. That is, the successor must sue the predecessor to recover for those losses. In those jurisdictions the successor should receive and review an accounting from the predecessor trustee and satisfy itself that the former trustee properly performed its duties, or sue to redress any deficiencies. Otherwise the successor is as responsible as is the predecessor for losses incurred by the predecessor. Trust instruments commonly relieve a successor trustee from the duty of inquiring into the administration of the trust by the prior trustee because of the understandable reluctance of successor trustees to assume this undertaking and potential liability, and to avoid the fees they charge for doing so. That particularly is true if the prior trustee was the settlor in a self-trusteed declaration of trust. UTC §812 obligates a successor trustee to redress only breaches "known" to the successor, and the §104 definition of "knowledge" suggests that the successor trustee generally is under no duty to investigate the former trustee's administration.

## Duty to Manage Property

Generally, a fiduciary is responsible for administering trust or estate assets by employing such care and skill as a person of ordinary prudence would use in managing their own property. In addition, a fiduciary with greater skills than a person of ordinary prudence is held to the higher obligation to use those special skills. This general duty can take on a myriad of forms.

One is *earmarking* trust assets, which is the process of holding title to assets in the name of the fiduciary as fiduciary. *Segregating* assets is the process of keeping trust or estate assets separate from the fiduciary's own assets. *Commingling* occurs when estate or trust assets are mixed with the fiduciary's personal assets. All of this is important because, among other things, the fiduciary may be held to a higher investment standard than it is with its own funds. To illustrate, T, as individual Trustee of the Jones Family Trust, deposits trust funds in Bank. The assets have been earmarked if the account into which the deposit is made is in the name of "T, as Trustee of the Jones Family Trust" (or just in the name of "the Trustee of the Jones Family Trust"). The trust funds have been segregated only if there are no funds of T in the account. Otherwise the trust assets have been commingled, which may make it impossible to judge whether T has properly managed the trust assets (as distinct from T's own funds). The fiduciary duty is to earmark and segregate. Although commingling usually is not a problem with corporate fiduciaries, it may be the single most common source of individual fiduciary liability (and attorney malfeasance as well), even if there is no theft or other impropriety attributable to the failure to segregate the funds.

Earmarking and segregation also are designed to protect beneficiaries from claims by the fiduciary's personal creditors against entity assets and to protect the fiduciary's personal creditors from claims by a fiduciary or the beneficiaries that the fiduciary's personal assets belong to the entity. This can be especially problematic because some bonds are "bearer bonds," meaning they are not registered in the owner's name but are simply payable to whoever has possession of them (the bearer). Similarly, for ease of transfer, registered securities and sometimes even land are held in nominee (or "street") name, meaning they are titled in the name of an entity other than the real owner so that sales and transfers can take place without the need for the real owner to sign instruments of transfer or to supply documentation as to the fiduciary's power to sell the property. Generally, fiduciaries may hold assets in these forms without breaching their fiduciary duty to earmark and segregate, provided that separate books and accounts are maintained that clearly identify the proper ownership of all assets.

Common trust funds are another widely accepted exception to the duty to earmark and segregate fiduciary assets. A common trust fund is a device similar to a mutual fund that is used by many bank trust departments to pool funds of many trusts and estates of which it serves as fiduciary. This allows for better diversification and for efficiencies of size in making investment decisions and trades. Thus, for example, ABC Bank, as personal representative of the Jones estate, may own 1 unit of ABC's common trust fund, which in turn may own stocks, bonds, or both of many different companies or other issuers of securities. If there are 100 units of the common trust fund outstanding, the Jones estate will receive one percent of all income, gains, and losses of the common trust fund and may liquidate its interest for one percent of the value of the fund. Statutes in most states, and federal banking regulations for national banks, permit the use of common trust funds unless the trust instrument prohibits investment in them (which would be rare).

The traditional view, still followed in some jurisdictions, is that a fiduciary that breaches the duty not to commingle or the duty to earmark is liable for losses incurred, regardless of whether the commingling or failure to earmark caused the loss. The modern view is that liability will be imposed only to the extent the breach caused the loss. When there has been such a breach, however, causation likely will be determined by resolving questions against the fiduciary who breached this duty. For example, T, as personal representative of the Jones estate, opened an investment account at ABC Brokerage with $1,000 of T's own funds and $1,000 of estate assets. Two investments of $1,000 were made, one in stock of X Company and one in stock of Y Company. The X Company stock increased in value to $1,200; the Y Company stock decreased in value to $700. Regardless of whether the account was opened in the name of T or the estate, the X Company stock likely would be allocated to the estate and the Y Company stock to T. If both stocks had declined in value to $700, the traditional view would surcharge T for the $300 loss to the estate. The modern view would not (assuming both investments otherwise were prudent).

Fiduciaries also should take reasonable steps to *safeguard assets*. For example, depending on the nature of the asset, valuable tangible and intangible personal property may need to be safely stored, perhaps in a bank safety deposit box. Thus, one of the first duties of a personal representative following the decedent's death or if a ward is removed to a care facility is to physically secure the personal residence and its contents. Again depending on the circumstances, the duty to manage prudently also may include *insuring* personal and real property against loss. And it is the fiduciary's duty to provide maintenance to preserve asset values. Further, the fiduciary's duties include timely *payment of* all income, excise, transfer, and property *taxes* because failure may result in liens that may spawn penalties, interest, and (ultimately) seizure or foreclosure.

Perhaps the most difficult asset for a fiduciary to manage is an *operating business*. In many jurisdictions, in the absence of specific authority the fiduciary does not have the power to continue an ongoing business beyond the period necessary to sell the business as a going concern or to wind up its affairs and liquidate its assets. A personal representative who continues a business beyond that period may be held personally liable for losses. Difficult questions can arise, even if there is authority to continue the business, such as what the fiduciary may or must do if the business is losing money and additional capital is required.

In some jurisdictions it does not matter whether the decedent conducted the business as a sole proprietorship or in another form, such as a corporation the stock of which the decedent owned. See, e.g., *In re Estate of Kurkowski*, 409 A.2d 357 (Pa. 1979), and *Estate of Baldwin*, 442 A.2d 529 (Me. 1982). In other jurisdictions holding corporate stock as an estate asset could be viewed as distinguishable from operating an ongoing business, because the role of a personal representative traditionally has been viewed as preserving estate assets for ultimate distribution to the beneficiaries, not making investment decisions for estate assets. To avoid potential liability, however, a personal representative should continue an ongoing business only with court authorization or the consent of all estate beneficiaries, based on full disclosure.

Similarly, if the assets of a trust include an interest in a closely held business, the first question is whether the trust instrument expressly or impliedly authorizes the trustee to retain the interest and operate the business. If not, it usually will be a breach for the trustee to do so. If retention is only authorized and not mandated the trustee's duty is to use prudence and care in deciding whether to retain the business interest. And in some cases the trustee also may be held liable for doing so even if retention is directed. See page 409.

## Delegation of Duties

The fiduciary relationship is one of trust and confidence. Fiduciaries are chosen by testators and settlors, wards and courts, because of such factors as the relationship with the fiduciary and the fiduciary's abilities and reputation. For these reasons, there are limitations on the ability of a fiduciary to delegate its duties to administer a trust or estate.

Although the traditional rule sometimes is referred to as a duty not to delegate, it either is impractical or impossible for a fiduciary personally to perform all trust administration functions (e.g., selling publicly traded securities without using a broker or performing difficult maintenance or repairs on improved property). Thus, some duties are delegable even under the most traditional view. The historic compromise is to allow delegation of ministerial duties, but not discretionary ones. A fiduciary who delegated discretionary duties was held liable for all resulting losses, regardless of the reasonableness of the delegation or the conduct of the delegate. A fiduciary who delegated ministerial duties was required to use prudence and care in selecting the delegate and in monitoring that work.

Even under this traditional view, a trustee who delegated discretionary duties was not liable for losses that were not caused by the delegation. For example, in *Shriners Hospitals for Crippled Children v. Gardiner*, 733 P.2d 1110 (Ariz. 1987), the trustee opened an investment account at a major brokerage firm and turned over all decision making for the funds to another, who then embezzled funds from the account. The trustee breached the duty to invest the trust assets when it completely delegated that responsibility (as opposed to obtaining investment advice from an expert but making the final investment decisions), but the case was remanded for a determination of how the embezzlement occurred and whether it was caused by the delegation (rather than, for example, the brokerage firm improperly allowing the delegate access to the funds in the account). The breach would not produce liability for the criminal act unless the one caused the other.

A more modern view of fiduciary delegation expressly allows duties to be delegated, without regard to their being ministerial or discretionary, but only to the extent that a prudent person would delegate them. Restatement (Third) of Trusts (Prudent Investor Rule) §171 comment f (1992); UTC §807. Although wholesale delegation of all duties is not permitted, hard and fast rules of which duties may be delegated and which may not are not provided. Rather, under the Restatement a duty may be delegated "when it is reasonably intended to further sound administration of the trust. . . . [C]onsideration should be given to all factors that are relevant to analyzing whether the fact and manner of delegation can reasonably be expected to contribute to the sound and efficient administration of the trust." Thus, a fiduciary must use care and prudence in exercising the discretion to delegate, both in selecting delegates and in supervising them. The decision to delegate is judicially reviewable only for abuse, based on a failure to exercise the required degree of care, skill, or caution. The Restatement (Third) also expressly contemplates delegation of investment authority. The fiduciary is directed by §227 to act with prudence in deciding whether and how to delegate authority over investments and in the selection and supervision of agents. Comment j to §227 goes further. It gives the fiduciary the power to delegate investment authority and, in some circumstances, may create a duty to do so. See page 408.

## Duty to Account

The essence of the fiduciary relationship is the management of property by the fiduciary for the benefit of the beneficiaries. Despite holding legal title to fiduciary assets, in a very real sense those assets do not "belong" to the fiduciary. Rather, the fiduciary administers the assets for their "real" owners in interest, who are the beneficiaries. Fundamental to the fiduciary's duties is the obligation to account (i.e., report) to the beneficiaries concerning management of the trust or estate. Without proper accountings no one would be able to properly police the administration or seek redress for errors.

Accounts are prepared on a periodic basis. Their purpose is to report on the fiduciary's administration for a given period of time (often a year). At a minimum, the account should report the assets (and liabilities, if any) at the beginning of the period; receipts and disbursements during the period; purchases, sales, exchanges, and other acquisitions and dispositions of assets during the period; and the assets (and liabilities, if any) at the end of the period. The assets reported as being held by the fiduciary at the beginning and end of the period are reconciled by the receipts, disbursements, and other information contained in the account (i.e., to oversimplify, beginning assets + receipts - disbursements = ending assets). Generally, beneficiaries are entitled to even more information concerning administration of the trust than the items that must, at a minimum, be included in an account. Thus, beneficiaries may request and are entitled to receive other information that may be useful to them in protecting their rights under the trust, and may inspect property and records of the trust or estate as appropriate.

Further, the fiduciary may have an affirmative duty to provide beneficiaries with material information concerning administration. For example, in *Allard v. Pacific National Bank*, 663 P.2d 104 (Wash. 1983), the trustee was given the "full power to . . . sell . . . the assets of the trust." It was held to have breached its fiduciary duty to inform the beneficiaries when it sold the trust's sole asset (commercial real estate in downtown Seattle) without first advising the beneficiaries. The court acknowledged that the trustee did not need the beneficiaries' consent to sell the property. But the beneficiaries had indicated a desire to keep the property and the court held that they should have been afforded the opportunity to outbid the party who bought it. (The trustee also was held to have breached its duty of care with respect to the sale by not taking appropriate steps to obtain the highest possible price for it, such as by having the property appraised.)

Some jurisdictions have statutes that require judicial accountings by personal representatives of estates and by trustees of testamentary trusts. These accountings typically are set for hearing, notice is given to the beneficiaries, and (absent a successful challenge) judicial approval of the accounts is rendered. In most circumstances this approval protects the fiduciary from future claims by beneficiaries. Generally, such an accounting that fails to adequately disclose matters material to administration of the entity will not foreclose later claims against the fiduciary with respect to those matters. Furthermore, even judicial approval of an accounting that disclosed everything the fiduciary knew to disclose may not protect the fiduciary from future claims. In *National Academy of Sciences v. Cambridge Trust Co.*, 346 N.E.2d 879 (Mass. 1976), for example, the settlor created a trust for his wife for her life or until her earlier remarriage, remainder to a charity. The widow remarried, but did not so inform the trustee, which continued distributions to her that were reported on accountings that were provided to the charity and approved by the court. The court's approval of the accountings did not preclude the charity's subsequent claim against the trustee because the accounts implicitly constituted representations of fact that the widow remained single and thus was the proper income beneficiary of the trust. Those representations were false, and they were made by the trustee as of its own knowledge. Because the trustee had not made reasonable efforts to determine their truth, its conduct constituted constructive fraud that allowed the charity to reopen the accountings.

There is no general requirement of judicial accountings for inter vivos trusts, nor in many jurisdictions even for testamentary trusts and estates. Rather, the accounts are provided directly to the beneficiaries. (Trustees and personal representatives nevertheless sometimes choose to account to the court to minimize the risk of future claims being made against them.) The real question raised is whether the fiduciary is protected from future claims if the beneficiaries approve an informal accounting. Generally, beneficiaries who do not approve an account will not be foreclosed from challenging it later regardless of its approval by other beneficiaries. The practical problem this presents is that trusts often have minor, unborn, and other contingent beneficiaries whose approval is difficult or impossible to obtain (perhaps a guardian ad litem could be appointed to approve accounts for them, but that entails a judicial process and a significant purpose of informal accountings is to avoid the time and expense of judicial proceedings for approval of accounts).

Trust instruments sometimes address the accounting issue by providing that approval by the current adult income beneficiaries bars *any* beneficiaries from later challenging the account. Because of the inherent conflicts of interest that often exist between income and remainder beneficiaries, however, some courts have refused to allow income beneficiaries to approve accounts on behalf of remainder beneficiaries, especially when the instrument does not expressly allow it. See, e.g., *In re Crane*, 41 N.Y.S.2d 940 (N.Y. 1943).

UTC §§105(b)(8) and (b)(9) are among the most controversial in the entire Code, prescribing mandatory duties to inform beneficiaries that a settlor may not alter. "Qualified beneficiaries" (generally, adult current and first line remainder beneficiaries) must be notified of the existence of the trust, the identity of the trustee, and their right to see periodic reports. Some legislatures have modified these provisions in unusual ways. For example, the District of Columbia § 19-1301.05(b) and (c) allows waiver of the beneficiaries' rights to receive information if the settlor appoints a representative to receive reports on the beneficiaries' behalf and then act in good faith to protect their interests.

## Duty to Invest

The traditional role of a decedent's personal representative is to wind up the estate. By contrast, the role of a ward's personal representative or of a trustee is to manage property on behalf of the ward or the trust beneficiaries. As a result, Restatement (Second) of Trusts §6 comment b flatly states that personal representatives ordinarily are not under a duty to invest estate assets to make them productive, unless there is a delay in distribution of the estate to the heirs or devisees. Restatement (Third) of Trusts §5 comment *c* is not as explicit, largely dodging the issue, which may indicate that there is a developing change of undefined parameters. *In re Estate of Kugler*, 344 N.W.2d 160 (Wis. 1984), may be indicative of the trend, it holding a personal representative responsible in surcharge for lost interest on estate funds deposited in noninterest bearing checking accounts for over eight years.

According to the court, a personal representative, although not a trustee, nevertheless has a duty "to reasonably invest estate funds." Even if personal representatives have such a limited duty to invest to make estate assets productive, their investment powers may be substantially more restricted than are those of trustees. For example, most states have statutes granting trustees rather broad investment authority, but many restrict permissible investments of estate assets by personal representatives (for example, to short term government obligations). Furthermore, personal representatives are under a duty to preserve estate assets (which may require sales of perishable property), but they generally are not under a duty to diversify. See *Estate of Beach*, 542 P.2d 994 (Cal. 1975), which distinguished between a personal representative and a trustee in this regard also, notwithstanding that the personal representative of the estate also was to serve as trustee of a testamentary trust that would be funded with estate assets at the close of estate administration. As a result of this dichotomy between the investment responsibilities of personal representatives and trustees, the following discussion is presented in terms of a trustee's duties, recognizing that the two standards may continue to converge over the course of your career. Generally, a trustee's duty to manage trust assets for the beneficiaries includes a duty to invest those assets prudently in a way that earns income, generates appreciation of principal to keep up with inflation, or both. The specific rules governing trust investments continue to evolve.

### *Legal Lists*

Reflecting a conservative focus on preserving trust principal, many states enacted statutes in the late 19th century and first part of the 20th century (when inflation was not as pronounced and its erosive effects on purchasing power not as well known) specifying permissible investments for trustees. These "legal lists" typically permitted investments only in government bonds and first mortgages on real estate. Common stocks frequently were prohibited. Today legal list statutes are quite uncommon and, where found, they are more diverse.

### *Prudent Person Rule*

Most states replaced legal list statutes with "prudent man" statutes and, more recently, with "prudent person" statutes (these differ by more than just gender neutrality) under which the trustee's investment obligation, and required general standard of conduct, is to exercise the skill and care the ordinarily prudent trustee would exercise in dealing with its own property (or, in some statutes, the property of another, which is a difference of more than just semantics also). Moreover, a trustee that has (or that represented that it has) special skills is held to the higher standard of a prudent trustee with those special skills. In theory, the exercise of a trustee's investment authority is judged without benefit of hindsight. The trustee's acts are weighed according to what the trustee knew or should have known at the time. Although the standard is one of conduct, not results, some decisions nevertheless appear to reflect the influence of hindsight, viewing the actual investment results.

Each investment is examined separately under the prudent person rule, without regard to other trust investments, to determine if it was prudent or speculative. The trustee has complied with its investment responsibilities if each decision was prudent and consistent with the terms of the trust. The trustee has breached its investment duties, however, if those investments were speculative and not expressly permitted by the instrument. The analysis is two-fold. The first step is to determine whether the type of investment was permitted. If so, the second question is whether the particular investment was permitted. Investments of certain types are impermissible under the prudent person rule as being inherently speculative. For example, Restatement (Second) of Trusts §227 comments f and h list the following as improper investments: (1) the purchase of securities for speculation, such as bonds selling at discounts because of uncertainty as to whether they will be paid at maturity; (2) the purchase of securities in start-up ventures; (3) the use of trust assets in carrying on a trade or business; (4) the purchase of land or other things for resale; and (5) second or other junior mortgages (unless the trustee is authorized or directed to sell land and it is reasonably necessary to take a second mortgage to make the sale). Common and preferred stocks are permitted in companies with regular earnings that pay regular dividends that reasonably may be expected to continue.

Under the prudent person rule, only prudent investments are proper. Depending on the circumstances even government bonds, first mortgages on land, and corporate bonds may be speculative and impermissible. Restatement (Second) of Trusts §227 comment o lists 10 factors the trustee should consider in evaluating a specific investment, in addition to principal preservation and income production. In general, the trustee is required to use care, skill, and caution in making an investment from within a permissible category of investments.

Most versions of the prudent person rule require trust funds to be invested to accomplish the dual goals of preserving principal and generating income. Whether either of these objectives is given primary consideration in a given case depends on the particular circumstances of the trust. Of growing concern in a long-term administration is the effect of inflation on the preservation of principal for the remainder beneficiary. Imagine that $100,000 is invested in bank certificates of deposit for 20 years and the interest earned is distributed entirely to the income beneficiary. Income will benefit the income beneficiary but the "real" value of the $100,000 of principal (in terms of the purchasing power to the remainder beneficiary) will be less than $50,000 in current dollars if inflation averages four percent per year for the 20 year period. The traditional view has been that a trustee is under no duty to increase the value of trust principal, even as necessary to keep up with inflation. As discussed at page 408, that view is changing.

The trustee's duty of loyalty is to administer the trust for the sole benefit of the beneficiaries. The trustee's investment duty is to produce income and preserve principal. In recent years one unresolved issue is whether investing trust assets in furtherance of social goals (such as not investing in the stock of companies that operate in ways that are particularly harmful to the environment, or that do business in countries with politically repressive policies) complies with these duties. Because the jury is still out on this issue, a cautious fiduciary will not pursue those objectives without the consent of all beneficiaries, which may be hard to obtain because of minor, unborn, and other contingent beneficiaries. Otherwise returns must be generated that approximate those available to less socially-conscious funds. Note, however, that in recent years the socially responsible mutual funds have outperformed many generic funds.

Trustees that are subject to the prudent person rule also are required to diversify their investments to reduce the risk of large losses. A trust with diversified investments does not have a disproportionately large part of its assets invested in a particular investment or type of investment. What constitutes adequate diversification of funds is at first a finance question, but the fact that a failure to diversify is a breach of fiduciary duty makes it a legal one as well. As discussed at page 407, diversification is a primary component of the trustee's duty under the new "prudent investor" standard. The Restatement (Third) of Trusts, which advances the new prudent investor standard, provides no guidance on what percentage of a trust's assets may be invested in a particular investment or investment type without running afoul of the diversification requirement, and we are loathe to hazard a guess whether something like ten or more different investments is adequate, no more than five percent in any one investment vehicle should be the benchmark, or whether two or three (or even one) well managed and diverse mutual funds would suffice.

A mutual fund is an investment vehicle in which many persons pool their assets for investment by the fund manager in a diversified portfolio of securities. Although mutual funds are subject to criticism (because usually investment in them delegates to the fund manager how the funds are invested), they are authorized by statute in a number of jurisdictions and are particularly useful for smaller trusts. Common trust funds operated by banks, discussed at page 397, serve the same diversification purpose for trust assets held by corporate trustees as mutual funds provide for investors like us or you. Note, however, that an investment in a mutual fund or common trust fund may provide only limited diversification. There are thousands of mutual funds on the market with a wide variety of investment objectives. For example, although there are mutual funds that attempt to provide in one asset a well diversified portfolio of securities, there also are mutual funds investing only in one type of security, such as gold stocks, the stocks of so-called "emerging" foreign markets (e.g., Brazil and Turkey), short-term U.S. government bonds, energy stocks, health care industry stocks, small company stocks, "junk" bonds, tax exempt bonds of Ohio, etc. Thus, the degree of diversification provided by a particular mutual fund will depend on the investment objectives of the fund.

An actively managed mutual fund is one for which the fund manager researches investment opportunities in an effort to provide the fund's shareholders with superior returns. By contrast, a passive mutual fund is one in which the investments are designed to track the performance of a specific index (such as the Standard & Poors 500, which consists of 500 large domestic corporations). Increased attention is being given to investment in these "index" funds because their costs are significantly less than those of actively managed funds and because of questions about the ability of active fund managers to "beat the market" by more than the additional recurring costs incurred by active funds.

A final factor to guide a trustee investing under either a prudent person rule (or, under the prudent investor rule discussed at page 407) is the trust's need for liquidity. The assets of a trust for a beneficiary with relatively large short term cash needs (e.g., a trust for the college education of a high school student) should be invested differently than the assets of a trust for a beneficiary without cash needs for the near future (e.g., a trust for the college education of a newborn).

*Estate of Collins*, 139 Cal. Rptr. 644 (Cal. Ct. App. 1977), was decided under the prudent person rule and illustrates how not to invest trust funds. The trustees (one of whom was the testator's lawyer) invested substantially all of a testamentary trust in a loan to real estate developers (who were clients of the lawyer/trustee) secured by a second deed of trust (similar to a mortgage) on a tract of land. The value of the land securing the loan declined, the borrowers defaulted on the loan, the holders of the first trust deed foreclosed, and the trust received no principal repayments on its loan. The trustees were surcharged for the loss, in large part because the concentration of the trust assets in the loan violated the trustee's duty to diversify. Furthermore, the loan was secured only by a second deed of trust, which is an imprudent "speculative" investment. Finally, the trustees did not properly investigate such matters as the value of the land securing the second trust deed or the credit worthiness of the borrowers.

## Prudent Investor Rule

The modern investments world has changed dramatically since the prudent person rule was produced, both in terms of the nature of available investment opportunities and the strategies for best taking advantage of them. The rules governing permissible trustee investments are responding to those changes through the development of the prudent investor rule, established by the Restatement (Third) of Trusts and the Uniform Prudent Investor Act. The underlying theoretical basis of the prudent investor rule is "modern portfolio theory," which focuses not on the prudent or speculative nature of individual investments but on the management of the portfolio as a whole. No investments are imprudent per se under the modern portfolio theory. Rather, each investment is evaluated in the context of the entire portfolio. Thus, an investment that would not be appropriate for consideration by a trustee under a legal list or the prudent person rule (e.g., options, futures, venture capital investments, and junior mortgages) *may* be proper under the prudent investor rule.

A trustee operating under the prudent investor rule has considerably more flexibility in designing an investment strategy than does a trustee governed by the prudent person rule (which still is in effect in many jurisdictions). Yet the prudent investor rule does not provide trustees with an unchecked ability to invest. Rather, the Restatement (Third) provides that trustees governed by the prudent investor rule are guided by the following principles (in addition to the fundamental proposition that no investment or technique is imprudent per se and that trust investments are to be evaluated in the context of the portfolio as a whole).

- Diversification: Absent special circumstances (e.g., significant adverse income tax consequences of sales to diversify or family held business interests), trustees are under a duty to diversify trust investments.

- Risk and Return: Somewhat analogous to the conventional wisdom that "you get what you pay for" is the truism of finance that higher returns generally are available from investments accompanied by higher risk. Under the prudent investor rule, the trustee must consider the risk/return trade-off in the context of the particular trust, its purposes, and its distribution requirements for its beneficiaries.

- Expenses: Along with the increased sophistication of the modern investment world are increased fees and costs for taking advantage of them. The prudent investor rule directs trustees to take them into account in devising an investment strategy and to avoid high cost investments that are not justified by the circumstances of the trust.

- Impartiality: The trustee's duty to invest trust assets impartially for the benefit of both the income and remainder beneficiaries includes a duty to consider the erosive effects of inflation on the purchasing power of the trust principal. The objective of preserving principal is retained, but under the prudent investor rule the "principal" to be preserved is its real, after-inflation purchasing power. Further, depending on the particular circumstances of the trust, the investment objective may be to maintain and then increase the purchasing power of the trust.

- Delegation: Finally, trustees under the prudent investor rule may have the authority to seek expert advice in making investment decisions. Indeed, they may have a *duty* to do so. That might be the case, for example, if the trustee has little or no investment experience or if the trust is large and sophisticated investment strategies are being followed. In delegating, however, the trustee must use prudence in selecting the delegate, establishing the terms of the delegation, and monitoring the delegate's conduct.

### *Effect of Governing Instrument Provisions on Investment Authority*

A trustee's investment authority may be restricted or expanded by the terms of the governing instrument. Occasionally a document will limit the trustee's investment authority to fixed income instruments (such as government securities) that provide steady income and safety of principal, but that do not protect the principal from the effects of inflation. For example, *In re Trusteeship Agreement with Mayo*, 105 N.W.2d 900 (Minn. 1960), involved trusts created in 1917 and 1919 that permitted investment in real estate mortgages and municipal bonds and prohibited investment in common stock. The court removed that restriction because inflation (the effects of which became known after the trusts were created) threatened to defeat the dominant purpose of the transferor, which was to prevent a loss of principal. On similar facts, however, an Ohio court refused to remove a similar restriction in *Toledo Trust Co. v. Toledo Hospital*, 187 N.E.2d 36 (Ohio 1962). In an age of increasingly long term trusts any kind of restriction is a significant problem, simply because no one can predict the future.

At the other end of the spectrum, a trust instrument may expand a trustee's investment authority in several different ways. For example, a trust instrument governed by the law of a jurisdiction that limits permissible investments (such as to first mortgages of land and government securities) may authorize the trustee to make investments permitted by the prudent person rule. Generally, such an expansion will be respected. Of more difficulty is a governing instrument that purports to authorize the trustee to make investments that would not satisfy the prudent person rule. According to Restatement (Second) of Trusts §227 comment u, such a provision will be respected (see, e.g., *Hoffman v. First Virginia Bank*, 263 S.E.2d 402 (Va. 1980)), but the provisions of the governing instrument are strictly construed against any such enlargement of investment authority. Further, not all investments would be proper even if the trustee is authorized to invest in securities that would not meet the prudent person rule. Rather, the trustee always is required to use care, skill, and caution in making the selection. Thus, in *Collins*, discussed at page 406, the trustees were liable for the loss occasioned by the second deed of trust investment, notwithstanding language in the instrument authorizing them to make investments not otherwise permissible for corporate trustees and stating that their discretion was absolute and their exercise was conclusive on all persons.

To illustrate, assume a trust instrument authorizes the trustee to invest in foreign certificates of deposit. The trustee does so and substantial losses occasioned by fluctuations in foreign currencies are incurred. If the beneficiary sues, the trustee will not necessarily be protected from liability by the authorization in the trust instrument, because authority to act does not mean authority to act imprudently. The trustee will be liable if it was imprudent as determined by a negligence standard (for example, in selecting the foreign certificates of deposit in which to invest, or in monitoring the investments selected). And the trustee could be strictly liable for resulting losses without regard to the trustee not having acted negligently if the instrument did not authorize the investments (and the prudent investor rule was not in effect). See *Republic National Bank v. Araujo*, 697 So.2d 164 (Fla. Ct. App. 1997).

Individuals often entrust assets that do not satisfy the prudent person rule or other standards governing permissible trust investments. A testator who creates a testamentary trust may own speculative assets. Documents frequently permit or require trustees to retain the original trust assets in an effort to prevent the trustee from being required to sell part or all of the assets and reinvest the proceeds in different investments to comply with the governing investment rules. A trustee that is *required* by the document to retain original investments is under a duty to do so and a sale of them would be a breach. Still, there may be a trap for the unwary fiduciary, because Restatement (Third) of Trusts §66 comment *e* provides that the trustee is under a duty to apply to the court for permission to deviate from the terms of the trust "if circumstances exist that would justify judicial action with respect to an *administrative* provision . . . if the trustee knows or should know of those circumstances and that substantial harm may result to the trust or its beneficiaries from adhering to the existing terms of the trust" (emphasis in original).

Thus, for example, D's estate was devised to T, in trust, for the benefit of D's descendants. D's most valuable asset was stock of a company that D controlled and that had a long history of operating profitably. D's will both authorized T to retain the stock and prohibited T from selling it. After D's death, the company began incurring significant losses that adversely affected the value of the stock. If continued losses appear likely, T would be well advised to seek instructions from the court on whether unanticipated circumstances have arisen that make it prudent to sell the stock to protect the value of the trust for the beneficiaries, all notwithstanding D's prohibition. See *In re Pulitzer*, 249 N.Y.S. 87 (Surr. Ct. 1931), in which the court determined it could modify the terms of a trust to permit the sale of corporate stock in this kind of situation.

Similarly, a trustee that is *authorized*, but not required, to retain original investments may not necessarily do so with impunity. Instead, the trustee will be required to exercise due care in deciding whether the authority should be exercised or the original investments nevertheless should be sold. Even if not expressed, the authority to retain may be implied by the circumstances of the trust and the relationship of the property to the transferor and the beneficiaries. Examples include stock in closely held family businesses and land used in family farming operations.

If the trustee is authorized or directed to retain corporate stock that changes form during the trust administration, the new stock may be retained if it is the substantial equivalent of the old. For example, the trust instrument for the ABC Trust authorizes the trustee to retain the stock of Family Corporation, Inc. (FCI). If FCI reorganizes to change from a Texas corporation to a Delaware corporation, the stock in the new entity will be the substantial equivalent of the stock in FCI and may be retained to the same extent the FCI stock could be retained. But assume that FCI is acquired by merger with Acquiring Company, Inc. (ACI), a larger corporation engaged in various businesses in addition to that of FCI. The ACI stock received by the trustee in the merger may not be covered by the retention provision in the trust instrument and the trustee may be obligated to sell the ACI stock if it is not an appropriate trust investment (or to sell part of it if necessary to properly diversify the trust's investments). For a case so holding, see *In re Mueller's Trust*, 135 N.W.2d 854 (Wis. 1965).

### Investment Losses and the Anti-Netting Rule

A trustee's liability for investment losses will depend on the circumstances. For example, there is no liability for loss if there is no breach of the duty of loyalty and a trustee's investments were prudent and authorized by the controlling statute (in a legal list jurisdiction), or if they were prudent (in a jurisdiction governed by the prudent person rule), or they were proper (in a jurisdiction governed by the prudent investor rule). But a trustee that breaches the investment duty under the appropriate standard generally will be liable personally for the loss. The significant issue then is whether gains may be offset against losses to reduce the trustee's liability. Offsetting is not allowed if the losses result from breaches and the gains from proper investments. Similarly, gains and losses may not be offset if they result from separate and distinct breaches. But if breaches that are not separate and distinct produce both gains and losses, the breaches essentially are treated as a single occurrence and netting is permitted to determine the net loss from the breach for which the trustee is liable. It is a factual inquiry whether conduct constitutes separate and distinct breaches rather than a single breach.

To illustrate, High Roller, trustee of the ABC Trust, "invests" $10,000 of the trust assets in casino slot machines and wins $5,000. High Roller takes the original $10,000 and the $5,000 of winnings to the track and loses $6,000 "investing" in horse race betting. If the anti-netting rule applies, High Roller is liable to the trust for the $6,000 loss and the trust keeps the original $10,000 and the $5,000 "gain." If not, the $5,000 gain offsets the $6,000 loss, leaving High Roller liable to the trust only for the $1,000 difference. Were the breaches separate and distinct? Should it matter whether they were "investments" made the same day, at the same facility, on a single trip? We doubt that netting would apply and imagine that High Roller should be held accountable for the entire $6,000 loss (thus recouping for the trust the original $10,000) *and* the $5,000 of slot machine winnings. Because of the nature of High Roller's conduct, the equities would not favor netting the gain against the loss. In fact, to allow the offset arguably would encourage additional breaches in an effort to make up the loss and avoid personal liability.

## Management Powers

Personal representatives had inherent powers at common law to collect the decedent's assets, pay claims, and make distributions to beneficiaries. But trustees were said to have no powers not granted by the trust. Today jurisdictions have statutes granting personal representatives and trustees alike powers to administer estates and trusts, with garden variety authority to do most things an outright owner of property may do. For example, unless the will provides otherwise (or the administration of the estate is court "supervised," which is the exception rather than the rule), in a UPC state a personal representative has broad administrative powers similar to those typically provided to trustees, exercisable without court approval. Many other state statutes grant trustees substantially more powers than personal representatives, as befits the long term administration expected of a trust and the relatively limited functions of a personal representative. For example, a trustee may be authorized to borrow money and to sell, lease, and mortgage trust assets. In many states personal representatives can do none of these without court approval.

### Liability to Third Parties

The administration of a trust can result in a trustee being personally liable to the beneficiaries if the trustee commits a breach of duty, and also being personally liable to third parties for contract and tort claims. Most newcomers to this area are surprised to learn that a common law trustee who entered into a contract with a third party in the course of the administration of the trust was personally liable to the third party for amounts due under the contract. This was true at common law even if (1) the trustee had the authority to enter into the contract and was properly performing trustee duties in doing so, (2) the third party knew of the existence of the trust, the trustee's role as trustee, and the identity of the beneficiaries, and (3) the contract identified the trust and provided that the trustee was entering into the contract in a representative capacity.

A trustee with personal liability may be indemnified by the trust if entering into the contract was part of a proper performance of fiduciary duties, but that is between the trustee and the trust. The contract party could look to the trustee personally. Thus, the harshness of the traditional common law rule was of no ultimate effect if the trustee had the authority to enter into the contract and did so prudently, and the trust had sufficient assets to satisfy its indemnification obligation to the trustee. Still, in the event of a contract dispute with a third party the traditional rules permitted the third party to pursue its claim against the trustee, after which the trustee had to press an indemnification claim against the trust.

At common law the only way for a trustee to avoid the possibility of personal liability to third parties with whom the trustee contracted was to include in the contract a specific provision that the trustee would have no personal liability under the contract. State laws such as UPC §7-306 reverse these traditional rules regarding a trustee's contract liability to third parties, if the contract was properly entered into in the course of the administration of the trust. Under the UPC a trustee will not be personally liable unless the contract expressly so provides, or the trustee did not reveal the representative capacity and identify the trust estate in the contract.

To illustrate, assume D's estate was devised to T, in trust, for the benefit of D's descendants. The principal asset of D's estate that T received from D's personal representative was a farm. D's will directed T to retain the farm and authorized T to conduct farming operations on it.

T hired laborers to work on the farm; ordered seed, fertilizer, and other supplies; arranged for various needed maintenance and improvements to the farm; and purchased on the installment basis equipment needed for the farm. Because of the weather, fewer crops were harvested than were expected. Low prices for the crops added to T's problems, as did a general decline in the value of farmland in the area. T was unable to meet the trust's obligations to the bank that loaned money to D, secured by a mortgage on the farm, and the bank foreclosed. T also was unable to pay third parties with whom T had contracted for goods and services for the farm.

At common law, T would be personally liable to those third parties for amounts due them under their contracts. The only exception to this would apply if the contracts with those third parties specifically provided otherwise. If the UPC is in effect, however, T will not be liable to the third parties, except to the extent the contracts so provide or if T did not reveal the representative capacity and identify the trust estate in the contracts. The net result is that at common law T is personally liable under the contracts, T is entitled to indemnification from the trust for amounts paid by T to the third parties, but T will suffer the loss if the trust has insufficient assets to satisfy the indemnification obligation. Under the UPC the third parties would suffer the loss to the extent the trust is inadequate to pay all the contract obligations.

In some respects the rules with respect to the tort liability of trustees to third parties are similar to the contract rules. At common law, a trustee was liable personally to third parties for torts committed in the course of trust administration to the same extent as if the trustee had owned the trust property individually. For these purposes, the principle of respondeat superior applied. Thus, the trustee also was responsible if a tort was committed in the administration of a trust by an employee or agent of the trustee. These rules applied regardless of whether the trustee violated any fiduciary duties in acting or in failing to act and regardless of a provision in the trust instrument purporting to exonerate the trustee from personal liability for torts committed in the course of trust administration.

Again, the trustee may be entitled to indemnification from the trust estate, but only if the tort liability was incurred by the trustee without fault. And again, state laws like UPC §7-306 reverse the common law rule. In a UPC jurisdiction, for example, a trustee is not personally liable for torts committed in the course of trust administration unless the trustee personally was at fault. So, for example, imagine that an asset of a trust that the trust instrument authorizes T to operate is an apartment complex. An employee hired by T to maintain the property negligently causes injury to a tenant. Under the common law T is personally liable to the tenant and may be indemnified from the trust. On the other hand, T is not personally liable under a statute like the UPC. Instead, the tenant's claim is against T only in a representative capacity as trustee of the trust. The important point is that any recovery will be limited to the trust assets.

Finally, under the Comprehensive Environmental Response, Compensation, and Liability Act (CERCLA), landowners and others can be held liable for the costs of cleaning up property contaminated by hazardous substances. The liability can be staggering in amount (many millions of dollars) and, generally, it is joint and several among those parties responsible for the clean-up costs (although there are rights of contribution). A very serious issue facing trustees and personal representatives has been whether they could be held personally liable for the trust or estate's share of the clean-up costs if the assets of the trust or estate were insufficient. In a landmark decision, *City of Phoenix v. Garbage Services Co.*, 827 F. Supp. 600 (D. Ariz. 1993) held that a trustee could be personally liable for CERCLA clean-up costs under certain circumstances. Widespread attention to *City of Phoenix* resulted in a 1996 amendment to CERCLA that exempts most garden-variety fiduciaries from most sources of personal CERCLA liability attributable to assets held in a fiduciary capacity (although all assets of the fiduciary entity may be subject to CERCLA liability). Among other reasons, however, this exemption from personal liability will not apply if the fiduciary's own negligence caused or contributed to the environmental tort.

### Cotrustees' Liability

One last point illustrates why using cotrustees often is not a savvy solution to one or another potential actor being deficient in one manner or skill or another. Cotrustees each have responsibility for 100 percent of the administration of the trust and they share joint and several liability for each trustee's breaches of fiduciary duty. As a result, knowledgeable trustees who serve with cotrustees each will charge a full trustee's fee, rather than dividing a single trustee's fee among them. In fact, because of the added work and responsibility of serving with a cotrustee (in terms of monitoring its activities), in some circumstances a professional trustee will charge more for serving as a cotrustee than to serve as sole trustee. This merely encourages the use of special purpose advisors or other "unofficial" participants to fill the gaps in the abilities or sensibilities of the one person best (but not perfectly) suited to be the fiduciary. Examples include investment or insurance advisors and distribution directors whose advice the fiduciary is to consider or is required to follow, all with appropriate indemnification and exoneration for errors attributable to the unofficial actor. This authorized or mandated delegation is permissible and may be more wise than naming cofiduciaries, none of whom is well suited for all of the fiduciary administration.

Under UTC §703(f) the general rule is that one trustee is not liable for actions taken by another trustee. By an exception in §703(g), however, each trustee must exercise reasonable care to prevent a cotrustee from committing, and to compel a cotrustee to redress, any serious breach of trust. In addition, each trustee must participate in the performance of any trustee function, and may not delegate to another trustee the performance of any function, that the settlor reasonably expected the trustees to perform jointly. UTC §703(c) and (e). Thus, there is a substantial risk that a trustee will be liable for actions taken by a cotrustee even under the UTC.

CHAPTER 19

# WEALTH TRANSFER TAXATION[*]

The federal and state tax rules that apply on the transfer of wealth are hardly central to your study of the state law that applies to the transmission of wealth at death or inter vivos, which is the primary focus of this book. Nevertheless, to give you an overview of how these taxes affect the estate plan in everyday situations, included here is a bare-bones summary of the primary rules and concepts under the federal wealth transfer taxes. Please note that a growing number of states have their own separate wealth transfer taxes (mostly just estate or inheritance taxes) but the state systems do not follow a general pattern. So it largely is necessary to ignore state death taxes in this material and focus entirely on the federal excise on the transfer of wealth, either inter vivos or at death. There are plenty of refinements to the following incomplete and cursory material of which an expert would want to be aware. So be prepared to do much more study when or if the time comes to invade the domain of tax sensitive estate planning.

Because of the way the Internal Revenue Code is structured, this material covers in the following order the estate tax inclusion rules, then the estate tax deduction rules, then the estate tax computation requirements, followed by the gift tax and then the generation-skipping transfer tax. This is not, necessarily, the most intuitive method of learning these rules, and it is not the way the Internal Revenue Code (IRC or Code) is oriented.

## Inclusion in the Gross Estate

A decedent's estate for wealth transfer tax purposes typically is different from and greater than the decedent's estate for state law probate purposes. The reason is simple. Many assets that pass at a decedent's death by will substitute are includible in the decedent's "gross estate" for tax purposes. See Chapter 6.

### §2033: the Probate Estate

Includible in a decedent's gross estate for estate tax purposes (meaning subject to tax) under §2033 is "all property to the extent of [the] decedent's interest at death." This means that a decedent's "walk-around" wealth is subject to tax at death. Think of this as the probate estate provision. What you own and pass under your will or by intestacy is includible under §2033.

Assets that arise at or after death are not §2033 includible. A simple illustration is the proceeds of a life insurance policy on the life of the decedent. (As discussed below, life insurance proceeds may, however, be includible in the gross estate for estate tax purposes under §2042.)

Similarly, assets that terminate at death are not includible under §2033. An example is property in which the decedent owned only a life estate measured by the decedent's own life, meaning that at death nothing remains of the decedent's entitlement to be transferred to others, and none of the value of the property producing the income is includible under §2033. However, the value of any income paid to the decedent during life and that increased the decedent's net worth at death *is* §2033 includible. Also note that the remainder following a life estate may be §2033 includible in the remainder beneficiary's gross estate, even if death precedes the life tenant, depending on whether the remainder was vested or contingent. If there is no stated or implied condition of survivorship the vested remainder would be includible, measured by the full value of the property reduced by the outstanding value of the remaining life estate (determined under actuarial tables that estimate the value of the life estate for the life tenant's remaining life). A special provision in the Code prevents having to pay the tax on a remainder interest until the prior interest terminates and the remainder becomes possessory.

Only assets that exist before and that survive the decedent's death are includible in the decedent's gross estate under §2033. Even then inclusion is not guaranteed. For example, beneficial ownership is required. Just legal title alone is not enough to require inclusion if the decedent was holding the legal title on behalf of someone else. We will see that in some cases the title as trustee could cause inclusion, but not under the bare-bones ownership inclusion provision of §2033.

Assets that arise as of (or because of) death are includible under §2033 if two tests are met: (1) there was a legal entitlement at death, and (2) the interest was transmissible by the decedent. One of two common examples of assets that arise because of death is a death benefit payable under an employee benefit plan only in the event of death. Under caselaw defeating the government's efforts to require inclusion of these benefits, the standard has developed that inclusion is avoided if the plan specifies the recipient (or precludes the employee from designating the beneficiary). An illustration of such death benefit only amounts are Social Security survivorship benefits payable to certain family members under Federal law and not subject to change by the decedent.

A second asset that arguably fits into this category of nonincludible wealth that arises as of or because of death is a wrongful death recovery. These come in two varieties. In a Lord Campbell Act (Death Act) state, the right of recovery is an original cause of action in the decedent's surviving family members for their loss caused by the defendant's tort. Any recovery is their property compensating them for their loss. It never belonged to or compensates the decedent. This form of recovery clearly is not includible. In a Connecticut Act (Survival Act) jurisdiction, the cause of action belongs to the decedent for his or her own loss and "survives" death to be prosecuted by the decedent's personal representative. The issue with these recoveries is whether the entitlement arose soon enough to be owned by the decedent as of the requisite moment of death, such that these recoveries are includible. Federal caselaw has determined that the answer is no, although the real rationale of the courts is that there should be symmetry among the Death Act and Survival Act recoveries and the former clearly are beyond the reach of the tax statute.

### Valuation

The valuation of includible property is a different issue than includibility. It is addressed by §§2031, 2032, and 2032A. The base rule is §2031, which includes the value of property "at the time of [the] decedent's death." Unless a special rule is applicable, the includible value is the property's "fair market value." Treas. Reg. §20.2031-1(b) defines this as the price at which an asset would change hands between a willing buyer and a willing seller, (1) based on a reasonable knowledge of all relevant facts, (2) both parties acting without compulsion, and (3) with the property being valued at its highest and best use, regardless of its actual use.

### Alternate Valuation

Under §2032 a taxpayer may elect an alternate valuation of includible property at the first to occur of six months after the decedent's death or an earlier postmortem disposition of the property. This provision was adopted following the stock market crash in 1929 because some decedents lost so much value between the date of death and the time for filing their estate tax returns (now nine months after death) that they did not have enough wealth remaining to pay the estate tax on the date of death value of the stock.

### Special Use Valuation

A reduced "special use" valuation of realty used in farming or in a trade or business is permitted by §2032A. This targeted relief provision allows qualified property to be taxed at its actual use versus its highest and best use. It is illustrated by comparing the value of farmland that sits in the path of urban development. As a crop generating asset it might be worth $2,000 per acre, but as the next subdivision it might fetch $20,000 per acre. If elaborate qualification rules are met, the actual use value of $2,000 per acre is used. The definition of farming is much broader than you might imagine and realty used in a business also can qualify for this politically popular provision.

### Special Valuation Rules

For gift tax purposes §§2701 and 2702 apply a very specialized valuation that may have a residual effect at death. The very highly technical application of these provisions places them well beyond this introductory summary.

### Determining Value

Methods to ascertain value include (1) actual sales of identical or comparable assets, (2) capitalization of earnings from the includible property, and (3) the purchase or replacement cost of the asset (not its lower liquidation value), which sometimes is referred to as the retail cost or the auction price. In each case, value is determined using the facts as of the date of death or the alternate valuation date, depending on whether §2031 is applicable or §2032 was elected.

The value of an asset included in a decedent's gross estate (or gifted during life) may reflect an adjustment from the value initially determined if one or more of a variety of circumstances exist. For example, large holdings may qualify for a blockage discount, meaning that if the decedent tried to unload the entire block held at death the market value would be depressed because there is not enough demand to absorb that amount of supply. To illustrate, assume D owned 400,000 of the 1 million shares of outstanding stock of ABC, Inc., a publicly traded company. The stock was trading for $10 per share on the date of D's death. If the personal representative of D's estate attempted to sell all 400,000 shares immediately, the blockage discount question is whether the market could absorb them without causing the price per share to fall. Like substantially all valuation questions, this is a question of fact and the opinions of expert appraisers, sometimes for the government as well as the taxpayer, frequently are determinative.

Control blocks of stock or similar interests may command a premium valuation because willing buyers would pay extra to be in control. For example, if the market price for a share of stock is $10, a buyer might pay $11 per share for a block of stock that represents control of the company. And on the flip side, minority interests in a closely held business may qualify for a discount because the buyer is not able to exercise control over the entity and has little opportunity to manage or govern the investment.

In addition, a discount may be available for illiquidity because an interest in a closely held business is not readily marketable. For example, consider D, who died owning 30% of the outstanding stock of XYZ, Inc., a closely held business. The value of the business as a whole on the date of D's death is determined to be $5,000,000. Because D's 30% minority interest is not readily marketable, its value might be discounted by (for example) 35% from its proportionate share of the value of the business as a whole. As such the value of D's 30% interest in XYZ, Inc. would be $975,000 rather than $1,500,000. [$5,000,000 × 30% = $1,500,000 × 35% = $525,000; $1,500,000 - 525,000 = $975,000.] Much current estate planning is directed at attempting to qualify for such discounts.

Similarly, fractional interests in certain assets are entitled to a discount that reflects the reduced marketability of something like an undivided half interest in Blackacre. These discounts often are in the 15 to 25% range, meaning that if Blackacre was worth $200,000 when the decedent died, and the decedent owned an undivided half interest in it, the decedent's half might have a value of $75,000 to $85,000, not $100,000.

A buy-sell agreement may peg values for federal estate tax purposes if it (1) sets a reasonable and bona fide price, based on facts and circumstances at the time of the agreement, regardless of the facts that exist and that inform value at the applicable valuation date; (2) obligates the decedent to sell; a simple option to sell will not suffice to lock in value, although it may be evidence probative of value; and (3) does not run afoul of §2703, which restricts the effect of a buy-sell agreement to establish value as between family members.

Treas. Reg. §20.7520 contains tables to value temporal interests: life estates, terms of years, remainder interests, and annuities. Value is based on life expectancy and income yield assumptions, and these kinds of split interests must be valued under these tables unless death is clearly imminent due to an incurable physical condition that is in an advanced state (meaning that there is a greater than 50% chance that death will occur within one year). Unless the exception is applicable, taxpayers and the government alike must use the predictions of value under the tables rather than wait to determine the actual yield and duration of such an interest.

Assets sold during estate administration may qualify for a Treas. Reg. §20.2053-3(d)(2) selling expense deduction that effectively reduces the amount includible to the liquidation value received in the sale rather than a higher replacement cost. But lacking an actual sale, the government's position is that replacement cost must be used to value an asset. For example, if you would pay $20,000 for a used car off the dealer's lot but it would fetch only $16,500 if you tried to sell it *to* that dealer, the replacement cost of $20,000 defines the amount includible. If the car *actually* is sold during administration of the estate the $16,500 liquidation value would apply by indirection, the differential being a deduction from the includible $20,000 value (if the requirements of §2053 are met). More on this at page 440.

Alternate valuation under §2032 presents the opportunity to value an asset six months after death (or upon an earlier disposition, meaning that the personal representative no longer is in control of the asset because it is not part of the estate; a mere change in the form of the asset will not toll the valuation date). Required is valuation of the same interest that was held at death, using facts and circumstances at the alternate valuation date. A change in the asset (such as replacement of includible stock with that of another corporation) could not be reflected in this valuation regime. But assume D's car was destroyed during administration of the estate. It is a total loss (there is no residual value and no insurance). The personal representative's alternative approaches to valuation and claiming the loss for income and estate tax purposes include (1) inclusion at the date of death value of the automobile and deduction of the loss for estate tax purposes under §2054, (2) inclusion at the date of death value and deduction for income tax purposes under §165, or (3) inclusion at the alternate value. Depending on a slew of other factors, any of the three alternatives might be preferable in any given case. That decision is just one of a number of postmortem estate planning elections that face a personal representative, attributable to the tax laws. Among other factors, postmortem estate planning must consider that distributions during probate administration will trigger the alternate valuation disposition rule if distribution occurs within six months of the decedent's death.

Under alternate valuation, changes due to the mere lapse of time (for example, a life estate that becomes less valuable over time) are not considered in determining value on the alternate valuation date. For example, assume Decedent (D) owned the remainder following a life estate in X. At death the underlying assets subject to the life estate were worth $130,000. Six months later their value was $100,000. At D's death X was closest to the age of 50 years. On the alternate valuation date six months later X was closer to the age of 51. The remainder interest factor for these ages under Treas. Reg. §20.7520 is .15 and .16 respectively. For alternate valuation purposes the change in value to $100,000 could be reflected in valuing D's interest, but not the change in the factor based on X's change in age, meaning that the estate tax value would be .15 × $100,000 (not .16 × $100,000) rather than the date of death value of .15 × $130,000. Note also that valuation of a temporal interest like these involves an interest factor that changes monthly and that factor may be updated when alternate valuation is selected.

To qualify for alternate valuation (1) the value of the estate must decrease and (2) estate and generation-skipping taxes payable by the estate also must decline. This latter requirement is designed to prevent a nontaxable estate from intentionally electing a higher alternate valuation to generate a higher basis for income tax purposes. That form of abuse also would be harmless to an estate that passes to charity or to a surviving spouse and qualifies for the charitable or marital deductions.

### The String Provisions

Certain inter vivos transfers may be includible in the transferor's gross estate at death. When that happens a mechanism effectively treats the transfer as if it never occurred during life. These transfers are includible under §§2035-2038, which sometimes are referred to as the "string" provisions because they look to see whether some form of enjoyment or control was retained (i.e., whether the gift was made "with strings attached"), or otherwise whether circumstances are such that the transfer should be disregarded. Each section applies to an inter vivos transfer for less than full and adequate consideration in money or money's worth, upon which the decedent as transferor may have paid a gift tax. Notwithstanding this treatment, application of these sections at death does not constitute double taxation, because of a "purge and credit" mechanism found in §2001(b).

To illustrate, assume the taxpayer (T) made an inter vivos transfer of $200,000 that will be subject to §2036(a)(2) inclusion (e.g., T conveyed property in trust and retained the ability to direct who among T's descendants would receive benefits from the trust). At death T's remaining estate includible under §2033 is $1,800,000. For estate tax purposes, the $200,000 inter vivos transfer will be ignored (i.e., it will not be included in the estate tax calculation as an adjusted taxable gift) and the §2036(a)(2) inclusion will result in the taxable estate being regarded as $2 million. Had there been no §2036(a)(2) inclusion, the same $200,000 gift would have been part of the adjusted taxable gift base for computing T's estate tax liability, and you might question why the estate tax rule is needed. The answer is valuation. If the transferred property grew in value between the time of the gift and T's death, the higher value would be included at death and the lower value would be purged from the gift tax base. The assumption is that values go up rather than down, because when these rules were created that was the assumed strategic advantage in making inter vivos transfers. Recognize that this is a two-edged sword, that in some cases the opposite is true, and that today such "estate freezing" gifts no longer serve the same purpose. We will explore those notions more when we study the gift tax and advantages of making gifts. See page 453.

### *§2035: The Three Year Rule*

Gone is a pre-1976 law that contained a rebuttable presumption that assets transferred within three years of death were testamentary in character and therefore includible in the gross estate. In its place is the present, absolute rule of §2035(a), coupled with a "gross up" rule in §2035(b). This straightforward "gross up" rule requires the decedent's estate to include all gift taxes paid by the decedent (or the decedent's estate) on any transfer made within three years of death. This avoids the so-called "DuPont effect" that takes advantage of the "tax exclusive" calculation of the gift tax, as compared to the "tax inclusive" calculation of the estate tax, both as discussed at page 453.

The rest of §2035 is not so pristine. For example, the key to §2035(a) is knowing whether a property interest transferred within three years before death has a much lower value inter vivos than it would cause to be included at death. If the answer is yes (technically, if the interest were retained and would cause inclusion under any of §§2036, 2037, 2038, or 2042), then §2035(a) is applicable to treat the inter vivos transfer made within three years of death as if it did not occur. Regarding the rest of §2035, a sophisticated analysis would inquire whether the decedent's estate seeks to qualify for nondividend treatment on a §303 stock redemption postmortem, for §2032A special use valuation, or for installment payment of estate tax under §6166, in which case further applications under §2035(c) are germane, but for our overview purposes there is no need to get into that complexity. There also is a §2035(d) full and adequate consideration exception that operates under special rules that make it very unlikely ever to be met, and two valuation rules that are worth knowing.

One is that §2035 includes the value at death of the transferred asset, less any consideration received on the transfer and any value received after the transfer that is attributable to the donee's own activities and contributions. In either case the objective is taxation as if no transfer had been made. The other is a completely wrong minded rule that income earned after the transfer but before death is not brought back into the transferor's gross estate (although stock on stock dividends may be and stock split shares definitely will be; recall our discussion of accessions in Chapter 9). This is error because, had the transfer not been made, the income would have been received by the transferor and that income would have increased the transferor's gross estate at death.

For lack of a better place to address it, also note another proximate to death rule that is somewhat the exact opposite of the §2035 three year rule. This is §1014(e), which applies for income tax purposes to transfers made within one year of a *donee's* death (not the donor's). The intent of making a gift to a dying individual is to cause inclusion in their gross estate at death (especially if they will pay no estate tax, because their estate is too small or qualifies for the marital deduction) and obtain the §1014 new basis at death for income tax capital gain computation purposes. The result of §1014(e) is denial of this new basis if the gifted asset passes back to the donor (or to the donor's spouse) when the donee dies. Just think of this second "transfer proximate to death" provision as designed to prevent another near death transfer abuse.

### §2036(a)(1): Retained Interests

Inter vivos transfers with retained controls or rights may cause the value of transferred property to be §2036(a) includible at death. Involved in §2036(a)(1) is a lifetime transfer with retained enjoyment for any of three periods: (1) for life (e.g., to X following a life estate in the taxpayer); (2) for a period that cannot be determined without reference to death (e.g., to X one week prior to the taxpayer's death); or (3) for a period that does not end before death (e.g., to X in 40 years, and the taxpayer was age 85 when the transfer was made and dies at age 90).

Also reached by §2036(a) are secondary life estates or retained interests (e.g., life estate to X, then to taxpayer for life, remainder to Y; this different situation would be relevant if the taxpayer predeceases X). In addition, the transfer with retention may be by indirection or agreement, which may be implied or unenforceable. A simple example would be a transfer of your house to your children, who just happen to allow you to continue to reside there until your death, notwithstanding that there was no formal reservation of a life estate or deed from them back to you. In addition, there are other more formal rules that may apply.

The paradigm illustration of this is Husband who creates a trust for Wife for life, remainder to X. Meanwhile Wife creates a trust for Husband for life, remainder also to X. This can trigger a "reciprocal trust" doctrine. Under it, if the parties (e.g., Husband and Wife) are in the same economic position as if each had created the trust the other created, the reciprocal trust doctrine applies to "uncross" the trusts and treat them as if each created the trust for their own benefit. The reversal of what they actually did occurs at the settlor level, meaning that Wife would be regarded as the settlor of the trust that Husband created for Wife's benefit, and Husband would be treated as the settlor of the trust Wife created for Husband's benefit. Thus, each would be regarded as having made a transfer with a retained life estate that would cause the property to be included in their gross estates under §2036(a)(1) at their respective deaths. If the trusts are of unequal size, the doctrine calls for inclusion of all of the smaller trust and a pro rata portion of the larger one.

To illustrate, assume:

| Transferor | | Beneficiary | Amount |
|---|---|---|---|
| H | ——Trust—— | W | $100,000 |
| W | ——Trust—— | H | $75,000 |

Here the smaller trust that W created for H would be treated as if H created it for H and 100% of it would be includible in H's gross estate at death. But the larger trust that H created for W would be treated as if W created it for W and this uncrossing would apply only to the extent of the 75% that represents mutual value at the time of creation. The remaining 25% would be respected as created by H.

The rationale for the reciprocal trust rule is based on the effect of the transfers, recognizing the adage that form should not prevail over substance. The test for application of the doctrine is simply whether the trusts were interrelated, meaning that they were substantially identical in terms and created at approximately the same time. And as shown in the example of unequal size trusts that will be uncrossed only in part, a given trust may have (or be treated as having) multiple contributions made by multiple individuals. For wealth transfer tax purposes each transferor will be regarded as having created a separate trust, and tracing of contributions is possible (although pro ration is proper if the identity of assets contributed is impossible to determine). To illustrate, if X contributed Blackacre and Y contributed IBM stock to a trust as to which each retained a life estate, those assets would be includible in their respective estates, and if those assets were sold but the proceeds were invested in identifiable assets, the replacement assets would be includible. On the other hand, if X contributed $10x and Y contributed $20x and the money was invested and reinvested so that no tracing is possible, inclusion to X would be ⅓ of the corpus at X's death.

The effect of retaining a discretionary income entitlement, as opposed to a mandatory distribution right, has been somewhat confused. If, for example, you retain only the opportunity to receive income if an independent trustee chooses to distribute any to you, the better reasoned result is that there is a sufficient retention to cause §2036(a)(1) to apply if your creditors may reach trust income under state law. Even with a spendthrift provision we know that under most state laws creditors could reach the full amount the trustee could distribute to you. See Chapter 13. So the courts likely will regard this as if you retained enjoyment of the entire trust income. But a court might accept an argument that all that should be includible is the amount of corpus needed to produce the limited amount of income that you might need. And Rev. Rul. 2004-64 highlighted the distinction between mandatory and discretionary distributions by an independent trustee and muddied these waters, particularly with respect to creditor protection trusts. As a result we are not sure what rules will apply to a discretionary trust in the future.

An additional area of uncertainty relates to trust distributions that could discharge your legal obligations. The Regulations suggest that you retain enjoyment by designating your dependent child as a beneficiary, because you have a legal obligation to support the child, that obligation is discharged by trust distributions to the child, and that makes you an indirect trust beneficiary. For reasons that are too involved for this discussion, the government's discharge of obligation theory is wrong and should be challenged, but it never has been and the only safe planning with respect to this provision is to draft so that distributions cannot be made that would have the effect of discharging the settlor's legal obligation of support. For more information see 2 Casner & Pennell, ESTATE PLANNING §7.1.1.10.1 (6th ed. 1999).

Let's consider one final quirk. If a taxpayer were to transfer an entire fee, first by conveying the remainder, followed by a gift of the retained life estate, the problem is that §2035(a)(2) could apply. If both transfers occur more than three years before the taxpayer's death, it will not matter that the transfer was in two stages. But §2035(a)(2) will apply and inclusion will result as if no transfer had been made if the second transfer was within three years of death. This means that getting it right by transferring the full fee simple in one step is important, especially because even a death bed no strings attached gift avoids §2035(a).

### *§2037: Reversionary Interests*

Like all the other string provisions, required for §2037 to apply is an inter vivos transfer for less than full and adequate consideration in money or money's worth. Meaning that this was a gift, usually subject to the gift tax, and again requiring the purge and credit mechanism of §2001(b)(2) to apply to avoid double taxation. In a §2037 case the retained interest that causes estate tax inclusion of transferred property is a reversion in corpus, either expressly reserved (not likely) or by operation of law (as in those future interest examples we studied in Chapter 15 in which there was a gap in the conveyance). Not subject to §2037 inclusion, however, is the mere possibility of inheriting from the donee.

This provision is different than §2033 inclusion of a retained reversion. Usually §2033 will apply (to the extent §2037 does not) because a reversion does not often meet all the requirements of §2037.

The additional §2037 requirement is that some other beneficiary's possession or enjoyment is contingent on surviving the decedent. For example, "O to X for life, and one year after X's death to Y, *if Y survives O.*" The one year reversion is a §2033 interest, but here the whole fee (less X's life estate) may be §2037 includible. Note, however, that the illustration of what is required shows why §2037 almost never applies. Instead, §2033 does in most cases in which a reversion is found. For example, "To S for life, remainder to C if living." Here there is no §2037 reversion because no one must survive the settlor to take. Instead, because there is a reversion, §2033 will require inclusion of its value, based on the actuarial likelihood that C will predecease S.

In addition, §2037 will apply only if the reversion (valued immediately before the decedent's death) is worth more than 5% of the value of the corpus in which the reversion exists. That is, based on the actuarial tables, there was at least a one-in-twenty chance of reverting to the decedent. The 5% requirement is measured against the portion that is contingent, which is the only part that is subject to §2037.

### §§2036(a)(2) and 2038(a)(1): Inter Vivos Transfers with Retained Powers

Involved here are retained powers to affect who (other than the decedent) will enjoy the benefits of property transferred inter vivos or when they will enjoy them. These provisions often are regarded as two peas from the same pod, and frequently they both will apply. In each case the theory that supports inclusion is that there are two benefits of wealth: personal enjoyment of it or control over someone else's enjoyment of it. We saw that §2036(a)(1) applies to the retention of personal enjoyment of it, and these two sections apply to retention of the other form of enjoyment: control over someone else's enjoyment. Notwithstanding their fundamental similarity (which may make you wonder why we need both provisions), there are several very important but sometimes subtle differences between these two provisions.

- For example, §2036(a)(2) involves a decedent's power to affect or designate the enjoyment of an interest that would cause §2036(a)(1) inclusion if enjoyed or retained by the decedent personally. The confusing aspect of this is that it only reaches powers to sprinkle, spray, or accumulate income, or control over the possession of nonincome producing corpus. A power affecting possession or enjoyment of income producing *corpus* is *not* subject to §2036(a)(2) (because retained possession or control of that income producing corpus — as opposed to its income — would not trigger §2036(a)(1)). Because this rule mirrors §2036(a)(1) enjoyment, the power also must exist for any of the periods that would cause §2036(a)(1) to apply (life, a period not ascertainable without reference to death, or a period that does not end before death).

- It is much easier to trigger §2038(a)(1). It involves a decedent's power to alter, amend, revoke, or terminate enjoyment of any interest that was transferred by the decedent. Simply a power to *prevent* enjoyment will suffice.

- "Retention" constitutes a difference between the two sections: §2036(a)(2) requires that the power was created by and retained by the decedent, but under §2038(a)(1) the source or manner of acquiring the power is irrelevant. So, for example, only §2038(a)(1) applies if a beneficiary with a power of appointment creates a power in the settlor to affect enjoyment of the property. To trigger §2036(a)(2) the settlor would have had to retain on creation of the trust the power to affect enjoyment. (Notice how the §2036(a)(2) rule trifles with the fiction for property law purposes that the exercise of a power of appointment merely involves the powerholder acting as the settlor's agent.)

- Another difference involves contingent or conditional powers, to which §2036(a)(2) can apply but §2038(a)(1) will not.

- The amount includible under each provision also can differ. Under §2036(a)(2), the amount includible is the amount that would be included if the decedent had retained a §2036(a)(1) enjoyment, being the full value of the portion spinning off the income that the decedent could control. Under §2038(a)(1), the amount includible is only the interest that is subject to the decedent's power. Thus, for example, a power to defer income would cause §2038(a)(1) inclusion of the value of the income interest. A power to alter the remainder beneficiary would cause §2038(a)(1) inclusion of the value of the remainder following whatever outstanding life estate cannot be altered.

There are a number of similarities between the two provisions as well:

- Both are inapplicable to the extent a transfer was for full and adequate consideration in money or money's worth.

- The existence of the power will suffice under each section, regardless of any inability (such as due to incompetence) to exercise it.

- The power to remove a trustee and appoint yourself is tantamount to having the trustee's powers. So is the power to remove and replace trustees at will, if the successor could be a related or subordinate party.

- Under each section joint powers and veto rights are the same as sole powers and direct powers to act.

- A power to merely alter the timing of enjoyment is sufficient under each provision.

- Discretion is required under each section. Thus, limiting the settlor's discretion with what is known as a definite external objective standard will protect against inclusion. We will consider an "ascertainable" standard in the context of powers of appointment and all you need to know here is that an ascertainable standard will serve this purpose as well. Because it is the more reliable of the two, the ascertainable standard is the "gold standard" for drafting. See page 435.

*United States v. Byrum*, 408 U.S. 125 (1972), and §2036(b) deal with an issue whether a transfer of stock with a retention of the voting rights is a §2036(a)(2) power for estate tax purposes. The Court said no and Congress disagreed by adopting §2036(b). It deals only with powers relating to a controlled corporation (meaning that the decedent had over 20% ownership at some point within three years of death). Thus, under §2036(b), retained voting rights over stock in a controlled corporation causes inclusion of the stock in the transferor's gross estate. Weird is that inclusion is under §2036(a)(1), not either of §2036(a)(2) or §2038(a)(1). The retained voting power is as if the settlor retained personal enjoyment and not control. Go figure — we cannot explain this.

### §2039: Retirement Benefits

Until 1984 retirement benefits were excluded. Today they are fully includible under §2039, which ostensibly applies to all annuities that survive the decedent owner's death. We totally lack guidance under this provision notwithstanding the passage of two decades since this 180 degree reversal in the rule. Suffice it to say that survivor annuities (those owned by the decedent that do not expire at death) are includible.

### §2040: Jointly Held Property

As a legal matter there are three times when joint tenancy or tenancy by the entirety property can be subject to wealth transfer tax: on creation or on termination during life, and at death. As a practical matter there almost never is inter vivos attention to these tax consequences, probably because the vast majority of concurrent ownership cases involve spouses and the event is nontaxable because of the unlimited gift tax marital deduction for spouses who are United States citizens. See page 448. So it is the testamentary element that is meaningful, and even then the marital deduction may eliminate any meaningful issues other than the income tax new basis at death rule (about which we are not primarily concerned in this Chapter).

The creation of a joint tenancy can be a taxable event for gift tax purposes, but not if the joint tenancy was unintentional (e.g., established for convenience) and no gift was intended. Alternatively, it is possible that a 100% gift was the intent, in which case a gift tax return may be required (but not likely to be filed). Intentional creation is a gift to the extent contributions are not equal, with possible application of §§2503 (annual exclusion) or 2523 (marital deduction) or both. Note, however, that the creation of a joint bank account with another does not constitute a gift unless and until the other person withdraws funds from the account with no obligation to account for the funds withdrawn.

To illustrate, D deposited $100,000 in a joint tenancy bank account with A, transferred title to Blackacre to D and D's spouse, S, as joint tenants with rights of survivorship, and transferred title to Whiteacre to D and A, as joint tenants with rights of survivorship. At the time of the transfers Blackacre and Whiteacre each had a fair market value of $100,000. The creation of the joint tenancy bank account with A was not a taxable gift because D could withdraw all of the funds from the account. Withdrawals by A for A's own use (and with no obligation by A to account for the withdrawals to D) would constitute taxable gifts. The transfer of Blackacre to D and S as joint tenants constituted a gift to S that qualified for the marital deduction and therefore was nontaxable. The transfer of Whiteacre to D and A as joint tenants constituted a gift to A of $50,000. Assuming no other gifts had been made by D to A during the year, $11,000 of the gift would be excluded from gift tax treatment by the gift tax annual exclusion.

Now consider that payment of a mortgage, taxes, expenses, or making improvements on a jointly held residence is a transfer subject to wealth transfer taxation if less than all tenants make the payments or they are made in proportions that do not match their contributions to ownership. Gracious! You can begin to understand why there is substantial noncompliance with the gift tax consequences of joint ownership. A gift also is made to the extent amounts received on inter vivos termination or distribution of jointly owned assets are less than the contribution made to acquire those assets (in each case using percentage ownership). So if X provided 50% of the consideration to acquire Blackacre but the proceeds from its sale are distributed 75% to co-owner Y, X would be making a gift of 25% on that distribution. If X had provided 75% of the consideration, there would have been a gift to Y at creation of 25%. A distribution of 50% to each on termination of the tenancy should not be another gift of 25%, but Y would be treated as having provided half the consideration only if X reported that original gift (which is not likely).

The estate tax consequences of a decedent's joint tenancy terminating at death will depend on how the tenancy was created and who the other tenants are. The §2040(a) rule is 100% inclusion of the full value of jointly held property (but not tenancy in common), subject to three exceptions.

- If the tenancy was created by a gift from a third party, whatever percentage ownership was designated by the donor is the portion includible in the deceased joint tenant's estate or, if no percentage was established by the donor, then only an equal share is includible. For example, D's parent, P, transferred Blackacre to D and D's siblings, B and S, as joint tenants with rights of survivorship. If P did not provide for unequal ownership by P's children, then on D's death one-third of the value of Blackacre will be included in D's gross estate. When either B or S next dies half will be includible. And when the survivor of the three dies §2033 will cause all of it to be includible. Overall this one property required 188% inclusion over the three lives, making it easy to see why joint tenancy with the right of survivorship is the single worst form of property ownership from a tax perspective.

- The second exception to 100% inclusion treatment for joint tenancy property is if the tenancy is a qualified joint interest, meaning a joint tenancy or tenancy by the entirety between only spouses. Only half is includible in the estate of the first spouse to die, and that half qualifies for the estate tax marital deduction. The net effect is that the new basis at death rule grants only a 50% basis increase (if the property has appreciated in value this is not as good a deal as if 100% were includible in the first spouse's estate, that full amount qualified for the estate tax marital deduction, and the survivor got a new basis in the entire property. So don't view the exception here as beneficial). Also note that total inclusion over both spouses' lives is: (1) 50% on creation, subject to the §2523 marital deduction; (2) 50% on the death of the first spouse to die, subject to the §2056 marital deduction; and (3) 100% on the surviving spouse's death or earlier disposition. Nothing was saved by the joint tenancy or tenancy by entireties ownership, and the basis result is worse than if the first spouse to die had held the entire title (again assuming the property has appreciated in value). To illustrate, assume that D owns Blackacre. Its fair market value is $100,000, but D's income tax basis in it is $20,000. If D devises Blackacre to D's spouse, S, it will be included in D's gross estate at $100,000 and S will obtain a new basis of $100,000 for income tax purposes. If, by contrast, D transfers title to Blackacre to D and S as joint tenants, at D's death $50,000 will be included in D's estate and S's basis would be only $60,000 (half of the original $20,000 basis plus half of the fair market value of the property at D's death).

- The third exception to full inclusion for joint tenancy property is if consideration was furnished for acquisition of the tenancy by the surviving tenant(s) (other than the decedent's surviving spouse). If so, the percent attributable to the survivor(s)' contributions (and not previously withdrawn) is not includible. For example, if Blackacre was purchased with the decedent's funds and title was taken in joint tenancy with J (not the decedent's spouse), 100% will be includible in the decedent's gross estate if the decedent dies first. If J were to die first, however, zero would be includible. The latter result looks pretty favorable, but remember that when the decedent dies second the full value of the property will be subject to inclusion (so there never is less than 100% inclusion in someone's estate). Moreover, if the decedent died first, 100% will be includible under §2033 on J's subsequent death or disposition of the property, which thus totals 200% subject to estate tax, depending on the order of deaths. That result again illustrates why jointly held property is the worst form of ownership for wealth transfer tax purposes.

This last consideration furnished rule requires attention to what qualifies as the separate consideration provided by a concurrent owner. For example, consideration that the surviving tenant acquired from the decedent for less than full and adequate consideration does not count if it is used by the surviving tenant to acquire a cotenancy with the decedent. If it did, the decedent would provide the consideration to the other co-owner and they together would acquire the property, changing its estate tax liability in the process. The tax system is not so easily jiggered. So, for example, assume that X gave Blackacre to Y, who subsequently transferred it into joint tenancy with X. When X dies first, 100% is includible because all of Y's consideration for the property ownership was acquired from X for less than full and adequate consideration in money or money's worth. Under the same facts, the result would be the very same even if Y sold Blackacre and used the proceeds to purchase Greenacre in joint tenancy with X.

There is an income earned exception, however, if the consideration furnished by a surviving tenant consisted of income earned on assets that had been given by the decedent to the surviving tenant. To illustrate, X gave IBM stock to Y and then Y, using dividends paid on that stock, purchased assets to be held in joint tenancy with X. When X dies none of that jointly held property would be includible in X's gross estate. Note that stock on stock dividends are not regarded as consideration furnished by the new holder of gifted stock. These are just a change in form of the underlying gifted stock. Thus, if the dividends used by Y to acquire jointly owned assets with X were dividends of IBM stock, instead of cash, they would not count as consideration furnished by Y. On X's death before Y the full value of the joint property would be includible in X's estate.

To make you more crazy, appreciation or gain on acquired consideration is clean consideration, counted as furnished by the new owner, provided that it was generated after acquisition and it was "realized" for income tax purposes (meaning there was a sale or exchange) before the new acquisition. Finally, improvements and additions paid for by the surviving cotenant may count as consideration furnished (depending on the source of the funds used by that surviving concurrent owner).

### §2041: Powers of Appointment

The reach of §2041 is to include property that the decedent never owned and never will. Instead, this property was subject to the decedent's general power of appointment, which may include:

- Powers to appoint property to the powerholder-decedent personally, to the powerholder's estate, or to creditors of either. In this respect, recall the property law definitions of powers of appointment and that the tax definition has been embraced for property law purposes by the Restatement (Third) of Property — Wills and Other Donative Transfers. See Chapter 14.

- Powers to withdraw are the same as a power to appoint to yourself and this also constitutes a general power of appointment. Also see Chapter 14.

- Powers to amend, if the powerholder may benefit personally.

- Certain other powers to indirectly benefit the powerholder personally, such as the power to appoint property to discharge a legal obligation of the powerholder-decedent (or so the government asserts, subject to the same defective theory noted at page 427).

Given their tax consequences, there are few reasons to create a taxable general power of appointment. One is to qualify for the §2056(b)(5) marital deduction in a trust that grants the surviving spouse all income annually for life and a general power of appointment. We will study this beginning at page 447. Another is to satisfy the §2503(c)(2)(B) qualified minor's trust exception requirement, or to constitute an interest in trust as qualifying as a present interest by granting a power of withdrawal (a *Crummey* power). See pages 458 and 457, respectively.

A third is to avoid generation-skipping transfer tax by intentionally incurring the estate or gift tax instead. Often there is a better way to accomplish this desirable objective, and also note that sometimes it is preferable to *incur* the generation-skipping tax. This is *way* beyond our introductory study.

A final reason to create a taxable general power is because the settlor wanted to give a beneficiary a right of withdrawal over a trust rather than forcing a mandatory distribution. Note that, with this one exception, general powers of appointment are the requisite "pay back" for a tax benefit given to the creator of the power. This final reason is just a wise alternative to what many thoughtless planners do (mandatory force-out distribution), as discussed in Chapter 14.

It is termination of a general power at death that is taxable under §2041. And possession of a general power (as opposed to the physical or mental ability to exercise it) will suffice to cause this §2041 inclusion. Exceptions to §2041 apply if the power was limited by an ascertainable standard (i.e., related to health, education, maintenance, or support), or the power was a joint power (or consent was required) in certain unlikely circumstances. Please be careful to note that the lifetime "five or five" limitation of §2514(e) (discussed at page 56) affords no estate tax protection with respect to a power that has not lapsed before death. This means that the amount subject to a power of withdrawal that has not yet lapsed is includible in the powerholder's estate, notwithstanding that the power is limited appropriately by the requisite $5,000 or 5% parameters and could lapse tax free during life. Read carefully §2041(b)(2), which only relates to an inter vivos lapse, *not* to lapse of such powers still available at the date of death.

To illustrate this last point, assume X transferred property to T in trust for the life of D. D may withdraw up to $20,000 per year but D does not exercise the power and the trust is worth $450,000 at D's death. Here the lifetime power of withdrawal is protected from untoward tax consequences on each year's lapse of the power by the 5% limitation under §2514(e), but that limitation is no protection at death and the amount subject to D's withdrawal on the date of death is includible.

Let's try a number of other examples that illustrate the §2041 consequences of a variety of powers of appointment.

First, assume that X transferred property to T in trust for the life of D. On D's death the property is distributable to such of D's children as D shall appoint. This is not a general power of appointment, because D may not appoint the property to D, D's estate, or the creditors of either. Thus, §2041 will not cause inclusion of the trust corpus in D's gross estate.

Next, assume that X transferred property to T in trust for the life of D. On D's death the property is distributable to such person or persons as

D shall appoint. This power is unlimited in scope and thus may be exercised in favor of D's estate or the creditors of D or D's estate. As such it will trigger inclusion in D's gross estate. Similarly, if X transferred property to T in trust for the life of D and provided that during D's life T shall distribute so much or all of the principal as D directs, this power also is unlimited in scope and is a general power of appointment, exercisable inter vivos but that will terminate at D's death and therefore also will cause estate tax inclusion.

Now let's consider a harder case. X transferred property to T in trust for the life of D. During D's life T shall distribute so much or all of the principal as D directs for D's "support, comfort, maintenance, or education." This power is limited by a standard (support, comfort, maintenance, or education) that arguably is not "ascertainable" (comfort is the term the regulations regard as too broad) but that some case law holds is sufficiently restricted. So there could be litigation over the estate tax inclusion of the trust corpus, and a prudent drafter would not use the arguably offensive term. If D's power was limited to directing distributions for D's "health, education, maintenance, and support" it would be limited by an ascertainable standard and would not cause inclusion at D's death.

Finally, a controversial example. X transferred property to D in trust for the life of D. During D's life D shall distribute so much or all of the principal to D or D's children as D deems necessary for the "health, education, support, or maintenance in reasonable comfort of any one or more of the class of beneficiaries," and all D's children are minors at the date of D's death. Here the quoted standard governing distributions is ascertainable. There would be no general power treatment if the power allowed D to appoint only for D's personal benefit. Unfortunately, the government's position here is that the power is also for D's *indirect* benefit through the ability to "discharge D's legal obligation of support" to D's children, and that the ascertainable standard is no protection. The logic of this last assertion is that an ascertainable standard only works if it relates exclusively to the needs of the powerholder. It is the discharge of obligation theory that is wrong in this treatment, because state law in most jurisdictions would not support the notion that distributions from the trust would have that effect, but that concept has never been presented by a taxpayer and no case under §2041 has ever considered it. See 2 Casner & Pennell, ESTATE PLANNING §7.1.1.10.1 (6th ed. 1999). So for the time being it would be best to consider this a general power for planning purposes and avoid it using a provision that precludes any distribution that would have the effect of discharging D's legal obligation to support the children.

### §2042: Proceeds of Life Insurance

The rule governing the inclusion of life insurance proceeds consists of two parts, numbered unlike the other estate tax rules (§2042(1) and (2), rather than (a) and (b)). Don't ask why. The easy rule is §2042(1), which requires inclusion of insurance proceeds under a policy on the life of the decedent to the extent payable to the insured-decedent's estate or available (even if they were not utilized) for payment of estate expenses, debts, or taxes. Much more detailed is §2042(2), which requires inclusion of insurance proceeds under a policy on the life of the decedent if the decedent possessed "incidents of ownership" over the insurance policy at any time within three years of death, regardless of to whom the proceeds were payable.

Incidents of ownership constitute economic enjoyment, benefit, or control over the policy or its proceeds, including powers:

- To change the beneficiary or the settlement option (the terms under which the proceeds are payable, such as in a lump sum, an annuity, a life estate and remainder, or other options).
- To surrender or cancel the policy.
- To assign, borrow against, or pledge the policy for a loan.
- To veto the exercise of incidents of ownership exercisable by another person, or jointly held incidents.
- An arguably closely related power to terminate employment is not itself an incident, even if it would cause termination of coverage because the insurance is employee group term coverage.

Note that a right to receive policy dividends is not an incident of ownership because dividends are regarded as excess premiums paid that the company did not need and therefore refunded, and the payment of premiums is not an incident of ownership in its own right (so getting some back also is not an incident).

As with a general power of appointment or §§2036 and 2038 powers, the mere existence or possession of incidents alone will suffice to cause inclusion, regardless of the actual physical or mental ability to exercise them. Incidents held by the insured in a fiduciary capacity (for example, as trustee of a trust that holds the insurance) has generated a long history of conflict that culminated in Rev. Rul. 84-179, which many casual observers believe eliminates the issue. Because it contains three caveats, wise planners will not name the insured to be fiduciary of a trust or an estate that holds insurance on the life of the insured.

Similarly, corporate owned incidents can be imputed to a decedent who controls the corporation through stock ownership. The developed rule is that incidents will not be imputed to the decedent to the extent the proceeds are payable to the corporation. Instead, the proceeds will increase the value of the business, which will indirectly increase the value of the decedent's stock ownership. Otherwise, a controlling shareholder will be deemed to possess the corporation's incidents of ownership to the extent the proceeds are payable to a third party (not the corporation). Finally, there is limited authority that a partnership will be treated essentially like a corporation for purposes of these rules, with the twist that one of several general partners will be deemed to be in control for purposes of imputing the partnership's incidents to the insured.

Don't lose sight of the reality that §2042 inclusion is about policies of insurance on the life of the decedent. Policies not on the decedent's life but that the decedent owned at death (on the life of someone else) are §2033 assets, includible not under §2042 at the face amount of the proceeds but, instead, at their value like any other asset (what you would pay to replace the policy — the single premium value, essentially).

Recall that the three year rule in §2035(a)(2) applies to insurance that is subject to §2042. So, a transfer of a policy on the insured's life, made within three years of the insured's death, will require inclusion of 100% of the proceeds paid at death. A limited exception applies, however, if someone other than the insured pays some premiums after the transfer. The unexpected *"Silverman"* rule is that only a pro rata portion of the proceeds are includible, with the excludible portion being represented by the portion of the total premiums paid by someone else compared to the total premiums paid on the policy. A transfer of the incidents of a policy more than three years before the insured's death is immune to estate tax if there are no incidents of ownership at death and no payment to the insured's estate. Payment of premiums by the decedent is irrelevant. The premium payment issue applies only if death occurs within the three year period of §2035(d)(2). And with respect to yearly renewable term insurance, each year's premium payment is not a new transfer, if the policy is automatically renewable. Otherwise, an irrevocable transfer more than three years before death is deemed to apply each year to a newly purchased policy represented by the annual renewal, with the three year rule applicable to each newly purchased policy.

### §2043: Consideration

Concepts about full and adequate consideration in money or money's worth are relevant at several points in the wealth transfer tax law. For example, as we've seen already, transfers for full and adequate consideration in money or money's worth are not subject to the string provisions in §§2035-2038. The question raised in that and other contexts is what constitutes full and adequate consideration in money or money's worth. Further, it is critical to know that consideration must be full and adequate. A peppercorn (or an amount even a peppercorn shy) will not do. Whether consideration in a given case is full and adequate is a fact question that may turn on sophisticated expert valuation testimony, depending on the circumstances.

Under §2516, which defines consideration for both gift and estate tax purposes, a spouse's support rights are consideration. Plus incorporation of an agreement for support or property settlement into a decree by a court with power to alter the terms of the agreement may constitute the agreed terms as valid consideration. We will visit the specifics again at page 455 under the gift tax discussion. In addition, here are three additional estate tax concepts relating to consideration. One is that obligations incurred during life for full and adequate consideration may be deductible under §2053(c)(1)(A).

A second is that it is important to measure full and adequate consideration against only interest(s) that are transferred. So, for example, if all the decedent transferred was a life estate in property, the consideration that would need to be full and adequate should be measured only against the value of the life estate and not the full fee simple absolute in the property. In such a case, however, §2702 may be applicable, in which case full and adequate consideration would be measured against the full value of the transferred property because that would be the amount of the deemed transfer for gift tax purposes. And *United States v. Allen*, 293 F.2d 916 (10th Cir. 1961), holds that full and adequate to avoid §2035(a) means an amount equal to what would be includible if no transfer were made. So, to avoid the three year rule on a transfer close to death of a §2036(a)(1) retained life estate would require sale for the full value of the otherwise includible trust, *not* just for the de minimis remaining value of the life estate at that near death moment.

The third concept is the "consideration offset" rule in §2043(a), which amounts to a deduction from the gross estate if consideration was received as part of a transfer that nevertheless is subject to estate tax inclusion (for example, because the consideration was not full and adequate). This rule reduces the amount includible by the amount of any inadequate consideration received, because we shouldn't ignore the transfer for estate tax purposes by inclusion of the transferred property, and then *respect* the same transfer by including the consideration that was received for the transfer. There is a disconcerting aspect of this rule, however, that can produce inequity. Inclusion is at the federal estate tax value of the transferred property (meaning any appreciation or depreciation during the period between the transfer and death is reflected), but the offset reduction is at the value of the consideration received, valued at the time of the transfer, not the federal estate tax value of the consideration received. This means that any appreciation or depreciation in the consideration received is *not* purged the way the underlying consideration is.

To illustrate, assume that §2036(a)(2) reaches a transfer of property that was worth $100,000 during life at the time of the transfer. Consideration of $60,000 was paid and this is inadequate to preclude application of §2036(a)(2). Also assume that the federal estate tax value of the transferred property is $150,000 and that the consideration also has grown 50% in value to $90,000. The consideration is owned at death and that $90,000 is §2033 includible. The §2036(a)(2) amount includible is the full $150,000 value of the transferred asset. And the reduction under the §2043(a) consideration offset rule is $60,000 because that was the value of the consideration at the time of the transfer. This means that the growth in both assets is includible in the estate, which is a totally wrong rule in policy. This is the law because of an "anti-tracing" rule designed to avoid having to identify the consideration received, as it may exist or may have been invested and reinvested between the date of the transfer and the date of death.

### Deductions from the Gross Estate

Deductible from the gross estate are funeral and administration expenses, debts, losses, gifts to charity, gifts to a surviving spouse, and death taxes paid to any state.

### *§§2053 and 2054: Deductions for Losses, Debts, and Expenses*

Losses due to casualty or theft that occur during the period of administration are deductible under §2054, but only to the extent they are neither compensated by insurance nor reflected in the alternate valuation of the asset. In estates large enough to be taxable it is uncommon to be uninsured and this deduction seldom is encountered.

Debts and expenses are deductible under §2053, which is the workhorse deduction of the entire estate tax because every estate is going to incur some items of deductible expense or have outstanding claims. For example, qualified deductible expenses and debts under §2053 include items such as:

- Funeral expenses (provided that state law does not impose them on a family member, such as a surviving spouse).

- Expenses of administration, subject to the limitations discussed at page 442, including fees of personal representatives, attorneys for the estate, trustee fees for acts that the personal representative otherwise would perform, accountants, investment advisors, appraisers, and selling expense commissions.

- Interest is deductible to the extent incurred on loans to the decedent before death, incurred on late payment of gift tax, incurred on deferred payment of estate tax under §§6161 and

6163 (but not §6166), and any other late payment interest (but not any penalty for late payment).

- Claims and debts that are personal obligations of the decedent, to the extent they are enforceable, bona fide, supported by full and adequate consideration in money or money's worth, and incurred in an arm's length transaction that does not represent a disguised attempt to shift wealth through a bogus claim with a deduction for it.

- Wealth transfer taxes paid to a state or foreign country may be deductible under §2053 in very rare cases but income and property taxes owed by the decedent at death are not deductible as taxes. They are deductible as debts. Most state death tax is §2058 deductible.

Administration expenses deductible under §2053 are restricted, based on the source of payment and the time within which payment is made. For example, expenses incurred with respect to "property subject to claims" (which the regulations regard as probate assets) are deductible to the extent they are paid out of probate assets at any time, plus to the extent they are paid out of nonprobate assets within nine months after death (plus any extensions to file the estate tax return). See §2053(c)(2). Expenses incurred with respect to property *not* subject to claims (nonprobate assets) are deductible to the extent they are paid within three years and nine months after death, regardless of the source of payment.

For example, assume the expenses of administration incurred on nonprobate assets equal $20,000, expenses of administration incurred on probate assets equal $60,000, and the includible assets of the estate include $50,000 of probate property and $200,000 of nonprobate property. In this case the expenses incurred on probate property exceed the probate property available to pay them, so at least the excess will be paid from nonprobate assets. To be certain of their deductibility, those expenses should be paid within nine months of the decedent's death. And the full $20,000 of expenses payable from nonprobate assets should be paid within three years and nine months of the decedent's death, in each case to preserve their deductibility. Only the portion of the $60,000 of probate expenses paid from the original $50,000 of probate assets would be deductible without regard to the time of their payment.

Many items that are §2053 deductible for estate tax purposes also are deductible by the estate for income tax purposes (as discussed in Chapter 20, an estate is a separate income tax paying entity). Under §642(g) the personal representative must elect whether to deduct those items on the income versus the estate tax return. They cannot be taken for both tax purposes (unless they constitute a very special form of "deductions in respect of a decedent" that we describe in Chapter 20). Commonly known as the "swing item" election, it turns out that this decision of how to reflect deductions is a piece of postmortem estate planning that raises some very troublesome consequences and implicates questions of fiduciary responsibility, again beyond the scope of this overview. It is worthy of mention, however, because in the real world this postmortem endeavor is not the realm for amateurs, and it cannot be ignored.

Several additional requirements must be met for an amount to be deductible under §2053. First, the amount deducted must be reasonable. This is a judicial gloss and it is consistent with income tax deduction principles. Second, the deductible items must be *allowable* under state law. This is not the same as "allowed" and a state court decree allowing the payment is not necessary. Indeed, with respect to expenses attributable to nonprobate assets a decree of approval probably could not be had. Moreover, a state court decree is not binding on the federal government. So about the only effect of a state court decree would be to limit the amount that could be deducted by establishing the maximum amount actually allowed by the state court.

Finally, the third requirement, imposed by the regulations, is that administration expenses must be "necessary" to proper administration. Although this has been the subject of extensive litigation, it now is so well regarded as valid that you can assume that the necessity requirement is a part of the federal jurisprudence. It creates a special dynamic with respect to attorney fees, which are deductible but only to the extent incurred for the proper settlement of the estate and not to the extent incurred for the primary benefit of the beneficiaries (because the latter would not meet the necessity requirement). This is a tough question in many cases because litigation or dispute resolution will benefit multiple parties. As a practical matter perhaps the most predictive element in whether attorney fees are deductible is who hired the lawyer. If it was the estate, the expense probably will be deductible. If it was a beneficiary, the opposite is likely to be true, regardless of the nature of the debate and extent to which its resolution was central to proper administration or distribution of the estate.

### §2055: The Charitable Deduction

Gifts to charity may be deductible under §2522 for gift tax purposes if made during life, or under §2055 for estate tax purposes if made at death. Unlike the income tax charitable deduction, there are no dollar or percentage limitations on the amount of the gift and estate tax charitable deductions. Thus, anyone may avoid the payment of all wealth transfer taxes by use of the charitable deduction regardless of the amount of their wealth. To qualify there are four basic requirements.

- Property must "pass" from the decedent or donor, basically meaning that it is taxable property of the decedent or donor.
- The interest must be qualified property, which also basically means it was includible in the decedent's gross estate or was taxable property of the donor.
- The recipient must be a qualified charity.
- The transfer is in a qualified format, which is where all the real action is. The requirements here are more technical than even the normal wealth transfer tax course would investigate, so we provide here only the most cursory description because you will not just "dabble" in this arena. Either you will be totally immersed in it or you should leave it alone entirely.

Qualified transfers come in three flavors, the last of which being the one that creates all the difficulty. The first is easy: an outright bequest to a qualified charity. The second is not very common but it also is relatively straightforward: a remainder interest (not in trust) in either a farm or a personal residence. The third is a qualified split interest trust. These rules are problematic because they are so highly technical and easy to mess up. Qualified trusts come in a number of varieties:

- A Charitable Remainder Unitrust (CRUT) provides that a percentage of the fair market value of the trust (determined *annually*) is payable as an annuity to a private beneficiary, either for the life of that beneficiary, or for a term not exceeding 20 years. The following remainder is distributed to a qualified charity. Available options include two that are quite popular for strategic planning purposes. One is to limit the annuity in any year to the available income, so that corpus need not be cannibalized to make the annuity payment if income is inadequate. That "net-income-only" option (a NICRUT) then can be coupled, but need not be, with a "deficiency make-up" provision (a NIMCRUT) that allows the trustee to make payments in future years from excess income to make up for any deficiency incurred in prior years under a net-income-only provision. Additions may be made at any time to any of the CRUTs (but not to the next variety, the annuity trust).
- A Charitable Remainder Annuity Trust (CRAT) pays an annual annuity equal to a fixed percentage of the trust's *initial* fair market value, either for the life of the beneficiary, or for a term not exceeding 20 years. There is no net income or deficiency catch-up option in these trusts.
- A Pooled Income Fund pays an annuity of a pro rata share of the fund's annual return, something like a mutual fund. About the

only difference is that pooled income funds are prohibited from investing in tax exempt investments.

- Qualified Terminable Interest Remainder Trusts are a mixture of a charitable and marital deduction trust and are discussed very briefly at page 448.

- A Charitable Lead Trust (CLAT or CLUT) is like the charitable remainder trust, only in reverse. The charity receives the annuity interest for a period of time and the remainder passes to a private beneficiary when the annuity is completed. The use of this format provides a charitable deduction for property that ultimately will return to the donor's family.

### §2056: The Marital Deduction

Gifts to a spouse may be deductible under §2523 for gift tax purposes if made during life, or under §2056 for estate tax purposes if made at death. If done properly the effect of the deduction is twofold. One is estate splitting, with the objective of either minimizing overall taxes, or deferring imposition of the ultimate liability until death of the surviving spouse.

Note, however, that using the marital deduction to defer taxes may *increase* the aggregate liability over both estates because all the wealth of the couple is combined and taxed at once in the survivor's estate. Historically this resulted in a higher impost under the progressive estate tax tables. The estate tax is slated to become a flat tax but it may not stay that way and, in a progressive tax system, deferral of the tax until the survivor's death causes "estate stacking" that generates a higher overall tax cost. Also note that the notion that this increase in tax is offset by the time-value of deferring payment of the government's tax dollars until the survivor dies is an exactly wrong concept, as illustrated in Pennell & Williamson, *The Economics of Prepaying Wealth Transfer Taxes*, 136 Trusts & Estates 49, 40, 52 (June, July, & August 1997). The other effect of proper marital deduction planning is lifetime shifting of income or appreciation (which will increase the donee spouse's estate instead of the donor's) or sheltering the applicable exclusion amount of the spouse with less wealth. This latter effect is the most critical because leaving unused unified credit in the estate of the first spouse to die is a cardinal sin if the couple has enough wealth to incur wealth transfer tax. The applicable exclusion amount is discussed at page 450.

Since 1981 the allowable deduction is 100% of any qualifying transfers to a surviving spouse during life or at death (or both). In essence, the wealth transfer taxes treat married individuals as a single economic unit and permit them to delay tax until they distribute the property to a third party. Because of the spouses' applicable credit amounts, however, using the authorized unlimited marital deduction seldom is wise planning for persons with relatively large estates. Instead, most well drafted marital deduction provisions take advantage of the deduction of no more than an "optimum" bequest. For example:

If my spouse survives me, I devise to (him/her/marital trust) the smallest pecuniary amount that, if allowed as a federal estate tax marital deduction, would result in the least possible federal estate tax being payable by reason of my death.

This approach would first "shelter" the deceased spouse's unified credit and only any excess wealth would qualify for the marital deduction. Examples of this form of planning can be found in 3 Casner & Pennell, ESTATE PLANNING §13.1.1 (6th ed. 2001).

There are four basic requisites to qualify for the estate tax marital deduction, of which three are pretty straightforward. First, the surviving spouse must be a U.S. citizen or, by virtue of §2056(d), a special form of qualifying trust must be used. Second, the decedent's spouse must survive the decedent (permitted either in actual fact or by virtue of a valid presumption of survivorship in circumstances such that the order of their deaths cannot be established by proof). In this regard, as we studied in Chapter 2, the Uniform Simultaneous Death Act provides a presumption that, between spouses, (1) jointly held assets pass as if owned half by each, and (2) with respect to each spouse's separately owned assets, each is deemed to be the survivor. The effect of these presumptions is to preclude property passing to the other spouse, which may be good for state law probate avoidance purposes but may be exactly the wrong result for marital deduction qualification purposes. Federal law permits the decedent's estate plan to alter this presumption by a provision that deems the spouse to have survived, thereby causing inclusion of property in the spouse's estate instead of the decedent's estate.

Whether the survivor is a "spouse" is determined under state law and any applicable decrees, looking to see whether a marriage or prior divorce is legitimate, but the government has indicated informally that it no longer will challenge this qualification on its own motion.

The third requirement is that the interest for which a marital deduction is sought must "pass" from the decedent to the surviving spouse. Two fundamental elements are involved here. One is that the property must be includible in the decedent's gross estate. Assets that are deemed to pass to the spouse (even though they do not pass through the probate estate of the decedent under state law) include joint tenancy, insurance payable to the spouse as beneficiary, §2041 general power of appointment property that passes to the spouse in default of or by virtue of exercise, property includible under §§2035-2038, annuities payable to the spouse and included in the decedent's estate under §2039, and even §2044 property or will contest settlements. With renunciation/disclaimer property, the treatment is as if the disclaimant had predeceased the decedent, with results applicable thereto. The other passing requisite is that the amount passing must be such that it will be includible in the spouse's gross estate at death (to the extent it is still held).

The fourth qualification requirement is where most litigation historically has centered. The interest passing to the spouse must be deductible. In this regard *all* interests are deductible *except* those falling into any of four categories:

- Assets not includible in the decedent's gross estate.
- Assets deducted under §2053.
- Assets deducted under §2054.
- Nondeductible terminable interests.

Terminable interests are where the shoe pinches, and deserve most of the attention in studying the wealth transfer tax marital deduction. And the first thing to remember is that **NOT ALL TERMINABLE INTERESTS ARE NONDEDUCTIBLE!!** This truth cannot be overstated.

An interest is terminable if it will terminate or fail on the occurrence or nonoccurrence of a contingency (for example, the most common being "on remarriage" of the surviving spouse), or on the lapse of time (the most common being death of the surviving spouse). The possibility of termination is determined at the decedent's death, based on the facts and possibilities that exist at that time.

Nondeductibility requires either that the interest was acquired by the decedent's fiduciary at the decedent's direction (yes, that's all it takes, and it does not make sense), *or* that all four of the following requirements are met (and this is where all the action is). (1) Another interest in the same property passes to a third party. (2) Enjoyment and possession in that third party follows the spouse's enjoyment or possession. (3) The interest passed from the decedent (not someone else) to that third party. (4) The interest passed for less than full and adequate consideration in money or money's worth. The following examples may help to distinguish deductible from nondeductible terminable interests.

- Decedent (D) named Spouse (S) as the beneficiary of insurance on D's life that is includible in D's gross estate at death. S elected an annuity settlement option with a refund feature payable to their children (e.g., S was to receive $X per month for life, but if S died before receiving $Y, their children would receive the difference between $Y and what S received). This is a terminable interest (because S's interest ends at S's death) and the refund does pass to a third party after S's enjoyment, but it is a deductible terminable interest because D did not create the terminable interest. S did.

- D's parent created a term of years in D, which D bequeathed to S at D's death before expiration of the term. This too is a terminable interest but it is deductible because D did not create it. D's parent did.

- D transferred property to a child, reserving a term of years that D then bequeathed to S at D's death before expiration of the term. This is a terminable interest and it is nondeductible because it meets all the requirements.

- But assume that D sold the property to the child, reserving the same term of years that D bequeathed to S. Now this is not nondeductible, albeit it is a terminable interest, because the full and adequate consideration transfer prevents it from meeting all four requirements.

- In the following deductible terminable interests the common characteristic is that nothing passes to a third party when the interest terminates: a patent or copyright; a life estate in Blackacre to S, remainder to S's estate; a joint and survivor annuity paying $5,000 per year to D and S until the death of the survivor of them.

In addition, due to statutory exceptions, three major forms of otherwise nondeductible terminable interests *are* deductible. The first is provided by §2056(b)(3), which permits a document to require up to six months' survivorship and, notwithstanding that failure to survive would terminate the interest, this terminable interest is deductible if the surviving spouse does not die within the survivorship period and therefore takes the interest. Thus authorized is a bequest "to S if S does not die within six months of my death." The rationale for using a survivorship provision is to prevent estate stacking (increased taxes attributable to lumping both estates together) if the surviving spouse is not going to live long enough to make the tax deferral attributable to qualifying for the deduction valuable enough to justify any increase in tax.

The second exception to the nondeductible terminable interest rule is under §2056(b)(5), which authorizes a trust providing the surviving spouse with a life estate and a general power of appointment. The requirements are two: (1) All income must be payable to the spouse annually. To hold unproductive property requires special (although easy) drafting. The income must be payable in the year in which it is received by the trust. Here state law trust accounting income is the key to the spouse's entitlement, not taxable income. (2) The spouse must have a power to appoint the full trust corpus to the spouse or to the spouse's estate, and the power must be exercisable by the spouse alone and in all events, meaning there can be no substantive restrictions on exercise. This general power of appointment will require §2041 inclusion in the spouse's gross estate at death and is the way Congress ensures that the wealth does not avoid tax in both spouses' estates.

The third primary exception to the nondeductible terminable interest rule is the most frequently used. Under §2056(b)(7) a qualified terminable interest property (QTIP) trust qualifies. It essentially is the §2056(b)(5) trust without the general power to appoint. That is, all income must be payable annually and no one may divest the spouse of income or corpus during life. Because a naked life estate would not otherwise cause inclusion in the spouse's estate at death, §2044 exists to require the "pay back" of subsequent taxation, and a timely election must be made that identifies this life estate as qualifying for the marital deduction. There also is a §2056(b)(8) qualified terminable interest charitable remainder trust that is permitted, but these are not often used.

A final form of trust also qualifies for the marital deduction but it is not an exception to the nondeductible terminable interest rule. Instead, this is not a terminable interest at all. Under this "estate trust" marital format the surviving spouse is entitled to income only in the trustee's discretion, with principal and accumulated but undistributed income payable to the spouse's estate at death. This is not a nondeductible terminable interest because nothing passes to a third party after S's enjoyment.

A final marital deduction qualification rule is §2056(d)(1), which disallows the marital deduction under §2056(a) if the decedent's surviving spouse is not a citizen of the United States. A "qualified domestic trust" (QDT) exception to this disallowance is provided by §2056(d)(2). Property held in a §2056A(a) QDT qualifies for a unique form of marital deduction. It is easiest to think of a QDT as a general power of appointment or QTIP marital deduction trust that requires the trustee to be a United States citizen or domestic corporation. An election must be made on the decedent's timely filed estate tax return to have the trust qualify for the marital deduction. And the trust must comply with any "requirements prescribe[d by regulations] to ensure the collection of any tax imposed" by §2056A(b). Wealth transfer tax is imposed by §2056A(b) on QDTs as if the decedent had died at the time of a triggering event and the taxable property was then includible in the decedent's estate. Like a gift tax computation, the amount by which the decedent's estate taxes would have been increased by inclusion of the property is the amount of tax that is to be paid (by the QDT). And the triggering events are any distribution from the QDT during the surviving spouse's overlife (other than the mandatory distributions of income required to qualify as a QDT), death of the surviving spouse, and any termination of the qualified status of the trust. Easy, but not forgettable, and you must ask each married client if they and their spouse are citizens, because it likely is malpractice if you fail to qualify a QDT for the marital deduction.

### §2058: Deduction for State Death Tax

Adopted in 2001 when the §2011 state death tax credit was repealed, §2058 permits deduction of estate, inheritance, legacy, or succession taxes paid to any of the 51 American jurisdictions at any time before four years after filing the federal estate tax return. We do not yet have any guidance regarding this provision.

### §2057: The Family-Owned Business Interest Deduction

Repealed in 2001, §2057 previously allowed a deduction for qualifying family-owned business interests that passed to qualified heirs. There were complex requirements that piggy backed largely on the §2032A special use valuation rule, and there is talk that this provision might be restored *if* Congress were to retain the estate tax rather than accelerate its repeal. Stay tuned.

### Computation and Payment of Estate Tax

Now that we have a general idea of what is includible in the gross and then taxable estates, let's look at a simple illustration of how the tax actually is computed. This calculation assumes the decedent died in 2005 and, for ease, we ignore state death taxes:

| | |
|---|---|
| Gross estate (§§2033 through 2044) | $7,300,000 |
| Taxable Estate (subtract §§2053-2056 deductions) | (750,000) |
| Add Adjusted Taxable Gifts | 100,000 |
| Total Tax Base | $6,650,000 |
| Tentative Tax on Total | $2,966,300 |
| Subtract Gift Tax Paid Post-1976 | 0 |
| Gross Estate Tax Payable | 2,966,300 |
| Subtract §§2010-2015 Credits | (555,800) |
| Net Tax Paid | 2,410,500 |

To be a taxable estate requires the total tax base to exceed the applicable exclusion amount, which is slated to increase from $1.5 million in 2005 until 2009, when it reaches $3.5 million, and then drop back to $1 million in 2011. As Congress tinkers with the potential for repeal of the estate tax these numbers will continue to change, but the basic inclusion, deduction, and calculation rules will remain the same.

### *Credits*

In general, credits reduce the tax to be paid, not the taxable estate (as would a deduction). This is thought to be more fair because credits are an offset to tax dollars owed and therefore have the same value to all taxpayers, regardless of the marginal bracket in which their estates are taxed. Deductions reduce the taxable estate and thereby reduce the amount taxable at the highest marginal bracket in a given estate, meaning they have a greater value to a larger taxable estate than to a smaller one. A number of credits are available to reduce the amount of estate tax that otherwise would be due.

For most donors and decedents, by far the most important and most commonly used credit is the unified credit, which shelters the §2010 "applicable exclusion amount" (so-called after the Taxpayer Relief Act of 1997). The applicable credit amount is the tax on the applicable exclusion amount it protects, which is scheduled to increase in accordance with the following table:

| Year | Applicable Exclusion Amount |
|------|------------------------------|
| 2005 | 1,500,000 |
| 2006 — 2008 | 2,000,000 |
| 2009 | 3,500,000 |

The unified credit always is available at death, regardless of gifts made during life that "used" the credit. Because the estate tax computation includes adjusted taxable gifts (the third line in the illustration at page 449), and then subtracts gift tax paid (the sixth line in the illustration at page 449), the effect of the lifetime use is as if there was a gift and no tax paid, causing the value of the gifted property to be included as part of the estate tax computation at death with no offsetting amount in the sixth line of the illustration. Under that vision, it is proper that the credit is available at death. This is one aspect of what is meant by the estate and gift taxes being "unified." Another is that a single tax rate schedule applies to both lifetime gifts and transfers at death.

Before 2005 every state had what was known as a "pick-up" tax in an amount equal to the §2011 state death tax credit. The same concept applied for the few state generation-skipping pick-up taxes. The effect was that the federal government gave the estate a credit for wealth transfer tax paid to the state, meaning that the federal tax bill was reduced dollar for dollar by the amount paid to the state. In effect, this was a form of revenue sharing with the states. Congress in 2001 phased out this credit and now the state wealth transfer tax picture is in turmoil as states attempt to replace this revenue. The §2058 deduction eases the bite of state death tax but we will see more estates shop for more favorable tax jurisdictions in the coming years unless this situation is reversed.

There also is a credit for any tax incurred on certain prior transfers. The §2013 "previously taxed property" credit reduces the tax burden of multiple rapid inclusions. This credit applies if a transferee dies within 10 years *after* (or 2 years *before*) the transferor, and the same property is includible in both estates. At this stage of our evaluation of inclusion provisions it is not easy to appreciate why an asset could be includible in both estates if the transferee dies *before* the transferor, so just imagine the more common circumstance of Parent leaving an estate subject to tax that passes to Child, who dies within ten years thereafter with the same property subject to tax again. The §2013 credit gives Child's estate a credit for tax paid on that same property in Parent's estate. Two limitations apply that effectively ensure that the property is taxed fully one time at whichever is the higher rate as between the two estates. And the credit phases out as the deaths occur less closely to each other within the 10 year period. In effect the available credit is reduced by 20% for every two years after the transferor's death the transferee dies. Thus, if the transferee dies within two years of the transferor, the credit is 100% of the amount determined. But if the transferee dies more than two years after but within four years of the transferor's death, the credit is only 80% of that amount, and if the transferee dies more than four years after the transferor but within six years after, the credit would be 60%, and so on.

### Payment of the Estate Tax

The decedent's estate tax return must be filed and the estate tax owed must be paid all within nine months after the decedent's death, with extensions of the time to pay permitted under §§6161, 6163, and 6166 in special cases. Today an automatic six month extension to file is routine, but it does *not* constitute an extension of the time to pay the tax (which can be an estimate). Don't make the mistake of not paying or getting a separate extension, because the estate tax will incur interest for late payment (and you likely will pay that out of your own pocket). Unless an extension is available, the time for payment is relatively short and often results in a fire sale mentality as the unprepared estate seeks to generate the requisite liquidity to pay the tax (because, after all, the government expects payment in *cash* and not in stuff the decedent owned at death).

For federal tax purposes, the primary burden of paying the tax is on the §2203 "executor" of the estate, and §2205 imposes the burden on the residue of the probate estate, the same as the abatement rules would in the absence of state law or a document provision to the contrary. In many states the burden instead is shifted to all recipients of estate taxable assets ("full apportionment") by statute or judicial opinion, and some states recognize that a will can apportion taxes incurred by nonprobate assets to the asset that generated the tax. In addition, the source for payment of the estate tax may be dictated by a will substitute, such as a revocable inter vivos trust, if it contains a valid tax clause, and Internal Revenue Code §§2206, 2207, 2207A, and 2207B are federal tax reimbursement rules. There is no consistency in these federal reimbursement rules. Some nonprobate assets (like life insurance proceeds payable to a third party) generate inclusion and therefore tax for which there is a federal right of reimbursement. This allows the personal representative (who pays the tax attributable to that asset under §2042) to recover the tax generated by that inclusion from the recipient. For life insurance payable to a third party and therefore includible, if at all, under §2042(2), §2206 grants such a right of reimbursement that allows the personal representative to force the insurance beneficiary to contribute a pro rata amount of the tax attributable to inclusion of the proceeds. There is a similar rule under §2207 with respect to §2041 general power of appointment property. And two others, §§2207A and 2207B, for §§2044 and 2036 inclusion. But there is no similar rule for other very common forms of includible property, like §2039 annuities or §2040 joint tenancy.

The point is that there are a variety of options and a crazy patchwork of state and federal rules, which together make drafting the tax payment provisions among the most likely to generate malpractice in all of the documents you prepare. And recall always that the personal representative of the estate has personal liability to the federal government if the tax is not paid when due and there is a transferee liability rule that permits the federal government to go after anyone holding property that was includible in the decedent's estate, until the federal government has been paid in full. Which is to say: Uncle *always* gets paid, no matter what the documents say.

## Gift Taxation

The federal gift tax exists to prevent estate tax avoidance. People would transfer wealth tax free before they die if we didn't have it. The overall objective of our "unified" wealth transfer tax system therefore is to impose the same aggregate taxes whether the taxpayer makes some, many, or no taxable lifetime transfers. Unified means that the calculation of a donor's gift tax liability, or a decedent's estate tax liability, is done on a cumulative basis, taking into account for each gift tax calculation all prior taxable transfers made by the donor and for estate tax calculation all taxable gifts made by the decedent after 1976. In either case, adding prior gifts to calculate current tax liability is done to determine the applicable marginal tax rate brackets. In each case the tax currently owed is the tax on the total cumulative taxable transfers, less any tax previously paid. And in theory this system intends for it not to matter if, when, or to what extent gifts are made. The aggregate tax should be the same.

Notwithstanding theories, however, significant advantages still exist under the present law for making gifts (and there is some theoretical support for subtle differences that encourage people to transfer wealth sooner rather than later). Among the advantages that exist, lifetime gifting allows a taxpayer to:

- Transfer future appreciation without paying tax on it (that is, we value gift property at its current value, rather than what it would be worth if the taxpayer died with it years later). In most but not all respects this advantage disappears under a flat tax after 2005.

- Transfer future income without paying income tax or wealth transfer tax on it (that is, we value the property at today's value, which reflects its income earning capability, but future income belongs and is taxed to the new owner).

- Transfer property to a spouse to take advantage (to "shelter") the spouse's applicable exclusion amount, generation-skipping transfer tax exemption, and to equalize estates (because the tax under a progressive rate tax system on two estates of half the size of their aggregate wealth is cheaper than the tax on one estate that holds all their wealth).

- Reduce the total amount that is subjected to tax. This is the so-called DuPont effect, which recognizes that the gift tax is incurred only on the assets transferred and not on the dollars used to pay the gift tax (a "tax exclusive" system) whereas the estate tax is incurred on all the taxpayer's wealth at death, including the dollars that will be used to pay the estate tax (a "tax inclusive" system). Gift tax dollars paid during life therefore reduce the gross estate tax free (unless §2035(b) is applicable because the taxpayer dies within three years of the gift). To illustrate this concept using simple (but not today accurate) numbers, assume a taxpayer had $100,000 of disposable wealth and wanted to transfer as much of it as possible, subject to a 50% wealth transfer tax rate. A lifetime gift of $66,666 would yield a gift tax of $33,333, together consuming the full amount the taxpayer was willing to relinquish. But if the taxpayer waited until death, the $100,000 would incur an estate tax of $50,000 and leave only that same amount for the taxpayer's beneficiary. The difference between the two taxes is the gift tax being computed on only the gift and not on the dollars used to pay the gift tax, while the estate tax is computed on the full $100,000, which includes the $50,000 that goes to the government in payment of the estate tax.

- Gifting also takes advantage of "relaxed" gift tax valuation rules. Audits of gift tax returns are far less common than of estate tax returns, and the method for valuing gifts differs in one significant respect. Gift tax is based on what the donee received. Estate tax is calculated on the basis of what the decedent devised. This difference is not appropriate but it flows from the government's own pronouncements and provides a huge advantage as illustrated by the following example. If a taxpayer owns all the stock in FamilyCo and transfers it at death to the taxpayer's five surviving children, the value of the stock will reflect the control block, undivided and without reference to who receives what. Contrariwise, however, if the taxpayer transfers the FamilyCo stock in five equal 20% blocks to the five children inter vivos, the gift tax will be incurred on each gift separately. Five times the tax on each 20% minority interest will be much less than the estate tax that would be incurred on 100% at death.

- Gifting also can take advantage of a rule that allows spouses to "split" their gifts, meaning that they can treat gifts by one of them as made in equal 50% shares by both of them. The gift splitting advantages include reduction of the effective rate at which either half is taxed, use of both spouses' applicable exclusion amounts, and taking advantage of two times the next gift tax opportunity, below.

- We also can reduce the gross estate through the gift tax annual exclusion, which allows every taxpayer to transfer as much as $11,000 per year (which amount increases in $1,000 increments, as indexed for inflation) to as many different donees as they want, with very few practical limitations.

- Gifts also avoid state wealth transfer tax virtually everywhere because few states have a separate gift tax.

- "Net gifts" also can reduce the gift tax liability by obligating the donee to pay the gift tax on the transfer, which reduces the value of the gift for gift tax valuation purposes.

- Finally, there are desirable family planning objectives served by inter vivos gifting (such as making a child financially independent, or giving a child an active interest in the family business as an incentive to remain involved in that enterprise).

### *"Gift"*

The gift tax definition of a "gift" is any property transferred for less than full and adequate consideration in money or money's worth. Required is a voluntary and complete transfer of property by an individual, not falling within the business transaction exception (discussed at page 456). The amount of the gift is the value of the transferred interest, to the extent it exceeds any consideration given. Important about this definition is that it does not equate with the income tax definition of a gift, nor does the estate tax description of a completed "gift" equate with the gift tax definition of a "gift." Thus, notwithstanding some cases suggesting that there should be pari materia as between the wealth transfer taxes especially, there is none. The same transfer may at once be a taxable gift for gift tax purposes but not be an effective gift that will shift the income tax liability on future income. And it may be complete enough to invoke the gift tax during life but not be complete enough to avoid the estate tax at death. About the only statement that it probably is fair to make is that a transfer cannot be sufficiently incomplete to avoid the gift tax on a transfer during life but be sufficiently complete to avoid the estate tax at death. Otherwise courts or litigants suggesting parity does or should exist are confused (or worse).

Unless the business transaction exception applies, a gift for gift tax purposes occurs if property is transferred for less than full and adequate consideration in money or money's worth. In this regard, a child's release of support rights is consideration. Marital property rights and property settlements have a special treatment as consideration for gift tax purposes. A spouse's release of property settlement rights generally is not consideration, but adequate consideration is found in a spouse's release of marital support rights (because the donor's estate would have been reduced by the support payments had they not been released). Consideration also exists under §2516, which applies if a transfer was made under a written agreement relative to a divorce that occurred within one year before or two years after the transfer. In addition, of long standing is the rule that any agreement that is incorporated into a court ordered decree of divorce or separate maintenance is involuntary and therefore not subject to gift tax.

The rationale for the consideration furnished exception to the gift tax is that only a diminution in net worth for ultimate estate tax purposes is meant to be taxed. A substitution of one property (consideration) for another (the transferred asset) does not present an abuse that the gift tax is meant to reach. So the only real question is whether the donee is giving something to the donor that will cause the donor's estate to be unreduced at death, in which case it counts as consideration that avoids the gift tax. In this vein, detriment to the donee is not consideration unless it constitutes a benefit in money or money's worth to the donor. For example, the donee's promise to quit drinking and doing drugs is not consideration for gift tax purposes, because it does not restore or maintain the donor's net worth.

Another matter about which much confusion is generated involves the concept of "donative intent." For §102 income tax exclusion purposes, there cannot be a gift unless donative intent exists. For gift tax purposes, however, donative intent is irrelevant in all but one very limited circumstance. Under the "business transaction exception," transfers made in the ordinary course of business are not taxable as gifts for gift tax purposes even though the consideration received for the transfer is less than full and adequate, if the taxpayer is able to prove that the transfer was bona fide, at arm's length, and free of donative intent. In other words, the taxpayer made a bad bargain in a business sense without any intent to make a donative transfer. For example, you pay too much for a used car, with no desire (and probably no knowledge) that you gave the seller too much money.

In addition to these basic gift tax definition elements, let's consider several that may not seem altogether intuitive. One is that the free use of property or services is not a taxable transfer for income tax purposes and may not be a gift for gift tax purposes either, but the "use" of cash for less than fair interest *is* subject to the gift tax, by virtue of §7872. So too, a cancellation or forgiveness of indebtedness is taxable as a gift by the creditor unless the business transaction exception applies. It may or may not be taxable §61(a)(12) income to the debtor. And a taxpayer's guarantee of another's debt may be a gift even if the guarantor never is obliged to make good on the indebtedness, the amount of the gift being the amount the debtor would have paid in an arm's length transaction for the same letter of credit or guarantee. These examples are a tad hard to embrace as taxable gifts because there is no tangible diminution in net worth as to which the gift tax should apply.

Qualified disclaimers are not gifts, but nonqualified disclaimers are treated as if the disclaimant received the property and made a taxable transfer of it. In the former examples this is the defining logic as well, foregoing interest or payment for a guarantee is the same as its acceptance followed by a gift. Whether a disclaimer qualifies is a function of §2518. It must be made within nine months following the transfer creating the interest (subject to a minority exception if the disclaimant is under the age of 21). It must be made without acceptance of benefits or enjoyment of the interest disclaimed. And the interest disclaimed must pass without direction by the disclaimant to a third party who would take it if the disclaimant had predeceased the transfer. By a special exception, the disclaimed interest may pass to a trust for the benefit of a transferor's surviving spouse, even if the spouse is the disclaimant, but otherwise there can be no future benefit to the disclaimant from disclaimed property.

Notwithstanding our focus on the donor's diminution in net worth, we need to remember another important concept that is highlighted by net gifts. In a net gift the donee pays the donor's gift tax, making the gift the value of the interest transferred less the amount of the gift tax paid by the donee (which requires a circular computation to determine). This reduces the gift tax value which reduces the gift tax liability, and may be desirable because the donee has the liquidity to pay the gift tax that the donor may be unable to pay. Note, however, that the donee's payment of gift tax converts the transfer into a part-sale, part-gift for income and gift tax purposes. The sale portion is the amount of gift tax paid, and the gift portion is the balance. A capital gain tax will be incurred if the sale price (the gift tax liability) exceeds the donor's basis in the entire property. Basis to the donee becomes the greater of cost (the gift tax paid) or the donor's carryover basis.

Finally, consider the gift tax "ed/med" exclusion before we come to the most important exception to taxable gift treatment. By §2503(e) payments of tuition or costs of medical care are not gifts. Required here is that the payments be made directly from the donor to the school or medical care provider. It is not adequate that the donor reimburse the student or patient's tuition or costs. Not required is that the donor owe any legal obligation to the beneficiary of these payments, so the theory of this exclusion is not so easy to pin down.

### The Annual Exclusion

The first $11,000 of qualifying transfers to each donee each year are ignored for gift tax purposes. This amount increases in increments of $1,000 to keep up with inflation after 1998. The most important aspect of this §2503(b) gift tax annual exclusion is that gifts to a third party of future interests do not qualify, meaning that the exclusion is not available to the extent the donee is not entitled to the present or immediate use, possession, or enjoyment of the transferred property. Required is an identifiable or separable portion or interest in property with an immediate unrestricted right that is not subject to any contingency or exercise (or withholding) of discretion. It is the right (as opposed to actual use, possession, or enjoyment) that is required.

*Crummey* clauses (typically granting to a trust beneficiary a power to withdraw money from a trust) will qualify a transfer to the trust as a present interest to qualify for the exclusion, if the donee knows of the withdrawal right and a reasonable time is allowed for its exercise. The withdrawal right is sufficient to convert an otherwise nonqualified future interest into a qualifying present interest even if the right to withdraw exists for only a limited time. Requiring the donee to act in some affirmative manner (for example, asking for the property to be distributed) is permissible if the donee is able to perform the act (including through a guardian, even if one has not yet been appointed) and the act is not one of independent significance (for example, the exclusion would be lost if the donee would lose a job or had to drop out of school if they exercised the power of withdrawal).

Lapse of the withdrawal right upon failure to withdraw is permissible and customary. Indeed, *Crummey* clause powers of withdrawal typically are used in the context of an insurance trust in which withdrawal is not anticipated. The donor adds money to the trust to be used to pay insurance policy premiums, and gives the beneficiaries withdrawal rights to qualify the money transfers as gift tax free by virtue of annual exclusions for each of the withdrawal power holders. The expectation is that none of the money will be withdrawn and therefore all of the contribution will be available to pay the insurance policy premiums.

Valuation is an issue for gift tax annual exclusion purposes, because it is necessary to determine what passes to the donee. Normally use of the actuarial tables under Treas. Reg. §25.7520 is mandatory with respect to valuing split interests such as life estates, terms certain, annuities, and remainder interests. Nonincome producing property will be valued lower if reinvestment in income producing assets is prohibited, and some authorities say the annual exclusion is not available at all unless the gifted property is income producing (the better reasoned result is that the exclusion is available if the donee can insist on reinvestment in income producing assets).

In addition, qualified minors' trusts under §2503(c) allow gift tax annual exclusion qualification of future interests held for the benefit of a minor. To qualify each of the following requirements must be met in an identifiable separable portion or interest of the trust. The trust beneficiary (donee) must be under age 21. The trustee must have discretion (without substantial restriction) to distribute income and principal to the donee before the donee reaches age 21. Income and principal must be made available to the donee at age 21 (actual distribution, a withdrawal right, or a general power to appoint all will suffice). And inclusion in the donee's estate must result if the donee dies before receiving distribution or becoming entitled to the power of appointment at age 21.

### Powers of Appointment

The exercise, release, or lapse of a general power of appointment may be a taxable gift. For this purpose the definition of a general power is taken from the estate tax law (a power that is exercisable in favor of any of the powerholder, the powerholder's estate, or creditors of either). The gift tax aspects of powers of appointment are essentially the same as the estate tax consequences discussed beginning at page 434, except for the application of §2514(e). The Code's logic is that the release or exercise inter vivos of a general power of appointment is taxable like any other gift. Further, a lapse of a general power of appointment is defined to be a release, meaning that it also is taxable. An exception applies for lapse purposes only, to the extent the amount subject to the power does not exceed $5,000 or 5% annually (the so-called "five or five" limitation). Also note that an otherwise taxable lapse or release will avoid gift tax to the extent the powerholder has any remaining power (such as a nongeneral power to appoint the lapse amount) because that gift is not yet complete. But beware the second clause of §2041(a)(2) in such a case. Refer back to page 435 regarding the estate tax consequences of these common powers, which many drafters wrongly assume have no tax consequence. Also see §678 (discussed in Chapter 20) regarding the income tax effect of these not quite harmless powers.

Among other important things to remember, an affirmative *release* of an inter vivos power of withdrawal is taxable even if the five or five limitation was employed, but the natural expiration of a power by its own terms is harmless to the extent of the five or five limitation. For this reason you should never counsel a beneficiary to submit a letter indicating that they do not intend to exercise powers of withdrawal. Merely let those powers lapse instead.

An unexpected source of gift tax liability also can arise if a powerholder has other interests in property that is subject to a power, because exercise of even a nongeneral power may be a gift of those other interests. For example, if a powerholder is the income beneficiary of a trust and exercises the power to appoint corpus to someone else, that exercise causes the powerholder to lose the income interest in the appointed corpus, constituting a taxable gift of only the income interest in that property. An exception may apply if the power to distribute to third parties is held in a fiduciary capacity and is limited by an ascertainable standard, but the primary message here is to not assume nongeneral powers are necessarily tax free. Further, as we will see when we discuss the generation-skipping transfer tax, the exercise of a nongeneral power of appointment also may be a generation-skipping taxable termination or distribution.

One final important gift tax concept is gift splitting. The Code permits married couples to effectively double the annual exclusion available to either of them, and to lower the marginal tax brackets applicable to a total gift, by treating transfers by one of them as made by both of them in equal shares. To be effective, the gift splitting provision in §2513 requires the spouses to split every gift made by either of them in the same calendar year.

## Generation-Skipping Transfer Tax

The generation-skipping transfer tax exists because of the perceived abuse possible under the estate tax, that a trust (such as a bypass or family trust) could be created for a beneficiary (such as a surviving spouse for life, and then for children for their lives) that provided all of the following benefits, without causing estate tax when that beneficiary died: all income, corpus in the trustee's unfettered discretion, corpus pursuant to the beneficiary's power of withdrawal limited by an ascertainable standard, corpus pursuant to the beneficiary's power of withdrawal without an ascertainable standard but only up to the $5,000 or 5% entitlement annually, a nongeneral inter vivos or testamentary (or both) power of appointment, and if you restrict the trustee's powers properly even the power to act as trustee. That is a lot of enjoyment and control without tax liability and, rather than alter the estate tax to change that result, Congress added the generation-skipping transfer tax instead.

To invoke this tax there must be a direct skip or a trust with "skip person" beneficiaries. A direct skip under §2612(c) is a transfer that is subject to estate or gift tax, made to or in trust for a skip person. And a skip person under §2613(a)(1) is any natural person with a present "interest" in the trust who is assigned to a generation more than one below the grantor. So, picture a trust with children as beneficiaries, followed by an interest in grandchildren. The grandchildren are the skip persons and it is the vision of children enjoying the trust for life and then the property going to the grandchildren without estate tax in the children's estates that Congress had in mind in enacting this tax.

Generation assignments are key to this tax and follow four general rules. First, lineal descendants of the grantor's grandparents are assigned to generations on the basis of consanguinity. So children are in the first generation below the grantor, grandchildren are in the second generation below, and so on. Second, relatives of the grantor's spouse (and former spouses) are assigned in the same manner, looking to the spouse's grandparents and their lineal descendants, relying on the rule that a grantor's spouse (or former spouse) is automatically assigned to the grantor's generation. Simply think of the grantor and any spouse as one person. Third, spouses of relatives are automatically assigned under the same logic to the same generation as the relative to whom they are (or at any prior time were) married. And fourth, all other beneficiaries are assigned on the basis of age, with spouses *not* automatically receiving the same generation assignment. Instead, this rule assumes that each generation is 25 years in length, and that the grantor is exactly in the middle of his or her generation. Thus, someone within 12.5 years of the grantor is deemed to be in the same generation as the grantor. Thereafter, every 25 years is a new generation. Someone over 12.5 years younger but not more than 37.5 years younger than the grantor is in the first generation below the grantor, while someone over 37.5 years younger but not more than 62.5 years younger than the grantor is in the second generation below, and so forth.

| Same Generation | *Grantor and Spouse* | Sibling and Spouse | Cousin and Spouse | Non-Relatives within 12.5 years of age |
|---|---|---|---|---|
| **First Level Below: Non-Skip Persons** | Child and Spouse | Niece or Nephew and Spouse | Cousin Once Removed and Spouse | Non-Relatives 12.5 to 37.5 years younger |
| **Second Level Below: Skip Persons** | Grandchild and Spouse | Grandniece or Grandnephew and Spouse | Cousin Twice Removed and Spouse | Non-Relatives 37.5 to 62.5 years younger |

The following examples of these rules illustrate generation-skipping trusts:

| This is a generation-skipping trust | Grantor ————> *In trust* | Child for life, remainder to child's descendants |
|---|---|---|
| This is not | Grantor ————> *In trust* | Spouse for life, remainder to child |
| This is a generation-skipping trust | Grantor ————> *In trust* | Spouse for life, remainder to child. Trustee discretion to spray income to descendants during spouse's overlife |
| This is a generation-skipping "direct skip" | Grantor ————> *In trust* | Grandchildren, until no living grandchild is under age 21, at which time distribution is to living grandchildren equally |

The Code also contemplates generation-skipping "trust equivalents": legal arrangements that have the same effect as a trust, such as a legal life estate to Child, remainder to Grandchild; or a life insurance policy settlement option or an annuity arrangement that benefited a child for life with remainder or refund to a grandchild.

To incur a generation-skipping tax, there must be a §2611(a) "generation-skipping taxable transfer," of which there are three types. The first, direct skips under §2612(c), include any transfer that is subject to the estate or gift tax, made to or in trust for the benefit of a skip person. For example, a grandparent's direct gift to a grandchild is a direct skip, subject to both the gift tax and the generation-skipping transfer tax. And like the gift tax, there is an exception if the direct skipping transfer is not a taxable gift for gift tax purposes under the annual exclusion or ed/med exclusion in §§2503(b) or 2503(e). For example, assume Grandparent gives Grandchild an outright gift of $11,000. Assuming Grandparent made no other gifts to Grandchild in that year, the gift qualifies for the gift tax annual exclusion and is excepted from generation-skipping transfer classification. (Certain additional requirements must be met for the gift to qualify for the generation-skipping transfer exception if the gift is made in trust and Grandchild is given a power to withdraw the gift to qualify it for the gift tax annual exclusion.)

There also is a predeceased ancestor rule under §2651(e), applicable to any transfer to or for the benefit of a skip person whose parent was a lineal descendant of the grantor's parent (or parent of the grantor's spouse, or the grantor's former spouse) and who is deceased. This exception applies to donees who are not descendants of the transferor only if, at the time of the transfer, the transferor has no living descendants and the exception applies to taxable distributions and taxable terminations, as well as to direct skips. The rationale for the exception is that there is no tax avoidance involved in transfers to a beneficiary whose parent no longer is alive (and therefore could not have been the logical beneficiary in a normal planning context).

The second form of taxable transfer is a taxable distribution under §2612(b). This is any distribution from a trust to a skip person. For example, a trustee's discretionary distribution of income or corpus to a grandchild from a trust being held for the grantor's child and descendants of that child would be a taxable distribution for generation-skipping transfer tax purposes.

The third form of taxable transfer is a taxable termination under §2612(a), which is the termination (by death, lapse, exercise, nonexercise, or otherwise) of any trust present interest, unless one of the two §2612(a)(1) exceptions apply. Under §2612(a)(1)(A) one exception applies if immediately after termination, a non-skip person has a present interest in the property that is more than nominal. So, in the preceding example, the death of a grandchild would not be a taxable termination if the child was alive. The *child's* death would constitute a taxable termination, but not if a sibling of the child (or some other nonskip person) also was a trust beneficiary. Neither death would constitute a taxable termination because of the other non-skip beneficial interests in that trust. The other exception exists under §2612(a)(1)(B). A taxable termination will be ignored if, "at no time after such termination may a distribution (including distributions on termination) be made from such trust to a skip person." An example would be the child's death with distribution to a charity rather than to a skip person.

## Amount of the Tax

Generation-skipping transfers are subject to tax at a flat rate equal to the maximum estate tax rate imposed under §2001. The lack of progressivity is designed to make the tax administerably easy, and when there was meaningful progressivity in the estate tax rates the result was to make it the most expensive wealth transfer tax alternative in many (but not all) cases. That spawned some planning designed to make the estate or gift tax apply instead of the generation-skipping transfer tax, which today likely is not very wise. Indeed, adept planners realize that there are more and better planning opportunities under the generation-skipping transfer tax than under the estate or gift taxes. But this is highly sophisticated work.

Under §2603(a), the tax is paid by the distributee in the case of a taxable distribution, the trustee in a taxable termination or a direct skip from a trust, or the transferor in a direct skip not from a trust. Further, §2603(b) provides that "unless otherwise directed pursuant to the governing instrument *by specific reference to the tax imposed by this chapter*, the tax imposed by this chapter on a generation-skipping transfer shall be charged to the property constituting such transfer" (emphasis supplied). A general tax clause directing payment of "all taxes caused by reason of my death" will not overcome this provision. And gift tax §2515 imposes a gift tax on the dollars used by the transferor to pay the direct skip tax inter vivos, to insure that these dollars don't escape gift tax liability.

Under §2621, the amount subject to tax in a taxable distribution is the amount received by the distributee. Because this tax is imposed on the distributee, this system of tax is similar to the estate tax (tax inclusive) system because dollars that the distributee uses to pay the tax are themselves subject to the tax. Further, if the trust pays the tax on behalf of the distributee, that payment of tax is an additional taxable distribution that also will be subject to the generation-skipping tax under §2621(b). Similarly, under §2622 the amount subject to tax in a taxable termination is the full amount subject to termination. Again, because the tax is paid out of this fund, the result here also is a tax inclusive system, because the dollars used to pay the tax are themselves subject to the tax.

Under §2623, however, the amount subject to tax in a direct skip is the value of property actually received by the transferee, as is the case in a gift tax (tax exclusive) computation. To illustrate, if a decedent leaves $1,000,000 of property in a direct skipping transfer at death, the direct skip subject to tax would be the $1,000,000 received by the beneficiary, not that amount plus any dollars used to pay the tax. Indeed, the amount of the taxable direct skip transfer is reduced by any federal or state estate or death tax that is paid out of the bequest. This produces a circular computation under the §2603(b) tax apportionment rules, in those cases in which the Code requires the tax to be paid out of the bequest, because you cannot know the taxable amount until you know the amount of the tax that will be paid from the transfer, and you cannot know the amount of the tax until you know the amount of the taxable transfer.

To solve this circularity problem the government has provided the following formula to determine the tax:

Tax = rate × [Fair Market Value ÷ (1 + rate of tax)]
Or  = Fair Market Value ÷ 3.1276595 [which is (1 + rate) ÷ rate]

Thus, if the taxpayer has $1,500,000 remaining after payment of estate tax to transfer in a direct skipping transfer, with the tax to be paid from that amount, the generation-skipping tax (assuming a 47% rate in 2005) would be $479,592 and the transfer would be $1,020,408, determined as

Tax = .47 × (1,500,000 ÷ 1.47)

The amount of the direct skip is the net amount passing (after payment of any wealth transfer tax), but if the donor is alive (and, therefore, incurs and must pay the tax), §2515 provides that the generation-skipping tax imposed on the direct skipping transfer is an added gift for gift tax purposes. In the prior example, if the transfer were made during life, the generation-skipping taxable amount would be $1,020,408, the tax on that amount would be $479,592 and, assuming the donor pays that tax, the taxable gift would be the aggregate of those two ($1,500,000, ignoring the annual exclusion and gift splitting, if they were applicable). No similar rule applies if the transferor makes the direct skip at death and the transferor's estate pays the tax. That is the right result because §2515 is essentially a gift tax "gross-up" rule (subjecting the generation-skipping tax dollars paid to gift tax). No similar rule is needed at death because the estate tax is a tax inclusive method of computation, which effectively imposes a gross-up result without the need for a special provision. That is, the full $1,500,000 in the prior example would be subject to estate tax without a special rule.

To many readers the foregoing is gobbledegoop, but illustrations that show the relative costs of the various forms of generation-skipping transfers graphically illustrate several important conclusions. One is that inter vivos transfers are cheaper for generation-skipping transfer tax purposes, just as they are for estate and gift tax purposes. And direct skips are cheaper than either taxable distributions or terminations. See 2 Casner & Pennell, ESTATE PLANNING §11.4.14.1 (6th ed. 1999). As discussed at page 466, the rules for automatic allocation of the generation-skipping exemption waste that valuable benefit on the cheapest transfers made (inter vivos direct skip transfers), which informs being aware of those rules to turn them off in appropriate cases. To make that determination, however, requires an accurate comparison of the various alternate transfers and their costs.

### Exceptions to the Tax

There are a variety of circumstances in which the otherwise applicable generation-skipping transfer tax is not imposed. One is the ed/med exclusion in §2611(b)(1), which grants an overall exemption under Chapter 13 for any transfer *from* a trust that would qualify as a gift tax free payment of medical expenses or tuition under §2503(e) if it was made by an individual. A second, under §2611(b)(2), applies to the extent property has already been generation-skipping taxed once at a given generation (or lower); it will not be taxed at that level again. To illustrate, imagine a trust for a child for life (at death there being a taxable termination), then for a grandchild's education and, if the child's spouse is still alive after the grandchild's education is complete, then back up to the spouse for life, finally distributing on the spouse's death to the child's descendants. Having been taxed once at the child level (i.e., the child's death would be a taxable termination, and the interest in the trust of the child's spouse would not prevent the taxable termination because it is not a present interest), this exception ensures against the trust being taxed at that level a second time at the death of the child's spouse. Under §2612(a)(1)(A), no taxable termination is deemed to occur at the end of the grandchild's education, when the interest of the grandchild terminates (at least until death of the spouse), because the spouse's interest (the spouse is the "non-skip person" referred to in that section) means that the property does not move down a generation.

The exceptions under §2612(a)(1)(A) and 2612(a)(1)(B) preclude taxable termination treatment if the property has stopped moving down the generational ladder (either permanently or just temporarily). For example, in a trust for Child and Grandchild with present interests at both generations, if Grandchild dies there will be no generation-skipping tax due because of the non-skip Child's continuing interest. A second example is a "pot" or "group" trust for children for life, with distribution to grandchildren only on the death of the last child to die. Here the death of any but the last child is not a taxable event because every child is a non-skip person and, while any child remains as a beneficiary, the exception in §2612(a)(1)(A) will apply. Further, if a trust were to be held after a child's death as a group trust for grandchildren until the last grandchild reached a specified age, and a grandchild died before the trust was distributed, the existence of any other living grandchild as a beneficiary would similarly prevent termination of the dying grandchild's interest from being a taxable event.

Yet another exception applies if a generation-skipping transfer occurs and the property involved in the transfer remains in trust. For purposes of determining if additional taxable generation-skipping transfers occur in the future the transferor is treated as being in the generation above the highest generation of beneficiaries of the trust. Thus, if Grandparent created a trust for Child for life, then for Grandchildren for their lives, remainder to Great-grandchildren, a taxable termination would occur at Child's death. Subsequent distributions to Grandchildren are not taxable distributions for generation-skipping tax purposes because the taxable termination caused by Child's death results in the transferor (Grandparent) being moved down to Child's generation. Distributions to Great-grandchildren while any Grandchildren are living would be taxable distributions, but the next taxable termination would not occur until the death of the survivor of the Grandchildren.

Finally, and most importantly, under §2631(a) all grantors have an exemption from the generation-skipping tax granted in the form of an "inclusion ratio" that is tied, under §2642, to the rate of tax for computation purposes. The amount of the exemption is equal to the estate tax applicable exclusion amount (e.g., $1.5 million in 2005). As a simple example of the operation of the §2642 "inclusion ratio" approach, assume a trust of $3,360,000, of which the transferor wishes to exempt $1,120,000 from the generation-skipping tax. The inclusion ratio would be determined by subtracting an "applicable fraction" from the number 1. The applicable fraction is ⅓, determined by taking the allocated exemption amount ($1,120,000) as the numerator and the value of the trust ($3,360,000) as the denominator. The resulting "inclusion ratio" of ⅔ is then multiplied against the rate of tax to determine the applicable rate of tax on all taxable transfers with respect to the trust in the future. Thus, in this example, if the maximum wealth transfer tax rate is 47%, the applicable rate would be 31.33% (⅔ times 47%). Accordingly, a $1,000 taxable distribution from the trust would generate a generation-skipping tax liability to the distributee in the amount of $313.33.

This example reveals that the trust is taxable in its entirety, at a reduced tax rate, unless the trust produces an inclusion ratio of zero from the outset. It almost always is better to create two trusts, one of the exact amount of the unused portion of the transferor's exemption to be made totally exempt, and the other to be totally taxable, and there are elaborate rules in the Regulations regarding the division (severance) of trusts for this purpose.

Failure to allocate the exemption will result in automatic allocation under §§2632(b) and (c) — in each case consuming enough exemption to cause the inclusion ratio to be zero, if possible. Allocation is made in the following order:

- seriatim to lifetime direct skips,
- then seriatim to lifetime nondirect skips,
- then pro rata to direct skips at the transferor's death,
- finally pro rata among all other generation-skipping transfers.

If you study the illustration at 2 Casner & Pennell, ESTATE PLANNING §11.4.14.1 (6th ed. 1999), you will notice that this priority uses the exemption on the least costly transfers, leaving more expensive transfers subject to tax. In each case the allocation can be prevented, if a better method can be identified. Because the automatic allocation rules could "waste" the exemption on the cheapest transfers made, conscious attention must be devoted to allocation of the exemption in the manner that produces the best results. This is a fiduciary function, and it might persuade you that taxes make fiduciary administration no place for amateurs, particularly when the wealth transfer taxes are involved.

CHAPTER 20

# INCOME TAXATION OF ESTATES, TRUSTS, GRANTORS AND BENEFICIARIES[*]

The income tax provisions that apply to estates and trusts, and their beneficiaries, are found in Subparts A-D of Part I of Subchapter J of the Internal Revenue Code (commonly referred to as just Sub J). In addition, a separate set of rules in Subpart E can trump all of the rest of Sub J, being the grantor trust rules that can cause a trust (but not an estate) to be regarded as a pass through entity with virtually all its tax consequences flowing to the grantor (or a third party treated as the grantor) for income tax purposes. Together these rules present various options and considerations that largely constitute the inter vivos and postmortem estate planning done by many estate and trust attorneys. This topic can support a separate stand alone course of study, so we're going to make this as simple and straightforward as the subject permits, with the understanding that you will definitely need to pay more attention to this when you specialize or do compliance in this arena.

Although for some purposes fiduciary entities are subject to pass through taxation similar to S corporations and partnerships, estates and trusts are treated as separate tax paying entities for income tax purposes and therefore must be considered separately. Estates and trusts file annual federal income tax returns (Form 1041) and may incur income tax on net earnings, capital gains, and other income that is not distributed currently to their beneficiaries. On the other hand, they are treated as conduits to the extent they pass "distributable net income" (DNI) to their beneficiaries on a current basis. In most respects income that is distributed to beneficiaries currently has the same character (tax exempt, capital versus ordinary, preference items for alternative minimum tax purposes, and such) in the beneficiaries' hands as it would on the fiduciary's return if it was not distributed.

As we will see, estates and trusts are subject to their own unique set of income tax rules, and any comparison to pass through entities or "conduit" taxation is a gross generalization. As the following material demonstrates, the operation of Subchapter J in its entirety is complex and remarkably technical.

---

[*] All section references in this Chapter are to the Internal Revenue Code unless specifically identified otherwise.

## Taxable Income

The taxable income of an estate or trust is generally the same as it is for an individual taxpayer. See §641(b). The principal differences between the tax treatment of the income of an estate or trust and that of an individual are the income tax deduction allowed to the entity under §§651(a) and 661(a) for distributions made (or required to be made) to beneficiaries, and the unlimited deduction allowable under §642(c) for amounts paid (or, in some circumstances, permanently set aside) for a charitable purpose. With few exceptions, any distribution made from an estate or trust to a beneficiary (whether made from current or accumulated income, or from principal) is treated as a distribution of current income to the extent of the entity's DNI. Under §643(c) the term "beneficiary" is as you would expect: an heir, a legatee, or a devisee. But under §643(a), DNI is a term of art, created by the tax law to serve a limited but pivotal role in the income taxation of estates and trusts. The primary function of DNI is to serve as a yardstick or measure, placing a limit on the amount of the entity's distributions deduction and on both the amount and the character of current income that is attributable to the income beneficiaries for taxation in the current year. DNI also serves as an element in a number of other rules that seldom are relevant these days, so we can defer an examination of the meaning and function of DNI because first we need to consider some special aspects of estate and trust taxable income, which is at the core of DNI.

### *Deduction in Lieu of Personal Exemption*

Estates and trusts are denied the §151 personal exemption afforded to individuals but are entitled instead to a §642(b) deduction in lieu of the personal exemption, granted in various amounts, all much less than the amount granted to individuals. For example, the deduction in lieu of an estate's personal exemption is $600, and the amount allowed to a trust is even less: $300 if the trustee is required to distribute all of the trust's income currently, and only $100 otherwise. §642(b). For this and most other purposes, the statutory reference to trust "income" means state law fiduciary accounting income and is to be contrasted with "taxable income," which is determined under the income tax rules. In most states fiduciary accounting income is determined under the Uniform Principal and Income Act or the Revised Uniform Principal and Income Act, under which capital gains and losses are excluded for most purposes from the determination of income for fiduciary accounting purposes.

Because §63(c) does not apply to an estate or trust, there also is no standard deduction or zero-bracket amount for fiduciary entities. Thus, every dollar of an estate or trust's net taxable income is subject to tax at the rates found in §1(e), which by far are the most onerous rates applicable to any taxpayer under the Code. Otherwise, with few exceptions, an estate or trust is permitted the same deductions that are allowed to individuals. One favorable discrimination in the taxation of fiduciary entities is §67(e), which specifies that the 2% (of adjusted gross income) loss of deductible miscellaneous itemized deductions for individuals will not apply with respect to "costs which are paid or incurred in connection with the administration of the estate or trust and would not have been incurred if the property were not held in such trust or estate." Some uncertainty exists with respect to the meaning of this provision in the context of deductible items that are attributable to expenses that would be incurred even if the property were not held in an estate or trust. For example, it seems clear that a fiduciary's costs to prepare the Form 1041 Fiduciary Income Tax Return are fully deductible, notwithstanding the 2% rule, because this return is necessary only because the property is held in a fiduciary capacity. But what about the fiduciary's own fees for administration of the entity?

Suppose for example that the grantor of a trust paid for investment advice prior to creation of the trust, but that the trustee of the trust provides investment counsel with respect to trust assets as part of the services it renders. If the trustee does not account or charge separately for this investment function, we don't know whether the full fee will be deductible, or whether the fiduciary must somehow allocate its fees to identify items of expense that might have been incurred if the property was not held in the trust. Most fiduciaries are assuming for the present that everything is deductible until the government establishes the contrary, and then clarifies the parameters of that rule. Compare *O'Neill Irrevocable Trust v. Commissioner*, 98 T.C. 227 (1992), rev'd, 994 F.2d 302 (6th Cir. 1993) (investment counseling fees paid to an outside advisor by individual trustees; the 2% rule did not apply), with *Mellon Bank v. United States*, 2000-2 U.S. Tax Cas. (CCH) ¶50,642 (Ct. Fed. Cl. 2000), aff'd, 265 F.3d 1275 (Fed. Cir. 2001), and *Scott v. United States*, 186 F. Supp. 2d 664 (E.D. Va. 2002), aff'd, 328 F.3d 132 (4th Cir. 2003) (which discredit *O'Neill*, saying it is not enough to determine that the expenses were incurred properly in a fiduciary context, nor that they were necessitated by the fiduciary duties involved, but instead requiring a determination whether the particular costs would have been incurred if a trust had not been involved, in which case the 2% rule applies).

Another important difference involves the charitable deduction. In lieu of the §170 deduction allowed to individuals for charitable contributions, which is subject to certain limitations based on the type of property transferred and character of the recipient, §642(c) allows an unlimited deduction to an estate or trust for any amount of its gross income that is paid for a charitable purpose or use. The deduction is allowed for amounts paid pursuant to a direction in the will or other governing instrument and for amounts paid pursuant to the exercise of fiduciary discretion granted in the instrument, including any current gross income of an *estate* that is permanently set aside for future charitable distribution. This §642(c)(2) set-aside deduction is not available to most trusts.

Finally, expenses of administration that are allowable as estate tax deductions under §2053 also may qualify as income tax deductions under §§162, 163, 165, or 212, as a reduction of the sales price in determining gain on the disposition of assets, or as §213 medical expenses deductible on the decedent's final income tax return. The decedent's personal representative must elect under §642(g) whether to take an income tax or an estate tax deduction (or some of each) with respect to these items, the object being to preclude utilization of the same expenditures to work double duty under each of the estate and income taxes.

## Distributable Net Income

Unique to the income taxation of trusts and estates is the concept of distributable net income. We begin our study of DNI by looking at why we need it, the primary purpose it serves. If you recall your basic income tax course you may remember that gifts of corpus are income tax free. If X gave or bequeathed property to Y, §102(a) provides that Y does not recognize gross income from the transfer. But §102(b) specifies that any income subsequently produced by the property *is* taxable to Y. Similarly, if X gratuitously gave or bequeathed income producing property to a trust for the benefit of Y, neither the transfer into the trust nor any subsequent distribution of the trust corpus to Y would constitute gross income to either Y or to the trustee. This is because §102 excludes gifts and inheritances from gross income, and it does not matter whether the property is transferred directly to the donee or beneficiary immediately or is held and distributed in the future through the medium of a trust.

On the other hand, however, income from gifted corpus is taxable. Income produced by the trust property subsequent to X's transfer should be subject to income taxation, either to the beneficiary or to the trust (as a separate entity). Moreover, the beneficiaries of a fiduciary entity should be taxed only on their distributive share of any *taxable* income of the entity, which requires that the tax exempt character of the estate or trust's income must be preserved. So the statutory challenge is to determine the extent to which distributions to beneficiaries are tax free distributions of corpus or of tax exempt income, as compared to taxable income produced by corpus that is not yet distributable. This identification of estate or trust distributions is geometrically more complex if distributions are made to multiple beneficiaries, especially if the nature of their beneficial interests vary (e.g., income and remainder beneficiaries). Since

1954, Subchapter J has used the concept of distributable net income as the device that determines the extent to which distributions to beneficiaries are taxable.

DNI is a tax term of art that has no meaning or use outside Subchapter J. Even within Subchapter J, the role of DNI is both limiting and limited, so it is best to keep it in proper perspective. First and foremost, DNI limits the amount of estate or trust distributions that may be treated as taxable income to the beneficiaries. §§652(a), 662(a). DNI also provides the basis for allocating various classes of income among the beneficiaries. §§652(b), 661(b), 662(b), and Treas. Reg. §§1.652(b)-2, 1.662(b)-2. Known as the character rules, this aspect of DNI's job is important because a distribution that is treated as *income* to a beneficiary is not necessarily *taxable* to the beneficiary, depending on the tax character of the item distributed (for example, interest from a state or municipal bond that is exempt from tax under §103, as opposed to taxable corporate bond interest). The character rule has the effect of treating the entity as a conduit through which income flows from its original source to the beneficiaries. This treatment requires an allocation of various classes of income ratably among beneficiaries according to the amount of DNI deemed received by each. In lieu of ratable sharing, the governing instrument specifically may allocate different classes of income to different beneficiaries, provided that the allocation has an economic effect independent of the income tax consequences of the allocation. See Treas. Reg. §1.652(b)-2(b).

DNI has a third function, limiting the maximum amount of income tax deduction allowed to an estate or trust under §§651(a) and 661(a) for distributions made to beneficiaries. We will see that this just precludes a fiduciary entity from being in a loss position for income tax purposes in any given year.

### *Determining DNI*

DNI is defined in §643(a) as the taxable income of the estate or trust for the tax year, with a number of adjustments. The first adjustment is the §643(a)(2) "add back" of the amount of the deduction in lieu of the personal exemption, allowed under §642(b) in computing taxable income. By this increase, distributable net income is larger than taxable income, meaning that a larger distributions deduction is available to the entity for current income distribution. Similarly, a larger amount is subject to inclusion in the taxable income of the beneficiaries of the estate or trust who received distributions, in each case because distributable net income is a cap on each. The net effect is to deny the benefit of the deduction in lieu of the personal exemption to the trust or estate beneficiaries. It serves only to reduce tax consequences to the entity.

The second adjustment is an additional add back, with a similar effect on DNI, dictated under §643(a)(5) for §103 tax exempt income. This add back serves to permit this form of tax favored income to pass through to the beneficiaries by increasing DNI, and thus increasing both the distributions deduction and the amount subject to inclusion at the beneficiary level. If distributed currently, the character pass through rules of the conduit system of taxation under §§652(b) and 662(b), discussed at page 480, permit the beneficiaries to enjoy the special status of income items that trigger this adjustment. However, because §§652(b) and 662(b) dictate a pro rata allocation of the character of all items included in DNI, distributions that generate deductions for the entity are also pro rated to various items of taxable and tax favored or exempt income, under Treas. Reg. §§1.643(a)-5(b), 1.652(c)-4, 1.661(b)-2, and 1.661(c)-2(d). Thus, care must be exercised to assure proper allocation of these items to the proper beneficiaries. Otherwise the government may attempt to allocate deductions to tax exempt income, which essentially wastes the deduction (the income and deductions balancing out) while the taxpayer attempts to allocate deductibles to receipt of taxable income to maximize their utility.

In addition to adding back the deduction in lieu of the personal exemption and tax exempt income in computing DNI, three items normally considered in the determination of taxable income are ignored for purposes of computing DNI. Thus, a third adjustment, dictated by §643(a)(1), is to ignore the distributions deduction allowed by §§651(a) and 661(a). Because that deduction is limited to the taxable portion of DNI, an unavoidable circularity otherwise would develop if DNI were equal to taxable income after allowance of the distributions deduction. The deduction would be limited by DNI and DNI would be dependent for computation on the amount of the deduction. So this modification is really just structural.

The fourth and fifth adjustments relate to items of taxable income that are allocated to fiduciary accounting principal and not currently distributed. Thus, for example, under §643(a)(3) and Treas. Reg. §1.643(a)-3, capital gains are ignored for purposes of computing DNI if they are allocated to corpus (either under the terms of the document or under a local law such as §3(b)(8) of both Uniform Principal and Income Acts) and not distributed or set aside for charity, along with capital losses used in computing taxable income. The effect is to reduce DNI and, correspondingly, to reduce the maximum distributions deduction, thereby causing these gains to be taxed to the entity in years when they are not distributed to the beneficiaries.

Similarly, but applicable only to simple trusts (defined at page 478) under §643(a)(4), taxable extraordinary or stock-on-stock dividends that are allocated to principal under the instrument or local law (see the

Uniform Acts §§3(b)(4) and (6)) and that are not currently distributed are excluded from DNI, again reducing the maximum distributions deduction and causing the tax thereon to fall on the entity. This is more complexity than you need to know.

The following example illustrates the foregoing adjustments in computing DNI. Assume a simple trust in which receipts and disbursements for the year include:

| | |
|---|---:|
| 1. Taxable Dividends, allocable to income | $25,000 |
| 2. Taxable Dividends, allocable to principal | 12,000 |
| 3. Taxable Interest | 15,000 |
| 4. Tax Exempt Interest | 10,000 |
| 5. Long Term Capital Gain | 7,000 |
| 6. Long Term Capital Loss | (2,000) |
| 7. Fiduciary Fees, charged to income | (5,000) |
| 8. Fiduciary Fees, charged to principal | (5,000) |

Fiduciary Accounting Income reflects the following items:

| | |
|---|---:|
| 1. Taxable Dividends | $25,000 |
| 3. Taxable Interest | 15,000 |
| 4. Tax Exempt Interest | 10,000 |
| 7. Fiduciary Fees | (5,000) |
| FAI = | $45,000 |

Taxable Income reflects the following items:

| | |
|---|---:|
| 1. Taxable Dividends, allocable to income | $25,000 |
| 2. Taxable Dividends, allocable to principal | 12,000 |
| 3. Taxable Interest | 15,000 |
| 5. Long Term Capital Gain | 7,000 |
| 6. Long Term Capital Loss | (2,000) |
| 7. 80% of Fiduciary Fees,[1] charged to income | (4,000) |
| 8. 80% of Fiduciary Fees, charged to principal | (4,000) |

Taxable Income = $49,000^2$

---

1. Fees are allocable in part to the tax exempt income and become nondeductible under §265. The portion deemed allocable to that income was based here on income allocable to the income account and is consistent with the illustration in Treas. Reg. §1.643(d)-2(a). It might be more appropriate to allocate based on all income, dividends, gains, and losses considered in computing taxable income, in which case the proper portion to exclude would be only 10 ÷ 67. A larger portion of the deduction is lost as illustrated in the regulation, which may explain the simplistic approach taken by the government.

Distributable Net Income is computed as:

| | |
|---|---:|
| Taxable Income | $49,000 |
| Less net long term capital gain[3] | (5,000) |
| Less dividends allocable to principal[4] | (12,000) |
| Plus tax exempt income, reduced by allocable fees[5] | 8,000 |

$$DNI = \$40,000$$

As illustrated, fiduciary accounting income, taxable income, and distributable net income each may differ during any given year. Fiduciary accounting income could exceed taxable income if deductible expenses were paid from principal or due to tax exempt interest or the deduction in lieu of the personal exemption; fiduciary accounting income could be less than taxable income if taxable items, such as capital gains or certain dividends, were allocable to principal. Taxable income could exceed DNI because the distributions deduction is ignored or because capital gains or taxable dividends are allocated to principal and thus excluded in computing DNI; taxable income could be less than DNI due to tax exempt income or the deduction in lieu of the personal exemption (all considered in computing taxable income but not in determining DNI). And there need be no correlation between fiduciary accounting income and DNI. Consequently, it could be hazardous to use short-cuts to determine the tax treatment of an estate or trust, by assuming a correlation between any of these three concepts.

### *Separate Share Rule*

In determining the amount of DNI of an estate or trust that is allocable to its beneficiaries, §663(c) provides that substantially independent and separately administered shares of a single trust or estate will be treated as separate trusts for their respective beneficiaries. Consequently, activity such as accumulations or distributions in one separate share will not affect application of the tax rules or the tax consequences of activity in other shares. Prior to 1997 the separate share rule applied only to trusts. Now it applies to estates as well. And it applies in each case regardless of how many beneficiaries there are of

---

2.  For ease, this figure has been computed before the §651(a) distributions deduction, with its §643(a)(1) adjustment, and before the §642(b) deduction, with its §643(a)(2) adjustment.

3.  Under §643(a)(3), reflecting items 5 and 6.

4.  Under §643(a)(4), reflecting item 2.

5.  Under §643(a)(5), reflecting items 4, 7, and 8.

any separate share or whether separate books of account are maintained for the separate shares. Treas. Reg. §1.663(c)-3.

### *Tax Years*

A final function of DNI is not very important for trust administration purposes, but it is relevant for estates, which are the only fiduciary entities with individuals as beneficiaries that routinely may have a tax year that is not a calendar year. Under §§652(c) and 662(c), if an estate or trust has a tax year that is different from that of its beneficiary, the amount of income potentially attributable to the beneficiary and the time of its inclusion in the beneficiary's gross income is based on the entity's income for the entity's tax year that ends during the beneficiary's tax year. To illustrate, assume the beneficiary is on a calendar year (most individuals are) and an estate is on a fiscal year that ends on January 31. Income distributed by the estate to the beneficiary on February 1 of year 1 is treated as the beneficiary's income in year 2 (the beneficiary's tax year in which the estate's tax year 1 ends — on January 31 of year 2). This means that the distribution will not be returned or tax paid on it until April 15 of year 3 at the earliest (unless estimated tax is being reported by the beneficiary on a quarterly basis).

This deferral opportunity has its downside at the end of administration, in which case a "bunching" of two years' worth of income may occur in a single year of the beneficiary. For example, in this illustration the prior year's income would be reported in the year of estate termination, plus the income of the year beginning February 1 and ending when the administration terminates in the same year. It also may occur at a beneficiary's death, because there is no tax year of the beneficiary with which or within which the distributing entity's tax year ends (the entity's tax year will end after the beneficiary's death unless the beneficiary happens to die on the last day of the distributing entity's tax year). Income paid to a beneficiary's estate or successors in interest after the beneficiary's death is taxable to those recipients as income in respect of a decedent under §691(a), which we study beginning at page 487.

Because fiscal years are still allowed for estates, careful attention is required to coordinate the tax year of the estate with the years of its beneficiaries. Selection of tax year is one item of postmortem tax planning customarily considered by the personal representative, and administration of even a simple, no frills estate can entail time consuming and often difficult details of this type that many planners and most beneficiaries do not recognize or appreciate. Similarly, for both estates and trusts, some discrétion exists in selecting when the last year of the entity will end for tax purposes. In this respect, both estates and trusts are deemed to continue to exist for a reasonable period necessary to perform the ordinary duties of administration and thereafter to distribute all but a reasonable reserve for contingent claims. Any attempt to unduly prolong administration (for example to force termination into a later tax year of the beneficiaries) will be disallowed and the entity will be deemed terminated when that reasonable time for administration has expired. Treas. Reg. §§1.641(b)-3(a), 1.641(b)-3(b).

### Simple Trusts

For income tax purposes, trusts commonly are divided into two groups: simple trusts and complex trusts. The terms "simple trust" and "complex trust" are not used in the Code, but they are common in tax parlance because they are used in the Regulations. See, e.g., Treas. Reg. §§1.651(a)-1, -2, -3; 1.651(b)-1; 1.652(a)-1; 1.661(a)-1. Curiously enough, although most tax lawyers who are familiar with this area of tax law routinely speak in terms of simple and complex trusts, the reality is that the distinction between them is of little significance today. With no exceptions of real merit, a simple trust and its beneficiaries would be taxed in an identical manner if the tax rules applicable to complex trusts (§§661-664) were applied. But the statutory provisions for simple trusts (§§651 and 652) are more concise, because much of the legislation needed for complex trusts need not apply to simple trusts.

In essence, then, the simple trust rules are the Reader's Digest version of the complex trust rules, stripped down to the bare essentials needed to deal with the form of trust that meets the requirements of §651(a) that the trust (a) must distribute all current income annually, (b) must make no distributions for the year in excess of the amount of current income, and (c) may make no charitable distributions or set asides. Notice that the trust must *require* distribution of all income currently, but not all income actually must *be* distributed to qualify. That is, even if income is not currently distributed, the fact that distribution is required will suffice to satisfy the all income requirement. Treas. Reg. §1.651(a)-1(b).

A trust might require distribution of income but not actually distribute it in a variety of circumstances. For example, often a trust's tax year ends with income on hand that is not distributable until the next periodic income distribution date (monthly, quarterly, semi-annually or whatever). This is proper administration of a trust and the Code recognizes it. Moreover, occasionally the beneficiary requests or authorizes a delay in the current distribution of income. And sometimes the trustee is unsure of the identity of the proper beneficiary and seeks instructions while withholding trust income pending a judicial determination. To avoid disqualification as a simple trust in any of these events, the tax rule intentionally does not require actual distribution of all income annually. It also does not require that the income entitlement of any given beneficiary be specified. For example, a trust that requires distribution of all income annually among a group of beneficiaries (a "sprinkle" trust), in whatever proportions the trustee selects, would be a simple trust even though no single beneficiary has a guaranteed entitlement.

As to the second requirement for qualification as a simple trust — that there be no distributions in excess of current income — the trustee need not be prohibited from distributing amounts in excess of current income. Rather, the trustee simply must ensure that only income is distributed in a given year, thus allowing the trust to be taxed as a simple trust for that year. This imposes a burden on the trustee to carefully monitor distributions, because expected tax consequences may be lost due to inadvertent excess distributions.

"Inadvertent" might seem to be an inappropriate term because you might think that even the most inexperienced trustee ought be able to tell whether a distribution exceeds income. Here, however, the difference between trust accounting income and income in a tax sense becomes important. For tax purposes, distributions made by a trust are income under §643(b) to the extent they do not exceed the amount of the current year's fiduciary accounting income. Whether they exceed DNI or match taxable income is irrelevant. That is, "income" *means* fiduciary accounting income, as determined by the fiduciary in good faith under the governing instrument and applicable local law. Thus, Treas. Reg. §1.651(a)-2(a) recognizes the validity of reserves to which income may be allocated without constituting a failure to distribute all current income annually.

So it is the *amount* of current income, rather than the actual identity of items received as income, that is determinative for simple trust qualification purposes, regardless of the source of that distribution for trust accounting purposes. See §651(a) (last sentence, referring to "amounts of income" described in §651(a)(1)). Distributions not in excess of the current year's fiduciary accounting income are "income" for purposes of applying the simple trust rules, and it is the amount of fiduciary accounting income, not the actual source of the distribution, that the trustee must monitor to ensure qualification as a simple trust. To illustrate, assume a trust has income of $1,000 for the current year and is required to distribute all income currently. A distribution of stock held in the trust with a fair market value of $1,000 would be regarded as a distribution of income, even though the stock was held as a part of trust corpus on the trust accounting ledger. Moreover, fiduciary accounting income may exceed either taxable income or DNI, so it is possible to distribute amounts of fiduciary accounting income in excess of what otherwise would be taxable to the trust, without losing the status of a simple trust.

## Tax Treatment of Simple Trusts

The tax treatment of a trust that qualifies as a simple trust is "conduit" taxation, effected under §§651(a) and 651(b) through the "distributions deduction," resulting in a tax wash to the trust. Distributions of fiduciary accounting income from the trust "carry out" DNI to the recipients thereof under §652(a) and Treas. Reg. §1.652(a)-1, and those recipients acquire the liability to pay tax on it. In computing its income tax liability for the year, a qualifying simple trust may deduct the amount of income it was required to distribute. However, under §651(b) the distributions deduction may not exceed distributable net income, computed without inclusion of the net amount of tax exempt income. This is to prevent a deduction larger than the trust's taxable income, which would put the trust in a loss position for tax purposes. To accomplish this result Treas. Reg. §1.651(b)-1 requires reduction of DNI by the amount of tax exempt interest income specified in §643(a)(5) (as adjusted by any deductions allocable to it). The effect of this adjustment is to limit the distributions deduction to the taxable portion of DNI so as not to put the trust in a loss position in computing its taxes for the year. The tax exempt quality of the income is not lost, however, because it carries over to the recipients by virtue of the character rule in §652(b).

The tax consequence of qualification as a simple trust to beneficiaries entitled to receive required distributions of income is §652(a) inclusion in income of the amount allowed as a deduction to the trust, whether the income actually was distributed or only required to be distributed. Distributions can exceed the allowable deduction, because fiduciary accounting income is greater than the taxable portion of DNI. When that occurs each recipient simply includes in income a pro rata portion of the amount of the deduction, based on the total distributions made by the trust.

So complete is the pass through of tax liability to the beneficiaries that, under §652(b) and Treas. Reg. §1.652(b)-1, amounts originally received by the trust retain their tax character (tax exempt income, capital gains, tax preference items, and so forth) when distributed to the beneficiaries. Moreover, the character of all amounts included in DNI, both income (including tax exempt income) and deductions, effectively is allocated pro rata to the recipients by §652(b) and Treas. Reg. §1.652(b)-2. This can be altered only by a provision of the governing instrument specifically mandating non pro rata distribution of various classes of income. Discretionary non pro rata distributions by the trustee of various classes of income do not alter this allocation. Treas. Reg. §1.652(b)-2(b)(1).

In short, the overall effect of both the distributions deduction and the inclusion rules is conduit taxation that taxes the beneficiaries generally as if the trust did not exist as an intermediary. The exception to this conclusion is the treatment of capital gains that are not treated under the instrument or local law as fiduciary accounting income. They are retained by and taxed to the simple trust.

## Estates and Complex Trusts

The complex trust rules of Subpart C (§§661-664) govern all estates, any trust that is not a simple trust for the year (because it either may accumulate income, provides for charity, or actually made distributions exceeding current income), and all trusts in the year of termination (because principal necessarily is distributed). But the tax consequences to the entity and beneficiary essentially are the same as the conduit tax treatment of a simple trust to the extent income of an estate or complex trust is currently distributed or is required to be distributed. The entity is entitled to a distributions deduction under §661(a), the beneficiaries include the deducted amounts under §662(a), and the character of each item in DNI carries through to the beneficiaries pro rata under §§661(b) and 662(b) (unless the governing instrument specifically dictates otherwise).

There is one notable difference between the distributions deduction for a complex trust and that for a simple trust. Both deductions cannot exceed the amount of DNI (see §651(b) and the last sentence of §661(a)) as reduced by tax exempt income (see the last sentence of §§651(b) and 661(c)). But the *amount* of DNI will differ by virtue of application only to simple trusts of §643(a)(4) (exclusion from DNI of taxable dividends allocable to principal). This special rule does not apply to complex trusts and it is not commonly encountered. Ignoring it at your slight peril, you can see why learning the one set of rules in Subpart C will suffice for all trusts and estates. Excepting this one slight variation, Subpart B really doesn't add anything.

One distinction is worthy of note but not any change to the suggestion that you don't need to learn two separate sets of rules. It is that a complex trust or an estate (unlike a simple trust) may make distributions of amounts in excess of the dollar amount of fiduciary accounting income (whether the distributed asset comes from fiduciary accounting income or principal). These distributions also are deemed to carry out income, to the extent of current DNI or prior years' accumulations of income (known as undistributed net income (UNI) and defined at page 483). These might generate additional distributions deductions for the estate or trust, and may require inclusion by the recipients under §662(a)(2).

To illustrate this difference between simple and complex trusts, assume a trust has $33,000 of fiduciary accounting income for the year, consisting of $24,000 of ordinary income and $9,000 of tax exempt income. The trustee is required to distribute all the income annually to B. If the trustee actually distributes more than $33,000 for the year, the trust would be a complex trust for that year. The distribution would carry out the $33,000 of DNI, of which $9,000 would be tax exempt to B and the trust would be entitled to a $24,000 distributions deduction (the taxable portion of DNI). In addition, the trust would have made either an accumulation distribution of UNI or a tax free distribution of corpus (or some of each) of the amount in excess of $33,000 that was distributed to B, making the trust complex. No additional distributions deduction would be available to the trust for this excess distribution, and the tax consequence to B would depend on the extent to which the distribution carried out UNI (which largely is irrelevant today). By way of comparison, if the trustee properly had distributed only $22,000 for the year, in this example the amounts distributed would be $^{24}/_{33} \times$ $22,000 of taxable income items and $^{9}/_{33} \times$ $22,000 of tax exempt income and the trust would be complex by virtue of accumulating the income that was not currently distributed. B would include taxable income of $^{24}/_{33} \times$ $22,000 ($16,000) and report tax exempt income of $^{9}/_{33} \times$ $22,000 ($6,000), and the trust would deduct the full $^{24}/_{33} \times$ $22,000 ($16,000) of taxable income that was distributed.

### In-Kind Distributions and Specific Bequests

Under §643(e) distributions in kind from a complex trust carry out income (either DNI, UNI, or a combination of both) only to the extent of the lesser of the distributed assets' adjusted basis or their fair market value. For example, distribution of stock worth $100 but with a basis of $80 can carry out (at most) the lesser $80 and only that amount could be includible in the beneficiary's income or be deducted by the entity. In addition, by §663(a)(1), excepted entirely from the income carryout rules applicable to complex trusts are transfers in satisfaction of a specific bequest, devise, or legacy payable in less than four installments, if not required to be satisfied only out of income. To constitute a "specific" disposition, the identity of the property conveyed, or the dollar amount of a pecuniary gift, must be ascertainable as of inception of the estate or trust. "Formula" bequests (for example, a marital deduction distribution that is tied to a concept such as a decedent's gross estate for Federal estate tax purposes) do not qualify as specific bequests the satisfaction of which will not carry out DNI. This is because they are dependent on variables (such as valuation and tax elections) that make them unascertainable until some time after the date of death. Treas. Reg. §1.663(a)-1(b). Further, in determining whether payment is to be made in less than four installments, the terms of the governing instrument, not actual administration, are determinative. Treas. Reg. §1.663(a)-1(c)(1).

### Accumulated Income

The principal difference between the taxation of simple trusts under Subpart B and the taxation of estates or complex trusts under Subpart C is attributable to accumulations of income in the latter. Only capital gains or other income properly allocable to corpus are taxed to a simple trust. All other income is offset completely by the distributions deduction and is thereby taxed through to the beneficiaries. In a complex trust or an estate, income that is accumulated rather than distributed will be taxed to the estate or trust because the distributions deduction is less than the total taxable income and, thus, does not wash out the full amount of income for the year. By virtue of this essential difference, the complex trust or estate as a separate taxpayer permits fragmentation of income between the beneficiaries and the entity.

At one time this fragmentation made it possible to reduce the tax paid by all. Now, however, the current rate schedule taxes trusts and estates with modest amounts of taxable income at the maximum income tax rate, so only a very modest potential reduction in tax is available by taxing some income to the entity and some to the beneficiary. Nevertheless, when the tax rates were more favorable it was recognized that this income fragmentation opportunity necessitated several concepts that are not applicable to simple trusts and that remain in the law.

Although the beneficiaries of complex trusts and estates still are taxed on income actually distributed, and the fiduciary receives a corresponding deduction for it (both identical to a simple trust), accumulated income (taxed to the entity) presents the potential for tax minimization. To deal with this factor, Subchapter J creates the concept of UNI and imposes seemingly complex rules known as the accumulation distribution and throwback rules. We will not demonstrate this but hope you will take our word for the fact that the rules are hard to decipher (this is one of those cases in which you really need to know what the Code is telling you before you can read it and figure out what it says). Their application also requires a good bit of tax related information about both the entity and the beneficiary for prior years. Still, the actual *operation* of a throwback computation itself is not as convoluted as many would have you believe. Furthermore, much more importantly, in 1997 Congress effectively repealed the accumulation distribution and throwback rules for 99% of all trusts. Although the provisions remain in the Code, they apply only to certain pre-1984 abusive multiple trusts, and to foreign trusts, so for our purposes the story of throwback is a dead letter and we won't bother you with any further details. Suffice it to say that simple and complex trusts are taxed virtually identically to the extent this complexity is gone.

## Multiple Trust Rule

A second rule applicable to complex trusts exists to minimize their use to fragment income into multiple separate taxpaying entities, each with its own separate rates and deduction in lieu of the personal exemption. By the "multiple trust" rule of §643(f), separate trusts are regarded as a single tax paying entity if they were created by substantially the same grantor or grantors, with substantially the same beneficiary or beneficiaries, and with a principal purpose to avoid taxes. Because of compression in tax brackets the old game to which §643(f) was directed also is a thing of the past, so we doubt you will encounter this either.

## Sixty-Five Day Rule

A third special rule originally limited to complex trusts (but now also applicable to estates) is a reflection of the fact that it may not be possible to know, as of year end, how much income must be distributed to avoid a trust accumulation. Thus, the "sixty-five day" rule of §663(b) permits complex trusts and estates to elect to treat distributions made within 65 days after year-end as distributions of DNI during the year just ended. The rule originally was applicable only to complex trusts because the object was to avoid accumulations that subsequently could be subject to the accumulation distribution and throwback rules, which applied only to complex trusts and not to estates or simple trusts. With the repeal of throwback for most trusts, and the equivalent treatment of estates and trusts, this rule now applies to both complex trusts and to estates. But with effective repeal of throwback the need for this rule also has waned (although it can be useful *if* the beneficiaries are in lower tax brackets than the entity and washing more income out to them proves to be desirable, based on information discovered in that 65 day period).

## The Tier Rules

A fourth concept, the "tier" rules, is made necessary in complex trusts by the ability to accumulate income for later distribution. The term "tier," which is not utilized in the Code or Regulations, refers to the distinction drawn in §§661(a)(1) and 661(a)(2) between amounts of income required to be distributed currently ("Tier 1" distributions) and other amounts properly paid, credited, or required to be distributed ("Tier 2" distributions).

To illustrate the importance of this concept, assume that a complex trust has $50,000 of fiduciary accounting income for the year but DNI of only $40,000 (due to an income tax deduction for expenses that were charged to principal for fiduciary accounting purposes). Also assume that the trustee must currently distribute all income in equal shares to beneficiaries A and B, and that the trustee also makes a discretionary distribution of $50,000 to B. Without the tier rules it would appear that, because A has received $25,000 while B has received $75,000, the $40,000 of DNI ought to be pro rated between them in proportions of $10,000 and $30,000 respectively. However, by virtue of the terms of the trust, it is apparent that A received half the current income, not just one-fourth, and should be taxed on half the DNI. The tier rules provide the mechanism for distinguishing between the various distributions to A and B to effect this treatment.

The technical definitions under the tier rules relate to distributions made by the trust. Under §661(a)(1), Tier 1 distributions are required current distributions of income (not in excess of DNI). So pervasive is the "required" distribution notion that, under §662(a)(1), a Tier 1 distribution is *treated* as having been made as required, resulting in DNI inclusion to the beneficiary, even if the distribution is not made in fact. Recall the comparable simple trust rule. Under §661(a)(2) and Treas. Reg. §1.661(a)-2(c), Tier 2 distributions are all other distributions, whether required or discretionary and whether made from current income, from accumulated income, or from corpus. So, in the preceding example, A and B are equal Tier 1 beneficiaries because the trustee must make current distribution of all income to them. Consequently, the $40,000 of DNI is pro rated equally between them under §662(a)(1) and Treas. Reg. §1.662(a)-2(b), rather than apportioned $10,000 to A and $30,000 to B. Any DNI remaining after satisfaction of all Tier 1 required current distributions of income similarly would be pro rated under §662(a)(2)(B) and Treas. Reg. §1.662(a)-3(c) among the Tier 2 beneficiaries on the basis of their Tier 2 distributions.

Only the amount of the Tier 2 distributions in excess of any DNI remaining after Tier 1 distributions would qualify as either a §665(b) accumulation distribution of prior years' UNI or a §102 tax-free distribution of principal. In the prior example, the $50,000 distributed to B is a Tier 2 distribution and may be taxable as UNI — if the trust has any (and if throwback applies) — or as a tax free distribution of corpus.

### *Separate Share Rule*

A final relevant concept under Subpart C is the separate share rule, mentioned at page 476, applicable under §663(c) to trusts and (only since 1997) to estates alike. By providing that substantially independent and separately administered shares of a single trust or estate will be treated as separate trusts for DNI allocation purposes, activity such as accumulations or distributions in one separate share do not affect application of the tier rules or the tax consequences of activity in other shares.

To summarize, DNI in both simple and complex trusts is carried out to trust beneficiaries by required current income distributions. Any remaining DNI is carried out by any other distributions made. DNI is shared pro rata by the recipients within any class or tier of distribution, and each item of income in DNI is shared pro rata within each class or tier (unless the governing instrument specifically provides otherwise).

### Distributions in Kind

Distributions from an estate or trust carry out income (first DNI, then UNI, to the extent either is available in the year of distribution), regardless of whether the distribution constitutes fiduciary accounting income or corpus and regardless of whether the fiduciary distributes cash or property in-kind. Section 643(e) limits the amount of income deemed distributed by a complex trust or an estate on a Tier 2 in-kind transfer of property, and establishes the basis of distributed property. Notice, however, that §643(e) establishes these special rules for distributions and basis only for purposes of §§661(a)(2) and 662(a)(2) (Tier 2 distributions) and has no application to simple trusts that are governed by §§651 and 652, nor to Tier 1 distributions that are governed by §§661(a)(1) and 662(a)(1). The reason for this is articulated more fully below, but the gist of it is that income equal to the fair market value of a distributed asset is carried out by distribution of an asset in-kind (to the extent there is sufficient DNI) if §643(e) does not apply. Meaning if distribution is a mandatory income entitlement (simple trust or Tier 1 from a complex trust). The only exception to this would be if the distribution qualifies as a specific bequest under §663(a)(1).

To the extent it *does* apply, §643(e)(2) limits the income carryout on an in-kind distribution to the lesser of (1) the asset's fair market value or (2) the adjusted basis of the asset (plus or minus any gain or loss realized on the distribution), with an election granted to the fiduciary under §643(e)(3) to intentionally incur gain or loss on the distribution. Further, adjusted basis to the distributee is a carryover of the distributing entity's basis (again, as adjusted for gain or loss realized on the distribution). To illustrate, consider an asset with a fair market value of $100 and an adjusted basis of $40. Distribution as a Tier 2 in-kind transfer would carry out income of $40, and basis to the distributee would be $40, being a carryover of the distributing entity's basis (with no adjustment for gain or loss because none was incurred on the distribution). The effect of §643(e) is that less income is carried out by a Tier 2 distribution of an appreciated asset in-kind.

To appreciate this rule, let's assume that a trustee wants to distribute $70 to a beneficiary. It could do so by distributing (1) an asset with a fair market value of $70 and a basis of any amount, (2) cash of $70, or (3) any combination of the two. Under §643(e) a Tier 2 distribution of cash will carry out up to $70 of DNI but a Tier 2 distribution in-kind will carry out no more DNI than the basis of the distributed asset. The justification for this limited DNI carry out is a feeling that it is inequitable to saddle a distributee with income equal to fair market value *plus* any unrealized appreciation represented by a basis that is lower than fair market value. That being the case, §643(e) need not apply to Tier 1 distributions governed by §§661(a)(1) and 662(a)(1) and to distributions from simple trusts governed by §§651 and 652 because those in-kind distributions are gain or loss realization events, as discussed next below. As a result fair market value and adjusted basis will be equal in the beneficiary's hands and DNI carryout will be that same amount (at least to the extent of DNI available for distribution).

### *Realization Events*

The carryover of basis and DNI carry out limitation of §643(e) is affected by distributions that otherwise generate a new basis. Gain or loss may be realized under Treas. Reg. §1.661(a)-2(f)(1) by distribution of an asset in-kind, with a concomitant adjustment to basis (to fair market value) if the distribution is in satisfaction of the distributee's right to receive some other asset (for example, if Blackacre were distributed instead of a specific bequest of stock), or the distribution is in satisfaction of the distributee's right to receive cash (for example, if Blackacre were distributed to satisfy a debt owed to a creditor or to satisfy a beneficiary's right to receive a specific legacy, or in satisfaction of a trustee's mandate to distribute an amount equal to all income annually). In either case, the income tax treatment is as if the proper asset or cash were distributed and then used to purchase the actual asset distributed, with gain or loss generated on that sale if the asset had unrealized appreciation or depreciation (and nonrecognition under the Code did not otherwise apply).

### Income and Deductions in Respect of a Decedent

Neither income in respect of a decedent (IRD) nor deductions in respect of a decedent (DRD) is a concept unique to the income taxation or administration of estates and trusts or the taxation of beneficiaries. Nevertheless, each applies to any taxpayer receiving income to which a decedent was entitled, or paying specified deductible expenses on the decedent's behalf. And IRD and DRD are common to fiduciary administration and the income taxation of trusts, estates, and beneficiaries. With respect to all taxpayers, the fundamental tax objective of both the IRD and DRD concepts is to maintain the same character of the income and deductions as if received or incurred by the decedent while alive. For fiduciary income tax purposes, any IRD received or

DRD incurred by an entity enters into the computation of its taxable income, and thus into the amount of DNI.

Broadly speaking, IRD is income earned by a decedent prior to death but not recognized for income tax purposes until after the decedent's death. Similarly, DRD consists of expenses or obligations incurred by the decedent prior to death and that would have been deductible by the decedent if they had been paid or properly accrued prior to death but they were paid by the estate or entitled beneficiary postmortem. Although there is no *statutory* definition of IRD, we know from Treas. Reg. §1.691(a)-2 that the government regards the following items as IRD:

- Compensation for the decedent's services, including a bonus voted after the decedent's death that the employer had no obligation to pay.
- Renewal commissions of a deceased life insurance agent.
- Accrued but unreported interest on Series EE United States Treasury Bonds.
- Dividends on stock owned by the decedent that were payable to shareholders of record on a date prior to the decedent's death.
- Alimony arrearages.
- Deferred compensation death payments made to beneficiaries under a qualified retirement plan.
- Capital gain on a sale made during the decedent's life and reported on an installment basis (the recipient of the right to receive those payments will continue to report them on the same basis as did the decedent).
- Distributive share of partnership income paid to a deceased partner for the partnership's taxable year in which death occurs, attributable to the period ending with the partner's death, is IRD even if the deceased partner made cash withdrawals from the partnership as an advance against that income. In addition, a share of profits for periods after the partner's death also can be IRD.

Helpful guidelines for identifying IRD refer to income that would have been taxable to the decedent had death not occurred prior to receipt. See Ferguson, Freeland & Ascher, FEDERAL INCOME TAXATION OF ESTATES, TRUSTS, AND BENEFICIARIES §3.3 at 3:10 (2d ed. 1993). Some cases refer to there being a legally significant arrangement that elevates the income above a mere expectancy and there being no outstanding economically material contingencies at the decedent's death. It is necessary to establish that the decedent, not the ultimate recipient, performed the substantive acts that spawned the entitlement to establish that the decedent would have received and included the income had death not intervened. Thus, the recipient's acquisition must be "passive," not due to efforts made to generate the right (as opposed to enforcing it) after the decedent's death.

### Tax Consequences of IRD

There are three primary tax consequences of an item being regarded as IRD, not all of which being disadvantageous, depending on the circumstances. First, income represented by the right to receive IRD is taxable in the year it is received. Second, under §691(a)(3), the character of the income is the same as if it was received by the decedent. And third, rather than a new basis at death, the item has a §1014(c) basis equal to what the decedent's basis would have been if living. This treatment is necessary because otherwise, to the extent of a new basis, the IRD would not be taxable as income as received. To illustrate, assume that D negotiated a sale of property prior to death that failed to close because of housing code violations. The sale was completed after D's death because the buyer agreed to take the property subject to the violations, in exchange for a $2,000 reduction in the purchase price. According to *Estate of Napolitano v. Commissioner*, 63 T.C.M. (CCH) 3092 (1992), the sale proceeds were not IRD because the sale was not complete prior to death. In this case avoiding an IRD label was a great result because D's basis in the property was $50,000 and the sale price was $240,000, so avoiding IRD treatment meant that a §1014(b) basis adjustment at death was available and the sale generated no gain.

### Deductions in Respect of a Decedent

As a counterpart to the rules governing income in respect of a decedent, a taxpayer who makes certain payments that would have been deductible if paid by a decedent prior to death is entitled to a §691(b) deduction in respect of the decedent. Those expenditures specifically are limited to §162 business expenses, §212 expenses of producing income or managing or safeguarding income producing property, §163 interest, and §164 deductible taxes (or the §27 credit for foreign taxes). In addition, the recipient of depletable property is entitled to any §611 percentage depletion attributable to income received therefrom, under Treas. Reg. §1.691(b)-1(b). In each case, the deduction is available to the recipient of property to which the expenditure is attributable, and without limitation by the otherwise applicable §642(g) rule denying double duty for deductions that may be taken on either the estate tax or estate income tax return. These deductions in respect of a decedent specifically are excepted from the operation of §642(g) because, had they been incurred by the decedent during life, they would have reduced the decedent's estate for estate tax purposes and still would have been deductible for income tax purposes.

### *Deduction for Taxes Attributable to IRD*

In addition to DRD, an income tax deduction is allowed under §691(c) for estate or generation-skipping transfer taxes attributable to IRD. This deduction is based on a theory that, had the income been received by the decedent during life, any income tax incurred on it would have been paid prior to imposition of the estate or generation-skipping transfer tax, resulting in a smaller estate subject to those taxes and, thus, less of those taxes being payable. Congress wanted to approximate that result without recomputing the estate or generation-skipping transfer tax after the income tax on the IRD has been computed. So Congress substituted an income tax deduction for the estate or generation-skipping transfer taxes attributable to the IRD. The general objective is to obtain a result that is administratively easier than recomputation of the wealth transfer tax and that approximates what would have happened if the IRD had been received during the decedent's life.

In some cases an item will be income no matter who receives it, so treatment as IRD carries no detriment and allows the §691(c) deduction that otherwise would not be available. In those cases it pays to argue in favor of IRD treatment, which shows that the IRD label is not always detrimental.

## Grantor Trust Rules

Subchapter J establishes a third category into which trusts may fall. Estates always are taxed as a complex trust and, by virtue of §671, cannot be subject to the following rules. But any trust (whether simple or complex) may be subject in whole or in part to this third category of rules, being Subpart E (§§671 through 679) of Part I of Subchapter J: the grantor trust rules. Trusts may be subject to Subpart E in some years or only to a limited extent but, to the extent the grantor trust rules apply, Subpart E overrides the balance of Subchapter J.

Fundamental to application of the grantor trust rules is possession of prohibited enjoyment or control of trust income or corpus by a grantor or, under the §678 pseudo grantor trust rule, someone treated as if they were the grantor. When Subpart E applies, the normal principles we just studied are supplanted by the grantor trust rules, and the applicable portion of the trust is said to be "ignored" for income tax purposes. To the extent this occurs, income, losses, deductions, and credits allocable to that portion of the trust are attributed to the grantor (actual or pseudo), rather than to the trust or its beneficiaries. These tax attributes retain their character in the grantor's hands, in most respects as if no trust had been created. Thus, for example, a trust loss would be the grantor's deduction, a distribution to charity would be treated as the grantor's contribution, capital gains in the trust would be aggregated with the grantor's capital gains and losses, and the statute of limitation for the trust may be that of the grantor.

The key to application of the grantor trust rules is whether the grantor enjoys any trust benefits, has retained so much control, or has left so many "strings" attached to the trust that the grantor should be regarded as the true owner of the trust property for income tax purposes. Accordingly, the grantor trust provisions read like a laundry list of powers and interests in the trust, any one of which is sufficient to invoke grantor trust treatment. By way of easiest example, a revocable inter vivos trust is a §676 grantor trust, which is fitting given that the trust does not really change the settlor's ownership or other tax posture with respect to trust assets. The most common powers and interests that will trigger grantor trust treatment under Subpart E include:

- Certain §674 powers in the grantor or the grantor's spouse (exercisable without the consent of an adverse party) to control some other beneficiary's enjoyment (subject to numerous exceptions).

- §675 administrative powers permitting the grantor or the grantor's spouse to deal at less than arm's length with the trust property.

- A §676 power in the grantor or the grantor's spouse to amend or revoke the trust.

- A §677 interest in income that may be used "for the benefit of the grantor," including income that may be paid to the grantor or to the grantor's spouse and income that is actually distributed to a person either the grantor or the grantor's spouse is obliged to support or maintain.

- A pseudo grantor trust, which is taxed by §678 as if someone other than the grantor was the grantor. Technically §678 is not a grantor trust provision because it applies only to someone other than the grantor who has (or, under proper circumstances, who has released or modified) certain powers. It is included in Subpart E and it is appropriate to consider it as part of the grantor trust rules, however, because it has the effect of treating that person as the owner of that portion of the trust as to which the power applies, just as if that person was a grantor who transferred property into the trust and retained certain powers or interests. Classic forms of exposure stem from five or five and *Crummey* withdrawal rights, along with inter vivos general powers of appointment, most often found in §2056(b)(5) marital deduction trusts or trusts for mature family members that permit withdrawal by the beneficiary as an alternative to mandatory termination when the beneficiary reaches a certain age.

There are other rules and exceptions, but for our purposes these are the ones on which planners tend to rely when they seek to make a trust subject to Subpart E. To appreciate why you might *want* to do so (by creating an intentionally defective grantor trust), consider the following perceived advantages of grantor trust planning:

- To the extent provided under the portion rules, all income, losses, deductions, credits, and other tax qualities of the trust are attributed to the grantor. Sometimes losses, deductions, and credits generated by the entity are more useful in the grantor's hands. It may be that the grantor is in a lower income tax bracket than the trust, or the grantor may need the income or gains generated by the trust to offset deductions, losses, or credits generated in the grantor's individual capacity that otherwise would be lost.

- The grantor wants to pay income tax on income distributed to someone else, which constitutes a gift tax free benefit from the grantor to that distributee.

- Various transactions involving the trust are deemed to be conducted with the grantor rather than with the trust. For example, a principal personal residence, owned by a marital deduction trust that is treated under §678 as a pseudo grantor trust, may be eligible for the §121 exclusion of gain on the trust's sale of the residence. Because the trust is treated as nonexistent, the tax result is the same as if the surviving spouse was the owner of the property and personally made the sale. Because it was used as the spouse's principal personal residence, it qualifies for the capital gain exclusion.

Grantor trust treatment may apply to an entire trust or only a portion. The Code provides that the grantor (or a pseudo grantor) is treated as the owner of only that portion of a trust as to which a requisite power or interest exists. Several different portions may be involved. For example, a grantor with a reversion or a power to revoke the trust in its entirety may be treated as the owner of the entire trust, meaning that every item of income, loss, deduction, and credit in the trust is attributed to that deemed owner. Similarly, the grantor (or any nonadverse party who is trustee) with unrestricted powers over income and corpus would generate entire trust portion treatment.

On the other hand, a grantor may be treated as the owner of only those items allocable to the fiduciary accounting income portion. For example, the grantor is treated as the current income beneficiary of only the ordinary income portion if the grantor possessed only an income interest. To illustrate, if taxable income allocable to the income account is $5,000, taxable income allocable to corpus is $2,000, and deductible expenses total $6,000, the current income beneficiary would be taxed on zero income and the excess deduction of $1,000 would reduce income allocable to corpus. That excess deduction would *not* pass through to the income beneficiary. As in a nongrantor trust, the excess deductions do not pass through to the beneficiaries except in the year of termination. §642(h). Essentially the calculation of the portion is based on a distributable net income analogue. Thus, a grantor who is deemed the owner of only the income portion would not be entitled to deductions in excess of ordinary income. This shows that grantor trust treatment is not the same as if no trust had been created, notwithstanding a frequent but sometimes inaccurate assumption about the application of the grantor trust rules.

Other portions include the corpus portion (all items not reflected in the ordinary income portion, meaning income, losses, deductions, and credits allocable or attributable to corpus, and all income earned thereon after accumulation as a part of corpus) and fractional portions that reflect rights that would cause one of the grantor trust rules to apply to less than all of the trust (for example, a right to receive half the income from a trust). In unusual circumstances the portion also may be a particular asset, such as generated by a power to vote closely held stock transferred to a trust, in which case the grantor must report the income, losses, deductions, and credits attributable to just that asset (along with a pro rata share of any deductions not specifically identifiable with respect to the asset but properly spread among all trust assets).

Often the most challenging grantor trust planning issue is how to make a trust taxable to the grantor or a pseudo grantor without encountering unwanted wealth transfer tax consequences. In this respect by far the most popular defect is the §675(4)(C) power to swap assets. This provision essentially authorizes any person not acting in a fiduciary capacity and without the consent of a fiduciary to exchange trust assets for a full and adequate consideration (to purchase trust assets for fair market value) with no wealth transfer tax exposure to the powerholder. Other common approaches work in situations involving married grantors who feel confident that the marriage will last because it is relatively easy to trigger grantor trust liability with an interest or power in the grantor's spouse that is only deemed to be an interest or power in the grantor. See the spousal unity rule in §672(e). This form of intentional grantor trust exposure will generate no wealth transfer tax consequence to the grantor (although care must be taken to avoid exposing the spouse to unexpected wealth transfer tax).

There is much more. For added guidance and self study regarding the grantor trust rules in particular, see 1 Casner & Pennell, ESTATE PLANNING §5.11 (6th ed. 1995), and Ferguson, Freeland, & Ascher,

FEDERAL INCOME TAXATION OF ESTATES, TRUSTS AND BENEFICIARIES ch. 10 (3d ed. 1999).

# CHAPTER 21

# ETHICS AND MALPRACTICE ISSUES

The vast majority of estate planners are of a personality type that makes them more sensitive than many attorneys to concerns about ethics, conflicts, and propriety. It is part of what drives them to specialize in this area of legal service. What some attorneys (including estate planners) seem to lack, however, is a sense of the issues and problems that can arise in the ethics arena. Moreover, the rules governing the legal profession are not about morality as much as they are guidelines and prohibitions that regulate the practice of law. Most relations involved in this arena fall under the law of agency, from which most of the obligations and prohibitions found in the ethical rules applicable to lawyers are derived. As such, this "law" is as susceptible to learning as the Internal Revenue Code or a local probate code.

This Chapter seeks to raise your level of consciousness about certain "predictable" ethical dilemmas in estate planning and fiduciary administration in situations that often generate problems or issues. In some situations the ethics issue is clear and the appropriate action easily is identifiable. In many other cases there is no "correct" response to the problems that are identified. In these circumstances, a good result is recognition of the problem, which must be considered in the context in which it arises. Although unsatisfactory, often conscious recognition and a sensitivity to these concerns is the best that can be expected.

This Chapter also illustrates that this area lacks clear answers and direction because the ethics rules weren't written by or for estate planners. Many of the existing rules don't apply or, if they do apply (which is arguable), they apply woodenly. Many ethics rules that were written from a conflict resolution perspective impose obligations and restrictions that are difficult or inappropriate in the planning context.

Many of these issues were addressed in the Restatement (Third) of the Law Governing Lawyers (Restatement), and improvements are developing all the time. Noted in place are changes in the Model Rules as proposed by the American Bar Association Commission on Evaluation of the Rules of Professional Conduct, commonly known as the Ethics 2000 Commission, Report with Recommendation to the House of Delegates (August 2001). Although these changes are not specifically relevant except as individual states ultimately adopt them, they spotlight issues of interest and concern.

Throughout this Chapter a healthy dose of hesitation seems appropriate, given the subjective and none too precise nature of many of the principles and rules discussed. Studies like that in Moore & Pennell, *Practicing What We Preach: Esoteric or Essential*, 27 U. Miami Inst. Est. Plan. ¶1200 (1993), and Moore & Pennell, *Survey of the Profession II*, 30 U. Miami Inst. Est. Plan. ¶1500 (1996), are interesting because they show how many estate planners (do not) address these rules, but beware. Minimal compliance or adherence to a "community standard" regarding various situations is not adequate. There is no reasonable level of compliance in the ethics arena that looks to what everyone else is doing, the way there is with respect to some aspects of malpractice liability. There is no community standard defense and no acceptable level of compliance short of full adherence to these rules.

Also note: This Chapter makes primary reference to the Model Rules of Professional Conduct promulgated by the American Bar Association. Although a small handful of states have not adopted those standards, they have been embraced in whole or in substantial part in virtually every state, replacing the Disciplinary Rules and Ethical Considerations of the American Bar Association's prior Model Code of Professional Conduct. A practitioner in a state that still imposes the Model Code standards will benefit from a consideration of the more recently developed Model Rules, because they establish minimum standards rather than the "aspirational" goals of the Model Code. In this respect, the Model Rules should be regarded as a *lesser* obligation than the Model Code. Everyone needs to be at least that respectful of the ethics concerns of our principal/agent relation. Moreover, because these are ethics rules, the professional is subject to being judged in the harshest possible light consistent with preserving the profession's responsibility (and opportunity) to govern itself. Finally, no responsible attorney will split hairs on which set of rules is applicable any more than someone knowingly would violate the spirit or the letter of a rule in reliance on an "audit lottery" view of ethics enforcement ("maybe you won't get caught").

In that regard, let's consider an often overlooked aspect of these rules. When there is a violation the appropriate punishment is not a damage award. Rather, it is a sanction (such as a "simple" reprimand, a suspension, or disbarment), for which there is no insurance! Instead, you and your dependents (including your employees and their dependents) pay a hefty price, usually in terms of lost income, which could result in foreclosure or other creditor action if you are unable to service debt obligations as a result. Frankly, you deserve to protect yourself (and all these others who depend on you) from being put in the line of fire because of an ethics allegation.

So one way to think about these rules is as *your* protection against the consequences of an ethics complaint (the same way we look upon the anonymous grading system as a protection against any allegation of impropriety in the academy). These rules are designed to protect *you* as much as they protect your clients from you. As you consider the information in this Chapter, it pays to remember how hard you are working as a lawyer, and to make a commitment not to risk your livelihood over silly aspects of noncompliance if the safe approach is easy to perform. Save your risk taking for challenges that are hard to address, because everyone who depends on you suffers if you can't prove that you did the right thing. You should protect all of them by doing all of this by the numbers, the way a good attorney does anything that is important.

Although compliance with every ethics rule is important, this Chapter does not address several obvious obligations (e.g., Model Rule 1.3 to serve clients diligently and Model Rule 1.4 to communicate with the client) that more than a few attorneys violate. These rules involve no real conceptual difficulty for estate planners, and can be addressed simply by paying attention. Instead, this material focuses on ethical issues confronting estate planners that usually fall under the following general categories: (1) conflicts of interest; (2) failure to exercise independent judgment; (3) violation of client confidences; (4) incompetent or inadequate representation; (5) excessive fees; (6) special estate administration concerns; (7) a general sense of duty to the "system"; and (8) misconduct involving solicitation and advertising.

## Conflicts of Interest

Easily the most important (and perhaps the most common, enduring, and troubling) ethical dilemmas facing estate planners are conflicts of interest. Compounding the difficulty of this issue is the fact that three separate provisions in the Model Rules speak to conflicts of interest, with differing standards or levels of conflict and different consent requisites.

For example, Model Rule 1.7(a)(1) deals with the representation of multiple clients whose interests are *directly adverse* to each other. This rule applies if an attorney is asked to bring suit against another active client of the attorney. The attorney's duty is to obtain the informed consent, confirmed in writing, of *each* client before undertaking the representation. Seldom is this rule applicable in a normal estate planning practice (except, perhaps, when a disappointed heir seeks to contest a will under which the attorney is acting as advisor to the personal representative).

Model Rule 1.7(a)(2) involves a similar conflict but applies if a client's interests are only *materially limited* by the attorney's representation of another client, a former client, a third person, or the lawyer's own personal interest. This rule *often* applies in a general estate planning practice. Under it, the attorney still must first obtain the informed consent, confirmed in writing, of each client whose representation may be affected. Usually this means that every mutually represented client must be consulted and must consent. In addition, both Rules 1.7(a)(1) and 1.7(a)(2) require the attorney to determine that the attorney will be able to provide competent and diligent representation to each affected client.

According to Comment 18 to Rule 1.7, regarding consent:

An informed consent requires that each affected client be aware of the relevant circumstances and of the material and reasonably foreseeable ways that the conflict could have adverse effects on the interests of that client. See Rule 1.0(e) (informed consent). The information required depends on the nature of the conflict and the nature of the risks involved. When representation of multiple clients in a single matter is undertaken, the information must include the implications of the common representation, including possible effects on loyalty, confidentiality and the attorney-client privilege and the advantages and risks involved.

According to Comment 20 to Rule 1.7, consent must be confirmed in writing, so as

to afford the client a reasonable opportunity to consider the risks and alternatives and to raise questions and concerns. . . . [T]he writing is required in order to impress upon clients the seriousness of the decision the client is being asked to make and to avoid disputes or ambiguities that might later occur in the absence of a writing.

Notice that neither Comment requires that the consent itself be in writing. It can be the product of an oral discussion and understanding. But a written follow up (confirmation) is required. Most estate planners commit the understanding or consent to writing just because the attorney ought to be able to prove the bona fides of the representation if the question arises (especially after a client's death). And again, let's make no mistake. It would be just plain stupid to have done the right thing in dealing with clients and not be able to prove it. Remember, your livelihood (and that of those who depend on you) can be at stake if you cannot defend yourself.

A third rule deals with a new client whose interests are *materially* adverse to those of a former client. Model Rule 1.9 requires the *former* client's consent before undertaking such a representation. The difficult aspect of this rule for most estate planners is determining whether a representation is complete so that the conflict is with a former client and Rule 1.7 is applicable in both cases — you need the new client's consent in all cases — so the only issue is whether Rule 1.7 or Rule 1.9 requires the existing or prior client's consent. Nevertheless, making a determination between these rules will not be very important because the obligations are so similar. Knowing that consents all around are required is the critical necessity.

### Representing Spouses

It does not seem to matter which of these varied standards and consent requirements applies in a given situation. To illustrate, consider the following hypothetical:

*Client has been represented for years by one of Attorney's partners; the firm has handled Client's substantial commercial and general corporate matters. Client is persuaded that it is time to have a new estate plan. Client makes an appointment to see Attorney and, at the initial meeting, appears with Spouse for their preliminary interview.*

The fundamental issue confronting Attorney at the outset of this representation is whether to represent both Client and Spouse and, if so, whether consents are required (and from whom). For our purposes the single most important realization is that the interests of Client and Spouse may not be identical, or even compatible, for a number of reasons. For example, the risk of conflict is significant if they may have:

- Separate assets (not uncommon even in community property jurisdictions), problems in characterizing property as separate or community property, or the need to create separate estates for both spouses to shelter tax benefits such as their unified credits and generation-skipping transfer tax exemptions.
- The right (in noncommunity property jurisdictions) to take a statutory forced heir share.
- ERISA-governed retirement benefit spousal annuity entitlements.
- An interest in using mirror image documents but an attraction to trusts that deny control to the surviving spouse.
- Children by another relation (now or potentially in the future).
- The risk of creditors of one spouse acquiring access to assets of the other spouse.
- The potential use of gift splitting.

And so on. Client and Spouse may be happy and harmonious in their objectives and plans, but either spouse may want planning that is not necessarily in the best interests of the other of them. There always is the *potential* for conflicts of interest in a representation of both spouses.

To illustrate, Attorney might advise Client to use a trust in lieu of a 100 percent outright disposition to Spouse if Client wants Spouse to leave it entirely to their common children at Spouse's later death. And Spouse might (justifiably) feel abused if Attorney talked Client out of leaving everything outright to Spouse. Alternatively, Attorney might feel obliged to advise Spouse on how to challenge Client's estate plan, whereas Attorney might at the same time be advising Client on how to move or settle assets in a form that precludes an effective spousal forced share election.

Based on the facts as they are revealed, there may be more or less reason to be concerned about the wisdom of Client's plan and the need to engage in certain forms of planning to guarantee its success. For example, Spouse may have a paramour (the soap opera type of illustration), children by a former marriage (the real life example), or charitable objectives that are not shared by Client (something most folks never would think to worry about until it has happened in their practice). But Attorney won't know any of this until after the representation has begun. Thus, the fundamental issue to be considered — theoretically even before Attorney hears one word from either Client or Spouse — is whether Attorney can even *begin* to represent both. Indeed, Attorney will not really know whether it is proper to represent both until Attorney has interviewed each, perhaps giving both the opportunity to speak with Attorney in private (which is something that many attorneys refuse to do, because they might actually discover a conflict. Does "don't ask, don't tell" make sense here?).

Restatement §201 describes a conflict of interest as "a substantial risk that the lawyer's representation of the client would be materially and adversely affected by . . . the lawyer's duties to another current client, a former client, or a third person." Restatement §211 uses essentially the same standard. Presumably the Restatement allows for the law of averages when it speaks of a "substantial risk." Neither the Model Code nor the Model Rules refer to such a "substantial risk," but Rule 1.7(a) employs the seemingly synonymous "significant" risk. Under each of these standards our question is whether a conflict waiver is needed. As you think about this issue, ask yourself why you would not just get one in all events.

Comment c(iii) to Restatement §201 defines "substantial" to mean that, "in the circumstances, the risk is significant and plausible, even if it is not certain or even probable that it will occur." More to the point, Restatement §211 comment c presents the following illustrations:

1. Husband and Wife consult Lawyer for estate-planning advice about a will for each of them. Lawyer has had professional dealings with the spouses, both separately and together, on several prior occasions. Lawyer knows them to be knowledgeable about their respective rights and interests, competent to make independent decisions if called for, and in accord on their common and individual objectives. Lawyer may represent both clients in the matter without obtaining consent (see §201). While each spouse theoretically could make a distribution different from the other's, including a less generous bequest to each other, those possibilities do not create a conflict of interest, and none reasonably appears to exist in the circumstances.

2. The same facts as in Illustration 1 except that lawyer has not previously met the spouses. Spouse A does most of the talking in the initial discussions with Lawyer. Spouse B, who owns significantly more property than Spouse A, appears to disagree with important positions of Spouse A but to be uncomfortable in expressing that disagreement and does not pursue them when Spouse A appears impatient and peremptory. Representation of both spouses would involve a conflict of interest. Lawyer may proceed to provide the requested legal assistance only with consent given under the limitations and conditions provided in §202.

3. The same facts as in Illustration 1 except that Lawyer has not previously met the spouses. But in this instance, unlike in Illustration 2, in discussions with the spouses, Lawyer asks questions and suggests options that reveal both Spouse A and Spouse B to be knowledgeable about their respective rights and interests, competent to make independent decisions if called for, and in accord on their common and individual objectives. Lawyer has adequately verified the absence of a conflict of interest and thus may represent both clients in the matter without obtaining consent (see §202).

Implicit in these illustrations is the assumption that conflicts do not necessarily exist between all spouses but that consent (presumably from both spouses) may be required under certain circumstances. If the spouses are in reasonable agreement about the terms of their respective wills, the Restatement suggests that no conflict exists that would create an ethics problem from the outset and that no mutual representation consent is yet required.

Illustration 2 suggests that not much needs to change before a sufficient conflict may be deemed to be a real potential between these spouses, requiring a mutual representation informed consent. How likely is it that you will be able to obtain such a consent when it becomes apparent that one is needed? As illustrated at page 520 with respect to confidences, mutual representations (and changes requested by one client without the knowledge of another) easily could create an ethics issue involving conflicts of interest long after the representation has begun.

In the context of the Model Rules, the potential for a conflict between spouses *presupposes* that Rule 1.7 is applicable. As a practical matter, at the outset of this representation the proper result is to obtain an informed consent from both Client and Spouse. The Restatement is merely creating cover for those lawyers who do not do so. And we would guess that you don't want to be the lawyer skittering around seeking cover when it hits the fan! You will be wise to take the precaution of obtaining their consent early, because doing so then will not be a problem (assuming there is no real conflict). If either spouse is unwilling to consent you may smoke out the fact that a conflict *does* exist, in which case you may be well advised not to even begin the representation. Indeed, in a case in which immediate facts suggest a real conflict, you might be well advised to *encourage* Spouse, as a new client, to seek independent representation (and in some cases Spouse might agree). If Spouse nevertheless remains comfortable with a mutual representation, you should obtain a written consent to that effect, as insurance against a future challenge.

In most cases both spouses will prefer to use one attorney, especially in single marriage situations or those in which only one of the spouses has any wealth. After all, hiring just one attorney is going to be expensive enough in terms of time, money, and aggravation, and Client and Spouse may not be all that eager to do estate planning in the first place. The Model Rules permit this mutual representation, provided the requisite inquiries and cautions are considered and consents are obtained. Sample joint representation letters are available in Engagement Letters: A Guide for Practitioners, a June 1999 monograph published by the Professional Standards Committee of the American College of Trust and Estate Counsel. Consult their website at actec.org

In addition to consent, the attorney should obtain an agreement regarding confidentiality of communications. The need for this can be illustrated by a simple modification of the hypothetical in which Client arrives alone for the initial interview. Client states that, although Client wants Attorney to draft estate plans for both Client and Spouse, today was not a good day for Spouse to be interviewed. Instead, Client proposes to tell Attorney what Spouse owns and what Spouse wants in Spouse's documents. In such a case, no responsible attorney should be willing to take Client's word for what Spouse would want. Independent verification of the facts is appropriate, perhaps by separately interviewing Spouse. If this works out such that Attorney is going to consult privately with each of Client and Spouse, then the possibility exists that secrets of each may be revealed to Attorney but not to the other spouse. If relevant to the plan of the other spouse, the issue then is whether Attorney may (or *must*) share those secrets with the ignorant spouse. A detailed discussion of this more knotty issue appears, beginning at page 520.

Now, let's consider a variation:

*Sometime long after another attorney drafted their estate plans, Client and Spouse were informed by their respective employers that the Retirement Equity Act of 1984 "requires some sort of spousal annuity" and, on consultation with their respective plan advisors, they learned that the beneficiary designations that their attorney originally arranged with them as part of their estate planning do not comply. They were, however, informed that a spousal waiver and consent will allow them to proceed with the planning that Attorney now recommends.*

Retirement benefits are important parts of many clients' total wealth. Attorney may represent Client and Spouse in the preparation of these documents, if Attorney recognizes the conflicts between what may be best for each as a surviving spouse and what each wants as their estate plan. Note, however, that waiver and consent may be desirable to the participant but likely are not in the nonparticipant spouse's best interests. See Chapter 10.

As a third example, consider:

*Client has children by a prior marriage, to whom Client makes gifts that Spouse splits for gift tax purposes. Each spouse uses the gift tax annual exclusion and (for larger gifts) consumes a portion of their unified credits to cover the gift tax cost of these transfers.*

Should Attorney in this case explain to Spouse that Spouse's unified credit is being used by Client and that Spouse may incur an estate tax at death, or a gift tax if Spouse subsequently wants to make other gifts? Indeed, should Attorney advise Spouse to seek compensation for the use of this credit? This lawyering might not be viewed kindly by Client, and again a potential conflict of interest exists.

Finally, closely related to the foregoing examples, but not quite a part of normal estate planning, is the situation in which Client comes to Attorney with plans to marry and asks for help in preparing a premarital agreement that will cover the spouses' rights if they divorce, or when one dies. Here Attorney would have a clear conflict of interest in representing both Client and the intended spouse. If you agree with this conclusion, that there is a clear conflict, but you're not yet convinced with respect to an already married couple, ask yourself what difference one day (their wedding day) makes? Planning done postmarital raises the same issues, so why would anyone think that representing spouses differs from representing potential, soon-to-be spouses?

### Dynastic Family Planning

The foregoing examples involved the most commonly recognized conflict of interest situation in estate planning: representing spouses. Less frequently encountered but easily more likely to present actual as opposed to only potential conflicts is the dynastic family plan illustrated by the following hypothetical:

*Daddy Warbucks is Attorney's client. Daddy's daughter, Annie, works for Warbucks Enterprises and she also is a client of Attorney. Daddy and Annie have heard cocktail party chatter about various gimmicks and schemes, they have some general business succession issues, income and wealth shifting objectives, and tax minimization concerns that they would like to consider. Daddy and Annie would like Attorney to represent them in a way that ensures an effective dynastic plan that will satisfy the needs of Daddy, Annie, and Annie's children.*

In this case what may be good for Annie as beneficiary of Daddy's estate may not be best in terms of minimizing the overall tax burdens or the succession of Daddy's estate.

To illustrate, income and wealth transfer taxes could be lower if Daddy made some direct bequests to Annie's children, entirely bypassing Annie. But Annie is likely to feel abused by a recommendation that "her" inheritance be given to someone else, even a natural object of Annie's bounty. (She might not, but you won't know in advance.) Similarly, Daddy may create a power of appointment in Annie for flexibility in dealing with yet unknown taxes or other changes in the law, but clearly may prefer that Annie never exercise it "needlessly." In drafting Annie's will, may (or must) Attorney advise Annie that the power exists? What if Daddy rejects Attorney's advice to discuss this with Annie? Annie may be no worse off for Attorney representing both Daddy and Annie than if she had retained some other attorney who might not know all (or any) of the specifics of Daddy's estate plan. However, the issue of "damages" is not relevant to the question whether a conflict between Daddy and Annie constitutes an ethical violation.

Further, if Annie was going to purchase stock from Daddy for what is thought to be full and adequate consideration but the transaction nevertheless runs the risk of part-sale, part-gift taxation, whose interests would Attorney represent in fashioning the contract of sale to avoid this result? And what if the contract imposes any gift tax incurred on Annie as a "net gift" arrangement (by which Annie would pay any gift tax incurred)? Would any of this depend on whether there are other beneficiaries of Daddy's estate? Any advice to Annie and Daddy regarding a buy-sell agreement could be troublesome. Especially tricky might be the question whether and how to purchase disability insurance to finance a disability purchase buy-sell agreement.

Under slightly different facts Attorney may realize that Daddy Warbucks might re-evaluate some of the planning that is being considered if Daddy knew some of the things about Annie's current marriage and her children that Attorney has deduced from Annie's plan. Indeed, it might come up in a different situation: what if Annie was about to be married and Daddy wanted Attorney to draft a prenuptial agreement for Annie and her intended, to protect Annie's Warbucks Enterprises stock in the case of a divorce?

The situation would pose even greater problems if Daddy, knowing that Annie otherwise would tend to procrastinate, offers to pay the fee for all the services Attorney renders for both Daddy and Annie. See page 509 dealing with Model Rule 1.8(f). Daddy might even offer to serve as an intermediary between Attorney and all the family members for purposes of gathering and relaying information that is essential, taking back and explaining all recommendations, and so forth.

Added issues of conflict and even the potential for a charge of undue influence might arise if Daddy has another child who is not active in the business or will be treated differently than Annie (for example, receiving different assets, or receiving a share in trust rather than outright). This would be even more troubling if Attorney represents Annie as well as Daddy. For a troubling example of this see *Hotz v. Minyard*, 403 S.E.2d 634 (S.C. 1991), in which the family attorney was sued for breach of fiduciary duty to the child who was treated badly by the decedent, based on the attorney-client relation of the attorney with *that* child.

A conflict of interest also can arise if an attorney attempts to represent both a corporation and some but not all shareholders, or represents all shareholders in preparing a buy-sell agreement, documents for incorporation of a business, or other general business matters. American Bar Association Standing Committee on Ethics and Professional Responsibility Informal Decision 564 (1962) involved an attorney who represented both a corporation and the executor of an estate that held stock of the corporation. The attorney was deemed to have a conflict of interest when the estate and the corporation became adversaries. But a quintessential example of dynastic representation involving conflicts of interest is *In re Estate of Halas, Jr.*, 512 N.E.2d 1276 (Ill. App. Ct. 1987), in which a major Chicago law firm represented the decedent's father as executor of the decedent's estate, as trustee of the decedent's testamentary trusts, as chief executive officer of the Chicago Bears football club (the family business) and individually; represented the business as corporate counsel; and represented the decedent's sister and her family. In its role as attorney for this dynasty the law firm recommended recapitalizations that the court concluded would benefit some family members but disadvantage others, including beneficiaries of the decedent's estate, to whom the court held the attorneys owed fiduciary duties through their representation of the personal representative.

Some estate planning attorneys have separately incorporated firms for consulting with family businesses because of the extent of family conflicts and some ethical dilemmas in situations such as these. In the legal or business advising involved, these attorneys strongly advocate common representation of families to minimize the extent of surprises, disappointment, and animosity about decisions that affect various members. In an effort to avoid the ethics rules that may apply, however, these attorneys will not represent family members as clients when also consulting with them as their business advisor. This may be a more conservative approach than necessary to the question of conflicts between clients in dynastic family business situations. It also may not succeed in preventing exposure to the ethics rules. Nevertheless, it is impressive that the potential for conflict is significant and potentially impossible of resolution within the dictates of the Model Rules.

## Which Rule Applies?

None of these representations is unusual, and the Ethics 2000 revision of the Model Rules more readily accommodates these mutual representations. The rules applicable to these situations make it clear that family counsel must obtain mutual informed consents, preferably at the outset of the representation, always confirmed in writing. This appears to be the only method to avoid concerns under each of the potentially applicable rules. As such, it is difficult to think of a reason not to obtain such consent and confirmation letters if they are available. Furthermore, it seems fair to ask why a responsible attorney would run the risk of committing an ethics violation in such a situation by engaging in the mutual representation if mutual consents are *not* obtainable.

A common comment made by attorneys in response to this suggestion is that it would be irresponsible for the attorney to raise issues of possible conflict if there is no reason to believe that there is a real conflict between the parties. The notion expressed appears to be that the mere mention of the possibility of conflict could "poison" an otherwise peaceful relationship and destroy the sense of mutual trust that existed between the clients before they consulted the attorney. According to this argument, the attorney should use objective independent judgment to determine whether it is in the clients' best interests to raise the possibility of conflict and that the attorney should not discuss conflict possibilities if the attorney independently determines that a real conflict is not likely, based on the facts and circumstances of the situation.

These attorneys would embrace a rule that consent is required only if an actual conflict exists and not if there is merely a potential for conflict in the particular situation. They also would advocate that an attorney should be entitled to presume that no conflict actually exists until it is made clear from the facts that this is not true. See *Report of the Special Study Committee on Professional Responsibility, Comments and Recommendations on the Lawyer's Duties in Representing Husband and Wife*, 28 Real Prop., Prob. & Trust J. 765, 777-780 (1994).

Whether this *ought* to be the approach taken by the Model Rules, and the ancillary problems raised by such a proposal, are interesting academic inquiries. But for *practical* purposes it is sufficient to note that it presently is not the rule, as is reasonably clear from reading the rules. The Restatement §211 examples quoted at page 500 are meant to give some comfort in the spousal representation arena because so many attorneys do not yet obtain the requisite consents at the outset of a representation. Similarly, Ethics 2000 Rule 1.7 Comment 8 stated: "The mere possibility of subsequent harm does not itself require disclosure and consent. The critical questions are the likelihood that a difference in interest will eventuate and, if it does, whether it will materially interfere with the lawyer's independent professional judgment . . . ."

Unfortunately, the need for those Restatement examples marking out an exception (and their limitation to the spousal representation context) may simply confirm the clear need in other situations to obtain the preemptive consent, even prior to discovery of an actual (as opposed to a potential) conflict. All this makes it dangerous to adopt the wait and see approach today. And if that is true, would you rely on a different result in representing spouses? Put another way, why *not* just get the consent? The answer may lie in the reality that an informed consent to a mutual representation requires the existing attorney to make a sufficient disclosure to guarantee that the clients perceive the possible risks of a mutual representation and, on the basis of an adequate understanding, give a truly informed and voluntary consent. Should you be unwilling? The persuasive fact is that lawyers who routinely make the disclosure have not reported problems of the "poison the well" variety.

### Other Common Conflicts

Two additional examples may help illustrate conflicts in estate planning that, if not already commonplace, certainly will become so:

*Child is a client of Attorney's firm and comes to Attorney asking Attorney to represent Elder, Child's aged parent, in the preparation of estate planning documents. In the course of an initial meeting Child reveals that Elder is in a nursing home located some distance away, that Elder is not able to travel, and that Elder is only sometimes able to sit and discuss business or other technical matters. Child offers to provide Attorney with any necessary information regarding assets and the desired dispositive plan. Child also states that Elder wants to give Child a durable power of attorney to facilitate annual exclusion gifting and other estate, tax, and general business planning.*

*Parent, a longstanding client of Attorney, comes to Attorney with Trust Officer (who represents a major corporate fiduciary that also is a client of Attorney's firm). They are seeking advice about Parent's child, Minor, who is the beneficiary of a trust (drafted many years ago by some other attorney who represented Minor's grandparent) that is scheduled to terminate at Minor's age 21, which is several months from now. Trust Officer and Parent feel strongly that Minor is not mature enough to handle the amount of money that will be distributed and wonder what kinds of "protection" are available to Minor. They ask Attorney to represent and advise Minor regarding the available options, and they assure Attorney that all fees will be paid by Parent. The likely recommendation is a rollover of the trust distribution directly into an irrevocable trust (or revocable with the consent of Parent or the trustee) that will be held for the benefit of Minor until termination and distribution to Minor at a more "reasonable" age.*

In the last example, imagine how the situation might differ if Minor does not yet know that the soon-to-be-distributed trust exists. That isn't uncommon.

A third example is not unique, but arises less frequently:

*Attorney represents Fiduciary, which was named as personal representative and trustee under the estate plan of Decedent. Attorney drafted the documents and is asked to advise beneficiaries under that plan in the course of the representation.*

A similar situation can exist if an attorney is asked to represent both the income and remainder beneficiaries of a trust, or several beneficiaries under a will. A related but more easily recognized conflicts issue arises if the drafter of an estate plan is later asked to represent a disappointed heir in a will contest.

### Obligations Imposed

In each case discussed in this Chapter the ethics rules require the attorney to determine at the outset what course of conduct is required before engaging in any of the requested representations. The first requisite under Model Rule 1.7 is to determine, based on a reasonable belief (whatever that means), that the representation will not adversely affect the relationship with the other client with whom a conflict may exist. Then, under Model Rule 1.7(b) (not as an alternative but as an additional requirement) the attorney must consult with both potentially injured clients to inform them of the possibility for conflict. Each affected client must be informed of the implications of the common representation and the risks and advantages involved.

Based on these consultations, the attorney must obtain an informed consent to the representation, confirmed in writing. If the conflict involves a client the attorney no longer actively represents, Model Rule 1.9 requires that the former client consent after consultation, again confirmed in writing. Although Rule 1.9 assumes that the new client will receive undivided attention and loyalty, making the new client's consent unnecessary, note that Rule 1.7 *also* requires the new client's consent.

If a mutual representation is contemplated (as would appear to be common with spouses or dynastic families), the attorney must conclude that the matters involved can be resolved compatibly to each client, in their respective best interests. In addition, if the attorney is unable to resolve their problems compatibly, the attorney must be confident that there will be no material prejudice to their interests. Further, the attorney must be confident that each client will be able to make adequately informed decisions in the course of the mutual representation, and the attorney must reasonably believe that the common representation can be undertaken impartially and without improper effect on the attorney's responsibilities to each client. Because the representation necessarily will be affected, the key here is whether it will be an *improper* effect.

Finally, each client must consent, the consent must be informed, confirmed in writing, and (presumably) given by a client who is capable of giving consent. See, e.g., Restatement §202(1). Thus, for example, in a mutual representation that requires the consent of Elder or Minor, it is questionable whether either can give an adequate consent and, although a guardian or conservator normally could consent on behalf of someone under disability, here that would seem to be inappropriate if the conflict is with the same person seeking to give the consent on their behalf. See Restatement §202, comment c(ii).

Full disclosure requires more than just informing the clients that the attorney is undertaking to represent both of them. Instead, the attorney must explain "the nature of the conflict of interest in such detail so that they can understand the reasons why it may be desirable for each to have independent counsel, with  undivided loyalty to the interest of each of them." *In re Boivin*, 533 P.2d 171, 174 (Or. 1975). This too may be impossible in practical application.

Another obligation is imposed if one of the clients will pay the attorney's fee for all of the collective engagements, which is pretty common in the spousal representation and may be common in dynastic and the other illustrated situations as well. Model Rule 1.8(f) requires the attorney to inform the nonpaying client that someone else is paying the fee, and the attorney must conclude that this does not create divided loyalties that interfere with the attorney's independent judgment. Further, the nonpaying client must give an informed consent to this arrangement. This rule does *not* require a written confirmation, but why would you not?

Oh, by the way, there are confidentiality issues with respect to these situations that we will address in due course. See page 519. They prove to be the devil in all of this and, when you understand them, they will change the way you resolve certain issues. So, it isn't time yet to decide how you will choose to practice in these varied situations.

### *Who Is the Client?*

The most beguiling issue in some of these cases is one the ethics rules do not address: who is the client? For example, if Child engages Attorney to represent the marginally capable Elder, or Parent asks Attorney to advise Minor, are the clients Elder and Minor (initially this seems obvious) or Child and Parent, who hire Attorney and seem to have the most interest in the representation? See, e.g., *In re Estate of Gillespie*, 903 P.2d 590 (Ariz. 1995) (Child obtained documents for Elder, who attorney never met); Indiana Ethics Opinion No. 2 (2001) (grandchild obtained documents for Elder, who attorney did not consult and who was represented by another attorney). And with Client and Spouse or Daddy and Annie, can the client be regarded as the spousal unit or the dynastic family, or is it each individual independently?

There appears to be no reason why Child and Parent cannot *also* be regarded as clients, but it probably cannot be claimed that Elder and Minor are *not* Attorney's clients. Thus, an informed consent must be obtained from them, reflecting their knowledge of the fact that Attorney is representing the interests of others who may not have the best interests of Elder and Minor in mind (or who may view the best interests of Elder and Minor differently than do Elder and Minor). Consequently, the ability of Elder or Minor to even give consent remains a problem. In addition, questions of undue influence may infect the planning independent of the ethics obligations involved. The bottom line: the ethics rules provide slim guidance other than to assume the informed consent of each affected individual is required and should be confirmed in writing.

As a reality check in this respect, it may be helpful to ask two questions posed by Boston attorney and tax ethics commentator, the late Fred Corneel: (1) who does the attorney think is the client, and (2) who do the clients think is their attorney? It is a pretty safe guess that a conflict exists if the attorney's vision of the role being played and the role the clients think the attorney is playing differ. Another indication of possible conflicts is if the attorney cares how a nonclient feels about a particular situation, which may indicate that there is a conflict of interest. A further danger signal is if the attorney's role has changed during the representation (for example, the attorney now represents both spouses after having represented only one, or vice versa).

Sometimes the answer to your question "who is the client" is obvious, albeit painful. For example, in the case of a premarital agreement, the client should be regarded as one or the other of the couple and the attorney probably commits malpractice by not insisting that the other obtain independent representation. See Springs & Bruce, *Marital Agreements: Uses, Techniques, and Tax Ramifications in the Estate Planning Context*, 21 U. Miami Inst. Est. Plan. ¶705.3 (1987). Failure to do so would be more than an ethical violation, because the surest way to ensure the effectiveness of a premarital agreement is to guarantee that both sides of the agreement have adequate *independent* representation. Thus, the spouse(s) desiring the agreement would be ill-served if the attorney did not insist on this measure as the most effective protection of the parties' best interests. Even if they are not willing to pay for two lawyers, normally the attorney should not accept "no" for an answer when recommending that they each employ independent counsel. And, if that recommendation is not accepted, the attorney still should regard only one of the parties as the client and should make it clear that the other was encouraged to obtain independent representation and voluntarily refused to do so. Indeed, some observers would argue that the attorney should withdraw entirely if they refuse the advised separate independent representation.

Finally, consider Model Rule 1.14, which deals with clients under disability. Comment 4 reads:

If a legal representative has already been appointed for the client, the lawyer should ordinarily look to the representative for decisions on behalf of the client. In matters involving a minor, whether the lawyer should look to the parents as natural guardians may depend on the type of proceeding or matter in which the lawyer is representing the minor. If the lawyer represents the guardian as distinct from the ward, and is aware that the guardian is acting adversely to the ward's interest, the lawyer may have an obligation to prevent or rectify the guardian's misconduct.

Materials added to this comment by Ethics 2000 may imply that the attorney also acts on behalf of the ward or that the ward is the attorney's de facto client. American Bar Association Standing Committee on Ethics and Professional Responsibility Informal Decision C-778 (1964) specifically dealt with this situation, the guardian having told the guardian's attorney that the guardian had misappropriated funds. The Decision determined that the attorney did not represent the ward and had no duty to the ward. The attorney was obliged, however, to advise the guardian to make amends, but could not reveal the misappropriation. The discussion beginning at page 533 reveals that this vision is not shared universally and the appropriate answer may be not nearly so clear.

New Rule 1.14(b) provides:

(b) When the lawyer reasonably believes that the client has diminished capacity, is at risk of substantial physical, financial or other harm unless action is taken and cannot adequately act in the client's own interest, the lawyer may take reasonably necessary protective action, including consulting with individuals or entities that have the ability to take action to protect the client and, in appropriate cases, seeking the appointment of a guardian ad litem, conservator or guardian.

Further, Comment 5 adds that:

If a lawyer reasonably believes that a client is at risk of substantial physical, financial or other harm unless action is taken, and that a normal client-lawyer relationship cannot be maintained as provided in paragraph (a) because the client lacks sufficient capacity to communicate or to make adequately considered decisions in connection with the representation, then paragraph (b) permits the lawyer to take protective measures deemed necessary. Such measures could include: consulting with family members, using a reconsideration period to permit clarification or improvement of circumstances, using voluntary surrogate decisionmaking tools such as durable powers of attorney or consulting with support groups, professional services, adult-protective agencies or other individuals or entities that have the ability to protect the client. In taking any protective action, the lawyer should be guided by such factors as the wishes and values of the client to the extent known, the client's best interests and the goals of intruding into the client's decisionmaking autonomy to the least extent feasible, maximizing client capacities and respecting the client's family and social connections.

Neither authority resolves the "who do you represent" imbroglio, nor is it clear what are the lawyer's duties if the ward is not meant to be a client.

As so viewed, at a minimum this situation creates another potential conflict for the attorney in the Elder or Minor cases. Were you waiting for an answer to these difficult questions, as if a ball exists that cleverly is being hidden from you? Were it so! Estate planners quite simply are groping in the dark on these unresolved questions. And no, you would *not* be better off not knowing that these questions exist! Ignorance here truly is not bliss. It is just all the more dangerous. So, what do you do? The best advice is to shun the conflict. Don't put yourself in harm's way, and praise the client (Child or Parent) who lets you stand aside and hires a truly independent attorney.

### Independent Judgment

The general ethics rules relating to an attorney's independence of judgment can create ethical problems for estate planners in some unexpected ways. Clearly subject to scrutiny is any attorney self dealing with an estate or trust under the attorney's administration. Model Rule 1.8(a) requires that all terms be fair and reasonable and fully disclosed in writing, and that the client consent in a signed writing recording the essential terms of the transaction and the lawyer's role in it. See Restatement §207. See also *Florida Bar v. White*, 368 So. 2d 1294 (Fla. 1979) (an attorney was suspended for buying land from a client at a price the client asked because, among other things, the attorney did not advise the client that the land might be worth more or that the client should obtain an independent appraisal or independent representation). This rule is not news to fiduciaries: avoiding self dealing is a clear responsibility under the law of fiduciary administration (although the ethical mandate here is less strict than the fiduciary prohibition).

Also well known to most estate planners is Model Rule 1.8(c), prohibiting an attorney from preparing

an instrument giving the lawyer or a person related to the lawyer any substantial gift unless the lawyer or other recipient of the gift is related to the client. For purposes of this paragraph, related persons include a spouse, child, grandchild, parent, grandparent or other relative or individual with whom the lawyer or the client maintains a close, familiar relationship.

Restatement §208 similarly precludes a lawyer from drafting an instrument effecting any gift from a client to the lawyer "unless the lawyer is a relative or other natural object of the client's generosity and the gift is not significantly disproportionate to those given other donees similarly related to the donor." The Restatement also precludes acceptance of a gift, regardless of who prepared the instrument of transfer, unless the gift is insubstantial, the attorney is a relative or other natural object of the client's bounty, or the client was encouraged to and had a reasonable opportunity to seek independent representation, which is a more lenient standard than the Model Rule (it is more akin to the older Model Code Ethical Consideration 5-5).

Although there is some room to wiggle in Rule 1.8(c), centering around the question of what is a "substantial" gift, the notion of whether a client is sufficiently "related to the donee" was addressed more clearly by Ethics 2000, and it will be clear enough what the rule prohibits in the vast majority of situations in which this issue might arise.

Any responsible estate planner ought to be able to reach a clear conclusion about whether to require separate representation if the client insists upon making a bequest to the attorney or a member of the attorney's family. For example, if the attorney feels uncomfortable about the appearance of the gift, it probably is too large to slip under the "substantial gift" threshold. But consider tough cases like *In re Boulger*, 637 N.W.2d 710 (N.D. 2001), in which the drafter was a life long friend of the decedent and only later became the decedent's attorney as well, had represented the decedent's business for years, and was made a remote contingent beneficiary but did not actually receive any bequest. The court held that the Rule does not invite debate about probabilities of various contingencies and held that a bright line rule requires sanctions to protect the public, notwithstanding the absence of evidence in the particular case of overreaching or undue influence.

Model Rule 1.8(a) also prohibits entering into a business transaction with a client or knowingly acquiring an ownership, possessory, security, or other pecuniary interest adverse to the client, unless the transaction and terms are fair and reasonable to the client, the essential terms are fully disclosed in writing to the client, the client is advised in writing of the desirability of seeking independent legal counsel on the transaction, and the client consents in writing.

In this regard, Comment b to Restatement §207 specifically states that "proving fraud or actual overreaching might be difficult. Hence, the law does not require such a showing on the part of a client." And Comment c gives the following illustration:

2. Lawyer represents the surviving Spouse of a long-time Client. Lawyer advises Spouse that farmland owned by the estate should be sold to pay taxes. Using the name of a business associate as purported buyer, Lawyer purchases the land from Spouse without disclosing Lawyer's involvement in the purchase. Even if the price is objectively fair, Lawyer has violated the requirement that Lawyer's identity be disclosed to the client.

In addition, related enough to this to be included in Model Rule 1.8(h) is the prohibition against agreeing with the client to a limitation of the attorney's liability to the client for malpractice unless the client is advised in writing about the desirability of being independently represented.

Less clear is whether this Rule 1.8(h) also would apply to an attorney who agrees to act as a fiduciary and, in that capacity, is exonerated or granted limited liability under the terms of a document that the attorney drafted. Comment 8 states that Rule 1.8 does not prohibit the lawyer from seeking to be named as fiduciary but is silent regarding normal exoneration language. Some authorities state that such a provision in the document itself may be ineffective for the intended purpose. See 3 Scott & Fratcher, The Law of Trusts §222.3 (4th ed. 1988); Annot., *Attorney at law: disciplinary proceedings based upon attorney's naming of himself or associate as executor or attorney for executor in will drafted by him*, 57 A.L.R.3d 703 (1974). But quite independent of that result is the issue whether the mere act of placing the provision in the trust constitutes an ethical violation for which the attorney also can be sanctioned, in addition to whatever liability would flow from the underlying violation as to which exoneration or limited liability was asserted.

### Ancillary Activities

Assume that Attorney also is a financial planner or sells insurance, and makes recommendations in the estate planning engagement regarding the purchase of products that Attorney sells. Although troublesome, is this activity sufficiently different that an ethical mandate clearly applies? The obvious issues of self dealing and lack of independent professional judgment probably cannot be ameliorated even if the nonlegal or ancillary activities of the attorney are performed in separate legal entities. Thus, Model Rule 5.7 appears to impose on the attorney in the nonlegal or ancillary activity the same rules of professional conduct imposed on the lawyer's provision of law-related services, unless the attorney takes "reasonable measures to assure that a person . . . knows that the . . . protections of the client-lawyer relationship do not exist."

In addition, Model Rule 1.8(a) presumably applies, requiring

- Disclosure of the possibility for conflict.
- That the client be advised of the desirability of seeking and be given a reasonable opportunity for independent representation.
- That the client consent in a signed writing.
- That all dealings be on absolutely fair and reasonable terms and be disclosed in a manner that can be reasonably understood by the client.

Quaere what are fair and reasonable terms and adequate disclosure. And how to make clients who are so informed and given the opportunity for independent representation feel free to go elsewhere without fear of offending the attorney or being treated as second class clients.

Even if this example seems clear, what about moving one step away:

*Attorney is licensed to sell insurance; because of that certification, when Attorney refers a client to another insurance agent Attorney customarily receives a portion of the sales commission from the other agent as a referral fee.*

*Attorney uses the same real estate broker to market realty held in any estate that Attorney probates, and the broker rebates a portion of the sales commission to Attorney as a referral fee.*

Do the same rules apply here as if Attorney sold the insurance directly to the client or acted as the real estate broker?

It is irrelevant to the ethics issue that the commission charged to the client in each case is no greater than if Attorney were not involved. An ethics violation can result even if there is no damage to the client. Yet these cases appear to be no different from receiving a referral from an insurance agent or fiduciary or being hired as a fiduciary's attorney. The fact that the attorney earns a fee for legal work as opposed to a mere referral is entirely irrelevant to the question whether the attorney's independent judgment might be impaired by the relationships involved. If any of these situations involves the potential for an impropriety in the absence of disclosure and consent, then presumably they all should be scrutinized for any impropriety under one or both of Rules 1.8 or 5.7.

As a final illustration that may give pause, consider the case in which, when asked for a deserving "contingent beneficiary" (to take if all named objects of the decedent's bounty fail to survive), an attorney recommends a particular charity with which the attorney is involved or interested. Presumably the attorney's independent judgment may be clouded in such a situation, and these facts should be regarded as no less problematical because a charity is involved and the attorney is not receiving a fee or otherwise being tangibly compensated. Disclosure of the personal interest should suffice, however, to absolve any possible ethics violation. To avoid prejudice to the attorney's charity, it might be appropriate to give an inquiring client a list of several deserving charities with a notation that the attorney is involved with or interested in one of them, without identifying which.

An important reminder is the law of agency, which applies totally independent of the ethics provisions that might apply in each of these situations. Most notable in this respect is the rule stated in §388 of the Restatement (Second) of Agency that "an agent who makes a profit in connection with transactions conducted by him on behalf of the principal is under a duty to give such profit to the principal" unless the principal and agent have agreed otherwise. The comment clarifies that this rule operates even if the agent "acted with perfect fairness to the principal and violated no duty of loyalty in receiving the amount." An ethics obligation thus appears to be the least of the agent's exposure.

Model Rule 5.7 has gone through numerous iterations that reveal a true conflict within the Bar relating to what rule ought to apply. A number of states have adopted their own rules concerning ancillary business activities, with varying degrees of success and controversy, all as revealed by the comments to Rule 5.7. Perhaps the only clear thing in this context is that there are numerous ways an attorney's independent judgment may be challenged and attorneys therefore should be cautious and vigilant about keeping track of the rules as they develop and change, in terms of their impact on the ancillary work that lawyers may perform.

### *Uncertain Scope*

Examples of two relatively common situations confronting estate planners help to illustrate the uncertain scope of the independent judgment rule. As revealed in Illinois State Bar Association Professional Ethics Opinion 90-2, Model Rule 1.7 applies if an attorney recommends a corporate fiduciary to a client without revealing that the fiduciary is a client of the attorney's firm. In fact, in that case the attorney was found guilty of an ethics violation for his insistence that the client name the fiduciary. But what if:

*Insurance Agent refers business to Attorney and Attorney reciprocates, based on a longstanding relationship. Alternatively, Attorney is contacted by Fiduciary to draft estate planning documents for Customer, who already has agreed to establish a trust arrangement with Fiduciary as trustee. As is common in the community, the unspoken policy is that Attorney will be hired to represent Fiduciary in its capacity as personal representative and trustee under Customer's estate plan.*

Although the multiple representation rules are not directly on point if the insurance agent or fiduciary are not clients of Attorney, a case can be made that an attorney should inform a client that the attorney's independent judgment may be affected by reciprocal relations such as these.

To illustrate that this is sensible, consider what the typical attorney would do if it was clear that the trust or insurance recommendation made by the referent is not appropriate under the circumstances. At least on a theoretical level there is an ethics issue in cases like this because, potentially, the attorney's independent judgment may be clouded. See Model Rule 5.4(c) (an attorney may not be influenced by the fiduciary that recommends or employs the attorney to represent a client). The closest authorities found on point conclude that there is an ethical violation in an analogous situation, not because of the independent judgment rule, but instead because the attorney's participation in a matter involving preparation of estate planning documents constitutes aiding in the unauthorized practice of law. See *In re Mid-America Living Trust Assoc. Inc.*, 927 S.W.2d 855 (Mo. 1996), and *Cincinnati Bar Association v. Kathman*, 748 N.E.2d 1091 (Ohio 2001), and their extensive collection of authority, both holding that trust mills are the unauthorized practice of law and that attorneys who assist in reviewing or drafting documents commit the violation of aiding the unauthorized practice, along with violation of the independent judgment rule attributable to fee sharing arrangements. A fine summary is *State and Local Action Against Trust Mills: The Unauthorized Practice of Law*, 27 ACTEC J. 162 (2001). Given the uncertain state of the law relative to unauthorized practice, it is questionable whether such a result would be reached consistently today. Whether our hypotheticals nevertheless would run afoul of the independent judgment admonition is not clear.

A related situation was presented in Oregon Legal Ethics Opinion 457 in 1981, involving a religious organization that referred members to an attorney "together with the proposed estate plan and distribution," all clearly in anticipation of receiving a bequest from the client. Stating that the attorney must be in a position of total fidelity to the client and not to the organization making the referral, the opinion recognized that it is permissible to accept referrals from a third party but that the opportunity for undue influence is significant if the referent is expecting a benefit in return.

Also not on point but worthy of consideration is authority stating that it would be a violation of the rules against solicitation if an attorney named him or her self as attorney for a fiduciary (or named him or her self as fiduciary). American Bar Association Standing Committee on Ethics & Professional Responsibility Formal Opinion 602 (1963). For more discussion of the solicitation issue see page 544. Although this was the case under Model Code Ethical Consideration 5-6 ("A lawyer should not consciously influence a client to name him as executor, trustee, or lawyer in an instrument"), that rule was not specifically incorporated in the Model Rules. And again, this ruling does not speak to our hypotheticals.

Although several rules come close to dealing with all of these hypotheticals, it is at least arguable that these cases do not pose an ethical violation under the Model Rules. At best they may be regarded as creating "the appearance of impropriety," which once was prohibited under the Model Code but also has been removed in the Model Rules and the Restatement, presumably because it was a catch-all rule with no definable boundaries. More would be required than just this general bromide about avoiding the appearance that something inappropriate is involved. As a practical matter, fiduciaries regularly engage the drafting attorney to represent the fiduciary as personal representative or trustee, without any formal obligation or agreement in advance. Most estate planners would be astounded by a suggestion that there is room for concern about impropriety in such a situation, even if it is not disclosed in writing to the client. Nevertheless, the rule regarding independence of judgment on its face seems relevant and therefore worthy of your respect and consideration.

### Preservation of Client Confidences

Certainly one of the easiest rules to state, and usually to follow, is Model Rule 1.6(a), which requires confidentiality of client communications and all confidential information acquired from or *about* the client relative to the representation. "The confidentiality rule, for example, applies not only to matters communicated in confidence *by* the client but also to all information relating to the representation, *whatever its source.*" Comment 3 to Model Rule 1.6(a) (emphasis added). In the estate planning context, this obligation extends to virtually all information regarding family, assets, dispositive pattern, and so forth. It extends to information acquired during a prospective client conference under new Rule 1.18 and exists even after the client's death. See American Bar Association Standing Committee on Ethics and Professional Responsibility Informal Opinion 1293 (1974).

Restatement §112(1) prohibits use or disclosure "if . . . doing so will adversely affect a material interest of the client or if the client has instructed the lawyer not to use or disclose such information"; this is a less rigid standard than the Model Rule imposes. But Comment c(i) to §112 states that adverse effects include "material frustration of the client's objectives . . . or material misfortune, disadvantage, or other prejudices to a client . . . [including] personal embarrassment that could be caused to a person of normal susceptibility and a normal interest in privacy."

Restatement §111 defines confidential client information to exclude only information "that is generally known" and only applies the confidence rule if information was acquired during the course of or as a result of the representation, which also is less restrictive than the Model Rule. But Comment b to §111 indicates that information from any source is included in the confidentiality prohibition, including nonprivileged sources and communications from a client not protected by the attorney-client privilege. Finally, Comment d to §111 states that "information is not generally known when a person interested in knowing the information could obtain it only by means of special knowledge or substantial difficulty or expense."

Notwithstanding these differences, at its most basic application this would appear to be a very easy rule to comprehend and apply, yet numerous attorneys share stories or trivia about clients as "cocktail chatter" in direct violation of this rule. This is not to say the rule is wrong (if it may be a bit overinclusive, surely it is better to err on that side), but it requires more thoughtful attention than some lawyers appear to give to it.

### Confidences in Representing Spouses

Far more problematic is the application of Model Rule 1.6(a) in a not uncommon client situation.

*Client and Spouse engaged Attorney for estate planning advice; Attorney agreed to represent them both only after informing them of potential conflicts of interest and obtaining their consent to the mutual representation. Wills were drafted for each that, contrary to Attorney's best judgment and advice, essentially leave everything to the survivor of Client and Spouse and by the survivor to their children. Several days (hours/months/years — it doesn't matter) after execution of their wills, Client calls Attorney to request a codicil making a "modest" bequest to Client's [fill in the blank: "child" (from a previously undisclosed liaison); "assistant, in recognition of long years of devoted service"; "close friend"; "personal trainer"; "paramour" (candor being the best policy)]. It is clear that Client would prefer that Spouse not know about this provision in Client's will. Indeed, Client indicates that Spouse would alter Spouse's will if Spouse knew about this deviation from their agreed plan.*

Or try a variation:

*Client calls to say that, quite unknown to Spouse, Client has discovered that Spouse has been unfaithful. Client is not going to seek a divorce ("because of the children" or perhaps "because of my political aspirations"), but Client wants to exclude Spouse from Client's estate plan. Again, for purposes of family harmony, Client insists that Attorney preserve the confidence.*

These facts may be a bit too dramatic, but the same issue can arise in numerous contexts. What if, for example, Spouse informs Attorney that Spouse plans to divorce Client as soon as a plan involving split gifting or credit shelter transfers from Client to Spouse is complete. Or Client calls to request a bequest to a relative who Spouse does not favor, to inform Attorney that Client has a nonmarital child of whom Spouse is unaware (roughly one in three births in America today is out of wedlock), or perhaps Client and Spouse have children by prior marriages who they agreed to treat equally but now Client wants to renege on that agreement and, in all these cases, *does not want Spouse to know*. Now Attorney is on the horns of a dilemma.

In a vacuum, Attorney's ethical obligation to Spouse probably dictates that Attorney inform Spouse of any changes to Client's plan that would affect the wisdom or the assumptions underlying Spouse's plan. At the very least, if Spouse were to come to Attorney at a later time to ask if Attorney knows of any reason to consider a change to Spouse's will, Attorney probably would have a duty to "suggest" that Spouse reconsider the outright and absolute nature of the bequest to Client. Attorney certainly would do so if Attorney's knowledge came from a nonprotected source. But Attorney's ethical obligation to Client may preclude Attorney from revealing the change Client requests and certainly would preclude Attorney from making the kind of slightly veiled comments to Spouse that might put Spouse on notice about Client's change of heart. So what should Attorney do?

First, Attorney could refuse to represent Client in drafting the codicil (and some ethics opinions state that the attorney *must* refuse to represent Client in any change that does not preserve or protect the best interests of Spouse). Even if Attorney does not do the requested work, Attorney still has knowledge that creates a conflict in further representing Spouse. And Client probably will go elsewhere and make the change, so Attorney's refusal will not protect Spouse in any way.

Second, Attorney could withdraw from representing Spouse, although Attorney probably cannot withdraw from representing just Spouse without raising some suspicions that ultimately might tip off Spouse. Moreover, Attorney might have a duty to Spouse *prior* to resignation.

A third alternative would be to withdraw from representing both Client and Spouse (indeed, this is probably the notion that most ethical lawyers would embrace as the least problematic) but, again, resignation might come too late to satisfy Attorney's duties to Spouse. Florida Bar Ethics Department Advisory Opinion 95-4 (1996) opined that Attorney *must* withdraw and cannot disclose the secret because the duty of confidentiality supersedes the duty to communicate all information relevant to the engagement. There is nothing to support the Florida conclusion that one ethics obligation is more important than or superior to another, and Attorney may be conflicted by turning tail on the innocent Spouse just to protect Client, who has the secret. The point is that Attorney may do wrong no matter what Attorney does now.

The Report of the Special Study Committee on Professional Responsibility, *Comments and Recommendations on the Lawyer's Duties in Representing Husband and Wife*, 28 Real Prop., Prob. & Trust J. 765, 783-793 (1994), addresses this situation, spinning a series of distinctions and a theory of permitted disclosure that requires exercise of attorney discretion that actually may magnify the attorney's exposure. It has been rejected by the American Bar Association Standing Committee on Ethics and Professional Responsibility and by the Florida Bar Ethics Department, which shows that even the best talent can go wrong in seeking to resolve such a dilemma. In this respect, Comment 31 to Rule 1.7 provides:

As to the duty of confidentiality, continued common representation will almost certainly be inadequate if one client asks the lawyer not to disclose to the other client information relevant to the common representation. This is so because the lawyer has an equal duty of loyalty to each client, and each client has the right to be informed of anything bearing on the representation that might affect that client's interest and the right to expect that the lawyer will use that information to that client's benefit. See Rule 1.4. The lawyer should, at the outset of the common representation and as part of the process of obtaining each client's informed consent, advise each client that information will be shared and that the lawyer will have to withdraw if one client decides that some matter material to the representation should be kept from the other. In limited circumstances, it may be appropriate for the lawyer to proceed with the representation when the clients have agreed, after being properly informed, that the lawyer will keep certain information confidential. . . .

Notice that this Comment assumes the mode of representation will be a joint or "common" representation rather than a concurrent separate representation. Quaere whether it also assumes that this duty cannot be altered by agreement? The last sentence appears to acknowledge that it may be altered. At a minimum the Comment seems to negate discretion in the attorney whether to reveal or hold the secret in confidence. The Comment appears to assume that either the attorney *will* disclose or *must* withdraw. Notice that Florida said that Attorney may *not* disclose and must withdraw. Given all this helpful guidance, is it clear to you what you should or may do in such a case? It is not clear to us, which is why it seems so important for you to reach an understanding at the outset of your representation, because surely you don't want to wrestle with all this once it hits the fan.

In that respect, let's think about how an estate planner gets into such a situation, and how it can be prevented. The problem posed relates directly to the fact that the attorney did not reach an understanding regarding confidences between Client and Spouse when the mutual representation began. Such an understanding might take any of at least three forms. The attorney could maintain the secrets of either client that are communicated to the attorney in confidence, notwithstanding that the ignorant spouse may not be as well represented as a result. The attorney could tell the other spouse of any secret that is revealed if the attorney, in the exercise of discretion, feels it is relevant to the other spouse, notwithstanding the otherwise improper violation of the confidences obligation. Or the attorney could in all events tell the other spouse of any secret that is revealed, notwithstanding the otherwise improper violation of the confidences obligation. Assuming such an agreement is reached with each spouse at the beginning of the representation, and that any of these approaches might be permissible, the issue then is, which is preferable?

The "priestly" approach of preserving all secrets ensures that either spouse will feel free to approach the attorney in confidence, to share information each feels unable to reveal in the presence of the other spouse. This ought to help ensure that the attorney's representation of each will be based on the most relevant information available.

One problem is that this approach can put the attorney in a box. In representing one of the spouses the attorney must maintain an independent judgment, unaffected by what has been learned in confidence from the other spouse. Thus, the difficult practical issue is whether Attorney will be able to avoid consciously or unconsciously pushing Client to a more circumspect plan if Spouse came to Attorney and let it be known that Spouse has a paramour that Spouse would like to benefit, and Client later comes to Attorney wanting to maintain a plan that is all "kisses and hugs" (obviously totally ignorant about Spouse's philandering).

In addition, the attorney may have trouble keeping track of and keeping a lid on information learned from one that is not known by the other. This may not be so difficult if the secret is a blockbuster, but what if it seems insignificant to the attorney (which is why withdrawal did not seem necessary) notwithstanding that it was important to the client? Would *you*, for example, remember that Client's codicil leaving a vase to Spouse's hated sibling is a bone of contention?

The "discretionary" approach was regarded by the Florida Bar Ethics Department Advisory Opinion 95-4 as corrupting and absolutely improper, stating that this is not a matter that the attorney may decide in the attorney's discretion. Comment 31 to Rule 1.7 also does not appear to regard this middle of the road approach as an option. And most attorneys faced with the issue whether to disclose will not know how to exercise that discretion. Indeed, if the secret is a doozie that might imperil the marriage, most estate planners will pull the covers up over their head and hope the problem rights itself or goes away without requiring action of any kind on the attorney's part. After all, estate planners are do-good types: they hope to fashion results that are a win-win for everyone involved, and they absolutely loathe the creation of unnecessary conflict. A few might swear that they would exercise the discretion and tell the innocent spouse, notwithstanding the probable fallout consequences, but they probably are lying to themselves about their ability or willingness to jump-start a family feud.

The mandatory "show and tell" approach may be preferable. It is favored by the overwhelming majority of estate planners in practice and seems to be anticipated by the Restatement and Ethics 2000 Reporters. Under this approach, the attorney might agree with each spouse that the attorney will not meet or speak alone with either spouse, or that any information acquired from either that is relevant to the other will be shared. The presumption in this approach is that fairness requires full sharing of information unless the clients specifically agree otherwise. Unfortunately, however, this approach discourages each spouse from approaching the attorney with secrets that might be relevant to their planning, which may mean that the attorney will do a less than complete job of best representing a spouse who has a relevant secret.

To address *this*, some attorneys require clients to agree in a written engagement letter to tell the attorney all matters that may affect the plan, as a precaution against malpractice if the client does not do so and the plan is flawed as a result. Others follow a slightly different approach when representing spouses by requiring them to inform the attorney of any fact or circumstance, any dispute or conflict, that might cause the attorney to have a conflict of interest in the dual representation. Quaere whether this truly is effective, even if it puts the clients on notice of the severity of the need for all relevant information. Nevertheless, the attorney escapes being in the middle of a terrible situation and essentially puts the monkey on the back of the spouse with the secret. Presumably the holder of the secret will go to another attorney if revelation of the secret is important to adequate representation, which takes care of the mutual representation problem in the right manner: the client decides what is best.

An unfortunate problem with the show and tell approach is that it is not in the best interests of the client. This approach is for the protection of the attorney, which may make it appear less than legitimate. Yet the priestly approach is criticized by some precisely because it exposes the attorney to liability. As a practical matter, if the innocent spouse is injured because the attorney knew the secret but did not share it, a jury might find the attorney negligent notwithstanding the letter of the mutual representation agreement.

An additional problem with the show and tell approach is the passage of time. What happens if, years after the representation, Client comes to Attorney and, forgetting the rule about secrets, tells Attorney about a child born out of wedlock, a torrid affair now going on, or something else that is relevant to Client and Spouse's planning? Now that Attorney knows the secret, must it be shared with Spouse?

Quaere whether a prior consent, given in the vacuum of a then happy marriage with no known secrets, is effective at a later date when a specific conflict-revealing secret is disclosed to the attorney. See American Bar Association Standing Committee on Ethics and Professional Responsibility Formal Opinion 372 (1993) (former waiver of objection to future conflicts of interest), suggesting that the answer is no. The opinion states that "if the waiver is to be effective with respect to a future conflict, it must contemplate that particular conflict with sufficient clarity so the client's consent can reasonably be viewed as having been fully informed" and that "courts are very reluctant to conclude from a prospective waiver an agreement by the client to waive rights of confidentiality." Comment 22 to Ethics 2000 Rule 1.7 states:

Whether a lawyer may properly request a client to waive conflicts that might arise in the future is subject to the test of [whether] . . . the client reasonably understands the material risks that the waiver entails. The more comprehensive the explanation of the adverse consequences of those representations, the greater the likelihood that the client will have the requisite understanding. Thus, if the client agrees to consent to a particular type of conflict with which the client is already familiar, then the consent ordinarily will be effective with regard to that type of conflict. If the consent is general and open-ended, then the consent ordinarily will be ineffective, because it is not reasonably likely that the client will have understood the material risks involved.

Another response might be that the representation has ended and, along with it, the obligations established in the mutual representation agreement. Quaere, however, whether this really is true. This scenario underscores the potential value of an "exit" letter that makes it clear to the client that the representation has ended and that all prior deals are off. See page 530 for a further discussion of "exit" letters.

Also note Model Rule 1.9, dealing with conflicts of interest involving former clients, which might apply in cases such as this. An exit letter may make it clear that the original Client and Spouse representation has ended. Attorney nevertheless may be unable to avoid the prohibitions of Model Rule 1.9 with respect to former clients once Client reveals the secret that persuades Attorney that Client and Spouse may have adverse interests. Client essentially becomes a new client with a "substantially related matter" with regard to a former client (Spouse) with arguably "materially adverse" interests. Will Client permit Attorney to consult with Spouse to determine whether Spouse will consent to Attorney's representation of Client on this matter? And would Spouse's consent be valid if something less than full disclosure is made? Maybe Attorney should just assume that withdrawal is the only viable option once the secrets bell has been rung. With an effective exit letter perhaps Attorney has no duty to Spouse flowing from the secret and the worst aspect of this situation is that Attorney must reject future work from Client.

Notably, Model Rule 1.9 does not define "matter" for purposes of this rule and the definition in Rule 1.11(d) clearly does not apply outside Rule 1.11 (and would not be appropriate even if it did). Neither does Rule 1.0 define the term. As a practical matter then, it may be that either the priestly or the show-and-tell approach will put an attorney in the position of having to withdraw from representing either spouse if a relevant secret is revealed. Withdrawal may alert the ignorant spouse that some problem exists, although not with any specificity.

None of this is avoidable unless the initial representation agreement anticipates these problems and can constitute a proper informed consent (which is questionable). And notice that the mutual representation aspect was relatively easy compared to these secrets aspects. The duty of confidentiality is a far more difficult aspect of mutual representations, yet many engagement letters deal with the conflict issue but say nothing about secrets.

Similar problems could arise in representing Child after having represented Parent, and unquestionably would preclude representing a will contestant after having represented the testator. At one time it may have been questionable whether the ethics rules were meant to apply this expansively in all of these common family estate planning situations. Today it seems pretty certain that the rules drafters have considered these types of situations and consciously have not provided any special exceptions. Nor is it apparent that the rules ought to differ.

### *Other Situations*

Several other situations raise confidentiality concerns. One that is obvious and not much different from the mutual representation of spouses is common representations among family members, such as a dynastic family situation. A second serious (and growing more common) concern relates to clients with diminished capacity.

*Attorney has represented the entire Client family since before Client's spouse died. Through friends and personal observation Attorney is aware that Client is "slipping" and that Client probably needs asset management and perhaps even a personal representative. Indeed, one of Client's children may be taking advantage of the situation financially, and Client may need extended, and costly, medical and custodial services.*

Model Rule 1.14(a) dictates that, if "a client's capacity to make adequately considered decisions in connection with a representation is diminished . . . the lawyer shall, as far as reasonably possible, maintain a normal client-lawyer relationship with the client." Then Model Rule 1.14(b) says that

when the lawyer reasonably believes that the client has diminished capacity, is at risk of substantial physical, financial or other harm unless action is taken and cannot adequately act in the client's own interest, the lawyer may take reasonably necessary protective action, including consulting with individuals or entities that have the ability to take action to protect the client and, in appropriate cases, seeking the appointment of a guardian ad litem, conservator or guardian.

This Rule is altered by Ethics 2000 to clarify that an attorney who reasonably believes that protective action is required does not breach the duty of loyalty or improperly violate the client's confidences by seeking appointment of a guardian or other protective action. Furthermore, Comment 8 to Rule 1.14 clarifies that "[w]hen taking protective action. . . the lawyer is impliedly authorized to make the necessary disclosures, even when the client directs the lawyer to the contrary."

Thus, for example, the court involved in the appointment may ask what caused the attorney to believe a guardian is required. The attorney may make needed disclosures if the answer is that the client wanted some weird dispositive provision, or it is clear that some less than meritorious (or even "normal") relationship is involved. Presumably the attorney may disclose even if doing so will put other family members on notice of affairs and facts that the client may reasonably have assumed would be kept confidential. Comments 2 and 8 to Rule 1.14 have been expanded, consistent with several ethics opinions that place the client's best interests (as determined by the attorney) above the absolute rule of confidentiality. Presumably these will trump other pronouncements, such as: "[i]f suggestions of a guardianship would require the use to the disadvantage of the client or the revelation of a confidence or other secret, such use or revelation would be improper." See, e.g., Standing Committee on Professional Responsibility and Conduct of the California State Bar Formal Opinion 1989-112 ("it is unethical for an attorney to institute conservatorship proceedings contrary to the client's wishes" because doing so would breach the duties of confidentiality and to avoid conflicting interests; the opinion did allow withdrawal).

Restatement §35(4) also allows the lawyer to seek an appointment "when doing so is practical and will advance the client's objectives or interests . . . ." This must be done consistent with §35(2), which addresses a lawyer representing a client "in a matter against the interests" of a guardian or other representative (see §35(3)), or a client for whom no guardian or other representative is available to act and whose ability to make adequately considered decisions is impaired. That lawyer "must, with respect to a matter within the scope of the representation, pursue the lawyer's reasonable view of the client's objectives or interests as the client would define them if able to make adequately considered decisions on the matter, *even if the client expresses* no wishes or gives *contrary instructions"* [emphasis added].

A related situation might involve a client, perhaps elderly or suffering a terminal disease, who the attorney suspects is abusing prescription drugs or, worse, is being overprescribed (for a variety of reasons, such as to make the client more "manageable"). Alcohol dependency also might prompt an attorney's concern over the client's welfare. The attorney must consider whether it is in the client's best interests to discuss it with the client's doctor (or, if necessary, with another doctor) without the client's consent if the attorney does not feel able to discuss the situation with the client directly. This issue is made all the more difficult by the fact that the client may not be competent to consent if the attorney's evaluation is correct.

Fortunately it is more clear today that two rules extend to these types of situations. One is Rule 1.6, which authorizes disclosures that are reasonably necessary to conduct the representation. The other is Rule 1.14, which authorizes protective action by the attorney on the client's behalf. For example, American Bar Association Standing Committee on Ethics and Professional Responsibility Informal Opinion 1500 (1983) authorized an attorney to disclose a client's intent to commit suicide, based on policy grounds placing the sanctity of human life above the attorney's ethical obligation regarding confidentiality. And id. 1530 (1989) authorized an attorney to communicate to an attending physician that the client appeared to be abusing drugs prescribed by that doctor. Quaere whether a similar balance routinely will be drawn in less dramatic or clear-cut situations.

The comments to Model Rule 1.14 now provide better guidance in any of these cases, although they still require an attorney to be thoughtful and wise. Consider new Comments 5-7:

5. If a lawyer reasonably believes that a client is at risk of substantial physical, financial or other harm unless action is taken, and that a normal client-lawyer relationship cannot be maintained as provided in paragraph (a) because the client lacks sufficient capacity to communicate or to make adequately considered decisions in connection with the representation, then paragraph (b) permits the lawyer to take protective measures deemed necessary. Such measures could include: consulting with family

members, using a reconsideration period to permit clarification or improvement of circumstances, using voluntary surrogate decisionmaking tools such as durable powers of attorney or consulting with support groups, professional services, adult-protective agencies or other individuals or entities that have the ability to protect the client. In taking any protective action, the lawyer should be guided by such factors as the wishes and values of the client to the extent known, the client's best interests and the goals of intruding into the client's decisionmaking autonomy to the least extent feasible, maximizing client capacities and respecting the client's family and social connections.

6. In determining the extent of the client's diminished capacity, the lawyer should consider and balance such factors as: the client's ability to articulate reasoning leading to a decision, variability of state of mind and ability to appreciate consequences of a decision; the substantive fairness of a decision; and the consistency of a decision with the known long-term commitments and values of the client. In appropriate circumstances, the lawyer may seek guidance from an appropriate diagnostician.

7. If a legal representative has not been appointed, the lawyer should consider whether appointment of a guardian ad litem, conservator or guardian is necessary to protect the client's interests. Thus, if a client with diminished capacity has substantial property that should be sold for the client's benefit, effective completion of the transaction may require appointment of a legal representative. . . . In many circumstances, however, appointment of a legal representative may be more expensive or traumatic for the client than circumstances in fact require. Evaluation of such circumstances is a matter entrusted to the professional judgment of the lawyer. In considering alternatives, however, the lawyer should be aware of any law that requires the lawyer to advocate the least restrictive action on behalf of the client.

## Adequate Representation

Model Rule 1.1 requires an attorney to be competent to perform the representation undertaken. The same requirement applies under Model Rule 5.3 to assistants employed by the attorney. Given the increasing complexity of the legal and other aspects of estate planning and fiduciary administration, it bears noting that an act might be malpractice and it also may constitute an ethical hickey for which sanctions by the Bar may be appropriate. Nevertheless, many attorneys still believe that anyone can draft a "simple will" notwithstanding the reality, in the current estate planning environment, that there are short wills and simple lawyers but probably no simple wills. The relevant question then is what to do about a representation that is over the head of a particular practitioner?

Probably the most important act a "general practitioner" can perform to protect against malpractice liability and the related ethical violation is to establish a good referral network to engage experts in areas in which the referring attorney is deficient. Similarly, even an "expert" may need to employ a consultant if the representation involves the law of another jurisdiction or ancillary issues about which estate planners normally are not experienced.

An attorney ought to address several ethics questions when crafting a referral agreement. One is issues of confidentiality of information (what may the referring attorney tell the expert without consent from the client). Notice that the older Model Code EC 2-22 states that an attorney should not associate another lawyer outside the firm without the client's consent. See also EC 4-2, which is softer in stating that the attorney should not "seek counsel" from another attorney without consent if the client's identity, confidences, or secrets might be revealed. The Model Rules do not contain these prohibitions, except to the extent Model Rule 1.5(e) addresses fee splitting. Another issue is who will communicate with the client in furtherance of the Rule 1.4 obligation to keep the client reasonably informed. A third ethics issue is how will the diligence requisite of Rule 1.3 be audited to ensure that the representation is proceeding properly. Additional issues slip into areas that are not necessarily ethics related, such as questions regarding fees, including what is reasonable, who is to determine the fee, who will do the billing, who suffers the loss if the client does not pay, and matters involving referral fees or fee splitting; piracy of the client's other business; and responsibility for mistakes, such as if the referring attorney passes along inaccurate information or the expert makes a blunder that the referring attorney is not competent to discover.

Adequate representation also involves questions regarding the scope of a representation. The ethical issue here is "when does the representation end"? Many estate planners now use engagement letters to specify the tasks that the attorney has undertaken to perform, along with a fee estimate that is addressed to those tasks. Some attorneys send an "exit" letter, usually with the final bill, informing the client that the assigned tasks and the representation have been completed. As with the initial engagement letter, the exit letter may make it clear that the attorney assumes no responsibility to inform the client of any changes in the law or otherwise that might require a reconsideration of the plans completed (unless the client chooses to pay for this added service). As discussed at page 525, another advantage of the exit letter is that it potentially reduces problems regarding on-going mutual representations. For example, if Client blurts out about Client's nonmarital child or paramour, the attorney might have no obligation to convey that information to Spouse because neither Client nor Spouse is the attorney's client with respect to the now completed estate planning representation.

From a practical perspective, these letters must be written carefully and with a great deal of tact to avoid severing a relationship that otherwise appropriately might continue into the future. Client relations require that an exit letter both encourage the client to think of the attorney as available for further consultations and make it clear that all prior representations are completed, at least for the moment. Unfortunately, with some (perhaps many) clients this may not be possible, because they are on-going clients for other matters and the representation of them as a client in general will not terminate. Moreover, some attorneys will continue to represent clients to keep them apprised of law changes, for an annual retainer that the exit letter can announce. In this respect the exit letter need not be a final termination but, instead, serves to inform the client about what has been done and what might be considered for the future. But does that turn off any shared secrets agreement?

Perhaps the best result of an exit letter is its ability to inform the client what (not) to expect from the attorney in the future. Aside from its law office economics and malpractice minimization attributes, note too what the exit letter suggests about the ethics world in which estate planners operate. The situation of an estate planner's representation differs from a typical litigation matter that ultimately comes to a rather definite closure. The ethics rules generally presume that representations come to such clean, definable endings, but estate planners and their clients often regard themselves as traveling through life together, dealing with changes as they develop. This ongoing relationship may illustrate that the applicable rules sometimes fail to reflect the reality of an estate planner's relation to clients.

## Fees

Model Rule 1.5 deals with fees, providing (among other things) three rules of particular relevance to estate planners.

First, the attorney's fee must be reasonable, based on a list of factors including the time and labor involved, the novelty and difficulty involved, the skill required to perform the service properly, the likelihood that this representation would preclude another representation, the amount customarily charged in the locality for similar services, and so forth. Not listed (although arguably it should be) is the time when payment will be received, recognizing that a delay (sometimes a significant period) may occur in probate and in some estate planning situations.

Johnston, *Estate Planners' Accountability in the Representation of Agricultural Clients*, 34 U. Kan. L. Rev. 611, 633-634 (1986), questions whether the tradition of providing estate planning documents at a loss in anticipation of receiving a windfall when representing the client's estate constitutes an ethical violation in two respects. One is because the lower fee may impel the attorney to do a less than adequate job at the front end, and the other is because the charge for representing the probate estate may be excessive, based on the factors noted. Moreover, an attorney may commit both malpractice and an ethical violation if probate avoidance otherwise might be appropriate but was not recommended because of such a fee-generation factor.

American Bar Association Standing Committee on Ethics and Professional Responsibility Informal Opinion 98 regarded it as unethical to offer to draft a will for free if the client would recommend to the personal representative that the drafter should be hired to represent the personal representative. The natural and unanswered question is at what price for drafting a will this improper form of solicitation is avoided. Moreover, a special concern with respect to fees arises if the attorney charges a flat percentage fee for assisting in probating a will and administration of an estate. Model Rule 1.5(a) requires a fee to be reasonable in relation to the work performed. Only one of many listed factors is the custom in the community for charging fees, which along with the ambiguous factor referring to the "labor" involved usually are the only objective factors supporting a percentage fee approach.

Second, if the attorney has not regularly represented the client the basis of the fee must be communicated to the client, "preferably in writing, before or within a reasonable time after commencing the representation." Ethics 2000 adds that this is not required with a regularly represented client who will be billed on the same basis or rate.

And third, fees may not be split between attorneys who are not in the same firm unless "the division is in proportion to services performed by each or each lawyer assumes joint responsibility for the representation; the client agrees to the arrangement, including the share each lawyer will receive, and the agreement is confirmed in writing; and the total fee is reasonable." This Rule addresses fee splitting and referral fee agreements between lawyers. It is not so clear, particularly in the context of Multiple Disciplinary Practices (MDPs), whether it speaks to fee splitting with nonattorneys such as financial planners, insurance agents, or accountants. But Model Rules 5.4(a) and 7.2(c) clearly prohibit such arrangements, which also present conflict of interest concerns that will present major controversial questions with which the Bar will wrestle for the foreseeable future in the context of MDPs.

The requirement in Model Rule 1.5(b) regarding a statement, "preferably in writing," specifying how fees will be computed is worthy of note because many (and probably most) estate planners do not abide by this dictate. Not so directly addressed by the Model Rules are a smattering of other related questions. One is illustrated by American Bar Association Standing Committee on Ethics and Professional Responsibility Informal Opinion 1517 (1986). The question involved was charging a corporate client for work performed for an individual shareholder, employee, or officer. The opinion notes the concern that the fee will end up being deducted for income tax purposes because the law firm charges the corporation, notwithstanding that it is not a deductible expenditure by the shareholder, employee, or officer. Another concern is that the corporation might be unaware that the individual essentially is using corporate funds to pay for personal services. The informal opinion concluded that charging the fee to the corporation is permissible, provided the basis of the fee is noted, indicating the portion of the fee that was for personal work for the individual involved. In this way the corporation can determine whether to treat this benefit as income or as a dividend to the individual, whether to deduct any part of the fee paid from the individual's salary or dividends, and whether any part of the fee was a proper charge to the corporation or deduction from its income for tax purposes. A related question might be whether to apportion an attorney's fee for postmortem estate planning that benefited beneficiaries rather than the estate proper.

## Fiduciary Administration Concerns

One significant and largely unanswered ethical issue haunts attorneys who engage in fiduciary administration, either as the fiduciary (trustee, personal representative, or guardian) or, more commonly, as the attorney engaged to assist in the administration of a fiduciary entity. The question is to whom do the attorney's duties and loyalties run, and with what ancillary or derivative obligations? Because this topic is addressed in gagging detail in Pennell, *Representations Involving Fiduciary Entities: Who Is the Client?*, 62 Fordham L. Rev. 1319-1356 (1994), and the *Report of the Special Study Committee on Professional Responsibility, Counseling the Fiduciary*, 28 Real Prop., Prob. & Trust J. 825 (1994), it is not discussed in anything more than bare bones detail here.

The unfortunate reality is that this issue is as confused and distressing as any to be found anywhere in the estate planning practice and the authorities and therefore the fundamental obligations are numerous and conflicting. The fortunate reality is that the attorney who anticipates the issue can dodge virtually all questions with a well drafted provision in an engagement letter, making it clear "who is the client" and avoiding in large part issues of spillover or ancillary duties. Doing so therefore necessarily is the first, last, and best advice on this topic.

In most situations this "who is the client" issue is of academic interest only, because the potential for a real conflict among the fiduciary, beneficiaries, and other claimants (such as creditors or disappointed heirs) never ripens into a real controversy. But in a small percentage of cases involving fiduciary administration, the real and present issue is whether an attorney who is engaged to advise the administration represents the fiduciary who hired the attorney, the beneficiaries of the fiduciary entity, or the entity itself. This issue is complicated geometrically if the attorney also acts as fiduciary and takes the position that the attorney also serves in a legal advisory role. "Who is the client" is a relevant question for a number of reasons, the most important being concerns about:

- **Confidentiality and work product privilege**. For example, if the fiduciary reveals to the attorney (or the attorney discovers in the course of the representation) that the fiduciary has made a mistake, or acted in a dishonest or criminal manner, may (or *must*) the attorney reveal this information to, or may it be discovered by, the beneficiaries or a court that supervises the administration? Or does the duty of confidentiality preclude such revelation? A fine summary of the law on this point is found in *Wells Fargo Bank v. Superior Court*, 990 P.2d 591 (Cal. 2000), and see Longan, *Middle-Class Lawyering in the Age of Alzheimer's: The Lawyer's Duties in Representing a Fiduciary*, 70 Fordham L. Rev. 902 (2001).

- **Conflicts of interest**. To whom do the attorney's loyalties belong if multiple fiduciaries are involved and they disagree, or if the fiduciary and the beneficiaries disagree (an easy illustration being over fees), or if the fiduciary is a creditor of the entity or one of several beneficiaries and their interests conflict, and does the attorney have a conflict of interest in the context of such a representation? *In re Estate of Fogelman*, 3 P.3d 1172 (Ariz. Ct. App. 2000), appears to say that representation of the fiduciary and creditors of the estate (in other matters) poses a conflict of interest. According to Kansas Bar Association Ethics Opinion 99-06, representation of a corporate fiduciary in its capacity as trustee or executor of a particular trust or estate also prevents the attorney from representing another party in an unrelated action against the same corporation in its corporate capacity. This opinion regarded as irrelevant the fact that the corporation is wearing a very different hat when acting as fiduciary than when it is engaged in the business of hiring and firing employees, engaging in commercial banking and consumer transactions of all types, dealing with its own shareholders, and the like.

- **Privity and the right to sue**. Although not specifically an ethics issue, the very closely related issue exists of the attorney's liability and the rights of various parties to assert a cause of action against the attorney, or to dismiss the attorney.

The identity of the client may be confused further if the attorney also represented the settlor of the trust or the decedent whose estate is being administered, or their families, any of which may justify various expectations about the attorney's role.

### *Confusion in Existing Authority*

Comment 27 to Model Rule 1.7 states that:

In estate [sic] administration the identity of the client may be unclear under the law of a particular jurisdiction. Under one view, the client is the fiduciary; under another view the client is the estate or trust, including its beneficiaries. In order to comply with conflict of interest rules, the lawyer should make clear the lawyer's relationship to the parties involved.

The limited authority on this issue is not consistent and virtually none comes from ethics disputes (the reported cases involve ancillary issues like fee disputes or evidentiary privilege). The comment appears to anticipate that the attorney may choose who will be the client by an indication communicated when entering into the relationship. Doing so in an engagement letter is easy and advisable, but experience suggests that few such engagement letters are used. See also Restatement §163, requiring that the attorney also make clear to others (such as beneficiaries) that they are not clients, if misunderstanding otherwise would be likely.

The "default rule," which applies absent an agreement otherwise, holds in the majority of situations that the fiduciary is the client, not the estate or trust, nor the beneficiaries or ward. However, the vast confusion in this area arises because so many cases imply duties (often akin to the fiduciary's own duties) that run from the attorney directly to the beneficiaries. See, e.g., Illinois State Bar Association Ethics Advisory Opinions 98-07 (1999) and 91-24 (1992), in which a guardian's attorney was required to take remedial action when the guardian filed false accountings that disguised misappropriations, with reliance on Rule 3.3 (candor to a tribunal) to justify disclosure in violation of the otherwise applicable duty of confidentiality. Nevertheless, the majority position found in case law and ethics opinions is to the effect that the lawyer's duties (if indeed they rise to that level) to the beneficiaries do not create a true lawyer-client relationship.

Just to illustrate how sloppy and disconcerting this awkward and ill-defined relation can be, 1 Hazard & Hodes, The Law of Lawyering: A Handbook on the Model Rules of Professional Conduct §1.3:108 (2d ed. 1990), stated that the fiduciary *entity* was the client and that the *fiduciary* was a "primary" client while the *beneficiaries* were "derivative" clients. Restatement of the Law Governing Lawyers §73(4) Comment h contains the following statement, consistent with this view:

A lawyer representing . . . a fiduciary . . . must sometimes use care to protect a beneficiary. This duty arises when the lawyer has knowledge of circumstances indicating that intervention is necessary to prevent or mitigate a violation of fiduciary duty by the lawyer's client. The duty should be recognized only when action by the lawyer would not violate the appropriate professional rules. . . . Because fiduciaries are generally obliged to pursue the interests of their beneficiaries, the duty does not subject the lawyer to conflicting or inconsistent duties. . . .

The duty recognized by Subsection (4) arises only when circumstances known to the lawyer make it clear that appropriate action by the lawyer is necessary to prevent or mitigate a breach of the client's fiduciary duty. This Subsection thus creates no duty of inquiry . . . [and] applies only to breaches constituting crime or fraud . . . and those in which the lawyer has assisted or is assisting the fiduciary.

Under Subsection (4) a lawyer is not liable for failing to take action that the lawyer reasonably believes to be forbidden by professional rules . . . . Thus, a lawyer is not liable for failing to disclose confidences when the lawyer reasonably believes that disclosure is forbidden . . . . For example, a lawyer is under no duty to disclose a prospective breach in a jurisdiction that allows disclosure only regarding a crime or fraud . . . . However, liability could result from failing to attempt to prevent the breach of fiduciary duty through means that do not entail disclosure. . . .

This formulation is unsatisfactory for a number of reasons, not the least of which being that the attorney often has an allegiance or loyalty to the beneficiaries rather than to the fiduciary. Indeed, the attorney may have a conflict of interest by virtue of having represented the decedent or settlor of an estate or trust and the surviving spouse or other family members who are beneficiaries of the entity.

Few courts have considered an alternative vision of the client representation that regards the entity (rather than the fiduciary or the beneficiaries) as the client. This probably is because of the historical notion that a decedent's estate or a trust does not have a jural existence (the civil procedure experts remind us that it is necessary to sue the personal representative or trustee, rather than the estate or trust), notwithstanding the fact that the entity exists for tax and other purposes. Nevertheless, an engagement letter that identifies the entity as a separate jural personality and treats it as the client has several important advantages.

One is to make clear the attorney's responsibilities to the various parties who have an interest in the administration. Rather than trying to establish the meaning and extent of fiduciary, derivative, or ancillary duties, the attorney knows that legal representation of a fiduciary entity is guided by the same focus as that which guides the fiduciary administration itself (the best interests of the entity) evaluated in an objective sense rather than with a view toward protection of some but not all of the various constituents or agents involved.

A second advantage is relevant in the very few cases in which actual fiduciary misconduct arises. The attorney avoids the question of the attorney's ability to reveal the fiduciary's breach of duty by regarding the entity as the client rather than the fiduciary. This confidentiality issue is distinct from the evidentiary privilege question whether a beneficiary who has become aware of the fiduciary action may discover from the attorney information about the breach. The entity-as-client approach also clarifies somewhat to whom the attorney owes fidelity if a conflict of interest arises.

A third advantage lies in the fact that the law surrounding questions that arise in representing other entities (such as corporations) is reasonably well developed and can be relied upon to inform the analogous issues that arise in the fiduciary context. In those cases in which the issue of fiduciary wrongdoing is raised, a rule that favors the fiduciary with confidentiality as the attorney's client protects the party least entitled to protection. Often that rule also conflicts with the beneficiaries' expectations, and may conflict with the attorney's own sentiments and former client representations.

Assume for the sake of this discussion that the attorney has not been hired in the wake of a fiduciary breach, with the fiduciary paying that lawyer out of its own funds in defense of its wrongdoing. Instead, this case involves the attorney who has been involved in the fiduciary administration from the beginning and discovers that the fiduciary either has committed (or is about to commit) a violation of its fiduciary duties. According to Hazard, *Rectification of Client Fraud: Death and Revival of a Professional Norm*, 33 Emory L.J. 271 (1984), the effect of the confidentiality obligation of Rule 1.6 under a regime that regards the fiduciary as the client is to force the attorney to abandon the representation to avoid being accused of participation or complicity in the fiduciary's wrongdoing. This does not serve the interests of the beneficiaries (who might rightly be regarded as the real parties in interest), it does not rectify the wrongdoing, and it leaves the attorney to draw the very difficult line of when withdrawal is required. Under the majority rule that regards the fiduciary as the client, the attorney's withdrawal may not even put the parties most entitled to protection on notice that they should seek representation of their own to investigate something that is amiss. Those individuals are not protected unless the attorney is able to signal knowledgeable beneficiaries that something is wrong by the manner in which a withdrawal is accomplished.

According to the majority approach, the attorney cannot disclose any information that reveals the wrongdoing if the fiduciary is the attorney's client. See American Bar Association Standing Committee on Ethics and Professional Responsibility Formal Opinion 94-380, which rejected a position that disclosure was impliedly authorized because of the fiduciary's obligations to the beneficiaries. That opinion stated that "[d]isclosure of client confidences is not impliedly authorized simply because the client owes duties to third parties." Thus, only the manner of withdrawal may constitute a warning that there is a problem.

Little logic supports a rule grounded in a duty of confidentiality to a wrongdoing fiduciary. The fiduciary is protected if the beneficiaries are too ignorant, impaired, or naïve to react if the attorney for a fiduciary learns of wrongdoing and can signal that a problem exists only by the manner of withdrawal. This charade would be eliminated if the attorney were permitted to notify beneficiaries (or, in appropriate cases, an appointing court) directly that a problem exists. That desirable objective can be achieved if an exception exists in Model Rule 1.6 for disclosures of fraudulent or criminal conduct, but that exception is not uniform among the states and may be of questionable application depending on the circumstances and the nature of the fiduciary action.

The better practice is to specify in the attorney's engagement letter that the fiduciary is merely a representative of the fiduciary entity and speaks on behalf of that entity to the extent the fiduciary is acting within the bounds of its duties. Under this approach, the entity proper is the client and the attorney's duties run to the entity, not to the fiduciary personally. Modeled after Model Rule 1.13 and Restatement of the Law Governing Lawyers §212 (dealing with representation of entities such as corporations), this approach regards the fiduciary as an agent of the client who may direct the attorney only to the extent the fiduciary is acting within the bounds of its authority. The fiduciary as an agent could not hide behind the attorney's duty of confidentiality to protect against disclosure of wrongdoing.

A fiduciary who is in trouble always can hire its own counsel, paying that attorney from its own funds, but such a fiduciary could not dismiss the entity's attorney in an effort to cover up wrongdoing. Moreover, the attorney who was aware of that wrongdoing could advise the fiduciary to make it right or to hire separate counsel, and the attorney then would be free to make disclosure to the true parties in interest.

To illustrate how such a representation would apply:

*Attorney represented Decedent (D) and D's surviving spouse (S) and drafted estate plans for both of them. D's plan named D's child (C) as executor of D's estate and as trustee of several following trusts that will be held for the primary benefit of S for life, remainder to D's descendants (C and C's siblings, and their descendants). During the course of administration Attorney discovers that C has made several decisions that work to the benefit of the remainder beneficiaries of the trusts, including C personally, and to the detriment of S. Attorney has advised C that these decisions were improper and recommended corrective action, but C has not followed Attorney's advice.*

Rather than merely withdraw from this representation, Attorney may remind C that Attorney represents D's estate (and perhaps also the following trusts) and not C personally. In that capacity, Attorney may disclose information relating to C's improper decisions and their effects to S, notwithstanding C's objections that Attorney is subject to the attorney-client privilege (meaning that Attorney could not be *forced* to divulge this information). Faced with this disclosure, C either will make the corrections recommended by Attorney or will hire counsel to represent C or all the remainder beneficiaries in arguing that the actions taken were proper. S also may need to hire counsel and, lacking a Rule 1.7 consent, Attorney should not represent any of these beneficiaries.

## Your Duty to the "System"

Several difficult (and perhaps unanswerable) questions arise in a general context that is here labeled the attorney's obligation to the legal "system." To illustrate, consider another hypothetical:

*Attorney's client is, at the very best, only periodically competent; in all likelihood if the question were raised a court would find the client to be unable to execute a will. Because everyone involved thinks it is in the best interest of the client and the client's family, however, a will has been prepared, which Attorney causes to be executed.*

The issue here is whether Attorney, as an officer of the court, has committed a violation of Model Rule 3.3 regarding candor to a tribunal. The alleged misconduct is causing to be put into motion the local law presumption that a will complying with all the formalities of the Wills Act is valid and the testator thereof competent. See, e.g., Uniform Probate Code §3-406(b). Use of a self-proving affidavit in a case such as this probably ensures that the question of proof never will be raised, meaning that the system may never get the opportunity to challenge the presumptions of validity and competence. In favor of allowing execution is the argument that the attorney is obliged to the client to make the best possible case, which in this situation may include giving the client the benefit of the doubt about capacity to execute and letting the system resolve the issue if ever raised. Clearly, however, there is a point at which a reasonable argument regarding capacity cannot be made and participation in an execution in that case would be improper. The issue is where to draw that line.

Although everyone involved may feel that execution is best, the attorney still has allowed the probate system to be deceived. The ethics rules regard this as improper, without room to wiggle under a theory that (like a "little white lie") no one is harmed. If there is a problem here, it may be in the probate code's unwavering prohibition of execution of a will without adequate capacity (although it is hard to conjure a flexible rule that would apply appropriately in all situations) or in the presumption of capacity that attends a formally executed will. The ethics rules merely preclude the attorney from intentionally bypassing the probate code restrictions by deceiving the court.

A far more likely and more troubling circumstance is illustrated by a second hypothetical:

*In the course of doing estate and gift tax planning for Donor, Attorney discovers that gifts were made in a prior year that should have been reported on a gift tax return, but were not.*

The issue here is Attorney's obligation with respect to the Internal Revenue Service concerning the deficiency in Donor's compliance with the gift tax laws. If the government can be likened to a tribunal, then Model Rule 3.3(a)(1) might be deemed to require disclosure of this material fact to avoid assisting Donor in a criminal or fraudulent act. In that regard, Ethics 2000 amends the definition of a "tribunal" to include an "administrative agency . . . acting in an adjudicative capacity." Quaere whether that would include the Internal Revenue Service, for example at an administrative level.

Circular 230 is the government's own rules regulating practice before it in the tax arena. See 31 C.F.R. §§10.0 to 10.93. Most significant to most estate planners is §10.34, which was amended in 1994 to more closely comply with the rules of §§6694 (understatement of income tax liability) and 6662 (accuracy related penalty). These rules impose ethical sanctions that may include disbarment or suspension from practice before the government and relate to all forms of returns, notwithstanding that the §6694 rules that inform the standards adopted relate only to income tax return preparation. Those rules used as a template for standard of practice dictates are indicated in bracketed references following each of the rules, which are reproduced in relevant part below:

(a) Standards of conduct—

(1) Realistic possibility standard. A practitioner may not sign a return as a preparer if the practitioner determines that the return contains a position that does not have a realistic possibility of being sustained on its merits (the realistic possibility standard) unless the position is not frivolous and is adequately disclosed. A practitioner may not advise a client to take a position on a return, or prepare a portion of a return on which a position is taken, unless

(i) The practitioner determines that the position satisfies the realistic possibility standard; or

(ii) The position is not frivolous and the practitioner advises the client of any opportunity to avoid the accuracy-related penalty in section 6662 . . . by adequately disclosing the position . . . . [§6694(a)(1)]

(2) Advising clients on potential penalties. A practitioner advising a client to take a position on a return, or preparing or signing a return as a preparer, must inform the client of the penalties reasonably likely to apply to the client [and] of any opportunity to avoid any such penalty by disclosure, if relevant, and of the requirements for adequate disclosure. This paragraph . . . applies even if the practitioner is not subject to a penalty with respect to the position.

(3) Relying on information furnished by clients. A practitioner . . . generally may rely in good faith without verification upon information furnished by the client. However, the practitioner may not ignore the implications of information furnished to, or actually known by, the practitioner, and must make reasonable inquiries if the information as furnished appears to be incorrect, inconsistent, or incomplete. [§6694(a)(2); Treas. Reg. §1.6694-1(e)]

(4) (i) Realistic possibility. A position is considered to have a realistic possibility of being sustained on its merits if a reasonable and well-informed analysis by a person knowledgeable in the tax law would lead such a person to conclude that the position has approximately a one in three, or greater, likelihood of being sustained on its merits. The authorities described in [Treas. Reg. §1.6662-4(d)(3)(iii)] . . . may be taken into account for purposes of this analysis. The possibility that a position will not be challenged by the Service (e.g., because the taxpayer's return may not be audited or because the issue may not be raised on audit) may not be

taken into account. [§6662(d)(2)(B)(i); Treas. Reg. §1.6694-2(b)(1)]

(ii) Frivolous. A position is frivolous if it is patently improper. [Treas. Reg. §1.6694-2(c)(2)]

(b) Standard of discipline. . . . [O]nly violations of this section that are willful, reckless, or a result of gross incompetence will subject a practitioner to suspension or disbarment from practice before the Service.

Notable about these rules is that a practitioner can be sanctioned either as a return preparer or for having advised a return preparer. They specifically negate consideration of the audit lottery in determining whether or how to report an item. And they dovetail into the substantial authority rules of §6662, which include only the Code, Regulations (proposed, temporary, and final), legislative history, cases, and administrative pronouncements from the government (revenue rulings, revenue procedures, private letter rulings, technical advice memoranda, general counsel memoranda, actions on decision, notices, and announcements). No other authority, no matter how reliable it may seem or how necessary resort to it may be in the absence of other guidance, may support the determination whether there was a one in three likelihood of success on the merits.

As with any rules relating to standards of practice in a professionalism or ethics arena rather than a malpractice forum, there is no community standard defense to a violation of these rules, and the ultimate sanction could be a loss of the right to practice, as to which insurance is no protection. As a consequence, these rules have real significance.

Circular 230 specifies in §10.21 that "[e]ach attorney . . . who knows that the client has not complied with the revenue laws . . . or has made an error in or omission from any return . . . shall advise the client promptly of the fact . . . ." Although Attorney is required to advise Donor to amend an erroneous return or to file a missing return, Circular 230 does *not* require Attorney to blow the whistle on Donor. Moreover, the better position regarding Model Rule 3.3 is that the government is not in the position of a tribunal in this respect, meaning that disclosure notwithstanding the Model Rule 1.6 obligation of confidentiality is not required. See American Bar Association Committee on Ethics and Professional Responsibility Formal Opinion 314 (1965).

Attorney must not, however, participate in any furtherance of that noncompliance. For example, if Donor makes another gift for which a return is required, Attorney may not simply report the latest gift as if the prior gifts had not been made. To do so would join Attorney with Donor in making a representation that no prior taxable gift was made that should be included in the adjusted taxable gifts base, which is untrue. By virtue of the Code §6701 aiding and abetting penalties, Attorney should not participate in filing a gift tax return for the latest gift if that return will be in error because the prior gifts were not reported.

Under Model Rule 1.16(b), Attorney may withdraw from the representation of Donor. Under Model Rule 4.1(a), Attorney probably *must* withdraw from at least that portion of the representation that involves filing an improper gift tax return. It is not enough to simply sit silent while Donor continues to mislead the government. This duty to withdraw from the representation would extend to any situation in which an attorney knows a client is committing a mistake (or, worse, a fraud) and is not willing to correct it after being advised to do so by the attorney. A good illustration would be an attorney representing a fiduciary who is improperly accounting, complying with the income tax, or making distributions, even after being advised by the attorney of the proper approach. In each of these cases it appears that the ethics rules work properly and that Circular 230 does not impose an inconsistent obligation. And, as a practical matter, do you *want* such a client?

A more intangible question is the obligation an estate planner owes to the general system of self assessment and compliance to avoid putting ideas in the mind of a client that the attorney believes to be insupportable under the tax laws, or to affirmatively counsel a client to avoid transactions that are not likely to succeed. The real issue is whether it is ethical to permit a client to play the audit lottery by taking a position or engaging in a transaction that never may be discovered by the government but that, if identified, would not produce the results the client desires. Although some authority exists in this respect in the tax shelter arena, there appears to be no other authority directly on point in "normal" tax planning situations. See Circular 230 §10.33. The difficult issue is knowing where to draw the line involved in Model Rule 1.2(d), which provides that:

A lawyer shall not counsel a client to engage, or assist a client, in conduct that the lawyer knows is criminal or fraudulent, but a lawyer may discuss the legal consequences of any proposed course of conduct with a client and may counsel or assist a client to make a good faith effort to determine the validity, scope, meaning or application of the law.

It probably is fair to state that an attorney who actively participates in planning that involves legal positions that are just plain wrong, has committed an ethical violation in addition to the Circular 230 violation if the position is not adequately disclosed in compliance mode, particularly if the only justification is that the government is not likely to discover the issue. See generally Model Rule 8.4(c). Short of that, however, the ethics rules provide no guidance in this darkest of gray areas, particularly if the client's activity is neither criminal nor fraudulent.

## Solicitation and Advertising

The last two items of potential misconduct for an estate planner noted here are related. Overreaching, duress, or solicitation of business is improper. This includes solicitations to name the attorney as a fiduciary or as attorney for a fiduciary named in a document. Being named as the fiduciary or as the attorney for the fiduciary is permissible, provided the attorney did not instigate the designation. American Bar Association Standing Committee on Ethics and Professional Responsibility Informal Decision 602 (1963); Virginia Legal Ethics Opinion 1515 (1994). New York State Bar Association Committee on Professional Ethics Opinion 481 (1978) states that the attorney may suggest that the client name the attorney if the circumstances

support a firm conviction that the client would request his lawyer to serve in that capacity if he were aware of the lawyer's willingness to accept the responsibility. Not only should the lawyer have enjoyed a long-standing relationship with the client, but it must also appear that the client is experiencing difficulty in selecting other persons qualified and competent to serve as executor.

See generally *Report of the Special Study Committee on Professional Responsibility, Preparation of Wills and Trusts that Name Drafting Lawyer as Fiduciary*, 28 Real Prop., Prob. & Trust L. 803, 821-822 (1994), which opines that, under Rule 1.8(h), it also may be improper to include a provision exculpating the drafter for negligence in acting as fiduciary. This should be true only if the exculpation provision is more protective than the attorney normally provides regardless of the identity of the fiduciary.

The hard part about this situation is proving there was no impropriety in the designation, especially because any statement by the client to that effect may be every bit as suspicious as the designation itself. Moreover, regular insertion of a provision designating the attorney as fiduciary for every client would be improper and may not be binding, no matter how it is worded. In addition, drafting a will for free provided that the client recommend that the drafter be hired as attorney for the personal representative also is improper.

Even in less severe cases, the practical reality is that being named as a fiduciary or as attorney for a fiduciary raises eyebrows. The presumption is that impropriety resulted in the designation unless the attorney can establish otherwise. And in any case, allowable fees are likely to be scrutinized carefully. See, e.g., *In re Estate of Weinstock*, 351 N.E.2d 647 (N.Y. Ct. App. 1976); *In re Estate of Thron*, 530 N.Y.S.2d

951, 955 (Surr. Ct. 1988), both involving appointment of two lawyers from the same firm as coexecutors, the court in *Thron* stating that "[t]he appointment of two or more members from the same law firm as co-executors in double commission cases, in almost every instance, can only be the product of gratitude, greed or ignorance."

Unsolicited retention of a will for safekeeping also arguably constitutes an ethical violation because it makes it more difficult for a client to engage another attorney if changes are desired in the future. Retaining the will also makes it harder for the testator's survivors to employ another attorney to represent the personal representative. Compare American Bar Association Standing Committee on Ethics and Professional Responsibility Informal Opinion 981 (1967) (authorizing the practice if done as an accommodation to the client), and Pennsylvania Bar Association Committee on Legal Ethics and Professional Responsibility Formal Opinion 2001-300 (concluding that the practice is not unethical if the client affirmatively requests the attorney to provide custody and the attorney informs the client in writing that the client may retrieve the document at any time and that the personal representative is under no obligation to hire the attorney postmortem), with State of Texas Professional Ethics Committee Opinion 280 (1964) (holding that use of a statement that a will was executed in duplicate and that one executed original was retained by the drafting attorney constitutes unauthorized solicitation of the probate representation). Quaere whether retention imposes a greater duty on the attorney to keep the client informed about law changes. It also may generate a duty under many states' laws to produce the will when the client dies. See, e.g., Uniform Probate Code §2-902. This duty may be more of an undertaking than the lawyer wishes to assume, as is the cost of providing fireproof security.

### Your Dilemma

Admittedly the existing ethics rules were not written primarily for the estate planning and fiduciary administration practice and, understandably, many of them make less than great sense in those contexts. Even those rules that are general enough to apply in those settings may not reflect the needs of clients for family planning representation. Worse, many rules that are appropriate in a litigation setting are inappropriate in a counseling practice. Nevertheless, the most important defensive tactics to protect against alleged ethical violations are common sense, unassailable honesty, disclosure, and knowing written consents regarding all conceivable conflicts of interest (especially including mutual representations), dissemination of confidential information, deemed solicitations (including designation as a fiduciary or its attorney), and fees.

As recommended by a respected attorney who speaks with wisdom about malpractice and ethics issues:

- Never enter into a business transaction with a client.

- Do not serve on the client's board of directors.

- Do not ever . . . attempt to put two clients into business together.

- Do not accept service as a fiduciary in a trust or will created by a client.

- Do not accept any engagement which might be in conflict with the interest of an existing client, no matter how lucrative the engagement might be.

- Honor the profession: avoid even the appearance of impropriety.

This attorney also admits that:

I did not always follow [this] advice. I . . . regret the result of each and every deviation I made. A pure professional relationship is one in which the lawyer, the accountant, the advisor, has nothing to gain from his or her relationship with the client other than a reasonable compensation for services fairly and objectively rendered.

### The Malpractice Aspect of All This

Theoretically a violation of the ethics rules is not tantamount to malpractice. Model Rules Scope Comment 20 states:

Violation of a Rule should not itself give rise to a cause of action against a lawyer nor should it create any presumption in such a case that a legal duty has been breached. In addition, violation of a Rule does not necessarily warrant any other nondisciplinary remedy, such as disqualification of a lawyer in pending litigation. The Rules are designed to provide guidance to lawyers and to provide a structure for regulating conduct through disciplinary agencies. They are not designed to be a basis for civil liability. Furthermore, the purpose of the Rules can be subverted when they are invoked by opposing parties as procedural weapons. The fact that a Rule is a just basis for a lawyer's self-assessment, or for sanctioning a lawyer under the administration of a disciplinary authority, does not imply that an antagonist in a collateral proceeding or transaction has standing to seek enforcement of the Rule. Nevertheless, since the Rules do establish standards of conduct by lawyers, a lawyer's violation of a Rule may be evidence of breach of the applicable standard of conduct.

An ethics violation is not necessarily an act of malpractice, because the ethics and malpractice concepts differ. Nevertheless, the same activity that constitutes an ethics violation also may constitute malpractice and cases may support attorney liability on the basis of an ethics violation. Moreover, some commentators and courts confuse the terminology (if not the concept) so that some refer to an attorney's violation of the ethical rules as malpractice or vice versa.

To guard against malpractice, some of the more common mistakes can be prevented (or the likelihood minimized) by taking the following steps:

1. Refer to a specialist matters that are out of the attorney's area of expertise (most especially including matters that involve the law of another jurisdiction). It is curious that the legal profession lags light years behind the medical profession in the area of referrals. No jury would excuse a podiatrist for malpractice in brain surgery; why would a fact finder be any more accepting of an inexperienced attorney who messes up in drafting any component of an estate plan?

2. Keep current. An attorney who attempts to practice in the estate planning arena without committing the time to regular review of developments (both tax and nontax related) is asking for trouble.

3. Establish routines, procedures, and guidelines, *and follow them.* An astounding number of malpractice cases involve situations in which seemingly simple functions were overlooked (like failing to provide the requisite number of witnesses to an execution supervised by an attorney, or having the wrong spouse sign a will prepared in a reciprocal will situation). Matters that seem routine easily can be overlooked without attention to detail, and the failure to properly perform routine matters is hard to defend.

4. Proofread documents *before* they go out. Estate planners want to rely on word processing notwithstanding the proclivity of computers to stutter or burp at the wrong moment, causing a provision to be omitted or jumbled. Frequently enough, a sentence or provision is omitted accidentally; the added time is well spent verifying that every paragraph is in place and says what it is supposed to say.

5. Obtain independent reviews of all unusual drafts. Even more dangerous than failing to include all necessary provisions is the proclivity to draft a provision and immediately send it to the client, without having a colleague review it to ascertain that it truly says what the drafter intended.

There is hardly a more dangerous trap in drafting than failing to have an unbiased set of eyes review a document. Even the best drafters will admit that it is all too easy to create a provision and, because the drafter knows what it is supposed to say, upon reviewing it conclude that it is clear, only to find that another person is not able to ascertain the drafter's intent. All drafters get too close to their work to see some of the mistakes or ambiguities created.

If another opinion is not available, then a wise drafter will try to set the document aside long enough to forget what the client wanted. The point is that the drafter should let the draft get old and cold (enough so that the drafter forgets), then re-read the draft, and then check it against the drafter's notes, all to verify that the document says what the drafter and the client originally intended. Gaining enough objectivity in this manner is difficult and requires time that many planners simply cannot make available.

By all means, when asking another reviewer to read a document, don't explain what the document is meant to say: have that person read it and explain what it said to them. The draft needs refinement if that explanation is not what the drafter and the client intended. Drafters who must review their own drafting seldom get this kind of disinterested, objective input, but waiting to review the document until the drafter has forgotten what the client intended (in hopes of accomplishing the same result) is the only effective method of accomplishing anything like the same result.

6. The review factor is only one of many reasons why it is bad business to do "rush" jobs. Although the ethical obligation is to avoid delay, the malpractice risk flows from too much haste. Sometimes an accelerated project cannot be avoided, but even then the client should be informed of the risks involved. The attorney is justified in informing the client that the time constraints imposed create risks and that the client cannot expect the same quality of service that a more reasonable time commitment would permit. Limiting the attorney's duty in such a case also may be permissible. See Restatement §30, but compare §76 (limiting duties is permissible, but limiting liability for malpractice in performing the attorney's duties is not).

7. Document the file, not only when a rush job creates the risk of error, but with respect to any aspect of the planning that might generate questions in the future. If recommendations were rejected by the client, document the fact that they were made and why they were not accepted. If special circumstances led to deviations from normal procedures or caused consideration of unusual factors, document what they were and what decisions were made (and why) and what consequences were anticipated. As with valuations, with

estate planning the attorney must be prepared to prove many years later that a proper job was done under the circumstances. Be sure to inform the client about dangers to anticipate in their future dealings (such as the need to revise the plan if an unmarried client with children marries again in the future or if a young client has or adopts a child).

8. In general, impose an affirmative obligation on clients to inform the attorney about their situation, about any unusual assets or relationships, and about all changes that might be relevant to the plan. Don't accept a client's refusal to provide needed information, or at the very least document that the request was made and refused and that the client was informed of the attendant risks. Moreover, don't take the client's word (or that of other advisors, such as an insurance agent or stock broker) for anything of substance that can be verified. Who owns life insurance, who is the designated beneficiary, what does a power of appointment provide, how is property titled (and the like), all can be verified and, more importantly, all can be misrepresented by individuals who don't understand the legal and practical issues involved.

9. Pay careful attention to the integration of documents and plans. For example, the tax payment provisions in a will and pour over trust, or the presumptions of survivorship in reciprocal wills, easily can be inconsistent and may defeat intent. To illustrate, one common glitch is each spouse leaving property to a third party if the other does not survive for X days, giving that person a windfall if one spouse survives but for fewer than X days. Another less common example is conducting an asset transfer for a client and failing to review the estate plan to determine whether that conveyance negates a specific disposition to a designated beneficiary (and potential plaintiff).

10.Be wary of "mixing and matching" or "cutting and pasting" documents. Especially with documents produced by others, the risk of including something that is inappropriate or, more likely, omitting something that is essential, increases geometrically when a drafter adopts material from sources that were not tailored for the task at hand. Marginally competent planners who don't know why a provision was included or can't find a guide to what provisions need to be included should try hard not to create their own documents. Instead, look for someone who has done this work, even if it is not perfect.

11.Try not to be the first kid on the block to try any new gimmick. Estate planners (particularly those more steeped in the tax side of it than the property or "people" side) seem to have an almost irresistible desire to embrace new techniques. Like the first several articles written about any new tax bill, there are bound to be mistakes made by those who are charting new ground. As the old chestnut says: "The second mouse gets the cheese." A client who can wait a while before jumping into a new routine almost always will be better served and the attorney will have less risk of overlooking something significant.

12. Be nice. Potential plaintiffs find it harder to sue attorneys who are likeable, helpful, sympathetic, responsive, and even polite. It is impossible to overstate the number of situations involving demonstrable blunders committed by planners who were in over their head, or distracted, or otherwise not able to do the job properly. Cases in which the family had a clear cause of action that they decided not to pursue against the attorney. Often their decision is based on no better reason than that the family felt charitable to an attorney who had been there for the decedent, perhaps someone the family was proud to regard as a friend. When all else fails, remember that Mama was right: "it don't cost nothin' to be nice."

# TABLE OF CASES

# TABLE OF INTERNAL REVENUE CODE SECTIONS
# AND TREASURY REGULATIONS

## *Treasury Regulations*

# TABLE OF MODEL RULES AND UNIFORM CODES

# TABLE OF RESTATEMENTS OF THE LAW

## Restatement (Third) of Restitution and Unjust Enrichment

## Restatement (Second) of Trusts

## Restatement (Third) of Trusts

## Restatement (Third) of Trusts (Prudent Investor Rule)

# INDEX